Bryan Beeckman
One or Two Translators?

Beihefte zur Zeitschrift für die alttestamentliche Wissenschaft

Edited by
John Barton, Reinhard G. Kratz, Nathan MacDonald,
Sara Milstein, and Markus Witte

Volume 549

Bryan Beeckman

One or Two Translators?

—

Translation Technique and Theology
of LXX Proverbs and Its Relation to LXX Job

DE GRUYTER

ISBN 978-3-11-104109-4
e-ISBN (PDF) 978-3-11-104158-2
e-ISBN (EPUB) 978-3-11-104207-7
ISSN 0934-2575

Library of Congress Control Number: 2023947843

Bibliographic information published by the Deutsche Nationalbibliothek
The Deutsche Nationalbibliothek lists this publication in the Deutsche Nationalbibliografie;
detailed bibliographic data are available on the internet at http://dnb.dnb.de.

Printing and binding: CPI books GmbH, Leck

www.degruyter.com

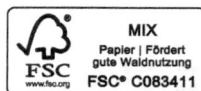

MIX
Papier | Fördert
gute Waldnutzung
FSC® C083411

In loving memory of Memuse

Foreword

This monograph is the published version of my doctoral dissertation. Writing a dissertation is an activity one cannot do alone. As a PhD researcher I found myself lucky to be surrounded by people who supported me in this exciting endeavour and who have, directly or indirectly, contributed to the final product of four, dare I say, fruitful years of academic research. Although my gratitude exceeds beyond the limits of what can be expressed by means of a written text, this foreword is a token of my gratefulness.

First and foremost, a word of thanks to two wonderful human beings, i.e., my promotors Prof. dr. Hans Ausloos and Prof. dr. Bénédicte Lemmelijn. They both embody the perfect image one has of a promotor. Just as *hapax legomena*, which are unique due to their oneness, so are my promotors who are unique and by whom I was blessed to have been guided. Not only did they support me during the writing process of the dissertation, they also supported me on a personal level. Without their continual support and kindness, I would not have been the scholar I am today. I am forever grateful that they were my two promotors of my doctoral dissertation and I want to express the hope that this collaboration is not the end but the beginning of an enduring partnership.

Next to my promotors, there are other professors from the academic community who deserve a token of my appreciation. The first one is Prof. dr. Johann Cook who has followed my career with utmost interest and who has created ample opportunities to boost my academic career. The assignment to co-author the *SBL Commentary on the Septuagint* volume of Proverbs, being the most exciting one. I am looking forward to further collaborate with him in the years to come. Another one is Prof. dr. Johan Lust. Not only did I enjoy our regular ping-pong games, I also appreciated the talks we had before, after or during the games. Many thanks to the members of my *comité d'accompagnement*, i.e., Prof. dr. Jean-Marie Auwers and Prof. dr. Brian Doyle, for their insightful remarks and their patience and endurance when reading my dissertation. A special thanks goes out to Prof. dr. Mathijs Lamberigts for giving me the opportunity to work as a science collaborator on a project of *Religie, zingeving en levensbeschouwing* before receiving a scholarship. During this year, I was blessed to work under the supervision of Prof. dr. Johan De Tavernier, whose company I have greatly appreciated during the last few years. Of course, I am blessed by having obtained funding by the *Fonds Spéciaux de Recherche* (FSR) to pursue a PhD and whose generous scholarship has enabled me to do what I love to do, i.e., doing research and working on a dissertation for four years.

https://doi.org/10.1515/9783111041582-202

Working at two faculties, i.e., the Faculté de theologie (UCLouvain) and Faculty of Theology and Religious Studies (KU Leuven), has the advantage of meeting a lot of warm people who have supported me during the writing process of the dissertation. In Louvain-la-Neuve, I had the pleasure of being surrounded with wonderful colleagues of the *Groupe de recherche Septante et critique textuelle*. I would like to thank Ellen, Camilla and Martinus for their great interest in my research and their presence during numerous conferences where I have presented one of my papers as well as their kind friendship. A special word of thanks goes out to Beatrice. We have started this adventure together and together we have come to the end of our journey. Her unconditional friendship and support were heart warming. I hope we can continue our academic journey together for many years to come. *Grazie mille!*

In Leuven, a place I like to call home, I had the honour of working with and getting to know many people from different departments. Between reading articles and books and writing the dissertation, I was lifted up by the 11 o'clock coffee breaks with my colleagues of the BAP-section, the talks with the people from the technical staff and the amusing lunches with the ATP-section. Also a word of thanks to Paul Kevers who I greatly appreciate and had the pleasure of working with for the *Vlaamse Bijbelstichting*.

Outside of academia, I found myself blessed of having a supportive group of friends who, all in their own unique way, contributed (directly and indirectly) to this monograph by being there for me, having drinks, listening to my DJ-sets and/or joining me on one of my many musical night life adventures. I would like to thank them for the warm friendship I received from them throughout the years.

A warm word of thanks goes out to the people working at De Gruyter who have assisted me with great patience during the preparation of this monograph. In particular, I want to thank Alice Meroz and Teodor Borsa for their excellent assistance and work.

I am forever in debt of the unconditional love and support I have received over the years from my family. My parents, Joanna and Luc, and their partners, resp. Dirk and Jeannine, have made me the man I am today. Without their faith in my potential, I would never have been where I am at this very moment in life. My gratitude for them exceeds the limits of this foreword and can, therefore, not be adequately captured into (written) sentences. Also my twin brother, Davy, his girlfriend Kimberly and their son Neill as well as my grandmother Anny, godfather Willy and his husband Valère deserve to be thanked for their support at the side lines.

Last but not least, a word of thanks to Stefan. *Liefde gaf jou duizend namen.* His love and encouragement is the fuel that keeps me going. He is the one that makes me whole. His family provided me with a home in the picturesque Limburg during weekends and have treated me as one of their own, for which I am truthfully grateful. Stefan, אני אוהב אותך.

Contents

Abbreviations

Series

AASFDHL	Annales Academiae Scientiarum Fennicae. Dissertationes Humanarum Litterarum
AASF	Suomalaisen Tiedeakatemian Toimituksia. Annales Academiae Scientiarum Fennicae
AcBib	Academia Biblica
AGJU	Arbeiten zur Geschichte des antiken Judentums und des Urchristentums
AOAT	Alter Orient und Altes Testament. Veröffentlichungen zur Kultur und Geschichte des Alten Orients und des Alten Testaments.
ATANT	Abhandlungen Zur Theologie Des Alten Und Neuen Testaments
BEATAJ	Beiträge zur Erforschung des Alten Testaments und des antiken Judentums
BETL	Bibliotheca Ephemeridum Theologicarum Lovaniensium
BHQ	Biblia Hebraica Quinta
BWANT	Beiträge zur Wissenschaft vom Alten und Neuen Testament
BZAW	Beihefte zur Zeitschrift für die alttestamentliche Wissenschaft
CBET	Contributions to Biblical Exegesis and Theology
CBOTS	Coniectanea Biblica. Old Testament Series
CBQMS	The Catholic Biblical Quarterly Monograph Series
CJEL	Commentaries on Early Jewish Literature
CTSRR	College Theology Society Resources in Religion
DCLS	Deuterocanonical and Cognate Literature Studies
EB.NS	Études Bibliques, Nouvelle Série
ICA	Initiations au christianisme ancien
JBLMS	Journal of Biblical Literature Monograph Series
JBS	Jerusalem Biblical Studies
JSOTSS	Journal for the Study of the Old Testament Supplement Series
KUSATU	Kleine Untersuchungen zur Sprache des Alten Testaments und seiner Umwelt
LUA	Lunds Universitets årsskrift
LXX.H	Handbuch zur Septuaginta / Handbook of the Septuagint
Med. KNAW	Mededelingen der Koninklijke Nederlandse akademie van wetenschappen
MOA	Die Wildrinder im alten Mesopotamien
MSU	Mitteilung des Septuaginta-Unternehmens der Akademie der Wissenschaften in Göttingen
OBO	Orbis Biblicus et Orientalis
OTS	Oudtestamentische Studiën/ Old Testament Studies
PFES	Publications of the Finnish Exegetical Society
PIRSB	Publications de l'Institut romand des sciences bibliques

https://doi.org/10.1515/9783111041582-204

SBLDS	Society of Biblical Literature. Dissertation Serie:
SBLEJIL	Society of Biblical Literature. Early Judaism and Its Literature
SBLSCS	Society of Biblical Literature. Septuagint and Cognate Studies
SJSJ	Supplements to the Journal for the Study of Judaism
SVT	Supplements to Vetus Testamentum
SVTP	Studia in Veteris Testamenti Pseudepigrapha
TECC	Textos y Estudios 'Cardinal Cisneros'
TSAJ	Texts and Studies in Ancient Judaism
VTS	Vetus Testamentum Supplements
WBC	World Biblical Commentary
WUNT	Wissenschaftliche Untersuchungen zum Neuen Testament

Journals

Bib	Biblica
BibInt	Biblical Interpretation
BIOSCS	The Bulletin of the International Organization of Septuagint and Cognate Studies
BT	The Bible Translator
BZ	Biblische Zeitschrift
CBQ	Catholic Biblical Quarterly
ETL	Ephemerides Theologicae Lovanienses
GRBS	Greek, Roman, and Byzantine Studies
HUCA	Hebrew Union College Annual
JECH	Journal of Early Christian History
JBL	Journal of Biblical Literature
JJS	Journal of Jewish Studies
JNSL	Journal of Northwest Semetic Languages
JSCS	Journal of Septuagint and Cognate Studies
JSJ	Journal for the Study of Judaism in the Persian, Hellenistic, and Roman Period
JTS	Journal of Theological Studies
HS	Hebrew Studies
OTE	Old Testament Essays
RB	Revue Biblique
ResQ	Restoration Quarterly
RevQ	Revue de Qumran
TZ	Theologische Zeitschrift
VT	Vetus Testamentum
ZAW	Zeitschrift für die Alttestamentliche Wissenschaft

Commentaries

AB	The Anchor Bible
ATD	Das Alte Testament Deutsch
BA	Bible d'Alexandrie
CEJL	Commentaries on Early Jewish Literature
HKAT	Handkommentar zum Alten Testament
ICC	The International Critical Commentary on the Holy Scriptures of the Old and New Testaments
KHC	Kurzer Hand-Commentar zum Alten Testament
NICOT	New International Commentary on the Old Testament
OTL	The Old Testament Library
SBLCS	Society of Biblical Literature Commentary on the Septuagint
SCS	Septuagint Commentary Series
WBC	Word Biblical Commentary

Texts, editions and translations

ArBib	The Aramaic Bible
BHS	Biblia Hebraica Stuttgartensia
BHQ	Biblia Hebraica Quinta
DJD	Discoveries in the Judean Desert
DSS	Dead Sea Scrolls
HBCE	The Hebrew Bible: A Critical Edition
LXX	Septuagint
MT	Masoretic text
NETS	New English Translation of the Septuagint
PTS	Patristische Texte und Studien

Dictionaries

BDB	Francis Brown, S. R. Driver & Charles A. Briggs' *A Hebrew and English Lexicon of the Old Testament*
DCH	David J. A. Clines's Dictionary of Classical Hebrew
GENESIUS	Wilhelm Genesius' Hebräischen und Aramäischen Handwörterbuch
GELS	Takamitsu Muraoka's A Greek-English Lexicon of the Septuagint
HALOT	William Holladay's A Concise Hebrew and Aramaic Lexicon of the Old Testament.
HTLS	Eberhard Bons' (ed.) Historical and Theological Lexicon of the Septuagint. Volume I: Alpha – Gamma
KBL	Ludwig Koehler & Walter Baumgartner's Hebräisches und Aramäisches Lexikon zum Alten Testament.

LEH	Johan Lust, Erik Eynikel & Katrin Hauspie's *Greek-English Lexicon of the Septuagint*
LSJ	Henry George Liddell, Robert Scott & Henry Stuart Jones's *A Greek-English Lexicon*
MSJ	Franco Montanari's The Brill Dictionary of Ancient Greek

Concordances

| **HR** | Edwin Hatch & Henry A. Redpath's Concordance to the Septuagint and Other Greek Versions of the Old Testament |

Other abbreviations

α´	Aquila
θ´	Theodotion
σ´	Symmachus
o´	οἱ ἑβδομήκοντα (Origen's LXX)
ε´	Quinta
※	asterisk

Introduction

In recent Septuagint (LXX) research a lot of attention has been given to the translators of the LXX and the translation technique(s) they applied to translate their Hebrew *Vorlage* into Greek. When using the term 'translation technique,' we denote the way in which the translator rendered his Hebrew *Vorlage* into Greek. However, this does not imply that the translator consciously opted for the application of one specific technique.[1] The study of the translation technique of

---

* This monograph follows the stream of thought as well as the research projects and articles of the research that has been conducted in the Centre for Septuagint Studies and Textual Criticism (CSSTC) (KU Leuven) and the Group de recherche 'Septante et critique textuelle' (UCLouvain). The centre has been founded by Prof. Dr. Johan Lust in 1988 at the Faculty of Theology and Religious Studies in Leuven and studies textual criticism and translation technique. Today, the centre in Leuven is supervised by Prof. Dr. Bénédicte Lemmelijn, whereas its French counterpart is supervised by Prof. Dr. Hans Ausloos. For more information regarding past and current research projects see http://theo.kuleuven.be/en/research/centres/centr_sept/, https://uclouvain.be/fr/instituts-recherche/rscs/sstc.html and Bénédicte Lemmelijn and Hans Ausloos, "Septuagint Studies in Louvain," in *The Present State of Old testament Studies in the Low Countries. A Collection of Old Testament Studies Published on the Occasion of the Seventy-Fifth Anniversary of the Oudtestamentisch Werkgezelschap*, ed. Klaas Spronk, OTS 69 (Leiden: Brill, 2016), 145–158. For more information regarding the content- and context-related approach that has been developed in Leuven, see, i.a., Hans Ausloos and Bénédicte Lemmelijn, "Content-Related Criteria in Characterising the LXX Translation Technique," in *Die Septuaginta. Texte, Theologien und Einflüsse. 2. Internationale Fachtagung veranstaltet von Septuaginta Deutsch (LXX.D), Wuppertal 23.-27. Juli 2008*, ed. Wolfgang Kraus, Martin Karrer and Martin Meiser, WUNT 252 (Tübingen: Mohr Siebeck, 2010), 356–376; Hans Ausloos and Bénédicte Lemmelijn, "Faithful Creativity Torn Between Freedom and Literalness in the Septuagint's Translations," *JNSL* 40.2 (2014): 53 –69.

1 Hereby, we follow the footsteps of the 'Finnish school' wherein Anneli Aejmelaeus plays a major role. In her article *What We Talk About When We Talk About Translation Technique*, she indicates what she means when speaking about translation technique: "I suggest that 'translation technique' be understood as simply designating the relationship between the text of the translation and its *Vorlage*. What is needed is a neutral term to denote the activity of the translator or the process of translation which led from the *Vorlage* to the translation, and I think that the term 'translation technique' actually suits this purpose very well. But 'translation technique' should not be thought of as a system acquired or developed or resorted to by the translators." Anneli Aejmelaeus, "What We Talk About When We Talk About Translation Technique," in *On the Trail of the Septuagint Translators. Collected Essays*, ed. Anneli Aejmelaeus, CBET 50 (Leuven — Paris — Dudley, MA: Peeters, 2007), 205–222, 205-206 (= Anneli Aejmelaeus, "What We Talk About When We Talk About Translation Technique," in *X Congress of the International Organization for Septuagint and Cognate Studies. Oslo, 1998*, ed. Bernard A. Taylor, SBLSCS 51 (Atlanta, GA: Society of Biblical Literature), 531–552). 205-206. In German the more

https://doi.org/10.1515/9783111041582-001

the LXX translators can, besides the knowledge about the LXX and its different books one might gain from it, help the discipline of textual criticism to come to a better assessment of the different textual witnesses.[2] By doing so, we can examine whether certain textual variants are to be ascribed to the translation technique(s) of the translator or to a different Hebrew *Vorlage* that differs from the *Vorlage* of the Masoretic Text (MT).

Different approaches

Due to the growing interest for these aspects, multiple approaches have been developed for studying the translation techniques of the LXX translators.[3] According to Bénédicte Lemmelijn we can distinguish two distinctive approaches: the quantitative and the qualitative approach.[4] Anneli Aejmelaeus, on the other hand, makes a threefold distinction:

> There is the more technical, statistical approach that interests itself in countable details of the relationship between the translation and its *Vorlage* [= quantitative approach]. There is the linguistic approach for which the main interest is the Greek language produced by

---

neutral term 'Übersetzungsweise' is used to denote the term 'translation technique.' Aejmelaeus has borrowed this term from her mentor Soisalon-Soininen. See Aejmelaeus, "What We Talk About," 205.

2 On the relationship between translation techniques and textual criticism see, e.g., Anneli Aejmelaeus, "What Can We Know about the Hebrew Vorlage of the Septuagint?," in *On the Trail of the Septuagint Translators. Collected Essays*, ed. Anneli Aejmelaeus, CBET 50 (Leuven − Paris − Dudley, MA: Peeters, 2007), 71–106.

3 See Anneli Aejmelaeus, "Translation Technique and the Intention of the Translator," in *On the Trail of the Septuagint Translators. Collected Essays*, ed. Anneli Aejmelaeus, CBET 50 (Leuven − Paris − Dudley, MA: Peeters, 2007), 59–69, 59: "This growing interest in translation techniques has brought about a diversity of studies that approach the common theme from different angles."

4 See Bénédicte Lemmelijn, "Two Methodological Trails in Recent Studies on the Translation Technique of the Septuagint," in *Helsinki Perspectives. On the Translation Technique of the Septuagint*, ed. Raija Sollamo and Seppo Sipilä, PFES 82 (Göttingen: Vandenhoeck & Ruprecht, 2001), 43–63; Bénédicte Lemmelijn, *A Plague of Texts? A Text-Critical Study of the So-Called 'Plague Narrative' in Exodus 7,14-11,10*, OTS 56 (Leiden − Boston: Brill, 2009), 96–125; Bénédicte Lemmelijn, "The Greek Rendering of Hebrew Hapax Legomena in LXX Proverbs and Job. A Clue to the Question of a Single Translator?," in *In the Footsteps of Sherlock Holmes. Studies in the Biblical Text in Honour of Anneli Aejmelaeus*, ed. in Timothy M. Law, Kristin De Troyer and Marketta Liljeström, CBET 72 (Leuven − Paris − Walpole, MA: Peeters, 2014), 133–150, 135–136.

the translators [= qualitative approach]. And there is the exegetical approach looking for interpretational elements in the translator's work.[5]

This third approach, which looks at content-related aspects of the translation, will be examined from a new and more specific approach: the so-called content- and context- related approach.

The quantitative approach was first introduced by James Barr in his work *The Topology of Literalism in Ancient Biblical Translations* and further elaborated by Emanuel Tov.[6] This approach takes the translation technique as study object and "different aspects of literalness as its starting point."[7] To examine whether a translator translated literal or not is more easy to determine than examining whether he translated freely.[8] This way, advocates of the quantitative approach

---

5 Aemelaeus, "Translation Technique and the Intention of the Translator," 59. See also A. Aejmelaeus, "What We Talk About," 205–222.

6 See, i.a., James Barr, *The Typology of Literalism in Ancient Biblical Translations*, MSU 15 (Göttingen: Vandenhoeck & Ruprecht, 1979); Emanuel Tov and Benjamin G. Wright, "Computer-Assisted Study of the Criteria for Assessing the Literalness of Translation Units in the LXX" *Textus* 12 (1985): 149–187 (= Emanuel Tov and Benjamin G. Wright, "Computer-Assisted Study of the Criteria for Assessing the Literalness of Translation Units in the LXX," in *The Greek and Hebrew Bible. Collected Essays on the Septuagint*, ed. Emanuel Tov, VTS 72 (Leiden: Brill, 1999), 219–237); Emanuel Tov, *The Text-Critical Use of the Septuagint in Biblical Research. Revised and Enlarged Second Edition*, JBS 8 (Jerusalem, Simor LTD., ²1997), 20–24; Emanuel Tov, *The Text-Critical Use of the Septuagint in Biblical Research. Third Edition, Completely Revised and Enlarged* (Winona Lake, IN: Eisenbrauns, 2015), 22–26; Emanuel Tov, "The Use of Computers in Biblical Research," in *Hebrew Bible, Greek Bible, and Qumran*, ed. Emanuel Tov, TSAJ 121 (Tübingen: Mohr Siebeck, 2008), 228–246. There are more scholars who follow the same methodological trail as Barr and Tov. See, e.g., Galen Marquis, "Consistency of Lexical Equivalents as a Criterion for the Evaluation of Translation Technique as Exemplified in the LXX of Ezekiel," in *VI Congress of the International Organization for Septuagint and Cognate Studies. Jerusalem, 1986*, ed. Claude E. Cox, SBLSCS 23 (Atlanta, GA: Scholars Press, 1987), 405–424; Benjamin G. Wright, "The Quantitative Representation of Elements. Evaluating 'Literalism' in the LXX," in *VI Congress of the International Organization for Septuagint and Cognate Studies. Jerusalem, 1986*, ed. Claude E. Cox, SBLSCS 23 (Atlanta, GA: Scholars Press, 1987), 311–335.

7 Lemmelijn, "Two Methodological Trails," 52. See also Anneli Aejmelaeus, "Introduction," in *On the Trail of the Septuagint Translators. Collected Essays*, ed. Anneli Aejmelaeus, CBET 50 (Leuven – Paris – Dudley, MA: Peeters, 2007), XIII–XVIII, XIII. For an overview of the different aspects of literalness as listed by Tov see Tov, *The Text-Critical Use of the Septuagint in Biblical Research*, 22–26.

8 Tov, *The Text-Critical Use of the Septuagint in Biblical Research*, 21: "When analysing translation techniques from the point of view of the translator's attitudes towards the Hebrew text, it is probably best to start from the criteria for literalness, not because literalness formed the basis of most translations, but rather because these criteria can be defined more easily than those for free renderings."

postulate that the degree of literalness of a certain book can be measured by means of statistic data and computer analysis.

On the other hand, there is the qualitative approach. This approach has been developed by the so-called 'Finnish or Helsinki school,' i.a., Raija Sollamo, Ilmari Soisalon-Soininen, Anneli Aejmelaeus and Seppo Sipilä.[9] Contrary to the study of the literalness of a translation, this approach focusses itself on the freedom of a translation. Instead of using computer techniques or statistics, as the quantitative approach, the qualitative approach performs its research by means of linguistic research.[10] "They posit that the study of the translation character of the Septuagint translations must take its starting point in the research of the way in which certain Hebrew grammatical features have been rendered in the Greek text."[11]

---

[9] For an overview of the works of these authors, see note 11 of the present chapter as well as chapter 1 of this book.

[10] Lemmelijn, "Two Methodological Trails," 49–51; Ausloos and Lemmelijn, "Content-Related Criteria in Characterising the LXX Translation Technique", 364–365.

[11] Lemmelijn, "Two Methodological Trails," 54–55. Examples of studies examining the Greek rendering of Hebrew grammatical features see, e.g., Raija Sollamo, *Renderings of Hebrew Semiprepositions in the Septuagint*, AASFDHL 19 (Helsinki: Suomalainen Tiedeakatemia, 1979); Raija Sollamo, "The LXX Renderings of the Infinitive Absolute Used with a Paronymous Finite Verb in the Pentateuch," in *La Septuaginta en la Investigación Contemporánea (V Congreso de la IOSCS)*, ed. Natalio Fernández Marcos, Textos y Estudios 'Cardinal Cisneros' 34 (Madrid: Instituto "Arias Montano," 1985), 101–113; Ilmari Soisalon-Soininen, "Renderings of Hebrew Comparative Expressions with מן in the Greek Pentateuch," in *Studien zur Septuaginta-Syntax*, ed. Ilmari Soisalon-Soininen, Anneli Aemelaeus and Raija Sollamo, AASF Series B 237 (Helsinki: Suomalainen Tiedeakatemia, 1987), 141–153; Anneli Aejmelaeus, "The Significance of Clause Connectors in the Syntactical and Translation-Technical Study of the Septuagint", in *On the Trail of the Septuagint Translators. Collected Essays*, ed. Anneli Aejmelaeus, CBET 50 (Leuven – Paris – Dudley, MA: Peeters, 2007), 43–57. Sometimes the Greek text is taken as a starting point in order to see how certain Greek grammatical features have been used to render the Hebrew *Vorlage*. See, e.g., Anneli Aejmelaeus, "Participium Coniunctum as a Criterion of Translation Technique," *VT* 32 (1982): 385–393 (= Anneli Aejmelaeus, "Participium Coniunctum as a Criterion of Translation Technique", in *On the Trail of the Septuagint Translators. Collected Essays*, ed. Anneli Aejmelaeus, CBET 50 (Leuven – Paris – Dudley, MA: Peeters, 2007), 1–10); Anneli Aejmelaeus, "Oti Causale in Septuaginal Greek," in *La Septuaginta en la Investigación Contemporánea (V Congreso de la IOSCS)*, ed. Natalio Fernández Marcos, Textos y Estudios 'Cardinal Cisneros' 34 (Madrid: Instituto "Arias Montano," 1985), 115–132 (= Anneli Aejmelaeus, "Oti Causale in Septuagintal Greek," in *On the Trail of the Septuagint Translators. Collected Essays*, ed. Anneli Aejmelaeus, CBET 50 (Leuven – Paris – Dudley, MA: Peeters, 2007), 11–29); Ilmari Soisalon-Soininen, "Der Gebrauch des genetivus absolutus in der Septuaginta," in in *Studien zur Septuaginta-Syntax*, ed. Ilmari Soisalon-Soininen, Anneli Aemelaeus and Raija Sollamo, AASF Series B 237 (Helsinki: Suomalainen Tiedeakatemia, 1987), 175–180;

Next to these two approaches a new approach that situates itself within the qualitative approach has been developed in Leuven the last decennium.[12] This approach focusses itself on content- and context-related criteria for the characterisation of the translation technique of the LXX books.[13] These criteria are based upon semantic situations which could have posed a difficulty for the LXX translator(s) and examine the way in which the translator(s) has/have dealt with them.[14] Examples of such difficult situations, that might serve as criteria, are, e.g., the rendering of Hebrew wordplay in the context of parallelism, Hebrew absolute *hapax legomena* and Hebrew wordplay in the context of aetiologies.[15] These situations are a challenge for the translator and forced him to make a specific choice of rendering.[16] "[…][T]he 'content- and context-related' approach could be compared to an artificially created laboratory situation in which a specific test is set up in order to elicit a reaction […]."[17] The translation of certain textual elements are being studied in order to describe

---

Anneli Aemelaeus, "Oti Recitativum in Septuagintal Greek," in *Studien zur Septuaginta. Robert Hanhart zu Ehren: aus Anlaß seines 65. Geburtstages*, ed Detlef Fraenkel, Udo Quast and John W. Wevers, MSU 20 (Göttingen: Vandenhoeck & Ruprecht, 1990), 74–82 (= Anneli Aemelaeus, "Oti Recitativum in Septuagintal Greek," in *On the Trail of the Septuagint Translators. Collected Essays*, ed. Anneli Aejmelaeus, CBET 50 (Leuven – Paris – Dudley, MA: Peeters, 2007), 30–41); Michael van der Meer, "The Use and Non-Use of the Particle οὖν in the Septuagint," in *In the Footsteps of Sherlock Holmes. Studies in the Biblical Text in Honour of Anneli Aejmelaeus*, ed. in Timothy M. Law, Kristin De Troyer and Marketta Liljeström, CBET 72 (Leuven – Paris – Walpole, MA: Peeters, 2014), 151–170; Ansi Voitila, "Μέλλω-Auxiliary Verb Construction in the Septuagint," in *In the Footsteps of Sherlock Holmes. Studies in the Biblical Text in Honour of Anneli Aejmelaeus*, ed. in Timothy M. Law, Kristin De Troyer and Marketta Liljeström, CBET 72 (Leuven – Paris – Walpole, MA: Peeters, 2014), 195–216.

12 The approach was introduced for the first time at the LXX.D-Tagung in Wuppertal in 2008. See Ausloos and Lemmelijn, "Content-Related Criteria in Characterising the LXX Translation Technique," 151, n. 25.

13 See Ausloos and Lemmelijn, "Content-Related Criteria in Characterising the LXX Translation Technique," 368.

14 See Lemmelijn, "The Greek Rendering of Hebrew Hapax Legomena," 137.

15 See, i.a., Ausloos and Lemmelijn, "Content-Related Criteria in Characterising the LXX Translation Technique;" Ausloos and Lemmelijn, "Faithful Creativity Torn Between Freedom and Literalness in the Septuagint's Translations," esp. 62–64; Lemmelijn, "The Greek Rendering of Hebrew Hapax Legomena," esp. 136–138; Lemmelijn and Ausloos, "Septuagint Studies in Louvain."

16 See Lemmelijn, "The Greek Rendering of Hebrew Hapax Legomena," 137.

17 "[…][T]he 'content- and context-related' approach could be compared to an artificially created laboratory situation in which a specific test is set up in order to elicit a reaction […]." Lemmelijn, "The Greek Rendering of Hebrew Hapax Legomena," 137.

and interpret the reaction, i.e., translation technique, of the translator in a very specific situation.[18]

The translation technique of LXX Proverbs

The present study will primarily focus itself on the characterisation of the translation technique of LXX Proverbs from the content- and context-related approach. Studies pertaining to the translation technique of LXX Proverbs are scarce. However, some effort has been made to analyse the translation technique of the LXX version of Proverbs. In this respect, the following scholars deserve credit for their valuable contribution to the research on LXX Proverbs: Paul de Lagarde,[19] Gillis Gerleman,[20] David-Marc d'Hammonville,[21] Michael V. Fox[22] and Johann Cook.[23] The latter can, in my opinion, be regarded as the most prominent scholar in research regarding LXX Proverbs today.[24]

---

18 See Lemmelijn, "The Greek Rendering of Hebrew Hapax Legomena," 137.

19 See Paul de Lagarde, *Anmerkungen zur Griechischen Übersetzung der Proverbien* (Leipzig: F. A. Brockhaus, 1863).

20 See Gillis Gerleman, *Studies in the Septuagint. III. The Book of Proverbs*, LUA 52.3 (Lund: Gleerup, 1956).

21 See David-Marc d'Hammonville, *Les Proverbes*, BA 17 (Paris: Les Éditions du Cerf, 2000).

22 See M. V. Fox, Proverbs. An Eclectic Edition with Introduction and Textual Commentary, HBCE 1 (Atlanta, GA: SBL Press, 2015).

23 Johann Cook is emeritus professor at the University of Stellenbosch (department Ancient Studies). He has published numerous articles on LXX Proverbs and is currently writing the SBL commentary on LXX Proverbs. The following references are a selection of his publications specifically concerning LXX Proverbs: Johann Cook, "Hellenistic Influence in the Septuagint Book of Proverbs," in *VII Congress of the International Organization for Septuagint and Cognate Studies. Leuven, 1989*, ed. Claude E. Cox, SBLSCS 31 (Atlanta, GA: Scholars Press, 1991), 341–353; Johann Cook, "The Dating of Septuagint Proverbs," *ETL* 69.4 (1993): 383–399; Johann Cook, "The Septuagint as Contextual Bible Translation. Alexandria or Jerusalem as Context for Proverbs?," *JNSL* 19 (1993): 25–39; Johann Cook, "A Comparison of Proverbs and Jeremiah in the Septuagint," *JNSL* 20.1 (1994): 49–58; Johann Cook, "'ishah zarah (Proverbs 1-9 Septuagint): A Metaphor for Foreign Wisdom?," *ZAW* 106/3 (1994): 458–476; Johann Cook, "The Septuagint Proverbs as a Jewish-Hellenistic Document," in *VIII Congress of the International Organization for Septuagint and Cognate Studies*, ed. Leonard J. Greenspoon Olivier Munnich, SBLSCS 41 (Atlanta, GA: Scholars Press, 1995), 349–365; Johann Cook, "Aspects of the Translation Technique Followed by the Translator of LXX Proverbs," *JNSL* 22.1 (1996): 143–153; Johann Cook, "The Hexaplaric Text, Double Translation and Other Textual Phenomena in the Septuagint (Proverbs)," *JNSL* 22.2 (1996): 129–140; Johann Cook, "Aspects of the Relationship between the Septuagint Versions of Proverbs and Job," in *IX Congress of the International Organization for Septuagint and Cognate Studies, Cambridge, 1995*, ed. B. A. Taylor, SBLSCS, 45 (Atlanta, GA: Scholars Press,

1997), 309–328; Johann Cook, "Contrasting as a Translation Technique in the LXX of Proverbs," in *The Quest for Context and Meaning. Studies in Biblical Intertextuality in Honor of James A. Sanders*, ed. Craig Evans and Shemaryahu Talmon (Leiden: Brill, 1997), 403–414; Johann Cook, "The Law in the Septuagint Proverbs," *JNSL* 23.1 (1997): 211–223; Johann Cook, *The Septuagint of Proverbs. Jewish and/or Hellenistic Proverbs? Concerning the Hellenistic Colouring of LXX Proverbs*, SVT 69 (Leiden — New York — Köln: Brill, 1997); Johann Cook, "Septuagint Proverbs and Canonization," in *Canonization & Decanonization. Papers Presented to the International Conference of the Leiden Institute for the Study of Religions (LISOR) Held at Leiden 9-10 January 1997*, ed. Arie van der Kooij and Karel van der Toorn (Leiden: Brill, 1998), 79–91; Johann Cook, "Apocalyptic Terminology in Septuagint Proverbs," *JNSL* 25.1 (1999): 251–264; Johann Cook, "Contextual Exegetical Interpretations in the Septuagint Proverbs," *JNSL* 25.2 (1999): 132–146; Johann Cook, "The Law of Moses in Septuagint Proverbs," *VT* 49.4 (1999): 448–461; Johann Cook, "Textual Problems in the Septuagint of Proverbs," *JNSL* 26.1 (2000): 171–179; Johann Cook, "Lexical Issues Septuagint of Proverbs," *JNSL* 26.2 (2000): 163–173; Johann Cook, "The Ideology of Septuagint Proverbs," in *X Congress of the International Organization for Septuagint and Cognate Studies. Oslo, 1998*, ed. Bernard A. Taylor, SBLSCS 51 (Atlanta, GA: Society of Biblical Literature, 2001), 463–479; Johann Cook, "Intertextual Relationships Between the Septuagint of Psalms and Proverbs," in *The Old Greek Psalter. Studies in Honour of Albert Pietersma*, ed. Robert V. J. Hiebert, Claude E. Cox and Peter J. Gentry, JSOTSS 332 (Sheffield: Sheffield Academic Press, 2001), 218–228; Johann Cook, "Towards a Computerised Exegetical Commentary of the Septuagint Version of Proverbs," in *Computer and Bible. The Stellenbosch AIBI-6 Conference: Proceedings of the Association Internationale Bible et Informatique 'From Alpha to Byte', University of Stellenbosch 17-21 July, 2002*, ed. Johann Cook (Leiden: Brill, 2002), 421–433; Johann Cook, "The Translator(s) of the Septuagint of Proverbs," *TC: A Journal of Biblical Textual Criticism* 7 (2002): http://rosetta.reltech.org/TC/v07/Cook2002.html; Johann Cook, "Unit Delimitation in the Book of Proverbs. In the Light of the Septuagint of Proverbs," in *Studies in Scriptural Unit Division*, ed. Marjo Korpel and Josef M. Oesch, Pericope 3 (Assen: Royal Van Gorcum, 2002), 46–65; Johann Cook, "The Greek of Proverbs. Evidence of a Recensionally Deviating Hebrew Text?," in *Emanuel. Studies in Hebrew Bible, Septuagint, and Dead Sea Scrolls in Honor of Emanuel Tov*, ed. Shalom M. Paul, Robert A. Kraft, Lawrence H. Schiffman and Weston W. Fields (Leiden — Boston: Brill, 2003), 605–618; Johann Cook, "The Theory and Practice of Textual Criticism. Reconstructing the Old Greek of Proverbs 8," *OTE* 17.4 (2004): 531–543; Johann Cook, "The Text-Critical Value of the Septuagint of Proverbs," in *Seeking Out the Wisdom of the Ancients. Essays in Honor of Michael V. Fox on the Occasion of His Sixty-Fifth Birthday*, ed. Ronald L. Troxel, Kelvin G. Friebel and Dennis R. Magary (Winona Lake, IN: Eisenbrauns, 2005), 409–419; Johann Cook, "Theological/Ideological Tendenz in the Septuagint. LXX Proverbs a Case Study," in *Interpreting Translation. Studies on the LXX and Ezekiel in Honour of Johan Lust*, ed. Florentino García Martínez and Marc Vervenne, BETL 192 (Leuven: Peeters – University Press, 2005), 65–79; Johann Cook, "Exegesis in the Septuagint of Proverbs," in *Stimulation from Leiden. Collected Communications to the XVIIIth Congress of the International Organisation for the Study of the Old Testament, Leiden 2004*, ed. Hermann M. Niemann and Matthias Augustin, BEATAJ 54 (Peter Lang: Frankfurt am Main, 2006), 187–198; Johann Cook, "Proverbs," in *A New English Translation of the Septuagint. And the Other Greek Translations Traditionally Included under That Title*, ed. Albert Pietersma and Benjamin G. Wright (New York, NY

In order to acquire an accurate *status quaestionis* concerning the characterisation of the translation technique of Proverbs, the results of the quantitative, quantitative and the Louvain approach as well as the results of the studies of Johann Cook will be examined and compared with one another in the first chapter of this monograph.[25] By examining these three approaches and comparing them, we follow the footsteps of Anneli Aejmelaeus who posits that multiple results of different approaches need to be compared with one another in order to come to a more nuanced and adequate image of the translators and the translation technique(s) they used to translate their Hebrew *Vorlage*.[26] By doing so, we will provide an exhaustive overview of the results of the study of the translation technique of LXX Proverbs in the present state of scholarship. This way, this *status quaestionis* will be the foundation of our further and own investigation with regard to the translation technique of LXX Proverbs.

After having analysed the scholarly opinions on the translation technique of LXX Proverbs, we will examine its translation technique by means of the content- and context- related approach. More specifically we will examine the Greek rendering of Hebrew *hapax legomena* in Proverbs. As already elaborately demonstrated by Hans Ausloos, Bénédicte Lemmelijn and Elke Verbeke, *hapax legomena* can be regarded as a content- and context- related criterion since they

---

— Oxford: Oxford University Press), 2007, 621–647; Johann Cook, "The Translator of the Septuagint of Proverbs. Is His Style the Result of Platonic and/or Stoic Influence?," in *Die Septuaginta. Texte, Kontexte, Lebenswelten. Internationale Fachtagung veranstaltet von Septuaginta Deutsch (LXX.D), Wuppertal 20.-23. Juli 2006*, ed. Martin Karrer, Wolfgang Kraus and Martin Meiser, WUNT 219 (Tübingen: Mohr Siebeck, 2008), 559–571; Johann Cook, "The Relevance of Exegetical Commentaries on the Septuagint. LXX Proverbs 1:1-7 as an Example," *OTE* 23.1 (2010): 28–43; Johann Cook, "Were the LXX Versions of Proverbs and Job Translated by the Same Person?," *HS* 51 (2010): 129–156; Johann Cook, "A Case Study of LXX Proverbs, LXX Job and 4 Maccabees," in *Die Septuaginta. Orte und Intentionen. 5. Internationale Fachtagung veranstaltet von Septuaginta Deutsch (LXX.D), Wuppertal 24.-27. Juli 2014*, ed. Siegfried Kreuzer et al., WUNT 361 (Tübingen: Mohr Siebeck, 2016), 59–77.

24 Although Johann Cook can be regarded as one of the most prominent scholars working on LXX Proverbs today and not a lot of monographs dealing specifically with LXX Proverbs have been published in recent years, it is worth mentioning that several scholars have focussed on LXX Proverbs for their doctoral dissertation. See, e.g., Lorenzo Cuppi, "Long Doublets in the Septuagint of the Book of Proverbs: With a History of the Research on the Greek Translations" (PhD diss. University of Durham, 2012); Silly Renaud, *Les grands mystères de la sagesse. Proverbes de Salomon 8 & 9 dans la version des Septante* (Paris: Les Belles Lettres, 2020).

25 Although the main focus will be on the different approaches and Johann Cook, it is self-evident that other secondary literature, especially works related to the translation technique of LXX Proverbs, will be integrated in the discussion.

26 See Aejmelaeus, "What We Talk About," 222.

might have posed a difficulty for the translator to render.[27] Thus, in the second chapter of this monograph, the Hebrew *hapax legemona* and their respective Greek rendering in Proverbs will be registered. Afterwards, these Greek translations will be analysed, discussed and evaluated in order to come to a more nuanced characterisation of the translation technique of LXX Proverbs.

Specific theology of the LXX?

Next to the question of the translation technique, recent LXX scholarship has paid more attention to the question of a specific theology of the LXX corpus[28]. Recently, however, several scholars have tried to characterise the theology of different individual LXX books.[29] With respect to the LXX version of Proverbs, it is once again Cook who has examined whether or not LXX Proverbs contains a

---

27 See Hans Ausloos and Bénédicte Lemmelijn, "Rendering Love. Hapax Legomena and the Characterisation of the Translation Technique of Song of Songs," in *Translating a Translation. The LXX and its Modern Translations in the Context of Early Judaism*, ed. Hans Ausloos et al., BETL 213 (Leuven – Paris – Dudley, MA: Peeters, 2008), 43–61; Hans Ausloos, "The Septuagint's Rendering of Hebrew Hapax Legomena and the Characterization of Its 'Translation Technique': The Case of Exodus," *Acta Patristica et Byzantina* 20 (2009): 360–376; Elke Verbeke, "The Use of Hebrew Hapax Legomena in Septuagint Studies. Preliminary Remarks on Methodology," in *Florilegium Lovaniense. Studies in Septuagint and Textual Criticism in Honour of Florentino García Martínez*, ed. Hans Ausloos, Bénédicte Lemmelijn and Marc Vervenne, BETL 224 (Leuven – Paris – Dudley, MA: Peeters, 2008), 507–521; Elke Verbeke, "Hebrew Hapax Legomena and their Greek Rendering in LXX Job" (PhD diss., KU Leuven, 2011); Hans Ausloos and Bénédicte Lemmelijn, "Characterizing the LXX Translation of Judges on the Basis of Content-Related Criteria. The Greek Rendering of Hebrew Absolute Hapax Legomena in Judg 3,12-30," in *After Qumran. Old and Modern Editions of the Biblical Texts – The Historical Books*, ed. Hans Ausloos, Bénédicte Lemmelijn and Julio Trebolle Barrera, BETL 246 (Leuven – Paris – Dudley, MA: Peeters, 2012), 171–192.
28 For a short overview on the development of the attention for a specific theology of the LXX, see Martin Rösel, "Towards a 'Theology of the Septuagint'," in *Septuagint Research. Issues and Challenges in the Study of the Greek Jewish Scriptures*, ed. Wolfgang Kraus and R. Glenn Wooden, SBLSCS 53 (Atlanta, GA: Society of Biblical Literature, 2006), 239–252, 240–241 (= Martin Rösel,, "Towards a 'Theology of the Septuagint'," in *Tradition and Innovation. English and German Studies on the Septuagint*, ed. Martin Rösel, SBLSCS 70 (Atlanta, GA: Society of Biblical Literature, 2018), 253–272).
29 In this regard, see especially the volume of *Handbuch zur Septuaginta* that deals with the theology of the LXX: Hans Ausloos and Bénédicte Lemmelijn, ed., *Die Theologie der Septuaginta / The Theology of the Septuagint*, LXX.H 5 (Gütersloh: Gütersloher Verlagshaus, 2020).

specific and different theology compared to its Hebrew counterpart.[30] In his view, the translator of LXX Proverbs was a conservative Jew who tried to put more emphasis on the Mosaic Law and tried to warn his readers against foreign (Hellenistic) wisdom.[31] Although Cook's study has shed more light on the specific theology of LXX Proverbs, it is the only study that has elaborately tried to do so.[32]

In order to contribute to a more precise and adequate description of the theology of LXX Proverbs, this study will look at the LXX verses in which ὁ κύριος and ὁ θεός have been attested and which have no counterpart in the Hebrew Masoretic Text (MT).[33] Thus, the present study will not look at the rendering of the Hebrew nouns יהוה or אלהים as such.

I am of the opinion that looking at the pluses containing ὁ κύριος and ὁ θεός, thus without any equivalent in the MT, will reveal more information on an alleged theology of the LXX translator,[34] since it is based on the explicit differ-

---

30 See, i.a., Cook, *The Septuagint of Proverbs*; Cook, "Contrasting as a Translation Technique;" Johann Cook, "Exegesis in the Septuagint," in *JNSL* 30.1 (2004): 1-19; Cook, "Exegesis in the Septuagint of Proverbs;" Johann Cook., "Towards a Formulation of a Theology of the Septuagint," in *Congress Volume Ljubljana 2007*, ed. André Lemaire, VTS 133 (Leiden – Boston, MA: Brill, 2010), 621–640; Johann Cook, "Interpreting the Septuagint," in *Congress Volume Stellenbosch 2016*, ed. Louis C. Jonker, Gideon R. Kotzé and Christl M. Maier, VTS 177 (Leiden – Boston, MA: Brill, 2017), 1–22.
31 See, i.a., Cook, "The Dating of Septuagint Proverbs," 397; Cook, "The Law of Moses in Septuagint Proverbs," 460; Cook, "The Translator of the Septuagint of Proverbs," 635–636.
32 Other scholars have (often briefly) touched upon the religious colouring and theology of LXX Proverbs but not as elaborated as Cook has done. See, e.g., Gerleman *Proverbs*, esp. 36–57; d'Hamonville, *Les Proverbes*, 113–128; Fox, *Proverbs*, 43–45. In the *Handbuch zur Septuaginta*, focusses on the theology of the LXX, there are several articles that deal with wisdom literature and thus also with Proverbs: Johann Cook, "Man Before God," in *Die Theologie der Septuaginta / The Theology of the Septuagint*, ed. Hans Ausloos and Bénédicte Lemmelijn, LXX.H 5 (Gütersloh: Gütersloher Verlagshaus, 2020), 301– 335; Markus Witte, "Weisheitsschriften," in *Die Theologie der Septuaginta / The Theology of the Septuagint*, ed. Hans Ausloos and Bénédicte Lemmelijn, LXX.H 5 (Gütersloh: Gütersloher Verlagshaus, 2020), 83–98; Frank Ueberschaer, "Weisheit," in *Die Theologie der Septuaginta / The Theology of the Septuagint*, ed. Hans Ausloos and Bénédicte Lemmelijn, LXX.H 5 (Gütersloh: Gütersloher Verlagshaus, 2020), 137–147.
33 Martin Rösel has stressed the importance of the study of the Greek rendering of the Hebrew designation of God. See Martin Rösel, "Towards a "Theology of the Septuagint," 245–248; Martin Rösel, "The Reading and Translation of the Divine Name in the Masoretic Tradition and the Greek Pentateuch – with an Appendix: Frank Shaw's Book on ΙΑΩ," in *Tradition and Innovation. English and German Studies on the Septuagint*, ed. Martin Rösel, SBLSCS 70 (Atlanta, GA: SBL, 2018), 291–315.
34 With the term 'plus', we denote a sentence or part of a sentence that is attested in the target text (here the LXX) but not in the source text (MT or Hebrew *Vorlage*). When a sentence or part

ences.[35] Moreover, the analysis of these extra attestations will also shed some light on the translation technique of the LXX translator. The theology of LXX Proverbs (and LXX Job, see below) will be the object of the third chapter.

Unum et unum sunt unum?

Besides providing a more nuanced characterisation of the translation technique and the theology of LXX Proverbs, this monograph also aims at providing an indicative but relevant answer to the question of a single translator for LXX Proverbs and LXX Job. This question has been introduced by Gillis Gerleman in his work *Studies in the Septuagint. I. The Book of Job* published in 1946.[36] According-ing to Gerleman, LXX Job and LXX Proverbs show some similarities regarding linguistics and vocabulary[37]. Later, in his work on LXX Proverbs,[38] he indicates other similarities between the two books, i.e., the use of the same expressions and the tendency to Hellenise biblical matters.[39] Once again he concludes that

---

of a sentence is attested in the source text but not in the target text, we talk about a 'minus.' These terms are being used descriptively and do not yet entail, in contrast to the terms 'addition' and 'omission,' any evaluation of a particular textual variant. See Lemmelijn, *A Plague of Texts*, 23, n. 84.

35 The focus on differences between MT and the LXX in order to detect a theology of a certain LXX book has been posited by several scholars. See, i.a., Evangelia Dafni, "Theologie der Sprache der Septuaginta," *TZ* 58 (2002): 315–328, 327; Anneli Aejmelaeus, "Von Sprache zur Theologie. Methodologische Überlegungen zur Theologie der Septuaginta," in *The Septuagint and Messia-nism*, ed. Michael A. Knibb, BETL 195 (Leuven: Peeters, 2006), 21–48, 30; Cook, "Towards the Formulation of a Theology of the Septuagint," 622; Hans Ausloos, "Sept défis posés à une theologie de la Septante," in *Congress Volume Stellenbosch 2016*, ed. Louis C. Jonker, Gideon R. Kotzé and Christl M. Maier, VTS 177 (Leiden – Boston, MA: Brill, 2017), 249–250; Hans Ausloos and Bénédicte Lemmelijn, "Theology or not? That's the Question. Is There Such a Thing as 'The Theology of the Septuagint'?," in *Die Theologie der Septuaginta / The Theology of the Septuagint*, ed. Hans Ausloos and Bénédicte Lemmelijn, LXX.H 5 (Gütersloh: Gütersloher Verlagshaus, 2020), 19–45.

36 "It seems incontestable that a distinct connection exists between Job and Proverbs in the LXX, a connection which cannot be satisfactorily explained by referring to the fact that both books belong to the same category, the literature of wisdom. This fact rather supports the pre-sumption that both translators originate from the same hand." Gillis Gerleman, *Studies in the Septuagint. I. The Book of Job*, LUA 43.2 (Lund: Gleerup, 1946), 16–17.

37 See Gerleman, *Job*, 15–17.

38 See Gerleman, *Proverbs*.

39 See Gerleman, *Proverbs*, 59-60.

both LXX Job and LXX Proverbs have been translated by one and the same person (or group of persons).[40]

Following Gerleman, other scholars have also tried to formulate an answer to the question of a single translator for LXX Job and LXX Proverbs. John G. Gammie was the first one to react against Gerleman. In his work *The Septuagint of Job. Its Poetic Style and Relationship to the Septuagint of Proverbs*,[41] he examines (a) several poetical and stylistic tendencies in LXX Job, which have not been examined in previous research and (b) reassesses the linguistic features which Gerleman has used to base his hypotheses upon.[42] The result is threefold:

> Some common background between Greek Proverbs and Greek Job may be granted on the basis of some similarities in poetic style and some shared vocabulary. (2) On the other hand, even when allowances are made for variations in style, diction, and vocabulary in the Hebrew originals, differences in style and in kind of openness to Greek culture in the translations are sufficient to cast doubt on the hypothesis of a common translator. (3) Most telling are the differences in diction (particles, prepositions, and the like) and in the manner in which the same Hebrew words are rendered so differently in Greek.[43]

According to Gammie, the second and third argument lead to the conclusion that LXX Job and LXX Proverbs were definitely not translated by one and the same translator or group of translators.[44] Johann Cook also shares the opinion of Gammie that both books were not translated by the same translator.[45]

---

40 Claude Cox posits that LXX Job and LXX Proverbs originated from the same group of translators. However, they were not written by the same translator because LXX Proverbs is not shortened, whereas LXX Job is. Therefore, both texts can be seen as different kinds of texts. See Claude E. Cox, "The Historical, Social & Literary Context of Old Greek Job," in *XII Congress of the International Organisation for Septuagint and Cognate Studies, Leiden, 2004*, ed. Melvin K. H. Peters, SBLSCS 54 (Atlanta, GA: Society of Biblical Literature, 2006), 105–116, 116. D'Hamonville shares Cox's opinion. See d'Hammonville, *Les Proverbes*, 139–141 (esp. 141): "[...][N]otre enquête lexicale ferait plutôt penser à deux traducteurs distincts mais issus d'un même milieu d'origine [...]."
41 John G. Gammie, "The Septuagint of Job. Its Poetic Style and Relationship to the Septuagint of Proverbs," *CBQ* 49.1 (1987): 14–31.
42 Gammie, "The Septuagint of Job," 15.
43 Gammie, "The Septuagint of Job," 30. The latter is also implied by Jan de Waard who argues that the Hebrew קֶרֶת is not known by the translator of Proverbs, contrary to the LXX translator of Job. See Jan de Waard, "Indices phonétiques hébreux dans et derrière le grec de la Septante de Proverbes," in *L'apport de la Septante aux études sur l'Antiquité*, ed. Jan Joosten and Philippe Le Moigne (ed.), Lectio Divina (Paris: Les Éditions du Cerf, 2005), 105–117, 107.
44 Gammie, "The Septuagint of Job," 30–31.
45 See Cook, "Aspects of the Relationship between the Septuagint Versions of Proverbs and Job," 328 and esp. Cook, "Were the LXX Versions of Proverbs and Job," 129–156. Cook argues

Nonetheless, there are scholars, e.g., Gilles Dorival, Julio Trebolle Barrera and Jean-Daniel Kaestli, who, explicitly or implicitly and contrary to Gammie and Cook, share the same opinion as Gerleman.[46]

On the basis of the above-mentioned analysis of the *status quaestionis* with regard to the question of a single translator for LXX Job and LXX Proverbs, it is clear that current scholarship is still undecided. Therefore, against this background, this monograph also aims at providing an indicative but relevant answer to the question of a single translator by comparing the results of the research on the Greek rendering of Hebrew *hapax legomena* in both LXX Job (Verbeke's study) and LXX Proverbs (present study).[47] However, since Verbeke has only analysed the Hebrew hapaxes in the speeches of Job and God, this monograph will also register and evaluate the Greek rendering of Hebrew *hapax legomena* in the prologue, the speeches of Job's friends and epilogue of Job. This in order to come to a more complete picture on how the LXX translator of Job rendered Hebrew hapaxes and to make a more accurate comparison with the results obtained in the study on the translation of Hebrew hapaxes in LXX Proverbs.

---

that the following criteria need to be analysed if one wants to answer the question of one or multiple translators: (a) linguistic criteria (*i.e.* lexical and syntactic/stylistic) and (b) arguments concerning content. In his article *Were the LXX Versions of Proverbs and Job Translated by the Same Person?* he only analyses the last criterion by examining the presentation of the concepts of wisdom and creation in LXX Proverbs and LXX Job. See Cook, "Aspects of the Relationship between the Septuagint Versions of Proverbs and Job," 132ff. The results of this study will be presented and discussed in chapter 1.

46 See Gilles Dorival, "L'Achèvement de la Septante dans le Judaïsme. De la faveur au rejet," in *La bible grecque des Septante. Du judaïsme hellénistique au christianisme ancient* (ICA), ed. Marguerite Harl, Gilles Dorival and Olivier Munnich (Paris: Cerf, 1988), 83–125, 105; Julio Trebolle Barrera, *The Jewish Bible and the Christian Bible. An Introduction to the History of the Bible* (Leiden – New York, NY – Köln: Brill; Grand Rapids, MI – Cambridge: Eerdmans, 1998), 319; Jean-Daniel Kaestli, "La formation et la structure du canon biblique. Que peut apporter l'étude de la septante," in *The Canon of Scripture in Jewish and Christian Tradition. Le Canon des Écritures dans les traditions juive et chrétienne*, ed. Philip S. Alexander and Jean-Daniel Kaestli, PIRSB 4 (Lausanne: Les Éditions du Zébre, 2007), 99–113, 106; Lemmelijn"The Greek Rendering of Hebrew Hapax Legomena," 135 (esp. n. 7).

47 For Verbeke's study on the Greek rendering of Hebrew *hapax legomena* in LXX Job see Verbeke, "Hebrew Hapax Legomena." The results of this study will be outlined in chapter 1 and chapter 2 of this monograph. For a preliminary comparison of the Greek rendering of Hebrew *hapax legomena* in LXX Job and LXX Proverbs see the pilot study of Bénédicte Lemmelijn: Lemmelijn, "The Greek Rendering of Hebrew Hapax Legomena."

Moreover, next to the analysis of the extra attestations of ὁ κύριος and ὁ θεός in LXX Proverbs, the same methodology will be applied for LXX Job and their results will be compared with one another in order to give a more accurate answer to the question of a single translator. By doing so, the comparison of the results on the translation technique and the theology of both books will provide an adequate answer to the question of a single translator.

1 *Status Quaestionis*: the characterisation of the translation technique of LXX Proverbs

As already indicated in the introduction, we can distinguish three approaches that enable us to characterise the translation technique of the different LXX translators: the quantitative, qualitative and content- and context-related approach. In this first chapter the results of these approaches with regard to LXX Proverbs will be examined and discussed. Next to these approaches we will also present the results of Johann Cook with regard to the translation technique of LXX Proverbs. Cook has extensively written on the subject and can therefore be seen as one of the most influential scholars on Proverbs nowadays. By doing so, this chapter aims at providing an exhaustive overview of the *status quaestionis* concerning the characterisation of the translation technique of Proverbs.

1.1 The quantitative approach

In this section the quantitative approach and its characterisation of the translation technique of LXX Proverbs will be discussed. This approach examines the degree of literalness of a given translation. According to some scholars, literalness can be measured objectively. Therefore, the degree of literalness is often measured and presented by means of statistic and computer data. The degree of literalness of LXX Proverbs can be measured by using this approach. Nonetheless, its seems that only James Barr and Emanuel Tov have examined the literal character of LXX Proverbs. Therefore, we will thoroughly analyse the quantitative approach and the way in which it characterises LXX Proverbs in the following sections. First, we will discuss the methodological framework of the approach as it is defined by James Barr and Emanuel Tov. Simultaneously, special attention will be given to the way in which these two authors have characterised the translation technique of LXX Proverbs.

1.1.1 James Barr

As indicated above, James Barr can be seen as the founding father of the quantitative approach. In his work *The Typology of Literalism in Ancient Biblical Trans-*

https://doi.org/10.1515/9783111041582-002

lations he examines how one can distinguish a literal from a free translation. This distinction can be made on the basis of the following criteria:[1]

(1) The division into elements or segments, and the sequence in which these elements are represented;
(2) The quantitative addition or subtraction of elements;
(3) Consistency or non-consistency in the rendering, i.e., the degree to which a particular versional term is used for all (or most) cases of a particular term of the original;
(4) Accuracy and level of semantic information, especially in cases of metaphor and idiom;
(5) Coded 'etymological' indication of formal/semantic relationships obtaining in the vocabulary of the original language;
(6) Level of text and level of analysis.

In the following section the above-mentioned criteria will be discussed with special attention for LXX Proverbs.

1.1.1.1 Barr's criteria for the determination of literalness
A The division into elements or segments, and the sequence in which these elements are represented

A literal translation shows the tendency to divide the text into word units and to translate these separately. On the one hand, the division may occur by translating every Hebrew element with a corresponding Greek element. This technique is called quantitative representation.[2] Another possibility is that the translator divides a Hebrew word that entails multiple words and translates it by corresponding Greek words. This practice is called segmentation.[3]

An example of segmentation is the translation of Hebrew temporal clauses (constructions containing ב + infinitive + noun or suffix) into Greek.[4] A free translation will start such sentences with a temporal adverb, e.g., ὅτε. Literal translations, on the other hand, will translate the Hebrew sentence word by

---

1 See Barr, *The Typology of Literalism*, 294. Staffan Olofsson also applies these 5 categories of Barr in order to characterise literal translations. See Staffan Olofsson, *The LXX Version. A Guide to the Translation Technique of the Septuagint*, CBOTS 30 (Stockholm: Almqvist och Wiksell, 1990), 12–26.
2 See Wright, "The Quantitative Representation of Elements. Evaluating 'Literalism' in the LXX," 314–315.
3 See Wright, "The Quantitative Representation of Elements," 315.
4 See Barr, The Typology of Literalism, 294–295.

word. This becomes visible in the rendering of the Hebrew 'ב + infinitive' to the Greek 'ἐν τῷ + infinitive'.

The degree with which the segmentation takes place differs according to the translation. In the worst case scenario, as is the case with the revision translation of Aquila, it leads to an incorrect representation of the *Vorlage* and by doing so the message the text wants to convey is distorted.[5] However, this may not be the case with every literal translation that divides and renders word units. In the majority of the cases, the meaning of the *Vorlage* is more or less preserved. Free translations exhibit a higher tendency to translate the sentence as one single unit without dividing it in exactly the same amount of word units.

Looking at the LXX translation of Proverbs, we can see that the translator did not divide the word units but instead translated them as one unit.[6] Concerning temporal clauses, the LXX translator of Proverbs follows the method ascribed to free translations.[7] He translates temporal clauses using adverbs such as ἡνίκα, ὅτε and ὡς (see, e.g., Prov 8:27-28).[8]

B   The quantitative addition or subtraction of elements

It often occurs that translations add or leave out words from the original text.[9] This gives the translation a less literal character. Literal translations try to render each linguistic element that is present in the original text. When elements that are not attested in the original text are being added or left out, we can characterise the translation as a free translation. Moreover, additions can often be seen as the exegetical activity of the translator.[10]

LXX Proverbs contains a lot of additions. Therefore, LXX Proverbs can be regarded as a free translation according to Barr. An example of such an addition is Prov 16:2:[11]

---

5 See Barr, *The Typology of Literalism*, 300. Barr denotes this type of literalism as 'extreme literalism'. For some examples hereof, taken from the translation of Aquila, see Barr, *The Typology of Literalism*, 26–27.

6 See Barr, The Typology of Literalism, 295.

7 See Barr, The Typology of Literalism, 295.

8 See Barr, The Typology of Literalism, 295.

9 See Barr, The Typology of Literalism, 303–304.

10 See Barr, *The Typology of Literalism*, 304: "Thus expansions are often not *mere* additions, they are exegetical provisions of context." Additions can, however, also be non-intentional 'mistakes' the copyist or scribe has made in the process of copying or translating the text. An example is dittography (i.e., the duplication of a letter, word or passage).

11 The English translation for the LXX version of Proverbs is taken from the NETS translation made by Johann Cook. See Johann Cook, "Proverbs," in *A New English Translation of the Septu-*

MT	LXX
כָּל־דַּרְכֵי־אִישׁ זַךְ בְּעֵינָיו וְתֹכֵן רוּחוֹת יְהוָה:	πάντα τὰ ἔργα τοῦ ταπεινοῦ φανερὰ παρὰ τῷ θεῷ, οἱ δὲ ἀσεβεῖς ἐν ἡμέρᾳ κακῇ ὀλοῦνται.
All one's ways may be pure in one's own eyes, but the Lord weighs the spirit.	All the works of the humble are manifest with God, but the impious shall perish in an evil day.

The second colon of Prov 16:2 in the LXX version, i.e., οἱ δὲ ἀσεβεῖς ἐν ἡμέρᾳ κακῇ ὀλοῦνται, is a major 'plus' that is absent in the Hebrew text.[12] This addition might be explained by the interpretative activity of the translator (see above) but can also be ascribed to a *Vorlage* that differed (substantially) from the one of MT.[13] The Hebrew *Vorlage* that the LXX translator had in front of him might have had additional verses that were not present in the *Vorlage* that has been used to form MT.

---

agint. And the Other Greek Translations Traditionally Included under That Title, ed. Albert Pietersma and Benjamin G. Wright (New York, NY — Oxford: Oxford University Press, 2007), 621–647. The English translation for the MT-version is taken from the NRSV.

12 With 'plus' we denote a sentence or part of a sentence that is attested in the target text but not in the source text. When a sentence or part of a sentence is attested in the source text but not in the target text, we talk about a 'minus'. These terms are being used descriptively and does not yet entail, in contrast to the terms 'addition' and 'omission', an evaluation of a particular textual variant. See Lemmelijn, *A Plague of Texts*, 23, n. 84.

13 See Emanuel Tov, "Recensional Differences Between the Masoretic Text and the Septuagint of Proverbs," in *The Greek & Hebrew Bible. Collected Essays on the Septuagint*, ed. Emanuel Tov (Leiden: Brill, 1999), 419–431. In this article, Tov talks about different revisions of a text that have emerged throughout the years. In my opinion, in current research that stresses the multi- and pluriformity of texts, it is better to speak of different versions of a text that existed next to each other and can be seen as equal to each other. See Hans Debel, "Rewritten Bible, Variant Literary Editions and OriginalText(s). Exploring the Implications of a Pluriform Outlook on the Scriptural Tradition," in *Changes in Scripture: Rewriting and Interpreting Authoritative Traditions in the Second Temple Period*, ed. Hanne von Weissenberg, Marko Martilla and Juha Pakkala, BZAW 419 (Berlin – New York, NY: Walter de Gruyter, 2011), 65–91. By using the word 'revision' Tov seems to consider the LXX version as a modification of the original Hebrew text which is, according to Tov, attested in MT. This gives the LXX an inferior and negative connotation.

C Consistency or non-consistency in the rendering, i.e., the degree to which a particular versional term is used for all (or most) cases of a particular term of the original

The degree of literalness can also be examined by investigating whether or not the LXX translator consequently and consistently used the same Greek word for a given Hebrew word.[14] In the LXX corpus, many Hebrew words are being rendered with the same Greek word. An example hereof is בְּרִית that is rendered into Greek by διαθήκη.[15] In this case, we cannot speak of literalness because it was custom in the context of the translator to consequently translate some Hebrew words by one and the same Greek word[16]. Literalness can only be detected when a Hebrew term entails multiple meanings[17]. When a word is translated by the same Greek word over and over again, without considering the immediate context of the verse, a translation can appear to be rigid and incorrect. In such a case, it is likely that the translator consciously opted to translate a Hebrew word consistently with the same Greek equivalent regardless of the immediate context[18]. LXX Proverbs uses multiple Greek equivalents to render the Hebrew word דרך, i.e., ὁδός, τρίβος and ἴχνος.[19] By doing so, the translator rendered his *Vorlage* in a free way. Nonetheless, Barr notes that the LXX translator often shows a lack of variation when rendering his Hebrew *Vorlage* into Greek. In this way, he translates the parallels דרך/ארח twice by the same Greek word, i.e., ὁδός or τρίβος.[20] Therefore, Barr argues that although LXX Proverbs shows some aspects of a free translation, it also contains some literal aspects.[21]

D Accuracy and level of semantic information, especially in cases of metaphor and idiom

The term whereby a certain word is translated does not always fully cover the meaning of the translated word.[22] In such a case, the translation detracts from the original on a semantical level. This can especially be observed from the

---

14 See Barr, The Typology of Literalism, 305.
15 More examples see Barr, *The Typology of Literalism*, 307.
16 See Barr, The Typology of Literalism, 306.
17 See Barr, The Typology of Literalism, 308.
18 See Barr, The Typology of Literalism, 311.
19 See Barr, The Typology of Literalism, 313.
20 See Barr, The Typology of Literalism, 313.
21 See Barr, *The Typology of Literalism*, 313: "The fact that the 'free' books like Proverbs contain substantial 'literal' elements as well fits in once again at this point."
22 See Barr, The Typology of Literalism, 314.

translation of metaphors.[23] When a translator is confronted with a metaphor he has two options: (a) He opts for a literal translation of the metaphor and thus preserves it, or (b) he chooses to explain the metaphor and thereby destroys it.[24] In the first case, the literal translation of a metaphor, the translator preserves the semantic-linguistic meaning of the word. A free translation, on the other hand, harms this meaning and opts for the reality whereto the metaphor refers. Literal translations are, therefore, often criticised for not adequately representing what the original text wanted to convey.[25]

Barr does not use an example taken from LXX Proverbs to demonstrate this category. However, it seems useful to apply this category on a metaphor from Proverbs (Prov 15:4) by following Barr's reasoning:

MT	LXX
מַרְפֵּא לָשׁוֹן עֵץ חַיִּים וְסֶלֶף בָּהּ שֶׁבֶר בְּרוּחַ׃	ἴασις γλώσσης δένδρον ζωῆς, ὁ δὲ συντηρῶν αὐτὴν πλησθήσεται πνεύματος.
A gentle tongue is a tree of life, but perverseness in it breaks the spirit.	A tongue's healing is a tree of life, and he who keeps it will be filled with spirit.

The LXX translator translated the first colon of the sentence in a literal way. In this part of the verse, the metaphor remains intact. The second colon, however, is translated more freely. The Hebrew reads 'but perverseness in it breaks the spirit', whereas the Greek attests 'he who keeps it will be filled with spirit'. Although the Greek is a free translation of the Hebrew, the metaphor and its mean-

---

23 See Lemmelijn's research on the translation of landscape and flora metaphors in Song of Songs: Bénédicte Lemmelijn, "Flora in Cantico Canticorum. Towards a More Precise Characterisation of Translation Technique in the LXX of Song of Songs," in *Scripture in Transition. Essays on Septuagint, Hebrew Bible, and Dead Sea Scrolls in Honour of Raija Sollamo*, ed. Anssi Voitila and Jutta Jokiranta, SJSJ 126 (Leiden: Brill, 2008), 27–51. See also the doctoral dissertation of Valérie Kabergs concerning wordplay on the basis of proper names in the Pentateuch and the Twelve Prophets as well as the doctoral dissertation of Marieke Dhont that analyses rhetorical features in Job: Valérie Kabergs, "Creativiteit in het spel? De Griekse weergave van expliciet Hebreeuws woordspel op basis van eigennamen in Pentateuch en Twaalf Profeten" (PhD diss., KU Leuven, 2014); Marieke Dhont, "The Language and Style of Old Greek Job in Context (PhD diss., UCLouvain – KU Leuven, 2016). For the published version of Dhont's thesis see Marieke Dhont, *Style and Context of Old Greek Job*, SJSJ 183 (Leiden – Boston, MA: Brill, 2017). Contrary to Tov, the content- and context-related approach does not evaluate the translation of metaphors quantitatively.
24 See Barr, The Typology of Literalism, 315.
25 See Barr, The Typology of Literalism, 317.

ing remain intact. Thus, in this verse the Greek translator handles his Hebrew
Vorlage in both a free and a literal way. Nonetheless, he preserves the meaning
of the metaphor. This example indicates that the category Barr has postulated is
not as sound. In my opinion, a free translation does not necessarily destroy the
meaning of a metaphor.

E   Coded 'etymological' indication of formal/semantic relationships obtaining in the vocabulary of the original language

Sometimes a Hebrew word is translated by a Greek word that resembles the
Hebrew word in form.[26] In some similar cases, e.g., לַיִשׁ ('lion') and the rare Greek
word λίς (lion), the meaning of the words are identical.[27] In other instances, it
can lead to a difference in meaning. An example hereof is אֵלוֹן ('tree') and αὐλών
('hollow').[28] Both meanings cannot be reconciled with one another. This technique was not very popular among ancient scribes and translators. It was often
applied when the *Vorlage* was obscure and when the translator had no idea
what the Hebrew word meant.[29]

There is another method that does not quantitatively render Hebrew consonants into corresponding Greek consonants but tries to render the Hebrew word
etymologically.[30] The translator often translated certain Hebrew words on the
basis of consonants he recognised from a different word which was a derivative
from the unknown word. This technique is called 'root-linked rendering.'[31] The

---

26 See Barr, The Typology of Literalism, 318.

27 See Barr, *The Typology of Literalism*, 319. Barr has borrowed this example from the Greek
translation of Job made by Aquila.

28 See Barr, *The Typology of Literalism*, 319. This example is also borrowed from Aquila.

29 See Barr, The Typology of Literalism, 319.

30 See Barr, The Typology of Literalism, 320.

31 See Emanuel Tov, "Did the Septuagint Translators Always Understand Their Hebrew
Text?," in *The Greek and Hebrew Bible. Collected Essays on the Septuagint*, ed. Emanuel Tov,
SVT 72 (Leiden – Boston, MA – Köln: Brill, 1999), 203–218, 216–217; Johan Lust, Erik Eynikel
and Katrin Hauspie, *Greek-English Lexicon of the Septuagint. Third Corrected Edition* (Stuttgart:
Deutsche Bibelgesellschaft, 2015), XXII. According to Tov, it is sometimes difficult to ascertain
if an etymological rendering expresses the concern of the translator to translate Hebrew word
pairs to equivalent Greek word pairs as consistent as possible or if it is the mere ignorance of the
translator concerning the meaning of a word. See Tov, "Did the Septuagint Translators Always
Understand Their Hebrew Text?," 217. The use of an etymological, 'root-linked', rendering can
be found when the translator was confronted with difficult words, e.g., *hapax legomena*. See
i.a. Ausloos and Lemmelijn, "Characterizing the LXX Translation;" Ausloos and Lemmelijn,
"Rendering Love;" Verbeke, "Hebrew Hapax Legomena," esp. 381–382. An etymological rendering also occurs in the case of wordplay: Hans Ausloos, "LXX's Rendering of Hebrew Proper

application of this technique can be seen in the rendering of בְּרֵאשִׁית in Gen 1:1 that has been translated to κεφάλαιον because בְּרֵאשִׁית is derived from the Hebrew word ראש ('head').[32]

LXX Proverbs also uses etymological renderings. An example can be found in the work of Barr:

> An interesting example is the rare word תַּחְבֻּלֹת, found only five times in Proverbs and once in Job. The Job example had no rendering in the original LXX, and Prov. 20.18 is also omitted from the Greek. But all four of the remaining examples (Prov. 1:5; 11:14; 12:5; 24:6) are rendered with κυβερνᾶν, κυβέρνησις. This was an etymology probably founded on the cognate understood as 'steersman, captain', found thrice in Ezek. 27.[33]

According to Barr, this indicates that a free translation, such as Proverbs, may also contain literal components.[34]

F   Level of text and level of analysis

The Hebrew text that was accessible for the translator could lead to another translation. There are two possible ways in which the translator had access to the text: (a) the non- vocalised text or (b) a combination of the written text with

---

Names and the Characterization of the Translation Technique of the Book of Judges," in *Scripture in Transition. Essays on Septuagint, Hebrew Bible, and Dead Sea Scrolls in Honour of Raija Sollamo*, ed. Anssi Voitila and Jutta Jokiranta, SJSJ 126 (Leiden: Brill, 2008), 53–71; Hans Ausloos, "The Septuagint's Rendering of Hebrew Toponyms as an Indication of the Translation Technique of the Book of Numbers," in *Florilegium Complutense. Textual Criticism and Dead Sea Scrolls Studies in Honour of Julio Trebolle Barrera*, ed. Andrés Piquer Otero and Pablo Torijano Morales, SJSJ 157 (Leiden: Brill, 2012), 35–50; Hans Ausloos and Bénédicte Lemmelijn, "Etymological Renderings in the Septuagint," in *Die Sprache der Septuaginta*, ed. Eberhard Bons and Jan Joosten, LXX.H 4 (Gütersloh: Gütersloher Verlag, 2016), 193–201; Hans Ausloos, Bénédicte Lemmelijn and Valérie Kabergs, "The Study of Aetiological Wordplay as a Content-Related Criterion in the Characterization of LXX Translation Technique," in *Die Septuaginta. Entstehung, Sprache, Geschichte. 3. Internationale Fachtagung veranstaltet von Septuaginta Deutsch (LXX.D), Wuppertal 22.-25.7.2010*, ed. Wolfgang Kraus and Martin Karrer, WUNT 286 (Tübingen: Mohr Siebeck, 2012), 273–294; Valérie Kabergs and Hans Ausloos, "Paronomasia or Wordplay? A Babylonian Confusion. Towards A Definition of Hebrew Wordplay," *Biblica* 93.1 (2012): 1–20; Kabergs, "Creativiteit in het spel?."

32 See Barr, The Typology of Literalism, 320.

33 Barr, The Typology of Literalism, 320.

34 Barr, The Typology of Literalism, 322.

the tradition of the pronunciation of that text.[35] A written text, without vocalisation, offers more possibilities for interpreting a text than a spoken text.[36]

Another possibility is that the LXX translator reads and translates different words more or less literal but organises them in a syntactic and free way.[37] According to Barr, this phenomenon also occurs in LXX Proverbs. An example is Prov 11:3a:

MT	LXX
תֻּמַּת יְשָׁרִים תַּנְחֵם	ἀποθανὼν δίκαιος ἔλιπεν μετάμελον.
The integrity of the upright guides them.	When a righteous person died, he left regret.

The translator translated the Hebrew words with Greek equivalents but the syntactic structure of the Greek version is a free composition from the hand of the translator.[38]

1.1.1.2 Conclusion

According to Barr, the line between the terms 'literal' and 'free' is often extremely vague. Therefore, one cannot simply categorise a translation as being literal without further explanation. A translation can be literal in some aspects. He argues that literalness as such does not exist. Rather, it is a matter of determining the 'aspects of literalness'. This is the case for most books of the LXX, including Proverbs. LXX Proverbs is a free translation that also applies literal methods. According to Barr, LXX Proverbs shows a lack of variation (see category 3), the use of etymological renderings (see category 5) and more or less a literal rendering of Hebrew words into Greek equivalents (see category 6).

Several other scholars, among which Emanuel Tov, followed in Barr's footsteps. His view on the literalness of a translation will be discussed in the next section.

---

35 Barr, The Typology of Literalism, 322.
36 See Barr, The Typology of Literalism, 322.
37 See Barr, The Typology of Literalism, 323.
38 See Barr, *The Typology of Literalism*, 323. MT attests the lexeme תֻּמַּת, whereas the LXX renders this lexeme with the Greek lexeme ἀποθανὼν. It is likely that the translator read the lexeme תמת in his non-vocalised Hebrew *Vorlage* as a form of מות ('to die').

1.1.2 Emanuel Tov

One of the most prominent scholars in the field of LXX studies and especially
the Hebrew Bible is Emanuel Tov. He argues that the literalness of a translation
can be examined objectively by means of statistics.[39] By using computers and
databases we can accurately identify individual LXX books as free or literal
translations. Tov, together with Robert Kraft, has developed a database of his
own, i.e., *Computer Assisted Tools for Septuagint/Scriptural Study (CATSS)*:[40]

> *CATSS*, contain[s] among other things, a running text of the LXX and MT, element by ele-
> ment, verse by verse, etc. It records 'formal' equivalents of the LXX and MT (as if the LXX
> were translated from MT) in col. a, and the 'presumed' equivalents of the LXX and its pre-
> sumed (retroverted) Hebrew *Vorlage* in col. b. This *Vorlage* is retroverted merely for select-
> ed words [...]. In the course of recording the equivalents of MT and the LXX, various types

---

39 See Tov and Wright, "Computer-Assisted Study." Tov indicates that he actually measures
the consistency of a translation instead of its literalness. Consistency, however, is an aspect of
literalness. The more consistent a translator was in translating his *Vorlage*, the more literal the
translation. See Tov and Wright, "Computer-Assisted Study," 153. There is a clear evolution
throughout Tov's work. See Bénédicte Lemmelijn, "What Are We Looking for in Doing Old
Testament Text-Critical Research?," *JNSL* 23.2 (1997): 69–80, 72: "[...][T]he view of one and the
same author can, consciously or not, change through the years [...]." In this publication, Lemmelijn examines the evolution in Tov's line of thought with regard to the concept of an *Urtext*.
Also with regard to the research concerning the degree of literalness by means of statistical
data, we can see an evolution in Tov's thinking. Throughout the years, his interest has been
shifted to the fifth category, i.e., linguistic adequacy of lexical choices, that he proposes to
study the degree of literalness (see below). This category examines the exegetical activity of the
translator and cannot be expressed in statistical data. See, e.g., Emanuel Tov, "Recensional
Differences Between the Masoretic Text and the Septuagint of Proverbs," in *Of Scribes and
Scrolls. Studies on the Hebrew Bible, Intertestamental Judaism, and Christian Origins Presented
to John Strugnell on the Occasion of His Sixtieth Birthday*, ed. Harold W. Attridge, John J. Collins
and Thomas H. Tobin, CTSRR 5 (Lanham, MD: University Press of America, 1990), 43–56.
40 See Robert A. Kraft and Emanuel Tov, "Computer-Assisted Tools for Septuagint Studies,"
BIOSCS 14 (1981): 22–40. For detailed information on how *CATSS* works, see, i.a., Tov and
BWright, "Computer-Assisted Study;" Emanuel Tov, "The CATSS Project. A Progress Report,"
in *VII Congress of the International Organization for Septuagint and Cognate Studies*, ed. Claude
E. Cox, SBLSCS 31 (Atlanta, GA: Scholars Press, 1991), 157–163; Emanuel Tov, "The Accordance
Search Program for the MT, LXX, and the CATSS Database," *BIOSCS* 30 (1997): 36–44; Emanuel
Tov, "A Computerized Database for Septuagint Research," in *The Greek and Hebrew Bible.
Collected Essays on the Septuagint*, ed. Emanuel Tov, VTS, 72 (Leiden: Brill, 1999), 31–51, 31–32;
Emanuel Tov, "The Use of Computers in Biblical Research," in *Hebrew Bible, Greek Bible, and
Qumran*, ed. Emanuel Tov, TSAJ 121 (Tübingen: Mohr Siebeck, 2008), 228–224.

of notes have been incorporated into the database which are of importance for the study of translation techniques.[41]

This database has been used by several scholars, i.a., Benjamin G. Wright and John R. Abercrombie,[42] to go beyond the theoretical framework as proposed by Barr and Tov.[43] It attempts to present the aspects of literalness on a major scale by means of statistical data.[44] Tov has postulated several criteria in order to distinguish literal translations from free translations, just as and in the footsteps of Barr.[45] He determines 5 criteria for the analysis of literalness from which the first four criteria can be measured statistically:[46]

(1) Internal consistency;
(2) The representation of constituents of Hebrew words by separate Greek equivalents;
(3) Word-order;
(4) Quantitative representation;
(5) Linguistic adequacy of lexical choices.

In the following sections, these 5 criteria will be discussed. Afterwards Tov's analysis of LXX Proverbs will be examined.

1.1.2.1 Tov's criteria for the determination of literalness
A   Internal consistency
Following Barr, Tov indicates that many LXX translators translated a certain Hebrew word consistently by the same Greek term.[47] Consistently translating a given Hebrew word or construction by the same Greek equivalent is called 'ste-

---

41 Tov and Wright, "Computer-Assisted Study," 221–222.

42 See, i.a., Wright, "The Quantitative Representation of Elements;" John R. Abercrombie, "A Computer-Assisted Study of A Textual Family in the Book of Ruth," *Textus* 13 (1986): 95–110.

43 See Wright, "The Quantitative Representation of Elements," 313-314: "While the works of Barr and Tov [...] primarily address the more theoretical aspects of 'literal' and 'free' translations and set out the general characteristics of literalism, few attempts have been made to quantify their recommendations on a large scale. This perhaps because of the large quantity of detailed information that would have to be examined for each translation. The greatest promise for pursuing this kind of study, it seems to me, is held out be the use of computer technology."

44 Wright, "The Quantitative Representation of Elements," 313.

45 See Tov, The Text-Critical Use of the Septuagint, 22–26.

46 See Tov, The Text-Critical Use of the Septuagint, 22.

47 See Tov, *The Text-Critical Use of the Septuagint*, 22. Barr describes this category under category 3 (Consistency or non-consistency in the rendering), see above.

reotyping.'[48] By means of statistical analyses, translations can be characterised as stereotyping translations. These analyses examine the consistency of translated words within the individual LXX books and compare them with the general vocabulary of the LXX.[49] The more a translation leans towards stereotypical renderings, the more this translation can be characterised as a literal translation.[50]

Also the etymological rendering of Hebrew words into Greek (see Barr, category 5), can, according to Tov, be included in this analysis.[51]

B   The representation of constituents of Hebrew words by separate Greek equivalents

Translators who aimed to render their *Vorlage* literally, tried to divide the Hebrew words in separate segments when possible and translated those segments by Greek equivalents.[52] An example hereof can be found above in the discussion of Barr's criteria, i.e., the division into elements or segments, and the sequence in which these elements are represented (the first category).

C   Word-order

Some translators deviated from the word-order of their Hebrew *Vorlage*, while others tried to be as close to the word-order as possible. The degree in which the word-order of the different LXX books differs with those in MT can be measured statistically.[53]

---

48 See Tov, *The Text-Critical Use of the Septuagint*, 22: "[...] consistent representation, often called 'stereo-typing' [...]."
49 See Tov, *The Text-Critical Use of the Septuagint*, 23–24. The results of these statistical analyses can be found in the *CATSS*-database.
50 See Tov, The Text-Critical Use of the Septuagint, 24.
51 See Tov, The Text-Critical Use of the Septuagint, 24.
52 See Tov, The Text-Critical Use of the Septuagint, 24.
53 See Tov, *The Text-Critical Use of the Septuagint*, 24. Galen Marquis also argues that the study of word order in a certain book can be a means to examine the degree of literalness. To point out the relevance of this kind of study, he has analysed the word order in LXX Ezekiel by means of statistical data. See Galen Marquis, "Word Order as a Criterion for the Evaluation of Translation Technique in the LXX and the Evaluation of Word-order Variants as Exemplified in LXX Ezekiel," *Textus* 13 (1986): 59–84; Marquis, "Consistency of Lexical Equivalents." However, Marquis goes very far in examining the degree of literalness by even integrating mathematical calculations. According to Lemmelijn, Marquis bases his methodology and results on questionable hypothetical constructions. This makes his results non-representative and can thus

D Quantitative representation

Literal translators will try to render each Hebrew element with a corresponding Greek element. Free translators, on the other hand, will often make additions to clarify the text or leave out several elements because they are being expressed by another word in the Greek translation.[54] The more adequate and accurate a translator translates, the more literal the translation will seem to be. This quantitative representation of Hebrew elements into Greek can be expressed statistically.[55]

E Linguistic adequacy of lexical choices

Translators tried to convey the meaning and message of their Hebrew *Vorlage* to their Greek target audience. In order to do this, some translators strived for high linguistic adequacy in the rendering of Hebrew words by paying attention to their form and meaning.[56] The more adequate a translator applied this method, the more literal the translation. However, this criterion cannot be measured statistically because the evaluation of the linguistic adequacy of the translator entails a subjective evaluation.[57] The meaning of a text as perceived by the translator is not exactly the same meaning it might have for us today. Moreover, "the modern evaluation of the linguistic background of the translations is subjective, for a rendering that according to one scholar reflects the translator's linguistic exegesis may be seen by another as reflecting content exegesis."[58]

1.1.2.2 Tov's analysis of the book of Proverbs

As co-founder of the *CATSS*-database, Tov has published an article together with Benjamin G. Wright wherein they analyse, amongst others, the LXX version of Proverbs by using this database.[59] Tov and Wright analyse the degree of literalness of the different LXX books on the basis of 5 criteria:[60]

---

not lead to a well-founded conclusion on the translation technique of the LXX books. See Lemmelijn, *A Plague of Texts?*, 120–122.
54 See Tov, The Text-Critical Use of the Septuagint, 24.
55 See Tov, The Text-Critical Use of the Septuagint, 24.
56 See Tov, The Text-Critical Use of the Septuagint, 25–26.
57 See Tov, The Text-Critical Use of the Septuagint, 26.
58 Tov, The Text-Critical Use of the Septuagint, 26.
59 Tov and Wright, "Computer-Assisted Study."
60 Tov and Wright, "Computer-Assisted Study", 158. The following books are being analysed: Judges (A text), Ruth, 1 Samuel, 2 Samuel, 2 Kings, Ezra, Nehemiah, Job 15, Psalms 30–65, Proverbs, Ecclesiastes, Song of Songs, Jeremiah, Lamentations, Ezekiel, Minor Prophets (individual

(a) The translation of the Hebrew proposition בּ by ἐν;
(b) The translation of the conjunction כִּי by ὅτι or διότι;
(c) The translation of the Hebrew 3rd person masculine singular suffix by αὐτός or ἑαυτος;
(d) The frequency of added prepositions in the LXX in accordance with the rules of the Greek language or translation habits;
(e) The relative frequency of the post-position particles δέ, μέν, οὖν and τέ in relation to καί.

The table below presents the results, in percentage, of these categories with regard to the LXX version of Proverbs and compares these percentages with the most literal and most fee translation according to each category:[61]

	בּ → ἐν	כִּי → ὅτι / διότι	/w and /yw → αὐτός /ἑαυτος	Added propositions	καί / δέ; καί / οὖν; καί / μέν; καί / τέ
Prov	30.3%	11.36%	57.49%	0.95%	121%; 0.81%; 2.6%; 0.61%
Most literal translation	92.4% (Qoh)	100% (Mal, Jonah, Joel Nah, Ezra, Hag, Obad, SoS)	100% (Joel, Nah)	/ (Qoh, Mal)	/ (Qoh, Nah, SoS; Sir, Zeph, Zach, SoS, Ruth, Qoh, Ps, Obad, Neh, Nah, Mal, Lam, Jonah, Joel, Jer, Hos, Hag, Hab, Ezek, Amos, MP; Zeph, Zach, SoS, 2 S, 1 S, Ruth, Qoh, Obad, Neh, Nah, Mal, Lam,

---

and together) and Wisdom of Jesus Sirach. See Tov and Wright, "Computer-Assisted Study," 157. By postulating these grammatical-linguistic criteria he follows the Finnish school. However, in comparison to the Finnish school, Tov will rather express the results quantitatively (statistically) instead of qualitatively.
61 Tov and Wright, "Computer-Assisted Study," 163, 167–168, 172, 176–177, 180–181. A complete overview of all the books that have been analysed by Tov and Wright can be found on these pages.

	ב → ἐν	כִּי → ὅτι / διότι	/w and /yw → αὐτός /ἑαυτος	Added propositions	καί / δέ; καί / οὖν; καί / μέν; καί / τέ
					Judg, Jonah, Joel, Jer, Hos, Hag, Hab, Amos; Amos, Ezek, Ezra, Hab, Hos, Jer, Joel, Jonah, Judg, 2 Kgs, Lam, Mal, Nah, Neh, Obad, Qoh, Ruth, SoS, Zeph, Job)
Most free translation	27.7% (Job)	11.36% (Prov)	57.49% (Prov)	0.95% (Prov)	121% (Prov); 2.6% (Job); 2.6% (Job and Prov); 2.1% (Hag)

When we compare the results of LXX Proverbs with the other books that have been analysed by Tov and Wright, it becomes clear that Proverbs is one of the most free translations.[62] On the basis of the above-mentioned results, the book of Job (chapters 1-5) is also regarded as a free translation.[63]

Not only has Tov studied the translation technique of LXX Proverbs by using the *CATSS*-database, he has also examined Proverbs without making use of statistics. In his article *Recensional Differences Between the Masoretic Text and the Septuagint of Proverbs*, he analyses the difference(s) between the MT-version and the LXX version of Proverbs.[64] According to Tov, the differences between the two versions can be ascribed to the exegetical activity of the LXX translator, on the one hand, and a Hebrew *Vorlage* that differed from the one of MT, on the other. With regard to our research, the exegetical activity of the translator is important in order to characterise the translation technique of the LXX translator. As has already been argued by Barr and Tov, the exegetical activity of the

---

62 Tov and Wright, "Computer-Assisted Study," 185–186.
63 See Tov and Wright, "Computer-Assisted Study," 185–186. Tov and Wright do not specify why they only analyse the first five chapters of the book of Job.
64 Tov, "Recensional Differences."

translator(s) is a characteristic of a free translation. The translator handles his *Vorlage* in a free way. He gives himself the freedom to provide the text with additional explanations, to add or leave out certain things and to adapt the structure of the text. The freedom which the translator applies is, among other things, visible in the translation of Hebrew doublets. According to Tov, the Greek text often offers a translation of one Hebrew verse, whereby one literal and one free translation of the verse are being given, instead of a translation of Hebrew doublets.[65] An example of this procedure can be found in Prov 4:10:

MT Prov 4:10b	LXX Prov 4:10b-c
וְיִרְבּוּ לְךָ שְׁנוֹת חַיִּים׃	καὶ πληθυνθήσεται ἔτη ζωῆς σου, ἵνα σοι γένωνται πολλαὶ ὁδοὶ βίου·
That the years of your life may be many.	And the years of your life shall be increased, that the ways of living may become many for you.

The first part of the verse (καὶ πληθυνθήσεται ἔτη ζωῆς σου) is a more or less literal translation of the Hebrew, while the second half of the verse (ἵνα σοι γένωνται πολλαὶ ὁδοὶ βίου) reflects a more free translation.[66]

In his article *A Textual-Exegetical Commentary on Three Chapters in the Septuagint*,[67] Tov defines the first chapter of LXX Proverbs as a free and paraphrasing translation.[68] Many differences between MT and the LXX are, according to Tov, to be ascribed to the exegesis of the translator.[69] This is, as already indicated above, an indication of a free translation.

---

65 Tov, "Recensional Differences," 44. The free translation of the verse can be ascribed to the original translation, whereas the literal translation of the verse would be a later addition. This addition would have been inserted by a reviser who found the original Greek text too free. Tov, "Recensional Differences," 44. However, parallelisms are not necessarily a characteristic of Greek poetry but rather of Hebrew poetry. Greek poetry did not deem it necessary to repeat something that was already said before, something which is typical for parallelisms. Although parallelism was not a literary feature in the broader Greek world, it is probable that it was recognised by Hellenistic Jews as such. See Dhont, *The Language and Style of Old Greek Job in Context*, 193–194.

66 See Tov, "Recensional Differences," 44.

67 Emanuel Tov, "A Textual-Exegetical Commentary on Three Chapters in the Septuagint," in *Scripture in Transition. Essays on Septuagint, Hebrew Bible, and Dead Sea Scrolls in Honour of Raija Sollamo*, ed. Ainssi Voitila and Jutta Jokiranta, SJSJ 126 (Leiden: Brill, 2008), 275–290.

68 See Tov, "A Textual-Exegetical Commentary," 276.

69 See Tov, "A Textual-Exegetical Commentary," 276.

1.1.2.3 Conclusion

Just as Barr, Tov has also postulated several criteria to distinguish literal LXX translations from free translations. Some of these categories correspond with those of Barr. Especially the category 'linguistic adequacy of lexical choices' is applicable to Tov's analysis of LXX Proverbs. In some of his articles, Tov defines LXX Proverbs as a free translation. For this, he bases himself on the exegetical activity of the LXX translator which indicates the free way in which the translator handled his Hebrew *Vorlage*.

Moreover, Tov, together with Wright, has analysed LXX Proverbs by using the *CATSS-* database. By means of this method, he examined the degree of literalness of the book of Proverbs. The statistic results of this study point out that LXX Proverbs is one of the more free translations in comparison to other LXX books.

1.1.3 Conclusion

The quantitative approach has tried to examine the degree of literalness for the different LXX books by means of several categories. As indicated in the analysis above, LXX Proverbs has also been studied by the quantitative approach.

Both Barr and Tov characterise LXX Proverbs as a free translation. Tov has examined LXX Proverbs in two different ways: on the one hand on the basis of the *CATSS*-database, on the other hand by analysing the differences between the MT- and the LXX-version of Proverbs. The first method tries to measure the degree of literalness of the individual LXX books on the basis of predetermined criteria. The second method attempts to ascertain the exegetical activity of the translator by a comparative study of both the Hebrew and the Greek text. Both studies have shown that LXX Proverbs is a free translation.

However, Barr warns us for the usage of the terminology, i.e., 'literal' and 'free', used to characterise the translation technique of the LXX translators. According to him, even a free translation as LXX Proverbs can exhibit traces of a literal translation. The literal aspect of the Greek translation of Proverbs can be observed by a lack of variation, the usage of etymological renderings and the more or less literal translation of Hebrew terms to Greek equivalents.

After having outlined the methodological framework of the quantitative approach and the way in which this method has characterised the translation technique of LXX Proverbs, we will give an overview of the characterisation of LXX Proverbs by the qualitative approach in the next section.

1.2 The qualitative approach

A second approach to analyse the translation technique of the LXX books is the qualitative approach. This approach examines how certain Hebrew grammatical features, e.g., conjunctions, word order, tenses, constructions with infinitive, *etc.*, are being translated into Greek.[70] By studying the syntax of the different LXX books the translation technique of the LXX translators can be analysed in order to compare the results of the different LXX books with one another.[71] In this approach the quality of the Greek translation plays a central role. By studying the syntax of the LXX and comparing it with the syntax of Koine Greek literature of the same age, a conclusion can be formulated with regard to the quality of the translation and thus also with regard to the competence of the LXX translator.[72]

In comparison to the quantitative approach, the qualitative approach only applies statistical data in order to support its linguistic research.[73] Raija Sollamo and Anneli Aejmelaeus warn us for the usage of statics in LXX research.[74] Quantitative research may seem adequate but in most of the cases it actually is not.[75] Aejmelaeus notices that it is impossible to statistically map the consistency of a translation with regard to vocabulary as Benjamin G. Wright and Galen Marquis

---

70 See Ilmari Soisalon-Soininen, *Die Infinitive in der Septuaginta*, AASF Series B 132 (Helsinki: Suomalainen Tiedeakatemia, 1965), 15 (= Ilmari Soisalon-Soininen, "Einleitung," in *Studien zur Septuaginta-Syntax*, ed. Ilmari Soisalon-Soininen, Anneli Aemelaeus and Raija Sollamo, AASF Series B 237 (Helsinki: Suomalainen Tiedeakatemia, 1987), 11–18, 18): "In den meisten Fällen ist es am besten, vom bestimmten hebräischen grammatischen Kategorien auszugehen und zu untersuchen, wie diese von den Septuaginta-Übersetzern wiedergegeben sind." Ilmari Soisalon-Soininen was the first scholar who introduced and applied this approach. Many scholars followed in his footsteps.
71 See Aejmelaeus, "What We Talk About," 207.
72 See Raija Sollamo, "Some 'Improper' Prepositions, such as ἐνώπιον, ἐναντίον, ἔναντι etc., in the Septuagint and Early Koine Greek," *VT* 25.4 (1975): 773–782, 775; Raija Sollamo, "The Study of Syntax and the Study of Translation Technique – What is the Difference?," in *Helsinki Perspectives on the Translation Technique of the Septuagint*, ed. Raija Sollamo and Seppo Sipilä (Helsinki: Finnish Exegetical Society; Göttingen: Vandenhoeck & Ruprecht), 2001, 32–41, 40.
73 See Raija Sollamo, *Renderings of Hebrew Semiprepositions in the Septuagint*, 280–281; Sollamo, "The Study of Syntax and the Study of Translation Technique," 37, 38 and 40; Aejmelaeus, "What We Talk About," 208–213.
74 See Sollamo, "The Study of Syntax and the Study of Translation Technique," 38; Aejmelaeus, "What We Talk About," 210.
75 See Aejmelaeus, "What We Talk About," 209.

have done in their research.[76] These results do not take into account the factors, e.g., context, which motivated the translator to opt for a certain translation.[77] By doing so, statistical data does not adequately describe the translation technique of the LXX translators. An example hereof can be found in the usage of the particle δέ as a translation of the Hebrew -ן in independent coordinate clauses in the Pentateuch:[78]

	δέ / -ן	percentage
Gen	777 / 3053	25.5%
Ex	312 / 1906	16.4%
Lev	30 / 1232	2.4%
Num	35 / 1660	2.1%
Deut	34 / 1273	2.7%

From the above-mentioned table, we can see a clear difference between the first two books and the last three books. This difference is not only visible in the above-mentioned data but also in the translational attitude of the respective translators. In Genesis and Exodus δέ is translated more free as an alternative for the conjunction καί, whereas in the last three books δέ is rather applied to express contrast.[79] Aejmelaeus argues that the translator of Genesis and Exodus exhibit the same attitude in relation to their *Vorlage* even though the usage of δέ as a rendering of -ן in independent coordinate clauses in Genesis is 8.9% more.[80]

Interesting to note is the study of Tov and Wright concerning the translation of -ן by a Greek conjunction in the LXX.[81] If we look at these results we get a different outcome for the books of Numeri and Deuteronomy than the results of Aejmelaeus' research:[82]

---

76 See Aejmelaeus, "What We Talk About," 212. For the studies of Galen Marquis and Benjamin G. Wright, see Galen Marquis, "Consistency of Lexical Equivalents," 405–424; Benjamin G. Wright, *No Small Difference. Sirach's Relationship to its Hebrew Parent Text*, SCS 26 (Atlanta, GA: Scholars Press, 1989), esp. 91–114.
77 See Aejmelaeus, "What We Talk About," 213.
78 Aejmelaeus, "What We Talk About," 216–217.
79 See Aejmelaeus, "What We Talk About," 217.
80 See Aejmelaeus, "What We Talk About," 217.
81 See Tov and Wright, "Computer-Assisted Study," 179–181.
82 Tov and Wright, "Computer-Assisted Study," 178–180; Aejmelaeus, "What We Talk About," 217, n. 27.

	δέ / καί	*percentage*
Num	74 / 2481	2.9%
Deut	99 / 2013	4.9%

According to Aejmelaeus, this difference can be explained by the fact that Tov and Wright did not take into account the different sorts of sentences.[83] By doing so, she demonstrates that the translation technique cannot simply be registered by statistical data, moreover, she indicates that a description of the translation technique by a LXX scholar is necessary.[84] The translation technique of the LXX books can, subsequently, be determined by studying each case individually case per case, something which statistical analyses tend not to do.[85] This does not entail that statistical data and results are redundant. However, they need to be applied to support or to summarise the results of linguistic research.[86] As indicated above, the translation technique of the LXX translators cannot be adequately measured but only be described.[87] The qualitative approach thus holds the opinion that the results of both quantitative and qualitative research need to be compared with one another in order to provide an accurate image of the translation technique of the individual LXX translators.[88] In the following sections an example will be given to demonstrate the method of the qualitative approach, i.e., Aejmelaeus' study of the causal ὅτι. Afterwards we will examine

how this approach has characterised the translation technique of LXX Proverbs.

---

83 See Aejmelaeus, "What We Talk About," 217, n. 27.

84 See Aejmelaeus, "What We Talk About," 217.

85 See Aejmelaeus, "What We Talk About," 213.

86 See Aejmelaeus, "What We Talk About," 213; Ilmari Soisalon-Soininen, "Methodologische Fragen der Erforschung der Septuaginta-Syntax," in *Studien zur Septuaginta-Syntax*, ed. Ilmari Soisalon-Soininen, Anneli Aemelaeus and Raija Sollamo, AASF Series B 237 (Helsinki: Suomalainen Tiedeakatemia, 1987), 40–52, 52.

87 See Aejmelaeus, "What We Talk About," 217.

88 See Aejmelaeus, "What We Talk About," 222.

1.2.1 The study of ὅτι *causale* as an example of the qualitative approach

In her article *Oti Causale in Septuagintal Greek*, Anneli Aejmelaeus examines the causal usage of ὅτι as a rendering of the Hebrew conjunction כי.[89] In a lot of languages, like Greek, several conjunctions are being used to distinguish different sorts of causality, i.e., direct and indirect.[90] The Greek conjunctions that are being applied to express direct causal sentences (subordinate clauses) that indicate a cause or reason, are ὅτι and διότι; ἐπεί and ἐπειδή.[91] Indirect causality, e.g., motivation and explanation, are being expressed by the conjunctions γάρ, ἐπεί and ὡς in coordinate clauses.[92] Hebrew has, in comparison to Greek, no extra conjunctions to express these nuances.[93] The conjunction כי is being applied in Hebrew to introduce both indirect as direct causal sentences.[94]

Aejmelaeus' study on the usage of ὅτι as a rendering of the Hebrew conjunction כי in the Pentateuch has indicated that half of the occurrences of ὅτι is used to express direct causality, on the one hand, and intermediary (or 'that' as the causal 'because'), on the other.[95] This usage is in accordance with the classical usage of ὅτι *causale*.[96] The other half is being used to express indirect causality.[97] As already indicated above, indirect causality is not expressed with ὅτι in Koine Greek but with other conjunctions, *i.a* γάρ. An example of the usage of ὅτι instead of γάρ can be found in Lev 24:22:

MT	LXX
מִשְׁפַּט אֶחָד יִהְיֶה לָכֶם כַּגֵּר כָּאֶזְרָח יִהְיֶה כִּי אֲנִי יְהוָה אֱלֹהֵיכֶם׃	δικαίωσις μία ἔσται τῷ προσηλύτῳ καὶ τῷ ἐγχωρίῳ, ὅτι ἐγώ εἰμι κύριος ὁ θεὸς ὑμῶν.

89 Annelie Aejmelaeus, "Oti Causale in Septuagintal Greek," in *On the Trail of the Septuagint Translators. Collected Essays*, ed. Anneli Aejmelaeus, CBET 50 (Leuven — Paris — Dudley, MA: Peeters, 2007), 11–29.
90 See Aejmelaeus, "Oti Causale in Septuagintal Greek," 12.
91 See Aejmelaeus, "Oti Causale in Septuagintal Greek," 12.
92 See Aejmelaeus, "Oti Causale in Septuagintal Greek," 12.
93 See Aejmelaeus, "Oti Causale in Septuagintal Greek," 12.
94 See Aejmelaeus, "Oti Causale in Septuagintal Greek," 12.
95 See Aejmelaeus, "Oti Causale in Septuagintal Greek," 12–14.
96 See Aejmelaeus, "Oti Causale in Septuagintal Greek," 14.
97 See Aejmelaeus, "Oti Causale in Septuagintal Greek," 14.

MT	LXX
You shall have one law for the alien and for the citizen: for I am the Lord your God.	There shall be one judgment for the guest and for the inhabitant of the country; for it is I who am the Lord your God.[98]

In the Hebrew version indirect causality, i.e., a motivation, is expressed, whereas the Greek expresses a direct causal relation that can be regarded as cause.[99]

Aejmelaeus also points out that ὅτι as a conjunction of indirect causal sentences does not occur in other literature such as the letter of Aristeas, 2 Maccabees and Philodemus' ΠΕΡΙ ΟΙΚΟΝΟΜΙΑΣ, The first book of Polybius' *Histories*, Theophrastus' *Characters* and Epicurus' *Three Epistles*.[100] In this literature, γάρ is being used as a causative conjunction in most of the cases.[101] The conjunction ὅτι is very rarely used.[102] In 2 Maccabees ὅτι *causale* is not even used once. This leads her to the conclusion that the usage of ὅτι as a translation of כִּי can be regarded as a Hebraism or even as a Septuagintism.[103]

Nevertheless, the LXX translators of the Pentateuch do not shun γάρ as a rendering of כִּי.[104] The percentages of the different books with regard to the correct translation of כִּי by γάρ or ὅτι are the following: "Gen 78%, Ex 96%, Lev 45%, Num 40% , Deut 32%."[105] From these results it is clear that the more the Pentateuch progresses, the less the translators paid attention to the correct translation of כִּי.[106] The more a translation applied the correct usage of γάρ or ὅτι as a translation of כִּי, the more free the translation was and the more the translator was familiar with the Greek language. In the Pentateuch, Exodus is the least literal translation as is clear from the percentages.

---

98 English translation taken from Dirk L. Büchner, "Leuitikon," in *A New English Translation of the Septuagint And the Other Greek Translations Traditionally Included Under That Title*, ed. Albert Pietersma and Benjamin G. Wright (New York, NY — Oxford: Oxford University Press, 2007), 82–106.
99 See Aejmelaeus, "Oti Causale in Septuagintal Greek," 15.
100 See Aejmelaeus, "Oti Causale in Septuagintal Greek," 17.
101 See Aejmelaeus, "Oti Causale in Septuagintal Greek," 17.
102 See Aejmelaeus, "Oti Causale in Septuagintal Greek," 17.
103 See Aejmelaeus, "Oti Causale in Septuagintal Greek," 18 and 29. A more frequent term that is used in contemporary scholarship to denote specific vocabulary that is only found in or stems from the LXX corpus is 'Septuagintalism.'
104 See Aejmelaeus, "Oti Causale in Septuagintal Greek," 19.
105 See Aejmelaeus, "Oti Causale in Septuagintal Greek," 20.
106 See Aejmelaeus, "Oti Causale in Septuagintal Greek," 20.

Aejmelaeus has indicated that the study of the usage of ὅτι *causale* in sentences where one should normally expect γάρ as a rendering of כִּי, can inform scholarship on the translation technique of the LXX translators. More free translations, which show the familiarity of the LXX translator with the Greek language, e.g., Exodus, rarely apply ὅτι *causale* on places where one would normally expect γάρ. Literal translations, which show that the translator did not fully master the Greek language, e.g., Deuteronomy, exhibit an abundant use of ὅτι *causale* instead of γάρ.

1.2.2 The characterisation of LXX Proverbs by the qualitative approach

The Finnish school who applied the qualitative approach on different LXX books has mainly focused its research on the Pentateuch.[107] However, LXX Proverbs is often briefly mentioned in their studies.

LXX Proverbs has also been characterised as a free translation by the qualitative approach.[108] Ilmari Soisalon-Soininen regards LXX Proverbs as a free translation on the basis of his study of the rendering of Hebrew infinitives. The freedom of the translator is, among other things, noticeable by the avoidance of the construction ἐν τῷ + infinitive as the rendering of the Hebrew construction ב + infinitive construct.[109] In the 26 cases where the construction ב + infinitive construct occurs in LXX Proverbs, the translator renders this construction 16 times with a subordinate clause, five times with a genitive absolutus and one

---

107 *See*, i.a., Ilmari Soisalon-Soininen, "Die Auslassung des Possessivpronomens im griechischen Pentateuch," in *Studien zur Septuaginta-Syntax*, ed. Ilmari Soisalon-Soininen, Anneli Aemelaeus and Raija Sollamo, AASF Series B 237 (Helsinki: Suomalainen Tiedeakatemia, 1987), 86–103; Raija Sollamo, *Repetition of the Possessive Pronouns in the Septuagint*, SCS 40 (Atlanta, GA: Scholars Press, 1995); Raija Sollamo, "Pleonastic Use of the Pronoun in Connection with the Relative Pronoun in the LXX of Leviticus, Numbers and Deuteronomy," *VIII Congress of the International Organization for Septuagint and Cognate Studies*, ed. in Leonard J. Greenspoon and Olivier Munnich, SBLSCS 41 (Atlanta, GA: Scholars Press, 1995), 43–62; Anneli Aejmelaeus, ed., *On the Trail of the Septuagint Translators. Collected Essays*, CBET 50 (Leuven – Paris – Dudley, MA: Peeters, 2007). The Pentateuch has been studied first because it has been translated first and is thus older than the rest of the LXX corpus. See Sollamo, "The Study of Syntax and the Study of Translation Technique," 35–36 and 40.
108 See, i.a., Soisalon-Soininen, "Methodologische Fragen," 44; Soisalon-Soininen, *Die Infinitive in der Septuaginta*, 158–159; Sollamo, *Renderings of Hebrew Semiprepositions in the Septuagint*, 284; Aemelaeus, "Oti Causale in Septuagintal Greek," 22.
109 See Soisalon-Soininen, "Der Gebrauch des genetivus absolutus in der Septuaginta," 178.

time with a participium conjunctum.[110] The usage of a subordinate clause as a rendering of ב + infinitive construct is more free than the Greek construction ἐν τῷ + infinitive.

Nevertheless, Soisalon-Soininen argues that this rendering is not as refined as the usage of the genitive absolutus.[111] The fact that the LXX translator of Proverbs uses a genitive absolutus 5 times to render the construction ב + infinitive construct testifies of the translator's profound knowledge of both languages.[112] The LXX translator of Proverbs also eliminates Hebrew infinitives with final meaning and replaces these with other terms.[113] In the Greek text, however, a lot of infinitives are attested that have no equivalent Hebrew infinitive.[114] These infinitives do not have a final meaning but are usually used as a(n) (direct) object.[115] Once more, the translator exhibits a profound knowledge of Greek in these cases. Soisalon-Soininen argues that:

> Trotz der großen Unterschiede zwischen den einzeln Übersetzern ist es möglich, eine scharfe Grenze zwischen der Übersetzungssprache und der ursprünglich auf Griechisch geschriebenen Bücher zu sehen. Nur bei Prov ist diese Grenze in mancher Hinsicht verwischt.[116]

The knowledge of Greek of the LXX translator of Proverbs is, according to Soisalon-Soininen, so profound that it does not make his translation look like a translation but like a decent written piece of Greek literature.

Raiji Sollamo also characterises LXX Proverbs as a free translation.[117] In her study of the translation of Hebrew 'semiprepositions', the Greek translation of Proverbs is also examined.[118] LXX Proverbs renders these 'semiprepositions' mostly in a free way. In this way, the translation of πρὸ προσώπου for the He-

---

110 See Soisalon-Soininen, "Der Gebrauch des genetivus absolutus in der Septuaginta," 178; Soisalon-Soininen, *Die Infinitive in der Septuaginta*, 188.

111 See Soisalon-Soininen, "Der Gebrauch des genetivus absolutus in der Septuaginta," 178.

112 See Soisalon-Soininen, "Der Gebrauch des genetivus absolutus in der Septuaginta," 158, 178 and 180.

113 See Soisalon-Soininen, Die Infinitive in der Septuaginta, 195.

114 See Soisalon-Soininen, Die Infinitive in der Septuaginta, 195.

115 See Soisalon-Soininen, *Die Infinitive in der Septuaginta*, 195. In 30 cases, the infinitive is used as an object. See Soisalon-Soininen, *Die Infinitive in der Septuaginta*, 194.

116 Soisalon-Soininen, Die Infinitive in der Septuaginta, 208.

117 See Sollamo, Renderings of Hebrew Semiprepositions in the Septuagint, 284.

118 The term 'semiprepositions' has been introduced by Carl Brockelman and indicates the combination of a preposition and a noun but its grammatical function is that of a preposition. See Sollamo, *Renderings of Hebrew Semiprepositions in the Septuagint*, 1; Johan Lust, "Syntax and Translation Greek," *ETL* 77.4 (2001): 395–401, 400.

brew לִפְנֵי, which is considered to be a Hebraism, is not being used by the LXX translator of Proverbs.[119] Sollamo also applies statistical data to support her research. On the basis of three criteria, i.e., the literal translation of common semiprepositions, the more free translation of common semiprepositions and the stereotypical rendering of semiprepositions, she categorises the LXX books into four groups.[120] The first group are the most free translations, the fourth group are the most slavish translations.[121] On the basis of the three criteria, LXX Proverbs, together with Esther, Exodus, Isaiah, Job and Daniel, has been categorised in the first group that entails the most free translations.[122] This group contains the most free translations of Hebrew semiprepositions, seldom or never uses Hebraisms and rarely stereotypes.[123]

Along with Soisalon-Soininen and Sollamo, Anneli Aejmelaeus has also characterised LXX Proverbs as a free translation although she has conducted more research on the LXX translation of the Pentateuch. As already mentioned earlier, she takes the usage of ὅτι *causale* on places where γάρ should have normally been used as a key to characterise the translation technique the LXX translators applied to render their Hebrew *Vorlage* into Greek. The LXX translator of Proverbs translates כי to ὅτι *causale* only six times in his translation, whereas he uses γάρ 56 times.[124] This way, with regard to this aspect of the translation technique, the Greek translation of Proverbs finds itself on the same level as the LXX translation of Exodus.[125]

1.2.3 Conclusion

The qualitative approach that is being applied by the Finnish school examines the Greek rendering of grammatical features that are characteristic for the Hebrew language. These syntactic aspects are being studied in the different LXX books and afterwards compared with Koine Greek literature of that time. By applying this method they aim to discern the quality of the LXX translation and try to define the translation technique of the LXX translators. Also the use of statistical data is being used by the qualitative approach. These data, however,

---

119 See Sollamo, Renderings of Hebrew Semiprepositions in the Septuagint, 70–71 and 80.
120 See Sollamo, Renderings of Hebrew Semiprepositions in the Septuagint, 280 et seq.
121 See Sollamo, Renderings of Hebrew Semiprepositions in the Septuagint, 284–287.
122 See Sollamo, Renderings of Hebrew Semiprepositions in the Septuagint, 284.
123 See Sollamo, Renderings of Hebrew Semiprepositions in the Septuagint, 285.
124 See Aejmelaeus, "Oti Causale in Septuagintal Greek", 22.
125 See Aejmelaeus, "Oti Causale in Septuagintal Greek", 22.

is merely used to support their linguistic analysis. Thus, quantitative research is not their primary concern.

Although the qualitative approach has mostly examined the LXX translation of the Pentateuch, other LXX books have been examined as well. LXX Proverbs, although briefly, has also been an object of their investigation in multiple publications. As indicated above, LXX Proverbs has been characterised as a free translation. The LXX translator tries hard to avoid Hebraisms. This way he (1) avoids the construction ἐν τῷ + infinitive as the rendering of the Hebrew construction ב + infinitive construct, (2) often uses γάρ as a rendering of כי instead of ὅτι *causale* and (3) avoids πρὸ προσώπου as the rendering for the Hebrew לְפְנֵי. Sollamo, Aejmelaeus and Soisalon-Soininen conclude that the translator of LXX Proverbs was someone who had a profound knowledge of the Greek language. According to them, the Greek translation of Proverbs does not resemble a translation but, concerning language, it shows strong resemblances with Koine Greek literature.

Now that we have examined the characterisation of the translation technique of LXX Proverbs by the quantitative and qualitative approach, we will first discuss the characterisation of LXX Proverbs by Johann Cook before we consider the content- and context-related approach and its results on the translation technique of LXX Proverbs.

1.3 Johann Cook

In scholarship the last decennia, Johann Cook is the scholar *par excellence* with regard to LXX Proverbs. He has published extensively on different themes concerning LXX Proverbs, e.g., the translation technique of the LXX translator,[126] the place of origin,[127] the dating[128] and the ideology/theology of LXX Proverbs.[129] Cook is one of the only scholars who has profoundly examined the translation

---

126 See, i.a., Johann Cook, "Following the Septuagint Translators," *JNSL* 22.2 (1996): 181–190; Cook, "Contrasting as a Translation Technique;" Johann Cook, "The Translator of the Septuagint of Proverbs."

127 See, i.a., Cook, "The Septuagint as Contextual Bible Translation."

128 See, i.a., Cook, "The Dating of Septuagint Proverbs."

129 See, i.a., Johann Cook, "Ideology and Translation Technique. Two Sides of the Same Coin?," in *Helsinki Perspectives on the Translation Technique of the Septuagint*, ed. Rajia Sollamo and Seppo Sipilä (Helsinki: Finnish Exegetical Society; Göttingen: Vandenhoeck & Ruprecht, 2001), 195–210; Cook, "The Ideology of Septuagint Proverbs;" Cook, "Theological/ideological Tendenz in the Septuagint."

technique of LXX Proverbs and can, for this reason, not be neglected in this study. Because we cannot categorise Cook's approach under the quantitative or qualitative approach, we will examine how he has analysed the translation technique of Proverbs in this part of our study.

1.3.1 Cook's analysis of the translation technique of LXX Proverbs

According to Cook, the translator of LXX Proverbs is a competent translator who handled his *Vorlage* in a free way.[130] To support this claim, Cook goes further than the Finnish school, i.e., beyond linguistic analysis. Moreover, he examines the ideology and the theology of the translator.[131] According to him, the translation technique of a translator cannot be determined by linguistic analysis alone, one should also take into account the exegesis the translator applied when he translated his Hebrew *Vorlage*.[132] Cook argues that the translator of Proverbs often opted for a certain translation on the basis of religious motives.[133] Throughout his work, he mostly makes a distinction between micro and macro level of a text. In the following sections we will discuss both levels as well as the ideology and theology of the translator in detail. By doing so we will try to provide an adequate image of the translation technique of LXX Proverbs as characterised by Cook.

1.3.1.1 Micro level
In his monograph *The Septuagint of Proverbs. Jewish and/or Hellenistic Proverbs? Concerning the Hellenistic Colouring of LXX Proverbs*, Cook examines six chapters (1; 2; 6; 8; 9 and 31) of LXX Proverbs with special attention to the translation technique of the LXX translator.[134] He carefully analyses the Greek text and observes the translator's (a) semantic approach, (b) syntactic approach and

---

130 Cook, *The Septuagint of Proverbs*, 317.
131 Cook, "Following the Septuagint Translators;" Cook, "Contrasting as a Translation Technique," 405; Cook, "Ideology and Translation Technique," 195. Aejmelaeus also shares the opinion that linguistic analysis can lead to a description of the theology of the LXX translators. She positions herself between two extremes, i.e., the statistical/quantitative approach and the theological approach. See Aejmelaeus, "What We Talk About," 208, 218–219.
132 Cook, *The Septuagint of Proverbs*, 30.
133 Cook, *The Septuagint of Proverbs*, 30.
134 Johann Cook, The Septuagint of Proverbs. Jewish and/or Hellenistic Proverbs? Concerning the Hellenistic Colouring of LXX Proverbs, SVT 69 (Leiden – New York – Köln: Brill, 1997).

(c) stylistic approach with regard to his Hebrew *Vorlage*.[135] These three approaches are situated, according to Cook, on the so- called micro level of the text. Out of his analyses he concludes that the translator had 'theological/ideological' motivations to render his *Vorlage* freely.[136] This approach will be discussed below.

A   The semantic approach

Cook characterises the translation technique of LXX Proverbs as a combination of unity and diversity.[137] On the one hand, the translator paraphrases his lexemes, on the other hand, he stereotypes them.[138]

With regard to the paraphrasing tendency, he renders some Hebrew lexemes by different Greek lexemes, whereas in other cases he uses only one Greek lexeme to render different Hebrew lexemes.[139] An example of the translation of a Hebrew lexeme by multiple Greek lexemes is אָרַב. This word occurs six times in Proverbs and is each time rendered with a different Greek word, i.e., κοινωνέω (Prov 1:11), ἐνεδρεύω (Prov 7:12), δόλιος (Prov 12:6), ἀπολεῖται (Prov 23:28) and μὴ προσαγάγῃς (Prov 24:15)[140]. An example of a Greek word that is used to translate multiple Hebrew words is παρανόμος ('the transgressor, the treacherous').[141] This word is used 73 times in the LXX, of which 25 times in LXX Proverbs.[142] The translator uses this Greek lexeme to render 11 different Hebrew words, i.e., בֶּגֶד (Prov 2:22; 11:6; 13:2; 22:12; 23:28; 25:19), לוֹז (Prov 3:32), רֵעַ (Prov 4:14), חָמָס (Prov 14:17; 16:29), אָוֶן (Prov 6:12; 17:4), בּוּשׁ (Prov 10:5), מְזִמָּה (Prov 12:2), פֶּשַׁע (Prov 19:11), זוּר (Prov 22:14), כְּסִיל (Prov 26:3) and רָשָׁע (Prov 19:12).[143]

---

135   Cook, *The Septuagint of Proverbs*, 31.
136   Cook, "Ideology and Translation Technique," 209.
137   Cook has introduced this designation for the translation technique of LXX Proverbs in, Cook, *The Septuagint of Proverbs*. This designation is also used multiple times in later works of Cook, i.a., Cook, "Ideology and Translation Technique," 197; Cook, "Theological/ideological Tendenz," 65; Cook, "The Translator(s) of the Septuagint of Proverbs," *TC: A Journal of Biblical Textual Criticism* 7 (2002): http://rosetta.reltech.org/TC/v07/Cook2002.html.
138   Cook, "Ideology and Translation Technique," 197.
139   Cook, "Ideology and Translation Technique," 208.
140   Cook, *The Septuagint of Proverbs*, 70. אָרַב also occurs in Prov 1:18. However, it has no equivalent in the LXX.
141   See Cook, "Ideology and Translation Technique," 200; LEH, 466.
142   See Cook, "Ideology and Translation Technique," 200.
143   See Cook, "Ideology and Translation Technique," 200. The other seven instances where παρανόμος is used are not attested in the Hebrew text and are thus considered a plus, i.e., Prov 1:18; 11:30; 14:9; 21:24; 28:17; 29:4 and 18.

In some cases, the translator uses only one accordingly Greek equivalent for a given Hebrew lexeme.[144] In this instance, one can speak of 'stereotyping.'[145] An example hereof is the usage of the lexeme σοφία.[146] This Greek word occurs 50 times in LXX Proverbs and is being used 34 times as an equivalent of חָכְמָה.[147] According to Cook, the LXX translator of Proverbs renders words that have to do with the concept of wisdom frequently with the same Greek word, e.g., φρόνησις (in connection with the Hebrew root בין), παιδεία (מוּסָר) and ἐντολή (מִצְוָה).[148] The tendency to stereotype is also being examined by the quantitative approach as is already mentioned earlier in the section on Emanuel Tov.

The translator of LXX Proverbs uses a substantial amount of Greek *hapax legomena* to render his Hebrew *Vorlage*.[149] This indicates a translator who mastered the Greek language very well.[150] According to Cook, many of these hapaxes are borrowed from classical Greek sources such as Aristotle and Plato.[151] An example hereof is ἐργάτις ('zealous') (Prov 6:8). This lexeme is also used in Aristotle's *Historia Animalium* (HA 627a12).[152] In both works, the LXX and *Historia Animalium*, the word is attested in connection with the image of the bee.[153] On the basis of this argument alone, it is impossible and unscientific to conclude that the translator of LXX translator of Proverbs knew and incorporated the work of Aristotle. Therefore, Cook postulates another argument to strengthen his findings. Aristotle connects the zealousness of bees with that of ants (οἱ μύρμηκες; HA 623b14) (HA 623b10-20). In the LXX version of Proverbs, the same

---

144 See Cook, "Ideology and Translation Technique," 201.

145 See Cook, "Ideology and Translation Technique," 201.

146 See Cook, "Ideology and Translation Technique," 201.

147 In all other cases, חָכְמָה is being translated by γνῶσις (2:6), ἐντολή (4:5), πηγὴ ζωῆς (18:4) and προσέχω (31:26). See Cook, "Ideology and Translation Technique," 201.

148 See Cook, "Ideology and Translation Technique," 201.

149 A complete list with Greek *hapax legomena* in LXX Proverbs can be found in Cook, "The Translator(s) of the Septuagint of Proverbs."

150 See Cook, *The Septuagint of Proverbs*, 317; Cook, "The Translator of the Septuagint of Proverbs. Is His Style the Result of Platonic and/or Stoic Influence?," 550; Cook, "A Case Study of LXX Proverbs, LXX Job and 4 Maccabees," 64.

151 See Cook, *The Septuagint of Proverbs*, 318–319; 335–342; Cook, "A Case Study of LXX Proverbs, LXX Job and 4 Maccabees," 64.

152 See Cook, *The Septuagint of Proverbs*, 165; Cook, "The Translator of the Septuagint of Proverbs. Is His Style the Result of Platonic and/or Stoic Influence?," 550.

153 See Cook, *The Septuagint of Proverbs*, 165. In *Historia Animalium* the plural form is used, namely ἐργάτιδες.

connection between bees and ants is being made.[154] Prov 6:6 encourages the lazy person to go to the ant and to observe its zealous ways in order to become wiser than the ant (Ἴθι πρὸς τὸν μύρμηκα, ὦ ὀκνηρέ, καὶ ζήλωσον ἰδὼν τὰς ὁδοὺς αὐτοῦ καὶ γενοῦ ἐκείνου σοφώτερος·). Two verses further, in Prov 6:8a, the lazy person is encouraged to go to the bee and to observe its zealousness and to look how serious she is in executing her work (ἢ πορεύθητι πρὸς τὴν μέλισσαν καὶ μάθε ὡς ἐργάτις ἐστὶν τήν τε ἐργασίαν ὡς σεμνὴν ποιεῖται). On the basis of these two comparisons, on the one hand the attestation of the and as the bee, and on the other hand the same order as the one in *Historia Animalium* that is being respected, Cook concludes that the LXX translator of Proverbs must have known the work of Aristotle and subsequently incorporated it in his translation.[155] However, according to Cook, the implementation of the ant and the bee in the LXX translation does not share the same meaning as in Aristotle's work, i.e., a description of the features of both insects.[156] Moreover, the translator used these images to clarify the Hebrew text, namely that wisdom is better than strength and that poverty can be combatted by zealousness.[157]

Out of the analysis above, it is clear, according to Cook, that the translator handles his *Vorlage* in a diverse way on the semantic level. By using a considerable amount of *hapax legomena* and the extensive Greek vocabulary that the translator applies to render Hebrew lexemes, the translator shows himself to be an expert in Greek language. Due to this profound knowledge of Greek, the translator was capable to clarify and nuance the meaning of his *Vorlage* for his target audience.

B The syntactic approach

On the syntactic level there are, according to Cook, also a considerable amount of differences between the MT- and LXX-version of Proverbs. These differences have to do with micro syntactic aspects, i.e., grammatical aspects such as num-

---

154 See Gerleman, *Proverbs*, 30–31; Ronald L. Giese, "Strength Through Wisdom and the Bee in LXX Prov 6,8[a-c]," *Biblica* 73.3 (1992) 404–411, 411.

155 See Cook, *The Septuagint of Proverbs*, 319. Although this might be the case, it is important to keep in mind that the image of the bee and the ant were common images in the time when the LXX translation of Proverbs was made. It is not necessarily so that the LXX translator of Proverbs was familiar with the works of Aristotle. It is more likely that they reflect the same Hellenistic milieu. In this respect, these images are also being used in other contemporary works of that time, e.g., the *Sentences of Pseudo-Phocylides*. See Pieter W. van der Horst, *The Sentences of Pseudo-Phocylides with Introduction and Commentary*, SVTP 4 (Leiden: Brill, 1978), 222-225.

156 See Cook, *The Septuagint of Proverbs*, 319.

157 See Cook, *The Septuagint of Proverbs*, 319.

ber, tenses, particles and even morphology, but also with macro syntactic aspects, such as the difference in verse and/or chapter structure.

Moreover, these adaptations that the translator brought about on micro syntactic level can influence the macro syntactic level.[158] An example hereof is Prov 1:28-32:

MT	LXX
אָז יִקְרָאֻנְנִי וְלֹא אֶעֱנֶה יְשַׁחֲרֻנְנִי וְלֹא יִמְצָאֻנְנִי: ²⁸	²⁸ ἔσται γὰρ ὅταν ἐπικαλέσησθέ με, ἐγὼ δὲ οὐκ
תַּחַת כִּי־שָׂנְאוּ דָעַת וְיִרְאַת יְהוָֹה לֹא בָחָרוּ: ²⁹	εἰσακούσομαι ὑμῶν·
לֹא־אָבוּ לַעֲצָתִי נָאֲצוּ כָּל־תּוֹכַחְתִּי: ³⁰	ζητήσουσίν με κακοὶ καὶ οὐχ εὑρήσουσιν.
וְיֹאכְלוּ מִפְּרִי דַרְכָּם וּמִמֹּעֲצֹתֵיהֶם יִשְׂבָּעוּ: ³¹	²⁹ ἐμίσησαν γὰρ σοφίαν, τὸν δὲ φόβον τοῦ
כִּי מְשׁוּבַת פְּתָיִם תַּהַרְגֵם וְשַׁלְוַת כְּסִילִים ³²	κυρίου οὐ προείλαντο
תְּאַבְּדֵם:	³⁰ οὐδὲ ἤθελον ἐμαῖς προσέχειν βουλαῖς,
	ἐμυκτήριζον δὲ ἐμοὺς ἐλέγχους.
	³¹ τοιγαροῦν ἔδονται τῆς ἑαυτῶν ὁδοῦ τοὺς
	καρποὺς καὶ τῆς ἑαυτῶν ἀσεβείας
	πλησθήσονται·
	³² ἀνθ᾽ ὧν γὰρ ἠδίκουν νηπίους,
	φονευθήσονται, καὶ ἐξετασμὸς ἀσεβεῖς ὀλεῖ.
	ὅτι ἐγώ εἰμι κύριος ὁ θεὸς ὑμῶν.
²⁸ Then they will call upon me, but I will not answer; they will seek me diligently, but will not find me.	²⁸ For it shall be when you call upon me, then I will not listen to you; evil people will seek me but will not find me,
²⁹ Because they hated knowledge and did not choose the fear of the Lord,	²⁹ For they hated wisdom and did not choose the fear of the Lord,
³⁰ would have none of my counsel, and despised all my reproof,	³⁰ nor were they willing to pay attention to my councils but despised my reproofs.
³¹ therefore they shall eat the fruit of their way and be sated with their own devices.	³¹ Therefore they will eat the fruits of their own way and be filled with their own impiety,
³² For waywardness kills the simple, and the complacency of fools destroys them.	³² for, because they would wrong the simple, they will be murdered and an inquiry will ruin the impious.

Cook observes that the contrast that the translator brings about between οἱ ἄκακοι (Prov 1:22) and οἱ κακοί (Prov 1:28) results in several syntactic adjustments in these passages.[159] This manifests itself in Prov 1:32.[160] The translator connects verse 32 with the previous verses by making οἱ κακοί subject of those

---

158 See Cook, *The Septuagint of Proverbs*, 104.
159 See Cook, *The Septuagint of Proverbs*, 104.
160 Cook, "Contrasting as a Translation Technique in the LXX of Proverbs," 407.

who have done injustice to the innocent starting from verse 28.[161] By the peculiar translation of Cook of Prov 1:32, namely: 'for the simple are killed by their turning away,'[162] these bad persons are being murdered in verse 32 and not the simple as indicated in MT.[163]

Because Cook ascribes all changes in syntax to the creativity and exegetical activity of the translator, it seems to be logical that he also ascribes the differences it brings about in the structure of the text to the translator instead of a different Hebrew *Vorlage*. The differences between MT Proverbs and LXX Proverbs on a macro level are being discussed elaborately below.

C Stylistic approach

According to Cook, the LXX translator of Proverbs shows himself to be an excellent stylist. He applies (1) rhyme, (2) dualisms or contrast, (3) alliterations, (4) special particles and (5) harmonisation to stylise his work.[164]

(1) The LXX translator tried to introduce rhyme in his translation. Some examples are Prov 1:1-3; Prov 1:11-13 and Prov 9:18. In Prov 1:1-3 the first word of verse 1, i.e., παροιμίαι, is being rhymed with infinitives that are being used in verses 2 and 3, i.e., γνῶναι, νοῆσαι (2x) and δέξασθαί.[165] According to Cook, this cannot be a coincidence and therefore he argues that the translator has consciously applied this out of stylistic motivations.[166] In Prov 1,11-13 we can find rhyme as well. Four times a conjunctive aorist 1st plural (-ωμεν) is being used: κρύψωμεν, καταπίωμεν, ἄρωμεν and πλήσωμεν.[167] In Prov 9:18 the translator tries to end the different colons with rhyme:

¹⁸ ὁ δὲ οὐκ οἶδεν ὅτι γηγενεῖς παρ' αὐτῇ ὄλλυνται,
καὶ ἐπὶ πέτευρον ᾅδου συναντᾷ.
¹⁸ᵃ ἀλλὰ ἀποπήδησον, μὴ ἐγχρονίσῃς ἐν τῷ τόπῳ
μηδὲ ἐπιστήσῃς τὸ σὸν ὄμμα πρὸς αὐτήν·
¹⁸ᵇ οὕτως γὰρ διαβήσῃ ὕδωρ ἀλλότριον
καὶ ὑπερβήσῃ ποταμὸν ἀλλότριον·
¹⁸ᶜ ἀπὸ δὲ ὕδατος ἀλλοτρίου ἀπόσχου
καὶ ἀπὸ πηγῆς ἀλλοτρίας μὴ πίῃς,

---

161 See Cook, *The Septuagint of Proverbs*, 96.
162 See Cook, *The Septuagint of Proverbs*, 96.
163 See Cook, *The Septuagint of Proverbs*, 96.
164 See Cook, *The Septuagint of Proverbs*, 64–65, 70–71, 83, 98, 105, 109, 121, 150–151 and 280.
165 See Cook, *The Septuagint of Proverbs*, 65; Cook, "Contrasting as a Translation Technique in the LXX of Proverbs," 407–408.
166 See Cook, *The Septuagint of Proverbs*, 65.
167 See Cook, *The Septuagint of Proverbs*, 83.

^{18d}ἵνα πολὺν ζήσῃς χρόνον,
προστεθῇ δέ σοι ἔτη ζωῆς.

In these verses rhyme is obviously present: ὄλλυνται rhymes with συναντᾷ, ἀλλότριον (2x) with χρόνον and πίῃς with ζωῆς.[168]

(2) Cook shows that the LXX translator of Proverbs uses dualisms more often than MT.[169] According to him, this indicates that contrasting by using dualisms is an important aspect of the translation technique of the translator[170]. Some examples of dualisms are: ἄκακος and ἄφρων (Prov 1:22); βουλὴ καλὴ and κακὴ βουλὴ (Prov 2:11.17); δίκαιος and ἄδικος (e.g., Prov 6:17; 25:29); κακός and σοφός (Prov 9:8); κακός and ἀγαθός (Prov 15:15), etc. Here again, Cook holds the opinion that these dualisms are being used because of religious motivations.[171] Cook even argues that the translator has made structural adaptations in the text on the basis of dualistic religious motives.[172] These adaptation are being discussed below.

(3) The usage of alliterations is a third example that shows the stylistic expertise of the translator. An example of an explicit addition by the LXX translator can be found in Prov 1:23:

MT	LXX
תָּשׁוּבוּ לְתוֹכַחְתִּי ^{23a}	^{23a} καὶ ὑπεύθυνοι ἐγένοντο ἐλέγχοις.
הִנֵּה אַבִּיעָה לָכֶם ^{23b}	^{23b} ἰδοὺ προήσομαι ὑμῖν ἐμῆς πνοῆς ῥῆσιν,
רוּחִי אוֹדִיעָה דְבָרַי אֶתְכֶם: ^{23c}	^{23c} διδάξω δὲ ὑμᾶς τὸν ἐμὸν λόγον.
^{23a} Give heed to my reproof;	^{23a} And they became liable to reproofs.
^{23b} I will pour out my thoughts to you;	^{23b} Look! I will bring forth to you the expression of my breath,
^{23c} I will make my words known to you.	^{23c} and I will teach you my word.

---

168 See Cook, *The Septuagint of Proverbs*, 280.
169 See Cook, "Contrasting as a Translation Technique in the LXX of Proverbs,", 409; Cook, "The Translator of the Septuagint of Proverbs. Is His Style the Result of Platonic and/or Stoic Influence?," 546.
170 See Cook, "Contrasting as a Translation Technique in the LXX of Proverbs," 409, 414; Cook, "Exegesis in the Septuagint of Proverbs," 193–196; Cook, "Theological/ideological Tendenz," 77. See also the study of Gerard Tauberschmidt with regard to parallelisms in LXX Proverbs: Gerhard Tauberschmidt, *Secondary Parallelism. A Study of Translation Technique in LXX Proverbs*, SBL 15 (Leiden: Brill, 2004).
171 See Cook, "Contrasting as a Translation Technique," 404–405.
172 See Cook, "Contrasting as a Translation Technique," 410 and 413–414.

The alliteration is not located on the first consonants (which is usually the case with alliteration) but on the vowel -ῇ of the words ἐμῆς πνοῆς ῥῆσιν of the second part of the verse.[173] In this verse we can speak of assonance instead of alliteration, something Cook does not point out. The word ῥῆσιν is not present in the Hebrew version and is, according to Cook, an addition of the translator to harmonise colons b and c (ῥῆσιν and λόγον) in order to obtain alliteration.[174] Cook argues, without further argumentation, that the translator uses ἐμῆς πνοῆς ῥῆσιν as an interpretation of רוּחִי on religious grounds.[175]

(4) The translator uses Greek particles in a creative way.[176] This way, the particles δέ and τέ of the first chapter are often used to enhance fluidity.[177]

(5) An example of harmonisation has already been given above when talking about alliterations in Prov 1:23, i.e., the addition of the word ῥῆσιν. The usage of the word λόγους as a rendering of the Hebrew in Prov 1:24 is also a sign that the translator harmonised the text in accordance with the context (in this case verse 23), according to Cook:[178]

MT	LXX
יַעַן קָרָאתִי וַתְּמָאֵנוּ נָטִיתִי יָדִי וְאֵין מַקְשִׁיב׃	ἐπειδὴ ἐκάλουν καὶ οὐχ ὑπηκούσατε καὶ ἐξέτεινον λόγους καὶ οὐ προσείχετε.
Because I have called and you refused, have stretched out my hand and no one heeded.	Since I would call but you did not heed. And I would prolong words but you were not paying attention.

Another example is Prov 9:16:

MT	LXX
מִי־פֶתִי יָסֻר הֵנָּה וַחֲסַר־לֵב וְאָמְרָה לּוֹ׃	Ὅς ἐστιν ὑμῶν ἀφρονέστατος, ἐκκλινάτω πρός με· ἐνδεέσι δὲ φρονήσεως παρακελεύομαι λέγουσα.

---

173 See Cook, *The Septuagint of Proverbs*, 87 and 98–99.
174 See Cook, *The Septuagint of Proverbs*, 87 and 98.
175 See Cook, *The Septuagint of Proverbs*, 99. Elsewhere he postulates the same thing without further argumentation. See Cook, "Contrasting as a Translation Technique," 409.
176 See Cook, "Contrasting as a Translation Technique," 407.
177 See Cook, "Contrasting as a Translation Technique," 407; Cook, *The Septuagint of Proverbs*, 101–102.
178 See Cook, "Contrasting as a Translation Technique," 408.

MT	LXX
You who are simple, turn in here!" And to those without sense she says.	He of you who is most foolish, let him turn aside to me, and to those that are in need of prudence I urge, saying.

Cook argues that this verse finds its origin in Prov 1:5: τῶνδε γὰρ ἀκούσας σοφὸς σοφώτερος ἔσται (for by hearing these things the wise will become wiser).[179] In this verse, Solomon says that the wise becomes wiser by listening (σοφὸς σοφώτερος). Parallel to this verse, Lady Folly says in Prov 9:16 that most fools (ὅς ἐστιν ὑμῶν ἀφρονέστατος) have to turn aside to her.[180] Cook considers this an example of internal harmonisation.[181] Although a superlative (σοφώτερος and ἀφρονέστατος) is being used in both verses, the comparison Cook makes is not very clear in my opinion. In his analysis, Cook does not take into account the possibility that these, according to him harmonised verses, were being attested in the Hebrew *Vorlage* of the LXX translator. According to me, the argument of Cook is unclear and therefore too weak to speak of internal harmonisation. The argument of harmonisation by the translator seems, in my opinion, to be stronger in Prov 1:24 whereby λόγους is being used as a rendering of the Hebrew word יָדִי. Consequently, verse 24b is not only harmonised with verse 23 but also with the previous colon 24a: ἐπειδὴ ἐκάλουν καὶ οὐχ ὑπηκούσατε (since I would call but you did not heed). It seems to me that the translator found colon b נָטִיתִי יָדִי (I have stretched out my hand) odd in the context of the previous verse (23) and colon (24a) where the Hebrew text speaks about the act of speaking. On the one hand, I can find myself in Cook's analysis when he argues that the translator has modified the Hebrew text of Prov 1:24b in order to harmonise the text with the immediate context, on the other hand, does Prov 9:16 not show any signs of internal harmonisation. Whether these verses were attested in this form in the Hebrew *Vorlage* of the LXX translator or whether they have been harmonised by the LXX translator must be discerned by further research.

The stylistic adaptations that the translator made were, according to Cook, not only stylistic but can also have originated from theological considerations, as is indicated multiple times above.[182] An example can be found in chapter 8. In

---

179 See Cook, *The Septuagint of Proverbs*, 277. According to Cook, Prov 9:16 can also be based on Prov 9:9 (δίδου σοφῷ ἀφορμήν, καὶ σοφώτερος ἔσται). See Cook, *The Septuagint of Proverbs*, 288.

180 See Cook, *The Septuagint of Proverbs*, 278.

181 See Cook, *The Septuagint of Proverbs*, 278.

182 See Cook, *The Septuagint of Proverbs*, 226.

verses 23-25, the translator uses the construction πρὸ τοῦ five times to introduce a temporal clause:[183]

²³ πρὸ τοῦ αἰῶνος ἐθεμελίωσέν με ἐν ἀρχῇ,
²⁴ πρὸ τοῦ τὴν γῆν ποιῆσαι
καὶ πρὸ τοῦ τὰς ἀβύσσους ποιῆσαι,
πρὸ τοῦ προελθεῖν τὰς πηγὰς τῶν ὑδάτων,
²⁵ πρὸ τοῦ ὄρη ἑδρασθῆναι,
πρὸ δὲ πάντων βουνῶν γεννᾷ με.

This construction is not present in the Hebrew text. Cook argues that this stylistic adaption also has an ideological foundation.[184] According to him, the translator uses this construction to emphasise that God is the sole Creator and that wisdom has been created first.[185] Moreover, by changing the subject of the verbs from a 1st person singular (which refers to wisdom) to a 3rd person singular (referring to God) in verses 23-25, God is presented as the only creator.[186] In verse 31 this statement is even sharpened: ὅτε εὐφραίνετο τὴν οἰκουμένην συντελέσας (when he rejoiced after he had completed the world).[187] By doing so, the translator wanted to prevent the misunderstanding that wisdom would have been involved in the creation of the cosmos.[188] The Hebrew text can be interpreted as such.

Just as the semantic approach, this approach demonstrates the profound knowledge of Greek the translator possessed.[189] The translator shows himself to be somebody who could play with the Greek language by enhancing parallelisms, using dualisms, creating rhyme, *etc.* Still, his stylistic approach was not being used merely for stylistic reasons. Moreover, he also applied this approach for religious intentions. He nuances or changes certain aspects of his *Vorlage* in order to convey the meaning of the text to his target audience in a more comprehensible way.

---

183 See Cook, *The Septuagint of Proverbs*, 226.
184 See Cook, *The Septuagint of Proverbs*, 224.
185 See Cook, *The Septuagint of Proverbs*, 224, 226. See also Cook, "Were the LXX Versions of Proverbs and Job," 156: Cook, "The Dating of Septuagint Proverbs," 396; Cook, "Aspects of the Relationship between the Septuagint Versions of Proverbs and Job," 324.
186 See Cook, "Were the LXX Versions of Proverbs and Job," 150–151, 156.
187 See Cook, "The Dating of Septuagint Proverbs," 396.
188 Cook, "Were the LXX Versions of Proverbs and Job," 156.
189 See Cook, *The Septuagint of Proverbs*, 317.

1.3.1.2 Macro level

It is commonly known that the structure of the chapters in the LXX version of Proverbs differ extensively from the MT-version. The structure of Proverbs in MT is mostly presented as follows:[190]

	verses	content
I	1:1-9:18	Prologue
II	10:1-22:16	Proverbs of Solomon
III	22:17-24:22	Words of the wise
IV	24:23-34	Also words of the wise
V	25:1-29:27	Hizkia's collection of proverbs of Solomon
VI	30:1-33	Words of Agur
VII	31:1-31	Words of Lemuel's mother

The LXX version attests another structure, namely:[191]

	verses	content
I-III	1:1-24:22	Prologue + Proverbs of Solomon + words of the wise
VI, part 1	30:1-14	Words of Agur (part 1)
IV	24:23-34	Also words of the wise
VI, part 2	30:15-33	Words of Agur (part 2)
VII, part 1	31:1-9	Words of Lemuel's mother (part 1)
V	25:1-29:27	Hizkia's collection of proverbs of Solomon
VII, part 2	31:10-31	Words of Lemuel's mother (part 2)

According to Cook, these differences can be ascribed to the activity of a creative translator who has rendered his *Vorlage* in a free and creative way.[192] The trans-

---

190 Cfr. Bryan Beeckman, "Voorbij vergeving? Een introductie in het boek Spreuken," *Ezra* 47 (2016) 109–119, 111; Eibert Tigchelaar, "Spreuken,", in *De Bijbel literair. Opbouw en gedachtegang van de bijbelse geschriften en hun onderlinge relaties*, ed. Jan Fokkelman and Wim Weren (Zoetermeer: Meinema; Kapellen: Pelckmans, 2003), 357–370, 358, also the numerous commentaries on Proverbs.

191 Beeckman, "Voorbij vergeving?," 112; Tov, "Recensional Differences," 429.

192 See Cook, "The Greek of Proverbs" 618; Johann Cook and Arie van der Kooij, *Law, Prophets, and Wisdom. On the Provenance of Translators and their Books in the Septuagint Version*, CBET 68 (Leuven, Peeters, 2012), 91, 94 and 105; Cook, "'ishah zarah," 460; Cook, "The Transla-

position of whole verses can be ascribed to the activity of the translator and thus not to a *Vorlage* that differed from the *Vorlage* of MT.[193] This way, Cook indicates, among other things, that some verses are intentionally re-arranged due to religious motives that are dualistic in nature.[194] An example is the LXX version of Prov 29:27 and 31:10:

LXX	NETS
[29,27] βδέλυγμα δικαίοις ἀνὴρ ἄδικος, βδέλυγμα δὲ ἀνόμῳ κατευθύνουσα ὁδός. [31,10] Γυναῖκα ἀνδρείαν τίς εὑρήσει; τιμιωτέρα δέ ἐστιν λίθων πολυτελῶν ἡ τοιαύτη.	[29,27] An unjust man is an abomination to the righteous, and the direct way is an abomination to the lawless. [31,10] Who can find a courageous wife? Yes, such a one is more precious than valuable jewels.

---

tor of the Septuagint of Proverbs," 547. See also the article of Hans Ausloos and Bénédicte Lemmelijn concerning the creativity of the LXX translators: Ausloos and Lemmelijn, "Faithful Creativity."

193 See, i.a., Cook, "The Greek of Proverbs," 618; Cook and van der Kooij, *Law, Prophets, and Wisdom*, 129; Cook, "The Ideology of Septuagint Proverbs," 467–469. Ruth Scoralick also shares the opinion that the transposition of verse scan be explained due to the freedom of the LXX transator. Ruth Scoralick, "Salomos griechische Gewänder. Beobachtungen zur Septuagintafassung des Sprichwörterbuches," in *Rettendes Wissen. Studien zum Fortgang weisheitlichen Denkens im Frühjudentum und im frühen Christentum*, ed. Karl Löning and Martin Faßnacht, AOAT 300 (Münster: Ugarit-Verlag, 2002), 43–75, 59: "Nach meiner Analyse sind sowohl der hebräische als auch der griechische Text planvoll angeordnet [...]. Der Septuagintatext weist dabei Gestaltungsprinzipien auf, die nur in der griechischen Fassung des Sprichwörterbuches möglich sind, insofern auf eine kreative Eigenleistung des Übersetzers hindeuten und die Annahme einer nicht überlieferten hebräischen Vorlage unwahrscheinlich machen." Paul de Lagarde, however, argues that the translator read the chapters, which were presented next to each other in adjacent columns, incorrectly and miscopied the verses. See de Lagarde, *Anmerkungen*, 51. Fox does not ascribe the differences in structure to the translator nor due to a different Hebrew *Vorlage* but to an accidental displacement of text by a later Greek of Hebrew scribe: "It is likely that the Septuagint's order resulted from accidental displacement [...]. This is unlikely to have happened by shuffling of leaves in a Greek codex [...], because the two [displaced] blocks are of different sizes. Possibly a copyist in Greek or Hebrew skipped over major blocks (perhaps by rolling up his scroll and then reopening too far along), after which he returned to incorporate the skipped material. In any case, the different large-scale ordering seen in G-Proverbs has no inherent connection to the translator's other changes and shows no signs of being the translator's doing." Fox, *Proverbs*, 38.

194 See Cook, "Contrasting as a Translation Technique," 410, 413; Cook, "Exegesis in the Septuagint of Proverbs," 188.

These verses follow each other in the LXX but not in MT.[195] According to Cook, we can see the creativity of the translator at work here: He re-arranges the verses in order to create a (moralising) dualism or contract, i.e., ἀνὴρ ἄδικος and γυναῖκα ἀνδρείαν, and because the ending of Prov 29 fitted better with Prov 31:10 instead of with the beginning of chapter 30.[196] The technique of contrasting is characteristic for the translation technique of LXX Proverbs, as mentioned earlier.[197] For these reasons Cook ascribes these adaptations on macro level to the translator's work.

By arguing that the transposition of verses can be explained due to the work of the translator, Cook's view is opposed to Tov who argues that the differences in verse order can be ascribed to a Hebrew *Vorlage* that differed from MT.[198] Tov sees the *Vorlage* of the LXX as a 'recension', indicating a revision of a text. According to Tov, the *Vorlage* used by the LXX translator of Proverbs reflects an editorial stage of the MT text.[199] I would like to argue for different versions of the text, that existed next to the each other and were of equal value. I want to consider all the textual witnesses as valuable witnesses since the different manuscripts can no longer be seen as deviations or errors from their 'original.'[200] In contrast to this view, it seems to me that Tov, when using the word 'recension,' sees the LXX version as a revision/reworking (which carries a rather negative connotation) of the 'original' Hebrew text, which would be attested in MT. In my view, this thesis can no longer be maintained.

---

195 MT attests another version than LXX: תּוֹעֲבַת צַדִּיקִים אִישׁ עָוֶל וְתוֹעֲבַת רָשָׁע יְשַׁר־דָּרֶךְ (The righteous know the rights of the poor; the wicked have no such understanding) (Prov 29:27); אֵשֶׁת־חַיִל מִי יִמְצָא וְרָחֹק מִפְּנִינִים מִכְרָהּ (A capable wife who can find? She is far more precious than jewels) (Prov 31:10).

196 See Cook, "Contrasting as a Translation Technique," 411-413; Cook, "The Ideology of Septuagint Proverbs," 469.

197 See Cook, "The Ideology of Septuagint Proverbs," 469.

198 See Tov, "Recensional Differences," 419–431. Also Richard Clifford shares Tov's opinion. See Richard J. Clifford, "Observations on the Text and Versions of Proverbs," in *Wisdom, You Are My Sister. Studies in Honor of Roland E. Murphy, O.Carm., on the Occasion of His Eightieth Birthday*, ed. Michael L. Barré, CBQMS 29 (Washington, DC: The Catholic Biblical Association of America, 1997), 47–61, 55; Richard J. Clifford, *Proverbs. A Commentary*, OTL (Louisville, KY: Westminster John Knox Press, 1999), 28. Gerard Tauberschmidt argues that the differences on a macro level can be ascribed to a different *Vorlage*. He does not make a statement on how this *Vorlage* factually looked like. See Tauberschmidt, *Secondary Parallelism*, 227.

199 See Tov, "Recensional Differences," 431; Tov, *Textual Criticism of the Hebrew Bible* (Minneapolis, MN: Fortress Press; Assen: Royal Van Gorcum, 1992²), 337.

200 See Bénédicte Lemmelijn, "Textual Criticism," in *Oxford Handbook of the Septuagint*, ed. Alison G. Salvesen and Timothy M. Law (Oxford: Oxford University Press, 2021), 709–721, 712–714.

Thus, Cook is careful when ascribing the differences in the Greek text toward the Hebrew text to a deviating *Vorlage*. Because of the fact that the Hebrew *Vorlage* of the LXX version of Proverbs has not been transmitted, we cannot be certain that the *Vorlage* differed from the text as attested in MT.[201] According to Cook, it is only possible to compare the LXX-version with the MT-version and draw conclusions on the basis of this comparison without postulating a different *Vorlage* which might or might not have existed. Therefore, he prefers to explain the difference between MT and the LXX due to the creativity of the LXX translator.[202] In my opinion it seems to be impossible to ascribe all the differences/variants to the creative mind of the translator. It seems to be improbable that a translator has relocated so many verses from one chapter to another. To endorse this claim I want to bring up an argument from the observation of the writing and copying methods in Antiquity.[203] In this period, papyrus scrolls were being used.[204] These scrolls lent themselves for a continuous reading that was intended for a 'start-to-finish'-reading that made it difficult to go from one chapter to another.[205] In the time wherein the LXX translation was being made, writing desks did not exist. These were only introduced around the 4th century. This caused scribes and translators to balance their scroll on their knee while their *Vorlage* was positioned elsewhere.[206] If one imagines this writing/copying technique, it seems highly improbable that the LXX translator of Proverbs trans-

---

201 See Cook, "Contrasting as a Translation Technique," 412.

202 Also in the case of LXX Job, Cook argues that it is the translator that modifies his text because there are no extant textual witnesses that attest a (shorter) Hebrew *Vorlage* of Job. See Cook, "Were the LXX Versions of Proverbs and Job," 148.

203 See also Bryan Beeckman, "Trails of a Different Vorlage."

204 Surprisingly, to my knowledge, no research has been conducted on the way in which the LXX translators handled their *Vorlage* and how this *Vorlage* must have factually looked like. However, there has been some historical research on the material and writing positions of scribes and copiers in Antiquity. Scholars dealing with the synoptic problem have integrated these results in their own research. See, i.a., Robert A. Derrenbacker, *Ancient Compositional Practices and the Synoptic Problem*, BETL 186 (Leuven – Paris – Dudley, MA: Peeters, 2005), esp. 30–39; Eric C. S. Eve, "The Synoptic Problem Without Q?", in *New studies in the Synoptic Problem. Oxford conference, April 2008. Essays in Honour of Christopher M. Tuckett*, ed. Paul Foster *et al.*, BETL 239 (Leuven – Paris – Walpole, MA: Peeters, 2011), 551–570, 565–569.

205 See Derrenbacker, *Ancient Compositional Practices and the Synoptic Problem*, 31: "[...] [A] "book roll" or scroll allowed the reader *continuous* or *sequential* access (as opposed to *random* access) to a particular document, with its design being most conductive to start-to-finish reading." Codices, on the other hand, do lend themselves for an *ad random* access and thus reading of a text. These were, however, only introduced since the first centuries CE. See Derrenbacker, *Ancient Compositional Practices and the Synoptic Problem*, 32.

206 See Derrenbacker, Ancient Compositional Practices and the Synoptic Problem, 37–38.

posed whole chapters and verses from one place to another. This would have cost the translator a lot of effort and would have been extremely time consuming.[207] I would deem it more credible to argue that the translators had a scroll (*Vorlage*) in front of them that had the same chapter order as is attested in the LXX. However, smaller variants can be ascribed to the work of the translator.[208]

1.3.2 The theology/ideology of the translator of LXX Proverbs

Out of the abovementioned analysis of Cook's view on the translation technique of LXX Proverbs, it is clear that he ascribes some of the adaptations the translator made to religious motives the translator held. Once more, Cook distinguishes the activity of the translator on two levels: macro and micro level.

1.3.2.1 Macro level
On a macro level, it has already been indicated that Cook ascribes the differences in chapters to the religious intentions of the translator instead of a different *Vorlage*. By placing Prov 31:10 after Prov 29:27 the translator creates an antithetical parallelism as is mostly the case in chapter 29.[209] Also the absence of the names of Lemuel and Agur in LXX Proverbs can be explained by the work of the translator according to Cook.[210] This happened intentionally because it seemed logical for the translator that all proverbs were only ascribed to Solomon as indicated in Prov 1:1 (Παροιμίαι Σαλωμῶντος υἱοῦ Δαυιδ, ὃς ἐβασίλευσεν ἐν Ισραηλ).[211]

1.3.2.2 Micro level
A characteristic of the translation technique of LXX Proverbs on micro level is, according to Cook, the tendency to 'religionise.'[212] He discerns three levels of

---

207 See also Derrenbacker, Ancient Compositional Practices and the Synoptic Problem, 31.
208 Tauberschmidt concludes that smaller variants are due to the activity of the translator but major variants due to the usage of a different *Vorlage*. However, he does not elaborate this hypothesis. See Tauberschmidt, *Secondary Parallelism*, 227.
209 See Cook, "The Ideology of Septuagint Proverbs," 468–469.
210 See Cook, "The Ideology of Septuagint Proverbs," 471; Cook, "Exegesis in the Septuagint of Proverbs," 189.
211 See Cook, "The Ideology of Septuagint Proverbs," 470–471.
212 See Cook, "Exegesis in the Septuagint of Proverbs."

religionising: (1) by adding the positive, (2) by adding the negative and (3) by contrasting.[213]

(1) An example whereby the translator adds religious nuances by the addition of the positive can be found in Prov 15:27-29:[214]

MT	LXX
²⁷ עֹכֵר בֵּיתוֹ בּוֹצֵעַ בָּצַע וְשׂוֹנֵא מַתָּנֹת יִחְיֶה:	²⁷ ἐξόλλυσιν ἑαυτὸν ὁ δωρολήμπτης, ὁ δὲ μισῶν δώρων λήμψεις σῴζεται. ²⁷ᵃ ἐλεημοσύναις καὶ πίστεσιν ἀποκαθαίρονται ἁμαρτίαι, τῷ δὲ φόβῳ κυρίου ἐκκλίνει πᾶς ἀπὸ κακοῦ.
²⁸ לֵב צַדִּיק יֶהְגֶּה לַעֲנוֹת וּפִי רְשָׁעִים יַבִּיעַ רָעוֹת:	²⁸ καρδίαι δικαίων μελετῶσιν πίστεις, στόμα δὲ ἀσεβῶν ἀποκρίνεται κακά. ²⁸ᵃ δεκταὶ παρὰ κυρίῳ ὁδοὶ ἀνθρώπων δικαίων, διὰ δὲ αὐτῶν καὶ οἱ ἐχθροὶ φίλοι γίνονται.
²⁹ רָחוֹק יְהוָה מֵרְשָׁעִים וּתְפִלַּת צַדִּיקִים יִשְׁמָע:	²⁹ μακρὰν ἀπέχει ὁ θεὸς ἀπὸ ἀσεβῶν, εὐχαῖς δὲ δικαίων ἐπακούει. ²⁹ᵃ κρείσσων ὀλίγη λῆμψις μετὰ δικαιοσύνης ἢ πολλὰ γενήματα μετὰ ἀδικίας. ²⁹ᵇ καρδία ἀνδρὸς λογιζέσθω δίκαια, ἵνα ὑπὸ τοῦ θεοῦ διορθωθῇ τὰ διαβήματα αὐτοῦ.
²⁷ Those who are greedy for unjust gain make trouble for their households, but those who hate bribes will live.	²⁷ A receiver of bribes destroys himself, but he who hates the receiving of bribes is saved. ²⁷ᵃ By acts of mercy and by faithfulness sins are purged, but by the fear of the Lord everyone turns away from evil.
²⁸ The mind of the righteous ponders how to answer, but the mouth of the wicked pours out evil.	²⁸ The hearts of the righteous ponder faithfulness, but the mouth of the impious answers evil things. ²⁸ᵃ The ways of righteous persons are acceptable to the Lord, and through them even enemies become friends.

213 See Cook, "Exegesis in the Septuagint of Proverbs," 189.
214 See Cook, "Exegesis in the Septuagint of Proverbs," 190. More examples, see Cook, "Exegesis in the Septuagint of Proverbs," 190–191.

MT	LXX
[29] The Lord is far from the wicked, but he hears the prayer of the righteous.	[29] God is far from the impious, but he hears the prayers of the righteous. [29a] Better is a small intake with righteousness than abundant produce with injustice. [29b] Let the heart of a man think righteous things, that his steps may be directed by God.

In the abovementioned verses we observe several plusses in comparison with the Hebrew text.[215] These plusses are, according to Cook, all additions made by the translator where the positive aspect is being (more) emphasised.[216] In verse 27, a verse is being added concerning the cleansing of sins by faith and good deeds (ἐλεημοσύναις καὶ πίστεσιν ἀποκαθαίρονται ἁμαρτίαι) and the fear of the Lord (φόβος κυρίου) is also being emphasised. Both terms, πίστις and φόβος κυρίου, have a religious connotation. The verse carries a positive meaning by the cleansing of sins (ἀποκαθαίρονται ἁμαρτίαι) and everyone who turns away from evil (ἐκκλίνει πᾶς ἀπὸ κακοῦ). Verse 28a emphasises that the righteous (δίκαιοι) are favoured by God and that even enemies become friends by them (διὰ δὲ αὐτῶν καὶ οἱ ἐχθροὶ φίλοι γίνονται).[217] This verse is obviously religiously coloured by the addition of the lexeme ὁ κύριος and οἱ δίκαιοι. The term οἱ δίκαιοι carries a positive meaning. Finally, there is also a positive addition in verse 29b whereby the righteous is being rewarded by God (ὁ θεός) by making the steps of his life straight (ὑπὸ τοῦ θεοῦ διορθωθῇ τὰ διαβήματα αὐτοῦ). This time the translator does not use the lexeme ὁ κύριος but ὁ θεός.

(2) Opposite to adding and emphasising the positive, there is the emphasise on the negative.[218] This procedure can also be found in LXX Proverbs. An example of this technique can be located in Prov 15:18:

---

215 Cook does not take into account the fact that these verses are being attested elsewhere in MT namely LXX Prov 15:27a = MT Prov 16:6; LXX Prov 15:28a = MT Prov 16:7; LXX Prov 15:29a = MT Prov 16:8; LXX Prov 15:29b = MT Prov 16:9. For a text-critical analysis of these verses see Beeckman, "Trails of a Different Vorlage," 571–591.
216 See Cook, "Exegesis in the Septuagint of Proverbs," 190.
217 In my article *Voorbij vergeving? Een introductie in het boek Spreuken*, I argue that the LXX translator radicalises the concept of forgiveness that is present in the Hebrew text (Prov 16:7) and replaces it by the concept of reconciliation. The translator goes further than his *Vorlage* and thereby shows another, more radical, theology. See Beeckman, "Voorbij vergeving?," 117–118.
218 See Cook, "Exegesis in the Septuagint of Proverbs," 191–193.

MT	LXX
אִישׁ חֵמָה יְגָרֶה מָדוֹן וְאֶרֶךְ אַפַּיִם יַשְׁקִיט רִיב׃	[18] ἀνὴρ θυμώδης παρασκευάζει μάχας, μακρόθυμος δὲ καὶ τὴν μέλλουσαν καταπραΰνει. [18a] μακρόθυμος ἀνὴρ κατασβέσει κρίσεις, ὁ δὲ ἀσεβὴς ἐγείρει μᾶλλον.
Those who are hot-tempered stir up strife, but those who are slow to anger calm contention.	[18] A passionate man stirs up fights, but he who is slow to anger appeases even an incipient one. [18a] A man slow to anger will extinguish disputes, but an impious person stirs them up exceedingly.

In the LXX version, the addition of verse 18a (μακρόθυμος ἀνὴρ κατασβέσει κρίσεις, ὁ δὲ ἀσεβὴς ἐγείρει μᾶλλον) once more emphasises that patience is a good virtue and that the impious stir up convictions. The translator uses the religiously coloured ὁ ἀσεβὴς to express the negative aspect of this verse.[219]

(3) Contrasting is, as indicated above, a preferred technique of the LXX translator. An example of this technique is the abovementioned βουλὴ καλὴ and κακὴ βουλὴ in Prov 2:11 and 17.

Furthermore, Cook observes on a micro level some more aspects that point to the ideology/theology and by this also the identity of the translator. A first observation is the role of the Law of Moses in LXX Proverbs.[220] Against the opinion of scholars such as Dick, Gerleman and Hengel, Cook observes that the Law of Moses plays a prominent role in LXX Proverbs.[221] According to him the role of the Law of Moses can be detected when looking at (1) the Hebrew and Greek lexemes that are being used to denote the Law, (2) pluses in the Greek text that emphasise the role of the Law and (3) parallels with certain Jewish writings in

---

219 See Cook, "Exegesis in the Septuagint of Proverbs," 192.
220 See especially Cook, "The Law of Moses in Septuagint Proverbs." See also Cook, "A Case Study of LXX Proverbs, LXX Job and 4 Maccabees," 63–64. For the discussion of the role of the Law of Moses in LXX Proverbs and its connection with its role in the works of Philo of Alexandria see Bryan Beeckman, "Apologetics Against the Devaluation of the Mosaic Law in Early Judaism? An Indication of An Anti-Hellenistic Stance in LXX Proverbs and the Works of Philo of Alexandria," *Scriptura* 117.1 (2018) 1–10.
221 See Cook, "The Law of Moses in Septuagint Proverbs," 448, 461.

relation to Prov 28:4 (οἱ δὲ ἀγαπῶντες τὸν νόμον περιβάλλουσιν ἑαυτοῖς τεῖχος/but those who love the law build a wall around themselves).[222]

(1) The Hebrew lexeme תּוֹרָה is attested 12 times in LXX Proverbs and is being translated by different Greek lexemes: νόμος (7x), θεσμός (2x), λόγος (1x), ἔννομος (1x) and νόμιμα (1x).[223] Cook argues that when the singular form of νόμος, θεσμός and λόγος is used, the translator intends the Law of Moses.[224] When the plural of these nouns is used the translator wants to convey a different meaning, i.e., the teachings of the parents.[225]

(2) In several passages the prominent role of the Law of Moses is attested. An example hereof is Prov 9:10 and 13:15:

MT 9:10	LXX 9:10
תְּחִלַּת חָכְמָה יִרְאַת יְהוָה וְדַעַת קְדֹשִׁים בִּינָה:	[10] ἀρχὴ σοφίας φόβος κυρίου, καὶ βουλὴ ἁγίων σύνεσις· [10a] τὸ γὰρ γνῶναι νόμον διανοίας ἐστὶν ἀγαθῆς·
The fear of the Lord is the be-ginning of wisdom, and the knowledge of the holy is understanding.	[10] The beginning of wisdom is the fear of the Lord, and counsel of the saints is understanding, [10a] for to know the law is the sign of a sound mind.

MT 13:15	LXX 13:15
שֵׂכֶל־טוֹב יִתֶּן־חֵן וְדֶרֶךְ בֹּגְדִים אֵיתָן:	σύνεσις ἀγαθὴ δίδωσιν χάριν, τὸ δὲ γνῶναι νόμον διανοίας ἐστὶν ἀγαθῆς, ὁδοὶ δὲ καταφρονούντων ἐν ἀπωλείᾳ.
Good understanding giveth favour, but the way of transgressors is hard.	Sound discretion wins favor, and to know the law is the sign of a sound mind, but the ways of scorners end in destruction.

---

222 See Cook, "The Law of Moses in Septuagint Proverbs," 448.
223 See Cook, "The Law of Moses in Septuagint Proverbs," 449.
224 See Cook, "The Law of Moses in Septuagint Proverbs," 449 and 451. An exception is Prov 4:2 (νόμος). See Cook, "The Law of Moses in Septuagint Proverbs," 451.
225 See Cook, "The Law of Moses in Septuagint Proverbs," 451.

The same plus is attested in both passages, namely τὸ γὰρ/δὲ γνῶναι νόμον διανοίας ἐστὶν ἀγαθῆς (and/for to know the law is the sign of a sound mind).[226] In chapter 9, several warnings are being given towards, *i.a.*, foreign wisdom and the devaluation of the Law.[227] This warning against the devaluation of the Law was an important feature of the ideology of the translator.[228] This is observed in Prov 9:10 and 13:15 where he stressed the importance of the law.[229] Cook ascribes these pluses to the historical milieu of the provenance of LXX Proverbs.[230] The LXX translation of Proverbs would have been written in a time where the influence of Hellenism was a threat for Jewish thought, which eventually led to a devaluation of the Torah by Jews.[231] An example of an Alexandrian Jew that renounced his religion is Dositheos son of Drimylos.[232] Some information about Dositheos can be found in the apocryphal book 3 Maccabees 1:3:

> [...] Dositheos, called the son of Drimylus, a Jew by race, [...] who later had abandoned the observance of the law and had become alienated from ancestral teachings.[233]

3 Maccabees does not depict a positive picture of the Gentiles. The aim of 3 Maccabees is polemical, apologetic, hortatory and etiological.[234] N. Clayton Croy writes: "The author exhorts readers to faithful adherence to the Torah, devotion to the Jerusalem temple, and resistance to the imposition of Gentile religious

---

226 See Cook, "The Law of Moses in Septuagint Proverbs," 455. Cook correctly observes the difference in meaning between γάρ and δέ: "The particle γάρ introduces a final clause, whereas δέ has a paratactical function". See Cook, "The Law of Moses in Septuagint Proverbs," 455.
227 See Cook, "The Law of Moses in Septuagint Proverbs," 456–457.
228 See Cook, "The Law of Moses in Septuagint Proverbs," 457.
229 See Cook, "The Law of Moses in Septuagint Proverbs," 457.
230 See Cook, "The Law of Moses in Septuagint Proverbs," 456.
231 See Cook, "The Dating of Septuagint Proverbs," 397; Cook, "'ishah zarah," 473–474; Cook, "Theological/ideological Tendenz," 77; Cook, "A Case Study of LXX Proverbs, LXX Job and 4 Maccabees," 64.
232 See Jospeh M. Modrzejewski, The Jews of Egypt. From Ramses II to Emperor Hadrian (Princeton: Princeton University Press, 1995), 56; Louis H. Feldman, Jew and Gentile in the Ancient World. Attitudes and Interactions from Alexander to Justinian (Princeton: Princeton University Press, 1993), 82 and Louis H. Feldman, Judaism and Hellenism Reconsidered, SJSJ 107 (Leiden – Boston: Brill, 2006), 68–69. Modrzejeweski refutes the modern critique of the non-authenticity of 3 Maccabees 1,3. On the basis of an extensive analysis of multiple Greek papyri and a demotic document, he comes to the conclusion that Dositheos son of Drimylos did exist. See Modrzejewski, The Jews of Egypt, 56–61.
233 See N. Clayton Croy, 3 Maccabees, SCS (Leiden: Brill, 2006), 3.
234 See Croy, 3 Maccabees, xix.

practices."[235] Taking the provenance of 3 Maccabees, i.e., Alexandria, into account, I want to argue, although cautiously, that it is possible that both LXX Proverbs and 3 Maccabees reflect a similar context.[236]

(3) The LXX translator in Prov 28:4 gives a specific interpretation of a central Jewish religious thought that is also present in Rabbinic literature; i.e., building a wall around the Torah:[237]

MT	LXX
עֹזְבֵי תוֹרָה יְהַלְלוּ רָשָׁע וְשֹׁמְרֵי תוֹרָה יִתְגָּרוּ בָם׃	οὕτως οἱ ἐγκαταλείποντες τὸν νόμον ἐγκωμιάζουσιν ἀσέβειαν, οἱ δὲ ἀγαπῶντες τὸν νόμον περιβάλλουσιν ἑαυτοῖς τεῖχος.
They that forsake the law praise the wicked, but such as keep the law contend with them.	So those who forsake the law praise impiety, but those who love the law build a wall around themselves.

This passage shows some similarities with other Jewish writings, i.e., Mishna, Talmud and the Letter of Aristeas.[238] Pirkei Avot indicates that a wall is being built around the Torah:

Moses received the *Torah* from Sinai, and handed it down to Joshua, and Joshua to the elders, and the elders to the prophets, and the prophets delivered it to the men of the Great Synagogue. They said three things, "Be deliberate in judgment; raise up many disciples; and make a fence about the *Torah*."[239]

The same expression is found in Midrash Rabba (Num. 8:X):

From this you can infer that the Torah has put a fence about its ordinances. We have learned elsewhere: Be deliberate in judgement, raise up many disciples, and make a fence

---

235 Croy, *3 Maccabees*, xix.
236 See Croy, *3 Maccabees*, xix.xiii; Beeckman, "Apologetics Against the Devaluation of the Mosaic Law in Early Judaism?," 4.
237 See Cook, "The Law of Moses in Septuagint Proverbs", 457; Cook, "Theological/ideological Tendenz," 75–76.
238 See Cook, "The Law of Moses in Septuagint Proverbs", 458–459.
239 Jospeh I. Gorfinkle, *The Sayings of the Jewish Fathers. Pirkei Abot* (July 2003); http://www.gutenberg.org/cache/epub/8547/pg8547-images.html (access 21.04.2017); See also Cook, "The Law of Moses in Septuagint Proverbs," *VT* 49.4 (1999): 448–461, 458.

around the Torah. How shall a man make a fence round his own affairs in the same way as the Torah make a fence round hers?[240]

In the LXX version of Proverbs, however, another interpretation of this theological tradition is found: The righteous have to build a wall around themselves.[241] A similar interpretation can be found in the Letter of Aristeas § 139:

συνθεωρήσας οὖν ἕκαστα σοφὸς ὢν ὁ νομοθέτης, ὑπὸ θεοῦ κατεσκευασμένος εἰς ἐπίγνωσιν τῶν ἀπάντων, περιέφραξεν ἡμᾶς ἀδιακόποις χάραξι καὶ σιδηροῖς τείχεσιν, ὅπως μηθενὶ τῶν ἄλλων ἐθνῶν ἐπιμισγώμεθα κατὰ μηδέν, ἁγνοὶ καθεστῶτες κατὰ σῶμα καὶ κατὰ ψυχήν, ἀπολελυμένοι ματαίων δοξῶν, τὸν μόνον θεὸν καὶ δυνατὸν σεβόμενοι παρ᾽ ὅλην τὴν πᾶσαν κτίσιν.[242]	Therefore the lawgiver, who was wise, contemplated each matter, being prepared by God for knowledge of all things, and he fenced us around with unbroken palisades and with iron walls so that we might not intermingle at all with other nations, being pure in both body and soul, having been set free from vain opinions, revering the only and powerful God above all of the entire creation.[243]

The lawgiver that is being mentioned in this passage and who has built the iron walls around the Jewish people is Moses.[244] Moses gave the Law, with moral regulations, to the Jewish people. This Law prohibited Jews to interfere with foreign nations. Cook and Wright recognise the shielding of Jews from pagans and other foreign nations.[245] According to Cook, this meaning is also conveyed in LXX Proverbs.[246]

Drawing on these three arguments, Cook rightly concludes that the Law of Moses has been given a prominent role in LXX Proverbs.[247] The LXX translator had a high regard for the Law and tried to convince his readers for the im-

---

240 Cook, "The Law of Moses in Septuagint Proverbs," 458.
241 See Cook, "The Law of Moses in Septuagint Proverbs," 459.
242 Henry G. Meecham, The Letter of Aristeas. A Linguistic Study with Special Reference to the Greek Bible (Manchester: Manchester University Press, 1935), 22.
243 Benjamin G. Wright, The Letter of Aristeas. 'Aristeas To Philocrates' Or 'On the Translation of the Law of the Jews', CEJL (Berlin: De Gruyter, 2015), 257.
244 See Wright, The Letter of Aristeas, 264.
245 See Cook, "The Law of Moses in Septuagint Proverbs," 459; Wright, *The Letter of Aristeas*, 264.
246 See Cook, "The Law of Moses in Septuagint Proverbs," 459.
247 See Cook, "The Law of Moses in Septuagint Proverbs," 459.

portance of this Law. According to Cook, the translator's target audience called the importance of the Law into question due to the influence of Hellenism.[248]

A second observation is the warning for strange, foreign wisdom in LXX Proverbs.[249] According to Cook אשה זרה (the foreign woman) in Proverbs, wherefore the text warns the reader multiple times in, *i.a.*, Prov 2; 5; 6; 7 and 9, is a metaphor for foreign wisdom.[250] This wisdom would be Greek philosophical thought that was being spread by the emerging Hellenism in the time that Proverbs was being translated into Greek *circa* 200 B.C.E.[251]

Consequently, Cook concludes that the LXX translator of Proverbs was a conservative Jew.[252] This is noticeable from the importance the translator placed on the Law of Moses as indicated above. The translator did everything to avoid misunderstanding and to make his text as comprehensible as possible for his target audience.[253] Subsequently, the translator would have been a conservative Jew who was hostile towards Greek philosophical thought, despite the fact that he had a profound knowledge of Greek.[254] These ideological and theological views bore their influence on the translation technique of the LXX translator of Proverbs. Therefore, this aspect needs to be taken into account when we want to characterise the translation technique of LXX Proverbs.

1.3.3 LXX Job and LXX Proverbs, two translators(?)

The question whether or not LXX Job and LXX Proverbs were translated by the same translator has been addressed by Cook. In multiple publications he

---

248 See Cook, "The Law of Moses in Septuagint Proverbs," 459; Cook, "The Dating of Septuagint Proverbs," 397; Cook, "Theological/ideological Tendenz," 76–77.
249 See Cook, "'ishah zarah;" Cook, "A Case Study of LXX Proverbs, LXX Job and 4 Maccabees,", 61–63.
250 See Cook, "'ishah zarah," 474; Cook, "The Translator of the Septuagint of Proverbs," 553–554.
251 See Cook, "'ishah zarah," 474–475; Cook, "Theological/ideological Tendenz," 77; Cook, "The Translator of the Septuagint of Proverbs," 555.
252 See, i.a., Cook, "The Dating of Septuagint Proverbs," 397; Cook, "The Translator of the Septuagint of Proverbs," 558.
253 See, i.a., Cook, "The Dating of Septuagint Proverbs," 397; Cook, "'ishah zarah," esp. 474–475.
254 Cook, "The Dating of Septuagint Proverbs," 391, 395, 397, 399; Cook, "The Law of Moses in Septuagint Proverbs," 461.

tries to formulate an adequate answer to the question on the basis of a thorough analysis.[255]

Cook goes beyond the lexical level and analyses several themes that are present in both books.[256] In his article *Were the LXX Versions of Proverbs and Job Translated by the Same Person?*, he examines the passages that deal with wisdom and creation in Proverbs and Job, i.e., Prov 8:20-36 and Job 28.

In Job 28, Cook observes a considerable amount of verses that are attested in MT but not in the Old Greek version of Job.[257] The analysed verses are Job 28:5-8.14-19.22a.26b:

MT	NRSV
28:5 אֶרֶץ מִמֶּנָּה יֵצֵא־לָחֶם וְתַחְתֶּיהָ נֶהְפַּךְ כְּמוֹ־אֵשׁ׃	28:5 As for the earth, out of it comes bread; but underneath it is turned up as by fire.
28:6 מְקוֹם־סַפִּיר אֲבָנֶיהָ וְעַפְרֹת זָהָב לוֹ׃	28:6 Its stones are the place of sapphires, and its dust contains gold.
28:7 נָתִיב לֹא־יְדָעוֹ עָיִט וְלֹא שְׁזָפַתּוּ עֵין אַיָּה׃	28:7 "That path no bird of prey knows, and the falcon's eye has not seen it.
28:8 לֹא־הִדְרִיכֻהוּ בְנֵי־שָׁחַץ לֹא־עָדָה עָלָיו שָׁחַל׃	28:8 The proud wild animals have not trodden it; the lion has not passed over it.
28:14 תְּהוֹם אָמַר לֹא בִי־הִיא וְיָם אָמַר אֵין עִמָּדִי׃	28:14 The deep says, 'It is not in me,' and the sea says, 'It is not with me.'
28:15 לֹא־יֻתַּן סְגוֹר תַּחְתֶּיהָ וְלֹא יִשָּׁקֵל כֶּסֶף מְחִירָהּ׃	28:15 It cannot be gotten for gold, and silver cannot be weighed out as its price.
28:16 לֹא־תְסֻלֶּה בְּכֶתֶם אוֹפִיר בְּשֹׁהַם יָקָר וְסַפִּיר׃	28:16 It cannot be valued in the gold of Ophir, in precious onyx or sapphire.
28:17 לֹא־יַעַרְכֶנָּה זָהָב וּזְכוֹכִית וּתְמוּרָתָהּ כְּלִי־פָז׃	28:17 Gold and glass cannot equal it, nor can it be exchanged for jewels of fine gold.
28:18 רָאמוֹת וְגָבִישׁ לֹא יִזָּכֵר וּמֶשֶׁךְ חָכְמָה מִפְּנִינִים׃	28:18 No mention shall be made of coral or of crystal; the price of wisdom is above pearls.
28:19 לֹא־יַעַרְכֶנָּה פִּטְדַת־כּוּשׁ בְּכֶתֶם טָהוֹר לֹא תְסֻלֶּה׃	28:19 The chrysolite of Ethiopia cannot compare with it, nor can it be valued in pure gold.
28:22a אֲבַדּוֹן וָמָוֶת אָמְרוּ	28:22a Abaddon and Death say,
28:26b וְדֶרֶךְ לַחֲזִיז קֹלוֹת׃	28:26b and a way for the thunderbolt;

---

255 See, i.a., Cook, "Aspects of the Relationship between the Septuagint Versions of Proverbs and Job;" Cook "Were the LXX Versions of Proverbs and Job"

256 See Cook, "Were the LXX Versions of Proverbs and Job," 132. He does not elaborate on the lexical level in this article because it has already been addressed by Gammie. See Cook, "Were the LXX Versions of Proverbs and Job," 132. However, he does so in his later work. See Johann Cook, "The Relationship Between the LXX Versions of Proverbs and Job."

257 See Cook, "Were the LXX Versions of Proverbs and Job," 135–148. These verses are denoted in the critical edition of Job with an asterisk.

Cook ascribes these minuses to the translator.[258] Here Cook rejects the hypothesis that the translator of LXX Job used a different *Vorlage* than MT, as he also argues for LXX Proverbs.[259] He claims that the translator omitted these verses, that have to do with mundane things, to 'spiritualise' the text.[260]

In Prov 8:20-36, wherein the same themes are being discussed as in Job 28, no verses are being omitted.[261] As indicated above, the translator nuances the meaning of the Hebrew text to avoid misunderstandings. By changing the person of the verbs, he emphasises that God is the sole actor in the creation process. Wisdom is being given a prominent role next to God, which is not clear in MT.[262] The translator tried to specify his *Vorlage* and tried to make the text more clear for his target audience, which for Cook is a characteristic of the translation technique of the LXX translator.[263] The translator tried to nuance the meaning of the Hebrew text to avoid any misunderstandings. By doing so the translator tried to specify his *Vorlage* for his target audience. This is, according to Cook, another characteristic of the translation technique of the LXX translator.

---

258 See Cook, "Were the LXX Versions of Proverbs and Job," 148. Just as Cook, Claude E. Cox ascribes the changes and omissions in the LXX text to the translational activity of the translator. According to him, these changes and omission cannot be explained due to a different *Vorlage*. This conclusion is based on 4 arguments: (1) the parts that are not attested in the Greek text do not differ from the rest of the Hebrew text. The translator was responsible for their omission; (2) the Greek text destroys parallelisms that are present in the Hebrew text. Because these are a characteristic of Hebrew poetry, these were also extant in the Hebrew *Vorlage* of the translator. Therefore, it is the translator who is responsible for their omission; (3), by the freedoms of the translation technique of the translator, it seems logical to ascribe omissions to the translator; (4) there are numerous associative translations in LXX Job that find their origin from Job or other LXX texts. Therefore, one can conclude that the *Vorlage* was a Greek text instead of a Hebrew text. See Claude E. Cox, "Does a Shorter Hebrew Parent Text Underlie Old Greek Job," in *In the Footsteps of Sherlock Holmes. Studies in the Biblical Text in Honour of Anneli Aejmelaeus*, ed. Timothy M. Law, Kristin De Troyer and Marketta Liljeström, CBET 72 (Leuven — Paris — Walpole, MA: Peeters, 2014), 451–462, esp. 461–462.
259 See Cook, "Were the LXX Versions of Proverbs and Job," 148.
260 See Cook, "Aspects of the Relationship between the Septuagint Versions of Proverbs and Job," 323.
261 See Cook, "Were the LXX Versions of Proverbs and Job," 156.
262 See Cook, "Were the LXX Versions of Proverbs and Job," 156; Cook, "Aspects of the Relationship between the Septuagint Versions of Proverbs and Job," 324.
263 See Cook, "Were the LXX Versions of Proverbs and Job," 156; Cook, *The Septuagint of Proverbs*, 319.

According to Cook, these differences between the LXX version of Job and Proverbs in the aforementioned passages with regard to the translation technique are significant.[264] While in LXX Proverbs there are mainly some differences on a micro level, e.g., the adaptation of personal endings of the verbs, there are differences on a macro level in LXX Job, i.e., the omission of whole verses.[265] Still, Cook does not deny the differences on macro level in Prov 8:20-36. In comparison to LXX Job, verses are being added and omitted.[266] An example of an addition can be found in Prov 8:21:

MT	LXX
לְהַנְחִיל אֹהֲבַי ׀ יֵשׁ וְאֹצְרֹתֵיהֶם אֲמַלֵּא׃	[21] ἵνα μερίσω τοῖς ἐμὲ ἀγαπῶσιν ὕπαρξιν καὶ τοὺς θησαυροὺς αὐτῶν ἐμπλήσω ἀγαθῶν. [21a] ἐὰν ἀναγγείλω ὑμῖν τὰ καθ' ἡμέραν γινόμενα, μνημονεύσω τὰ ἐξ αἰῶνος ἀριθμῆσαι.
Endowing with wealth those who love me, and filling their treasuries.	[21] In order that I may apportion possessions to those who love me and fill there treasuries with good things. [21a] If I report to you the things that happen daily, I will remember to enumerate the things of old.

Cook does not ascribe this plus to a different *Vorlage* but to the translation technique of the LXX translator.[267] According to him, the translator has added this part of the verse as a bridge between verses 11-21 and 22-36.[268] In my opinion, this plus can, however, be explained due to a *Vorlage* that differs from MT. Therefore, the plus does not necessarily have to be ascribed to the translator.

An example of an omission can be found in Prov 8:29:

MT	LXX
בְּשׂוּמוֹ לַיָּם ׀ חֻקּוֹ וּמַיִם לֹא יַעַבְרוּ־פִיו בְּחוּקוֹ מוֹסְדֵי אָרֶץ׃	καὶ ἰσχυρὰ ἐποίει τὰ θεμέλια τῆς γῆς.

---

264 See Cook, "Were the LXX Versions of Proverbs and Job," 156.
265 See Cook, "Were the LXX Versions of Proverbs and Job," 156.
266 See Cook, "Were the LXX Versions of Proverbs and Job," 156.
267 Cook, "Aspects of the Relationship between the Septuagint Versions of Proverbs and Job," 318.
268 Cook, "Aspects of the Relationship between the Septuagint Versions of Proverbs and Job," 318; See Cook, "Were the LXX Versions of Proverbs and Job," 149.

MT	LXX
When he assigned to the sea its limit, so that the waters might not transgress his command, when he marked out the foundations of the earth.	When he made strong the foundations of the earth.

Still, these differences on macro level between the MT and the LXX version of Proverbs are, surprisingly, not that significant for Cook to integrate them in his conclusion. He simply ascribes them to the complex textual transmission history of Proverbs.[269]

On the basis of this analysis, Cook concludes that it is improbable that LXX Job and LXX Proverbs were translated by the same translator or group of translators.[270] The translator of LXX Job modified his text on macro level by omitting a considerable amount of verses, while the translator of LXX Proverbs only modified chapter 8 on micro level. According to Cook, this denotes another approach toward the rendering of the *Vorlage*. Because Cook does not underscore the hypothesis of a different *Vorlage*, his argument can be perceived as being logical. However, when the omissions are being explained due to a different Hebrew *Vorlage* instead of due to the translational activity of the translator, Cook's argument of a different translator of LXX Job and LXX Proverbs can be refuted. One can also pose the question why Cook does not take the transpositions on macro level into consideration for his argument. When this is accounted for and we continue to follow Cook's reasoning, one might conclude that both translators modified their text on a macro level. This way one can conclude that both translators exhibit the same attitude towards their *Vorlage* and that both LXX Job and LXX Proverbs might have been translated by one and the same translator.

Looking at the nuances the LXX translator inserted on micro level, some similarities can be detected. In LXX Job God is attributed a more prominent role than in MT, just as is the case in LXX Proverbs.[271] In LXX Job 28:3-11.23-28, God is the subject of the verses while the miner is the subject in MT.[272] Cook also indicated that the same characteristic of the translation technique of LXX Proverbs,

269 See Cook, "Were the LXX Versions of Proverbs and Job," 156; Cook, "Aspects of the Relationship between the Septuagint Versions of Proverbs and Job," 328.
270 See Cook, "Were the LXX Versions of Proverbs and Job," 156.
271 See Cook, "Were the LXX Versions of Proverbs and Job," 146; Cook, "Aspects of the Relationship between the Septuagint Versions of Proverbs and Job," 323.
272 See Cook, "Were the LXX Versions of Proverbs and Job," 136, 137, 139 and 146.

i.e., religious nuancing, can also be found in LXX Job.[273] In Job 28:4 an example of this characteristic is found:

MT	LXX
הַנִּשְׁכָּחִים מִנִּי־רָגֶל דַּלּוּ מֵאֱנוֹשׁ נָעוּ׃	οἱ δὲ ἐπιλανθανόμενοι ὁδὸν δικαίαν ἠσθένησαν ἐκ βροτῶν.
they are forgotten by travellers, they sway suspended, remote from people.[274]	And those of mortals who kept forgetting the righteous way became weak.[275]

Cook considers the addition of ὁδὸν δικαίαν (the righteous way) as an example of religious nuancing.[276] These two modifications, the emphasis of God as actor in the creation process and the tendency of religious nuancing, are characteristics of the translation technique of both LXX Job as LXX Proverbs. Taking these arguments into account and accepting the hypothesis of a different *Vorlage* that explains the differences on macro level (*contra* Cook) can be an indication for the fact that LXX Job and LXX Proverbs were translated by one and the same person.

1.3.4 Conclusion

After a thorough analysis of the characterisation of the translation technique of LXX Proverbs by Johann Cook, we can formulate a conclusion. It is clear that Cook has examined the translation technique of LXX Proverbs much more profound than other scholars. On the basis of the above analyses we can, therefore,

---

273 See Cook, "Were the LXX Versions of Proverbs and Job," 137 and 146.

274 This passage is hard to translate. Scholars have tried to come up with a decent translation for this verse. Some even posited that the Masoretes have misread their unvocalised Hebrew text and have, therefore, proposed several emendations. For an elaborated discussion with regard to all proposed emendations concerning this passage, see David J. A. Clines, *Job 21-37b*, WBC 18a (Mexico City: Thomas Nelson, 2006), 896–898.

275 English translation from Claude E. Cox, "Iob," in *A New English Translation of the Septuagint. And the Other Greek Translations Traditionally Included under That Title*, ed. Albert Pietersma and Benjamin G. Wright (New York, NY — Oxford: Oxford University Press, 2007), 667–696.

276 See Cook, "Were the LXX Versions of Proverbs and Job," 137 and 146.

sketch a more adequate image of the translation technique as well as of the identity of the translator.

The first important observation that can be made is the methodological out-set of Cook. In comparison to Tov's view - which I hold myself as well – that the differences on macro level, i.e., the transposition of whole verses, can be as-cribed to a different *Vorlage*, Cook ascribes these to the activity of the translator. He radically rejects the hypotheses of a different *Vorlage* because there is no textual witness that attests such a different *Vorlage*.

Out of the above mentioned assertion, he draws the following conclusion concerning the translation technique of the LXX translator of Proverbs: The translator handles his *Vorlage* in a free and creative way, both on micro as on macro level.

Cook characterises the translation technique of LXX Proverbs both as one of unity as of diversity. The translator paraphrases and stereotypes lexemes. More-over, the translator shows himself to be an excellent stylist by applying harmo-nisation, alliteration, dualisms, rhyme and the creative usage if particles. By doing so, the translator shows a profound knowledge of Greek language.

Also on macro level we can see the creativity of the translator at work, ac-cording to Cook. He ascribes the transpositions of whole verses to the creative freedom of the translator and not, as other scholars tend to do, to a different *Vorlage*. As I have argued above, this seems to be improbable taken into ac-count the material nature of the scroll and the way in which manuscripts were being copied/translated in the centuries B.C.E.

The translator does not only take into account the stylistic aspect to modify the text. He also brings about changes on the basis of religious/ideological mo-tivations. These religious/ideological motivations are an expression of the the-ology/ideology of the translator. This way, the translator pays a lot of attention to the Law of Moses, which is not as much emphasised in the Hebrew version. Consequently, Cook goes even further by stating that the translator must have been a conservative Jew. This means that he nuanced the meaning of the He-brew text and tried to make the meaning comprehensible and clear for his target audience to avoid any misunderstanding. This is, e.g., the case in the verses concerning creation and wisdom in Prov 8. In this passage God is postulated as the sole Creator while wisdom is active next to God. The Hebrew text leaves room for another interpretation. The translator also warns his readers for for-eign wisdom by applying the metaphor of the strange/foreign woman (אשה זרה). According to Coo , this foreign wisdom would have been Greek philosophical thought which many Jews found interesting and tempting at the beginning of the Hellenistic period. A danger of this Hellenising trend (read 'foreign wisdom') is, according to the translator, the devaluation or undervaluation of the Law. The translator also has the tendency to religionise his text by adding positive or negative aspects or by contrasting. The latter is, according to Cook, an important characteristic of the translation technique of LXX Proverbs;

Cook gives a negative answer to the question whether or not LXX Job and LXX Proverbs were translated by the same person. According to him it is improbable that these books were translated by one and the same translator or group of translators. He draws this conclusion on the basis of his research of the translation of passages reflecting shared themes in both books, respectively wisdom and creation. The differences in both books are, according to Cook, significant. While the translator of LXX Job omitted a considerable amount of verses in his translation of the passages concerning wisdom and creation, LXX Proverbs does not omit verses in the passages reflecting the same themes. On the basis of these arguments, Cook concludes that both books do not exhibit the same translation technique and therefore both books cannot have been translated by one and the same person. As I have indicated in the analysis, Cook does not take into account the transpositions of verses on a macro level. When he would take these into account, he would come to the conclusion that LXX Job and LXX Proverbs are of the same hand. Cook's argument can also be refuted when the hypothesis of a different *Vorlage* is postulated and the minuses and plusses in both LXX Job and LXX Proverbs are explained within the framework of this hypothesis.

After having discussed the results concerning the translation technique of LXX Proverbs of the quantitative and qualitative approach as well as Johann Cook's analysis, we will examine the content- and context-related approach and its results on LXX Proverbs' translation technique in the next section.

1.4 The content- and context-related approach

About a decade ago, a new approach to analyse the translation technique of the LXX books has been developed in Leuven: the so-called content- and context-related approach. This approach can be situated in line with the qualitative approaches but goes further than the examination of grammatical and linguistic aspects of a text.[277] It examines the Greek translation on the basis of the way in which specific content- and context-related criteria have been rendered. These

---

277 See Ausloos and Lemmelijn, "Content-Related Criteria in Characterising the LXX Translation Technique," 368.

aspects, then, function as criteria for the characterisation of the translation technique of the individual LXX books. These criteria are, e.g., the rendering of Hebrew *hapax legomena*, Hebrew wordplay in the context of parallelism, aetiologies (toponyms and proper names), specific jargon and certain stylistic characteristics.[278] These aspects are being examined because they confronted the LXX translators with a challenge; they form situations that forced them to opt consciously for a specific rendering.[279] By doing so, one can detect how the LXX translators translated their Hebrew *Vorlage*. Afterwards the results of the content- and context-related approach need to be compared *ad intra* and subsequently *ad extra*.[280] *Ad intra*, the results of all content- and context-related criteria within one and the same LXX book can be compared with one another.[281] Afterwards these results can be compared *ad extra* with the other LXX books.[282] As a final step these results of the *ad intra* and *ad extra* comparison need to be related to the results of the quantitative and qualitative approach.[283] This way, the translation technique of the different LXX books can be described more adequately and in a more nuanced way.

The content- and context-related approach does not employ the traditional terms 'literal' and 'free' to characterise the translation of the LXX books. Next to the faithfulness with which certain LXX translators have translated their *Vorlage*, the study of content- and context-related criteria has shown that some translators handled their *Vorlage* in a creative way.[284] When the LXX translators were confronted with aspects in their *Vorlage* that were difficult to render, they often

---

278 See Ausloos and Lemmelijn, "Content-Related Criteria in Characterising the LXX Translation Technique," 368.

279 See Lemmelijn, "The Greek Rendering of Hebrew Hapax Legomena," 137.

280 See Lemmelijn, "The Greek Rendering of Hebrew Hapax Legomena," 137–138.

281 See Lemmelijn, "The Greek Rendering of Hebrew Hapax Legomena," 137.

282 See Lemmelijn, "The Greek Rendering of Hebrew Hapax Legomena," 137.

283 See Lemmelijn, "The Greek Rendering of Hebrew Hapax Legomena," 138.

284 See Ausloos and Lemmelijn, "Faithful Creativity," 62–64. For the faithfulness of LXX translation see Aejmelaeus, "The Significance of Clause Connectors in the Syntactical and Translation-Technical Study of the Septuagint," 278: "Changing the structure of a clause or a phrase, and by so doing replacing an un-Greek expression by a genuine Greek one closely corresponding to the meaning of the original, is quite a different thing from being recklessly free and paying less attention to the correspondence with the original. A distinction should be made between literalness and faithfulness. A good free rendering is a faithful rendering;" Soisalon-Soininen, "Die Auslassung des Possessivpronomens im griechischen Pentateuch," 88: "Sie haben den Text möglichst getreu wiedergeben wollen, nicht aber wortwörtlich [...]."

translated them by a faithful Greek equivalent that shows extraordinary creativity.[285]

In this section we will focus ourselves on the study of *hapax legomena* as a content- and context-related criterion, the characterisation of LXX Proverbs by the content- and context-related approach as well as the relationship between LXX Proverbs and LXX Job as defined by this approach.

1.4.1 The study of *hapax legomena* as a content- and context-related criterion

The study of Hebrew *hapax legomena* and their Greek rendering is a criterion that has been applied by the content- and context-related approach to characterise the translation technique of the different LXX translators in a more nuanced way.[286] These words, derived from the Greek ἅπαξ λεγόμενα, are words that are only attested once in a given corpus. The study of *hapax legomena* is not without methodological problems.[287] The answer on the question what a *hapax legomenon* is, determines the research about it. This way, one needs to take into account "the corpus from which they must come, that part of the corpus' vocabulary to be checked for a word appearing once, and the criteria defining 'one-ness' which are applied to that vocabulary."[288] With regard to our research concerning the translation technique of the LXX translators, more specifically the Greek rendering of Hebrew *hapax legomena*, we can ask the question which corpus needs to be considered as the object of the research: the

285 See Ausloos and Lemmelijn, "Faithful Creativity," 63.
286 See Ausloos and Lemmelijn, "Rendering Love"; Hans Ausloos, "The Septuagint's Rendering of Hebrew Hapax Legomena and the Characterization of Its 'Translation Technique'. The Case of Exodus," *Acta Patristica et Byzantina* 20 (2009): 360–376; Verbeke, "Hebrew Hapax Legomena;" Ausloos and Lemmelijn, "Characterizing the LXX Translation;" Lemmelijn, "The Greek Rendering of Hebrew Hapax Legomena."
287 In her doctoral dissertation on the Greek rendering of Hebrew *hapax legomena* in Job, Elke Verbeke has dedicated an entire chapter on methodological issues concerning the notion of a *hapax legomenon*. Very helpful in this regard is the overview of the *status quaestionis* on the way in which the term *hapax legomenon* has been perceived and used in research. Moreover, she has also examined the study of *hapax legomena* in other fields than Old Testament studies, such as New Testament, masora, Hebrew lexicography and rabbinic literature as well as extra-biblical approaches (i.e., psycho-sociology and pedagogy, classical philology and linguistics). See Verbeke, "Hebrew Hapax Legomena," 5–85. Our goal here is not to repeat the research of Verbeke but rather to summarise her overview and, if necessary, ameliorate her working definition of what a hapax is.
288 Greenspahn, Hapax Legomena in Biblical Hebrew, 17.

whole Hebrew Bible or a single book.[289] The content- and context-related approach takes the *hapax legomena* of the whole Hebrew Bible as a point of departure of its study.[290] Furthermore, a distinction is made between absolute and non-absolute *hapax legomena*.[291] Non-absolute *hapax legomena* are words that only occur once in a certain corpus but that might be linked to existing lexemes.[292] Absolute *hapax legomena* are words that only occur once but that cannot be linked to existing lexemes.[293] The content- and context-related approach focusses itself mainly, but not exclusively, on the study of absolute *hapax legomena*. Due to their unicity, these absolute *hapax legomena* confronted the translator with a challenge. They forced him to opt for a certain translation. This reaction is being studied by the content- and context-related approach in order to acquire an image of the translation technique of the LXX translators. Although the main focus of this approach lies on the analysis of the Greek rendering of Hebrew absolute *hapax legomena*, the present study will also evaluate the translation of non-absolute hapaxes. This way, this study hopes to provide a more accurate image of the way in which the translator has dealt with (possible) difficult Hebrew words.

Thus far, the content- and context-related approach has applied the rendering of Hebrew *hapax legomena* for the study of the translation technique of LXX version of Exodus, Judges, Song of Songs, Job and (in a preliminary way) Proverbs. In the sections below the results of Song of Songs, Exodus and Judges will be examined. LXX Proverbs will, as a main study object of this dissertation, be discussed separately under section 4.2 and subsequently be compared with the results of the studies concerning *hapax legomena* in LXX Job.

1.4.1.1 *Hapax legomena* in the LXX version of Song of Songs

In their article *Rendering Love: Hapax Legomena and the Characterisation of the Translation technique of Song of Songs*, Hans Ausloos and Bénédicte Lemmelijn

---

289 See Verbeke, "The Use of Hebrew Hapax Legomena in Septuagint Studies," 514–516. For an exhaustive application of the content- and context-related approach with regard to the Greek rendering of Hebrew *hapax legomena* in LXX Job, see Elke Verbeke's dissertation *Hebrew Hapax Legomena and their Greek Rendering in LXX Job*.

290 See, i.a., Verbeke, "The Use of Hebrew Hapax Legomena in Septuagint Studies," 509.

291 See, i.a., Casanowicz *et al*, "Hapax Legomena. Biblical Data," 226; Greenspahn, *Hapax Legomena in Biblical Hebrew*, 22–23; Ausloos and Lemmelijn, "Rendering Love," 44.

292 See, i.a., Ausloos and Lemmelijn, "Rendering Love," 44.

293 See Greenspahn, *Hapax Legomena in Biblical Hebrew*, 22–23; Ausloos and Lemmelijn, "Rendering Love," 44.

examine the translation technique of LXX Song of Songs on the basis of the Greek rendering of Hebrew absolute *hapax legomena* in LXX Song of Songs[294]. This study, which was the first impulse for the development of the content- and context-related criteriology, has shown that the LXX translator of Song of Songs aimed at finding an adequate translation for the Hebrew *hapax legomena* he was confronted with while translating his *Vorlage*.[295] He rarely transliterated the hapaxes, as is the case in Song 4:14:[296]

MT	LXX
נֵרְדְּ ׀ וְכַרְכֹּם קָנֶה ׀ ק נְמֹון	νάρδος καὶ κρόκος, κάλαμος καὶ κιννάμωμον.
Nard and saffron, calamus and cinnamon.	Nard and saffron, calamus and cinnamon.[297]

The Hebrew hapax in this verse is כַּרְכֹּם that has been rendered by the LXX translator to κρόκος.[298] According to Ausloos and Lemmelijn, the translator had difficulties rendering this word because he did not know the meaning of the word[299]. The LXX translator has misread the last consonant of the hapax, i.e., as a ס instead of a closing –ם, that is why he opted for the Greek word κρόκος as a rendering of כַּרְכֹּם.[300] Although the Greek is a transliteration of the Hebrew, it is still an existing Greek word meaning 'saffron.'[301] Ausloos and Lemmelijn conclude

---

294 See Ausloos and Lemmelijn, "Rendering Love."

295 See Ausloos and Lemmelijn, "Rendering Love," 61.

296 See Ausloos and Lemmelijn, "Rendering Love," 54–55 and 61.

297 English translation taken from the NETS translation of Song of Songs by Jay C. Treat. See Jay C. Treat, "Song of Songs," in *A New English Translation of the Septuagint And the Other Greek Translations Traditionally Included Under That Title*, ed. Albert Pietersma and Benjamijn G. Wright (New York, NY — Oxford: Oxford University Press, 2007), 657–666.

298 נֵרְדְּ, כַּרְכֹּם, קָנֶה and קִנָּמֹון are also being discussed in the article of Lemmelijn concerning the translation of Hebrew flora- and landscape metaphors in LXX Song of Songs, see Lemmelijn, "Flora in Cantico Canticorum," 44, 46–48.

299 See Ausloos and Lemmelijn, "Rendering Love," 54.

300 See Ausloos and Lemmelijn, "Rendering Love," 54.

301 See Ausloos and Lemmelijn, "Rendering Love," 54. In contrast to Marvin H. Pope who argues that the term כַּרְכֹּם is borrowed from Sanskrit (*kurkuma*) and Johan Lust, Erik Eynikel and Katrin Hauspie (leh) who argue that κρόκος is a Semitic loanword from כַּרְכֹּם, Ausloos and Lemmelijn argue that κρόκος was already attests in Homeric literature. The sequence of the consonants כ and ר is, according to them, no characteristic of Semitic languages. See Ausloos and Lemmelijn, "Rendering Love," 54; Marvin H. Pope, *Song of Songs. An New Translation with Introduction and Commentary*, AB 7c (New York, NY — London — Toronto — Sydney — Auckland: Doubleday, 1977), 493; LEH, 46.

that the LXX translator of Song of Songs did not merely transliterate this Hebrew hapax but instead consciously opted for an existing Greek word whenever this was possible.[302] According to Ausloos and Lemmelijn, in Song 4:14 the translator only transliterated the Hebrew word נֵרְדְּ to νάρδος while for קִנָּמוֹן and כַּרְכֹּם he used an existing Greek word that indeed resembles a transliteration of the Hebrew.[303] In that sentence the transliteration is not that strong.[304]

As an alternative for transliteration, the translator searched for an adequate Greek translation that connected semantically and sometimes even phonetically with the Hebrew text and its context.[305] An example of a semantic and phonetic translation can be found in Song 3:9:

MT	LXX
אַפִּרְיוֹן עָשָׂה לוֹ הַמֶּלֶךְ שְׁלֹמֹה	φορεῖον ἐποίησεν ἑαυτῷ ὁ βασιλεὺς Σαλωμων.
King Solomon made himself a palanquin from the wood of Lebanon.	King Salomon made himself a palanquin from Lebanon's trees.

When we look at the rendering of אַפִּרְיוֹן with φορεῖον we could argue that the translator has transliterated the Hebrew word. According to Lemmelijn and Ausloos, however, this is not the case because the translator did not transliterate the first letter of the Hebrew lexeme (א).[306] According to them, the lexeme φορεῖον as a rendering of אַפִּרְיוֹן indicates a creative translator.[307] While translating, the translator took into account the immediate context of his translation. By using φορεῖον he connects this verse with Song 3:7 (ἰδοὺ ἡ κλίνη τοῦ Σαλωμων)

---

302 See Ausloos and Lemmelijn, "Rendering Love," 55.

303 See Ausloos and Lemmelijn, "Rendering Love," 55. The rendering of κιννάμωμον for קַנָּמוֹן is namely a Greek word that is attested in Herodotus. See Ausloos and Lemmelijn, "Rendering Love," 54.

304 Nevertheless, I have my reservations about this. It might be that the translator was not aware of the fact that these words were used in the Greek world and that he indeed just transliterated his Hebrew text. It might also be, as Lemmelijn and Ausloos indicate (see Ausloos and Lemmelijn, "Rendering Love," 54 and n. 42), that the Hellenistic and Ancient Near Eastern culture had good contact with each other and that these Greek words are Semitic loanwords. When these two arguments are taken into account, we can argue that the translator transliterated instead of avoiding transliteration by using Greek words that resembled Hebrew words in form.

305 See Ausloos and Lemmelijn, "Rendering Love," 54.

306 See Ausloos and Lemmelijn, "Rendering Love," 54.

307 See Ausloos and Lemmelijn, "Rendering Love," 54.

where something portable is being suggested.[308] The translator aimed at representing the Hebrew word in an adequate way by using a Greek word that is close to the meaning and phonetics of the Hebrew word.[309]

From the translation of the examined *hapax legomena* in Song of Songs the following can be argued:

> [The LXX translator of Canticles] offered idiomatic Greek constructions, took care of stylistic characteristics and offered variation, played with assimilation and aimed rather at an understandable text than at a literal rendering of enigmatic words. Thus, he shows himself capable of searching for creative solutions in translating a Hebrew poem into a Greek one.[310]

The result of their study of the Greek rendering of Hebrew *hapax legomena*, as well as Lemmelijn's study with regard to the rendering of flora and landscape metaphors in LXX Song of Songs, is that the LXX translation of Song of Songs is not as slavish as has been assumed in LXX research.[311] On the contrary, the LXX translator handled his *Vorlage* in a free and creative but also faithful way.[312]

1.4.1.2 *Hapax legomena* in the LXX version of Exodus

In his article *The Septuagint's Rendering of Hebrew Hapax Legomena and the Characterization of Its 'Translation Technique'. The Case of Exodus*, Hans Ausloos examines the Greek rendering of Hebrew absolute *hapax legomena*, 11 in total, in LXX Exodus.[313] His analysis has indicated that the LXX translator of Exodus is a creative translator who remained faithful to his Hebrew *Vorlage*.[314] In order to find a decent translation equivalent for the Hebrew hapax, the LXX translator of Exodus often bases himself on the context of the verse. An example hereof can be found in Exod 16:14.[315]

---

308 See Ausloos and Lemmelijn, "Rendering Love," 54.
309 See Ausloos and Lemmelijn, "Rendering Love," 54.
310 Ausloos and Lemmelijn, "Rendering Love," 61.
311 See Ausloos and Lemmelijn, "Rendering Love," 60; Lemmelijn, "Faithful Creativity," 51.
312 Ausloos and Lemmelijn, "Rendering Love," 60; Lemmelijn, "Faithful Creativity," 51.
313 See Ausloos, "The Septuagint's Rendering of Hebrew Hapax Legomena and the Characterization of Its 'Translation Technique'. The Case of Exodus," esp. 362–370.
314 See Ausloos, "The Septuagint's Rendering of Hebrew Hapax Legomena and the Characterization of Its 'Translation Technique'. The Case of Exodus," 371. This conclusion is in line with other studies with regard to the translation technique of LXX Exodus.
315 The hapax חספס in this verse is attested as an absolute hapax by Greenspahn but not by Casanowicz. For a discussion on the application of the terms absolute and non-absolute by these two authors see chapter 2 of this book.

MT	LXX
וַתַּעַל שִׁכְבַת הַטָּל וְהִנֵּה עַל־פְּנֵי הַמִּדְבָּר דַּק מְחֻסְפָּס דַּק כַּכְּפֹר עַל־הָאָרֶץ:	καὶ ἰδοὺ ἐπὶ πρόσωπον τῆς ἐρήμου λεπτὸν ὡσεὶ κόριον λευκὸν ὡσεὶ πάγος ἐπὶ τῆς γῆς.
When the layer of dew lifted, there on the surface of the wilderness was a fine flaky substance, as fine as frost on the ground.	And look, upon the surface of the wilderness was something fine like coriander, white like frost on the ground.[316]

According to Ausloos, the rendering of the Hebrew hapax חספס with the Greek noun κόριον is based upon a harmonisation with Exod 16:31, wherein manna is depicted as כְּזֶרַע גַּד/σπέρμα κορίου (coriander seed), or *vice versa*.[317]

Next to contextual renderings, the LXX translator also draws on homophony (Exod 30:34) to render the Hebrew hapax (חֶלְבְּנָה).[318] Furthermore, he also uses Greek *hapax legomena* to translate the Hebrew absolute hapaxes.[319] This is the case in Exod 9:31; 12:4; 16:31; 30:34.[320]

1.4.1.3 *Hapax legomena* in LXX Judges

An impulse for the study of the translation technique of LXX Judges by means of the content- and context-related approach can be found in a study of the rendering of Hebrew *hapax legomena* in Judg 3:12-20 by Ausloos and Lemmelijn.[321] One of the *hapax legomena* that is being examined is located in Judg 3:16:

---

316 For the English translation of LXX Exodus see Larry J. Perkins, "Exodus," in *A New English Translation of the Septuagint. And the Other Greek Translations Traditionally Included under That Title*, ed. Albert Pietersma and Benjamin G. Wright (New York, NY — Oxford: Oxford University Press, 2007), 43–81.

317 See Ausloos, "The Septuagint's Rendering of Hebrew Hapax Legomena and the Characterization of Its 'Translation Technique'," 366.

318 For a discussion of this hapax see Ausloos, "The Septuagint's Rendering of Hebrew Hapax Legomena and the Characterization of Its 'Translation Technique'," 369–370.

319 See Ausloos, "The Septuagint's Rendering of Hebrew Hapax Legomena and the Characterization of Its 'Translation Technique'," 371.

320 For an elaborate discussion of the Hebrew hapaxes and their respective Greek rendering in these verses, see Ausloos, "The Septuagint's Rendering of Hebrew Hapax Legomena and the Characterization of Its 'Translation Technique'," 363–364 (Exod 9:31), 365 (Exod 12:4), 366–367 (Exod 16:31), 369–370 (Exod 30:34).

321 See their article Ausloos and Lemmelijn, "Characterizing the LXX Translation."

MT	LXX
וַיַּעַשׂ לוֹ אֵהוּד חֶרֶב וְלָהּ שְׁנֵי פֵיוֹת גֹּמֶד אָרְכָּהּ	καὶ ἐποίησεν ἑαυτῷ Αωδ μάχαιραν δίστομον, σπιθαμῆς τὸ μῆκος.
Ehud made for himself a sword with two edges, a cubit in length.	And Aod made for himself a double-bladed dagger, a span in length.[322]

The hapax in this verse is the word גֹּמֶד, that expresses the length of the murder weapon that Ehud used to kill Eglon. Many scholars have tried to come up with a possible meaning of this word.[323] In the search of a possible meaning, two things are taken into account: (1) the murder weapon needed to be big enough to pierce fat Elon with a deadly consequence, (2) the weapon must have been from a certain size that enabled Ehud to carry it unnoticed in the throne room.[324] The unit that expresses גֹּמֶד must take into account these two things. Although there are several speculations regarding the exact unit for expressing גֹּמֶד, current research still remains undecided on this point.[325]

When we look at the LXX translation, we can see that the translator rendered גֹּמֶד with σπιθαμή. This Greek length unit is mostly rendered as 'span.'[326] A span is a length between the tip of the pinkie and the thumb in stretched out position which more or less measures 23 cm.[327] Moreover, the LXX translator has translated the Hebrew word חֶרֶב (sword) with μάχαιρα meaning 'dagger'.

This analysis leads to the conclusion that the LXX translator of Judges has tried to take into account the content and context of the story when he was confronted with the Hebrew hapax גֹּמֶד.[328] This way the LXX translator exhibits a free translation technique that, nonetheless, remains faithful to the meaning of his *Vorlage*.[329] This stands in contrast to the results *ad extra* of the quantitative and qualitative approach with regard to LXX Judges. The quantitative results

---

322 English translation from Philip E. Satterthwaite, "Judges," in *A New English Translation of the Septuagint. And the Other Greek Translations Traditionally Included under That Title*, ed. Albert Pietersma and Benjamin G. Wright (New York, NY — Oxford: Oxford University Press, 2007), 195–238.
323 For an elaborated overview see Ausloos and Lemmelijn, "Characterizing the LXX Translation," 176–178.
324 See Ausloos and Lemmelijn, "Characterizing the LXX Translation," 176–177.
325 See Ausloos and Lemmelijn, "Characterizing the LXX Translation," 178.
326 See Ausloos and Lemmelijn, "Characterizing the LXX Translation," 180.
327 See LEH, 563; Ausloos and Lemmelijn, "Characterizing the LXX Translation," 180.
328 See Ausloos and Lemmelijn, "Characterizing the LXX Translation," 181.
329 See Ausloos and Lemmelijn, "Characterizing the LXX Translation," 181 and p. 189.

show a literal translator at work who tried to remain as close as possible to his Hebrew *Vorlage*.[330] Qualitative research has tried to nuance this statement by arguing that the LXX translator took his context into account when translating his *Vorlage*.[331] However, this approach still characterises LXX Judges as being a literal translation.[332] The comparison *ad intra* of the results of the content- and context-related approach concerning the translation of Hebrew aetiologies and *hapax legomena* in LXX Judges argue for the revision of the argument of LXX Judges being a literal translation.[333] The studies of Ausloos and Lemmelijn have indicated that the translator of LXX Judges was a competent and creative translator who has tried to represent and render difficult Hebrew words as adequately as possible by taken into account the content and context of the text, instead of rendering his *Vorlage* in a merely literal sense.[334]

1.4.2 The characterisation of the translation technique of LXX Proverbs by the content- and context-related approach and its relation with LXX Job

In her pilot article *The Greek Rendering of Hebrew Hapax Legomena in LXX Proverbs and Job: A Clue to the Question of A Single Translator*, Lemmelijn examines the translation of Hebrew *hapax legomena* in LXX Job and LXX Proverbs to provide an indicative answer to the question whether or not both books were translated by the same person[335]. In this section we will first discuss the characterisation of the translation technique of LXX Proverbs on the basis of the content- and context-related approach. Afterwards we will examine the (preliminary) results of the comparison between LXX Job and LXX Proverbs with regard to the rendering of Hebrew *hapax legomena*.

---

330 See Ausloos and Lemmelijn, "Characterizing the LXX Translation," 181.
331 See Ausloos and Lemmelijn, "Characterizing the LXX Translation," 190–191.
332 See Ausloos and Lemmelijn, "Characterizing the LXX Translation," 191.
333 See Ausloos and Lemmelijn, "Characterizing the LXX Translation," 191. For the study of the Greek rendering of Hebrew aetiologies in LXX Judges see Ausloos, "LXX's Rendering of Hebrew Proper Names."
334 See Ausloos and Lemmelijn, "Characterizing the LXX Translation," 191.
335 Lemmelijn, "The Greek Rendering of Hebrew Hapax Legomena."

1.4.2.1 *Hapax legomena* in LXX Proverbs

As a 'testcase' and an impulse for further exhaustive research, Lemmelijn examines the non-absolute *hapax legomenon* לְזוּת in Prov 4:24:[336]

MT	LXX
הָסֵר מִמְּךָ עִקְּשׁוּת פֶּה וּלְזוּת שְׂפָתַיִם הַרְחֵק מִמֶּךָּ:	περίελε σεαυτοῦ σκολιὸν στόμα καὶ ἄδικα χείλη μακρὰν ἀπὸ σοῦ ἄπωσαι.
Put away from you crooked speech, and put devious talk far from you.	Remove from yourself a crooked mouth, and thrust unjust lips far away from you.

A first observation is made on the verse itself. The LXX translator does not transliterate his *Vorlage*. In the contrary, he tries to modify and enhance the poetical structure of the verse without diminishing the meaning of the Hebrew text.[337] An example of the enhancement of parallelisms can be found on the level of the grammatical number of the lexemes used in Prov 4:24. The Hebrew lexeme שָׂפָה is attested as a *dualis*, לְזוּת as a singular form, while both Greek lexemes (ἄδικα χείλη) are attested in the plural form.[338] This creates a stronger parallelism with the previous colon whereby the lexemes are attested in a singular form in Hebrew (עִקְּשׁוּת פֶּה) as well as in Greek (σκολιὸν στόμα).[339]

A second observation concerns the meaning of לְזוּת in relation to the context of Prov 4:24. Both לְזוּת and עִקְּשׁוּת as well as the verbs where they are derived from, לוז and שקע, are (almost) exclusively attested in Proverbs.[340] On the basis of this similarity and because both constitute a parallelism, Lemmelijn indicates that the Greek translation of לְזוּת should also be examined in relation to the meaning of the lexeme עִקְּשׁוּת.[341] Both lexemes carry a double meaning, i.e., 'deviation' and 'to do bad or evil things.'[342] It is possible that both meanings are being conveyed by both lexemes.[343]

---

336 The hapax is non-absolute because scholars have argued that the lexeme is derived from the verb לוז ('to turn away'). See Lemmelijn, "The Greek Rendering of Hebrew Hapax Legomena," 143.

337 See Lemmelijn, "The Greek Rendering of Hebrew Hapax Legomena," 142.

338 See Lemmelijn, "The Greek Rendering of Hebrew Hapax Legomena," 141–142.

339 See Lemmelijn, "The Greek Rendering of Hebrew Hapax Legomena," 142.

340 See Lemmelijn, "The Greek Rendering of Hebrew Hapax Legomena," 144.

341 See Lemmelijn, "The Greek Rendering of Hebrew Hapax Legomena," 144.

342 See Lemmelijn, "The Greek Rendering of Hebrew Hapax Legomena," 144–145.

343 See Lemmelijn, "The Greek Rendering of Hebrew Hapax Legomena," 144–145.

Against the background of these observations, Lemmelijn investigates the Greek translation of the Hebrew hapax לָזוּת. As a starting point she examines the translations of the verb לוז in LXX Proverbs. This verb is attested in the following verses:[344]

Prov 2:15	עִקְּשִׁים וּנְלוֹזִים	σκολιαὶ καὶ καμπύλαι
Prov 3:21	אַל־יָלֻזוּ	μὴ παραρρυῇς
Prov 3:32	נָלוֹז	πᾶς παράνομος,
	וְאֶת־יְשָׁרִים	ἐν δὲ δικαίοις
Prov 4:21	אַל־יַלִּיזוּ	μὴ ἐκλίπωσίν
Prov 14:2	וּנְלוֹז דְּרָכָיו	ὁ δὲ σκολιάζων ταῖς ὁδοῖς

In Prov 2:15, לוז and שקע are attested together just as in Prov 4:24. Still, the LXX translator translates לוז by another Greek lexeme, i.e., καμπύλαι (to bent)[345].

The verb לוז is being translated in Prov 3:21 by another verb, παραρρυῇς (> παραρρέω: to be careless, to neglect).[346] This meaning is definitely not the same as the meaning of ἄδικα in Prov 4:24.

In Prov 3:32 the adjective παράνομος (unrighteous) is used as a translation of לוז.[347]This translation is close to the meaning of the lexeme ἄδικα. Furthermore, Lemmelijn observes that לוז/παράνομος is being contrasted with יְשָׁרִים/δικαίοις and that the Hebrew also carries the double meaning as is found in Prov 4:24.[348]

Just like in Prov 3:21, the LXX translator renders לוז as a verb (ἐκλίπωσίν > ἐκλείπω: forsaken, destitute) that is not close in meaning to ἄδικα.[349]

In Prov 14:2, the LXX translator uses the Greek word σκολιάζων as a translation of לוז. This word has the same root as σκολιὸν (Prov 4:24) that is the rendering of עִקְּשׁוּת. According to Lemmelijn, this indicates that the translator considered לוז and שקע as being synonyms.[350]

---

344 Table cited from Lemmelijn, "The Greek Rendering of Hebrew Hapax Legomena," 145.
345 See Lemmelijn, "The Greek Rendering of Hebrew Hapax Legomena,"145; LEH, 467: 'winding, bent, crooked (ways of dealing).'
346 See Lemmelijn, "The Greek Rendering of Hebrew Hapax Legomena," 146; LEH, p. 467: 'to be careless, to neglect.'
347 See LEH, 466: 'lawless.'
348 See Lemmelijn, "The Greek Rendering of Hebrew Hapax Legomena," 146.
349 See Lemmelijn, "The Greek Rendering of Hebrew Hapax Legomena," 146; LEH, 183: 'forsaken, destitute.'
350 See Lemmelijn, "The Greek Rendering of Hebrew Hapax Legomena," 146.

On the basis of the above analysis of the translation of the verb לוז in LXX Proverbs, it is clear that ἄδικα is not used as a translation of לוז. Even in Prov 2:15, where the same combination of לוז and עקש is attested as in Prov 4:24, he used another Greek equivalent[351]. In Prov 3:32, παράνομος is contrasted with δικαίοις. This makes the rendering of לְזוּת by ἄδικα a logical one[352]. According to Lemmelijn this leads to the following matter: or the LXX translator knew the hapax לְזוּת, or he did not know the hapax.[353] In the latter case, the question can be raised whether the translator knew the verb לוז and based his translation of the hapax on this verb.[354] Lemmelijn argues that this is not the case because the LXX translator did not translate the verb לוז by ἄδικα.[355]

From the analysis of the translation of the Hebrew hapax לוז, Lemmelijn concludes that the translator of LXX Proverbs stays true to his *Vorlage*, but translates it in a creative way by rendering the Hebrew parallelisms to Greek parallelisms.[356] In the next section the result of this research will be compared with the research regarding the translation technique of LXX Job.

1.4.2.2 Hapax legomena in LXX Job

In her doctoral dissertation *The Rendering of Hebrew Hapax Legomena in LXX Job*, Elke Verbeke has studied the translation technique of LXX Job by looking at the rendering of the Hebrew *hapax legomena*.[357] Her research has shown that the translator of LXX Job rendered the Hebrew hapax *legomena*, present in his *Vorlage*, in diverse ways. She makes a distinction between OG Job and the text of Job as presented with an asterisk in Ziegler.[358] Concerning the translation of the translation of Hebrew *hapax legomena* in OG Job she makes the following observations:

---

351 See Lemmelijn, "The Greek Rendering of Hebrew Hapax Legomena," 146.
352 See Lemmelijn, "The Greek Rendering of Hebrew Hapax Legomena," 146–147.
353 See Lemmelijn, "The Greek Rendering of Hebrew Hapax Legomena," 147.
354 See Lemmelijn, "The Greek Rendering of Hebrew Hapax Legomena," 147.
355 See Lemmelijn, "The Greek Rendering of Hebrew Hapax Legomena," 147.
356 See Lemmelijn, "The Greek Rendering of Hebrew Hapax Legomena," 147 and 149; Ausloos and Lemmelijn, "Faithful Creativity," 66.
357 This research has been conducted within the Centre for Septuagint Studies and Textual Criticism (CSSTC), Leuven, under the supervision of Prof. dr. Bénédicte Lemmelijn. It takes the content- and context-related approach as a method to study the rendering of Hebrew *hapax legomena* in LXX Job.
358 See Verbeke, "Hebrew Hapax Legomena," 404–405.

(1) The LXX translator of Job consistently rendered some hapaxes according to their root.[359] The term 'consistency' does not have the same meaning in Verbeke's dissertation as in the quantitative approach applied by James Barr and Emanuel Tov.[360] According to the quantitative method, consistency is as a sign of literalness because a translator consistently renders a Hebrew word with one and the same Greek lexeme. Verbeke notes that one cannot speak of consistency as a sign of literalness if the lexeme under consideration is a *hapax legomenon*.[361] She bases her argument on the observations made by Staffan Olofsson who remarks that a consistent translation often uses the most adequate Greek rendering and, further, the less a Hebrew lexeme occurs, the less we can speak about consistency as a characteristic of literalness.[362] On consistent renderings in the case of non-absolute *hapax legomena* Verbeke writes:

> [...] [A] special kind of consistency occurs when the translator was confronted with non-absolute hapaxes. The translation more than once exhibits cases in which a hapax is rendered by a translation equivalent of a more common Hebrew word that looks quite similar to the hapax. As such, 'consistent rendering' is understood in this study as the rendering in which the LXX translator recognizes the hapax as a unique derivation of a more common root and bases himself on the common rendering of that root in order to provide a kind of consistent translation of the hapax. In fact, this type of consistency should be understood as so-called 'root-linked renderings' or 'etymological guesses.'[363]

Verbeke takes, in contrast to the quantitative approach, consistency as the translation on the basis of root constructions.

(2) In the speeches of Job to God there are 19 *hapax legomena* that have been rendered on the basis of a similar Hebrew word whereby the root is not the same.[364] In some cases, the translator adapts parallelisms to make his translation qualitatively better. This is the case in Job 6:10:[365]

---

359 See Verbeke, "Hebrew Hapax Legomena," 402–403.
360 See Verbeke, "Hebrew Hapax Legomena," 376–383.
361 See Verbeke, "Hebrew Hapax Legomena," 381.
362 See Verbeke, "Hebrew Hapax Legomena," 378–381; Staffan Olofsson, "Consistency as a Translation Technique," in *Translation Technique and Theological Exegesis. Collected Essays on the Septuagint Version*, ed. Staffan Olofsson, CBOTS 57 (Winona Lake, IN: Eisenbrauns, 2009), 50–66, 51–63.
363 Verbeke, "Hebrew Hapax Legomena," 381.
364 See Verbeke, "Hebrew Hapax Legomena," 385–389, 403.
365 See Verbeke, "Hebrew Hapax Legomena," 403.

MT	LXX
וּתְהִי עוֹד ׀ נֶחָמָתִי וַאֲסַלְּדָה בְחִילָה לֹא יַחְמוֹל	εἴη δέ μου πόλις τάφος, ἐφ' ἧς ἐπὶ τειχέων ἡλλόμην ἐπ' αὐτῆς, οὐ μὴ φείσωμαι·
This would be my consolation; I would even exult in unrelenting pain.	And may my city, whose walls I used to leap upon, be my grave, I will not spare myself.

Verbeke argues that the LXX translator rendered the Hebrew hapax חִילָה with τεῖχος on the basis of a misreading of עוֹד in the first colon of the verse.[366] The LXX translator would have read עוֹד as עִיר (city) and has therefore rendered it with the Greek lexeme πόλις (city).[367] To create parallelism, the translator has read חִילָה as חֵילָה (his wall).[368]

(3) The LXX translator of Job often made use of contextual exegesis and *parallelismus membrorum* te discover the meaning of a hapax.[369] Contextual exegesis, in the work of Verbeke, denotes the translation of a Hebrew word with a Greek equivalent based on the context of the verse.[370] Furthermore, rooting the Greek translation in the parallelisms that are present in the Hebrew text can also be regarded as a form of contextual exegesis.[371] As I already indicted above, the translator tried to preserve Hebrew parallelisms.

Concerning the material attested in Ziegler's critical edition indicated with an asterisk, Verbeke makes the following two observations: (1) there are no omissions present in this material and (2) transliterations of Hebrew words to Greek only occur in these passages.[372] An example of a transliteration can be observed in Job 28:18 where the LXX translator rendered גָּבִישׁ with γαβις.[373] As indicated, transliteration is a characteristic of a literal translation.

Verbeke concludes that the translation technique of LXX Job reflects two different ways of translation the Hebrew *Vorlage*.[374] On the one hand, there is a

---

366 See Verbeke, "Hebrew Hapax Legomena," 211. This is a non-intentional modification of the translator. See Verbeke, "Hebrew Hapax Legomena," 386.
367 See Verbeke, "Hebrew Hapax Legomena," 212.
368 See Verbeke, "Hebrew Hapax Legomena," 212. This can be regarded as an intentional change made by the translator. He manipulated his *Vorlage* to create parallelism. See Verbeke, "Hebrew Hapax Legomena," 386.
369 See Verbeke, "Hebrew Hapax Legomena," 403.
370 See Verbeke, "Hebrew Hapax Legomena," 391.
371 See Verbeke, "Hebrew Hapax Legomena," 391–392.
372 See Verbeke, "Hebrew Hapax Legomena," 405.
373 See Verbeke, "Hebrew Hapax Legomena," 405.
374 See Verbeke, "Hebrew Hapax Legomena," 415.

free and creative translator at work in OG Job, on the other hand, there is a more literal translator at work in the asterisked material.[375]

1.4.2.3 The relationship between LXX Proverbs and LXX Job

The relationship between LXX Job and LXX Proverbs has only been studied preliminary by the content- and context-related approach by looking at the Greek translation of Hebrew *hapax legomena*. By comparing aforementioned results of the limited research on the translation technique of LXX Proverbs with the exhaustive results of Elke Verbeke concerning the translation technique of LXX Job, Lemmelijn is able to give an indicative but relevant answer to the question whether both books have been translated by the same person.[376]

As indicated above, the LXX translator of Proverbs is rendering the hapax in Prov 4:24 on the basis of Hebrew parallelism. Making use of contextual exegesis and more specifically looking at *parallelismus membrorum* to render a Hebrew *hapax legomena* to Greek, is, according to Verbeke, also a characteristic of the LXX translator of Job. Therefore Lemmelijn concludes, contrary to Cook, that LXX Proverbs and LXX Job might have been the work of one and the same translator.[377]

It is evident that this pilot study needs to be complemented with further and exhaustive research into the translation technique of LXX Proverbs as well as LXX Job. Lemmelijn has only studied one hapax in her study and therefore a study concerning all hapaxes is necessary in order to come to a more adequate image of the LXX translator's translation technique. The results of that study can, consequently, be compared with the results of Elke Verbeke's study on the Greek rendering of Hebrew *hapax legomena* in LXX Job. This way we will acquire a more nuanced and adequate image of the translation technique of both books and will we be able to formulate an indicative but relevant answer to the question of a single translator. This is what this dissertation aims to do.

1.4.3 Conclusion

The content- and context-related approach has delivered some innovative and important insights into the translation techniques of the different LXX books by

---

375 See Verbeke, "Hebrew Hapax Legomena," 415.
376 See Lemmelijn, "The Greek Rendering of Hebrew Hapax Legomena," 140.
377 See Lemmelijn, "The Greek Rendering of Hebrew Hapax Legomena," 147.

means of the examination of content- and context-related criteria, e.g., the Greek rendering of Hebrew *hapax legomena*, Hebrew wordplay in the context of parallelism, aetiologies. Although preliminary, the LXX version of Proverbs has also been examined by this approach. The pilot study of Lemmelijn concerning the Greek rendering of Hebrew *hapax legomena* in LXX Proverbs has indicated that the translator has rendered his *Vorlage* in a free and creative but still faithful way. When opting for a specific choice of rendering he often takes the context and Hebrew parallelism into account. This specific way of rendering is also found in LXX Job. This leads Lemmelijn to conclude that LXX Job and LXX Proverbs might have been translated by one and the same translator.

1.5 Conclusion

In this chapter we have provided an exhaustive overview of the *status quaestionis* with regard to the translation technique of LXX Proverbs. As point of departure, we made use of the distinction made by Bénédicte Lemmelijn, i.e., the quantitative, qualitative and content- and context-related approach. Next to these approaches, this chapter has also examined the works of Johann Cook since he is the most prominent scholar with regard to LXX Proverbs nowadays. In this section, a conclusion on the basis of the above mentioned results will be formulated.

1.5.1 LXX Proverbs: a free/creative translation

All approaches agree on the fact that LXX Proverbs can be regarded as a free translation. However, James Barr warns us for the terminology 'free' since free translations, such as LXX Proverbs, are not free from literal aspects. Still, LXX Proverbs can be characterised as free translation on the basis of the following criteria:

(1) The quantitative and qualitative approach have shown that the LXX translator of Proverbs applies different Greek equivalents than literal translations. Some characteristics of literal translations are (a) the translation of the Hebrew proposition ב by ἐν, (b) the translation of the conjunction כי by ὅτι or διότι, (c) the translation of the Hebrew 3rd person masculine singular suffix by αὐτός or ἑαυτος, (d) the frequency of added prepositions in the LXX in accordance with the rules of the Greek language or translation habits, (e) the relative frequency of the post-position particles δέ, μέν, οὖν and τέ in relation to καί, (f) the construction ἐν τῷ + infinitive as the rendering of the Hebrew construction ב

+ infinitive construct, (g) the translation of πρὸ προσώπου for the Hebrew לִפְנֵי,
(h) ὅτι *causale* as a rendering of the Hebrew conjunction כי . These renderings
and constructions are usually shunned by the LXX translator of Proverbs. According to the qualitative approach, by avoiding these hebraisms, the Greek
translation of Proverbs exhibits some similarities with Koine Greek literature.

It has also been demonstrated that the LXX translator of Proverbs uses multiple Greek equivalents for one and the same Hebrew lexeme. This variegated
approach for rendering his Hebrew *Vorlage* together with the use of multiple
Greek *hapax legomena*, rhyme, dualisms or contrast, alliterations, special particles and harmonisation indicates, according to Cook, that the LXX translator of
Proverbs was a skilled stylist who was well-versed in Greek language.

(2) The LXX translation of Proverbs exhibits a specific exegesis. According
to Barr, Tov and Cook, this exegesis can be seen on macro level in the many
transpositions of verses and chapters as well as omissions. This also demonstrates the freedom with which the LXX translator handled his Hebrew *Vorlage*.
As I have indicated above, I do not fully agree on this point. According to me,
these transpositions testify of a *Vorlage* that differs from MT. Taking into account the way of writing and copying in Antiquity, it seems improbable that the
translator has made these changes himself. However, some small changes on
micro level can be explained due to the creative mind of the LXX translator.

Cook argues that LXX Proverbs also exhibits the ideology and theology of
the translator on micro level. On the basis of a study of the concepts of law
(νόμος) and the foreign woman (אשה זרה), he argues that the LXX translator of
Proverbs reacts against the Hellenistic tendency whereby Jews would devaluate
the Mosaic law. Because of this tendency, the translator gave a more prominent
role to the Mosaic law in his translation and warned his readers against foreign
wisdom.

(3) Next to the terms 'literal' and 'free', the content- and context-related approach has invented a different term to characterise the LXX translations, i.e.,
'creative'. The above study on the *status quaestionis* with regard to LXX Proverbs and the study on the Greek rendering of Hebrew *hapax legomena* in Proverbs have indicated that the LXX translator of Proverbs has rendered his *Vorlage*
in a free and creative way. He translated difficult words that were attested in his
Vorlage into Greek based on the context of the verse and, in the case of hapaxes,
he also based his rendering on *parallelismus membrorum*. He often enhanced
the poetical structure of the Hebrew by adapting the parallelisms by means
of a (stronger) contrast. This exhibits the freedom and creativity of the
LXX translator.

1.5.2 Unum et unum sunt unum?

As is clear from the introduction and the present chapter of this dissertation, many scholars have tried to answer the question whether LXX Job and LXX Proverbs were translated by one and the same translator. We have presented and examined the results of Cook and Lemmelijn with regard to this question above. On the basis of their studies we could conclude, however preliminary, the following:

Cook answers the question whether LXX Job and LXX Proverbs were translated by one and the same person negatively. On the basis of the analysis of shared themes, i.e., wisdom and creation, in both works he concludes that LXX Job and LXX Proverbs cannot be ascribed to the same translator. LXX Job omits a significant amount of verses in the passage that deals with wisdom and creation, whereas this is not the case in LXX Proverbs. As indicated above, Cook's argument can be refuted when the transpositions on macro level in LXX Proverbs are taken into account. This way, we can observe that both LXX Job and LXX Proverbs show radical differences in structure and composition when compared to MT. When Cook would take this into account, as he does in his other studies, and would ascribe these differences on macro level to the activity of the translator, he would come to the conclusion that both books stem from the same translator.

Contrary to Cook, Lemmelijn argues, though on the basis of a very limited and preliminary study, that LXX Job and LXX Proverbs have been translated by one and the same translator. She draws this conclusion based on an exemplary study of some Hebrew *hapax legomena* in both books. Both LXX Job and LXX Proverbs exhibit a free and creative translation technique whereby the translator often draws upon contextual exegesis and *parallelismus membrorum* in order to render the Hebrew hapaxes in his *Vorlage*.

Having provided a *status questionis* on the translation technique of the LXX translator of Proverbs and the question of a single translator for both Proverbs and Job, the next chapter will analyse the Greek rendering of Hebrew *hapax legomena* in LXX Proverbs and the remaining sections of LXX Job which have not been examined by Verbeke. By doing so, a more nuanced characterisation of the translation technique of both books as well as a more indicative answer to the question of a single translation will be obtained.

2 The Greek rendering of Hebrew *hapax legomena* in LXX Proverbs and LXX Job

As outlined in the introduction of this monograph, this research will mainly focus on the Greek rendering of Hebrew *hapax legomena* in LXX Proverbs. The present chapter will therefore pay attention to the registration and evaluation of the Hebrew *hapax legomena* and their respective Greek rendering in LXX Proverbs in order to obtain a more nuanced image of the translation technique of the LXX translator.

Next to the description of the translation technique of LXX Proverbs on the basis of the examination of the Greek rendering of Hebrew *hapax legomena*, this chapter will also deal with the Greek rendering of Hebrew *hapax legomena* in LXX Job. The results of the present study on LXX Proverbs will be compared to both Verbeke's as well as the present study on LXX Job, in order to discern whether both translations were translated by the same translator.

2.1 The Greek rendering of Hebrew *hapax legomena* in LXX Proverbs

Before we can analyse the Greek rendering of the Hebrew *hapax legomena* in Proverbs and characterise translation technique of the LXX translator, we will first have to register all the Hebrew *hapax legomena* and their respective Greek rendering.

In her unpublished doctoral dissertation on the Greek rendering of Hebrew *hapax legomena* in Job, Elke Verbeke prepared a list containing all the Hebrew *hapax legomena* that are attested in the Hebrew Bible.[1] This list presents an

---

* This chapter is based on several presentations which have been published or accepted for publication in peer-reviewed journals. With regard to the Greek rendering of Hebrew *hapax legomena* in LXX Proverbs, see Bryan Beeckman, "De (Pro)verb(i)is Raris: The Greek Rendering of Hebrew Absolute Hapax Legomena in LXX-Proverbs," in *The Septuagint South of Alexandria*, ed. Johann Cook and Gideon Kotzé, VTS 193 (Leiden: Brill, 2022), 153–174. For the Greek rendering of Hebrew *hapax legomena* in the speeches of Job's friends, see Bryan Beeckman, "Verba Rara Amicorum Iob: The Greek Rendering of Hebrew Absolute Hapax Legomena in the Speeches of Eliphaz, Bildad and Elihu in LXX Job," *HTS Teologiese Studies/Theological Studies* 77.1 (2021): 1–8. For both excursuses dealing with the Greek rendering of Hebrew animal, plant, floral and herb names, see Bryan Beeckman, "Proverbia de Animalibus. The Greek Rendering of Hebrew Animal Names in Proverbs," *ZAW* 131.2 (2019): 257–270; Bryan Beeckman, "Animalia

https://doi.org/10.1515/9783111041582-003

updated version of all the Hebrew *hapax legomena* of the Hebrew Bible based upon BibleWorks and the works of Greenspahn, Casanowicz and Lisowsky.[2] Moreover, the list provides an overview of the absolute and non-absolute *hapax legomena* according to the consulted works. This distinction will also be made in our registration of the Hebrew *hapax legomena* in Proverbs.

First, for the sake of completeness, Verbeke's list of Hebrew *hapax legomena* will be presented. This way we can distinguish whether a certain word can be regarded as a *hapax* or not and if it is indeed a hapax whether it can be labelled as an absolute or non-absolute *hapax legomenon*. By doing so, we can filter out the redundant material present in the list and provide a new list containing only those words which might be labelled as a hapax with a high degree of certainty. This registration will function as the foundation for the evaluation.

2.1.1 The registration of Hebrew *hapax legomena* in Proverbs

2.1.1.1 Registration of Hebrew *hapax legomena* in Proverbs according to Verbeke

Verbeke has recorded 94 Hebrew *hapax legomena* in Proverbs.[3] Her registration, with minor corrections, will be presented below. In order to correctly interpret the table, the following legend is applicable:[4]

---

in Libro Iob: The Greek Rendering of Hebrew Animal Names in LXX Job," in *XVII Congress of the International Organisation for Septuagint and Cognate Studies, Aberdeen, 2019*, ed. Michael van der Meer, Martin Rösel and Gideon Kotzé, SBLSCS 76 (Atlanta, GA: SBL Press, 2022), 255–284; Bryan Beeckman, "Unitas Vegetabilium? The Greek Rendering of Hebrew Floral, Plant and Herb Names in LXX-Proverbs and LXX-Job," *JSCS* 53 (2020): 19–41. Some parts have not been published but have been presented at conferences, see "De (Pro)verb(i)is Raris 2.0: The Greek Rendering of Hebrew Non-Absolute Hapax Legomena in LXX-Proverbs" (presented at the *The Septuagint—Prophetic Words, Textual Worlds and Versions (LXX.D 8th International Conference)*, Wuppertal (online), 18 Jul 2021-21 Jul 2021) and "Verba Rara Amicorum Iob 2.0: The Greek Rendering of Hebrew Non-Absolute Hapax Legomena in the Speeches of Eliphaz, Bildad, Zophar and Elihu in LXX Job" (presented at the *Society of Biblical Literature Annual Meeting 2021*, San Antonio, Texas, Online, 20 Nov 2021-23 Nov 2021).

1 See Verbeke, "Hebrew Hapax Legomena," 77–128.
2 See Casanowicz *et al*, "Hapax Legomena;" Gerhard Lisowsky, *Konkordanz zum hebräischen Alten Testament* (Stuttgart: Württembergische Bibelanstalt, 1958); Greenspahn, *Hapax Legomena*; *BibleWorks 10.0.5.302* (BibleWorks. Software for Biblical Exegesis and Research, 2016). Verbeke used an earlier version of BibleWorks: *BibleWorks 7.0* (BibleWorks. Software for Biblical Exegesis and Research, 2007). For an overview of Verbeke's methodology on the selection of hapaxes in BibleWorks, see Verbeke, "Hapax Legomena," 61–63.
3 See Verbeke, "Hebrew Hapax Legomena," 119–122.

Lis	Lisowsky
BW	BibleWorks
Cas	Casanowicz
Gr	Greenspahn
na	non-absolute
a	absolute
+	hapax according to BW
-	not attested

Verse	Word	Lis[5]	BW	Cas	Gr
1:22	פֶּתִי	na	-	-	-
1:27	שָׁאֲוָה	-	+	-	na
2:18	שׁוּחַ	na	-	-	-
3:8	רִפְאוּת	na	+	-	na
3:8	שֹׁר	-	-	-	na
3:15	פְּנִיִּים	-	+	-	-
3:26	לְכֶד	na	+	-	na
4:24	לְזוּת	na	+	a	na
5:19	יַעֲלָה	na	+	-	na
7:16	אֵטוּן	a	+	a	a
7:16	חֲטֻבוֹת	a	+	a	-
7:16	רבד	na	+	-	na
7:18	אֹהַב	-	+	-	na

---

4 When a word is attested but not a *hapax* in Lisowsky's work, Verbeke uses the *siglum* '/'. If a certain word is not registered as a *hapax* by BibleWorks, Casanowicz or Greenspahn, she uses the *siglum* '-'. However, it seems unnecessary to add an extra *siglum* to indicate that the word is not a *hapax*. It is clear that Lisowsky's concordance attests all Hebrew words that are present in the Hebrew Bible. Therefore, we will only use '-' as a *siglum* for words that are not considered to be a *hapax* according to a certain author or BibleWorks.

5 Lisowsky does not apply the term *hapax legomenon* in his concordance. Verbeke has recorded every word that is listed with only one reference in Lisowsky's concordance as being a hapax. Non-absolute hapax *legomena* are words where Lisowsky has tried to indicate a Hebrew root wherefrom the lemma is derived. For absolute *hapax legomena*, there is no root mentioned. See Verbeke, "Hebrew Hapax Legomena," 186–187, n. 669.

Verse	Word	Lis⁵	BW	Cas	Gr
7:20	כֵּסֶא	-	-	-	na
7:21	חֵלֶק	na	-	-	-
8:6	מִפְתָּח	na	+	-	na
8:13	גֵּאָה	na	+	-	na⁶
8:18	עָתֵק	na	+	-	-
8:22	מִפְעָל	-	+	-	na
9:3	גַּף	a	-	-	-
9:13	כְּסִילוּת	na	+	-	na
9:13	פְּתַיּוּת	na	+	-	na
10:3	הַוָּה	-	-	a	-
11:2	צָנוּעַ	na	+	-	-
11:15	תּוֹקְעִים	na	+⁷	-	-
12:18	בטא/ה	-	-	-	a
12:18	מַדְקֵרָה	na	+	-	na
12:26	תוּר	-	-	-	na
12:27	חרך	a	+	a	na
14:10	מֹרָה	-	-	-	na
14:28	רָזוֹן	na	-	-	-
15:19	חֵדֶק	/	-	-	na
15:19	מְשֻׂכָה	na	+	-	na
16:1	מַעֲרָךְ	na	+	-	na
16:4	מַעֲנֶה	na	-	-	-
16:18	כִּשָּׁלוֹן	na	+	-	na
16:26	אכף	na	+	-	na
16:27	צָרֵב	na	+	-	-
16:30	עצה	a	+	a	na
17:22	גֵּהָה	na	+	-	na

---

6 Verbeke correctly points out the reference mistake in the work of Greenspahn. Instead of 8:13 Greenspahn has 7:13. See Verbeke, "Hebrew Hapax Legomena," 69; Greenspahn, *Hapax Legomena*, 188.

7 It must be noted that the provided list of BibleWorks by Verbeke needs some small corrections. A simple 'search on lemma' for a word that is not indicated as a hapax by BibleWorks in Verbeke's list resulted one time in a different outcome, e.g., Prov 11:15. Therefore, the table is updated in this respect and provides a more adequate representation of the hapaxes according to BibleWorks. The same might be concluded about מִיץ in 30:33. However, this word occurs three times in the same verse and, thus, cannot be considered a hapax.

Verse	Word	Lis[5]	BW	Cas	Gr
17:25	מֶמֶר	na	+	-	na
19:15	עַצְלָה	na	+	-	-
19:18	מוּת	-	-	-	na
19:19	[8] גְּרָל	-	+	-	na
20:20	אֶשׁוּן	a	+	-	na
21:8	הֲפַכְפַּךְ	na	+	-[9]	na
21:8	וָזָר	a	+	a[10]	a
21:14	כפה	a	+	a	a
22:21	קֹשְׁטְ	a	+	-	na
22:29	חָשֹׁךְ	na	+	-	na
23:2	לֹעַ	na	+	a	na
23:2	שֹׂכֵין	na	+	a	na
23:7	שָׁעַר	na	+	a	na
23:21	נוּמָה	na	+	-	na
23:28	חֶתֶף	na	+	-	na
23:29	אֲבוֹי	-	+	-	a
23:29	חַכְלִלוּת	na	+	-	na
23:32	צִפְעֹנִי	-	+	-	-
23:34	חִבֵּל	na	+	-	na
24:11	מוֹט	-	-	-	na
25:10	חסד	na	-	-	-
25:11	אֹפֶן	a	+	a	na[11]
25:13	צִנָּה	a	-	-	-
25:18	מֵפִיץ	na	+	-	na
25:26	רפשׂ	-	+	-	-
25:28	מַעְצוֹר	na	+	-	na
26:8	מַרְגֵּמָה	na	+	-	na
26:11	קֵא	na	+	-	-
26:14	צִיר	a	-	-	-

---

8 In Verbeke's list, the verb גרל is mentioned, See Verbeke, "Hebrew Hapax Legomena," 120. However, the hapax concerns גְּרָל.

9 Verbeke records this as a hapax in Casanowicz but it is not present in Casanowicz's list.

10 Verbeke does not record this as a hapax although it is attested in Casanowicz's list.

11 Greenspahn wrongly records Prov 25:4 for the Hebrew lexeme אֹפֶן. See Greenspahn, *Hapax Legomena*, 187.

Verse	Word	Lis[5]	BW	Cas	Gr
26:18	זֵק	na	-	-	-
26:18	להה	a	+	a	-
26:26	מַשָּׁאוֹן	na	+	-	na
26:28	מִדְחֶה	na	+	-	na
27:3	נֵטֶל	na	+	-	na
27:4	אַכְזְרִיּוּת	na	+	-	na
27:15	סַגְרִיר	a	+	-	na
27:20	אֲבַדּוֹ	na	+	-	na
27:21	מַהֲלָל	na	+	-	na
27:22	כתש	na	+[12]	-	-
27:22	עֱלִי	na	+	a	na
28:10	שְׁחוּת	na	+	-	na
28:19	רֵישׁ	-	-	-	na
29:13	תֹּךְ	-	-	-	na
29:18	אָשֵׁר	-	+	-	-
29:21	מְנוֹן	a	+	a	a
29:21	פנק	a	+	a	a
30:15	עֲלוּקָה	a	+	a[13]	a
30:28	שְׂמָמִית	a	+	a	a
30:31	אַלְקוּם	a	+	a?[14]	a[15]
30:31	זַרְזִיר	a	+	a	a?[16]
30:33	מִיץ	-	-	-	na
31:8	חֲלוֹף	na	+	-	na
31:19	כִּישׁוֹר	a	+	a	na
31:27	עֲצְלוּת	na	+	-	na

---

12 Not in Verbeke's list.

13 The question mark is not attested in Verbeke's list although it is mentioned in Casanowicz's list.

14 Question mark attested in Casanowicz's list, not in Verbeke's.

15 Verbeke records this as 'a?' meaning that it is indicated with a question mark in Greenspahn. However, this is not correct. No question mark is found in Greenspahn.

16 Apparently, Verbeke has switched the question mark of both hapaxes in Prov 30:31. In Greenspahn זַרְזִיר is marked with a question mark whereas אַלְקוּם is not.

2.1.1.2 Registration of Hebrew *hapax legomena* and their Greek rendering in Proverbs

As is apparent from the table above not all words have been labelled as a hapax by Casanowicz, Greenspahn, Lisowsky or Bibleworks together. Therefore, the following rules-of-thumb will be applied in this research:

(a) The words that have been labelled as a *hapax* by one author and BibleWorks or two, three or all of the authors and/or BibleWorks can be regarded as a hapax (absolute or non-absolute);

(b) Those who are only labelled as a *hapax legomenon* by only one author or BibleWorks will not be regarded as a hapax, since the others, i.e., the majority, agree that it is not a hapax.

Therefore, the latter cases will not be registered nor analysed in this work. These words, 25 in total, that will not be discussed are the following:

Verse	Word[17]	Lis	BW	Cas	Gr
1:22	פֶּתִי	na	-	-	-
2:18	שׁוּחַ	na	-	-	-
3:8	שֹׁר	-	-	-	na
3:15	פְּנִיִּים	-	+	-	-
7:20	כֶּסֶא	-	-	-	na
7:21	חֵלֶק	na	-	-	-
9:3	גַּף	a	-	-	-
10:3	הַוָּה	-	-	a	-
12:18	בטא/ה	-	-	-	a
12:26	תּוּר	-	-	-	na
14:10	מֹרָה	-	-	-	na
14:28	רָזוֹן	na	-	-	-
15:19	חֶדֶק	/	-	-	na
16:4	מֵעֲנֶה	na	-	-	-
19:18	מוּת	-	-	-	na
23:32	צִפְעֹנִי	-	+	-	-
24:11	מוֹט	-	-	-	na

---

17 Every word will be presented in the same way they are presented in Hebrew lexicons, i.e., every word is vocalised except verbs.

Verse	Word[17]	Lis	BW	Cas	Gr
25:10	חֶסֶד	na	-	-	-
25:13	צִנָּה	a	-	-	-
25:26	רָפַשׂ	-	+	-	-
26:14	צִיר	a	-	-	-
26:18	זֵק	na	-	-	-
28:19	רֵישׁ	-	-	-	na
29:13	תֹּךְ	-	-	-	na
29:18	אֲשֶׁר	-	+	-	-

In order to enhance the analysis, we will make a distinction between absolute and non-absolute *hapax legomena*. This distinction will help us to better characterise the translation technique in the analysis since absolute *hapax legomena* might have posed a greater difficulty for the LXX translator to render. The list made by Verbeke attests the difference between non-absolute and absolute hapaxes. However, this distinction is only explicitly made by Greenspahn.[18] Casanowicz, Lisowsky and BibleWorks do not make this distinction. Lisowsky, moreover, does not use the term *hapax legomena* but he does mention the possible Hebrew root a word is derived from. Casanowicz has only recorded the absolute *hapax legomena* in his list. Therefore, the following rules-of-thumb will be applied for the distinction between non-absolute and absolute hapaxes in this monograph:

(a) If all three authors agree on whether a certain hapax is absolute or non-absolute, we can record it as such. E.g., אָטוּן (7:16) => a (Lis, Cas, Gr) => a;

(b) If two of the three authors agree on whether a certain hapax is absolute or non-absolute, we can record it as such. E.g., לְזוּת (4:24) => na (Lis, Gr) + a (Cas) => na;

(c) If the *hapax legomenon* is only attested by two of the three authors and they do not agree on whether the hapax is absolute or non-absolute, then the decision will be made in favour of Greenspahn being the younger one and incorporating and interpreting the earlier views on *hapax legomena*.[19] E.g. אִישׁוֹן (20:20) => a (Lis) + na (Gr) => na;

---

18 See Greenspahn, *Hapax Legomena*, 22–23 as well as his lists of absolute and non-absolute *hapax legomena*, see Greenspahn, *Hapax Legomena*, 183–198.

19 This only occurs in three cases (Prov 20:20; 22:21; 27:15). In these instances, there is only a disagreement between Lisowsky and Greenspahn. In all these cases, Lisowsky records the

(d) If the hapax is only recorded by one of the authors and BibleWorks, the decision will be made in favour of this one author since BibleWorks does not make the distinction between absolute and non-absolute. E.g.: אֹהֶב (7:18) => na (Gr) => na.

In the next sections the remaining hapaxes will thus be divided into two categories, i.e., absolute and non-absolute, taking into the aforementioned rule of thumb.

In the registration below, the Hebrew hapaxes and their respective Greek rendering in the LXX version of Proverbs will be presented. For the Hebrew versions the *Biblia Hebraica Quinta* (BHQ) is used for the Masoretic Text (MT) and the *Discoveries in the Judean Desert* for the Qumran fragments where applicable.[20] For the LXX version we are limited to Rahlfs' version of the text since the Göttingen edition is still in production.[21]

A   Registration of absolute Hebrew hapax legomena and their Greek rendering in Proverbs

Based upon the rules of thumb presented above, there are 16 Hebrew absolute *hapax legomena* in total in Proverbs.

Verse	MT LXX		DSS
7:16	אֵטוּן	στρώννυμι	/
7:16	חֲטֻבוֹת	ἀμφίταπος	/
12:27	חרך	ἐπιτυγχάνω	/
16:30	עצה	στηρίζω	/

word as an absolute hapaxes, whereas Greenspahn records it as non-absolute. Casanowicz does not record these hapaxes. Since he did only list absolute hapaxes, Casanowicz disagrees with Lisowsky in the aforementioned instances. Thus, Greenspahn's classification seems to be the correct one.

20 For the BHQ of Proverbs see Jan de Waard, ed., *Proverbs*, BHQ 17 (Stuttgart: Deutsche Bibelgesellschaft, 2008) (= BHQ). Some manuscripts found at the Dead Sea excavation sites have preserved a small amount of fragments of Proverbs namely 4QProv[a] (= 4Q102; containing 1:27–2:1), 4QProv[b] (= 4Q103; containing 13:6b-9; 14:6-10; 14:31-15:8 and 15:19b-31) and 4Q271 (containing 15:8). See Eugene Ulrich *et al.*, ed., *Qumran Cave 4, XI. Psalms to Chronicles*, DJD XVI (Oxford: Clarendon Press, 2000), 181–186; Joseph M. Baumgarten, *Qumran Cave 4 XIII. The Damascus Document (4Q266-273)*, DJD XVIII (Oxford: Clarendon Press, 1996), 181.

21 For the text of Rahlfs, see Alfred Rahlfs, ed., *Septuaginta. Id est Vetus Testamentum Graece iuxta LXX Interpretes* (Stuttgart: Deutsche Bibelgesellschaft, 2006).

Verse	MT	LXX	DSS
21:8	זָר	σκολιός	/
21:14	כפה	ἀνατρέπω	/
23:29	אֲבוֹי	θόρυβος	/
25:11	אֹפֶן	/	/
26:18	להה	/	/
29:21	מָנוֹן	ὀδυνάω	/
29:21	פנק	κατασπαταλάω	/
30:15	עֲלוּקָה	βδέλλα	/
30:28	שְׂמָמִית	καλαβώτης	/
30:31	אַלְקוּם	δημηγορέω	/
30:31	זַרְזִיר	ἀλέκτωρ	/
31:19	כִּישׁוֹר	συμφέρω	/

B Registration of non-absolute Hebrew hapax legomena and their Greek rendering in Proverbs

There are 52 Hebrew non-absolute *hapax legomena* in total in Proverbs.

Verse	MT	LXX	DSS
1:27	שַׁאֲוָה	ἄφνω	/[22]
3:8	רִפְאוּת	ἴασις	/
3:26	לֶכֶד	σαλεύω	/
4:24	לְזוּת	ἄδικος	/
5:19	יַעֲלָה	πῶλος	/
7:16	רבד	τείνω	/
7:18	אֹהַב	ἔρως	/
8:6	מִפְתָּח	ἀναφέρω	/
8:13	גֵּאָה	ὕβρις	/
8:18	עָתֵק	πολύς	/
8:22	מִפְעָל	ἔργον	/
9:13	כְּסִילוּת	ἄφρων	/
9:13	פְּתַיּוּת	ψωμός	/

---

22 Although verse 1:27 is attested in 4QProv[a], it only attests a part of 1:27c: וצוקה צרה עליכם בבא. See DJD XVI, 182.

Verse	MT	LXX	DSS
11:2	צָנוּעַ	στόμαδὲταπεινῶν	/
11:15	תּוֹקְעִים	ἦχος	/
12:18	מַדְקְרָה	τιτρώσκω	/
15:19	מְשֻׂכָה	ἄκανθα	/[23]
16:1	מַעֲרָךְ	/	/
16:18	כִּשָּׁלוֹן	πτῶμα	/
16:26	אכף	ἐκβιάζω	/
16:27	צָרֵב	θησαυρίζω	/
17:22	גֵּהָה	/	/
17:25	מֶמֶר	ὀδύνη	/
19:15	עַצְלָה	ὀκνηρός (18,8)	/
19:19	גְּרָל	πολύς	/
20:20	אֱשׁוּן	κόρη (20,9a)	/
21:8	הֲפַכְפַּךְ	σκολιός	/
22:21	קֹשְׁטְ	ἀληθής	/
22:29	חָשֻׁךְ	ἀνδράσι νωθροῖς	/
23:2	לֹעַ	/	/
23:2	שָׂכִּין	/	/
23:7	שֵׁעָר	καταπίοι τρίχα	/
23:21	נוּמָה	ὑπνώδης	/
23:28	חֶתֶף	συντόμως	/
23:29	חַכְלִלוּת	πέλειος	/
23:34	חִבֵּל	κυβερνήτης	/
25:18	מֵפִיץ	ῥόπαλον	/
25:28	מַעְצוֹר	μετὰ βουλῆς	/
26:8	מַרְגֵּמָה	σφενδόνη	/
26:11	קֵא	ἔμετος	/
26:26	מַשָּׁאוֹן	δόλος	/
26:28	מִדְחֶה	ἀκαταστασία	/
27:3	נֵטֶל	δυσβάστακτος	/
27:4	אַכְזְרִיּוּת	ἀνελεήμων	/
27:15	סַגְרִיר	χειμερινός	/

---

23 4Prov[b] attests Prov 15:19–31. However, only the last word (סוללה) of 15:19 is preserved. See DJD XVI, 186.

Verse	MT	LXX	DSS
27:20	אֲבַדּוֹ	ἀπώλεια	/
27:21	מַהֲלֵל	ἐγκωμιάζω	/
27:22	כָּתֵשׁ	μαστιγόω	/
27:22	עֱלִי	συνέδριον?	/
28:10	שְׁחוּת	διαφθορά	/
31:8	חֲלוֹף	ὑγιῶς	/
31:27	עַצְלוּת	ὀκνηρός	/

Now that we have registered all Hebrew (absolute and non-absolute) *hapax legomena* and their respective Greek rendering in Proverbs, we can begin to evaluate the Greek translation in order to characterise the translation technique of the LXX translator. This will be the subject of the next sections.

2.1.2 The evaluation of the Hebrew *hapax legomena* and their Greek rendering in LXX Proverbs

After the registration of the Hebrew *hapax legomena* and their respective Greek rendering in Proverbs, we can now start with the evaluation of these renderings in order to characterise the LXX translator's translation technique. The evaluation of the different renderings will form the major part of this research. Every Hebrew hapax, absolute and non-absolute, and their Greek translation will be analysed, discussed and evaluated.

Before we begin with the evaluation of the Greek rendering of Hebrew *hapax legomena*, it is important to note that the meaning of the Hebrew hapaxes is often obscure. While the meaning of non-absolute *hapax legomena* might be derived from existing Hebrew roots, this is not the case for absolute *hapax legomena*. In order to grasp the meaning of these words, multiple dictionaries and scholarly works will be consulted.[24] In the case of absolute hapaxes, although

---

24 The following Hebrew lexicons have been consulted: Wilhelm Gesenius, *Hebräischen und Aramäischen Handwörterbuch* (Leipzig: Verlag von F. C. W. Vogel, 1921[17]) (= GESENIUS); Ludwig Koehler and Walter Baumgartner, *Hebräisches und Aramäisches Lexikon zum Alten Testament. Unveranderter Nachdruck der Dritten Auflage (1967–1995)* (Leiden – Boston, Brill, 2004) (= KBL); Francis Brown, Samuel R. Driver and Charles A. Briggs, *The New Brown – Driver – Briggs – Gesenius Hebrew and English Lexicon with an Appendix Containing the Biblical Aramaic* (Peabody, MA: Hendrickson Publishers, 1979) (= BDB); William L. Holladay, *A Concise Hebrew and*

their meaning cannot be derived from an existing Hebrew root, scholars have often pointed at their affiliation with cognate languages such as Aramaic, Arabic and Syriac. If this is the case, their meaning can often be derived from these. However, we need to bear in mind that in some cases dictionaries often depend upon the translated versions of the Hebrew Bible.[25] Therefore, we need to be careful in our assessment of the correct meaning of the Hebrew words under examination. Moreover, as Ausloos, Lemmelijn and Verbeke have also correctly articulated,[26] the focus of this research is not on *hapax legomena* as such but rather on the way in which the LXX translator has rendered his Hebrew *Vorlage* into Greek. The evaluation will also point out whether or not the LXX translator was familiar with the Hebrew hapax.

First, all 16 absolute *hapax legomena* will be evaluated. Since these hapaxes might have posed the greatest difficulty for the LXX translator to render, they can be regarded as the most interesting hapaxes. Therefore, their Greek rendering will be the greatest *locus* to study the translation technique of the LXX translator.

Aramaic Lexicon of the Old Testament. Based upon the Lexical Work of Ludwig Koehler and Walter Baumgartner (Leiden: Boston – Köln, Brill, 2000) (= HALOT); David J. A. Clines, *The Dictionary of Classical Hebrew Volume I–IX* (Sheffield Academic Press: Sheffield, 1993-2016) (= DCH). However, preference to DCH is given in this work. For the sake of clarity, the volume number after each reference of DCH is given. For the Greek lexicons, the following are consulted: Takamitsu Muraoka, *A Greek-English Lexicon of the Septuagint* (Leuven – Paris – Walpole, MA: Peeters, 2009) (= GELS); Johan Lust, Erik Eynikel and Katrin Hauspie, *Greek-English Lexicon of the Septuagint. Third Corrected Edition* (Stuttgart: Deutsche Bibelgesellschaft, 2015) (= LEH); Franco Montanari, *The Brill Dictionary of Ancient Greek* (Brill: Leiden, 2015) (= MGS). Especially gels and lust will be referred to. Also when necessary Henry G. Liddell, Robert Scott and Henry S. Jones, *A Greek-English Lexicon. Ninth Revised Edition* (Oxford: Clarendon Press, 1996) (= *The Online Liddell-Scott-Jones Greek-English Lexicon*, http://stephanus.tlg.uci.edu/lsj/) (= LSJ), has been consulted. Hatch & Redpath's *Concordance to the Septuagint* is used as a concordance of the LXX, see Edwin Hatch and Henry A. Redpath, *A Concordance to the Septuagint. And the Other Greek Versions of the Old Testament (Including the Apocryphal Books). Second Edition* (Grand Rapids, MI: Baker Book House Company, 1998) (= HR).

25 See Takamitsu Muraoka, "Hebrew Hapax Legomena and Septuagint Lexicography," in *VII Congress of the International Organization for Septuagint and Cognate Studies. Leuven, 1989*, ed. Claude E. Cox, SBLSCS 31 (Atlanta, GA: Scholars Press, 1991), 205–222, 212; Hans Ausloos, "Hapax Legomena, the Septuagint, and Hebrew Lexicography," in *XIV Congress of the International Oganization for Septuagint and Cognate Studies. Helsinki, 2010*, ed. Melvin K. H. Peters, SBLSCS 51 (Atlanta, GA: SBL Press, 2013), 291–300, 294, 300.

26 See Ausloos, 'The Septuagint's Rendering of Hebrew Hapax Legomena and the Characterization of Its 'Translation Technique," 362; Lemmelijn, "The Greek Rendering of Hebrew Hapax Legomena," 137; Verbeke, "Hapax Legomena," lxii.

Consequently, we will deal with the Greek rendering of the 52 non-absolute *hapax legomena* in Proverbs. Although they might not have posed such a great difficulty as absolute hapaxes for the LXX translator, their analysis will shed some light on how the translator dealt with them.

The results of the analysis and evaluation of every hapax and its Greek rendering in the LXX of Proverbs will enable us to achieve a more nuanced characterisation of the translation technique of LXX Proverbs. This characterisation will be presented in the final stage of this section.

2.1.2.1 Evaluation of the Greek rendering of Hebrew absolute *hapax legomena* in Proverbs

As is can be observed from the registration above, there are 16 absolute *hapax legomna* in Proverbs. These will be examined in this section.

A אֵטוּן and חֲטֻבוֹת (Prov 7:16)

MT	LXX
מַרְבַדִּים רָבַדְתִּי עַרְשִׂי חֲטֻבוֹת אֵטוּן מִצְרָיִם:	κειρίαις τέτακα τὴν κλίνην μου, ἀμφιτάποις δὲ ἔστρωκα τοῖς ἀπ᾽ Αἰγύπτου.
I have decked my couch with coverings, colored spreads of Egyptian linen.[27]	With coverings I have spread my couch, and with double tapestry from Egypt I have decked it.[28]

In 7:16, two absolute Hebrew *hapax legomena* are found, *i.e.* אֵטוּן and חֲטֻבוֹת. The Hebrew noun אֵטוּן is commonly translated into English with 'linen.'[29] The LXX translator rendered it by the Greek verb στρώννυμι (to spread),[30] more specifically a 1st person singular perfect (ἔστρωκα). As Michael V. Fox, David-Marc d'Hamonville and Gerhard Tauberschmidt have indicated,[31] the LXX translator

---

27 For the English translation of the Hebrew text, the New Revised Standard Version (NRSV) is used. Here too, one must be cautious when looking at the English translation of hapaxes since they are often based upon the Greek or other ancient versions.
28 The English translation of the LXX is taken from the New English Translation of the Septuagint (NETS). For LXX Proverbs, see Cook, "Proverbs."
29 See GESENIUS, 27; HALOT, 11.
30 See GELS, 640; LEH, 574.
31 Fox, *Proverbs*, 145; d'Hamonville, *Les Proverbes*, 201–202; Tauberschmidt, *Secondary Parallelism*, 221. However, Fox argues that στρώννυμι is used as a rendering of חֲטֻבוֹת instead of אֵטוּן. See Fox, *Proverbs*, 145.

has tried to render this *hapax* by enhancing the parallelism with the first colon of the verse, i.e., ערשי רבדתי מרבדים/κειρίαις τέτακα τὴν κλίνην μου, and this especially with the verb רבדתי which he also rendered by a 1st person singular perfect, i.e., τέτακα. Indeed, it is highly plausible that the LXX translator rendered the hapax by a Greek perfect form in order to enhance parallelism,[32] since this is one of the trails of his translation technique.[33] According to BHQ,[34] the LXX translator based his rendering on the Hebrew root נטה ('to spread out').[35] However, this seems far off from the word אֵטוּן. Therefore, this seems to be implausible.

The other *hapax* in this verse, i.e., חֲטֻבוֹת ('coloured, embroidered fabric'),[36] is rendered to ἀμφίταπος ('rug or carpet with pile on both sides'), both in Hebrew as in Greek in plural.[37] This rendering conveys one of the meanings of the Hebrew hapax, i.e., embroidered fabric. Therefore, it is an adequate translation of the hapax.

B חרך (Prov 12:27)

MT	LXX
לֹא־יַחֲרֹךְ רְמִיָּה צֵידוֹ וְהוֹן־אָדָם יָקָר חָרוּץ׃	οὐκ ἐπιτεύξεται δόλιος θήρας, κτῆμα δὲ τίμιον ἀνὴρ καθαρός.
The lazy do not roast their game, but the diligent obtain precious wealth.	The deceitful will obtain no game, but a pure man a valuable possession.

---

32 Moreover, rendering a hapax relying on parallelism is not an uncommon practice among LXX translators. In her study on the rendering of Hebrew *hapax legomena* in LXX Job, Verbeke has argued that the translator often resorted to contextual exegesis, more specifically, reliance of parallelism to render the Hebrew hapaxes. See Verbeke, "Hebrew Hapax Legomena," 393–394.

33 See, i.a., Tauberschmidt, *Secondary Parallelism*, 228; Fox, *Proverbs*, 52–54; Beeckman, "Trails of a Different Vorlage," 585; Bryan Beeckman, "De Nominibus Sacris: Theological Exegesis in Verses of LXX Proverbs Containing ὁ κύριος Without Any Counterpart in MT?," *RB* 128.4 (2021): 501–524, 520.

34 See BHQ, 14.

35 See GESENIUS, 500; HALOT, 235.

36 See GESENIUS, 224; HALOT, 101.

37 See Al Wolters, *Proverbs. A Commentary Based on Paroimiai in Codex Vaticanus*, SCS (Leiden – Boston, MA: Brill, 2020), 161. Al Wolters, following, *i.a.*, LSJ and GELS, disagrees with LEH which only records 'double-sided.' See GELS, 33; LEH, 34.

The Hebrew hapax חרך is rendered by ἐπιτυγχάνω ('to attain, to be successful') in Prov 12:27.[38] The thought expressed in the first stich deals with the image of hunting due to the attestation of the word צַיִד ('hunting, game, food').[39] Clearly, since the lazy or deceitful is mentioned in this verse and since the negative particle לֹא is attested, the colon must express something negative with regard to the lazy/deceitful and his ability to hunt. Given this context, the translation of 'to attain,' 'to obtain' or even better 'to succeed' seems to be a good, although perhaps not accurate, translation for the Hebrew verb חרך. Therefore, to LXX translator's choice to opt for ἐπιτυγχάνω seems logical and plausibly, it is therefore an adequate translation for the hapax חרך.

C   עצה (Prov 16:30)

MT	LXX
עֹצֶה עֵינָיו לַחְשֹׁב תַּהְפֻּכוֹת קֹרֵץ שְׂפָתָיו כִּלָּה רָעָה:	στηρίζων ὀφθαλμοὺς αὐτοῦ λογίζεται διεστραμμένα, ὁρίζει δὲ τοῖς χείλεσιν αὐτοῦ πάντα τὰ κακά, οὗτος κάμινός ἐστιν κακίας.
One who winks the eyes plans perverse things; one who compresses the lips brings evil to pass.	He who fixes his eyes considers perverse things, and he marks out with his lips all evil; he is a furnace of evil.

The LXX version of this verse is longer than its Hebrew counterpart due to the plus οὗτος κάμινός ἐστιν κακίας[40]. The hapax in this verse, עצה ('to contract, to narrow'),[41] is rendered by στηρίζω ('to fix') in the LXX.[42] The word pair στηρίζω and ὀφθαλμός, attested in this verse, occurs elsewhere in the LXX, i.e., Amos

---

38 See GELS, 285, LEH, 237.

39 See HALOT, 305. See also the Hebrew noun צַיָּד (hunter) which occurs in Jer 16:16. HALOT mentions that this noun is also attested in Prov 6:5. This is incorrect. Gesenius only mentions its attestation in Jeremiah which is correct. See GESENIUS, 681. Moreover, Prov 12:27 is, remarkably, not mentioned in HALOT next to the entry צַיִד.

40 I consciously use the neutral term 'plus' here since the word 'addition' already implies an evaluation, i.e., an addition by the LXX translator or a (later) scribe. See Lemmelijn, *A Plague of Texts?*, 23, n. 84. However, in order to call it an addition, one should evaluate this variant in light of the textual evidence and the translator's translation technique. Since we are only interested in the Greek rendering of the Hebrew hapax, we will not provide a text-critical analysis of this plus.

41 See GESENIUS, 610; HALOT, 280.

42 See GELS, 636–637, LEH, 569–570.

9:4, Jer 24:6 and Prov 27:20. In the two former, στηρίζω is used as a rendering of שׂים ('to set') and in Prov 27:20 it is a plus. The expression 'to fix ones eyes' is also attested in other extant Greek texts. More specifically, it was used in a medical context in the writings of Galenus (129-199), i.e., *De locis affectis libri vi* and *De musculorum dissectione ad tirones*.[43] D'Hamonville argues, though carefully, that the translation of the verbs עצה and קרץ into στηρίζω and ὁρίζω might be influenced by assonance.[44] However, he does not indicate which Greek verb has been altered to create the said assonance. Since קרץ is never translated by ὁρίζω in other LXX books, and in Prov 6:13 and 10:10, it is rendered by the verb ἐννεύω ('to nod'), the translator must have been familiar with the meaning of the Hebrew hapax עצה and rendered it by στηρίζω. Consequently, and it might indeed have been in order to create assonance, he opted for ὁρίζω instead of ἐννεύω which he used in other instances as a translation for קרץ.

D וְזֵר (Prov 21:8)

MT	LXX
הֲפַכְפַּךְ דֶּרֶךְ אִישׁ וָזָר וְזַךְ יָשָׁר פָּעֳלֽוֹ׃	πρὸς τοὺς σκολιοὺς σκολιὰς ὁδοὺς ἀποστέλλει ὁ θεός· ἁγνὰ γὰρ καὶ ὀρθὰ τὰ ἔργα αὐτοῦ.
The way of the guilty is crooked, but the conduct of the pure is right.	To the crooked God sends crooked ways, for his works are pure and upright.

Fox notes that the Hebrew of this verse is obscure.[45] Moreover, the LXX version differs from MT and contains a plus, *i.e.* ἀποστέλλει ὁ θεός. I have argued, see below, that the LXX translator deliberately added ἀποστέλλει ὁ θεός to nuance that it is God who sends crooked ways to the crooked, whereby God becomes the actor of the verse.[46]

43 Karl G. Kühn, "De musculorum dissectione ad tirones," in *Claudii Galeni Opera Omnia*, ed. Karl G. Kühn (Cambridge: Cambridge University Press, 2011), 926–1026, 932. In the Latin translation the word '*confero*' (to bring together) is used.
44 See d'Hamonville, *Les Proverbes*, 258. According to Gillis Gerleman this is one of the characteristics of the translator's translation technique. See Gerleman, *Proverbs*, 12 (examples can be found on p. 12–13).
45 See Fox, *Proverbs*, 289.
46 See Bryan Beeckman, "De Nomine Dei: Theological Exegesis in Verses of the Septuagint Version of Proverbs Containing ὁ θεός Without Any Counterpart in the Masoretic Text?," *Louvain studies* 43.4 (2020): 372–387, 382.

Concerning the hapax וָזָר, there has been much debate about its meaning.[47] According to Wilhelm Gesenius, the meaning of the word can be derived from the Arabic وَزَرَ (*wazara*, 'to bear a burden'), وَزِرَ (*wazira*, 'to be guilty') or زَوِرَ (*zawira*, 'to be crooked').[48] However, Arnold B. Ehrlich argues that it is unlikely that the initial *wav* belongs to the root of the word, since Hebrew words beginning with *wav* are scarce (in most of the cases it is a proper name).[49] Moreover, Wilhelm Nowack adds that there is no trace of such a derivative root in neither Hebrew, Aramaic or Syriac.[50] Thus, we are prompt to believe that the original Hebrew text read זר (strange) and that the initial *wav* might have originated due to dittography with the next word זור.[51] Thus, the *Vorlage* of the LXX translator probably attested זר instead of זור. Taking this into account, the LXX translator rendering אִישׁ וָזָר by σκολιός does not seem to be odd. Moreover, by doing so, he created assonance with σκολιούς.[52]

E   כפה (Prov 21:14)

MT	LXX
מַתָּן בַּסֵּתֶר יִכְפֶּה־אָף וְשֹׁחַד בַּחֵק חֵמָה עַזָּה:	δόσις λάθριος ἀνατρέπει ὀργάς, δώρων δὲ ὁ φειδόμενος θυμὸν ἐγείρει ἰσχυρόν.
A gift in secret averts anger; and a concealed bribe in the bosom, strong wrath.	A secret gift averts anger, but he who is sparing with gifts arouses fierce wrath.

---

47 See BHQ, 49*–50*.
48 See GESENIUS, 190; HALOT, 85.
49 See Arnold B. Ehrlich, Randglossen zur hebräischen Bibel. Textkritisches, sprachliches und sachliches. Sechter Band: Psalmen, Spruche und Hiob (Hildesheim: Georg Olms Verlagbuchhandlung, 1968), 122. See also BHQ, 50*.
50 Wilhelm G. H. Nowack, *Sprüche, Prediger und Hoheslied überzetst und erklärt*, HzAT II.3 (Göttingen: Vandenhoeck & Ruprecht, 1989), 121. See also BHQ, 50*.
51 See Fox, *Proverbs*, 289. Antoine Jean Baumgartner mentions that זר is attested in two manuscripts, see Antoine J. Baumgartner, "Étude critique sur l'état du texte du livre des Proverbes d'après les principals traductions anciennes" (PhD diss., University of Leipzig, 1890), 192. However, he does not indicate which manuscripts and nor the *Biblia Hebraica Stuttgartensia* (BHS) nor BHQ have a mention of a variant reading in their critical apparatus.
52 Gerleman also lists this verse in his examples of assonance in LXX Proverbs, see Gerleman, *Proverbs*, 13.

Whereas the Hebrew version attests a synonymous parallelism, the Greek attests an antithetical parallelism.[53] Moreover, as Fox has indicated, the LXX translation shuns bribery throughout his translation (see Prov 17:8; 15:27 and 19:24).[54] This is also the case in this verse.[55]

The hapax in this verse, i.e., יְכַפֶּה, is commonly translated by 'to overturn, avert, bend,' a meaning derived from the Arabic root كَفَأَ (*kafa'a*), Aramaic כפא and Assyrian *kipû*.[56] Scholars agree on the fact that the LXX probably read יכפר ('assuages') instead of יכפה, reading a ר instead of a ה.[57] The LXX translator has rendered it by the verb ἀνατρέπω ('turn back, turn around').[58] This verb is used in other places in the LXX as a translation for different Hebrew verbs denoting getting rid of something in a negative sense, i.e., דחה ('to overturn;' Ps 118 [LXX 117]:13), הדף ('to shove, drive away;' Prov 10:3), רחק ('to remove;' Eccl 12:6). Therefore, the LXX translation of ἀνατρέπω for יְכַפֶּה, whether the latter or יכפר was attested in the translator's *Vorlage*, seems to be accurate since both words express 'to get rid of' or 'to diminish something.'

F אֲבוֹי (Prov 23:29)

MT	LXX
לְמִי אוֹי לְמִי אֲבוֹי לְמִי מִדְיָנִים לְמִי שִׂיחַ לְמִי פְּצָעִים חִנָּם לְמִי חַכְלִלוּת עֵינָיִם:	τίνι οὐαί; τίνι θόρυβος; τίνι κρίσις; τίνι ἀηδίαι καὶ λέσχαι; τίνι συντρίμματα διὰ κενῆς; τίνος πέλειοι οἱ ὀφθαλμοί;
Who has woe? Who has sorrow? Who has strife? Who has complaining? Who has wounds without cause? Who has redness of eyes?	Who has woe? Who has trouble? Who has strife? Who has vexations and squabbles? Who has wounds without reason? Who has blood-shot eyes?

---

53 See d'Hamonville, *Les Proverbes*, 279; Fox, *Proverbs*, 292; Tauberschmidt, *Secondary Parallelism*, 46–47. According to Tauberschmidt, the LXX translator of Proverbs was fond of antithetical parallelism. See Tauberschmidt, *Secondary Parallelism*, 47.
54 See Fox, *Proverbs*, 256.
55 See Fox, *Proverbs*, 292.
56 See GESENIUS, 358; HALOT, 162. This meaning is based upon the Arabic root كَفَأَ, Aramaic כפא and Assyrian *kipû*. See also Gerrit D. Wildeboer, *Die Sprüche*, KHCAT (Freiburg – Leipzig – Tübingen: Mohr Siebeck, 1897), 62.
57 See, e.g., Wildeboer, *Die Sprüche*, 62; Ehrlich, *Randglossen*, 124; Fox, *Proverbs*, 291; BHQ, 38.
58 This is a literal translation proposed by Wolters in his commentary on the Vaticanus (B) text of Proverbs. See Wolters, *Proverbs*, 218–219. The original meaning is 'to stir up, to arouse.' However, Wolters says that the context of the verse does not allow the meaning 'to arouse.' See Wolters, *Proverbs*, 218. Others lexicons translate it to 'to turn back, to overthrow.' See GELS, 47; LEH, 44–45.

The hapax אֲבוֹי is commonly rendered by 'woe' (interjection) or 'uneasiness.'[59] None of the lexica or commentators has discussed its rendering in the LXX, i.e., θόρυβος. This noun denotes 'noise, tumult, confusion.'[60] Whatever the translation of the noun might be, the LXX translator did not transliterate it as he did with אוֹי/οὐαί. Therefore, he (a) must have known the exact meaning of the Hebrew word and/or (b) he must have avoided the repetition of using another interjection and thus opted for a noun that fitted the context of the verse. Giving the translator's tendency to avoid repetition,[61] the latter option seems to be the most plausible one.

G אֹפֶן (Prov 25:11)

MT	LXX
תַּפּוּחֵי זָהָב בְּמַשְׂכִּיּוֹת כֶּסֶף דָּבָר דָּבֻר עַל־אָפְנָיו:	μῆλον χρυσοῦν ἐν ὁρμίσκῳ σαρδίου, οὕτως εἰπεῖν λόγον.
A word fitly spoken is like apples of gold in a setting of silver.	As an apple of gold in a necklace of Sardian stone, so it is to speak a word.

The LXX translation does not provide a rendering for the hapax אֹפֶן ('a word spoken at the right time').[62] Fox argues that the LXX translator has skipped the difficult phrase עַל־אָפְניו ('at the right time').[63] De Waard argues that it is not rendered due to lexical ignorance.[64] However, when one looks at the different renderings of the particle עַל, it is in a few instances (*i.e.* Prov 19:12; 25:11; 25:20; 26:11; 26:14 and 26:17) translated by the adverb οὕτως in LXX Proverbs. Thus, since עַל is rendered by οὕτως in Prov 25:11, Fox's conclusion that the translator avoided עַל־אָפניו because it was too difficult to render becomes questionable. Moreover, if אֹפֶן does convey 'a word spoken at the right time,' it expresses the

---

59 See GESENIUS, 3; HALOT, 1. The Vulgate translates it as the Aramaic 'his father' (אבוהי). See Fox, *Proverbs*, 317.
60 See GELS, 331; LEH, 278.
61 See Beeckman, "Proverbia de Animalibus," 265; Beeckman, "Unitas Vegetabilium?," 29–30.
62 See GESENIUS, 59–60; HALOT, 25.
63 See Fox, *Proverbs*, 334. The other commentaries do not explain this non-rendering.
64 See Jan de Waard, "Lexical Ignorance and the Ancient Versions of Proverbs," in *Sôfer Mahîr. Essays in Honour of Adrian Schenker Offered by the Editors of Biblia Hebraica Quinta*, ed. Yohanan A. P. Goldman, Arie van der Kooij and Richard D. Weis, SVT 110 (Leiden – Boston, MA: Brill, 2006), 261–268, 261.

same thought as the preceding דְּבַר דָּבָר ('a spoken word'). Since the LXX translator often did not translate certain Hebrew words or opted for a different Greek lexeme to avoid repetition (see above), it seems more likely to assume that he did not render אַף not because of his difficulty or ignorance, *contra* Fox and de Waard, but on the basis of stylistic reasons.

H   לֹהֵהַּ (Prov 26:18)

MT	LXX
כְּמִתְלַהְלֵהַּ הַיֹּרֶה זִקִּים חִצִּים וָמָוֶת:	ὥσπερ οἱ ἰώμενοι προβάλλουσιν λόγους εἰς ἀνθρώπους, ὁ δὲ ἀπαντήσας τῷ λόγῳ πρῶτος ὑποσκελισθήσεται.
Like a maniac who shoots deadly firebrands and arrows.	As those who are being treated propound tales to people and he who encounters the tale will be the first to be tripped up.

The obscure and difficult Greek text does not correspond to the Hebrew. The hapax לֹהֵהַּ in this verse means 'to act like a madmen.'[65] It has no rendering in the LXX.

Fox argues that the LXX translator has created a whole new proverb.[66] However, as I have argued,[67] it seems highly improbable that the LXX translator would have created a whole new proverb. Moreover, when an explanation of this sort is given, no single scholar explains why the translator would have done so and why he would have opted for the specific chosen wording. In my opinion, a whole additional proverb (not a single additional colon or verse) reflects a different Hebrew *Vorlage*.[68]

---

65 See GESENIUS, 379; HALOT, 173. According to Gerrit D. Wildeboer and Crawford H. Toy the word is an Armaism. See Wildeboer, *Sprüche*, 77; Crawford H. Toy, *A Critical and Exegetical Commentary on the Book of Proverbs*, ICC (Edinburgh: T&T Clark, ²1904), 481.

66 See Fox, *Proverbs*, 347. D'Hamonville only explains the Greek wording and does not explain the deviation from the Hebrew text. See d'Hamonville, *Les Proverbes*, 319–320.

67 See Beeckman, "De Nominibus Sacris," 517.

68 See Beeckman, "De Nominibus Sacris," 517. Cook does not agree on this matter since he ascribes everything to the creative mind of the translator and does not postulate a different *Vorlage* because we have no extant textual material of this *Vorlage*. See, e.g., Cook, "Contrasting as a Translation Technique," 412. However, given the enormous amount of transpositions and additions in LXX Proverbs *vis-à-vis* MT as well as the scribal practices in Antiquity

I מָנוֹן and פנק (Prov 29:21)

MT	LXX
מְפַנֵּק מִנֹּעַר עַבְדּוֹ וְאַחֲרִיתוֹ יִהְיֶה מָנוֹן:	ὃς κατασπαταλᾷ ἐκ παιδός οἰκέτης ἔσται, ἔσχατον δὲ ὀδυνηθήσεται ἐφ' ἑαυτῷ.
A slave pampered from childhood will come to a bad end.	He who lives luxuriously from his childhood will be a domestic, but in the end he will be grieved over himself.

In Prov 29:11, two absolute *hapax legomena* can be found, i.e., מָנוֹן and פנק. The former, מָ, is more obscure and difficult than the latter.[69] Gesenius translates the noun מָנוֹן as 'ungrateful.'[70] Gottfried Kuhn argues that the original Hebrew read שמנון ('fat person') and that the *shin* dropped out.[71] He elaborates that this word was commonly used since the word שמנוניתא ('fatness') is an existing Aramaic word.[72] The LXX renders it by the verb ὀδυνάω ('to cause pain, to grieve').[73] Fox argues that this is a contextual guess by the LXX translator to translate מָנוֹן by ὀδυνηθήσεται ἐφ' ἑαυτῷ.[74] According to BHQ and Gerrit D. Wildeboer, the LXX translator has read the word מאנון stemming from אנן ('to complain').[75] This might be a correct explanation since the verb ὀδυνάω expresses the same thought more or less.

The other *hapax*, פנק, commonly translated into English as 'to pamper,'[76] has been understood as a passive form by the translator making him render it by a passive form of the verb κατασπαταλάω (to live in excessive comfort, to be spoilt),[77] thus making it an adequate rendering.[78] Since he understood this ha-

---

('start-to-finish' reading and usage of scrolls), it is impossible to ascribe everything to the translator's own doing. See Beeckman, "Trails of a Different Vorlage," 587.

69 Nor d'Hamonville or Fox comment on its rendering. See d'Hamonville, *Les Proverbes*, 335; Fox, *Proverbs*, 376.

70 See GESENIUS, 436. HALOT does not attest this noun.

71 See Gottfried Kühn, *Beiträge zur Erklärung des Salomonischen Spruchbuches*, BWANT III.16 (Stuttgart: W. Kohlhammer Verlag, 1931), 76.

72 See Kühn, *Beiträge*, 76.

73 See GELS, 486; LEH, 427.

74 See Fox, *Proverbs*, 376.

75 See BHQ, 54; Wildeboer, *Sprüche*, 83.

76 See GESENIUS, 650; HALOT, 294. GESENIUS attests the Aramaic and Arabic roots it is derived from.

77 See Fox, *Proverbs*, 376. The verb κατασπαταλάω also occurs in Amos 6:4. According to LEH it is a neologism. For the lexicon entries of κατασπαταλάω see LEH, 326 and GELS, 383.

pax as a passive, his choice to render מָנוֹן with a passive form of ὀδυνάω seems obvious considering his attention to literary style (see above), in which he enhances parallelism.

J עֲלוּקָה (Prov 30:15)

MT	LXX
לַעֲלוּקָה שְׁתֵּי בָנוֹת הַב הַב שָׁלוֹשׁ הֵנָּה לֹא תִשְׂבַּעְנָה אַרְבַּע לֹא־אָמְרוּ הוֹן׃	τῇ βδέλλη τρεῖς θυγατέρες ἦσαν ἀγαπήσει, ἀγαπώμεναι καὶ αἱ τρεῖς αὗται οὐκ ἐνεπίμπλασαν αὐτήν, καὶ ἡ τετάρτη οὐκ ἠρκέσθη εἰπεῖν Ἱκανόν.
The leech has two daughters; "Give, give," they cry. Three things are never satisfied.	The leech has three lovingly beloved daughters, but these three did not satisfy her, and the fourth was not pleased to say, "It is enough."

The hapax עֲלוּקָה means 'leech.'[79] In the LXX, the hapax has been translated into βδέλλα which is, in its turn, a Greek *hapax legomenon* in the LXX.[80] However, it does appear in other Greek works such as Herodotus' *Historiae*, Aristotle's *De incessu animalium*, Theocritus' *Idyllia* and Nicander's *Alexipharmaca*.[81] I have has already indicated elsewhere that the LXX rendering of עֲלוּקָה by βδέλλα is an adequate one.[82] The adequate rendering of most Hebrew animal names by a corresponding Greek equivalent shows the LXX translator's familiarity with both Hebrew and Greek.[83]

D'Hamonville notes that the verb σπαταλάω is used specifically for the spoiling of children. See d'Hamonville, *Les Proverbes*, 335.

78 See also de Waard, "Lexical Ignorance and the Ancient Versions of Proverbs," 262.

79 See GESENIUS, 591; HALOT, 274. This meaning is derived from the Aramaic and Arabic and is also the post-Biblical meaning of the word. See Ernst Bertheau, *Die Sprüche Salomo's* (Leipzig: Verlag von S. Hirzel, 1883), 170.

80 See GELS, 115; LEH, 105.

81 See LSJ, 312.

82 See Beeckman, "Proverbia de Animalibus," 262–263. However, I did not discuss the hapax in detail.

83 See Beeckman, "Proverbia de Animalibus," 269.

K שְׂמָמִית (Prov 30:28)

MT	LXX
שְׂמָמִית בְּיָדַיִם תְּתַפֵּשׂ וְהִיא בְּהֵיכְלֵי מֶלֶךְ: פ	καὶ καλαβώτης χερσὶν ἐρειδόμενος καὶ εὐάλωτος ὢν κατοικεῖ ἐν ὀχυρώμασιν βασιλέως.
the lizard can be grasped in the hand, yet it is found in kings' palaces.	and the lizard, though dependent on its hands and being easily caught, it lives in the king's fortresses.

The meaning of the hapax שְׂמָמִית has been the object of debate for many years. Some have proposed 'lizard,' whereas others argue that it means 'spider.'[84] Currently, scholars agree that it means 'lizard.'[85] Therefore, the LXX translator's rendering of שְׂמָמִית by καλαβώτης ('lizard') seems to be an adequate translation.[86] This is in line with the general tendency of the LXX translator to adequately render the Hebrew animal names by an appropriate Greek lexeme (as indicated above).

L אַלְקוּם and זַרְזִיר (Prov 30:31)

MT	LXX
זַרְזִיר מָתְנַיִם אוֹ־תָיִשׁ וּמֶלֶךְ אַלְקוּם עִמּוֹ:	καὶ ἀλέκτωρ ἐμπεριπατῶν θηλείαις εὔψυχος καὶ τράγος ἡγούμενος αἰπολίου καὶ βασιλεὺς δημηγορῶν ἐν ἔθνει.
the strutting rooster, the he-goat, and a king striding before his people.	also a cock strutting courageously among the hens, and the he-goat leading the herd, and a king making a speech in a nation.

In Prov 30:31, two absolute hapaxes are attested, i.e., אַלְקוּם and זַרְזִיר. The Hebrew lexeme אַלְקוּם probably means 'war people, military levy.'[87] Scholars agree that

---

84 For an elaborated discussion on the history of the interpretation of שְׂמָמִית, see Tova Forti, *Animal Imagery in the Book of Proverbs*, VTS 118 (Leiden – Boston, MA: Brill, 2008), 116–117.
85 See Forti, *Animal Imagery in the Book of Proverbs*, 116–117; Fox, *Proverbs*, 387; GELS, 358; LEH, 301. Tova Forti specifies the type of lizard, i.e., house gecko. See Forti, *Animal Imagery in the Book of Proverbs*, 116–117.
86 See Beeckman, "Proverbia de Animalibus," 262–263.
87 See GESENIUS, 45; HALOT, 18.

the LXX translator has read אל קום ('standing before') instead of אלקום ('military levy, irresistible').[88] Therefore, he rendered it with δημηγορέω ('to speak in public'), which seems an appropriate rendering for the probable misreading of the hapax.[89] One could argue that this might be a form of metathesis. However, אֶלְקוּם was also read as קום אל by other translations such as the Peshitta, targum and Vulgate.[90]

The other Hebrew hapax, זַרְזִיר, is a sort of animal which is translated to 'rooster, cock' or sometimes also as 'greyhound,' the former being accepted by most contemporary commentators.[91] As already argued in another contribution,[92] the LXX rendering of ἀλέκτωρ ('cock') seems to be an adequate rendering.[93]

M כִּישׁוֹר (Prov 31:19)

MT	LXX
יָדֶיהָ שִׁלְּחָה בַכִּישׁוֹר וְכַפֶּיהָ תָּמְכוּ פָלֶךְ:	τοὺς πήχεις αὐτῆς ἐκτείνει ἐπὶ τὰ συμφέροντα, τὰς δὲ χεῖρας αὐτῆς ἐρείδει εἰς ἄτρακτον.
She puts her hands to the distaff, and her hands hold the spindle.	She extends her forearms to what is profitable, and she strengthens her hands at the spindle.

The Hebrew noun and *hapax* כִּישׁוֹר is translated into English by 'spindle-whorl.'[94] The LXX translator, however, renders this noun with a participle of the verb συμφέρω ('to be useful').[95] According to Fox, this rendering is based upon the

---

88 See BHQ, 56; Fox, *Proverbs*, 387.
89 See GELS, 147; LEH, 134. This verb only occurs once elsewhere in the LXX, i.e., 4 Macc 5:15.
90 See BHQ, 56.
91 See GESENIUS, 206; HALOT, 92; Forti, *Animal Imagery in the Book of Proverbs*, 119. However, after his analysis, Forti concludes that she simply does not know what the word means. For an elaborate discussion on the interpretation of זַרְזִיר, see Franz J. Delitzsch, *Biblical Commentary on the Proverbs of Solomon. Vol. II*, trans. Matthew G. Easton (Edinburgh: T&T Clark, 1875), 306–309. Gerleman argues that the translator's rendering of זַרְזִיר by ἀλέκτωρ is a conjectural rendering that emphasises the Greek character of the translation. See Gerleman, *Proverbs*, 31.
92 See Beeckman, "Proverbia de Animalibus," 262–263.
93 See GELS, 25; LEH, 25.
94 See GESENIUS, 344; HALOT, 156. More specifically, 'small disk at the bottom of the spindle to give momentum to the spin.' HALOT, 156.
95 See GELS, 649; LEH, 584.

verb כשר ('to be useful').[96] If this is the case, the translator (a) did either not understand the hapax and sought his refuge to a known word with a similar root or (b) he read the word as derived from כשר instead of בְּיְשׁוֹר. However, contrary to several scholars who believe that the LXX translator did not understand the word,[97] it seems more likely that he has read the word as בכושרת (from כשר).

N Conclusion

Having analysed the 16 absolute Hebrew *hapax legomena* in Proverbs and their Greek rendering in the LXX version, we can formulate the following (preliminary) conclusions with regard to the translation technique of the LXX translator:

(a) No hapax has been transliterated by the LXX translator;
(b) Several absolute Hebrew *hapax legomena* have been rendered by an adequate Greek lexeme (i.e., Prov 7:16; 12:27; 21:14; 29:21; 30:15; 30:28 and 30:31);
(c) In some cases, the LXX translator has read his Hebrew *Vorlage* differently resulting in a different translation (i.e., Prov 29:21; 30:31 and 31:19). In 31:19 the translator resorted to a known Hebrew word in order to render the hapax;
(d) Sometimes, he has opted for a specific rendering on the basis of stylistic motivations such as assonance (i.e., Prov 16:30 and 21:8), avoidance of repetition (i.e., Prov 23:29 and 25:11) or enhancement of parallelism (i.e., Prov 7:16 and 29:21);
(e) In the instances in whiche the LXX does not render the Hebrew hapax (Prov 25:11 and 26:18), this can be explained on the basis of the probable intention to avoid repetition (25:11) or against the background of a diverging Hebrew *Vorlage* (26:18).

From the conclusions above, it can be observed that the LXX translator of Proverbs was well-versed in both Hebrew and Greek. This enabled him to render Hebrew absolute *hapax legomena*, which might have been difficult to comprehend and to translate, by an adequate Greek equivalent or to render them in order to improve the poetical structure of the Greek text.

---

96 See Fox, *Proverbs*, 395. More specifically, he read בבשרת, see de Lagarde, *Anmerkungen*, 91; Baumgartner, "Étude critique," 245.
97 See Wildeboer, *Sprüche*, 91; Bertheau, *Die Sprüche Salomo's*, 178.

2.1.2.2 Evaluation of the Greek rendering of Hebrew non-absolute
  hapax legomena in Proverbs

As noted above, there are 52 non-absolute Hebrew *hapax legomena* in Proverbs. In this section, we will analyse each hapax and their Greek rendering in the LXX.

A שַׁאֲוָה (Prov 1:27)

MT	LXX	4QProvᵃ
בְּבֹא (כְשָׁאֲוָה) [כְשׁוֹאָה]ׂ פַּחְדְּכֶם וְאֵידְכֶם כְּסוּפָה יֶאֱתֶה בְּבֹא עֲלֵיכֶם צָרָה וְצוּקָה:	καὶ ὡς ἂν ἀφίκηται ὑμῖν ἄφνω θόρυβος, ἡ δὲ καταστροφὴ ὁμοίως καταιγίδι παρῇ, καὶ ὅταν ἔρχηται ὑμῖν θλῖψις καὶ πολιορκία, ἢ ὅταν ἔρχηται ὑμῖν ὄλεθρος.	בבא עליכם צרה וצוקה
when panic strikes you like a storm, and your calamity comes like a whirlwind when distress and anguish come upon you.	Yes, when confusion strikes you unexpectedly and destruction arrives like a whirlwind and when affliction and siege come upon you or when ruin comes upon you.	distress and anguish come upon you.[98]

Both BibleWorks and Greenspahn record שַׁאֲוָה as a non-absolute *hapax legomenon* in Prov 1:27. However, for this word, there is a *qere* (כְשׁוֹאָה) and a *ketiv* (כְשָׁאֲוָה/כשאוה) reading. It is the *ketiv* reading that is recorded as a non-absolute *hapax*. Both BHQ and Fox argue for the *qere* being the original one.[99] According to Fox, the *ketiv* is "a mechanical error."[100] Thus, the *qere* variant, i.e., כְשׁוֹאָה, is the correct variant reading. The word שׁוֹאָה occurs multiple times in the Hebrew Bible (i.e., Job 30:3; 30:14; 38:27; Ps 35[LXX 34]:8; 63[LXX 62]:10; Prov 3:25; Isa 10:3; 47:11; Ezek 38:9 and Zeph 1:15) and cannot be considered a (non-absolute) *hapax legomenon*.

---

98 Own translation.
99 See BHQ, 4; Fox, *Proverbs*, 26, 90 and 91.
100 Fox, *Proverbs*, 91.

B רִפְאוּת **(Prov 3:8)**

MT	LXX
רִפְאוּת תְּהִי לְשָׁרֶּךָ וְשִׁקּוּי לְעַצְמוֹתֶיךָ׃	τότε ἴασις ἔσται τῷ σώματί σου καὶ ἐπιμέλεια τοῖς ὀστέοις σου.
It will be a healing for your flesh and a refreshment for your body.	Then it will be a healing to your body and treatment for your bones.

The hapax רִפְאוּת ('healing, cure,' > רפא ['to heal, to cure'])[101] is rendered by the Greek noun ἴασις (healing).[102] The LXX translated provided an adequate rendering for the Hebrew non-absolute hapax רִפְאוּת.[103]

C לֶכֶד **(Prov 3:26)**

MT	LXX
כִּי־יְהוָה יִהְיֶה בְכִסְלֶךָ וְשָׁמַר רַגְלְךָ מִלֶּכֶד׃	ὁ γὰρ κύριος ἔσται ἐπὶ πασῶν ὁδῶν σου καὶ ἐρείσει σὸν πόδα ἵνα μὴ σαλευθῇς.
for the Lord will be your confidence and will keep your foot from being caught.	For the Lord will be over all your ways and he will support your foot in order that you may not be unsettled.

The Hebrew noun לֶכֶד, regarded as an non-absolute *hapax legomenon*, is derived from the verb לכד ('to capture') and thus means 'capture.'[104] The LXX renders this noun with the Greek verb σαλεύω ('to shake, to loose equilibrium').[105] Antoine Jean Baumgartner argues that this is a bad rendering.[106] According to d'Hamonville, since σαλεύω is only used here in LXX Proverbs, the usage in LXX Proverbs reflects Ps 16(LXX 15):8.[107] However, both Cook and Jan Joosten, who have written on the intertextuality between LXX Proverbs and LXX Psalms, do not indicate Prov 3:26 as

---

101 See DCH, vol. VII, 536.
102 See GELS, 336; LEH, 283.
103 The term 'adequate rendering' denotes a (literal) rendering whereby the Hebrew word has been rendered by a corresponding Greek equivalent that shares the same meaning as the Hebrew. The term 'non-adequate rendering' denotes a non-literal rendering.
104 See DCH, vol. IV, 547.
105 See GELS, 616; LEH, 547.
106 See Baumgartner, "*Étude critique*," 50.
107 See d'Hamonville, *Les Proverbes*, 179.

an example whereby LXX Proverbs quotes or alludes to LXX Psalms.[108] Nonetheless, one can see various intertextual references in the second colon of the verse:

(a) ἐρείδω + πούς: This word pair occurs one time in the LXX (in the verse under discussion) and multiple times in earlier Greek sources, *i.e.* Hippocrates' *De articulis* (section 58, line 27) , Democritus' *Fragmenta* (fragment 228, line 4) and Asclepiades' *Fragmenta* (fragment 21b, line 7) , though not in a religious context as is the case in Proverbs.

(b) σαλεύω + πούς: This word pair is attested in several verses of the LXX, i.e., 4 Kgdms 21:8; 2 Chr 33:8; Ps 37(MT 38):17 and Ps 72(MT 73):2. Earlier Greek sources also attest this word pair but only in the context of biology/kinematics, cfr. Aristotle's *Problemata* (883a, 34) and Theophrastus' *Fragmenta* (fragment 7, section 11, line 7) .

(c) ἵνα μὴ + σαλεύω: This phrase occurs in Ps 15(MT 16):8; Ps 16(MT 17):5; Is 40:20. The attestations in Psalms concern a religious image that is related to God, just as in Proverbs. In Isaiah, on the other hand, it concerns the image of idols.

Thus, since the phrase ἵνα μὴ + σαλεύω occurs twice in LXX Psalms in a religious context that also refers (explicitly or implicitly) to the Lord, it might be that the LXX translator of Proverbs had these verses of LXX Psalms in mind when rendering his Hebrew *Vorlage*. By doing so, he explains the metaphorical image of MT of the foot being caught.[109] The Lord, who is always there, is the one who will support you in order that you will not be unsettled.

D לְזוּת **(Prov 4:24)**

MT	LXX
הָסֵר מִמְּךָ עִקְּשׁוּת פֶּה וּלְזוּת שְׂפָתַיִם הַרְחֵק מִמֶּךָּ׃	περίελε σεαυτοῦ σκολιὸν στόμα καὶ ἄδικα χείλη μακρὰν ἀπὸ σοῦ ἄπωσαι.
Put away from you crooked speech, and put devious talk far from you.	Remove from yourself a crooked mouth, and thrust unjust lips far away from you.

---

108 See Johann Cook, "Intertextual Relationships Between the Septuagint of Psalms and Proverbs;" Jan Joosten, "The Relation of the Septuagint of Proverbs to the Septuagint of Psalms," in *Septuagint, Sages and Scripture. Studies in Honour of Johann Cook*, ed. Randall X. Gauthier, Gideon Kotzé and Gert Steyn, VTS 172 (Leiden: Brill, 2016), 99–107.
109 See Fox, *Proverbs*, 104.

The noun לְזוּת, denoting 'perversity', is a derivative of the verbלוז ('to depart, to be devious').[110] The verb לוז occurs 5 times in Proverbs and is rendered by a variety of Greek lexemes in the LXX: καμπύλος (2:15), παραρρέω (3:21), πᾶς παράνομος (3:32), ἐκλείπω (4:21) and σκολιάζω (14:2). In Prov 4:24, its derivative noun לְזוּת is rendered by the adjective ἄδικος ('unjust, unrighteous'). This lexeme is used abundantly (18x) in LXX Proverbs and applied to render a variety of Hebrew lexemes: לְזוּת (4:24), שֶׁקֶר (6:17.19; 11:18; 12:17.19; 13:5; 14:5; 29:12), תַּהְפּוּכָה (10:31), אָוֶן (10:31), בְּלֹא מִשְׁפָּט (13:23), רַע (15:26), גּוֹרָל (16:33), (17:1), רֶשַׁע (17:15), רֶשַׁע (17:15) and עָוֶל (29:27).

As already indicated in chapter 1, Lemmelijn has extensively examined the Greek rendering of לְזוּת. According to her, the hapax illustrates the creativity of the translator on a stylistic and linguistic level whereby the translator resorted to contextual exegesis in order to render the Hebrew hapax and by doing so preserved the meaning of the Hebrew and the parallelism of the verse.[111] Although her analysis is accurate and valuable, she did not note the religious motives the translator might have had to use this specific lexeme. According to Cook, the LXX of Proverbs exhibits a religionising tendency that is also apparent in the dualism between ἄδικος and δίκαιος (see *e.g.* 6:17; 16:33).[112] However, he does not explicitly specify what this religious tendency entails. A possible explanation, given by Dorota Hartman, is that the adjective in the LXX "is used in the context of transgression" whereby the "transgressor is at the same time violator of the divine law, and ἄδικος becomes the equivalent of ἀσεβής."[113] This thesis might be correct since the word pair and dualism ἀσεβής and δίκαιος occurs multiple times in LXX Proverbs (e.g., 3:33; 10:3.6.7.11.16.20.24.25.28.30.32; 11:8.9.31; 13:5; 14:32; 21:26; 28:1; 29:7). Although this dualism is not found in the verse under discussion, the

110 See DCH, vol. IV, 523 and 531.
111 See Lemmelijn, "The Greek Rendering of Hebrew Hapax Legomena," 140–147.
112 See, e.g., Cook, *The Septuagint of Proverbs*, 177–178; Cook, "Exegesis in the Septuagint of Proverbs," 196; Theo A. W. van der Louw, Transformations in the Septuagint. Towards an Interaction of Septuagint Studies and Translation Studies, CBET 47 (Leuven – Paris – Walpole, MA: Peeters, 2007), 309. See also chapter 1. Moreover, d'Hamonville notes that the translator has applied these dualisms in order to amplify the effect of the text. He also notes that the LXX has also added δίκαιος and its derivative lexemes abundantly where the Hebrew text does not attest a word derived from the Hebrew root צדק. See d'Hamonville, *Les Proverbes*, 82. Michael Brennan Dick calls these dualisms 'ethical dualisms,' see Michael B. Dick, "The Ethics of the Old Greek Book of Proverbs," in The Studia Philonica Annual. Studies in Hellenistic Judaism Volume II 1990, ed. David T. Runia, Brown Judaic Studies 226 (Atlanta, GA: Scholars Press, 1991), 20–50.
113 Eberhard Bons, Historical and Theological Lexicon of the Septuagint. Volume I: Alpha – Gamma (Tübingen: Mohr Siebeck, 2020), 202 (= HTLS).

dualism ἄδικος and δίκαιος can be found when taking verse 25 into consideration. There, the LXX translator used δίκαιος as a rendering of ישר ('to make straight, just, to be straight').[114] Moreover, δίκαιος is used as an adjective with the noun χεῖλος in LXX Proverbs, i.e., χείλη δίκαια (10:18 and 16:13), as is the case for ἄδικος in 4:24. The image of (un)just lips was a familiar image to the LXX translator of Proverbs which he employed in three instances in his translation.

Thus, apart from Lemmelijn's conclusion that the LXX translator resorted to contextual exegesis and stylistic motivations to render the Hebrew *hapax* under discussion, he also introduced one of his preferred dualisms in Prov 4:24-25 and by doing so, created a better and antithetic parallelism between the two verses. Moreover, the use of the lexeme ἄδικος adds a religious/moralising nuance and contrast to the verse which is not present in the Hebrew text.

E   יַעֲלָה (Prov 5:19)

MT	LXX
אַיֶּלֶת אֲהָבִים וְיַעֲלַת־חֵן דַּדֶּיהָ יְרַוֻּךָ בְכָל־עֵת בְּאַהֲבָתָהּ תִּשְׁגֶּה תָמִיד:	ἔλαφος φιλίας καὶ πῶλος σῶν χαρίτων ὁμιλείτω σοι, ἡ δὲ ἰδία ἡγείσθω σου καὶ συνέστω σοι ἐν παντὶ καιρῷ ἐν γὰρ τῇ ταύτης φιλίᾳ συμπεριφερόμενος πολλοστὸς ἔσῃ.
A lovely deer, a graceful doe. May her breasts satisfy you at all times; may you be intoxicated always by her love.	Let the fawn of your love and the foal of your favors consort with you, and let her be considered your very own and be with you on every occasion, for while indulging in her love you will be increased immeasurably.

The hapax יַעֲלָה, meaning 'female mountain-goat, wild she-goat,'[115] is rendered by πῶλος ('colt of a horse, foal of an ass, any young animal') in the LXX.[116] I have commented on this hapax in an article dealing with the Greek rendering of Hebrew animal names in Proverbs.[117] There I have argued that although the main thought of the Hebrew verse, i.e., to be indulged or intoxicated by love, is

---

114 See DCH, vol. VI, 339; KBL, 413–414. δίκαιος is used 7 times to render a Hebrew lexeme of the root ישר in LXX Proverbs. See HR, 331.
115 See DCH, vol. IV, 242; KBL, 389.
116 See GELS, 609; LEH, 539.
117 See Beeckman, "Proverbia de Animalibus." See also Excursus I below.

preserved in the Greek, the LXX translator probably had a diverging Hebrew *Vorlage* since the Greek is totally different from MT.[118]

F   רבד (Prov 7:16)

MT	LXX
מַרְבַדִּים רָבַדְתִּי עַרְשִׂי חֲטֻבוֹת אֵטוּן מִצְרָיִם:	κειρίαις τέτακα τὴν κλίνην μου, ἀμφιτάποις δὲ ἔστρωκα τοῖς ἀπ' Αἰγύπτου.
I have decked my couch with coverings, colored spreads of Egyptian linen.	With coverings I have spread my couch, and with double tapestry from Egypt I have decked it.

Next to two absolute *hapax legomena*, אֵטוּן and חֲטֻבוֹת (see above), verse 16 of chapter 17 also attests a non-absolute *hapax legomenon*, i.e., רבד. This verb, meaning 'to deck (with), to spread with,'[119] only occurs in Prov 7:16 but its meaning is derived from several emendated attestations in Amos 3:12; 1 Sam 9:25 and Ezek 23:41.[120]

The LXX translator rendered רבד by τείνω ('to pull tight, to stretch out and extend, to spread').[121] In the LXX, this verb is used 9 times in different contexts: (a) to denote the stretching of a bow (τόξον) (see 1 Chr 5:18; 8:40; 3 Macc 5:25; Jer 27:14 and 28:3 [2x]), (b) stretching of arms (Ezek 30:22) and (c) to pull tight a couch or curtains (see Prov 7:16 and Esth 1:6). In his commentary on the Vaticanus text of LXX Proverbs, Al Wolters argues that τείνω needs to be understood as 'to pull tight' instead of 'to spread' as proposed by Cook in NETS.[122] According to him, κειρία, used in Prov 7:16, is a synonym of τόνος ('that by which a thing is stretched, or that which can itself be stretched, cord, brace, band').[123] Nonetheless, by using τείνω as a rendering of רבד, the image of the Hebrew stich (i.e., to make up or to spread a bed or couch) is preserved.

---

118 See Beeckman, "Proverbia de Animalibus," 263–264.
119 See DCH, vol. VII, 395.
120 See DCH, vol. VII, 395.
121 See LEH, 607–608; GELS, 673.
122 See Wolters, *Proverbs*, 160–161.
123 See LSJ, 107219–107221.

Moreover, as I have argued above, the LXX translator has enhanced the parallelism in this verse by using two 1ˢᵗ perfect singular verbs, i.e., τέτακα and ἔστρωκα.[124] This syntactic parallelism is absent in MT.

G אֹהַב (Prov 7:18)

MT	LXX
לְכָה נִרְוֶה דֹדִים עַד־הַבֹּקֶר נִתְעַלְּסָה בָּאֳהָבִים:	ἐλθὲ καὶ ἀπολαύσωμεν φιλίας ἕως ὄρθρου, δεῦρο καὶ ἐγκυλισθῶμεν ἔρωτι.
Come, let us take our fill of love until morning; let us delight ourselves with love.	Come, and let us enjoy love until the early morning; come here, and let us embrace in love.

The non-absolute hapax, אֹהַב, is derived from the verb אהב ('to love') and carries the meaning 'display of love.'[125] In the LXX it is rendered by ἔρως, 'sexual passion, love (between the sexes),'[126] which only occurs in LXX Proverbs (7:18 and 30:16)[127]. In 30:16, it is used together with γυνή as a rendering of וְעֹצֶר רָחַם.

Vladimir Olivero has exemplary argued that the reference to ἔρως, ᾅδης, τάρταρος and γῆ in LXX Prov 30:16 is based upon Hesiod's Theogony.[128] By doing so, the LXX translator conveyed the meaning of his source text but adapted it in order to make it more intelligible for his target audience.[129] Olivero argues that there could be an intertextual reference between 30:16 and chapter 7 that depicts the greedy love and lust of 30:16 in 7:18 and the mention of ᾅδης in 7:27.[130] However, the choice of the translator to opt for ἔρως as a rendering of אֹהַב, was most probably motivated by the parallelistic structure of the verse. It has already been noted by several scholars that the Greek verse preservers a

---

124 See also d'Hamonville, *Les Proverbes*, 201–202.
125 See DCH, vol. I, 141.
126 See GELS, 293; LEH, 244; see also LSJ, 44008–44010.
127 Interestingly, Aquila (αʹ) and Theodotion (θʹ) both have ἀγάπη instead of ἔρως in 7:18. For 25:51 (30:16) αʹ has ἐποχὴ μήτρας and Symmachus (σʹ) συνοχὴ μήτρας instead of ἔρως γυναικός. See Frederick Field, *Origenis Hexaplorum quae supersunt sive veterum interpretum Graecorum in totum vetus testamentum fragmenta. Tomus 2 Jobus – Malachias* (Oxonii: Typographeo Clarendoniano, 1875), 324.
128 See Vladimir Olivero, "A Genealogy of Lust. The Use of Hesiod's Theogony in the LXX Translation of the Book of Proverbs," *Textus* 30 (2021): 28–42. Vladimir Olivero follows the numbering of Henry Barclay Swete's critical edition of the LXX. Therefore, Prov 30:16 is presented as Prov 24:51 in his article. For the sake of clarity, Rahlfs' numbering will be used here.
129 See Olivero, "A Genealogy of Lust," 41.
130 See Olivero, "A Genealogy of Lust," 37.

better parallelism than its Hebrew counterpart by adding δεῦρο (// ἐλθὲ).[131] In the Hebrew text, there are two lexemes that denote 'love,' i.e., דּוֹד and אֹהַב. In the first stich, דּוֹד has been rendered by φιλία ('love, friendship, intense attachment to and predilection towards somebody or something').[132] The noun φιλία is used 9 times in LXX Proverbs as a rendering of אָהַב (5:19), אַהֲבָה (5:19; 10:12; 15:17; 17:9 and 27:5), דּוֹד (7:18), מֵרֵעַ (19:7) and one time as a plus (25:10). Surprisingly, the noun ἀγάπη, contrary to ἀγαπάω which is used 23 times, is not employed by the translator of LXX Proverbs.[133] In Prov 7:18, it seems that the translator used the lexeme ἔρως instead of φιλία to render אֹהַב (a) for the sake of variety in order to preserve the variety of lexemes denoting 'love' attested in the Hebrew text (דּוֹד and אֹהַב), (b) to avoid repetition since he already used φιλία in the first stich of the verse and (c) in order to create a better parallelism and enhancing the contrast between the two stichs of the verse since φιλία denotes a different type of love than ἔρως.[134]

H   מִפְתָּח (Prov 8:6)

MT	LXX
שִׁמְעוּ כִּי־נְגִידִים אֲדַבֵּר וּמִפְתַּח שְׂפָתַי מֵישָׁרִים:	εἰσακούσατέ μου, σεμνὰ γὰρ ἐρῶ καὶ ἀνοίσω ἀπὸ χειλέων ὀρθά.

---

131 See d'Hamonville, *Les Proverbes*, 202; Tauberschmidt, *Secondary Parallelism*, 94.

132 See GELS, 715–716; LEH, 647;

133 The recensions, i.e., α′, θ′ and σ′, on the other hand do use ἀγάπη. According to S. Paul Swinn, the LXX translator presumably avoided ἀγάπη on the basis of literary motivations, *i.e.* the noun being a recent development within Koine at the time of the translation of Proverbs. See S. Paul Swinn, "ἀγαπᾶν in the Septuagint," in *Melbourne Symposium on Septuagint Lexicography*, ed. Takamitsu Muraoka, SBLSCS 28 (Atlanta, GA: Scholars Press, 1990), 49–82, 72 and 74.

134 That variety and avoidance of repetition is a trait of the translation technique of the LXX translator of Proverbs has been demonstrated by several scholars. See Fox, *Proverbs*, 425 (where examples of enhancement of variety are given); d'Hamonville, *Les Proverbes*, 68 (although according to d'Hamonville it is only in a few instances that variation occurs). and also Beeckman, "Unitas Vegitabilium?," 38; Beeckman, "Proverbia de Animalibus," 265. In the context of Prov 7:15, James Barr has also noted that the use of the term ἔρως and derivative lexemes by the LXX translator of Proverbs is motivated by his devotedness to variety. See James Barr, "Words for Love in Biblical Greek", in *The Glory of Christ in the New Testament. Studies in Christology in Memory of George Bradford Caird*, ed. Lincoln D. Hurst and N. Tom Wright (Oxford: Clarendon Press, 1987), 3–18, 10–11, esp. 11. The observation that φιλία and ἔρως form a good parallel is also observed by d'Hamonville. See d'Hamonville, *Les Proverbes*, 202

MT	LXX
Hear, for I will speak noble things, and from my lips will come what is right.	Listen to me, for I will talk about serious things, and I will bring forth from my lips what is right.

The non-absolute hapax מִפְתָּח ('opening'; > פתח, 'to open') occurs only here in the Hebrew Bible but is also attested in 1 QS X 4 (= 4QS^d IX 1, למפתח).[135] The LXX renders it with a future form (ἀνοίσω) of ἀναφέρω. Aquila (α΄), Theodotion (θ΄), Symmachus (σ΄) and the Quinta (ε΄; the fifth Greek translation) read the noun ἄνοιγμα ('opening'), which is closer to the Hebrew text[136]. The Syro-Hexapla has a reading that attests the Syriac translation of ἀνοίξω, from the verb ἀνοίγω.[137] As also noted by d'Hamonville, some manuscripts attest variant readings: ἀνοίγω (A) and ἀνοίξω (V).[138]

Tauberschmidt argues that the LXX translator provided an enhanced parallel structure by opting for ἀνοίσω as a parallel of ἐρῶ.[139] Indeed, given the translator's tendency to enhance parallelism, this might explain the tense of the verb used. However, this does not explain the choice of the verb in question, i.e., ἀναφέρω. The lexeme ἀναφέρω has a plurality of meanings whereby the one in Prov 8:6 denotes 'to utter.'[140] According to HTLS, ἀναφέρω is used "in a more administrative sense" in Prov 8:6, in accordance with its attestations in several papyri fragments.[141] However, considering the context of Prov 8:6, I fail to see the connection with the administrative context since no legal or administrative jargon is used in chapter 8.

Moreover, the verb ἀναφέρω is only used once in LXX Proverbs. When rendering Hebrew verb forms from the root פתח, the LXX translator used ἀνοίγω (see Prov 31:8; 31:9; 31:28), the same verb as attested in A, V and in Syriac in

---

135 See DCH, vol. V, 434. For 1QS, see Sarianna Metso, *The Community Rule. A Critical Edition with Translation*, EJL 51 (Atlanta, GA: SBL Press, 2019), 50–51. For 4QS^d (= 4Q258) see Philip S. Alexander and Geza Vermes, ed., *Qumran Qave 4 XIX. Serek Ha-Yahad and Two Related Texts*, DJD XXVI (Oxford: Clarendon Press, 1998), 121.

136 See Field, Origenis Hexaplorum (Tom. II), 325.

137 See Field, Origenis Hexaplorum (Tom. II), 325, n. 6.

138 See d'Hamonville, *Les Proverbes*, 205.

139 See Tauberschmidt, *Secondary Parallelism*, 97. This is, more or less, also what Fox asserts. He argues that the LXX translator opted for Fox asserts that the LXX opted for ἀναφέρω to smoothen out the Hebrew text which has sudden shifts in tense and number. See Fox, *Proverbs*, 151 (see also 118).

140 See GELS, 47–48, esp. 47; LEH translates it with 'to speak.' See LEH, 45. See also MGS, 159–160, esp. 160 ('to emit, pronounce' in the context of speech and voice).

141 HTLS, 701, see also 698–699 for the papyri references and usage.

Syro-Hexapla. It might be that the original LXX text attested a derived form of ἀνοίγω, i.e., ἀνοίγω (indicative present, 1ˢᵗ singular, ἀνοίγω; attested in A), ἄνοιγμα (the derivative noun, attested in α´, σ´, θ´ and ε´) or even ἀνοίξω (indicative future, 1ˢᵗ singular, ἀνοίγω; as preserved in Syriac in Syro-Hexapla). The latter would, on the basis of the poetic inclinations of the translator (see above), be the most likely reading in order to enhance the parallelism with ἐρῶ.[142] It might also be that a scribal error occurred whereby the *gamma* of ἀνοίγω was read as a *sigma* and thus changed the word to ἀνοίσω (or *vice versa*), although this seems unlikely since it is not mentioned as an interchange in Francis Thomas Grignac's list of possible interchanges.[143] Moreover, ἀνοίγω is never used with the preposition ἀπό + genitive, whereas ἀναφέρω occurs ample times with ἀπό.[144] Therefore, the original LXX must have read ἀνοίσω (which was later on revised by the recensions to ἄνοιγμα in order to bring the text more closely to the Hebrew). Most probably, the LXX translator opted for ἀναφέρω on the basis of מפתח, which he read as a verb form of פתח (see the piel participle + prep. כמפתח in 1 Kgs 20:11);[145] but decided not to render it with ἀνοίγω but with ἀναφέρω which fitted the context of the verse. Moreover, as already noted above, he rendered it with the future form in order to enhance the parallelism with ἐρῶ of the first stich of the verse.

I   גֵּאָה **(Prov 8:13)**

MT	LXX
יִרְאַת יְהֹוָה שְׂנֹאת רָע גֵּאָה וְגָאוֹן וְדֶרֶךְ רָע וּפִי תַהְפֻּכוֹת שָׂנֵאתִי׃	φόβος κυρίου μισεῖ ἀδικίαν, ὕβριν τε καὶ ὑπερηφανίαν καὶ ὁδοὺς πονηρῶν· μεμίσηκα δὲ ἐγὼ διεστραμμένας ὁδοὺς κακῶν.

---

142 Antoine Jean Baumgartner indicates that ἀνοίξω is attested in different manuscripts without indicating which. He also states that this reading is the most correct one. However, he does not say whether it is the most correct one of being attested in the original LXX text or the most correct as a rendering of the Hebrew text. See Baumgartner, "Étude critique," 83.

143 See Francis T. Grignac, *A Grammar of the Greek Papyri of the Roman and Byzantine Periods. Volume I: Phonology*, Testi e documenti per lo studio dell'antichità 55 (Milan: Instituto Editoriale Cisalpino – La Goliardica, 1976). Although this is not noted by Grignac, a confusion between the *sigma* and the *gamma* is observed in Medieval uncial manuscripts of Pindar. See Douglas Young, "Some Types of Scribal Error in Manuscripts of Pindar," *Greek, Roman and Byzantine Studies* 6.4 (2002): 247–273, 248.

144 A search on a combination of both lemma's in the full corpus of *Thesaurus Linguae Graecae* (TLG) makes this clear.

145 I would like to thank my colleague dr. Beatrice Bonanno for pointing this reference out.

MT	LXX
The fear of the Lord is hatred of evil. Pride and arrogance and the way of evil and perverted speech I hate.	The fear of the Lord hates injustice, also pride and arrogance and the ways of the wicked; yes, it is I who hate the perverse ways of evil people.

The Hebrew non-absolute hapax in verse 13 of chapter 8 is גֵּאָה, a derivative noun from the verb גאה ('to rise, to be exalted') that means 'pride.'[146] The LXX translator renders this hapax with the Greek lexeme ὕβρις ('pride, arrogance, insolence'),[147] a noun that is used 11 times in LXX Proverbs to render לָצוֹן (1:22), גֵּאָה (8:13), זָדוֹן (11:2; 13:10), גַּאֲוָה (14:3; 29:23), גָּאוֹן (16:18), זָר (14:10), - (19:10; 21:4) and מוּת (19:18)[148]. In 4 instances, the LXX translator rendered a lexeme derived from the root גאה with ὕβρις.

Prov 8:13, attests two Hebrew lexemes that share the root גאה, i.e., גֵּאָה and גָּאוֹן. Although the latter is translated by ὕβρις in 16:18, in 8:13 it is rendered by the noun ὑπερηφανία ('arrogance, pride').[149] This noun is only attested here in LXX Proverbs but is often used throughout the LXX as a rendering of Hebrew lexemes from the root גאה (see, e.g., Ps 17[LXX 16]:10; 31[LXX 30]:18; Amos 8:7; Isa 16:6).[150] Thus, the LXX translator of Proverbs must have opted for ὕβρις, his preferred equivalent for the rendering of a noun of the root גאה, as a rendering of the hapax גֵּאָה and consequently, and in order to avoid repetition of the same lexeme, chose ὑπερηφανία to translate גָּאוֹן.

J עָתֵק **(Prov 8:18)**

MT	LXX
עֹשֶׁר־וְכָבוֹד אִתִּי הוֹן עָתֵק וּצְדָקָה:	πλοῦτος καὶ δόξα ἐμοὶ ὑπάρχει καὶ κτῆσις πολλῶν καὶ δικαιοσύνη.
Riches and honor are with me, enduring wealth and prosperity.	Wealth and honor are at my disposal, and the acquisition of many things and justice.

---

146 See DCH, vol. II, 292.
147 See GELS, 692; LEH, 625.
148 For the instances in 14:10; 19:10 and 18, HR is not sure what the Hebrew equivalent is. See HR, 1380. However, CATSS does record an equivalent for 14:10 and 19:18.
149 See GELS, 698; LEH, 630.
150 See HR, 1409–1410 for full list.

In Prov 8:18 the non-absolute hapax עָתֵק is attested. This adjective, derived from the root עתק which indicates 'to move, to advance,' 'to speak arrogantly,' 'to become old,' 'to remove,' 'to transcribe' or 'to thrive, to prosper,'[151] can be translated by 'enduring.'[152] In the LXX, the adjective has been rendered by the adjective πολύς, which Baumgartner labels as a bad rendering.[153] The recensions attest other readings for the word-pair κτῆσις πολλῶν: α΄ has ὕπαρξις μετ' εἰρήνης, σ΄ has βίος παλαιός and θ΄ has ὕπαρξις παλαιά.[154] Both σ΄ and θ΄ based themselves upon עַתִּיק which only occurs in Dan 7:9; 7:13 and 7:22 and where it is rendered by παλαιός in all three instances.[155] The LXX rendering πολύς for עָתֵק is indeed puzzling. In Prov 25:1 the verb עתק is attested and is translated by the Greek hapax ἐκγράφω ('to write out [and copy something that is already written]').[156] This is the only instance in the Hebrew Bible where עתק is interpreted as 'to transcribe' or 'to copy.'

Concerning our hapax in 8:18, it seems that the LXX translator found its attestation in the context of the verse odd and therefore sought to make the Greek text more legible. When confronted with the noun עתק in his *Vorlage*, the LXX translator might have had עָתָק ('arrogant') in mind.[157] This noun occurs 4 times in the Hebrew Bible and is rendered by ἀδικία ('act contravening law, iniquity,' wrongdoing, injustice;' Ps 75[LXX 74]:6 and 94[LXX 93]:4), ἀνομία ('act [or its consequences] which is in breach of law,' 'transgression, evil [conduct], iniquity, wickedness;' Ps 31[LXX 30]:19) and the neologism μεγαλορρημοσύνη ('boastful talk,' 'big talking, boasting;' 1 Sam 2:3).[158] These lexemes denote a negative meaning and would not have fitted the context whereby Wisdom is proclaiming her many gifts. Therefore, the LXX translator opted for πολύς which definitely fits well with κτῆσις ('that which is or has been acquired,' 'acquisition, possession, property') as well as the overall context of the verse.[159]

---

151 See DCH, vol. VI, 641–642.
152 See DCH, vol. VI, 642. KBL translates it as 'hereditary,' see KBL, 748.
153 See Baumgartner, "Étude critique," 86: "עָתֵק est mal trad. par πολλῶν."
154 See Field, Origenis Hexaplorum (Tom. II), 326.
155 See HR, 1051.
156 See GELS, 205; LEH, 178.
157 See DCH, 642.
158 See resp. GELS, 10–11, 55 and 444; LEH, 10, 51–52 and 388.
159 See GELS, 416; LEH, 358.

K מִפְעָל (Prov 8:22)

MT	LXX
יְהֹוָה קָנָנִי רֵאשִׁית דַּרְכּוֹ קֶדֶם מִפְעָלָיו מֵאָז׃	κύριος ἔκτισέν με ἀρχὴν ὁδῶν αὐτοῦ εἰς ἔργα αὐτοῦ.
The Lord created me at the beginning of his work, the first of his acts of long ago.	The Lord created me as the beginning of his ways, for the sake of his works.

The Hebrew hapax מִפְעָל denoting 'deed, work,'[160] is labelled as a hapax in Bi-bleWorks and Greenspahn. The latter has categorised the word as non-absolute. However, the word is also attested in Ps 46(LXX 45):9; 66(LXX 65):5 and Sir 15:15 and 16:12. Thus, although the word is labelled as a hapax by Greenspahn and Bibleworks, we can conclude that the word is not a hapax. Moreover, it's rendering does not pose any problems. In LXX Proverbs, מִפְעָל is rendered by ἔργον ('work'), just as in Psalms and Sirach.

Nonetheless, there is something remarkably about this verse. The Hebrew מֵאָז ('from that time') is not rendered in the LXX and קֶדֶם ('front, beginning') is not represented as well.[161] One might wonder why the LXX translator did not render these Hebrew words. It seems that either he found those words redundant since they entail a repetition of רֵאשִׁית ('beginning'), or that he wanted to convey the image that wisdom was necessary to be created first for the sake of the Lord's works of creation. The latter seems plausible since the explanation of the purpose of wisdom as the first to be created, seems to be absent in MT. Thus, in the LXX, wisdom in chapter 8 is characterised as an instrument which is created first by God in order to create the rest of the creation. Indeed, Cook is correct in asserting that the LXX translator wants to avoid misunderstanding about the role wisdom plays during creation.[162] However, he fails to note that wisdom is used by God as an instrument to perform creational acts.

---

160 See DCH, vol. V, 432.
161 Surprisingly, Cook has not addressed this minus in LXX Prov 8:22 in his article dealing with Prov 8. See Cook, "Were the LXX Versions of Proverbs and Job," 150.
162 See Cook, "Were the LXX Versions of Proverbs and Job," 156.

L פְּתַיּוּת and כְּסִילוּת (Prov 9:13)

MT	LXX
אֵשֶׁת כְּסִילוּת הֹמִיָּה פְּתַיּוּת וּבַל־יָדְעָה מָּה:	Γυνὴ ἄφρων καὶ θρασεῖα ἐνδεὴς ψωμοῦ γίνεται, ἢ οὐκ ἐπίσταται αἰσχύνην.
The foolish woman is loud; she is ignorant and knows nothing.	A foolish and audacious woman who knows no shame comes in need of a morsel of food.

In Prov 9:13 the Hebrew hapaxes כְּסִילוּת and פְּתַיּוּת occur. The first hapax, כְּסִילוּת, is considered to be a noun derived from the verb כסל ('to be foolish') and bears the meaning 'stupidity.'[163] In the LXX it is rendered by the adjective ἄφρων ('foolish, crazy, silly, sinful').[164] This adjective is used 133 times in the LXX corpus, of which 74 occurrences in LXX Proverbs. In the majority of attestations in LXX Proverbs, it is used to render כְּסִיל ('fool').[165] Thus, the rendering of כְּסִילוּת by ἄφρων seems to be a consistent rendering. Moreover, it might even be that the LXX translator read ותהמי כסיל (cfr. Ps 42[LXX 41]:6) instead of כסילות המיה. This would explain the conjunction καί that has no counterpart in MT.

The second hapax in Prov 9:13 is פְּתַיּוּת. This noun means 'simpleness' and is derived from the Hebrew root פתה ('to be simple, to be enticed').[166] In the LXX, the hapax is rendered by ψωμός ('morsel, bit, small piece of food'),[167] a word which occurs four times in Proverbs (9:13; 17:1; 23:8 and 28:21). In 17:1; 23:8 and 28:21 it is used as a rendering of פַּת ('piece of bread').[168] Thus, the LXX translator must have read פַּת in 9:13 and consequently rendered it by ψωμός as he did in other instances in his translation.[169]

163 See DCH, vol. IV, 444.
164 See GELS, 109; LEH, 99.
165 See HR, 186–187.
166 See DCH, vol. VI, 810.
167 See GELS, 745; LEH, 675.
168 See DCH, vol. VI, 796–797. HR wrongly indicates 23:7 instead of 23:8. Therefore it notes that ψωμός in this case has no Hebrew equivalent. See HR, 1490.
169 See Fox, *Proverbs*, 169.

M צָנוּעַ (Prov 11:2)

MT	LXX
בָּא־זָדוֹן וַיָּבֹא קָלוֹן וְאֶת־צְנוּעִים חָכְמָה:	οὗ ἐὰν εἰσέλθῃ ὕβρις ἐκεῖ καὶ ἀτιμία· στόμα δὲ ταπεινῶν μελετᾷ σοφίαν.
When pride comes, then comes disgrace; but wisdom is with the humble.	Where pride enters, there will also be disgrace, but the mouth of the humble attends to wisdom.

The Hebrew hapax in this verse is צָנוּעַ ('humble, modest' [adj.], 'the humble one, the modest one' [noun] > צנע, 'to be humble, to be modest').[170] This word also occurs in the Hebrew text of Sirach (34:22 and 42:8) where it is used as an adjective.[171] In Proverbs it is used as a noun. The LXX translator renders it by ταπεινός ('humble').[172] This Greek lexeme is used four times in LXX Proverbs: 3:14 (עָנִי); 11:2 (צָנוּעַ); 16:2 (עַיִן) and 30:14 (עָנִי). In 16:2, it is likely a misreading of the translator of עָנִי ('poor, afflicted, humble') instead of עַיִן ('eye'). Concerning our hapax, there are two possible explanations: (1) the LXX translator misread צָנוּעַ as a form of עָנִי, or (2) the LXX translator derived צָנוּעַ from צנע and thus understood its meaning. On the basis of the textual material, it is hard to decide which explanation is the most plausible. Nonetheless, by using ταπεινός the meaning of the Hebrew verse is, nonetheless, preserved.

N תּוֹקְעִים (Prov 11:15)

MT	LXX
רַע־יֵרוֹעַ כִּי־עָרַב זָר וְשֹׂנֵא תֹקְעִים בּוֹטֵחַ:	πονηρὸς κακοποιεῖ ὅταν συμμείξῃ δικαίῳ, μισεῖ δὲ ἦχον ἀσφαλείας.
To guarantee loans for a stranger brings trouble, but there is safety in refusing to do so.	A wicked person does evil whenever he mingles with a righteous person, and he hates the sound of security.

---

170 See DCH, vol. VII, 135.

171 See DCH, vol. VII, 135. For the Hebrew of Ben Sirach, see Pancratius C. Beentjes, The Book of Ben Sira in Hebrew. A Text Edition of All Extant Hebrew Manuscripts and a Synopsis of All Parallel Hebrew Ben Sira Texts, SVT 68 (Leiden: Brill, 1997), 167 (Sir 42:8 MS B, 34:22 is not attested); Ze'ev Ben-Ḥayyim, The Book of Ben Sira. Text, Concordance and an Analysis of the Vocabulary, The Historical Dictionary of the Hebrew Bible (Jerusalem: The Academy of the Hebrew Language and the Shrine of the Book, 1973), 263.

172 See GELS, 669–670; LEH, 605.

The Hebrew word תִּוְקָעִים denotes 'handshake' and is a derivative of תקע ('thrust, fasten, blow, sound an alarm').[173] In the LXX it is rendered by ἦχος ('sound').[174] According to BHQ, d'Hamonville and Fox, the LXX translator has read תֶּקַע ('blast').[175] Indeed, when looking at the Hebrew underlying ἦχος in the rest of the LXX we find one other instances where ἦχος is used as a rendering of תֶּקַע, i.e., Ps 150:3.[176] Thus, the LXX translator must have read תִּוְקָעִים as a form of תֶּקַע and rendered it by the Greek equivalent ἦχος.

O מַדְקֵרָה (Prov 12:18)

MT	LXX
יֵשׁ בּוֹטֶה כְּמַדְקְרוֹת חָרֶב וּלְשׁוֹן חֲכָמִים מַרְפֵּא:	εἰσὶν οἳ λέγοντες τιτρώσκουσιν μαχαίρᾳ, γλῶσσαι δὲ σοφῶν ἰῶνται.
Rash words are like sword thrusts, but the tongue of the wise brings healing.	Some, when they speak, wound with a dagger, but the tongues of wise men heal.

The word pair כְּמַדְקְרוֹת, containing the hapax מַדְקֵרָה ('piercing,' > דקר ['to pierce']),[177] is rendered by the LXX translator by a present indicative 3rd plural of τιτρώσκω ('to wound, to pierce').[178] Thus, the LXX treats the hapax, a plural noun, as a plural verb, probably from דקר. Although τιτρώσκω is never used as a translation of דקר, in other LXX books דקר is translated by a variety of Greek lexemes: ἀποκεντέω ('to pierce through;' Num 25:8; 1 Sam 31:4 [2x]), ἐκκεντέω ('to pierce;' Judg 9:54; 1 Chr 10:4; Jer 37:10; Lam 4:9), ἡττάω ('to be inferior;' Isa 13:15), κατακεντέω ('to be defeated;' Jer 51:4), κατορχέομαι ('to dance in triumph over;' Zech 12:10), συμποδίζω ('to bind the feet together;' Zech 13:3). As is evident from this list, the majority of instances have been rendered by a Greek

---

173 See DCH, vol. VIII, 610, 672–674.
174 See GELS, 332; LEH, 268.
175 See BHQ, 21; d'Hamonville, *Les Proverbes*, 225; Fox, *Proverbs*, 189. In HR it is noted that ἦχος is a rendering of תֶּקַע. See HR, 630.
176 In the majority of instances, it is used as a rendering of הָמוֹן ('sound, murmur'). See HR, 630–631.
177 See DCH, vol. V, 149.
178 See GELS, 682; LEH, 615. Both NETS and Wolters translate it with 'to strew.' See Wolters, *Proverbs*, 65. In the versions, σ´ and θ´ attest κέντημα ('point [of a weapon], prick, puncture') instead of τιτρώσκω. The fifth column of the Hexapla, i.e., the Septuagint (ο´), attests τιτρώσκουσι. See Field, *Origenis Hexaplorum (Tom. II)*, 335.

lexeme denoting 'to pierce.' Thus, the LXX translation of τιτρώσκω for מַדְקֵרָה is indeed based upon the verb דקר.

Moreover, since the LXX translator rendered מַדְקֵרָה (attested in plural) by a plural verb, he rendered the singular noun מַרְפֵּא ('a healing, cure') by a plural form of the verb ἰάομαι ('to heal'). By doing so, he created a better parallelism between the two stichs of the verse.

P מְשֻׂכָה (Prov 15:19)

MT	LXX	4QProv^b
דֶּרֶךְ עָצֵל כִּמְשֻׂכַת חָדֶק וְאֹרַח יְשָׁרִים סְלֻלָה׃	ὁδοὶ ἀεργῶν ἐστρωμέναι ἀκάνθαις, αἱ δὲ τῶν ἀνδρείων τετριμμέναι.	סוללה
The way of the lazy is overgrown with thorns, but the path of the upright is a level highway.	The ways of the idle are strewn with thorns, but those of the courageous are beaten.	Smoothed.[179]

In Prov 15:19, the hapax מְשֻׂכָה is attested in MT. 4QProv^b only attests סוללה, the last part of 15:19,[180] and thus not the hapax under examination. The word מְשֻׂכָה, or מְשׂוּכָה, denotes 'hedge [of briar]' and might be derived from שׂוּךְ 'to hedge about, to obstruct, to fence in.'[181]

In the LXX, the hapax is rendered by a perfect passive participle of στρώννυμι/στρωννύω ('to spread, to bring down, to lay low, to place something over a wide surface').[182] This verb is used nine times in the LXX and in most of the cases it is used to denote 'spreading of a couch' (cfr. Jdt 12:15; Prov 7:16; Job 17:13 and Ezek 23:41). In the New Testament, it is used to describe the strewing of branches on the road (cfr. Mt 21:8; Mk 11:8), which confirms the image of strewing plant-like things on the road as is the case in Prov 15:19.

BHS notes that the Hebrew underlying the LXX's ἐστρωμέναι is מְשֻׂכֶת, from שׂכך ('to cover').[183] It is not unlikely to presume that this reading might have

---

179 Own translation.
180 The editors of DJD are not certain whether this reading is an orthographic difference *vis-à-vis* MT or a variant reading. See DJD XVI, 186. Fox regards the reading of 4QProv^b as the elder reading. See Fox, *Proverbs*, 237.
181 See DCH, vol. V, 501 and 503.
182 See GELS, 640; LEH, 574. The version agree on this reading. Only σ΄ has a different translation, i.e., ὥσπερ (כ) φραγμὸς (משבת) ('like a fence'). See Field, *Origenis Hexaplorum (Tom. II)*, 342.
183 See BHS, 1295; DCH, vol. V, 150.

been in the translator's *Vorlage* or that the translator has read it differently,[184] since כמשכת and משכבת look similar. The only difference is the transposition from the first *khaf* of כמשכת after the *sin* or after the *khaf* in משכבת. Given the translator's inclination for metathesis,[185] this transposition of vowels seems to be highly plausible. It seems that the LXX translator has provided a consistent rendering of the hapax which also fits the context of the verse.

Moreover, as Tauberschmidt has indicated, the LXX provides a better parallel than its Hebrew counterpart due to the word pair ἀεργῶν ('sluggards') and ἀνδρείων ('the diligent').[186] This word pair is also used in Prov 13:4. The enhancement of parallelism can also be observed in the usage of the plural throughout the verse, which is absent in MT.

Q מַעֲרָךְ (Prov 16:1)

MT	LXX
לְאָדָם מַעַרְכֵי־לֵב וּמֵיְהֹוָה מַעֲנֵה לָשׁוֹן: /	/
The plans of the mind belong to mortals, but	
the answer of the tongue is from the Lord.	

As I have argued elsewhere,[187] the LXX does not have a reading for MT 16:1, not even transposed, due to a diverging *Vorlage*.

---

184 Crawford H. Toy argues that the LXX translator read מְסֻכֶּבֶת, see Toy, *Proverbs*, 312.

185 See Jan de Waard, "Metathesis as a Translation Technique?," in *Traducere navem: Festschrift für Katharina Reiß zum 70. Geburtstag*, ed. Justa Holz-Mänttäri and Christiane Nord, Studia translatologica 3 (Tampere: Finland, University of Tampere, 1993), 249–260; Jan de Waard, "The Septuagint of Proverbs as a Translational Model?," *The Bible Translator* 50.3 (1999): 304–314, 312; Richard J. Clifford, "Observations on the Text and Versions of Proverbs," in *Wisdom, You Are My Sister. Studies in Honour of Roland E. Murphy, O.Carm., on the Occasion of His Eightieth Birthday*, ed. Michael L. Barré, CBQMS 29 (Washington, DC: The Catholic Biblical Association of America, 1997), 47–61, 54–55. Jan de Waard did not list 15:19 as a case of metathesis in his article "Metathesis as a Translation Technique?," since his list is not exhaustive.

186 See Tauberschmidt, *Secondary Parallelism*, 205–206.

187 See Beeckman, "Trails of a Different Vorlage," 588.

R כִּשָּׁלוֹן (Prov 16:18)

MT	LXX
לִפְנֵי־שֶׁבֶר גָּאוֹן וְלִפְנֵי כִשָּׁלוֹן גֹּבַהּ רוּחַ׃	πρὸ συντριβῆς ἡγεῖται ὕβρις, πρὸ δὲ πτώματος κακοφροσύνη.
Pride goes before destruction, and a haughty spirit before a fall.	Pride goes before ruin, and malice before a fall.

The Hebrew word כִּשָּׁלוֹן, 'stumbling' from כשל 'to stumble,'[188] occurs in Prov 16:18 but also in 1QH 17,25 and Sir 25:23.[189] In the LXX it is rendered by πτῶμα ('fall, disaster, misfortune, fallen body, corpse, downfall, ruin').[190] The meaning of the Greek term employed by the translator agrees with the meaning of the hapax, i.e., stumbling/fall. Moreover, the Hebrew word מִכְשׁוֹל ('stumbling block, obstacle'), which also stems from the Hebrew root כשל, is rendered by πτῶμα in Isa 8:14.[191] Thus, the translator understood the hapax כִּשָּׁלוֹן and rendered it by an adequate Greek lexeme.

S אכף (Prov 16:26)

MT	LXX
נֶפֶשׁ עָמֵל עָמְלָה לּוֹ כִּי־אָכַף עָלָיו פִּיהוּ׃	ἀνὴρ ἐν πόνοις πονεῖ ἑαυτῷ καὶ ἐκβιάζεται ἑαυτοῦ τὴν ἀπώλειαν, ὁ μέντοι σκολιὸς ἐπὶ τῷ ἑαυτοῦ στόματι φορεῖ τὴν ἀπώλειαν.
The appetite of workers works for them; their hunger urges them on.	A man at labor labors for himself and fences off his own destruction, but the crooked carries destruction in his own mouth.

---

188 See DCH, vol. IV, 470.
189 See DCH, vol. IV, 470. DCH notes Sir 25:22 but it is 25:23 (כה,כג), see Ben- Ḥayyim, *The Book of Ben Sira*, 180; Solomon Schechter, "A Further Fragment of Ben Sira. Prefatory Note," *The Jewish Quarterly Review* 12.3 (1900): 456–465, 465; Beentjes, *The Book of Ben Sira in Hebrew*, 99. Also for 1QH, DCH is incorrect. He notes 9,25 whereas it is 17,25, see Eileen M. Schuller and Carol A. Newsom, *The Hodayot (Thanksgiving Psalms): A Study Edition of 1QHª*, SBLEJIL 36 (Atlanta, GA: Society of Biblical Literature, 2012), 54.
190 See GELS, 606–607; LEH, 536.
191 See DCH, vol. V, 275.

Prov 16:26 has a plus which is not present in MT, i.e., ὁ μέντοι σκολιὸς ἐπὶ τῷ ἑαυτοῦ στόματι φορεῖ τὴν ἀπώλειαν. According to Fox, this plus is due to the translator who was not able to make sense of כי־אכף עליו פיהו (whereby he read פיהו as פידו).[192] However, in an article dealing with hexaplaric material in Proverbs, Charles T. Fritsch has indicated that the plus Prov 16:26 can be regarded as hexaplaric based upon its categorisation as such in the Syro-Hexapla.[193] Fox did not take this into account although he is aware of Fritsch's work.[194] However, taking the parallelistic structure of 16:26 and 27 without the plus into consideration, the thesis of Fritsch the most plausible one:

LXX 16:26	LXX 16:27
ἀνὴρ ἐν πόνοις πονεῖ ἑαυτῷ καὶ ἐκβιάζεται ἑαυτοῦ τὴν ἀπώλειαν.	ἀνὴρ ἄφρων ὀρύσσει ἑαυτῷ κακά ἐπὶ δὲ τῶν ἑαυτοῦ χειλέων θησαυρίζει πῦρ.
A man at labor labors for himself and fences off his own destruction.	A foolish man digs up evil for himself, and treasures fire on his own lips.

Our hapax under consideration, i.e., אכף ('to press,' > אֶכֶף 'pressure'),[195] is attested here in 16:26 and in Sir 46:5 where it is rendered by rendered by θλίβω ('to [op]press').[196] In LXX Proverbs it is translated by ἐκβιάζω ('to force [out], to do violence to').[197] This Greek verb occurs only four times in the LXX and is used to render three different Hebrew lexemes, i.e., ירש ('to take possession of [something];' Judg 14:15), נקש ('to entrap;' Ps 38[LXX 37]:13) and אכף ('to press;' Prov 16:26).[198] It also occurs in Wis 14:19 and Sus 1:19.

---

192 See Fox, *Proverbs*, 251.
193 See Charles T. Fritsch, "The Treatment of the Hexaplaric Signs in the Syro-Hexaplar of Proverbs," *JBL* 72.3 (1953): 169–181, 176.
194 See Fox, *Proverbs*, 36, n.2.
195 See DCH, vol. I, 249.
196 See Beentjes, The Book of Ben Sira in Hebrew, 82 (MS B).
197 See GELS, 204; LEH, 178. The nets translation of 'to fence off' seems to be a contextual translation. A more literal rendering would be 'A man at labor labors for himself and *forces out/expels* his own destruction.' Wolters translates it by 'A man who is hard at work works hard for himself, and keeps his ruin at bay.' See Wolters, *Proverbs*, 71 and 200. This is, in my opinion, a better translation than the one proposed in NETS.
198 According to HR it also occurs in Esth 7:8, see HR, 421. However, LXX Esther attests βιάζομαι, Aʹ- and *L*-text (7:11) attest ἐκβιάζω as a rendering of MT's כבש ('to subdue, to subjugate'), see Robert Hanhart, *Esther*, Septuaginta. Vetus Testamentum Graecum. Auctoritate Academiae Scientiarum Gottingensis editum VIII.3 (Göttingen: Vandenhoeck & Ruprecht, 1966), 183–184.

The reading of פִּיהוּ ('his mouth') as פִּידוֹ ('his misfortune'), which the translator rendered by ἑαυτοῦ τὴν ἀπώλειαν, caused the translator to opt for a verb
that fitted the context. The translation 'A man at labor labors for himself and
presses/urges his own destruction,' would be a weird in this context since destruction does not befall the man that labours for himself. Moreover, the antith-
esis comes in verse 27 (see below), whereby the foolish man (ἀνὴρ ἄφρων) is
mentioned. Therefore, the translator provided ἐκβιάζω as a contextual rendering of אכף based upon a (mis)reading of פִּיהוּ as פִּידוֹ.

T צָרֶב (Prov 16:27)

MT	LXX
אִישׁ בְּלִיַּעַל כֹּרֶה רָעָה וְעַל־שְׂפָתָיו כְּאֵשׁ צָרֶבֶת:	ἀνὴρ ἄφρων ὀρύσσει ἑαυτῷ κακά, ἐπὶ δὲ τῶν ἑαυτοῦ χειλέων θησαυρίζει πῦρ.
Scoundrels concoct evil, and their speech is like a scorching fire.	A foolish man digs up evil for himself, and treasures fire on his own lips.

In the LXX, the Hebrew hapax צָרֶב ('burning, scorching,' > צרב 'to burn'),[199] is
rendered by θησαυρίζω ('to store [up], to lay up, to treasure, to hoard').[200] This
Greek verb is used to render three different Hebrew lexemes throughout the
LXX: אצר ('to store up'), צבר ('to heap up, to pile up') and צפן ('to hide, to be
stored up').

The resemblance of צבר, which occurs in Zech 9:3 and Ps 39(LXX 38):7, and
our hapax צָרֶב is striking. Once again, we detect a clear case of metathesis: the
translator has shifted the *resj* and *bet*.[201] Fox notes that the translator must have
ignored the final *tav* of צברת since this form is grammatically impossible.[202]
Baumgartner indicates that the translator read צברה, instead of צברת proposed
by Fox, which seems to be more plausible.[203] However, both Fox and Baumgartner did not elaborate on why the translator read צברת/ה instead of צרבת.

---

199 See DCH, vol. VII, 157.
200 See GELS, 330; LEH, 276.
201 See Jan de Waard, "Some Unusual Translation Techniques Employed by the Greek Trans-
lator(s) of Proverbs," in *Helsinki Perspectives. On the Translation Technique of the Septuagint*,
ed. Raija Sollamo and Seppo Sipilä, PFES 82 (Göttingen: Vandenhoeck & Ruprecht, 2001), 185–
193, 186.
202 See Fox, *Proverbs*, 252.
203 See Baumgartner, "Étude critique," 157.

Although d'Hamonville does not observe the metathesis, he does give a possible solution to why the translator transposed the letters to form צברת. According to him, the LXX translator wanted to harmonise stich b of 16:27 with stich a of the same verse and also wanted to construct a parallel with the previous verse, i.e., 16:26.[204] Indeed, as already argued above, the LXX translator enhanced the antithetic parallelistic structure of verses 26 and 27.[205] Not only does he contrast the man at labour (ἀνὴρ ἐν πόνοις) with the foolish man (ἀνὴρ ἄφρων), in verse 27 he treats the adjective צָרֶבֶת as a verb (צבר) and translates it by θησαυρίζω. This way, the second stich of verse 27 also attests a verb, which is absent in MT. This enhances the parallelistic structure of stichs a and b of verse 27 as well as the parallelism between verses 26 and 27.

U   גֵּהָה (17:22)

MT	LXX
לֵב שָׂמֵחַ יֵיטִב גֵּהָה וְרוּחַ נְכֵאָה תְּיַבֶּשׁ־גָּרֶם׃	καρδία εὐφραινομένη εὐεκτεῖν ποιεῖ, ἀνδρὸς δὲ λυπηροῦ ξηραίνεται τὰ ὀστᾶ.
A cheerful heart is a good medicine, but a downcast spirit dries up the bones.	A cheerful heart promotes well-being, but the bones of a depressed man dry up.

The hapax גֵּהָה denotes 'healing' (> גהה, 'to heal').[206] However, several scholars have suggested to emendate this hapax to גְּוִיָּה ('body') on the basis of its translation in the Peshitta and the Targum.[207] The LXX reads εὐεκτεῖν ποιεῖ as a rendering of יֵיטִב גֵּהָה. The Greek εὐεκτέω ('to be in good health, to promote good health, to be in sound condition') is a hapax in the LXX.[208] Its noun εὐεξία ('good physical condition, good health') also occurs only one time in the LXX corpus, i.e., in Sir 30:15.[209] Remarkably, the Hebrew טובה (feminine singular of טוב 'good, pleasing desirable') in Sir 30:15 is rendered by the adjective and ha-

---

204 See d'Hamonville, *Les Proverbes*, 257.
205 See Gerleman, *Proverbs*, 20. See also Clifford, "Observations on the Text and Versions of Proverbs," 55.
206 See DCH, vol. II, 328. The verb גהה is also a hapax and occurs in Hos 5:13.
207 See Toy, *Proverbs*, 350; Wildeboer, *Sprüche*, 52; See also DCH, vol. II, 334. Fox presents גֵּהָה in his eclectic edition and does not even comment on 17:22. See Fox, *Proverbs*, 260.
208 See GELS, 298; LEH, 248. It does appear elsewhere in Ancient Greek literature, see LSJ, 44941.
209 See GELS, 298; LEH, 248. Like the verbal form, it also appears elsewhere in Ancient Greek sources, see LSJ, 44984.

pax εὔρωστος ('strong, stout').[210] Thus, rendering a Hebrew word stemming from the root טוב by a Greek by word with the prefix εὐ- ('good') was not unusual. Moreover, the choice to render יֵיטַב by εὐεκτέω might also have been triggered by שָׂמֵחַ/εὐφραινομένη, which causes alliteration, i.e., a stylistic device used by the translator throughout his translation.[211] Moreover, יֵיטַב has not only been rendered by εὐεκτεῖν, but by εὐεκτεῖν ποιεῖ. The *hiphil*, which expresses a periphrastic causative, is often translated by ποιέω + verb.[212] In Job 5:18, יַכְאִיב (*hiphil* imperfect 3rd masculine singular) has been rendered by ἀλγεῖν ποιει. The same grammatical structure, i.e., infinitive + ποιέω is used to render the *hiphil* imperfect 3rd masculine singular in Prov 17:22 as well. Thus, יֵיטַב גֵּהָה is represented in the LXX by εὐεκτεῖν ποιεῖ, our hapax גֵּהָה is not represented.[213]

Concerning the rendering of the hapax גֵּהָה, if יֵיטַב has been rendered by εὐεκτεῖν ποιεῖ, why did the translator not translate גֵּהָה? When confronted with either ייטב גהה ('will do good [like] a healing') or the emendated ייטב גויה ('will do good [to] a body'), the translator opted for εὐεκτέω ποιεῖ in order to enhance the literary character of the translation, *i.e.* alliteration with εὐφραινομένη. Moreover, εὐεκτέω ποιεῖ captures the meaning of both ייטב גהה and ייטב גויה.

V מֵמֶר (Prov 17:25)

MT	LXX
כַּעַס לְאָבִיו בֵּן כְּסִיל וּמֶמֶר לְיוֹלַדְתּוֹ:	ὀργὴ πατρὶ υἱὸς ἄφρων καὶ ὀδύνη τῇ τεκούσῃ αὐτοῦ.
Foolish children are a grief to their father and bitterness to her who bore them.	A foolish son is a cause of anger to his father and a grief to her who bore him.

---

210 See GELS, 305; LEH, 253. For the Hebrew text of Sir 30:15, see Beentjes, *The Book of Ben Sira in Hebrew*, 54 (MS B).

211 See Gerleman, *Proverbs*, 12; Cook, *The Septuagint of Proverbs*, 98–99 and chapter 1 of this monograph.

212 See Emanuel Tov, "The Representation of the Causative Aspects of the Hiph'il in the LXX A Study in Translation Technique," *Biblica* 63.3 (1982): 417–424, 422.

213 This is something that other scholars have overlooked. Some scholars share the opinion that גֵּהָה is represented by εὐεκτεῖν. See, e.g., Toy, *Proverbs*, 350; CATSS. De Waard indicates, correctly, that the hapax is not represented in the LXX. See BHQ, 32. Neither Fox nor d'Hamonville comment on the translation of the hapax.

The Hebrew מֶמֶר, meaning 'bitterness' which is derived from מרר ('to be bitter, to make bitter'),[214] is rendered by the LXX translator by ὀδύνη ('pain, grief, suffering').[215] The other translations record πικραίνω (α´ & σ´) and πικρασμός (θ´)[216], which is closer to the Hebrew. The noun ὀδύνη is used 6 times to render a word stemming from the root מרר: מַר ('drop, bitter;' Job 3:7; Amos 8:10; Mic 1:12; Isa 38:15), מֶמֶר ('bitterness;' Prov 17:25), מרר ('to be bitter, to make bitter;' Zech 12:10) and מְרִירוּת ('bitterness;' Ezek 21:11).[217] In the context of Prov 17:25 stich b, the choice to render מרר by ὀδύνη seems to fit the context better since 'a bitterness to her who bore him' seems to be odd. Moreover, the translator was also moved by stylistic considerations. By opting for ὀδύνη as a rendering of מֶמֶר, he created rhyme with ὀργὴ, which is consistently used as a rendering of כַּעַס in LXX Proverbs (12:16; 17:25 and 27:3, except in 21:19 where it is rendered by the cognate ὀργίλος).[218]

W עַצְלָה (Prov 19:15)

MT	LXX
עַצְלָה תַּפִּיל תַּרְדֵּמָה וְנֶפֶשׁ רְמִיָּה תִרְעָב׃	δειλία κατέχει ἀνδρογύναιον, ψυχὴ δὲ ἀεργοῦ πεινάσει.
Laziness brings on deep sleep; an idle person will suffer hunger.	Timidity restrains the effeminate, and the soul of the idle will suffer hunger.

This verse has often been discussed due to its attestation of the rare word ἀνδρογύναιος ('[like an] effeminate man'),[219] which is a Greek hapax in the LXX.[220] Although this form only occurs in B and in Sinaiticus (א),[221] it is present-

---

214 See DCH, vol. V, 333 and 493–494.

215 See GELS, 486; LEH, 427.

216 See Field, Origenis Hexaplorum (Tom. II), 346.

217 See HR, 967.

218 For rhyme as a trait of the translator's translation technique, see Gerleman, *Proverbs*, 13–14; Cook, *The Septuagint of Proverbs*, 64–65; Cook, "Contrasting as a Translation Technique," 407–408; as well as chapter 1 of this book.

219 See LEH, 46. This word is listed as a neologism in LEH. GELS does not list this lexeme. Prov 19:15 is listed under the lexeme ἀνδρογύνον. See GELS, 49.

220 According to Cook, this lexeme also occurs in Prov 18:18, See Cook, *The Septuagint of Proverbs*, 76. Although he probably means 18, he is still incorrect.

221 However, a (later) scribe indicated two dots on top of αι, thus indicating a correction. See Constantine von Tischendorf, ed., *Bibliorum Codex Sinaiticus Petropolitanus. III Veteris Testamenti pars posterior* (Hildesheim: Georg Olms Verlag, 1969), 49.

ed in Rahlfs' main text. More likely, the original LXX read ἀνδρογύνον,[222] which is attested in Codex Alexandrinus (A),[223] Origen's LXX (o´),[224] and is also used in Prov 18:8. Moreover, ἀνδρογύναιος is only attested in LXX Prov 19:15 and in Athanasius' *De sancta trinitate*.[225] D'Hamoville has argued that the usage of ἀνδρογύν(αι)ος in LXX Proverbs reflects Plato's *Symposium* 189de.[226] However, the majority of other scholars do not accept this hypothesis.[227] Nonetheless, all authors agree that LXX Prov 19:15 reflects LXX Prov 18:8:

MT	LXX
דִּבְרֵי נִרְגָּן כְּמִתְלַהֲמִים וְהֵם יָרְדוּ חַדְרֵי־בָטֶן:	ὀκνηροὺς καταβάλλει φόβος ψυχαὶ δὲ ἀνδρογύνων πεινάσουσιν.
The words of a whisperer are like delicious morsels; they go down into the inner parts of the body.	Fear casts down the timid, and the souls of the effeminate will suffer hunger.

The Hebrew of 18:8 does not correspond with its Greek counterpart. Interestingly, MT 18:8 has an exact doublet in 26:22, which is (more or less) rendered adequately in LXX 26:22. Moreover, the Greek of 18:8 reflects the Hebrew of 19:15:

MT 19:15	LXX 18:8
עַצְלָה	ὀκνηροὺς (cfr. עַצְלוּת/ὀκνηρός [Prov 31:27]; עָצֵל/ὀκνηρός [*e.g.* Prov 6:6.9; 11:16])
תַּפִּיל	καταβάλλει (cfr. 2 Sam 20:15; 2 Chr 32:21; Prov 7:26)
תַּרְדֵּמָה	φόβος (cfr. Job 4:13; 33:15)
וְנֶפֶשׁ	ψυχαὶ δὲ (standard equivalent in LXX and Proverbs)
רְמִיָּה	ἀνδρογύνων
תִרְעָב	πεινάσουσιν (cfr. standard equivalent, see also Prov 6:30; 25:21)

---

222 See also Peter Walters, *The Text of the Septuagint. Its Corruptions and their Emendation*, ed. David W. Gooding (Cambridge: University Press, 1973), 121–122.

223 See British Museum, The Codex Alexandrinus (Royal MS. 1 D. V-VIII) in Reduced photographic Facsimile. Old Testament Part IV I Esdras-Ecclesiasticus (London: The Trustees of the British Museum, 1957), Proverbs xviii. 12-xix. 20 (23).

224 See Field, Origenis Hexaplorum (Tom. II), 350.

225 See Henry G. Liddell, Robert Scott and Henry S. Jones, *Greek-English Lexicon. A Supplement*, ed. E. A. Barber with the Assistance of P. Maas, M. Scheller and M. L. West (Oxford: Clarendon Press, 1968), 14; TLG (online).

226 See d'Hamonville, *Les Proverbes*, 108–110 and 269–270.

227 See Fox, *Proverbs*, 275; Wolters, *Proverbs*, 209.

As can be observed from the table above, the only questionable rendering is רְמִיָּה/ ἀνδρογύνων.[228] Nonetheless, the rest of the translation seems to be consistent renderings (apart from the shift from singular to plural for some lexemes). On the basis of the observations that MT 18:8 = MT 26:22; MT 19:15 = LXX 18:8; MT 26:22 = LXX 26:22 and LXX 19:15 does not correspond with a reading in MT, we can assume that the LXX translator (a) had a diverging *Vorlage* in 19:15, or (b) the same reading as MT 19:15 and opted for a different translation because he already provided a translation of this Hebrew verse in 18:8.[229] However, it is hard to discern which possibility is the most likely.[230]

If we take the conclusion that MT 19:15 = LXX 18:8 into account, then our hapax עַצְלָה, meaning 'sluggishness, idleness' from the root עצל ('to be sluggish').[231] is rendered in the LXX by ὀκνηρός ('idle, lazy, slothful, sluggish, habitually disinclined to work') instead of δειλία ('fearfulness, timidity, cowardice') of LXX 19:15.[232] The adjective ὀκνηρός only occurs 15 times in the LXX: 3x in Sirach and 12x(!) in Proverbs. In Proverbs it is always used as rendering of עָצֵל. Only in 31:27 it is used as a translation of the Hebrew non-absolute hapax עַצְלוּת (see below) and in 11:16 it has no Hebrew counterpart. Thus, the LXX translator must have opted to render עַצְלָה with his preferred lexeme for עָצֵל, i.e., ὀκνηρός.

X   גָּרֵל (Prov 19:19)

MT	LXX
גְּרָל־חֵמָה נֹשֵׂא עֹנֶשׁ כִּי אִם־תַּצִּיל וְעֹוד תּוֹסִף׃	κακόφρων ἀνὴρ πολλὰ ζημιωθήσεται· ἐὰν δὲ λοιμεύηται καὶ τὴν ψυχὴν αὐτοῦ προσθήσει.
A violent tempered person will pay the penalty; if you effect a rescue, you will only have to do it again.	A malicious man will be severely punished, and if he causes injury, he will even add his soul.

---

228 De Waard argues that the LXX text of 18:8 "reflects partially" MT 19:15. See BHQ, 47*. However, as is evident from the table, LXX 18:8 almost completely represents MT 19:15.

229 The latter explanation can also be complemented by a misreading of the translator. Perhaps he skipped from 18:8 to 19:15 and first rendered 19:15. When he came to the actual Hebrew of 19:15 he decided to provide a different translation because he already rendered the Hebrew in 18:8.

230 Also Fox underscores this difficulty. See Fox, *Proverbs*, 266.

231 See DCH, vol. VI, 533.

232 See GELS, 141 and 491–492; LEH, 129 and 432.

As can be observed, the Greek presents a different rendering than MT. The hapax under discussion is גְּרֵל ('a lot,' > גרל 'to cast lot').[233] This word has a *ketiv* (גרל) and a *qere* (גְּדֵל) variant.[234] The *ketiv* is most likely a orthographic error.[235] The LXX translator rendered the first stich as follows:

MT	LXX
גְּדֵל	πολλά
חֵמָה	κακόφρων
נֹשֵׂא	ἀνήρ
עֹנֶשׁ	ζημιωθήσεται

The translator read עֹנֶשׁ as the verb עָנַשׁ ('to be fined, to pay penalty') which he rendered by ζημιόω ('to suffer loss, damage'), a verb which he always employed as a rendering of ענשׁ (see Prov 17:26; 21:11 and 22:3).[236] The verb נשׂא ('to lift, to carry'), has been translated by ἀνήρ, which seems strange. However, the translator applied metathesis to form אנשׁ ('man'),[237] from אִישׁ, which he rendered by ἀνήρ elsewhere (see Prov 24:1; 28:5; 29:8 and 29:10). The Hebrew חֵמָה has been rendered by the rare κακόφρων ('ill-minded, of bad spirit, malignant') which only occurs twice in the LXX (Prov 11:22 and 19:19).[238]

Concerning our hapax, the LXX translator rendered גְּרֵל/גְּדֵל by πολλά.[239] It is clear that he (or his *Vorlage*) read the *qere* variant, *i.e.* גְּדֵל > גָּדוֹל ('great'), since

---

233 This translation is based upon the noun גּוֹרֵל. The hapax גְּרֵל is not attested in DCH. See DCH, vol. II, 337–338 and 375. Also BDB does not mention this word. Both GESENIUS and KBL do not give a translation but indicate that it is a form of either גּוֹרֵל or גרל. See GESENIUS, p. 148; KBL, 193. De Lagarde also shares this opinion. See de Lagarde, *Anmerkungen*, 63.

234 See BHQ, 35.

235 See Fox, *Proverbs*, 276.

236 In Prov 27:12, ענשׁ has been translated by ζημία ('damage, loss'), which is cognate to the verb ζημιόω.

237 In his article on metathesis in LXX Proverbs, de Waard has also discussed Prov 19:19. In the second stich, the translator has read לֵץ instead of נצל and rendered it by λοιμεύομαι. De Waard argues that לֵץ is always rendered by λοιμεύομαι in Proverbs. This is impossible since this verb occurs only once in LXX Proverbs. Nonetheless, his conclusion regarding metathesis is correct since the Hebrew לֵץ is often rendered by λοιμός, a cognate of λοιμεύομαι. See de Waard, "Metathesis as a Translation Technique?," 252; see also Baumgartner, "Étude critique," 178. However, de Waard does not note the metathesis נשׂא => אנשׁ.

238 See GELS, 357; LEH, 301.

239 According to Baumgartner, the LXX translator read גבר and consequently translated it by ἀνήρ, see Baumgartner, "Étude critique," 178. However, he does not explain the attestation of

גָּדוֹל is often translated throughout the LXX by πολύς (cfr. Gen 29:27; 1 Chr 28:5; Jer 38[MT 31]:8; Ezek 37:10; Dan 11:13). Thus, the LXX translator provided an adequate Greek equivalent for גְּדָל, which cannot be considered a hapax.

Y   אֵשׁוּן (Prov 20:20)

MT	LXX 20:9a
מְקַלֵּל אָבִיו וְאִמּוֹ יִדְעַךְ נֵרוֹ בֶּאֱשׁוּן חֹשֶׁךְ׃	κακολογοῦντος πατέρα ἢ μητέρα σβεσθήσεται λαμπτήρ, αἱ δὲ κόραι τῶν ὀφθαλμῶν αὐτοῦ ὄψονται σκότος.
If you curse father or mother, your lamp will go out in utter darkness.	The lamp of one who curses father or mother will be extinguished, and the pupils of his eyes will see darkness.

Just as was the case in Prov 19:19 (see above), we have a *qere* (בֶּאֱשׁוּן) and a *ketiv* (באישון) of the hapax under discussion.[240] Most authors agree that the LXX translator has rendered the *ketiv*,[241] i.e., אישון, and thus not the hapax אֵשׁוּן ('beginning').[242] In the LXX, אִישׁוֹן ('pupil') is rendered by κόρη ('pupil of the eye'), which is the standard Greek equivalent.[243]

Z   הֲפַכְפַּךְ (Prov 21:8)

MT	LXX
הֲפַכְפַּךְ דֶּרֶךְ אִישׁ וָזָר וְזַךְ יָשָׁר פָּעֳלוֹ׃	πρὸς τοὺς σκολιοὺς σκολιὰς ὁδοὺς ἀποστέλλει ὁ θεός· ἁγνὰ γὰρ καὶ ὀρθὰ τὰ ἔργα αὐτοῦ.

πολλά in this verse. Moreover, it makes more sense that the LXX translator read אנש instead of נשא and rendered it by ἀνήρ. Both Fox and de Waard agree that πολλά is a rendering of the *qere*. See Fox, *Proverbs*, 276; BHQ, 48*. Σ has the neologism μεγαλόθυμος for גְּדָל־חֵמָה, which brings it closer to the Hebrew. See Field, *Origenis Hexaplorum (Tom. II)*, 350.

240 See BHQ, 36.
241 See Fox, *Proverbs*, 285; BHQ, 36. Baumgartner and d'Hammonville, on the other hand, argue that the LXX translator did not know how to render the construction בֶּאֱשׁוּן חֹשֶׁךְ, see Baumgartner, "Étude critique," 187–188; d'Hamonville, *Les Proverbes*, 274.
242 See DCH, vol. I, 412.
243 See DCH, vol. I, 237; GELS, 408; LEH, 351. The Hebrew אִישׁוֹן only occurs five times in the Hebrew Bible and is rendered four times by κόρη (Deut 32:10; Ps 17[LXX 16]:8; Prov 7:2 and 20:20), see HR, 779.

MT	LXX
The way of the guilty is crooked, but the conduct of the pure is right.	To the crooked God sends crooked ways, for his works are pure and upright.

In this verse ἀποστέλλει ὁ θεός is added which emphasises God's agency *vis-à-vis* MT.[244] The hapax in this verse is הֲפַכְפַּךְ ('crooked').[245] In the LXX it is rendered by the adjective σκολιός ('crooked').[246] The hapax reminds of the Hebrew noun תַּהְפּוּכָה ('perversity'),[247] which is translated twice in LXX Proverbs by σκολιός, i.e., in Prov 16:28 and 23:33. Thus, the translator must have read הֲפַכְפַּךְ as a cognate of תַּהְפּוּכָה.

AA   קֹשְׁטְ (Prov 22:21)

MT	LXX
לְהוֹדִיעֲךָ קֹשְׁטְ אִמְרֵי אֱמֶת לְהָשִׁיב אֲמָרִים אֱמֶת לְשֹׁלְחֶיךָ׃ פ	διδάσκω οὖν σε ἀληθῆ λόγον καὶ γνῶσιν ἀγαθὴν ὑπακούειν τοῦ ἀποκρίνεσθαι λόγους ἀληθείας τοῖς προβαλλομένοις σοι.
To show you what is right and true, so that you may give a true answer to those who sent you?	Therefore I teach you a true word and good knowledge to heed in order that you may answer words of truth to them who question you.

According to de Waard and Fox,[248] the hapax קֹשְׁטְ ('truth,' > קֶשֶׁט 'bow, truth') is rendered by ἀληθής ('truthful, trusty, being in accordance with the true state of affairs').[249] However, Baumgartner has argued that γνῶσιν ἀγαθὴν ὑπακούειν is a paraphrase of קֹשְׁטְ, without giving further explanation.[250] Thus, this gives us the following equivalents:

---

244 See Beeckman, "De Nomine Dei," 382. For an elaborate discussion, see chapter 3.
245 See DCH, vol. II, 582.
246 See GELS, 408; LEH, 351.
247 See DCH, vol. VII, 587.
248 See Fox, *Proverbs*, 306; BHQ, 40.
249 See DCH, vol. VII, 336; GELS, 25; LEH, 26.
250 See Baumgartner, "Étude critique," 203. According to d'Hamonville, the hapax is rendered by γνῶσις, see d'Hamonville, *Les Proverbes*, 287. However, he does not give an explanation for the translation of the rest of the first stich.

MT	LXX
לְהוֹדִיעֲךָ	διδάσκω οὖν σε
קֹשְׁטְ	καὶ γνῶσιν ἀγαθὴν ὑπακούειν
אִמְרֵי	λόγον
אֱמֶת	ἀληθῆ
לְהָשִׁיב	ἀποκρίνεσθαι
אֲמָרִים	λόγους
אֱמֶת	ἀληθείας
לְשֹׁלְחֶיךָ	τοῖς προβαλλομένοις σοι

This might be plausible since אֱמֶת ('firmness, faithfulness, truth'), is rendered in LXX Proverbs by πίστις/πιστός or ἀλήθεια. Moreover, the verb ὑπακούω is often used as a translation of קשׁב in LXX Proverbs (cfr. Prov 2:2; 17:4 and 29:14), which shares a resemblance with קֹשְׁטְ. The addition of καὶ γνῶσιν ἀγαθὴν is an elaboration of Prov 22:20, where דַּעַת/γνῶσις is mentioned:

MT	LXX
הֲלֹא כָתַבְתִּי לְךָ שָׁלִישִׁים בְּמוֹעֵצֹת וָדָעַת:	καὶ σὺ δὲ ἀπόγραψαι αὐτὰ σεαυτῷ τρισσῶς εἰς βουλὴν καὶ γνῶσιν ἐπὶ τὸ πλάτος τῆς καρδίας σου.
Have I not written for you thirty sayings of admonition and knowledge.	Now then, copy them for yourself three times over, for counsel and knowledge on the surface of your heart.

Thus, indeed, Baumgartner was correct in arguing that קֹשְׁטְ has been paraphrased by καὶ γνῶσιν ἀγαθὴν ὑπακούειν in the LXX. The LXX translator has read קֹשְׁטְ as קשׁב and translated it by ὑπακούειν.[251] Consequently, he added γνῶσιν ἀγαθὴν to elaborate on the image of Prov 22:20.

---

251 According to Clifford, the change of the triliteral root is a trait of the translation technique of the LXX translator, see Clifford, "Observations on the Text and Versions of Proverbs," 54. However, it is not certain whether the translator read קשׁב instead of קֹשְׁטְ deliberately or not. He probably struggled with קֹשְׁטְ and opted to render it by ὑπακούω as he did for קשׁב elsewhere.

BB חָשֻׁךְ (Prov 22:29)

MT	LXX
חָזִיתָ אִישׁ| מָהִיר בִּמְלַאכְתּוֹ לִפְנֵי־מְלָכִים יִתְיַצָּב בַּל־ יִתְיַצֵּב לִפְנֵי חֲשֻׁכִּים: פ	ὁρατικὸν ἄνδρα καὶ ὀξὺν ἐν τοῖς ἔργοις αὐτοῦ βασιλεῦσι δεῖ παρεστάναι καὶ μὴ παρεστάναι ἀνδράσι νωθροῖς.
Do you see those who are skillful in their work? They will serve kings; they will not serve common people.	A man with vision and skilled in his work should serve before kings and should not serve slothful men.

The hapax in Prov 22:29 is חָשֻׁךְ ('obscure [one],' > חשׁך ['to be dark']).[252] The LXX translator opted for ἀνδράσι νωθροῖς ('slothful men') as a translation of the hapax.[253] The adjective νωθρός ('slothful, lazy, sluggish') is only used here and in Sir 4:29 and 11:29 in the LXX.[254] In 12:8, the LXX uses a neologism νωθροκάρδιος (νωθρός + καρδία, 'slow of mind, stupid, unintelligent') as a rendering of נעוה־לב ('perverse mind').[255]

It seems that the LXX translator opted for ἀνδράσι on the basis of βασιλεῦσι to create rhyme (assonance). Moreover, the choice to add νωθροῖς is possibly prompted by the context of the verse, i.e., skilled man and kings *versus* slothful men, as well as assonance with τοῖς ἔργοις. Nonetheless, ἀνδράσι νωθροῖς seems to be an interpretative rendering of חֲשֻׁכִּים.

CC לֹעַ and שַׂכִּין (Prov 23:2)

MT	LXX
וְשַׂמְתָּ שַׂכִּין בְּלֹעֶךָ אִם־בַּעַל נֶפֶשׁ אָתָּה:	καὶ ἐπίβαλλε τὴν χεῖρά σου εἰδὼς ὅτι τοιαῦτά σε δεῖ παρασκευάσαι.
And put a knife to your throat if you have a big appetite.	And extend your hand, since you know that you will have to prepare such things.

---

252 See DCH, vol. III, 331.

253 Wolters translates ἀνδράσι νωθροῖς by 'listless men,' see Wolters, *Proverbs*, 89. In his commentary, he does not explain his choice. For his commentary on Prov 22:29, see Wolters, *Proverbs*, 225. The meaning 'listless' is not even mentioned in LSJ (see LSJ, 73697). In the context of the verse, 'slothful' is a decent translation.

254 See GELS, 479; LEH, 422.

255 See GELS, 479; LEH, 422.

The two hapaxes in this verse, i.e., שַׂכִּין ('knife,' > סכן ['to cut']) and לֹעַ ('throat,' > לעע ['to swallow']),[256] are located in the first stich. In the LXX they are not rendered at all.[257] According to Baumgartner, the LXX translator had difficulties translating these two hapaxes and had to resort to the second stich of the verse in order to come up with an intelligible rendering.[258] Among similar lines, Fox states that the translator found the image of 'putting a knife to one's own throat' weird and therefore affirmed that it is good to eat the things that have been given to you (verse 1).[259] He asserts that LXX 23:2a ≈ MT 23:2a; LXX 23:2b ≠ MT; LXX 23:3a = MT 23:2b; LXX 23:3b = MT 23:3a and LXX 23:3c ≈ MT 23:3b[260]. D'Hamonville, on the other hand, claims that the LXX translator has provided a psychological reasoning instead of rendering the hapaxes.[261] Although not explained, he probably is referring to παρασκευάζω ('to prepare oneself/something), which might also be understood in a non-psychological sense.[262]

All of these commentators are correct in observing that the LXX translator struggled with either the hapaxes or the meaning the Hebrew wants to convey. However, none of them have commented on ἐπίβαλλε τὴν χεῖρά σου, which can be considered the substitute for stich a of MT 23:2 that contains both hapaxes. The expression ἐπιβάλλω + χείρ (+ personal preposition) occurs multiple times throughout the LXX, i.a., Gen 22:12; 46:4; Exod 7:4; Deut 12:18; 15:10; 28:8.20; 2 Sam 18:12. Strikingly, in Deut 12:18, it is used in the context of eating as is the case in Prov 23:2:

---

256 See DCH, vol. VIII, 149; DCH, vol. IV, 554.
257 See Baumgartner, "Étude critique," 204; Bruce K. Waltke, *The Book of Proverbs 15-31*, NICOT (Grand Rapids, MI – Cambridge: Willam B. Eerdmans Publishing Company, 2005), 226; Fox, *Proverbs*, 309; d'Hamonville, *Les Proverbes*, 289. Both hapaxes are rendered in α΄ (καὶ θήσεις μάχαριαν ἐν καταπόσει σου) and θ΄ ([καὶ] θήσεις μάχαριαν τῷ λάρυγγί σου). See Field, *Origenis Hexaplorum (Tom. II)*, 57.
258 See Baumgartner, "Étude critique," 204–205.
259 See Fox, *Proverbs*, 309.
260 See Fox, *Proverbs*, 309.
261 See d'Hamonville, *Les Proverbes*, 289.
262 Fox notes that it is unclear what 'to prepare' wants to convey in this verse, see Fox, *Proverbs*, 309. Throughout the LXX, this verb is only employed 16 times. Most of the times it is applied to denote the preparation for war. In 2 Macc 2:27 it is used in the sense of 'preparing a banquet,' which is not psychological. Even in LXX Proverbs, the non-psychological use of παρασκευάζω can be found. Prov 29:5 speaks of preparing a net before his friends (ὃς παρασκευάζεται ἐπὶ πρόσωπον τοῦ ἑαυτοῦ φίλου δίκτυον).

MT[263]	LXX[264]
כִּי אִם־לִפְנֵי֩ יְהוָ֨ה אֱלֹהֶ֜יךָ תֹּאכְלֶ֗נּוּ בַּמָּקוֹם֙ אֲשֶׁ֣ר יִבְחַ֣ר יְהוָ֣ה אֱלֹהֶ֗יךָ בּוֹ֙ אַתָּ֤ה וּבִנְךָ֙ וּבִתֶּ֔ךָ וְעַבְדְּךָ֖ וַאֲמָתֶ֑ךָ וְהַלֵּוִ֞י אֲשֶׁ֣ר בִּשְׁעָרֶ֗יךָ וְשָׂמַחְתָּ֗ לִפְנֵי֙ יְהוָ֣ה אֱלֹהֶ֔יךָ בְּכֹ֖ל מִשְׁלַ֥ח יָדֶֽךָ׃	ἀλλ' ἢ ἐναντίον κυρίου τοῦ θεοῦ σου φάγῃ αὐτὰ ἐν τῷ τόπῳ, ᾧ ἂν ἐκλέξηται κύριος ὁ θεός σου αὐτῷ, σὺ καὶ ὁ υἱός σου καὶ ἡ θυγάτηρ σου, ὁ παῖς σου καὶ ἡ παιδίσκη σου, καὶ ὁ προσήλυτος ὁ ἐν ταῖς πόλεσιν ὑμῶν καὶ εὐφρανθήσῃ ἐναντίον κυρίου τοῦ θεοῦ σου ἐπὶ πάντα, οὗ ἂν ἐπιβάλῃς τὴν χεῖρά σου.
These you shall eat in the presence of the Lord your God at the place that the Lord your God will choose, you together with your son and your daughter, your male and female slaves, and the Levites resident in your towns, rejoicing in the presence of the Lord your God in all your undertakings.	But these you shall eat in the presence of the Lord your God at the place, that which the Lord your God may choose, you and your son and your daughter, your male slave and your female slave and the guest in your cities, and you shall be joyful in the presence of the Lord your God in all things where you may put your hand.[265]

Here, οὗ ἂν ἐπιβάλῃς τὴν χεῖρά σου is used to render מִשְׁלַח יָדֶךָ. The phrase οὗ ἂν ἐπιβάλῃς τὴν χεῖρά σου occurs six times in LXX Deuteronomy and is always used in the context of a rejoicing or blessing (or a curse in 28:20) upon the things where men may put their hands on, i.e., the works and products of men.[266] If we look at Prov 23:1-2, the same context might be applicable as well:

ἐὰν καθίσῃς δειπνεῖν ἐπὶ τραπέζης δυναστῶν νοητῶς νόει τὰ παρατιθέμενά σοι.	If you sit down to eat at the table of rulers, [attend attentively to the dishes set before you],[267]

263 For the Hebrew text of Deuteronomy, see Carmel McCarthy, *Deuteronomy*, BHQ 5 (Stuttgart: Deutsche Bibelgesellschaft, 2007).
264 Greek text from John W. Wevers, *Deuteronomium*, Septuaginta. Vetus Testamentum Graecum. Auctoritate Academiae Scientiarum Gottingensis editum III.2 (Göttingen: Vandenhoeck & Ruprecht, 1977).
265 English translation from nets, see Melvin K. H. Peters, "Deuteronomion," in *A New English Translation of the Septuagint And the Other Greek Translations Traditionally Included Under That Title*, ed. Albert Pietersma and Benjamin G. Wright (New York, NY — Oxford: Oxford University Press, 2007), 141–173.
266 See. John W. Wevers, *Notes on the Greek Text of Deuteronomy*, SCS 39 (Altlanta, GA: Scholars Press, 1995), 210 and 217.
267 nets has 'observe carefully what has been set for you.' However, Wolters has argued that from the usage of νοητῶς νόει it does not follow that νοητῶς denotes 'carefully' in this verse. See Wolters, *Proverbs*, 89 and esp. 225.

καὶ ἐπίβαλλε τὴν χεῖρά σου εἰδὼς ὅτι τοιαῦτά σε δεῖ παρασκευάσαι.	and extend your hand, since you know that you will have to prepare such things.

When sitting at the table of rulers, you have to give attention to the food that is set in front of you. Consequently, when you put your hand on them, they will be blessed, since you know you will have to prepare the same kind of food.

DD שׁער (Prov 23:7)

MT	LXX
כִּי כְּמוֹ־שָׁעַר בְּנַפְשׁוֹ כֶּן־הוּא אֱכֹל וּשְׁתֵה יֹאמַר לָךְ וְלִבּוֹ בַּל־עִמָּךְ׃	ὃν τρόπον γὰρ εἴ τις καταπίοι τρίχα, οὕτως ἐσθίει καὶ πίνει.
For like a hair in the throat, so are they. "Eat and drink!" they say to you; but they do not mean it.	For in the same manner as one swallows a hair so he eats and drinks.

The hapax שׁער denotes 'to calculate' (> שָׁעַר ['measure']).[268] The LXX has θρίξ ('hair'),[269] which is prompted by reading שֵׂעָר ('hair') instead of שׁער ('to calculate').[270] Moreover, not only did the LXX translator opt for θρίξ but also for καταπίνω ('to swallow down, to gulp'),[271] which is an equivalent for שׁער ('to whirl away') (cfr. Ps 57[MT 58]:10).[272] Thus, the hapax in our verse is rendered by the double translation καταπίοι τρίχα.[273]

---

268 See DCH, vol. VIII, 519 and 525.

269 See GELS, 279; LEH, 422.

270 See DCH, vol. VIII, 175. All commentators agree on this point, see Baumgartner, "Étude critique," 205; d'Hamonville, *Les Proverbes*,289;Fox, *Proverbs*, 311; Dominique Barthélemy, *Critique textuelle de l'Ancien Testament. Tome 5: Job, Proverbes, Qohélet et Cantique des Cantiques*, OBO 50.5 (Fribourg – Göttingen : Academic Press – Vandenhoeck & Ruprecht, 2015), 696–697. The first one to make this observation was Jäger, see Johann G. Jäger, *Observationes in Proverbiorum Salomonis versionem Alexandrinam* (Meldorpi et Lipsiae: Apud Reinhold Iacob Boie, 1788), 163.

271 See GELS, 380; LEH, 323.

272 See DCH, vol. VIII, 174–175.

273 See de Waard, "Some Unusual Translation Techniques Employed by the Greek Translator(s) of Proverbs," 191; BHQ, 41; Fox, *Proverbs*, 311.

EE נוּמָה (Prov 23:21)

MT	LXX
כִּי־סֹבֵא וְזוֹלֵל יִוָּרֵשׁ וּקְרָעִים תַּלְבִּישׁ נוּמָה:	πᾶς γὰρ μέθυσος καὶ πορνοκόπος πτωχεύσει, καὶ ἐνδύσεται διερρηγμένα καὶ ῥακώδη πᾶς ὑπνώδης.
For the drunkard and the glutton will come to poverty, and drowsiness will clothe them with rags.	For every drunkard and glutton will become poor, and every sluggard will clothe himself with tatters and rags.

The hapax נוּמָה, meaning 'drowsiness, slumber' derived from נום ('to be drowsy'),[274] is rendered in LXX Proverbs by the Greek hapax ὑπνώδης ('drowsy, fond of sleep').[275] The verb נום occurs six times in the LXX and is rendered by νυστάζω ('to become drowsy'; Ps 121[LXX 120]:3.4; Isa 5:27; 56:10 and Nah 3:18) and ὑπνόω ('to fall asleep, to put to sleep'; Ps 76[LXX 75]:5). The former occurs in Prov 6:10 (תְּנוּמָה) and 24:33 (תְּנוּמָה). The latter is also used in Prov 3:24 (שֵׁנָה); 4:16 (יִשָׁן) and 6:10 (שֵׁנָה). The noun νυσταγμός ('dozing, drowsiness') does not occur in Proverbs but is used by α´ as a substitute for ὑπνώδης in Prov 23:21.[276] It is clear that the rendering of the hapax נוּמָה in Prov 23:21 by the hapax ὑπνώδης is an adequate rendering. The LXX translator definitely understood its meaning.

FF חֶתֶף (Prov 23:28)

MT	LXX
אַף־הִיא כְּחֶתֶף תֶּאֱרֹב וּבוֹגְדִים בְּאָדָם תּוֹסִף:	οὗτος γὰρ συντόμως ἀπολεῖται, καὶ πᾶς παράνομος ἀναλωθήσεται.
She lies in wait like a robber and increases the number of the faithless.	For it will quickly perish, and every transgressor will be destroyed.

In Prov 23:28, the hapax חֶתֶף ('robber, robbery, prey', > חתף ['to snatch away']) is attested.[277] The LXX translates it by συντόμως ('suddenly, quickly, speedily,

---

274 See DCH, vol. V, 641.

275 See GELS, 700; LEH, 633. Wolters is correct in noting that the Greek adjective means 'sleepy, drowsy' and translates it by 'sleepyhead' in this verse instead of NETS's 'sluggard.' See Wolters, *Proverbs*, 91 and 228.

276 See Field, Origenis Hexaplorum (Tom. II), 358.

277 See DCH, vol. III, 337.

without delay'),[278] an adverb that only occurs in 3 Macc 5:25 and Prov 13:23 elsewhere.

De Waard is the only scholar who has given a reasonable explanation for the rendering of חֶתֶף by συντόμως.[279] He argues that the LXX translator was not aware of the meaning of the hapax and therefore applied metathesis (see 15:19 and 16:27 above) and rendered בפתע ('in an instant,' > פֶּתַע).[280] He underscores this conclusion by emphasising the ב/כ confusion and the interchange of ח and ע by the translator of LXX Proverbs.[281] Indeed, since metathesis is a characteristic of the translator's translation technique, it is possible that he rendered בפתע instead of כחתף by συντόμως, which is a good rendering of בפתע.

GG חַכְלִלוּת (Prov 23:29)

MT	LXX
לְמִי אוֹי לְמִי אֲבוֹי לְמִי מִדְיָנִים| לְמִי שִׂיחַ לְמִי פְּצָעִים חִנָּם לְמִי חַכְלִלוּת עֵינָיִם:	τίνι οὐαί; τίνι θόρυβος; τίνι κρίσις; τίνι ἀηδίαι; καὶ λέσχαι τίνι συντρίμματα; διὰ κενῆς τίνος πέλειοι οἱ ὀφθαλμοί;
Who has woe? Who has sorrow? Who has strife? Who has complaining? Who has wounds without cause? Who has redness of eyes?	Who has woe? Who has trouble? Who has strife? Who has vexations and squabbles? Who has wounds without reason? Who has blood-shot eyes?

The LXX has the Greek hapax πέλειος ('livid, pale, black and blue') as a rendering of the Hebrew hapax חַכְלִלוּת ('dullness', sparkle, redness').[282] For πέλειος GELS has 'livid', LEH 'pale.'[283] However, it is better to translate it by 'black and blue' since the context of the verse deals with a drunkard and πέλειοι οἱ

---

278 See GELS, 661; LEH, 596.
279 Fox does not take into account de Waard's analysis and, wrongly, asserts that συντόμως is a reasonable rendering of כחתף. See Fox, *Proverbs*, 317. D'Hamonville plainly states that the LXX presents a different rendering of MT without mentioning the hapax. See d'hamonville, *Les Proverbes*, 292.
280 See BHQ, 51* and 43. See also Jan de Waard, "Difference in Vorlage or Lexical Ignorance: a Dilemma in the Old Greek of Proverbs," *JSJ* 38.1 (2007): 1–8, 6–7. For the meaning of פֶּתַע, see DCH, vol. VI, 812.
281 See BHQ, 51*.
282 See DCH, vol. III, 218. DCH has חַכְלִילוּת instead of חַכְלִלוּת, which is probably a mistake since the *yod* is not attested in MT. See BHQ, 43.
283 See GELS, p. 543; LEH, 478.

ὀφθαλμοί refers to a black eye.[284] Wolters translates it as such, *i.e.* 'Whose eyes are black and blue?.'[285] Thus, given the context of the drunkard, which is evoked in Prov 23:20-21 and elaborated in Prov 23:30-31, the translation of πέλειος for חַכְלִלוּת seems accurate.

HH חִבֵּל (Prov 23:34)

MT	LXX
וְהָיִיתָ כְּשֹׁכֵב בְּלֶב־יָם וּכְשֹׁכֵב בְּרֹאשׁ חִבֵּל׃	καὶ κατακείσῃ ὥσπερ ἐν καρδίᾳ θαλάσσης καὶ ὥσπερ κυβερνήτης ἐν πολλῷ κλύδωνι.
You will be like one who lies down in the midst of the sea, like one who lies on the top of a mast.	And you will lie as in the heart of the sea and like a navigator in a large wave.

The hapax חִבֵּל ('mast, tackle, rigging,' > חבל ['to bind']) is rendered in the LXX by κυβερνήτης ('steersman, captain, pilot [of ship]').[286] This Greek lexeme is used four times in the LXX, i.e., 4 Macc 7:1; Prov 23:34; Ezek 27:8.27.28. In Ezekiel it is used to render חֹבֵל ('sailor, pilot').[287] Indeed, scholars have noted that the LXX translator read חֹבֵל instead of חִבֵּל, which explains the choice of κυβερνήτης.[288] By doing so, the rendering seems to be adequate.

II מֵפִיץ (Prov 25:18)

MT	LXX
מֵפִיץ וְחֶרֶב וְחֵץ שָׁנוּן אִישׁ עֹנֶה בְרֵעֵהוּ עֵד שָׁקֶר׃	ῥόπαλον καὶ μάχαιρα καὶ τόξευμα ἀκιδωτόν, οὕτως καὶ ἀνὴρ ὁ καταμαρτυρῶν τοῦ φίλου αὐτοῦ μαρτυρίαν ψευδῆ.

---

284 See Wolters, *Proverbs*, 228. Moreover, there are multiple orthographic differences of the word in the textual transmission, *i.e.* πέλειοι, πελιοὶ and πελιδνοί. These differences do not matter since they are different variants or biforms of the same word. See Wolters, *Proverbs*, 228.

285 See Wolters, *Proverbs*, 93.

286 See DCH, vol. III, 150 and 152; GELS, 417; LEH, 358.

287 See DCH, vol. III, 152.

288 See Jäger, *Observationes in Proverbiorum*, 170; Fox, *Proverbs*, 319. Moreover, the rendering of בראש by ἐν πολλῷ κλύδωνι is based upon a reading of ברעש or בשער (interchange א/ע and metathesis). See Jäger, *Observationes in Proverbiorum*, 170; Baumgartner, "Étude critique," 211; BHQ, 51*.

MT	LXX
Like a war club, a sword, or a sharp arrow is one who bears false witness against a neighbor.	Pointed is a nail and a dagger and an arrow; so also is a man who bears false witness against his friend.

The hapax מֵפִיץ ('scatterer, disperser', > פוּץ ['to be scattered']) is attested at the beginning of Prov 25:18.[289] De Lagarde has proposed the emendation מַפֵּץ ('club, hammer'),[290] a lexeme which occurs in Jer 51[LXX 28]:20. However, both Baumgartner as Dominique Barthélemy are not in favour of this emendation.[291] Nevertheless, when looking at the LXX, the translator has the Greek hapax ῥόπαλον ('club, cudgel'),[292] which seems to indicate that the translator read מַפֵּץ instead of מֵפִיץ. Moreover, when looking at the translation of the rest of the verse, it can be observed that the translator has provided a consistent, one-on-one, rendering of each Hebrew lexeme:

MT	LXX
מֵפִיץ	ῥόπαλον
וְחֶרֶב	καὶ μάχαιρα
וְחֵץ	καὶ τόξευμα
שָׁנוּן	ἀκιδωτόν
/	οὕτως καὶ
אִישׁ	ἀνὴρ ὁ
עֹנֶה	καταμαρτυρῶν
בְרֵעֵהוּ	τοῦ φίλου αὐτοῦ
עֵד	μαρτυρίαν
שָׁקֶר	ψευδῆ

This observation is an additional argument that the LXX translator read מַפֵּץ instead of מֵפִיץ and, consequently rendered it by ῥόπαλον. Moreover, ῥόπαλον

---

289 See DCH, vol. V, 431.

290 See de Lagarde, *Anmerkungen*, 82. For the meaning of מַפֵּץ, see DCH, vol. V, 433.

291 See Baumgartner, "Étude critique," 221; Barthélemy, *Critique textuelle de l'Ancien Testament. Tome 5*, 725–727, esp. 727. Baumgartner does not prefer this emendation since מַפֵּץ occurs only in Jer 51[LXX 28]:20 where it is rendered by διασκορπίζω ('to scatter'). Barthélemy gives מַפֵּץ the benefit of the doubt but states that מֵפִיץ is the most preferred reading.

292 See GELS, 615; LEH, 544. nets has, incorrectly, 'nail' which is probably based upon the Latin *clavus*. See Wolters, *Proverbs*, 247.

fits the context which lists a series of weapons, i.e., a sword (μάχαιρα) and an arrow (τόξευμα).

JJ מַעְצוֹר (Prov 25:28)

MT	LXX
עִיר פְּרוּצָה אֵין חוֹמָה אִישׁ אֲשֶׁר אֵין מַעְצָר לְרוּחוֹ:	ὥσπερ πόλις τὰ τείχη καταβεβλημένη καὶ ἀτείχιστος, οὕτως ἀνὴρ ὃς οὐ μετὰ βουλῆς τι πράσσει.
Like a city breached, without walls, is one who lacks self-control.	As a city is with its walls cast down and unfortified, so is a man who does everything without counsel.

The hapax מַעְצוֹר, denoting 'stopping, restraint, impediment' (> עצר ['to stop']),[293] is translated by the LXX translator by μετὰ βουλῆς ('with counsel'). Johann Gottlob Jäger was the first to indicate that the LXX translator has read מעצה ('with counsel,' > עֵצָה ['counsel']), in his source text.[294] Both de Waard and Fox agree with his observation.[295] Indeed, עֵצָה is often rendered by βουλή throughout the LXX and also in Prov 1:25.30; 8:14; 19:21; 20:5 and 21:30.[296] The translation of מעצה by μετὰ βουλῆς prompted the LXX translator to skip לרוחו and to substitute it with τι πράσσει in order to fit the context and complete the comparison with the first stich.[297]

KK מַרְגֵּמָה (Prov 26:8)

MT	LXX
כִּצְרוֹר אֶבֶן בְּמַרְגֵּמָה כֵּן־נוֹתֵן לִכְסִיל כָּבוֹד:	ὃς ἀποδεσμεύει λίθον ἐν σφενδόνῃ, ὅμοιός ἐστιν τῷ διδόντι ἄφρονι δόξαν.
It is like binding a stone in a sling to give honor to a fool.	He who ties down a stone in a sling is like him who gives glory to a fool.

---

293 See DCH, vol. V, 410.
294 See Jäger, *Observationes in Proverbiorum*, 185. For עֵצָה, see DCH, vol. VI, 528–531.
295 See BHQ, 52*; Fox, *Proverbs*, 340.
296 See HR, 22–228.
297 See BHQ, 52*; Fox, *Proverbs*, 340.

The hapax in this verse concerns the word מַרְגֵּמָה ('sling, heap of stones', > רגם ['to stone']).[298] The LXX has σφενδόνη ('sling [as a weapon], bullet, stone') as a rendering of the hapax.[299] This lexeme is used seven times elsewhere in the LXX, i.e., 1 Kingdoms 17:40; 25:29; 2 Chr 26:14; Jdt 9:7; 1 Macc 6:51; Sir 47:4; Zech 9:15, where it is a rendering of קֶלַע ('sling') in the instances where we have an extant Hebrew text.[300] Just as was the case in 25:18 (see above), the Greek provides a consistent rendering of the Hebrew:

MT	LXX
כִּצְרוֹר	ὅς ἀποδεσμεύει (> כִּצְרֵר)[301]
אֶבֶן	λίθον
בְּמַרְגֵּמָה	ἐν σφενδόνῃ
כֵּן־נוֹתֵן	ὅμοιός ἐστιν τῷ διδόντι
לִכְסִיל	ἄφρονι
כָּבוֹד	δόξαν

Thus, we might assume that מַרְגֵּמָה/σφενδόνη is an adequate rendering.

LL קֵא (Prov 26:11)

MT	LXX
כְּכֶלֶב שָׁב עַל־קֵאוֹ כְּסִיל שׁוֹנֶה בְאִוַּלְתּוֹ׃	ὥσπερ κύων ὅταν ἐπέλθῃ ἐπὶ τὸν ἑαυτοῦ ἔμετον καὶ μισητὸς γένηται, οὕτως ἄφρων τῇ ἑαυτοῦ κακίᾳ ἀναστρέψας ἐπὶ τὴν ἑαυτοῦ ἁμαρτίαν. [11a] ἔστιν αἰσχύνη ἐπάγουσα ἁμαρτίαν, καὶ ἔστιν αἰσχύνη δόξα καὶ χάρις.
Like a dog that returns to its vomit is a fool who reverts to his folly.	Like a dog, when he returns to his vomit, also becomes the more hated, so is a fool, when by his own wickedness, he returns to his own sin. [11a] There is a sense of shame that leads to sin, and there is a sense of shame that is glory and grace.

---

298 See DCH, vol. V, 478.
299 See GELS, 665; LEH, 600.
300 This is also the case for its attestation in Sirach. See Beentjes, *The Book of Ben Sira in Hebrew*, 83.
301 See BHQ, 48; Fox, *Proverbs*, 343.

Prov 26:11 has a plus in the LXX *vis-à-vis* MT: ἔστιν αἰσχύνη ἐπάγουσα ἁμαρτίαν καὶ ἔστιν αἰσχύνη δόξα καὶ χάρις. This verse also occurs in Sir 4:21, albeit slightly different: ἔστιν γὰρ αἰσχύνη ἐπάγουσα ἁμαρτίαν καὶ ἔστιν αἰσχύνη δόξα καὶ χάρις.[302] This quotation is regarded as a later insertion.[303]

The hapax קֵא, 'vomit, vomited thing' > קיא ('to vomit'),[304] is rendered by the hapax ἔμετος ('vomit') in LXX Proverbs[305]. This seems to be an adequate rendering of the Hebrew hapax. However, the LXX translator apparently felt the need to elaborate and explicate the image of the Hebrew since he has added καὶ μισητὸς γένηται.[306] Afterwards, the same is done in the second stich concerning the fool, i.e., τῇ ἑαυτοῦ κακίᾳ.[307]

MM מַשָּׁאוֹן (Prov 26:26)

MT	LXX
תִּכַּסֶּה שִׂנְאָה בְּמַשָּׁאוֹן תִּגָּלֶה רָעָתוֹ בְקָהָל:	ὁ κρύπτων ἔχθραν συνίστησιν δόλον, ἐκκαλύπτει δὲ τὰς ἑαυτοῦ ἁμαρτίας εὔγνωστος ἐν συνεδρίοις.

---

302 See Jäger, *Observationes in Proverbiorum*, 188; de Lagarde, *Anmerkungen*, 85; Baumgartner, "Étude critique," 225–226; d'Hamonville, *Les Proverbes*, 318; Fox, *Proverbs*, 345. Wolters argues that this verse "found its way into LXX Proverbs from Sir[ach]." He does not specify whether the insertion is made by the translator or during the textual transmission of the Greek text. See Wolters, *Proverbs*, 250. Strikingly, Cook does not mention this parallel in his article dealing with the relationship between LXX Proverbs and Sirach, see Johann Cook, "The Relationship Between the Wisdom of Jesus Ben Sira and the Septuagint Version of Proverbs," in *Construction, Coherence and Connotations: Studies on the Septuagint, Apocryphal and Cognate Literature. Papers Presented at the Association for the Study of the Septuagint in South Africa International Conference at the Faculty of Theology, North-West University, Potchefstroom, South Africa (28-30 August 2015)*, ed. Pierre. J. Jordaan and Nicholas P. L. Allen, DCLS 34 (Berlin – Boston, MA: De Gruyter, 2016), 11–26.
303 See d'Hamonville, *Les Proverbes*, 318; Fox, *Proverbs*, 345.
304 See DCH, vol. VII, 169. DCH notes that 4QJub[h] 61,2 (4Q223-224) perhaps also attests this hapax. However, 4QJub[h] does not attest this verse, see Harold Attridge *et al.*, ed., *Qumran Cave 4 VIII. Parabiblical Texts, Part 1*, DJD XIII (Oxford: Clarendon Press, 1994), 95–140.
305 See GELS, 226; LEH, 195. LEH translates it by 'vomiting' in line with LSJ, 35165.
306 See Fox, *Proverbs*, 345.
307 According to Jäger, τῇ ἑαυτοῦ κακίᾳ and ἐπὶ τὴν ἑαυτοῦ ἁμαρτίαν can be considered a double translation of באולתו. See Jäger, *Observationes in Proverbiorum*, 188. However, it seems that the LXX translator deliberately added τῇ ἑαυτοῦ κακίᾳ in line with the addition καὶ μισητὸς γένηται in the first stich of the verse in order to explain the image that is attested in the Hebrew.

MT	LXX
Though hatred is covered with guile, the enemy's wickedness will be exposed in the assembly.	He who conceals enmity contrives deceit, but he exposes his own sins, being well- known in the councils.

The Hebrew מַשָּׁאוֹן ('deception,' > נשא ['to deceive']) is rendered by δόλος ('deception, deceit, craft, treachery') in the LXX.[308] In LXX Proverbs, δόλος is used 7 times (Prov 10:10; 12:5.20; 16:28; 26:23.24.26), in the instances where it is not a plus (10:10; 16:28; 26:23), it is used as a rendering of מִרְמָה ('deceit, treachery').

As noted by d'Hamonville, this verse reprises several themes of preceding verses by using the exact same lexemes: ἔχθρα (26:24), δόλος (26:23 and 24) and (ἐκ)καλύπτω (26:23).[309] Thus, the rendering of מַשָּׁאוֹן by δόλος, is not surprising giving since מַשָּׁאוֹן shares the same meaning as מִרְמָה which is translated by δόλος elsewhere in LXX Proverbs and, in the context of 26:26, especially in 26:24. Moreover, by rendering תְּכַסֶּה as a participle (ὁ κρύπτων > מְכַסֶּה),[310] the LXX translator had to add a verb, i.e., συνίστημι ('to contrive'), in order to form a legible Greek sentence.

NN מִדְחֶה (Prov 26:28)

MT	LXX
לְשׁוֹן־שֶׁקֶר יִשְׂנָא דַכָּיו וּפֶה חָלָק יַעֲשֶׂה מִדְחֶה:	γλῶσσα ψευδὴς μισεῖ ἀλήθειαν, στόμα δὲ ἄστεγον ποιεῖ ἀκαταστασίας.
A lying tongue hates its victims, and a flattering mouth works ruin.	A false tongue hates truth, and an unguarded mouth works instability.

The Hebrew מִדְחֶה denotes 'downfall, ruin' (> דחה ['to push']).[311] The LXX translator applied the rare word ἀκαταστασία ('instability, confusion'),[312] which only

---

308 See DCH, vol. V, 507; GELS, 175; LEH, 159.

309 See d'Hamonville, *Les Proverbes*, 321; Fox, *Proverbs*, 349–350.

310 See BHQ, 49 and 53*; Fox, *Proverbs*, 350. The Vulgate, Targum and Peshitta also read מְכַסֶּה.

311 See DCH, vol. V, 146.

312 See GELS, 20; LEH, 20. It also appears in Sir 26:27, presented in Ziegler's critical edition in a smaller font, but this verse belongs to a later Greek recension. See Joseph Ziegler, *Sapientia Salomonis*, Septuaginta. Vetus Testamentum Graecum. Auctoritate Academiae Scientiarum Gottingensis editum XII.1 (Göttingen: Vandenhoeck & Ruprecht, 1962), 249.

occurs here and in Tob 4:13, as a rendering of the hapax. When comparing the Hebrew and Greek of this verse, we can see a one-on-one rendering of each word (cfr. 25:18 and 26:8 above):

MT	LXX
לְשׁוֹן	γλῶσσα
שֶׁקֶר	ψευδὴς
יִשְׂנָא	μισεῖ
דַּכָּיו	ἀλήθειαν
וּפֶה	στόμα δὲ
חָלָק	ἄστεγον
יַעֲשֶׂה	ποιεῖ
מִדְחֶה	ἀκαταστασίας

At first sight, the only odd rendering in this verse seems to be דַּכָּיו/ἀλήθειαν. However, scholars have pointed at the fact that the LXX translator opted for ἀλήθεια based upon a reading of the Aramaic דכי ('pure').[313] The LXX translator must have understood the meaning of the hapax and, consequently, rendered it by an adequate equivalent, i.e., the equally rare word ἀκαταστασία.[314]

OO נֵטֶל (Prov 27:3)

MT	LXX
כֹּבֶד־אֶבֶן וְנֵטֶל הַחוֹל וְכַעַס אֱוִיל כָּבֵד מִשְּׁנֵיהֶם:	βαρὺ λίθος καὶ δυσβάστακτον ἄμμος, ὀργὴ δὲ ἄφρονος βαρυτέρα ἀμφοτέρων.
A stone is heavy, and sand is weighty, but a fool's provocation is heavier than both.	A stone is heavy and sand is weighty, but the rage of a fool is heavier than both.

---

313 See, e.g., Baumgartner, "Études critique," 227; BHQ, 49 and 53*; Fox, *Proverbs*, 350; Barthélemy, *Critique textuelle de l'Ancien Testament. Tome 5*, 745. Baumgartner also leaves the possibility of a derivation from the Hebrew זכה, see Baumgartner, "Études critique," 227. Fox, following Baumgartner, records דכא. However, this is probably a mistake since דכא means 'chamber.' See Edward M. Cook, *Dictionary of Qumran Aramaic* (University Park, PA: Penn State University Press, 2015), 54.

314 According to Gerleman, ἄστεγον and ἀκαταστασίας can be regarded as alliteration introduced by the translator. See Gerleman, *Proverbs*, 12-13.

In Prov 27:3 the hapax נֵטֶל ('weight', > נטל ['to lift, to lay upon, to take away']) occurs.[315]

Just as was the case in 26:28 (see above), the LXX translator rendered the hapax by a rare Greek word, *i.e.* the LXX *hapax legomenon* δυσβάστακτος ('difficult to carry').[316] Once more, the resemblance between the Hebrew and Greek equivalents is striking:

MT	LXX
כֹּבֶד	βαρὺ
אֶבֶן	λίθος
וְנֵטֶל	καὶ δυσβάστακτον
הַחוֹל	ἄμμος
וְכַעַס	ὀργὴ δὲ
אֱוִיל	ἄφρονος
כָּבֵד	βαρυτέρα
מִשְּׁנֵיהֶם	ἀμφοτέρων

The LXX translator understood the meaning of each word in this verse and provided a literal, one-on-one, translation of the Hebrew.[317]

PP אַכְזְרִיּוּת (Prov 27:4)

MT	LXX
אַכְזְרִיּוּת חֵמָה וְשֶׁטֶף אָף וּמִי יַעֲמֹד לִפְנֵי קִנְאָה:	ἀνελεήμων θυμὸς καὶ ὀξεῖα ὀργή, ἀλλ' οὐδένα ὑφίσταται ζῆλος.
Wrath is cruel, anger is overwhelming, but who is able to stand before jealousy?	Wrath is merciless and anger is passionate, but jealousy can bear no one.

---

315 See DCH, vol. V, 676. According to dch, the verb נטל might also express the meaning of 'weigh' based upon its attestation in Arad ostracon 60,1. See DCH, vol. V, 676.

316 See GELS, 180; LEH, 163. LEH records this as a neologism and translates it by 'cumbersome, intolerable.' LSJ notes 'intolerable, grievous to be borne,' see LSJ, 29665.

317 This is also evident when looking at the works of commentators. Jäger, Fox, Barthélémy and Wolters do not comment on this verse. D'Hamonville briefly indicates the LXX hapax and its attestation in the New Testament. See d'Hamonville, *Les Proverbes*, 323. Baumgartner makes some small observations on the Peshitta and the targum. See Baumgartner, "Étude critique," 227.

The hapax אַכְזְרִיּוּת ('cruelty,' > אַכְזָר ['cruel']),[318] has been translated by ἀνελεήμων ('merciless, without mercy') in LXX Proverbs.[319] The Greek adjective ἀνελεήμων occurs 11 times in the LXX: Prov 5:9; 11:17; 12:10; 17:11; 27:4; Job 19:13; Wis 12:5; 19:1; Sir 13:12; 35:22 and 37:11. In the verses for which we have a Hebrew counterpart, it is used as a rendering of אַכְזָרִי ('cruel').[320] Since אַכְזָרִי has been rendered consequently by ἀνελεήμων in LXX Proverbs, it is reasonable to assume that the translator translated אַכְזְרִיּוּת by ἀνελεήμων taking אַכְזְרִיּוּת to stem from אַכְזָרִי.

QQ סַגְרִיר (Prov 27:15)

MT	LXX
דֶּלֶף טוֹרֵד בְּיוֹם סַגְרִיר וְאֵשֶׁת מִדְיָנִים נִשְׁתָּוָה׃	σταγόνες ἐκβάλλουσιν ἄνθρωπον ἐν ἡμέρᾳ χειμερινῇ ἐκ τοῦ οἴκου αὐτοῦ, ὡσαύτως καὶ γυνὴ λοίδορος ἐκ τοῦ ἰδίου οἴκου.
A continual dripping on a rainy day and a contentious wife are alike.	Drops on a rainy day drive a person from his house, likewise also an abusive wife, from his very own house.

The Hebrew סַגְרִיר, denoting 'heavy rain, cloudburst,'[321] is rendered in the LXX by χειμερινός ('pertaining to winter, winter, wintry, stormy').[322] The adjective χειμερινός is used scarcely throughout the LXX: 1 Es 9:11; Ezr 10:13 (גֶּשֶׁם, 'rain, shower'); Prov 17:25 (סַגְרִיר); Wis 16:29 (Codex A and א); Zech 10:1 (גֶּשֶׁם); Jer 36(LXX 43):22 (חֹרֶף, 'harvest time, autumn'). The translation of סַגְרִיר by χειμερινός both denoting harsh weather conditions, seems appropriate.

Tauberschmidt has rightly indicated that the LXX translator has created a better parallelism than MT in this verse.[323] He has added ἐκβάλλουσιν ἄνθρωπον and ἐκ τοῦ οἴκου αὐτοῦ and by doing so he elaborated and explained the image

---

318 See DCH, vol. I, 240.
319 See GELS, 49; LEH, 47.
320 This is also the case for Sir 13:12; 35:22 (35:20 in BibleWorks; 35:18 according to HR, 86) and 37:11, see Beentjes, *The Book of Ben Sira in Hebrew*, 41 (MS B), 61 (MS B) and 64 (MS B and D). In Job 19:13, the Hebrew reads אַךְ־זָרוּ which the translator obviously read as אַכְזָרִי.
321 See DCH, vol. VI,. 121. DCH does not note the root of which this hapax is derived from.
322 See GELS, 730; LEH, 661. Wolters translates it by 'stormy,' see Wolters, *Proverbs*, 113. This is also one of the meanings noted in LSJ. See LSJ, 116546.
323 See Tauberschmidt, *Secondary Parallelism*, 73. In 19:13, the same phrase as in 27:15, i.e., ודלף טרד, occurs. However, there it is rendered completely different and has been converted into another image than MT.

which is attested in the Hebrew.[324] Against this background, the plus ἐκ τοῦ ἰδίου οἴκου in the second stich cannot be considered as a wrong repetition of ἐκ τοῦ οἴκου αὐτοῦ of the 1ˢᵗ stich, as Baumgartner asserts,[325] but has to be regarded as an addition of the translator to enhance the parallelistic structure of the verse.

RR אֲבַדּוֹ (Prov 27:20)

MT	LXX
שְׁאוֹל וַאֲבַדֹּה לֹא תִשְׂבַּעְנָה וְעֵינֵי הָאָדָם לֹא תִשְׂבַּעְנָה:	ᾅδης καὶ ἀπώλεια οὐκ ἐμπίμπλανται, ὡσαύτως καὶ οἱ ὀφθαλμοὶ τῶν ἀνθρώπων ἄπληστοι. ²⁰ᵃ βδέλυγμα κυρίῳ στηρίζων ὀφθαλμόν, καὶ οἱ ἀπαίδευτοι ἀκρατεῖς γλώσσῃ.
Sheol and Abaddon are never satisfied, and human eyes are never satisfied.	Hades and destruction are never satisfied; likewise insatiable are the eyes of people. ²⁰ᵃ An abomination to the Lord is a person who fixates his eye, also the uneducated, unable to control their tongue.

Verse 27:20 contains a plus. As I have argued elsewhere, this plus can be ascribed to the translator since it contains vocabulary which is characteristic of the LXX translator of Proverbs.[326]

The hapax אֲבַדֹּ is a form of אֲבַדּוֹן which means 'destruction, Abaddon.'[327] In 27:20 וַאֲבַדֹּ is the *qere* variant, ואבדה, which is also a form of אֲבַדּוֹן, is the *ketiv*.[328] The LXX has rendered this word by ἀπώλεια ('destruction, annihilation, loss [of property]').[329] Throughout the LXX this word has been used to render Hebrew words from the root אבד 'to be destroyed.'[330] Also in LXX Proverbs it is used to render words like אבד (11:10; 28:28) and אֲבַדּוֹן (15:11). Thus, the translation of אֲבַדֹּ (*qere*) or וַאֲבַדֹּה (*ketiv*), whatever the translator must have read, by ἀπώλεια is an adequate translation in line with other the Greek rendering of Hebrew words from the root אבד in the rest of LXX Proverbs.

---

324 See also Baumgartner, "Étude critique," 228.
325 See Baumgartner, "Étude critique," 228.
326 See Beeckman, "De Nomine Dei," 217–519. See also chapter 3 of this monograph.
327 See DCH, vol. I, 101.
328 See BHQ, 50.
329 See GELS, 88–89; LEH, 79.
330 See HR, 151–152.

SS מַהֲלָל (Prov 27:21)

MT	LXX
מַצְרֵף לַכֶּסֶף וְכוּר לַזָּהָב וְאִישׁ לְפִי מַהֲלָלוֹ:	δοκίμιον ἀργύρῳ καὶ χρυσῷ πύρωσις, ἀνὴρ δὲ δοκιμάζεται διὰ στόματος ἐγκωμιαζόντων αὐτόν. ²¹ᵃ καρδία ἀνόμου ἐκζητεῖ κακά, καρδία δὲ εὐθὴς ἐκζητεῖ γνῶσιν.
The crucible is for silver, and the furnace is for gold, so a person is tested by being praised.	Burning is a test for silver and gold, but a man is tested by the mouth of them who praise him. ²¹ᵃ The heart of a lawless person seeks out evil, but an upright heart seeks out knowledge.

Once more, as was the case in the previous verse (see above), there is a plus: καρδία ἀνόμου ἐκζητεῖ κακά καρδία δὲ εὐθὴς ἐκζητεῖ γνῶσιν. The addition is also attested in the Peshitta and, although slightly different, in the Vulgate.[331] Scholars have asserted that this addition also belongs to the LXX text.[332] Indeed, given the attestation of the word εὐθής, which occurs only in Judg 21:25; Jdt 8:11; Wis 9:9 and two times in Proverbs (21:29 and 27:21), we might assume that this verse belonged to the original Greek text.

The hapax in this verse is מַהֲלָל, meaning 'praise, reputation' > הלל ('to praise').[333] The LXX translator provided the translation ἐγκωμιάζω ('to praise, to laud, to extol, to eulogise') for this hapax.[334] This verb only occurs in LXX Proverbs 12:8; 27:2.21; 28:4 and 29:2. In 12:8; 27:2 and 28:4 it is a translation of הלל ('to praise'). The translator has read מהלליו, instead of MT's מַהֲלָלוֹ, and rendered it by ἐγκωμιαζόντων αὐτόν in accordance with the rest of his translation.[335] Moreover, the variant מהלליו also appears in Hebrew manuscripts described by

331 See Fox, *Proverbs*, 358. The Vulgate reads 'cor iniqui exquiret mala cor autem rectum exquiret scientiam.' See Bonifatius Fischer *et al.*, ed., *Biblia Sacra. Iuxta Vulgatam Versionem. Tomus II: Proverbia – Apocalypsis*, red. Robert weber (Stuttgart: Württembergische Bibelanstalt, 1969), 982.

332 See d'Hamonville, *Les Proverbes*, 326; Fox, *Proverbs*, 358. Fox even gives a retroversion of the Greek into Hebrew. Baumgartner declares that it is impossible to know whether the additions in verses 20 and 21 belonged to the original Greek text. See Baumgartner, "Étude critique," 230.

333 See DCH, vol. V, 164.

334 See GELS, 188; LEH, 170.

335 See BHQ, 50; Fox, *Proverbs*, 357.

Benjamin Kennicott and Giovanni de Rossi.[336] Also the Peshitta and the Targum have read this form.[337]

כתש TT and עֲלִי (Prov 27:22)

MT	LXX
אִם תִּכְתּוֹשׁ־אֶת־הָאֱוִיל ׀ בַּמַּכְתֵּשׁ בְּתוֹךְ הָרִיפוֹת בַּעֱלִי לֹא־תָסוּר מֵעָלָיו אִוַּלְתּוֹ׃ פ	ἐὰν μαστιγοῖς ἄφρονα ἐν μέσῳ συνεδρίου ἀτιμάζων, οὐ μὴ περιέλῃς τὴν ἀφροσύνην αὐτοῦ.
Rush a fool in a mortar with a pestle along with crushed grain, but the folly will not be driven out.	If you beat a fool when he is disgraced in the council, you will never remove his folly.

This verse contains two hapaxes, i.e., כתש ('to pound,' > מַכְתֵּשׁ ['mortar']) and עֲלִי ('pestle,' > עלה ['to go up']).[338] As can be observed, the LXX presents another reading for this verse than MT:

MT	LXX
אִם	ἐὰν
תִּכְתּוֹשׁ	μαστιγοῖς
אֶת־הָאֱוִיל	ἄφρονα
בַּמַּכְתֵּשׁ	/
בְּתוֹךְ	ἐν μέσῳ
הָרִיפוֹת	! (ἀτιμάζων)[339]
בַּעֱלִי	συνεδρίου
(הָרִיפוֹת) !	ἀτιμάζων
לֹא	οὐ μὴ
תָסוּר	περιέλῃς (> תָּסִיר)[340]
מֵעָלָיו	/
אִוַּלְתּוֹ	τὴν ἀφροσύνην αὐτοῦ

---

336 See BHQ, 50.
337 See BHQ, 50.
338 See resp. DCH, vol. IV, 478; DCH, vol. VI, 421.
339 ἀτιμάζων is the result of a reading of חֶרְפוֹת (> חֶרְפָּה, 'reproach, shame, disgrace') instead of הָרִיפוֹת. See Baumgartner, "Étude critique," 230; DCH, vol. III, 321–322.
340 See Fox, *Proverbs*, 358.

Both d'Hamonville and Fox have argued that the variant reading of the LXX has to be explained by the LXX translator's interpretational activity who has politicised this verse.[341] Fox adds that the translator has explicated the metaphor attested in the Hebrew and added the theme of συνέδριον ('council, assembly, group of people formally gathered to discuss matters and take decisions') which also occurs in Prov 11:13; 15:22; 22:10 (2x); 24:8; 26:26 and 31:23.[342] Indeed, this word is characteristic of LXX Proverbs since it is used only 4 times elsewhere in the LXX: 2 Macc 14:5; Ps 25(MT 26):4; PsSol 4:1 and Jer 15:17.[343] In Prov 27:22, συνέδριον can be considered a rendering of בַּעֲלִי, which the translator read as a word stemming from the root עלה ('to go up') and which denoted 'elevated place, place of the high assembly.'[344] Nonetheless, given the fact that the LXX translator provided a different interpretation of the verse than MT, it seems that he struggled to render the difficult Hebrew verse.

As can be observed, the hapax כתש is rendered in the LXX by μαστιγόω ('to [beat with a] whip, to flog, to punish, to chastise').[345] Although this verb is used to render נכה ('to smite, to strike down') in LXX Proverbs,[346] both נכה and כתש express the meaning of beating/pounding something/someone (by force). Moreover, the usage of μαστιγόω in 27:22 fits the political interpretation the translator gave to this verse. Furthermore, due to its orthographic resemblance with תְּכְתּוֹשׁ, which he rendered by μαστιγοῖς, the LXX translator might have skipped over בַּמַּכְתֵּשׁ. Furthermore, when he would have rendered מַכְתֵּשׁ, the image he created into Greek would not have made sense.

---

341 See d'Hamonville, *Les Proverbes*, 326; Fox, *Proverbs*, 358.

342 See Fox, *Proverbs*, 358; GELS, 654; LEH, 589.

343 According to Cook, this lexeme, amongst others, is typical for LXX Proverbs and does not occur in LXX Job and is an indication of a different translation for both books. See Cook, "The Relationship Between the LXX Versions of Proverbs and Job," 153. The phrase 'in the midst of the assembly' occurs also in the Targum. See John F. Healey, *The Targum of Proverbs. Introduction, Apparatus, and Notes*, The Aramaic Bible 15 (Edinburgh: T & T Clark, 1991), 56.

344 See Baumgartner, "Étude critique," 230. However, it must be noted that Baumgartner believes that συνέδριον is a rendering of בַּמַּכְתֵּשׁ and that בַּעֲלִי is not attested in the LXX. See Baumgartner, "Étude critique," 230. However, as Barthélemy asserts, the LXX, Peshitta and Targum have interpreted עֲלִי as גֹּרֶן, a designation for the Sanhedrin which is confirmed by other scholars. See Barthélemy, *Critique textuelle de l'Ancien Testament. Tome 5*, 754.

345 See GELS, 442; LEH, 385.

346 See HR, 898.

UU שְׁחוּת (Prov 28:10)

MT	LXX
מַשְׁגֶּה יְשָׁרִ֨ים| בְּדֶ֣רֶךְ רָ֗ע בִּשְׁחוּת֥וֹ הֽוּא־יִפּ֑וֹל וּתְמִימִ֗ים יִנְחֲלוּ־טֽוֹב:	ὃς πλανᾷ εὐθεῖς ἐν ὁδῷ κακῇ, εἰς διαφθορὰν αὐτὸς ἐμπεσεῖται· οἱ δὲ [ἄμωμοι διελοῦνται] ἀγαθὰ καὶ οὐκ εἰσελεύσονται εἰς αὐτά³⁴⁷.
Those who mislead the upright into evil ways will fall into pits of their own making, but the blameless will have a goodly inheritance.	He who misleads the upright into an evil way will himself fall into destruction. And the lawless will pass through good things but will not enter into them.

The Hebrew hapax in Prov 28:10 is שְׁחוּת which means 'pit' (> שׁוח ['to sink']).³⁴⁸ The LXX has rendered this hapax by διαφθορά ('destruction, corruption').³⁴⁹ This lexeme is, almost always, used in the LXX as a rendering of שַׁחַת ('pit, grave').³⁵⁰ Thus, the translation of שַׁחַת by διαφθορά was common practice. Moreover, in Job 33:28 בשחת is rendered by εἰς διαφθορὰν. Thus the translator of Proverbs must have read בשחתו and, consequently, translated it by εἰς διαφθορὰν αὐτὸς.³⁵¹

VV חֲלוֹף (Prov 31:8)

MT	LXX
פְּתַח־פִּ֥יךָ לְאִלֵּ֑ם אֶל־דִּ֝֗ין כָּל־בְּנֵ֥י חֲלֽוֹף:	ἄνοιγε σὸν στόμα λόγῳ θεοῦ καὶ κρῖνε πάντας ὑγιῶς.
Speak out for those who cannot speak, for the rights of all the destitute.	Open your mouth with a divine word, and judge all fairly.

---

347 Rahlfs has ἄνομοι διελεύσονται ἀγαθά. However, based upon textual evidence, scholars such as de Lagarde, Barthélemy and de Waard have argued that οἱ δὲ ἄμωμοι διελοῦνται ἀγαθὰ represents the original Greek. See de Lagarde, *Anmerkungen*, 88; BHQ, 54*; Barthélemy, *Critique textuelle de l'Ancien Testament. Tome 5*, 763.

348 See DCH, vol. VIII, 319.

349 See GELS, 162–163; LEH, 149.

350 See HR, 315. LEH also notes that it is a stereotypical rendering of שַׁחַת See LEH, 149.

351 Fox argues that the LXX translator read בְּשְׁחוּתוֹ ('in his corruption') instead of בְּשְׁחוּתוֹ ('in his pit'). See Fox, *Proverbs*, 363. However, he fails to observe that שַׁחַת by διαφθορά was a common translation throughout the LXX corpus.

In Prov 31:8 there is a plus, i.e., θεοῦ, which is added by the translator to emphasise the divine provenance of the conveyed teachings in chapter 31.[352]

The phrase בְּנֵי חֲלוֹף, which contains the hapax in this verse, i.e., חֲלוֹף (meaning 'passing away, opposition, foolishness'),[353] is rendered in the LXX by the hapax ὑγιῶς ('soundly, fairly, by exercising sound mind').[354] In connection with ὑγιῶς, d'Hamonville refers to the attestation of ὑγιῶς κρίνειν in Plato's *Politeia* 409a.[355] However, based upon this resemblances, we cannot conclude any textual connection between LXX Proverbs and Plato's *Politeia*.[356] Moreover, no scholar has provided a decent explaining why the translator opted for ὑγιῶς as a rendering of בְּנֵי חֲלוֹף. Nonetheless, a possible solution might be found when looking at the LXX of the first stich of the next verse, i.e., 31:9:

LXX	NETS
ἄνοιγε σὸν στόμα καὶ κρῖνε δικαίως.	Open your mouth, and judge justly.

This verse is a literal translation of MT's פְּתַח־פִּיךָ שְׁפָט־צֶדֶק and has a strong resemblance with Prov 31:8. As can be observed, the adverbs ὑγιῶς and δικαίως rhyme, which is absent in the Hebrew. The translator, probably having trouble translating בְּנֵי חֲלוֹף must have rendered it by ὑγιῶς in order to create rhyme with the next verse where he opted for δικαίως as a translation of צֶדֶק. Thus, the translation of the hapax חֲלוֹף was, most likely, prompted by stylistic considerations.[357]

---

352 See Beeckman, "De Nomine Dei," 386. See also chapter 3.

353 See DCH, vol. III, 231. DCH does not give a cognate or derivative word for this hapax.

354 See GELS, 692; LEH, 625.

355 See d'Hamonville, *Les Proverbes*, 309.

356 See Fox, *Proverbs*, 392. Fox is correct in pointing out that d'Hamonville's observation does not explain the LXX rendering. De Waard, on the other hand, leaves the possibility of intertextuality open. See BHQ, 57*.

357 D'Hamonville points out the rhythmic character of the adverbs but does not conclude that the translator might have been prompted by stylistic motivations to render the hapax by ὑγιῶς. See d'Hamonville, *Les Proverbes*, 309. Tauberschmidt has indicated that by the addition of λόγῳ θεοῦ, the near-synonymous parallelism of 31:8 has been destroyed. However, although he indicates that the translator might have had the liberty to drop the parallelism due to the similarity between verse 8 and 9, he did not notice the obvious rhyme between the adverbs ὑγιῶς and δικαίως, contrary to d'Hamonville. See Tauberschmidt, *Secondary Parallelism*, 127.

WW עֲצָלוּת (Prov 31:27)

MT	LXX
צוֹפִיָּה הֲלִיכוֹת בֵּיתָהּ וְלֶחֶם עַצְלוּת לֹא תֹאכֵל׃	στεγναὶ διατριβαὶ οἴκων αὐτῆς, σῖτα δὲ ὀκνηρὰ οὐκ ἔφαγεν.
She looks well to the ways of her household, and does not eat the bread of idleness.	The way she ran her household was careful, and she did not eat the bread of idleness.

The last non-absolute hapax concerns the word עֲצְלוּת ('idleness,' > עָצֵל ['to be sluggish']).[358] The LXX has rendered it by ὀκνηρός ('idle, lazy, sluggish, slothful, habitually disinclined to work'),[359] an adjective only used in LXX Proverbs and Sirach. In Proverbs, it is always used as a translation of עָצֵל ('sluggish, lazy').[360] The LXX translator read עֲצָלוּתas a plural form of עָצֵל and, consequently, translated it by the plural form of ὀκνηρός, i.e., ὀκνηρὰ, which only occurs here in the LXX. Thus, the translator had no problem understanding and rendering the hapax עֲצָלוּת.

XX Conclusion

Having analysed the 52 Hebrew non-absolute hapax legomena and their Greek rendering in Proverbs, we can draw the following conclusions with regards to the translation technique of the LXX translator:

(a) As was the case for the absolute hapaxes, no hapax has been transliterated. Moreover, the majority of the hapaxes have been rendered by an adequate Greek equivalent. Often, these renderings are based upon an existing Hebrew word of the same root as the hapax (i.e., root-linked renderings) (9:13; 11:2.15; 12:18; 19:15; 21:8; 23:34; 25:18; 27:4.20.21; 28:10; 31:27). It must be noted that in two instances, i.e., 23:34 and 25:18, the translator read the Hebrew word *Vorlage* differently than MT. Nonetheless, he provided an adequate Greek equivalent for the word he read.

(b) Remarkably, in three instances (26:28; 27:3.21), the translator opted for a rare Greek word or Greek hapax to render the Hebrew non-absolute hapax. This is an indication that he did understand his Hebrew source text and had no difficulty in rendering those hapaxes when confronted with them;

---

358 See DCH, vol. VI, 533.
359 See GELS, 491–492; LEH, 432..
360 See HR, 985.

(c) Upon closer examination, four hapaxes cannot be labelled as a hapax although other scholars have labelled it as such. In three instances, the translator rendered the *qere* (1:27; 19:19) or *ketiv* (20:20) variant of the Hebrew word. In one instance, the so-called hapax also occurs elsewhere in the Hebrew Bible (8:22);

(d) For a vast number of hapaxes, the translator resorted to contextual exegesis when opting for a certain Greek variant (4:24; 8:6.18; 15:19; 16:26; 22:29; 23:2.29; 25:28);

(e) As have been observed by other scholars as well, the LXX translator often enhanced the poetic structure of his translation *vis-à-vis* MT. This can also be observed in the verses where a non-absolute hapax is attested. In several verses he enhanced the parallelistic structure of the Greek (4:24; 7:16.18; 12:18; 15:19; 16:27; 27:15), avoided repetition and opted for variation (7:18; 8:13) and introduced rhyme (17:22 [alliteration], 17:25; 31:8; 22:29 [assonance]);

(f) In some instances, the translator has applied metathesis in order to render the Hebrew hapax (15:19; 16:27; 23:28);

(g) In 23:7 the translator provided a double translation as a translation of the hapax;

(h) It has been observed that the LXX translator made some intertextual references to other LXX books when rendering his Hebrew hapax: 3:26 (LXX Psalms) and 23:2 (LXX Deuteronomy);

(i) In three instances, the translator explained or elaborated the image preserved in the Hebrew text (3:26; 4:24; 26:11). In 4:24, he even inserted one of his preferred dualisms, i.e., ἄδικος and δίκαιος;

(j) The translator rarely struggled to render a Hebrew non-absolute hapax. We have observed three verses wherein the translator might have had difficulties with the hapax: 23:2; 27:22 and 31:8. However, in these instances, he did manage to render the Hebrew into a decent Greek verse by applying contextual exegesis (23:2), inserting a politicising image (27:22) or creating rhyme (31:8);

(k) Two hapaxes have been misread by the LXX translator and thus rendered differently (11:2 and 22:21);

(l) Only in a few cases did the translator not render the Hebrew hapax. In 5:19 and 16:1 the non-rendering can be explained due to a diverging Hebrew *Vorlage*. For 17:22 he skipped the hapax in order to create rhyme and for 25:28 we concluded that he did not render the hapax based on the context of the verse.

2.2 The Greek rendering of Hebrew *hapax legomena* in LXX Job

As already noted in the introduction of this book, Verbeke has dedicated a whole dissertation on the Greek rendering of Hebrew *hapax legomena* in LXX Job. However, although her dissertation is entitled *Hebrew Hapax Legomena and their Greek Rendering in LXX Job*, it is misleading. In her work, she has only examined the hapaxes which are attested in the speeches of Job and God. Therefore, in order to make a decent comparison between the results of the Greek rendering of Hebrew *hapax legomena* in both books, the remaining hapaxes in Job need to be analysed as well. The parts of Job that still need to be examined are (1) the prologue (chapters 1-2), (2) the speeches of Eliphaz, Bildad, Zophar and Elihu aka Job's friends (chapters 4, 8, 11, 15, 18, 20, 21, 22, 25, 32-37) (3) and the epilogue (chapter 42).

In the following sections, we will first register the Hebrew *hapax legomena* and their Greek rendering in these parts of Job. Afterwards, their Greek rendering will be evaluated in order to draw conclusions with regard to the translation technique of the LXX translator of Job.

2.2.1 The registration of Hebrew *hapax legomena* in Job

2.2.1.1 Registration of Hebrew *hapax legomena* in Job according to Verbeke
In the parts of the book of Job we still need to analyse, Verbeke has recorded 53 *hapax legomena* in total:

Verse	Word	Lis	BW	Cas	Gr
2:8	גָּרַד	a	+	-	a
4:10	נָתַע	a	+	a	a
4:18	תָּהֳלָה	a	+	a	a
8:6	נְוֶה	na	-	-	-
8:14	יָקוֹט	a	-	-	na
8:16	רָטֹב	na	+	-	na
8:21	מלה	a	-	-	-
11:17	עוּף	a	-	-	-
11:20	מַפַּח	na	+	-	na
15:12	רזם	a	+	a	a
15:24	כִּידוֹר	a	+	a	na
15:27	פִּימָה	a	+	a	na

Verse	Word	Lis	BW	Cas	Gr
15:29	מִנְלֶה	a	+	a	a?[361]
15:31	שׁו	-	-	-	na
15:32	רען	na	+	a	na
18:2	קֵנֶץ	a	+	a	a
18:3	טמה	a	+	a	a
18:5	שָׁבִיב	a	+	-	na
18:10	מַלְכֹּדֶת	na	+	-	na
20:6	שִׂיא	na	+	-	na
20:18	יָגֵע	na	+	-	na
20:22	שָׂפֵק	na	+	a	na
20:25	גֵּוָה[362]	na	-	-	-
22:20	קִים	na	+	-	a
22:24	אוֹפִיר[363]	a	-	-	-
22:29	שַׁח	na	+	-	na
25:5	אהל	-	+	a	-
32:19	אוֹב	na	-[364]	-	-
33:7	אֶכֶף	na	+	-	na
33:9	חַף	na	+	a	na
33:16	מֹסָר	-	+	-	na
33:20	זהם	a	+	a	a
33:24	פדע	a	+	a	a
33:25	רטפש	a	+	a	a
34:8	חֶבְרָה	na	+	-	na
34:25	מַעְבָּד	na	+	-	na
34:36	אָבִי	na[365]	+	a	na

---

361 The *siglum* '?' is added by Greenspahn because he is not sure if it concerns an absolute hapax or not. See Greenspahn, *Hapax Legomena*, 185.

362 In Verbeke's list, גוה is mentioned, see Verbeke, "Hebrew Hapax Legomena," 116. However, it concerns the noun גֵּוָה.

363 This word is also attested unvocalised in Verbeke's list, see Verbeke, "Hebrew Hapax Legomena," 116.

364 Verbeke records nothing here, see Verbeke, "Hebrew Hapax Legomena," 117. However, when searching on the lemma in BibleWorks, multiple attestations can be found. Thus, BibleWorks does not regard this word as a hapax.

365 There is some doubt regarding אָבִי in 34:36. Greenspahn records it as non-absolute, Casanowicz has it in his list of absolute hapaxes and BibleWorks records it as a hapax. However, in

Verse	Word	Lis	BW	Cas	Gr
35:15	פַּשׁ	a	+	a	a
36:18	סֵפֶק	na	+	-	na
36:19	מַאֲמָץ	na	+	-	na
36:27	נֵטֶף	na	+	-	na
37:4	עקב	a	-	-	-
37:6	הוה	na	-	-	-
37:9	מְזָרִים	na	+	a	na
37:11	רִי	na	+	-	na
37:11	טרח	na	+	-	na
37:12	מְסִבָּה	-	+	-	na
37:16	מִפְלָאוֹת	na	+	-	na
37:16	מִפְלָשׂ	na	+	-	a
37:18	רָאִי	na	+	-	na
37:21	בָּהִיר	na	+	-	na
42:13	שִׁבְעָנָה	-	+	-	-
42:14	יְמִימָה [366]	-	-	-	na

2.2.1.2 Registration of Hebrew *hapax legomena* and their Greek rendering in Job

As we did for Proverbs above, the same rules-of-thumb will be applied to the hapaxes in the prologue and epilogue of Job as well as the speeches of Job's friends, in order to discern whether a certain word is a hapax and if so whether it can be considered an absolute or non-absolute hapax. On the basis of the first rule-of-thumb, which enables us to discern whether a certain word can be labelled a hapax or not, the following 11 words cannot be considered a hapax and will therefore not be analysed:

Verbeke's list, the attestation in Lisowsky is marked with a question mark ('?'). See Verbeke, "Hebrew Hapax Legomena," 118. This means that it is not sure whether it is mentioned or not. See Verbeke, "Hebrew Hapax Legomena," 76. In Lisowsky, the word is mentioned but without any biblical references. See Lisowsky, *Konkordanz*, 12. However, since Greenspahn labels it as a non-absolute against Casanowicz, the hapax will be considered a non-absolute hapax (see rule-of-thumb II).

366 Unvocalised in Verbeke's list, see Verbeke, "Hebrew Hapax Legomena," 119.

Verse	Word	Lis	BW	Cas	Gr
8:6	נֹוֶה	na	-	-	-
8:21	מִלָּה	a	-	-	-
11:17	עוּף	a	-	-	-
15:31	שָׁו	-	-	-	na
20:25	גֵּוָה	na	-	-	-
22:24	אוֹפִיר	a	-	-	-
32:19	אוֹב	na	-	-	-
37:4	עָקַב	a	-	-	-
37:6	הֹוֵה	na	-	-	-
42:13	שִׁבְעָנָה	-	+	-	-
42:14	יְמִימָה [367]	-	-	-	na

Moreover, since we are only interested in the translational activity of the LXX translator, verses which are part of the asterisked material in the Greek text, indicated by the *siglum* '⁂' in Ziegler's edition of the Greek text of Job, will not be analysed because the renderings in those verses do not belong to the activity of the original translator of the book.[368] Those verses are the following (10 in total, 11 hapaxes):

Verse	MT	LXX	DSS
15:27	פִּימָה	⁂	/
18:10	מַלְכֹּדֶת	⁂	/
22:20	קִים	⁂	*lacuna* (11QtgJob)
22:29	שַׁח	⁂	/
35:15	פַּשׁ	⁂	*lacuna* (11QtgJob)
36:19	מַאֲמָץ	⁂	מאמצי (4QJob[a])

---

367 Unvocalised in Verbeke's list, see Verbeke, "Hebrew Hapax Legomena," 119.

368 Some scholars have failed to distinguish the asterisked material from the OG text. See Claude E. Cox, "Some Things Biblical Scholars Should Know about the Septuagint," *Restoration Quarterly* 56 (2014): 85–98, 88–89. For the delimitation of the asterisked material, the following works have been consulted: Joseph Ziegler, *Job*, Septuaginta. Vetus Testamentum Graecum. Auctoritate Academiae Scientiarum Gottingensis editum XI.4 (Göttingen: Vandenhoeck & Ruprecht, 1982); Peter J. Gentry, *The Asterisked Materials in the Greek Job*, SBLSCS 38 (Atlanta, GA: Scholars Press, 1995), see list p. 31. Peter Gentry's work presents an updated and corrected list of the asterisked material of Ziegler's text.

Verse	MT LXX	DSS
37:11	רִי ※	בהון (11QtgJob)
37:11	טרח ※	ימרק (11QtgJob)
37:12	מְסִבָּה ※	אמר ישמעון לה (11QtgJob)
37:18	רְאִי ※	כמח[זיה (11QtgJob)
37:21	בָּהִיר ※	/

In the next section, the remaining hapaxes and their Greek rendering will be registered. For MT BHS has been used since BHQ of Job, which is being prepared by Robert Althann, has not been published yet.[369] For the LXX text the Göttingen edition prepared by Ziegler has been consulted.[370] Where applicable, the attestations in the Qumran scrolls (DSS) are attested as well.[371] For the Qumran Scrolls the *siglum* '/' indicates that the verse is not attested in DSS. Whenever a certain verse is attested in the manuscript, but the word is not attested due to *lacunae* in the manuscript, it is indicated by '*lacuna*'.

A Registration of absolute Hebrew *hapax legomena* and their Greek rendering in Job

Based upon the rules-of-thumb presented above and having discarded the verses which belong to the asterisked material in the Greek text of Job, there are 12 Hebrew absolute *hapax legomena* in the speeches of Job's friends, one in the prologue and none in the epilogue. This leaves us with 13 absolute *hapax legomena*, that will be evaluated in here:

---

369 See Karl Elliger *et al.*, *Biblia Hebraica Stuttgartensia* (Stuttgart: Deutsche Bibelstiftung, ⁵1977).

370 See Ziegler, *Job*.

371 The book of Job is attested in 2QJob, 4QPaleoJob[c], 4QJob[a] and 4QJob[b], see Maurice Baillet, Józef T. Millik and Roland de Vaux, ed., *Les 'petites grottes' de Qumrân*, DJD III (Oxford: Clarendon Press, 1962), 71; Patrick W. Skehan, Eeugene Ulrich and Judith E. Sanderson, ed., *Qumran Cave 4 IV. Palaeo-Hebrew and Greek Biblical Manuscripts*, DJD IX (Oxford: Clarendon Press, 1992), 155–167; Eugene Ulrich *et al.*, ed., *Qumran Cave 4 XI. Psalms to Chronicles*, DJD XVI (Oxford: Clarendon Press, 2000), 171–180. A Targum version of Job (4QtgJob and11QtgJob) has also been found. See Józef T. Milik, *Qumrân grotte 4 II. Tefillin, Mezuzot et Targums (4Q128-4Q157)*, DJD VI (Oxford: Clarendon Press, 1977), 90 and Johannes P. M. van der Ploeg and Adam S. van der Woude, ed., *Le Targum de Job de la grotte xi de Qumrân* (Leiden: Brill, 1971); Florentino García Martínez, Eibert Tigchelaar and Adam S. van der Woude, ed., *Qumran Cave 11 II. 11Q2–18, 11Q20–31*, DJD XXIII (Oxford: Clarendon Press, 1998), 79–180.

Verse	MT	LXX	DSS
2:8	גֵּרֶד	ξύω	/
4:10	נִתָּע	σβέννυμι	/
4:18	תָּהֳלָה	σκολιός	*lacuna* (4QtgJob [4Q157])
15:12	רֵזַם	ἐπιφέρω	/
15:24	כִּידוֹר	πίπτω	/
15:29	מִנְלֵה	σκιά	/
18:2	קֵנֶץ	οὐ(?) παύω	סוף (11QtgJob)
18:3	טמה	σιωπάω	דמינא (11QtgJob)
25:5	אהל	ἐπιφαύσκω	זכי[(11QtgJob)
33:20	זהם	οὐ μὴ δύνηται προσδέξασθαι	/
33:24	פדע	/	פצהי (11QtgJob)/*lacuna* (4QJob^a [4Q99])
33:25	רטפש	ἀπαλύνω	בשרו (4QJob^a [4Q99])/*lacuna* (11QtgJob)
37:16	מִפְלֵשׂ	διάκρισις	להלבש{ו}א (11QtgJob)

B Registration of non-absolute Hebrew *hapax legomena* and their Greek rendering in Job

Based upon the rules-of-thumb and leaving out the verses which belong to the asterisked material in the Greek text of Job, there are 18 non-absolute *hapax legomena* in the speeches of Job's friends and none in the prologue or epilogue of Job. This leaves us with 18 Hebrew non-absolute hapaxes which will be evaluated in order to examine the translation technique of the LXX translator of Job:

Verse	MT	LXX	DSS
8:14	יָקוֹט	ἀοίκητος ἔσται?	/
8:16	רָטֹב	ὑγρός	*lacuna* (4QJob^b)
11:20	מַפָּח	ἀπώλεια	/
15:32	רַעֲנָן	πυκάζω	/
18:5	שָׁבִיב	φλόξ	/
20:6	שִׂיא	αὐτοῦ τὰ δῶρα	*lacuna* (11QtgJob)
20:18	יָגָע	κοπιάω	/
20:22	שֶׂפֶק	πληρόω	/
33:7	אֶכֶף	χείρ	*lacuna* (11QtgJob)
33:9	חַף	ἄμεμπτος	ונקא[א (11QtgJob)

Verse	MT	LXX	DSS
33:16	מוֹסָר	ἐν εἴδεσιν φόβου τοιούτοις	]רה[(11QtgJob)
34:8	חֶבְרָה	κοινωνέω	ומתחבר (11QtgJob)
34:25	מַעֲבָד	ἔργον	עבדהון (11QtgJob)
34:36	אָבִי	οὐ μὴν δὲ ἀλλά	/
36:18	סֵפֶק	δι' ἀσέβειαν	lacuna (4QJobᵃ)
36:27	נֵטֶף	σταγών	lacuna (4QJobᵃ)
37:9	מְזָרִים	ἀκρωτήριον	/
37:16	מִפְלָאוֹת	ἐξαίσιος	גבורה (11QtgJob)

2.2.2 The evaluation of the Greek rendering of Hebrew absolute *hapax legomena* in Job

Now that we have registered the Hebrew *hapax legomena* and their Greek rendering in the prologue, speeches of Job's friends and epilogue, we will evaluate their Greek rendering. First all the absolute hapaxes will be evaluate. Afterwards, the non-absolute hapaxes will be examined and evaluated.

2.2.2.1 Evaluation of the Greek rendering of Hebrew absolute *hapax legomena* in Job

In this section, the registered 13 absolute *hapax legomena* and their Greek rendering in LXX Job will be evaluated.

A גרד (Job 2:8)

MT	LXX
וַיִּקַּח־לוֹ חֶרֶשׂ לְהִתְגָּרֵד בּוֹ וְהוּא יֹשֵׁב בְּתוֹךְ־הָאֵפֶר:	καὶ ἔλαβεν ὄστρακον, ἵνα τὸν ἰχῶρα ξύῃ, καὶ ἐκάθητο ἐπὶ τῆς κοπρίας ἔξω τῆς πόλεως.
He took a potsherd with which to scrape himself, and sat among the ashes.[372]	And he took a potsherd, so that he could scrape away the pus, and sat on the rubbish heap outside the city.[373]

---

372 English translation of Hebrew text taken from NRSV.
373 English translation of the LXX taken from NETS. The LXX version of Job has been translated by Claude C. E. Cox, "Iob," in *A New English Translation of the Septuagint. And the Other*

The Hebrew hapax גרד denotes 'to be bare, to scratch oneself.'[374] The word also occurs in 11QT 49,12 and also in Rabbinic Hebrew, Aramaic, Syriac and Arabic.[375] In the LXX it is rendered by ξύω ('to scrape away'),[376] which only occurs in LXX Job 2:8 and 7:5. In the latter it is used as a translation of רגע ('to stop, to crust over') but the translator might have read גרע ('to omit, to diminish').[377] The rendering of גרד by ξύω is an adequate rendering and is unproblematic. Noteworthy, in connection with ξύω, the LXX translator has added ἰχώρ ('pus') in both 2:8 and 7:5 to enhance the morbidity of the image which is absent in MT.

B נתע (Job 4:10)

MT	LXX
שַׁאֲגַת אַרְיֵה וְקוֹל שָׁחַל וְשִׁנֵּי כְפִירִים נִתָּעוּ׃	σθένος λέοντος φωνὴ δὲ λεαίνης γαυρίαμα δὲ δρακόντων ἐσβέσθη.
The roar of the lion, the voice of the fierce lion, and the teeth of the young lions are broken.	The strength of the lion and the voice of the lioness and the pride of dragons was extinguished.

The LXX presents a different reading than MT in this verse. Noteworthy is the rendering of כְּפִיר by δράκων.[378] However, what is of interest here, is the rendering of the Hebrew hapax נתע by the Greek lexeme σβέννυμι ('to quench, to put out, to extinguish, to cause or cease burning or being aflame').[379] Scholars agree that נתע is an Aramaic form of the verb נתץ ('to tear down,' 'to break up,' 'to

Greek Translations Traditionally Included under That Title, ed. Albert Pietersma and Benjamin G. Wright (New York, NY ── Oxford: Oxford University Press, 2007), 667–696.

374 See DCH, vol. II, 374.

375 See DCH, vol. II, 374; Yigael Yadin, *The Temple Scroll. Volume Two: Text and Commentary* (Jerusalem: The Israel Exploration Society – The Institute of Archaeology of the Hebrew University of Jerusalem – The Shrine of the Book, 1983), 215; Edouard Dhorme, *A Commentary on the Book of Job* (London: Thomas Nelson & Sons, 1967), 18–19; Choon-Leong Seow, *Job 1-21. Interpretation and Commentary*, Illuminations, (Grand Rapids, MI – Cambridge: Eerdmans, 2013), 304. Yigael Yadin asserts that the verb has a different meaning in the Temple Scroll than it has in the Bible. However, he also translates it by 'to scrape.' Thus, it does not have another meaning than in Job 2:8. Another connotation cannot be excluded. See Yadin, *The Temple Scroll. Volume Two*, 215.

376 See GELS, 482; LEH, 425.

377 See Dhorme, A Commentary on the Book of Job, 100.

378 See Beeckman, "Animalia in Libro Iob," 263–266.

379 See GELS, 618; LEH, 549.

demolish').[380] Choon-Leong Seow classifies it among the Hebrew lexemes that have a root starting with נת, indicating 'elimination or removal.'[381] Therefore, the LXX's rendering of σβέννυμι, also denoting elimination or extinguishing, seems to be an adequate rendering. This lexeme is used throughout LXX Job to translate different Hebrew lexemes, i.e., עלל (16:15), דעך (18:5.6; 21:17), נבא (30:8), ספק (34:26) and כנע (40:12). According to Joseph Ziegler,[382] σβέννυμι is a favourite lexeme of LXX Job to render obscure or difficult Hebrew lexemes.[383] However, in this case, it seems that the LXX translator has understood the general meaning of the Hebrew hapax.

C   תׇּהֳלָה (Job 4:18)

MT	LXX	4QtgJob
הֵן בַּעֲבָדָיו לֹא יַאֲמִין וּבְמַלְאָכָיו יָשִׂים תׇּהֳלָה:	εἰ κατὰ παίδων αὐτοῦ οὐ πιστεύει κατὰ δὲ ἀγγέλων αὐτοῦ σκολιόν τι ἐπενόησεν.	ובמלאכו]הי ישים
Even in his servants he puts no trust, and his angels he charges with error.	Whether he believes charges against his servants, who knows, but he took note of any crookedness in his angels.	and against [his] angels [he charges[384]

The hapax תׇּהֳלָה ('error') is rendered by the Greek σκολιός ('not straight, crooked, bent') in this verse.[385] It is not preserved in 4QtgJob. Several scholars think that the hapax stems from the root הלל ('be foolish').[386] Apparently, σ' has understood it this way and rendered it by ματαιότητα (> ματαιότης; 'folly, vanity,

---

380 See Georg Beer, *Der Text des Buches Job* (Marburg: N. G. Elwertsche Verlagsbuchandlung, 1897), 47; BDB, 683; Seow, *Job 1-21*, 397.
381 See Seow, *Job 1-21*, 397.
382 See Joseph Ziegler, *Der textkritische Wert der Septuaginta des Buches Job*, Miscellaneis Biblicis II (Pontifico Instituto Biblico: Rome, 1934), 277–296, 284.
383 See also Verbeke, "Hebrew Hapax Legomena," 254.
384 Translated from the French translation of Émile Puech: 'et à [ses] anges[*Il impute*." Émile Puech, "Le targum de Job de la grotte 4: 4Q157 = 4QtgJob," *Revue de Qumran* 32.1 (2020): 135–141, 138.
385 See DCH, vol. VIII, 549; GELS, 626; LEH, 558.
386 Beer, *Der Text des Buches Job*, 27; Dhorme, *A Commentary on the Book of Job*, 53; DCH, vol. VIII, 594. The root הלל entails multiple meanings. The most commonly known is 'to sing, to praise, to shout exultingly' but it can also mean 'to act like a madman, folly' and 'to begin to shine' (see Job 25:5 below) . See KBL, 235–236.

uselessness'),[387] a lexeme used abundantly in both LXX Psalms and Ecclesiastes and once in Proverbs. If those scholars are correct, then תְּהֳלָה must be regarded as a non-absolute *hapax legomenon* instead of an absolute hapax although Greenspahn, Casanowicz and Lisowsky all agree that it is an absolute hapax.[388]

When the hapax can be understood as a derivative from the root הלל, the rendering of σ′ reflects a more adequate translation than LXX's σκολιός. Nonetheless, the meaning of σκολιός pertains to the same semantic field as הלל, since crookedness can be considered a consequence of folly.[389] Moreover, the LXX translator has rendered the second colon of this verse rather literally, providing a Greek equivalent for each Hebrew lexeme and thus more or less quantitively representing the Hebrew:

MT	LXX
וּבְמַלְאָכָיו	δὲ ἀγγέλων αὐτοῦ
יָשִׂים	ἐπενόησεν
תָּהֳלָה	σκολιόν τι

The addition of the indefinite neutral pronoun τί ('any') which accompanies σκολιόν, is an addition by the LXX translator to emphasise that no single error or any crooked ways of God's angels are left unnoticed. By doing so, the LXX translation seems to stress the omniscience of God.[390]

D   רֹזֵם (Job 15:12)

MT	LXX
מַה־יִּקָּחֲךָ לִבֶּךָ וּמַה־יִּרְזְמוּן עֵינֶיךָ:	τί ἐτόλμησεν ἡ καρδία σου ἢ τί ἐπήνεγκαν οἱ ὀφθαλμοί σου.

---

387 See Field, Origenis Hexaplorum (Tom. II), 11.
388 See Verbeke, "Hebrew Hapax Legomena," 114.
389 See Claude E. Cox, *Iob*, SBLCS (forthcoming). I would like to express my gratitude to Claude E. Cox for giving me access to his unpublished manuscript of his SBL commentary on LXX Job.
390 That the LXX translator of Job made some theological nuances with respect to the figure of God is also observed by Cook. See Cook and van der Kooij, *Law, Prophets, and Wisdom*, 182–183.

MT	LXX
Why does your heart carry you away, and why do your eyes flash.	What did your heart dare, or what did your eyes set themselves upon.

The LXX represents the Hebrew quantitively in this verse. The Hebrew hapax רֹזם ('to wink, to fail, to become weak') is rendered here by the Greek verb ἐπιφέρω ('to bring, to put, to lay upon, to aim at').[391] The verb רֹזם has possibly been derived from the Aramaic verb רמז ('to indicate [through a physical motion], signal, to wink').[392] Edouard Paul Dhorme has postulated the retroversion ירומון as being the Hebrew *Vorlage* of the LXX.[393] However, Seow argues that this retroversion is difficult to explain when taking all the manuscript evidence into account.[394] He thinks that the LXX translator understood the Hebrew as 'to stare' (cognate to the Arabic *razama*).[395] Thus, given Seow's argumentation and considering the LXX translator's quantitative representation in this verse, it is reasonable to assume that the LXX translator has rendered the Hebrew hapax with a corresponding Greek equivalent, i.e., ἐπιφέρω.

E   כִּידוֹר (Job 15:24)

MT	LXX
יְבַעֲתֻהוּ צַר וּמְצוּקָה תִּתְקְפֵהוּ כְּמֶלֶךְ עָתִיד לַכִּידוֹר׃	ἀνάγκη δὲ καὶ θλῖψις αὐτὸν καθέξει ὥσπερ στρατηγὸς πρωτοστάτης πίπτων.
Distress and anguish terrify them; they prevail against them, like a king prepared for battle.	And distress and anguish will take hold of him; he will be like a general falling in the front rank.

So far, no one has given a well-argued answer to the question why the translator has opted for πίπτω ('to move downward, to fall defeated or exhausted in battle, to collapse, to win notice, to perish') as a rendering of כִּידוֹר ('attack').[396] The hapax might have an affiliation with the Syriac (*kdr*, 'to disturb'), Akkadian

---

391 See DCH, vol. IV, 391; GELS, 286; LEH, 238.
392 See BDB, 931.
393 See Dhorme, A Commentary on the Book of Job, 212–213.
394 See Seow, *Job 1-21*, 714.
395 See Seow, *Job 1-21*, 714.
396 See DCH, vol. VII, 459; GELS, 558–559; LEH, 493.

(*kadāru*, 'to be overbearing, arrogant, spirited;' *kadru*, 'aggressive;' *kadrūtu*, 'aggressiveness') or Arabic (*kadara*, 'to throw down, to disturb, afflict, distress').[397] Therefore, Seow concludes that the term "should probably be understood to mean 'aggression, attack, combat'."[398] Claude E. Cox argues that the LXX translator has interpreted the *hapax* in the same line of thought as the (Rabbinic) Targum's interpretation, *i.e.* 'for battle', 'to die in battle.'[399]

In MT, distress and anguish are the subject of this verse. They are the ones that prevail against the wicked/impious like a king ready for battle. However, in contrast to MT, the subject of the verse in the LXX remains the impious as introduced at the beginning of the cluster (15:20). Thus, although the LXX renders the verse differently and perhaps even struggled to translate the hapax, it seems that he has opted for a rendering that was fitting with the context of the verse. This kind of contextual rendering is a technique favoured by the LXX translator to render Hebrew *hapax legomena*, as has been demonstrated by Verbeke in her dissertation.[400]

F   מִנְלֶה (Job 15:29)

MT	LXX
לֹא־יֶעְשַׁר וְלֹא־יָקוּם חֵילוֹ וְלֹא־יִטֶּה לָאָרֶץ מִנְלָם׃	οὔτε μὴ πλουτισθῇ οὔτε μὴ μείνῃ αὐτοῦ τὰ ὑπάρχοντα οὐ μὴ βάλῃ ἐπὶ τὴν γῆν σκιάν.
They will not be rich, and their wealth will not endure, nor will they strike root in the earth.	Neither shall he ever become rich, nor shall his possessions last. He shall not cast a shadow upon the ground.

The LXX renders the hapax מִנְלֶה ('acquisition,' > נלה 'to obtain') by the Greek noun σκιά ('shade, shadow, greater or smaller area darkened by an object blocking the light, darkness').[401] According to Seow, מִנְלֶה either means 'possession' or 'root.'[402] Within the context of the verse in which there is an emphasis on plant

397 See Seow, *Job 1-21*, 719.
398 eow, *Job 1-21*, 719. See also BDB, 461; DCH, vol. IV, 391.
399 See Cox, *Iob* (forthcoming). The Aramaic reads: 'Distress and anguish terrify him; they *surround* him like a king who is ready for *the bier.*' Some variants read '... like one who is ready *to be surrounded by legions*' (Original italicisation). See Céline Mangan, *The Targum of Job*, The Aramaic Bible 15 (Edinburgh: T&T Clark, 1991), 47.
400 See Verbeke, "Hebrew Hapax Legomena," 390–394.
401 See DCH, vol. V, 354; GELS, 624; LEH, 556.
402 See Seow, *Job 1-21*, 722–723.

metaphors,[403] the translation of 'roots' seems to make more sense. Looking at the LXX, one might think that the metaphorical language pertaining to plants in the Hebrew text of 15:28-35 has not been preserved in the LXX verse under discussion. However, the LXX does preserve the metaphor, since a tree can cast a shadow upon the ground (this has been interpreted as such by Olympiodorus (Diaconus) in his *Commentarii in Job*).[404] Gerleman asserts that the translator has been influenced by the ancient tradition that the dead do not cast any shadow, which is attested in the writings of Plutarch.[405]

Moreover, it seems that the LXX translator has tried to fit this verse into the context of the first colon of the next verse (15:30) which reads:

MT	LXX
לֹא־יָסוּר ׀ מִנִּי־חֹשֶׁךְ	οὐδὲ μὴ ἐκφύγη τὸ σκότος.
They will not escape from darkness.	Nor shall he escape darkness.

In this verse, the noun σκότος ('darkness') is used as a rendering of חֹשֶׁךְ ('darkness'). Both lexemes, σκότος and σκιά, pertain to the same semantic domain and are even orthographically closely linked to one another. Moreover, σκότος and σκιά often appear as a word pair in the LXX in general (e.g., Ps 106(MT 107):10.14; Od 9:79; Jer 13:16) and even occurs three times in LXX Job (3:5; 12:22 and 28:3). Thus, the choice to render the obscure word מִנְלֶה by the Greek lexeme σκιά might have stemmed from the immediate context of 15:29, i.e., 15:30, in order to create the word pair σκότος/σκιά. Once more, as was the case with 15:24 (see above), the Hebrew hapax has been rendered by means of contextual exegesis. This has been generally overlooked by commentators.

G קֶנֶץ (Job 18:2)

MT	LXX	11QtgJob
עַד־אָנָה ׀ תְּשִׂימוּן קִנְצֵי לְמִלִּין תָּבִינוּ וְאַחַר נְדַבֵּר׃	μέχρι τίνος οὐ παύσῃ ἐπίσχες ἵνα καὶ αὐτοὶ λαλήσωμεν.	עד אמת[י תשוא סוף למלא]

403 See, e.g., Johan de Joode, Metaphorical Landscapes and the Theology of the Book of Job. An Analysis of Job's Spatial Metaphors, VTS 179 (Leiden – Boston, MA: Brill, 2018), 101–102.
404 See Ursulina Hagedorn and Dieter Hagedorn, ed., *Olympiodor, Diakon von Alexandria – Kommentar zu Iob*, PTS 24 (Berlin: De Gruyter, 1984), 142–143.
405 See Gerleman, *Job*, 38–39.

MT	LXX	11QtgJob
How long will you hunt for words? Consider, and then we shall speak.	How long before you stop? Hold back, so that we too can speak.	[Whe]n will you stop speaking? [[406]

The hapax under discussion is קֵנֶץ. Commentators have offered different transla-tions for this word, e.g., 'fetters, bonds, shackles,'[407] 'traps, snares,'[408] and 'end.'[409] 11QtgJob has סוף ('stop') for MT's קֵנֶץ. Moreover, the noun קֵנֶץ can "be regarded as an equivalent of קץ" ('end').[410] Taking this into account, it is highly plausible that the hapax indeed means 'end' or 'stop.'

The editors of DJD XXIII note that παύσῃ is LXX's rendering of 11QtgJob's תשוא and MT's תְּשִׂימָוּן (> שׂים ['to set, to put']).[411] However, it seems that the LXX translator has opted to render וֻן קִנְצֵי-תְשִׂימ by οὐ παύσῃ. The translation of the first stich in Greek reads (literally): 'How long will you not stop?,' a question from Bildad following the extensive speech of Job, requesition him to stop speak-ing so that Job's friends can say something as well. It is hard to discern whether the translator rendered קֵנֶץ or שׂים by παύσῃ. Nevertheless, given the fact that תְּשִׂימָוּן קִנְצֵי denotes 'to put a stop,' the translator's choice to render it with παύω ('to stop') offers a very adequate rendering.

H טמה **(Job 18:3)**

MT	LXX	11QtgJob
מַדּוּעַ נֶחְשַׁבְנוּ כַבְּהֵמָה נִטְמִינוּ בְּעֵינֵיכֶם:	διὰ τί ὥσπερ τετράποδα σεσιωπήκαμεν ἐναντίον σου.	לב[עירא דמינא]
Why are we counted as cat-tle? Why are we stupid in your sight?	Why have we, like quadrupeds, been silent before you?	[] do we resemble [ca]ttle? [

406 Translation of 11QtgJob taken from DJD XXIII, 79–180.
407 See Dhorme, A Commentary on the Book of Job, 257.
408 See Albert Schultens, *Liber Jobi: cum nova versione ad Hebraeum fontem et commentario perpetuo* (Lugduni Batavorum: apud J. Lusac, 1737), 435 [Lat. *laqueus*]; BDB, 890.
409 See KBL, 846; Seow, *Job 1-21*, 779, see 779–780 for a full discussion.
410 Dhorme, *A Commentary on the Book of Job*, 257; see also KBL, 844; DCH, vol. VII, 271.
411 See DJD XXIII, 91.

In Job 18:3, the Greek σιωπάω ('to keep quiet, not speaking, to cease, to fail, to be silent') for the Hebrew hapax טמה ('to be impure, to be regarded as unclean') of MT can be explained on the basis of the fragmentary attestation of this verse in 11QtgJob.[412] 11QtgJob attests דמינא, which reflects a form of the verb דמה ('to resemble').[413] Next to the meaning 'to resemble, to be like,' the verb דמה can also denote 'be silent, still.'[414] Moreover, the LXX translator of Job uses σιωπάω in 29:21 and 30:27 to render the Hebrew דמם, which is a parallel form of דמה.[415] Given the 11QtgJob fragment, the Hebrew *Vorlage* of the LXX probably had a reading that preserved a form of דמה whereby the LXX translator interpreted as denoting 'be silent, still.'

Thus, it seems that the LXX translator offers an adequate rendering of the Hebrew verb that was attested in his *Vorlage*, i.e., דמה, which is attested in MT as טמה. How this specific reading of MT came about reaches beyond the scope of this research, since we are solely interested in the LXX translator's attitude towards his parent text.

I   אהל (Job 25:5)

MT	LXX	11QtgJob
הֶן עַד־יָרֵחַ וְלֹא יַאֲהִיל וְכוֹכָבִים לֹא־ זַכּוּ בְעֵינָיו:	εἰ σελήνῃ συντάσσει καὶ οὐκ ἐπιφαύσκει ἄστρα δὲ οὐ καθαρὰ ἐναντίον αὐτοῦ.	[זכי וכוכביא לא]
If even the moon is not bright and the stars are not pure in his sight.	If he instructs the moon, then it does not shine, and the stars are not pure before him.	[] pure, and the stars are not [

The Hebrew hapax אהל in Job 25:5 is to be understood as a derivative of the Hebrew root הלל ('to shine').[416] Just as in Job 31:26 and 41:10, the LXX translator rendered this verb with ἐπιφαύσκω ('to shine out, to emit light and be bright'),[417] which only occurs in the LXX of Job (in the New Testament, it is only used once, namely in Eph 5:14), thus providing an adequate translation. Since this hapax

---

412 See DCH, vol. III, 371; GELS, 622; LEH, 554.
413 See DJD XXIII, 91.
414 See KBL, 213; BDB, 199.
415 See KBL, 213.
416 See Dhorme, *A Commentary on the Book of Job*, 369; BDB, 14; DCH, vol. I, 142.
417 See GELS, 286; LEH, 238.

might be linked to an existing Hebrew root, we cannot label it as an absolute *hapax legomenon* (as is the case with 4:18, see above).[418]

J   זהם (Job 33:20)

MT	LXX
וְזִהֲמַתּוּ חַיָּתוֹ לָחֶם וְנַפְשׁוֹ מַאֲכַל תַּאֲוָה:	πᾶν δὲ βρωτὸν σίτου οὐ μὴ δύνηται προσδέξασθαι.
So that their lives loathe bread, and their appetites dainty food.	And he shall not be able to take any edible bit of food.

The LXX only attests the first stich of verse 33:20. Stich b, i.e., καὶ ἡ ψυχὴ αὐτοῦ βρῶσιν ἐπιθυμήσει, is marked with an asterisk and is not part of OG.

The Greek text of the LXX offers a completely different translation of the Hebrew text attested in MT. Concerning the hapax under examination, i.e., זהם (which means 'be foul, loathsome, to abhor', from the Aramaic זהים 'foul'),[419] Dhorme and Georg Beer argue that the Hebrew text originally read זְהֵמָה instead of זְהֲמַתּוּ.[420] Nonetheless, the LXX rendering does not provide an exact quantitative representation of the Hebrew of MT, but rather a paraphrastic one since the hapax in 33:20 is represented by the phrase οὐ μὴ δύνηται προσδέξασθαι (he will not be able to take/receive). If the translator paraphrased the Hebrew, he understood the hapax as 'something that cannot be eaten.' The negative connotation of זהם is thereby represented by the construction οὐ μὴ. However, it is hard to tell whether the LXX translator has provided a paraphrastic rendering of his Hebrew *Vorlage* which might have resembled MT or whether his *Vorlage* has actually differed from MT.

---

418 The authors that worked on the registration of hapaxes in the Hebrew Bible do not agree whether אהל is a hapax or not. Only BibleWorks and Casanowicz label it as such (the latter labels it as an absolute hapax. See Verbeke, "Hebrew Hapax Legomena," 117.
419 See BDB, 263; DCH, vol. III, 93.
420 See Dhorme, A Commentary on the Book of Job, 498; Beer, Der Text des Buches Job, 211.

K פדע (Job 33:24)

MT	LXX	11QtgJob	4QJob[a]
וַיְחֻנֶּנּוּ וַיֹּאמֶר פְּדָעֵהוּ מֵרֶדֶת שַׁחַת מָצָאתִי כֹפֶר:	ἀνθέξεται τοῦ μὴ πεσεῖν αὐτὸν εἰς θάνατον ἀνανεώσει δὲ αὐτοῦ τὸ σῶμα ὥσπερ ἀλοιφὴν ἐπὶ τοίχου τὰ δὲ ὀστᾶ αὐτοῦ ἐμπλήσει μυελοῦ.	ת] לא[חב מן פצהי ויאמר אשה ישנקנה ויתמלין גרמוהי מוח]	פדעהו [מר]מ[ויא וגננ]ויח מצאתי שחת מרדת כפר]
And he is gracious to that person, and says, 'Deliver him from going down into the Pit; I have found a ransom.	He will provide support so that he does not fall into death and renew his body like paint does a wall and fill his bones with marrow.	And he will say: 'Save him from ha[rm] of fire strangles him. And [his bones] will be filled [with mar- row.]	And he is gracious to that person, and says, 'Deliver him from going down into the Pit; I have found a ransom.

According to Seow, the Hebrew hapax פדע should be read as פרע ('to loose, to free' and also possibly 'ransom'), since this is attested in MSS[Kenn 206,454] and because the *dalet* and *reš* were "graphically similar [...] in the paleo-Hebrew script."[421] The hapax is attested in MT; in 4QJob[a] there is a *lacuna*. 11QtgJob, on the other hand, records פצהי which means 'to deliver, to save.'[422] According to the editors of DJD, this reading is based upon the reading of MT's פדעהו as פדהו.[423]

The LXX provides a completely different reading from MT. One might think that the translator has elaborated this verse, since the Hebrew text is considerably shorter than the Greek one. However, the suggestion of the editors of DJD that 11QtgJob probably lacks two hemistichs that are missing in MT, implies that it might have reflected the Hebrew *Vorlage* of the LXX translator.[424] Even if this is the case, the LXX does not provide a rendering for פדעהו (MT) or פדהו

---

421 Choon-Leong Seow, "Putative Hapax Legomena in the Book of Job," in Studien zur hebrä- ischen Bibel und ihrer Nachgeschichte. Beiträge der 32. Internationalen Ökumenischen Konfe- renz der Hebräischlehrenden, Frankfurt a.m. 2009, ed. Johannes F. Diehl and Markus Witte, KUSATU 12.13 (Kamen: Hartmut Spenner, 2011), 145–182, 168.
422 DCH and BDB translate פדע by 'deliver.' See DCH, vol. VI, 655; BDB, 804.
423 See DJD XXIII, 132. See also Homer Heater, *A Septuagint Translation Technique in the Book of Job*, CBQMS 11 (Washington, DC: The Catholic Biblical Association of America, 1982), 105.
424 See DJD XXIII, 132.

(11QtgJob).[425] In this verse, it seems that the LXX translator has ignored the hapax (perhaps because he did not know its meaning). Instead, he has elaborated on the negative image of flesh and bones that is introduced in 33:21 and contrasted it with a positive image in 33:24b:

33:21 (LXX)	33:24b (LXX)
ἕως ἂν σαπῶσιν αὐτοῦ αἱ σάρκες καὶ ἀποδείξῃ τὰ ὀστᾶ αὐτοῦ κενά.	δὲ αὐτοῦ τὸ σῶμα ὥσπερ ἀλοιφὴν ἐπὶ τοίχου τὰ δὲ ὀστᾶ αὐτοῦ ἐμπλήσει μυελοῦ.
Until his flesh rots and he shows his bones to be bare.	And renew his body like paint does a wall and fill his bones with marrow.

This contrasting elaboration of the image of the renewed body and bones is absent in MT's version of 33:24.

L   רטפש (Job 33:25)

MT	LXX	11QtgJob	4QJob^a
רֻטֲפַשׁ בְּשָׂרוֹ מִנֹּעַר יָשׁוּב לִימֵי עֲלוּמָיו:	ἀπαλυνεῖ δὲ αὐτοῦ τὰς σάρκας ὥσπερ νηπίου ἀποκαταστήσει δὲ αὐτὸν ἀνδρωθέντα ἐν ἀνθρώποις.	מן[עולים ותב ליומי עלימ]ותה	[ ] בשרו מנער] ישוב לימי עלומין[
Let his flesh become fresh with youth; let him return to the days of his youthful vigor."	And will make his flesh soft like an infant's and restore him full-grown among people.	] than that of a youth, and he will return to the days of [his] you[th.	[ ] his flesh become fresh with youth; [let him return to the days of his youthful vigor."]

In 4QJob^a, the last letters of the first word are attested, although they are barely readable. The editors of DJD XVI suggest that it cannot be a *šin*, but rather a *reš-waw* construction.[426] Thus, 4QJob^a probably had a different reading for MT's רֻטֲפַשׁ. However, since the complete word is not attested, it is hard to discern what the word might have been. It might as well be a dittography of בשרו.

---

425 Contrary to Homer Heater, who believes it has been rendered in the LXX. However, he does not indicate the Greek equivalent of the Hebrew hapax. See Heater, *A Septuagint Translation Technique*, 105.
426 See DJD XVI, 174.

The LXX renders רָטַפֵשׁ ('to be fresh') by ἀπαλύνω ('to soften, to make tender').[427] The verb ἀπαλύνω only occurs three times in the LXX, i.e., 4 Kingdoms 22:19, Ps 54:22 and Job 33:25, as a rendering of the Hebrew verb רכך ('to be tender'). Seow argues that is possible that the *reš* is a dittograph and that the root is טפש ('be unsensible, unfeeling', and often also translated by 'be fat'), which also occurs in Ps 119(LXX 118):70.[428] However, one might argue that the fragmentary 4QJob[a] attests *khaf-waw* and that the *Vorlage* of the LXX translator recorded רכו as is the case in Ps 55(LXX 54):22. When looking at the fragment (i.e., plate 1116, fragment 5) itself,[429] one can detect a little dot of ink under the *waw* that might reflect the presence of a *khaf*, certainly when compared to other *khafs* by the scribe's hand (see, e.g., Job 32:4 in 4QJob[a]). Thus, the LXX's *Vorlage* might have attested רכך and consequently, the LXX translator provided an adequate rendering (i.e., ἀπαλύνω).

M מִפְלָשׂ (Job 37:16)

MT	LXX	11QtgJob
הֲתֵדַע עַל־מִפְלְשֵׂי־עָב מִפְלָאוֹת תְּמִים דֵּעִים׃	ἐπίσταται δὲ διάκρισιν νεφῶν ἐξαίσια δὲ πτώματα πονηρῶν.	[התנ]דע להלבש{ו}א עננה גבורה
Do you know the balancings of the clouds, the wondrous works of the one whose knowledge is perfect.	And he understands the division of the clouds and the extraordinary falls of the wicked.	[Do you kn]ow how to clothe His cloud with might?

The Hebrew hapax מִפְלָשׂ has been rendered by the lexeme διάκρισις ('separation, dissolution') into Greek.[430] MT attests a plural form whereas the LXX has a singular form. Only Greenspahn records this hapax as an absolute hapax (it is not present in Casanowicz's list and Lisowsky labels it as a non-absolute ha-

427 See DCH, vol. VII, 477; GELS, 64; LEH, 60.
428 See Seow, "Putative Hapax Legomena in the Book of Job," 169–170. See also BDB, 936; Dhorme, *A Commentary on the Book of Job*, 503 and especially M. A. Altschüller, "Einige textkritische Bemerkungen zum Alten Testamente," in *ZAW* 6.1 (1886): 211–213, 212. Altschüller is the one who introduced this idea.
429 See *Dead Sea Scrolls Digital Library* (https://www.deadseascrolls.org.il/explore-the-archive/image/B-368375). DJD XVI has a different labeling, i.e., plate XXI, fragment 4. See DJD XVI, PLATE XXI.
430 See GELS, 153; LEH, 139.

pax).[431] However, the meaning of the hapax can be derived from the root פלס ('to smooth, to level, to balance').[432] Therefore, just as was the case with תְּהֳלָה (4:18) and אהל (Job 25:5), this absolute hapax cannot be labelled as such. It should rather be considered as a non-absolute hapax.

Dhorme has suggested that the LXX read מִפְלָשׂ as a form of פרשׂ ('to make distinct, to divide').[433] This might be plausible since, as Cox argues,[434] the derivative verb of διάκρισις, i.e., διακρίνω ('to decide, to judge, to distinguish'), is also used in Lev 24:12 as a rendering of פרשׂ. By doing so, LXX provided an adequate rendering of the Hebrew lexeme. Moreover, in 37:15, the LXX refers to the creation of light out of darkness (φῶς ποιήσας ἐκ σκότους), which entails a division (i.e., light vs. darkness). Thus, the choice of the translator to render מִפְלָשׂ by διάκρισις also reflects his stylistic attention for the literary context.

N Conclusion

Having analysed the Greek rendering of the Hebrew absolute *hapax legomena* in the speeches of Eliphaz, Bildad and Elihu in LXX Job, we can draw the following conclusions with regard to the translation technique of the LXX translator:

(a) Most hapaxes have been rendered by an adequate Greek equivalent by the LXX translator. This is the case for the *hapax legomena* in 2:8 (גרד), 4:10 (נתע), 4:18 (תְּהֳלָה), 15:12 (רזם), 18:2 (קֶנֶץ) and 25:5 (אהל). In 2:8 he elaborated on the image found in the Hebrew text.

It must be noted that the examination has indicated that three of the hapaxes which were considered absolute at the outset of this study on the basis of earlier research, i.e., תְּהֳלָה (4:18), אהל (25:5) and מִפְלָשׂ (37:16), should actually be labelled non-absolute *hapax legomena*, since our analysis indicated that their meaning might be derived from an existing Hebrew root;

(b) Some Hebrew hapaxes have been rendered into Greek by drawing upon contextual exegesis, i.e., כִּידוֹר (15:24), מִנְלֶה (15:29) and in a lesser degree also מִפְלָשׂ (37:16). This observation confirms the results of Verbeke on the Greek rendering of Hebrew *hapax legomena* in the speeches of Job and God. Therefore, it can indeed be considered a specific trait of the LXX translator of Job;

---

431 See registration above.
432 See DCH, vol. VI, 432; BDB, 814.
433 See Dhorme, A Commentary on the Book of Job, 568.
434 See Cox, *Iob* (forthcoming).

(c) In one instance, the LXX does not provide a Greek rendering for the Hebrew hapax, i.e., פדע (33:24). Instead, he contrasted the image of flesh and bones in 33:21 and thereby enhanced its imagery;

(d) In two cases, i.e., טמה (18:3) and רטפש (33:25), the LXX translator of Job probably had a Hebrew *Vorlage* that differed from the text attested in MT. In 33:20, the extant textual material does not allow any decision on whether the LXX translator paraphrased the Hebrew text or whether it rather had a diverging *Vorlage*.

These results point toward a translator who employed a variety of techniques to render possibly difficult Hebrew words. Although some of these words might have posed a challenge, the LXX translator never resorted to transliteration and has always aimed at providing an intelligible rendering of the Hebrew text, e.g., by employing contextual exegesis.

2.2.2.2 Evaluation of the Greek rendering of Hebrew non-absolute *hapax legomena* in Job

In this section, the registered 18 non-absolute *hapax legomena* and their Greek rendering in LXX Job will be evaluated.

A יָקוֹט (Job 8:14)

MT	LXX
אֲשֶׁר־יָקוֹט כִּסְלוֹ וּבֵית עַכָּבִישׁ מִבְטַחוֹ׃	ἀοίκητος γὰρ αὐτοῦ ἔσται ὁ οἶκος, ἀράχνη δὲ αὐτοῦ ἀποβήσεται ἡ σκηνή.
Their confidence is gossamer, a spider's house their trust.	For his house will be uninhabited, and his tent will prove to be a spider's web.

The noun יָקוֹט can be derived from the root קוט ('to break, to snap') and denotes 'gossamer.'[435] In the LXX, this hapax seems to have been rendered by the phrase ἀοίκητος ἔσται ('he/she/it will be uninhabited').[436]

The translation of the whole verse seems to be odd. Some lexemes, עַכָּבִישׁ/ἀράχνη and בַּיִת/οἶκος, have been rendered adequately with a corresponding Greek lexeme but בַּיִת/οἶκος has been transposed to the first stich. For the

---

435 See DCH, vol. VII, 213; DCH, vol. IV, 273.
436 See GELS, 62; LEH, 58.

other Hebrew lexeme, the Greek equivalents do not match. It seems that the LXX translator deliberately changed the meaning of the verse. A possible solution can be found when looking at the following verse (8:15) which reads:

MT	LXX
יִשָּׁעֵן עַל־בֵּיתוֹ וְלֹא יַעֲמֹד יַחֲזִיק בּוֹ וְלֹא יָקוּם:	ἐὰν ὑπερείσῃ τὴν οἰκίαν αὐτοῦ, οὐ μὴ στῇ· ἐπιλαβομένου δὲ αὐτοῦ οὐ μὴ ὑπομείνῃ.
If one leans against its house, it will not stand; if one lays hold of it, it will not endure.	If he props up his house, it will not stand, and when he lays hold of it, it will not remain.

In this verse, the image of the house, which started in 8:14, is elaborated. The LXX translator shifted the 'spider's house' in 8:14 to 'his (i.e., the impious) house' which enhances the image of the house of the impious being desolated and fragile. By doing so, the LXX translator created a more coherent text.

Thus, with regard to our hapax, we can conclude that the LXX translator skipped over the hapax. Not necessarily because he did not know the word in question, but in order to enhance the image regarding the house of the impious in verses 14-15 and to create a more coherent textual unity.

B רָטֹב (Job 8:16)

MT	LXX
רָטֹב הוּא לִפְנֵי־שָׁמֶשׁ וְעַל גַּנָּתוֹ יֹנַקְתּוֹ תֵצֵא:	ὑγρὸς γάρ ἐστιν ὑπὸ ἡλίου, καὶ ἐκ σαπρίας αὐτοῦ ὁ ῥάδαμνος αὐτοῦ ἐξελεύσεται.
The wicked thrive before the sun, and their shoots spread over the garden.	For he is languid beneath the sun and his shoot will spread forth out of his rottenness.

The Hebrew word רָטֹב ('moist, lush, full of sap') is an adjective derived from the verb רטב ('to be wet, to be moist'),[437] whose meaning can be derived from the Akkadian word *raṭbu* ('moist').[438] In the LXX it is rendered by ὑγρός ('moist'),[439]

---

437 See DCH, vol. VII, 477.

438 See Robert D. Biggs *et al.*, ed., *The Assyrian Dictionary of the Oriental institute of the University of Chicago. Volume 14. R* (Chicago, IL, Oriental Institute, 1999), 218. Choon-Leong Seow gives the verb *ruṭṭubu* ('soaked') as a reference. See Seow, *Job 1-21*, 534. However, the word

an adjective only used in Judg 16:7.9 and Sir 39:13. In Judges it is used as a rendering of לַח ('moist, fresh').[440]

Job 24:8 attests the verb רטב which is labelled as a non-absolute *hapax legomenon* as well.[441] The LXX does not have a reading but the asterisked material presents the Greek verb ὑγραίνω ('to become wet'), a hapax in the LXX, as a rendering of the Hebrew.[442] In her analysis of רטב, Verbeke has argued that the Greek verb used in the asterisked material represents a consistent rendering since the rendering is in line with רָטֹב/ὑγρός in 8:16.[443] However, she did not take the Assyrian *raṭbu/ruṭṭubu* into account. This, however, is a more conclusive argument to argue that the rendering of רָטֹב by ὑγρός in 8:16 and רטב by ὑγραίνω in 24:8 are consistent renderings.

C   מַפֵּחַ (Job 11:20)

MT	LXX
וְעֵינֵי רְשָׁעִים תִּכְלֶינָה וּמָנוֹס אָבַד מִנְהֶם וְתִקְוָתָם מַפַּח־ נָפֶשׁ׃	σωτηρία δὲ αὐτοὺς ἀπολείψει· ἡ γὰρ ἐλπὶς αὐτῶν ἀπώλεια, ὀφθαλμοὶ δὲ ἀσεβῶν τακήσονται.
But the eyes of the wicked will fail; all way of escape will be lost to them, and their hope is to breathe their last.	But deliverance will fail them, for their hope is destruction, and the eyes of the impious will waste away.

The word מַפֵּחַ, denoting 'expiring, breathing out,'[444] only occurs here in Job 11:20 but also in Sir 30:12c.[445] Nonetheless, since Sirach does not belong to the Hebrew Bible, it is labelled by Lisowsky, Greenspahn and BibleWorks as a (non-absolute) *hapax legomenon*.[446] Sir 30:12c is not rendered into Greek thus we

---

raṭbu, which is an adjective, is a better argument in favour for the meaning 'moist' for the hapax רָטֹב.

439 See GELS, 693; LEH, 627.
440 See DCH, vol. IV, 531.
441 See Verbeke, "Hebrew Hapax Legomena," 117.
442 See GELS, 693; LEH, 627.
443 See Verbeke, "Hebrew Hapax Legomena," 283.
444 See DCH, vol. V, 430–431.
445 See Beentjes, The Book of Ben Sira in Hebrew, 54.
446 See Verbeke, "Hebrew Hapax Legomena," 115.

cannot see how it is rendered there. When looking at the LXX rendering 11:20, it is clear that the Greek does not follow the Hebrew ordering:[447]

MT	LXX
וְעֵינֵי רְשָׁעִים תִּכְלֶינָה	ὀφθαλμοὶ δὲ ἀσεβῶν τακήσονται
וּמָנוֹס אָבַד מִנְהֶם	σωτηρία δὲ αὐτοὺς ἀπολείψει
וְתִקְוָתָם מַפַּח־נָפֶשׁ	ἡ γὰρ ἐλπὶς αὐτῶν ἀπώλεια

The word-pair מפח־נפשׁ ('expiration of the soul/life'),[448] containing the non-absolute hapax מַפַּח, is attested in the third stich of the Hebrew verse and is rendered by ἀπώλεια ('destruction, termination of life') in the LXX.[449] The noun ἀπώλεια is used 5 times in LXX Job for a variety of Hebrew lexemes: מַפַּח (11:20), רֶגַע (20:5), יְבוּל (20:28), - (27:7), דְּאָבָה (41:14).[450] Homer Heater has noted that the use of ἀπώλεια in 11:20 has been influenced by 8:13, i.e., וְתִקְוַת חָנֵף תֹּאבֵד/ἐλπὶς γὰρ ἀσεβοῦς ἀπολεῖται.[451] The attestation of both תִּקְוָה ('hope') and אבד ('to destroy') in 11:20 might have motivated the LXX translator to look at 8:13 where both words are attested as well.[452] Although he uses the verb ἀπόλλυμι ('to destroy') in 8:13, the resemblances between the two verses are striking:

8:13	11:20
ἐλπὶς γὰρ ἀσεβοῦς ἀπολεῖται	ἡ γὰρ ἐλπὶς αὐτῶν ἀπώλεια

Moreover, although the Hebrew word-pair מפח־נפשׁ of 11:20 is not rendered in a literal way, the choice of rendering it by ἀπώλεια seems to be an adequate rendering since 'expiration of the soul/life' denotes 'destruction.'[453] Thus, the rendering of the Hebrew hapax מַפַּח by ἀπώλεια in 11:20 can be regarded as a consistent rendering that preserves the meaning of the Hebrew and which is prompted by 8:13.

---

447 See Beer, Der Text des Buches Job, 70–71; Heater, A Septuagint Translation Technique, 59.
448 Which is the same as in Sir 30:12.
449 See GELS, 88–89; LEH, 79.
450 An additional five times in the asterisk material: 21:30; 26:6; 28:22; 30:12 and 31:3.
451 See Heater, A Septuagint Translation Technique, 59, 82–83.
452 See Heater, A Septuagint Translation Technique, 59.
453 See Cox, *Iob* (forthcoming).

D רען (Job 15:32)

MT	LXX
בְּלֹא־יוֹמוֹ תִּמָּלֵא וְכִפָּתוֹ לֹא רַעֲנָנָה׃	ἡ τομὴ αὐτοῦ πρὸ ὥρας φθαρήσεται, καὶ ὁ ῥάδαμνος αὐτοῦ οὐ μὴ πυκάσῃ.
It will be paid in full before their time, and their branch will not be green.	His stump will perish before its time, and his branch will provide no cover.

The Hebrew hapax רען ('to be luxuriant, to be green'), whose meaning is derived from the adjective רַעֲנָן ('luxuriant, leafy'),[454] is rendered in Job 15:32 by the verb πυκάζω ('to overshadow, to protect, to be thickly covered').[455] The Greek verb πυκάζω occurs four times in the LXX, i.e., 3 Macc 4:5; Ps 117(MT 118):27; Job 15:32 and Hos 14:9. Remarkably, it is used as a participle (πυκάζουσα) as a translation of the adjective רַעֲנָן in Hos 14:9. Therefore, the rendering of רען by πυκάζω seems to be an adequate rendering.

E שָׁבִיב (Job 18:5)

MT	LXX
גַּם אוֹר רְשָׁעִים יִדְעָךְ וְלֹא־יִגַּהּ שְׁבִיב אִשּׁוֹ׃	καὶ φῶς ἀσεβῶν σβεσθήσεται, καὶ οὐκ ἀποβήσεται αὐτῶν ἡ φλόξ.
Surely the light of the wicked is put out, and the flame of their fire does not shine.	Yes, the light of the impious will be put out, and their flame will not do well.

Although the hapax in this verse, i.e., שָׁבִיב ('flame, spark'),[456] does not occur in the Hebrew Bible elsewhere, it is attested in extra-biblical texts such as 1QH XI,21; XI,31; XVI,21 and 4QBerᵃ 1.ii,3.[457] It is also attested in the Hebrew version of Sirach, i.e., Sir 8:10 and 45:19.[458] In the Greek text of Sirach, שָׁבִיב is rendered

---

454 See DCH, vol. VII, 529.

455 See GELS, 607; LEH, 537.

456 See DCH, vol. VIII, 236.

457 See DCH, vol. VIII, 236. For the attestations of שָׁבִיב in 1QH, see Schuller and Newsom, *The Hodayot*, 36, 46 and 54 (the numbering of the attestations of this work is used). DCH does not mention the last attestation. For its attestation in 4QBerᵃ, see Esther Eshel *et. al.*, ed., *Qumran Cave 4 VI. Poetical and Liturgical Texts, Part 1*, DJD XI (Oxford: Clarendon Press, 1998), 12.

458 See DCH, vol. VIII, 236. For the text of Sirach, see Beentjes, *The Book of Ben Sira in Hebrew*, 32 and 81.

by φλόξ ('flame') in these two verses.[459] Also in Job, the Greek has φλόξ for the hapax שָׁבִיב. Since both lexemes denote the same thing, i.e., flame, and since both Sirach and Job render שָׁבִיב by φλόξ, we can conclude that the LXX translator of Job understood this Hebrew word and, consequently, rendered it adequately.

F שִׂיא (Job 20:6)

MT	LXX
אִם־יַעֲלֶה לַשָּׁמַיִם שִׂיאוֹ וְרֹאשׁוֹ לָעָב יַגִּיעַ׃	ἐὰν ἀναβῇ εἰς οὐρανὸν αὐτοῦ τὰ δῶρα, ἡ δὲ θυσία αὐτοῦ νεφῶν ἅψηται.
Even though they mount up high as the heavens, and their head reaches to the clouds.	Even if his gifts go up to heaven and his sacrifices touch the clouds.

The Hebrew hapax שִׂיא 'height, head, desire, loftiness,'[460] is rendered in the LXX by αὐτοῦ τὰ δῶρα ('his gifts'). The recensions (α´, θ´ and σ´) attest ἔπαρμα αὐτοῦ.[461] Various scholars have indicated that the LXX translator read 'his gifts' from שַׁי ('gift') instead of שִׂיא ('height, head, desire, loftiness').[462] Moreover, שַׁי has been rendered by δῶρα in Ps 68(LXX 67):30; 76(LXX 75):12 and Isa 18:7. Indeed, a misreading of שִׂיא as 'his gifts' is the only and most plausible explanation to explain LXX's rendering of αὐτοῦ τὰ δῶρα.

G יֶגַע (Job 20:18)

MT	LXX
מֵשִׁיב יָגָע וְלֹא יִבְלָע כְּחֵיל תְּמוּרָתוֹ וְלֹא יַעֲלֹס׃	εἰς κενὰ καὶ μάταια ἐκοπίασεν πλοῦτον, ἐξ οὗ οὐ γεύσεται, ὥσπερ στρίφνος ἀμάσητος ἀκατάποτος.

---

459 See GELS, 717; LEH, 650. The Greek word φλόξ also occurs in Si 21:9 and 28:22. However, a Hebrew text of these verses has not been found.
460 See DCH, vol. VIII, 123. The latter meaning has also been proposed by Seow. See Seow, *Job 1-21*, 850.
461 See Field, Origenis Hexaplorum (Tom. II), 37.
462 See Beer, Der Text des Buches Hiob, 132; Dhorme, A Commentary on the Book of Job, 292; Seow, Job 1-21, 850.

MT	LXX
They will give back the fruit of their toil, and will not swallow it down; from the profit of their trading they will get no enjoyment.	Vainly and foolishly he has toiled for wealth of which he will not taste; it will be like something tough, unchewable, impossible to swallow.

In Job 20:18, יָגָע ('gain'),[463] a noun derived from the verb יגע ('to be weary, to toil, to labour'),[464] is rendered by the verb κοπιάω ('to become exhausted, to work hard, to toil, to labour').[465] Although the noun occurs only here in the Hebrew Bible, the verb יגע, its adjectives יָגֵעַ, יָגִיעַ and the noun יְגִיעַ occur ample time.

Throughout the LXX, the verb יגע is often rendered by the verb κοπιάω.[466] The verb κοπιάω only occurs two times in LXX Job, i.e., 2:9 (-) and 20:18 (יָגָע), and one time in the asterisked material, i.e., 39:16 (יָגִיעַ). For the noun, LXX Job uses ἔργα as a rendering (see 10:3 and 39:11). However, the adjective יָגִיעַ is translated by κατάκοπος ('[very] weary') in 3:17 which is a derivative of the verb κοπιάω. Thus, instead of reading the noun יָגָע, the LXX translator must have read the verb יגע and rendered it by the common rendering κοπιάω.

H שֶׁפֶק (Job 20:22)

MT	LXX
בִּמְלֹאות שִׂפְקוֹ יֵצֶר לוֹ כָּל־יַד עָמֵל תְּבוֹאֶנּוּ:	ὅταν δὲ δοκῇ ἤδη πεπληρῶσθαι, θλιβήσεται, πᾶσα δὲ ἀνάγκη ἐπ᾽ αὐτὸν ἐπελεύσεται.
In full sufficiency they will be in distress; all the force of misery will come upon them.	But just when he thinks he has fully satisfied himself, he will be afflicted, and every distress will come upon him.

The first stich of Job 20:22 (בִּמְלֹאות שִׂפְקוֹ) is rendered by ὅταν δὲ δοκῇ ἤδη πεπληρῶσθαι. Since מלא ('to be full, to fill') is very often rendered by πληρόω ('to fill, to fulfil') in the LXX, we might assume that πληρόω is used as an equivalent of מלא in Job 20:22 as well. However, the verb מלא is mostly rendered by the verb ἐμπίπλημι (3:15; 8:21; 15:21; 22:18; 23:4 and 38:39) or the adjective πλήρης (21:24; 32:18 and 39:2) in LXX Job. Πληρόω is only used as a rendering of

---

463 See DCH, vol. IV, 81.
464 See DCH, vol. IV, 80–81.
465 See GELS, 406–407; LEH, 350.
466 For a full list, see HR, 778.

מלא in 20:23 which belongs to the asterisked material. Thus, although the rest of the LXX seems to regard πληρόω as an equivalent of מלא, the LXX translator of Job does not employ this equivalent but opts for ἐμπίπλημι or πλήρης. The attestation of πληρόω in Job 20:22 is most probably not a rendering of מלא.

The non-absolute hapax שֶׂפֶק denotes 'sufficiency, abundance' is probably derived from either שפק ('to be sufficient') or סֶפֶק ('abundance').[467] Edouard Dhorme argues that the translator read a form of the Aramaic ספק ('to doubt') and therefore rendered it by δοκέω.[468] However, as already pointed out by Homer Heater, the phrase ὅταν δοκῇ ἤδη ('just when he thinks') occurs three times in Job (15:21; 20:7 and 20:22) in similar contexts, i.e., the fate of the wicked.[469] In 15:21 and 20:7 ἤδη is not used as a rendering for a form of ספק, but to render בשלום (15:21) and כגללו (20:7).

The most plausible argumentation for the rendering of בִּמְלֹאות שִׂפְקוֹ by ὅταν δὲ δοκῇ ἤδη πεπληρῶσθαι might be that: (a) the translator wanted to harmonise this verse with previous passages, i.e., 15:21 and 20:7, and therefore opted for the phrase ὅταν δοκῇ ἤδη; (b) and he must have thought that מלא ('to be full, to fill') and שֶׂפֶק ('sufficiency, abundance') (more or less) meant the same thing and therefore provided one equivalent, i.e., πεπληρῶσθαι, for both Hebrew terms.

I אֶכֶף (Job 33:7)

MT	LXX
הִנֵּה אֵמָתִי לֹא תְבַעֲתֶךָּ וְאַכְפִּי עָלֶיךָ לֹא־יִכְבָּד׃	οὐχ ὁ φόβος μού σε στροβήσει, οὐδὲ ἡ χείρ μου βαρεῖα ἔσται ἐπὶ σοί.
No fear of me need terrify you; my pressure will not be heavy on you.	No fear of me will send you spinning, nor will my hand be heavy on you.

The Hebrew אכפי from the hapax אֶכֶף, meaning 'pressure' and derived from אכף, is translated by ἡ χείρ μου ('my hand').[470] In line with other commentators before him, Dhorme argues that this translation is prompted by a reading of וכפי ('and my hand,' > כַּף, 'hand') instead of ואכפי ('and my pressure').[471] Indeed,

467 See DCH, vol. VIII, 180; DCH, vol. VI, 184.
468 See Dhorme, A Commentary on the Book of Job, 301.
469 See Heater, A Septuagint Translation Technique, 68–69.
470 See DCH, vol. I, 249.
471 See Dhorme, A Commentary on the Book of Job, 489.

when looking at the Greek rendering of כַּף in LXX Job, it is rendered by χείρ in 8 of the 13 instances (i.e., 9:30; 10:3; 11:13; 13:14.21; 16:17; 31:7 and 40:32). For the other instances, it is rendered by ἀπό + gen. in connection to πούς (2:7), δάκτυλος (29:9) and three times there is no equivalent in the LXX but only in the asterisked material (22:30; 27:23 and 36:32). Thus, the suggestion that the translator read וכפי instead of ואכפי and consequently rendered it by (οὐ)δὲ ἡ χείρ μου makes sense considering his tendency to translate כַּף consistently by χείρ.

J   חַף (Job 33:9)

MT	LXX	11QtgJob
זַךְ אֲנִי בְּלִי פָשַׁע חַף אָנֹכִי וְלֹא עָוֹן לִי׃	διότι λέγεις Καθαρός εἰμι οὐχ ἁμαρτών, ἄμεμπτος δέ εἰμι, οὐ γὰρ ἠνόμησα.	[זכ]י אנה ולא חטא לי ונקא]
You say, 'I am clean, without transgression; I am pure, and there is no iniquity in me.	That you say, 'I am pure, since I have done no wrong, and I am blameless, for I did not act lawlessly.	['Pu]re am I, and I have no sin; and innocent [472

The Hebrew hapax חַף, translated by 'pure,'[473] is rendered by the adjective ἄμεμπτος ('irreproachable [morally], blameless') in LXX Job.[474] According to the editors of DJD, the fragment of 11QtgJob corresponds to MT.[475] However, they add that the word attested in 11QtgJob is נקי which means 'innocent, clean, blameless' in Hebrew and 'clean' in Aramaic dialects[476]. The adjective ἄμεμπτος used in Job 33:9, occurs mostly in LXX Job.[477] Strikingly, it is used as a rendering of נָקִי in Job 22:19. Therefore, it might be that the *Vorlage* of the translator attested נקי instead of חַף. Therefore, he rendered it by ἄμεμπτος as he did in 22:19.

---

472 Translation from DJD XXIII, 129.
473 See DCH, vol. III, 285. According to Dhorme, the hapax stems from the root חפף which means 'to wash' in New Hebrew and has a parallel in Syriac (חוף, 'to wash') and Akkadian (ḫâpu, 'to clean'). See Dhorme, *A Commentary on the Book of Job*, 490. Consequently, he argues that the Hebrew hapax denotes "'clean" in the moral sense". See Dhorme, *A Commentary on the Book of Job*, 490.
474 See GELS, 32; LEH, 350.
475 See DJD XXIII, 130.
476 See DJD XXIII, 130. See also DCH, vol. V, 750–751.
477 For all the attestations, see HR, 65.

K   מוֹסֵר (Job 33:16)

MT	LXX	11QtgJob
אָז יִגְלֶה אֹזֶן אֲנָשִׁים וּבְמֹסָרָם יַחְתֹּם׃	τότε ἀνακαλύπτει νοῦν ἀνθρώπων, ἐν εἴδεσιν φόβου τοιούτοις αὐτοὺς ἐξεφόβησεν.	[רה]
Then he opens their ears, and terrifies them with warnings.	Then he lays bare the human mind; he frightened them with such scary apparitions.	/[478]

MT attests the hapax מוֹסֵר ('bond') in Job 33:16.[479] 11QtgJob only attest the top of two letters which the editors of DJD have identified as רה, although the letters are very hard to discern on the basis of the fragment.[480] Thus, the fragment does not help our examination of the hapax.

The LXX does not render this hapax with only one word, but by a whole phrase: ἐν εἴδεσιν φόβου τοιούτοις. On the basis of the LXX reading, and especially the noun εἶδος ('vision, shape, appearance'),[481] several scholars have proposed the emendation וּבמראים (> מַרְאֶה, 'sight, appearance').[482] The Hebrew מַרְאֶה is often rendered by εἶδος throughout the LXX[483]. However, this does not explain adequately why the translator opted for ἐν εἴδεσιν φόβου τοιούτοις. It might be that the LXX translator rendered ἐν εἴδεσιν φόβου τοιούτοις as a translation of ובמראים. The Greek word φόβος often functions as a rendering of מוֹרָא ('fear'),[484] which resembles מַרְאֶה. That these words were confusing to the LXX translators can be observed in the rendering of מוֹרָא by ὅραμα ('what is seen, sight, vision, spectacle'),[485] which has more or less the same meaning as εἶδος, in Deut 4:34; 26:8 and Jer 32(LXX 39):21. Thus, it might be that the LXX transla-

---

478 No translation is provided since only two letters of the verse are (partially) preserved. See DJD XXIII, 129.

479 See DCH, vol. V, 177.

480 See DJD XXIII, 130.

481 See GELS, 192; LEH, 173.

482 See Dhorme, *A Commentary on the Book of Job*, 494–495. For an overview, see David J. A. Clines, *Job 21-37*, WBC 18a (Nashville, TN: Thomas Nelson, 2006), 695–696. For the meaning of the Hebrew word, see DCH, vol. V, 474–476.

483 See HR, 375–376.

484 See DCH, vol. V, 187–188. The rendering of מוֹרָא by φόβος occurs in Deut 11:25; Isa 8:12.13; Mal 1:6 and 2:5.

485 See GELS, 502; LEH, 443.

tor was not certain whether the Hebrew read a form of מֻרְאֶה or מוֹרָא and thus provided a double translation.[486]

L חֶבְרָה (Job 34:8)

MT	LXX	11QtgJob
וְאָרַח לְחֶבְרָה עִם־פֹּעֲלֵי אָוֶן וְלָלֶכֶת עִם־אַנְשֵׁי־רֶשַׁע:	οὐχ ἁμαρτών οὐδὲ ἀσεβήσας ἢ ὁδοῦ κοινωνήσας μετὰ ποιούντων τὰ ἄνομα τοῦ πορευθῆναι μετὰ ἀσεβῶν.	ומתחבר לעברי שקרא] רש]ע
who goes in company with evildoers and walks with the wicked?	Seeing that I have not sinned or acted impiously or shared a way with doers of lawless acts, to walk with the impious.	And keeps company with wrongdoers [ev]il?[487]

MT of Job 34:8 records the hapax חֶבְרָה ('company, community').[488] In 11QtgJob attests ומתחבר for MT's וְאָרַח לְחֶבְרָה and thus attests a form of the verb חבר ('to join') instead of the noun which is considered a hapax.[489] The LXX has κοινωνέω ('to have in common, to share, to take part in,') as a rendering of the hapax.[490]

Throughout the LXX, the verb κοινωνέω occurs 13 times: 2 Chr 20:35; 2 Macc 5:20; 14:25; 3 Macc 2:31; 4:11; Prov 1:11; Ecc 9:4; Job 34:8; Wis 6:23; Sir 13:1.2 and 13:17. In all these cases where we have a preserved Hebrew text,[491] except in Prov 1:11,[492] it is a rendering of the Hebrew verb חבר ('to join'). Thus, the LXX translator has interpreted לחברה as a verb, as is the case in 11QtgJob, and rendered it by the standard equivalent κοινωνέω.

---

486 On double translations in LXX Job, see Marieke Dhont, "Double Translations in Old Greek Job," in Die Septuaginta – Orte und Intentionen. 5. Internationale Fachtagung veranstaltet von Septuaginta Deutsch (LXX.D), Wuppertal 24.–27. Juli 2014, ed. Siegfried Kruezer et al., WUNT 361 (Tübingen: Mohr Siebeck, 2016), 475–490.

487 Translation taken from DJD XXIII, 134.

488 See DCH, vol. III, 156.

489 See DJD XXIII, 135. For the translation of חבר, see DCH, vol. III, 153–154.

490 See GELS, 403; LEH, 346.

491 The LXX translator of Proverbs has rendered ארב ('to lie in wait, to ambush') by κοινωνέω in Prov 11:1. However, he might have read חבר instead of ארב.

492 This is also the case in Sir 13:1.2 (2x) and 13:17. See Beentjes, *The Book of Ben Sira in Hebrew*, 40–41.

M   מַעֲבָד (Job 34:25)

MT	LXX	11QtgJob
לָכֵן יַכִּיר מַעְבָּדֵיהֶם וְהָפַךְ לַיְלָה וְיִדַּכָּאוּ׃	ὁ γνωρίζων αὐτῶν τὰ ἔργα.	יחכ]ם עבדהון
Thus, knowing their works, he overturns them in the night, and they are crushed.	He who reveals their deeds.	He kno]ws their work.[493]

In Job 34:25, the LXX does not present the second stich of MT (וְהָפַךְ לַיְלָה וְיִדַּכָּאוּ). Although it is attested in the asterisked material (καὶ στρέψει νύκτα καὶ ταπεινωθήσονται), the second stich is also absent from 11QtgJob where verse 26 immediately follows 25a.[494]

The hapax under discussion, מַעֲבָד ('deed' > עבד, 'to do, to serve, to work'),[495] is located in the first stich that is also attested in 11QtgJob as עבדהון. The LXX renders the construction מעבדיהם by αὐτῶν τὰ ἔργα. The Greek ἔργον ('work, deed') is used ample times in the LXX corpus as an equivalent for nouns from the root עבד, e.g., עֲבֹדָה and עֲבֹדָה, meaning 'work, deed.'[496] In Job 1:3, the noun עֲבֻדָּה is also rendered by ἔργον. Thus, the LXX translator knew the word מַעֲבָד and or derived its meaning from its root עבד and, consequently, rendered it by the adequate equivalent ἔργον. Moreover, the *Vorlage* of the LXX translator might also have read something similar to עבדהון of 11QtgJob, which is plausible since 11QtgJob agrees with the LXX In 34:25 since both do not attest stich b.

N   אָבִי (Job 34:36)

MT	LXX
אָבִי יִבָּחֵן אִיּוֹב עַד־נֶצַח עַל־תְּשֻׁבֹת בְּאַנְשֵׁי־אָוֶן׃	οὐ μὴν δὲ ἀλλὰ μάθε, Ἰώβ, μὴ δῷς ἔτι ἀνταπόκρισιν ὥσπερ οἱ ἄφρονες.
Would that Job were tried to the limit, because his answers are those of the wicked.	Nonetheless, learn O Iob! No longer give a response as fools do.

---

493 Translation taken from DJD XXIII, 136.
494 See DJD XXIII, 135.
495 See DCH, vol. V, 378–379.
496 For an overview of the attestations, see HR, 541–544.

The interjection אֲבִי ('alas') is the hapax in this verse.[497] In the LXX it is rendered by the collection of particles οὐ μὴν δὲ ἀλλά which also occurs elsewhere in Job (2:5; 5:8; 12:6; 13:3; 17:10; 21:17; 27:7; 33:1 and 34:36),[498] which seem to be a trait of the translator to connect different parts of the book together.[499] In most of these verses (2:5; 5:8; 13:3; 17:10 and 33:1), the collection of particles is used to render אוּלָם ('but, indeed'). In the rest of the cases, it is added twice (12:6 and 27:7) and used as a rendering כמה (21:17).

For 34:36, Dhorme has proposed that the translator read אֲבָל ('indeed, however, alas').[500] However, it might also have been אֲבוֹי ('alas') as in Prov 23:39,[501] as Johann Georg Ernst Hoffmann has proposed.[502] On the basis of the extant textual material, it is hard to discern which of the two proposed readings is more preferable. Nonetheless, both are interjections and might have motivated the translator to opt for his preferred particle collection οὐ μὴν δὲ ἀλλά as he did to render the interjection אוּלָם.

O סֶפֶק (Job 36:18)

MT	LXX	4QJob[a]
כִּי־חֵמָה פֶּן־יְסִיתְךָ בְסָפֶק וְרָב־כֹּפֶר אַל־יַטֶּךָ׃	θυμὸς δὲ ἐπ᾽ ἀσεβεῖς ἔσται δι᾽ ἀσέβειαν δώρων, ὧν ἐδέχοντο ἐπ᾽ ἀδικίαις.	[כי]חמה פן יסיתך [ ] אל יטכה
Beware that wrath does not entice you into scoffing, and do not let the greatness of the ransom turn you aside.	But wrath will fall on the impious on account of the impiety of gifts they would receive for injustices.	[Beware that] wrath does not entice you [ ] not let you turn aside.

The Hebrew word סֶפֶק ('scoffing, scorning'),[503] has probably been rendered in the LXX by δι᾽ ἀσέβειαν ('on account of the impiety'). 4QJob[a] has one minor variant reading, יטכה, and follows MT.

---

497 See DCH, vol. I, 102.
498 Next to 9 attestations in LXX Job, it only occurs in 3 Macc 5:50 and 4 Macc 15:9.
499 See Claude E. Cox, "Tying It All Together: The Use of Particles in Old Greek Job," *BIOSCS* 38 (2005): 41–54, esp. 49.
500 See Dhorme, A Commentary on the Book of Job, 527.
501 See Johann G. E. Hoffmann, *Hiob* (Kiel: C. F. Haeseler, 1891), 99.
502 See DCH, vol. I, 102.
503 See DCH, vol. VI, 184.

It is hard to see how the LXX translator rendered this verse. The attestation of ἀδικία can be explained on the basis of the previous verse. Verse 36:17 reads οὐχ ὑστερήσει δὲ ἀπὸ δικαίων κρίμα ('Yes, justice will not be wanting for those in the right'). The use of ἀδικία in verse 18 thus comes as no surprise since it is a good parallel with δίκαιος. In order to enhance the parallelistic image, verse 18 deals with the impious (ἀσεβεῖς), which is lacking in the Hebrew text. By doing so, he adds a theological/ethical nuance that is not present in MT: the pious will receive justice (36:17), the impious will receive wrath on account of the injustices they do (36:18).

With regard to the unusual δι' ἀσέβειαν δώρων, we can see a parallel with Job 8:20 where it is stated that the Lord will not accept the gift/bribe (δῶρον) from the impious (ἀσεβής), which resonates in 36:18:

LXX	NETS
ὁ γὰρ κύριος οὐ μὴ ἀποποιήσηται τὸν ἄκακον, πᾶν δὲ δῶρον ἀσεβοῦς οὐ δέξεται.	For the Lord will not reject the blameless person, but no gift will he accept from the impious.

The same nouns are used together in Exod 23:7:

LXX	NETS
ἀπὸ παντὸς ῥήματος ἀδίκου ἀποστήσῃ· ἀθῷον καὶ δίκαιον οὐκ ἀποκτενεῖς, καὶ οὐ δικαιώσεις τὸν ἀσεβῆ ἕνεκεν δώρων.[504]	From every unjust thing said you shall keep away. An innocent and just person you shall not kill, and you shall not acquit the impious person for the sake of bribes.

Thus, the attestation of δι' ἀσέβειαν δώρων and δῶρον ἀσεβοῦς in LXX Job might be an allusion to Exod 23:7 where it is stated that impious people will not be exonerated on account of bribes.

It is hard to discern whether the LXX translator had a *Vorlage* similar to the text of MT or not. Although he rendered חֵמָה by θυμός, the rest of the verse seems to be an interpretation which is based upon verse 17 and an allusion to 8:20 and possibly also Exod 23:7.

---

504 See John W. Wevers, *Exodus*, Septuaginta. Vetus Testamentum Graecum. Auctoritate Academicae Scientiarum Gottingensis editum II.1 (Göttingen: Vandenhoeck & Ruprecht, 1991), 267.

P נֶטֶף (Job 36:27)

MT	LXX
כִּי יְגָרַע נִטְפֵי־מָיִם יָזֹקּוּ מָטָר לְאֵדוֹ:	ἀριθμηταὶ δὲ αὐτῷ σταγόνες ὑετοῦ.
For he draws up the drops of water; he distills his mist in rain,	But to him raindrops are numbered.

The second stich of 36:27 (יָזֹקּוּ מָטָר לְאֵדוֹ) is not attested in the LXX. The asterisked material reads καὶ ἐπιχυθήσονται ὑετῷ εἰς νεφέλην.

The hapax נֶטֶף, meaning 'drop' derived from the verb נטף ('to drip'),[505] is rendered by σταγών ('drop of water, raindrop') in the LXX.[506] The noun σταγών occurs only 8 times elsewhere in the LXX: 4 Macc 10:8; Ps 64(MT 65):11 (רְבִיבִים); Ps 71(MT 72):6 (רְבִיבִים); Prov 27:15 (דֶּלֶף); Sir 1:2; 18:10; Mic 2:11 (נטף) and Isa 40:15 (מַר). Remarkably, the hiphil participle of נטף, i.e., מַטִּיף, which occurs in Mic 2:11 is rendered by σταγών. Thus, the rendering of נֶטֶף by σταγών in Job 36:27 seems to be an adequate rendering. The translator knew the hapax or the verb נטף and provided a decent Greek equivalent.

Q מְזָרִים (Job 37:9)

MT	LXX
מִן־הַחֶדֶר תָּבוֹא סוּפָה וּמִמְּזָרִים קָרָה:	ἐκ ταμιείων ἐπέρχονται δῖναι, ἀπὸ δὲ ἀκρωτηρίων ψῦχος.
From its chamber comes the whirlwind, and cold from the scattering winds.	From their chambers whirlwinds come, and cold from the peaks.

In 37:9, the hapax מְזָרִים ('press, scatterers, north wind' > זרם, 'to scatter') is attested.[507] The LXX has ἀκρωτήριον ('extremities, farthest end, mountain peak') as a rendering.[508] In the Syro-Hexapla, α´ and θ´ transliterate the Hebrew and have Μαζοριμ.[509] When looking at the representation of the Hebrew into Greek, we can observe an almost quantitative representation:

---

505 See DCH, vol. V, 678–679.
506 See GELS, 632; LEH, 565.
507 See DCH, vol. V, 212.
508 See GELS, 23; LEH, 24.
509 See Ziegler, *Iob*, 380. Also scholars and modern translators have found the hapax difficult to translate and have suggested various emendations and translations. For an overview, see Clines, *Job 21-37*, 840.

MT	LXX
מִן־הַחֶדֶר	ἐκ ταμιείων
תָּבוֹא	ἐπέρχονται
סוּפָה	δῖναι
וּמִמְּזָרִים	ἀπὸ δὲ ἀκρωτηρίων
קָרָה	ψῦχος

The only thing that differs is the change from the singular (Hebrew) to the plural (Greek) in the first stich, which is probably introduced to create a better parallelism between the first and second stich in the Greek text.

Given the quantitative representation of the Hebrew into Greek, one can assume that the LXX translator either knew the meaning of מְזָרִים or tried to come up with a rendering that fitted the context. Moreover, the Greek ἀκρωτήριον is used only five times in the LXX to render a diversity of Hebrew lexemes: כְּרָע (Lev 4:11), שֵׁן (1 Sam 14:4 [2x]), מְזָרִים (Job 37:9) and קָצֶה (Ezek 25:9). Thus, it is hard to decide whether the translator knew the word or derived its meaning from the context of the verse.

Nonetheless, the translator's choice to opt for ἀκρωτήριον, which denotes a place or space, in 37:9 fits the context of the verse, since in the first stich ταμιεῖον ('room') also denotes a space or place. Therefore, by opting for ἀκρωτήριον the parallelism of the verse is enhanced.

R מִפְלָאוֹת (Job 37:16)

MT	LXX	11QtgJob
הֲתֵדַע עַל־מִפְלְשֵׂי־עָב מִפְלָאוֹת תְּמִים דֵּעִים:	ἐπίσταται δὲ διάκρισιν νεφῶν, ἐξαίσια δὲ πτώματα πονηρῶν.	[התג]דע להלבש{ו}א עננה גבורה [ ] ארו הוא ידע מדע]א
Do you know the balancings of the clouds, the wondrous works of the one whose knowledge is perfect.	And he understands the division of the clouds and the extraordinary falls of the wicked.	[Do you kn]ow how to clothe His cloud with might? [ ] Behold, it is He who has knowledge.[510]

In my article on the Greek rendering of Hebrew absolute *hapax legomena* in the speeches of Job's friends, I have already touched upon another hapax in 37:16,

---

510 See DJD XXIII, 147. 16b has been transposed after verse 17.

i.e., מִפְלָשׂ ('poising, balancing').[511] The hapax under discussion is מִפְלָאוֹת ('won-drous work'),[512] derived from פלא ('to be wonderful').[513] 11QtgJob reads גבורה ('might'). The LXX has rendered this lexeme by ἐξαίσιος ('extraordinary, re-markable'),[514] a lexeme that only occurs in LXX Job: שֶׁמֶץ (4:12), פלא (5:9; 9:10), פִּתְאֹם (9:23; 22:10), צֶלַע (18:12), שִׂמְחָה (20:5), - (34:24) and מִפְלָאוֹת (37:16).[515] Given the fact that the LXX translator rendered פלא to ἐξαίσιος in 5:9 and 9:10, we can assume that the rendering of מִפְלָאוֹת, whose meaning can be derived from פלא, by the same Greek lexeme is an adequate rendering.[516]

S Conclusion

Having analysed the Greek rendering of the Hebrew non-absolute *hapax le-gomena* in the speeches of Job's friend in LXX Job, we can draw the following conclusions with regard to the translation technique of the LXX translator:

(a) Most of the Hebrew hapaxes have been rendered by an adequate Greek lexeme. This is the case in 8:16; 11:20; 15:32; 18:5; 20:18; 33:7.9; 34:8.25.36; 36:27 and 37:16. Some of these renderings are in line with the translator's own choice of equivalents for certain Hebrew words. This is the case in 33:9; 34:25.36 and 37:16. It is also important to note that in 33:9; 34:8.25 the reading of the LXX is corroborated by the fragments of 11QtgJob;

(b) In some instances the LXX translator skipped over the hapax and rendered the verse on the basis of stylistic motivations which are based upon the (immediate) context (cfr. contextual exegesis) such as the enhancement of parallelism (36:18 and 37:9), harmonisation (20:22), enhancing of the image

---

511 See Beeckman, "Verba Rara Amicorum Iob," 6–7. Although the hapax can be labelled as an absolute hapax according to the rules-of-thumb, I have concluded that the hapax must be considered a non-absolute hapax since its meaning can be derived from an existing Hebrew root. See Beeckman, "Verba Rara Amicorum Iob," 7.

512 See DCH, vol. V, 431. The entry in DCH is not מִפְלָאוֹת but מִפְלָאָה.

513 See DCH, vol. V, 431; DCH, vol. VI, 683–686.

514 See GELS, 245; LEH, 209. Dhorme, however, argues that מִפְלָאוֹת has been rendered by ἐξαίσιος and πτῶμα and considers it to be a double-translation. See Dhorme, *A Commentary on the Book of Job*, 570. Heater is correct in arguing that מִפְלָאוֹת has been rendered by ἐξαίσιος alone. See Heater, *A Septuagint Translation Technique*, 120 and 135.

515 See HR, 486.

516 See also Heater, *A Septuagint Translation Technique*, 68. According to Heater, the Greek rendering of 37:16 has been influenced by the Greek rendering of 18:12 where πτῶμα also oc-curs next to ἐξαίσιος. See Heater, *A Septuagint Translation Technique*, 68 and 120.

of the text (8:14) and creating a better and coherent textual unity (8:14).[517] Moreover, in 36:18 a theological/ethical nuance is present in the Greek text that is absent from MT, i.e., the pious will receive justice, whereas the impious will receive wrath on account of the injustices they do.

(c) In two cases he did not wholly understand the Hebrew hapax. However, instead of transliterating, he resorted to double translation (33:16) and provided one Greek equivalent for two Hebrew words (20:22).

(d) In 20:6, he has misread his *Vorlage* and provided a different rendering.

As is clear from the analysis and conclusions, the LXX translator understood most of the non-absolute hapaxes discussed in this study (11 out of 18). When he did not understand the meaning of the hapax, he never transliterated but provided a creative solution which often led to a stylistically better text.

Having analysed the absolute and non-absolute *hapax legomena* in LXX Proverbs and LXX Job, we can now compare the results in order to give an indicate answer on the question of a single translator for both books.

2.3 A comparison of the translation technique of LXX Proverbs and Job with regard to Hebrew *hapax legomena*

In the previous sections we have analysed and evaluated the Hebrew *hapax legomena* and their Greek rendering in LXX Proverbs and Job. These analyses have obtained results on the translation technique of both books. However, as already indicated, this book also aims at providing an (indicative) answer to the question of a single translator of both Proverbs and Job. In order to do so, this section will compare the results of the study on the Greek rendering of Hebrew hapaxes in both books.

2.3.1 LXX Proverbs' attitude towards *hapax legomena*

This study, being the first of its kind to have systematically examined the Greek rendering of Hebrew hapaxes in LXX Proverbs, have shed some light on the translator's attitude towards *hapax legomena*. As has been observed, no hapax

---

517 Contextual exegesis is a trait of the LXX translator of Job, certainly in connection with the Greek rendering of Hebrew *hapax legomena*. See Verbeke, "Hebrew Hapax Legomena," 390–394.

has been transliterated by the LXX translator. Moreover, the majority of the hapaxes have been rendered by an adequate Greek lexeme. This indicates that the translator was familiar with the Hebrew word.

Often, the translator made use of contextual exegesis in to render the Hebrew hapaxes (e.g., 4:24; 8:6.18; 15:19; 16:26; 22:29; 23:2.29; 25:28). In a vast number of instances, the translator was motived by stylistic considerations when rendering the hapax into Greek. The stylistic tendencies observed in this work are (a) the enhancement of parallelistic structure of the verse (e.g., 7:16; 29:21), (b) the avoidance of repetition and thus creating variation (e.g., 7:18; 8:13; 23:29; 25:11) and (c) the introduction of rhyme (alliteration and assonance) (e.g., 16:30; 17:22.25; 21:8; 22:29). These techniques are an indication of the translator's fondness to not only create a decent translation and make his text legible for his target audience, but also to create a stylistic Greek text.

In several instances, the LXX translator has rendered the Hebrew hapax by a Greek lexeme he used elsewhere to render Hebrew words of the same root (i.e., root-linked renderings) (e.g., 9:13; 11:2.15; 12:18; 19:15; 21:8; 23:34; 25:18; 27:4.20.21; 28:10; 31:27). Whether these root-linked renderings attest of the translator's ignorance of the meaning of the hapax is debatable and cannot be satisfactorily determined. Nonetheless, these root-linked renderings do fit the context of the verse wherein they occur. Thus, the opting for a root-linked rendering reveal a translator who either knew the word or took the context of the verse into consideration.

It has been observed that the LXX translator often explained or elaborated the image which is attested in MT (3:26; 4:24; 26:11). This explanation resulted in a religious/moralising nuance in 4:24. Seldomly, the translator made intertextual references to other LXX books (3:26 and 23:2).

In some instances, the translator misread his *Vorlage* and provided a different translation than the Hebrew (e.g., 11:2; 22:21; 29:21; 30:31; 31:19). However, sometimes the translator applied metathesis to make sense of the Hebrew text and rendered it accordingly (e.g., 15:19; 16:27; 23:28).

Several hapaxes have not been rendered by the translator. Some of those can be ascribed to a diverging Hebrew *Vorlage* (e.g., 5:19; 16:1; 26:18). In the instances where those renderings who cannot be ascribed to another *Vorlage*, the translator nonetheless tried to make a legible Greek text (e.g., 25:11; 17:22; 25:28).

2.3.2 LXX Job's attitude towards *hapax legomena*

In her study on the Greek rendering of Hebrew *hapax legomena* in the speeches of Job and God, Verbeke has concluded that:[518]
(1) no hapax has been transliterated by the LXX translator;
(2) sometimes the translator did not render the hapax;[519]
(3) the translator provided an adequate/consistent rendering for several hapaxes and, thus, had no problem with the Hebrew in his source text;[520]
(4) in some instances, the translator resorted to contextual exegesis in order to translate the *hapax legomenon*;
(5) some translations are root-linked translations;
(6) the translator often gives an approximate translation or a paraphrase;
(7) sometimes the Greek points to a diverging *Vorlage*.[521]

Since Verbeke has not examined all the Hebrew hapaxes and their Greek rendering in Job, this study has registered and examined the remaining hapaxes which are found in the prologue and speeches of Job's friends. The results of this examination has provided a more complete picture of the way the translator dealt with *hapax legomena*.

The majority of the hapaxes has been rendered by an adequate Greek lexeme. Some of these renderings are root-linked renderings and are in line with the translator's choice of Greek words for those lexemes (cfr. Verbeke) (e.g., 33:9; 34:25.36 and 37:16).

Some hapaxes have been rendered by drawing upon contextual exegesis (cfr. Verbeke) (e.g., 15:24.29; 37:16).

In some cases he struggled to render the hapax (3:16; 20:22) or misread his *Vorlage* (20:6). The hapaxes which he probably did not fully understand were not transliterated. Instead, the LXX translator provided a double translation (33:16) or one Greek equivalent for two Hebrew lexemes (20:22).

---

518 For a full and exhaustive overview with examples, see Verbeke, "Hebrew Hapax Legomena," 367–407.
519 She labels the non-renderings as 'omissions.' See Verbeke, "Hebrew Hapax Legomena," 370-372.
520 Verbeke makes two different categories for 'consistent renderings' and 'no problem with the Hebrew text.' See Verbeke, "Hebrew Hapax Legomena," 376–385 and 397–398.
521 Verbeke adds another category, i.e., variant types and unclear renderings, to indicate renderings which cannot be categorised or properly evaluated. However, this category does not shed a lot of light on the overall technique of the LXX translator and is, therefore, not listed here.

In some instances, the hapax is not rendered in the LXX and has been skipped over. The LXX translator did render the verse creatively and was motivated by stylistic considerations based upon the context of the verse. Examples thereof are (1) the enhancement of parallelism (e.g., 36:18; 37:9), harmonisation (e.g., 20:22), the enhancement of the image of the text (e.g., 8:14), contrasting (e.g., 33:24) and creating a better and coherent textual unity (e.g., 8:14; 33:24).

Some non-renderings might be explained due to a different *Vorlage* (e.g., 18:3; 33:25).

2.3.3 LXX Proverbs and Job: a same translator?

From the above conclusions, it is clear that LXX Proverbs and Job share similar techniques to handle Hebrew hapaxes. A first similarity worth noting is that no hapax has been transliterated and both have rendered the majority of Hebrew hapaxes by an adequate Greek lexeme. This is an indication that both translators were highly proficient in both Hebrew and Greek. Moreover, this also demonstrates that although hapaxes are words which are only attested in a certain corpus, their usage outside this corpus might have been more common than one would expect. Therefore, although their meaning might sometimes be obscure to contemporary readers and scholars, it was not necessarily so for Hebrew speakers and readers in the time the Hebrew Bible was written or translated into Greek.

Both books attest several renderings which are root-linked. As indicated above, it is hard to discern whether these renderings elicit the translator's ignorance of the meaning of the hapax. Certainly since these renderings do fit the context wherein they are used.

For both books it has been observed that some renderings are made on the basis of contextual exegesis and stylistic motivations. The enhancement of parallelism and imagery is present in both Proverbs and Job. However, on the basis of the study of hapaxes, it seems that the inclination to insert rhyme is a trait which is unique to Proverbs. However, Gammie has convincedly demonstrated the occurrence of rhyme (i.e., alliteration and assonance) in LXX Job.[522]

From the results, it is clear that there is only one double translation found in the rendering of *hapax legomena* in Job, which is not found in Proverbs. It has indeed been noted that Job contains several double translations.[523] However,

---

522 See Gammie, "The Septuagint of Job," 16–19.
523 See, esp. Dhont, "Double Translations in Old Greek Job."

although no double translation in Proverbs has been found, scholars agree that double translations can be found in LXX Proverbs.[524] The same goes for harmonisation and contrasting.[525]

The LXX translator of Proverbs applied metathesis to render several hapaxes. This technique has not been observed in LXX Job's treatment of *hapax legomena*. However, just as was the case for double translations, metathesis has been detected in other parts of LXX Job.[526]

Taking the above observations and similarities, it is clear that both LXX Proverbs and Job exhibit the same translation techniques. Although some differences between their approach to render Hebrew *hapax legomena* can be observed (i.e., creating rhyme [Proverbs], metathesis [Proverbs], double translation [Job], harmonisation [Job], contrasting [Job]), these techniques have also been applied in the other book elsewhere. Thus, to answer the question of a single translator for Job and Proverbs, on the basis of the examination of the Greek rendering of Hebrew *hapax legomena*, it can be concluded that both books were either translated by a single translator or that they stemmed from the same milieu/group of translators.

Having examined one content- and context-related criterion, i.e., Hebrew *hapax legomena*, we have given an indicate answer to the question of a single translator. However, in order to come to a more nuanced answer, more content- and context-related criteria need to be analysed in both books and their results compared with one another. Therefore, the two following excursuses will analyse the Greek rendering of Hebrew animal names and floral, plant and herb names in LXX Proverbs and Job in order to obtain a more nuanced characterisation of their translation technique as well as a more profound answer to the question of a single translator.

---

524 See Fritsch, "The Treatment of the Hexaplaric Signs," 44; Johann Cook, "The Hexaplaric Text," 132–136; de Waard, "Some Unusual Translation Techniques," 190.
525 See, e.g., Cook, *The Septuagint of Proverbs*, i.a., 57, 85, 88, 259 and 290; Cook, "Contrasting as a Translation Technique in the LXX of Proverbs."
526 See Annette Y. Reed, "Job as Jobab: The Interpretation of Job in LXX Job 42:17b-e," *JBL* 120.1 (2001): 31–55, 38–40; Cox, "Iob," 668; Claude E. Cox, "Job," in *The T&T Clark Companion to the Septuagint*, ed. James K. Aitken (London – New York, NY: Bloomsbury T&T Clark, 2015), 385–400, 388.

2.4 Excursus I: the Greek rendering of Hebrew animal names in LXX Proverbs and Job

Within the framework of the content- and context-related approach (outlined in chapter 1), I have proposed a new criterion to examine the translation technique of the LXX translators: the Greek rendering of Hebrew animal names. This criterion, which is jargon-defined vocabulary, has not been systematically examined in LXX studies.[527] However, I am of the opinion that fauna vocabulary could have posed a difficulty for the LXX translator since it indeed quite often concerns very specific vocabulary (as is the case in flora and herb names). Therefore, analysing the rendering of Hebrew animal names could shed light on the translation technique of the LXX translator.[528]

Against this background, and as a first of its kind, this excursus will systematically register and evaluate the Greek rendering of animal names in LXX Proverbs and LXX Job in order to come to a more accurate image of the translation technique of the LXX translator of both books. Moreover, since this monograph also aims at providing an answer to the question of a single translator for both books, the results of the analyses of the Greek rendering of Hebrew animal names in both books will be compared with one another in order to give a more indicative answer to the question of a single translator.

2.4.1 The registration of Hebrew animal names in Proverbs and Job

2.4.1.1 Registration of Hebrew animal names and their Greek rendering in Proverbs

In order to evaluate the Greek rendering of Hebrew animal names in Proverbs, I will first register the Hebrew animal names and their respective Greek rendering

---

[527] In the past, some studies have looked at animal imagery in the Book of Proverbs: Paul B. Likeng, "Animal Imagery in Proverbs," *The Bible Translator* 49.2 (1998): 225–232; Tova L. Forti, "Animal Images in the Book of Proverbs," *Biblica* 77.1 (1996): 48–63; Forti, *Animal Imagery in the Book of Proverbs*. However, none of these works explicitly focus on the rendering of Hebrew animal names in the LXX. Tova L. Forti only briefly touches upon the translation of the LXX in several cases in her monograph *Animal Imagery in the Book of Proverbs*. However, she does not elaborate on the translation technique of the LXX translator.

[528] Note that we are not interested in general designations of groups of animals (e.g., flock, cattle, wild animals, four-footed animals, etc.), but rather specific animal names since they might have posed a greater difficulty for the translator due to their specific nature.

by making a synopsis in which all extant textual witnesses are listed.[529] Since there are no manuscripts found in the Judean desert that attest the verses of Proverbs in which animal names occur, we will look only at MT and the LXX.

Verse	MT[530]	LXX[531]
1:17	כָּנָף (wing/winged creature)	πτερωτός (winged creature)
5:19	אַיֶּלֶת (deer)	ἔλαφος (deer, hind)
5:19	יַעֲלָה (female ibex/wild she-goat)[532]	πῶλος (colt)
6:5	צְבִי (gazelle)	δορκάς (deer, gazelle)
6:5	צִפּוֹר (bird)	ὄρνεον (bird)
6:6	נְמָלָה (ant)	μύρμηξ (ant)
7:22	שׁוֹר (bull, ox)	βοῦς (cow, cattle)
7:23	צִפּוֹר (bird)	ὄρνεον (bird)
11:22	חֲזִיר (wild boar)	ὗς (wild swine)
14:4	אֶלֶף (cattle)	βοῦς (cow, cattle)
14:4	שׁוֹר (bull, ox)	βοῦς (cow, cattle)
15:17	שׁוֹר (bull, ox)	μόσχος (the young of cattle, calf)
17:12	דֹּב (bear)	/
19:12	כְּפִיר (young lion)	λέων (lion)
20:2	כְּפִיר (young lion)	λέων (lion)
21:31	סוּס (horse)	ἵππος (horse)
22:13	אֲרִי (lion)	λέων (lion)
23:5	נֶשֶׁר (eagle, vulture)	ἀετός (eagle)

---

529 A list of animal names in Proverbs has been provided by Paul Bitjick Likeng. See Likeng, "Animal Imagery in Proverbs,", 228–229. See also the index of Tova L. Forti with corresponding (transcribed) Hebrew names: Forti, *Animal Imagery in the Book of Proverbs*, 191. Although these lists are helpful, some remarks have to be made. The first remark concerns the list of Paul Likeng. This list contains all references to animal imagery. Therefore, it also notes the attestation of honey in the Book of Proverbs. According to Likeng Proverbs also attests a stag (7:22). MT does not attest the Hebrew word for stag. Likeng has probably based himself on a translation of the Book of Proverbs, e.g., NRSV, which wrongly translates עֶבֶס as stag. The second remark concerns the index of Forti. This index contains animal names that are not attested in the Book of Proverbs but are attested in other LXX books. Examples hereof are the words 'fly' (Qohelet) and 'moth' (Psalms).
530 English translation taken from HALOT and DCH.
531 Translation of the Greek words taken from LEH.
532 DCH translates יַעֲלָה with 'wild she-goat,' whereas HALOT renders it to 'female ibex.' See DCH, vol. IV, 242; HALOT, 12.

Verse	MT[530]	LXX[531]
23:32	נָחָשׁ (snake)	ὄφις (snake, serpent)
23:32	צִפְעֹנִי ([venomous] snake, viper)	κεράστης (horned serpent)
26:2	צִפּוֹר (bird)	ὄρνεον (bird)
26:3	סוּס (horse)	ἵππος (horse)
26:3	חֲמוֹר (ass, donkey)	ὄνος (ass, donkey)
26:11	כֶּלֶב (dog)	κύων (dog)
26:13	שַׁחַל (lion-cub)	/
26:13	אֲרִי (lion)	λέων (lion)
26:17	כֶּלֶב (dog)	κύων (dog)
27:8	צִפּוֹר (bird)	ὄρνεον (bird)
27:26	כֶּבֶשׂ (lamb/young ram)	πρόβατον (sheep)
27:27	עֵז (goat)	/
28:1	כְּפִיר (young lion)	λέων (lion)
28:15	אֲרִי (lion)	λέων (lion)
28:15	דֹּב (bear)	λύκος (wolf)
30:15	עֲלוּקָה (leech)	βδέλλα (leech)
30:17	עֹרֵב (raven)	κόραξ (raven)
30:17	נֶשֶׁר (eagle, vulture)	ἀετός (eagle)
30:19	נֶשֶׁר (eagle, vulture)	ἀετός (eagle)
30:25	נְמָלָה (ant)	μύρμηξ (ant)
30:26	שָׁפָן (coney/rock badger)[533]	χοιρογρύλλιος (rabbit, coney)
30:27	אַרְבֶּה (locust)	ἀκρίς (locust)
30:28	שְׂמָמִית (gecko)[534]	καλαβώτης (gecko, spotted lizard)
30:30	לַיִשׁ (lion)	σκύμνος λέοντος (young lion)

---

533 DCH attests the translation 'rock badger' for שָׁפָן, whereas HALOT records 'coney.' See DCH, vol. VIII, 544; HALOT, 381. However, DCH also attests the translation of 'coney' for the Hebrew noun שָׁפָן elsewhere under the lemma שְׂמָמִית. Therefore, I am more inclined to translate שָׁפָן by 'coney.'

534 שְׂמָמִית is a *hapax legomenon* in the Hebrew Bible. Its meaning had been contested throughout the ages. Some have even suggested the meaning of 'spider' (see, e.g., DCH, vol. VIII, 167). For an overview on the history of the meaning of שְׂמָמִית, see Forti, *Animal Imagery in the Book of Proverbs*, 116–117. In the *Commentary on the Book of Proverbs Attributed to John Chrysostom* the Greek reads ἀσκαλαβώτης. This attestation does not form a significant variation. See Bryan Beeckman, "Traces of Proverbs in Patristic Writings. Tracing Back Proverbs' Greek Rendered Hebrew Hapax Legomena in the Commentary on the Book of Proverbs Attributed to John Chrysostom," *JECH* 7.2 (2017): 40–53, 51.

Verse	MT[530]	LXX[531]
30:31	זַרְזִיר (cock)	ἀλέκτωρ (cock)
30:31	תַּיִשׁ (he-goat)	τράγος (he-goat)

2.4.1.2 Registration of Hebrew animal names and their Greek rendering in Job

Compared to Proverbs, more animal names are attested in Job[535]. There are 75 animal occurrences in Job. All these instances are listed in the table below. Although we are interested in the translational activity of the LXX translator, the asterisked material will be indicated by the *siglum* '⁂' in the LXX column for the sake of completeness[536]. However, as was the case for the hapaxes, we will not evaluate them. Where applicable, the attestations in the Qumran scrolls (DSS) are attested as well.

Verse	MT	LXX	DSS
1:3	צֹאן (sheep)	πρόβατον (sheep)	/
1:3	גָּמָל (camel)	κάμηλος (camel)[537]	/
1:3	בָּקָר (cow)	βοῦς (cow)	/
1:3	אָתוֹן (female donkey)	ὄνος θήλεια (female donkey)	/
1:14	בָּקָר (cow)	βοῦς (cow)	/
1:14	אָתוֹן (female donkey)	ὄνος θήλεια (female donkey)	/
1:16	צֹאן (sheep)	πρόβατον (sheep)	/
1:17	גָּמָל (camel)	κάμηλος (camel)	/
3:8	לִוְיָתָן (Leviathan, sea-monster)	κῆτος (sea monster, huge fish, cetecea)	/
4:10	אַרְיֵה (lion)	λέων (lion)	/
4:10	שַׁחַל (lion-cub)	λέαινα (lioness)	/
4:10	כְּפִיר (young lion)	δράκων (dragon, serpent)	/
4:11	לַיִשׁ (lion)	μυρμηκολέων (ant-lion)[538]	/
4:11	לָבִיא (lioness)	λέων (lion)	/

---

535 A complete list of all attestations of animals can be found in Lesley C. F. Deysel, "Animal Names and Categorisation in the Hebrew Bible. A Textual and Cognitive Approach" (PhD diss., University of Pretoria, 2017), 290–316.

536 For the delimitation of the asterisked material, the following works have been consulted: Ziegler, *Job*; Gentry, *The Asterisked Materials in the Greek Job*, 31.

537 According to LEH this is a Semitic loanword, see LEH, 304.

538 LEH records this as a neologism, see LEH, 410.

Verse	MT	LXX	DSS
4:19	עָשׁ (moth)	σής (moth)	/
6:5	פֶּרֶא (zebra, wild donkey)	ὄνος ἄγριος (wild donkey)	/
6:5	שׁוֹר (bull, ox, steer)	βοῦς (cow)	/
7:5	רִמָּה (maggot)	σκώληξ ([wood]worm)	/
7:12	תַּנִּין (monster, sea-dragon, serpent)	δράκων (dragon, serpent)	/
8:14	עַכָּבִישׁ (spider)	ἀράχνη (spider)	/
10:16	שַׁחַל (lion-cub)	λέων (lion)	/
11:12	פֶּרֶא (zebra, wild donkey)	ὄνος ἐρημίτης (desert donkey)	/
12:7	עוֹף (bird)	πετεινός (winged creature, bird)	/
12:8	דָּג (fish)	/※	/
13:28	אֲכָלוֹ עָשׁ (moth-eaten)	σητόβρωτος (moth-eaten)[539]	/
17:14	רִמָּה (maggot)	σαπρία (decay, decayed matter)	lacuna
20:14	פֶּתֶן (asp, cobra)	ἀσπίς (asp, serpent)※	/
20:16	פֶּתֶן (asp, cobra)	δράκων (dragon, serpent)	/
20:16	אֶפְעֶה (snake)	ὄφις (snake, serpent)	/
21:10	שׁוֹר (bull, ox, steer)	βοῦς (cow)	lacuna
21:10	פָּרָה (cow)	ἐν γαστρὶ ἔχουσα (the one having in the belly = the pregnant one)	הריתהו (the one of them who is pregnant)
21:11	צֹאן (sheep)	πρόβατον αἰώνιος (eternal sheep)	/
21:26	רִמָּה (maggot)	σαπρία (decay, decayed matter)	lacuna
24:3	חֲמוֹר (donkey)	ὑποζύγιον (draught animal, beast of burden, ass, mule or horse)	/
24:3	שׁוֹר (bull, ox, steer)	βοῦς (cow)	/
24:5	פֶּרֶא (zebra, wild donkey)	ὄνος (donkey)	/
24:20	רִמָּה (maggot)	/	/
25:6	רִמָּה (maggot)	σαπρία (decay, decayed matter)	lacuna
25:6	תּוֹלֵעָה (maggot, worm, vine-weevil)	/※	[תולע]תא (maggot, worm, vine-weevil)
26:12	רַהַב (Rahab)	κῆτος (sea monster, huge fish, cetecea)	lacuna
26:13	נָחָשׁ (snake)	δράκων (dragon, serpent)	תנין (sea-monster, sea-

---

539 LEH records this as a neologism, see LEH, 552.

Verse	MT	LXX	DSS
			dragon, serpent)
28:7	עַיִט (birds of prey)	πετεινός (winged creature, bird)⸪	lacuna
28:7	אַיָּה (falcon)	/⸪	lacuna
28:8	שַׁחַל (lion-cub)	/⸪	lacuna
28:21	עוֹף (bird)	/⸪	עוֹף (bird)
29:18	חוֹל (phoenix, palm-tree)	φοῖνιξ (phoenix, date palm, date)[540]	/
30:1	כֶּלֶב (dog)	κύων (dog)	כלב (dog)
30:29	תַּן (jackal)	σειρήν (siren, demon of the dead living in the desert)[541]	lacuna
30:29	יַעֲנָה (ostrich, kind of owl)	στρουθός (sparrow, ostrich)	יענה (ostrich, kind of owl)
31:20	כֶּבֶשׂ (young ram)	ἀμνός (lamb)	lacuna
35:11	עוֹף (bird)	πετεινός (winged creature, bird)	צפר (bird)
38:39	לָבִיא (lioness)	λέων (lion)	/
38:39	כְּפִיר (young lion)	δράκων (dragon, serpent)	/
38:41	עֹרֵב (raven)	κόραξ (raven)	/
39:1	יַעֲלֵי־סָלַע (mountain goat)	/⸪	יעלי כפא
39:1	אַיָּלָה (doe of a fallow deer)	/⸪	lacuna
39:5	פֶּרֶא (zebra, wild donkey)	ὄνος ἄγριος (wild donkey)	פראה (zebra, wild donkey)
39:5	עָרוֹד (wild ass)	/	ערדא (donkey)
39:9	רְאֵם (wild ox)[542]	μονόκερως (unicorn)	ראמ[א] (wild ox)
39:13	רְנָנִים (female ostriches)	/⸪	/
39:18	חֲסִידָה (stork, heron)	ασιδα (transliteration) ⸪	/
39:18	סוּס (horse)	/⸪	/
39:19	סוּס (horse)	ἵππος (horse)	/

---

540 LEH only records 'date palm, date.' However, according to Gerleman, the Greek word is also ambiguous and can also mean phoenix just as its Hebrew counterpart. See Gerleman, *Job*, 44–46.

541 LEH notes that this Greek equivalent is often used to translate Hebrew animal names such as ostriches, desert owls and jackals, see LEH, 550.

542 Dictionaries, such as KBL, will only identify רְאֵם as a 'wild ox' on the basis of the article *Beduinisches zum Alten und Neuen Testament* of Johan J. Hess. See Johan J. Hess, "Beduinisches zum Alten und Neuen Testament," *ZAW* 35 (1915): 120–136, 121. The identification of the רְאֵם with the oryx has been noted by several scholars. See, e.g., Charles M. Doughty, *Travels in Arabia Deserta* (London: Jonathan Cape – The Medici Society Limited, 1924), 327–328.

Verse	MT	LXX	DSS
39:20	אַרְבֶּה (locust)	/	lacuna
39:26	נֵץ (falcon)	ἱέραξ (hawk, falcon)	נצא (falcon)
39:27	נֶשֶׁר (eagle, vulture)	ἀετός (eagle)	נש[רא] (eagle, vulture)
40:15	בְּהֵמוֹת (hippopotamus, crocodile)	θηρίον (wild animal, beast, monster)	/
40:15	בָּקָר (cow)	βοῦς (cow)	/
40:25	לִוְיָתָן (Leviathan, sea-monster)	δράκων (dragon, serpent)	תנין (sea-monster, sea-dragon, serpent)
41:5	צִפּוֹר (bird)	ὄρνεον (bird)	/
42:8	פַּר (young bull)	μόσχος (the young of cattle, calf, young bull)	/
42:8	אַיִל (ram)	κριός (ram)	/
42:12	צֹאן (sheep)	πρόβατον (sheep)	/
42:12	גָּמָל (camel)	κάμηλος (camel)	/
42:12	בָּקָר (cow)	βοῦς (cow)	/
42:12	אָתוֹן (female donkey)	ὄνος θήλεια (female donkey)	/

2.4.2 The evaluation of the Greek rendering of Hebrew animal names in Proverbs and Job

2.4.2.1 Evaluation of the Greek rendering of Hebrew animal names in Proverbs
Looking at the synopsis provided above, we can see that almost all animal names are rendered by an adequate Greek equivalent. Some renderings, however, do not attest an adequate Greek equivalent (יַעֲלָה/πῶλος [5:19]; דֹּב/λύκος [28:15]),[543] exhibit a potential lack of variation (שַׁחַל/לַיִשׁ, אֲרִי, כְּפִיר/λέων [19:12; 20:2; 22:13; 26:13; 28:1.15; 30:30]); or are not even rendered at all (דֹּב [17:12]; שַׁחַל [26:13]; עַז [27:27]). In this section, I will try to evaluate these renderings by taking the translation technique of the LXX translator into account.

---

543 One could argue that כֶּבֶשׂ/πρόβατον (27:26) could also be considered an inadequate rendering since the Greek equivalent of כֶּבֶשׂ is ἀμνός (see, e.g., Job 31:20; Ezra 8:35; Exod 29:38). Though, in the context of the verse which deals with lambs (MT) or sheep (LXX) providing for clothing, the meaning remains the same.

A Inadequate renderings

I Prov 5:19

In verse 19 of chapter 5, MT attests the animal name יַעֲלָה meaning 'female ibex, wild she-goat'. This word is a *hapax legomenon* in the Hebrew Bible. The LXX renders it with the word πῶλος which means 'colt.' In order to properly evaluate this variant rendering, the whole context of the verse has to be taken into account:

MT	LXX
אַיֶּלֶת אֲהָבִים וְיַעֲלַת־חֵן דַּדֶּיהָ יְרַוֻּךָ בְכָל־עֵת בְּאַהֲבָתָהּ תִּשְׁגֶּה תָמִיד:	ἔλαφος φιλίας καὶ πῶλος σῶν χαρίτων ὁμιλείτω σοι, ἡ δὲ ἰδία ἡγείσθω σου καὶ συνέστω σοι ἐν παντὶ καιρῷ ἐν γὰρ τῇ ταύτης φιλίᾳ συμπεριφερόμενος πολλοστὸς ἔσῃ.
A lovely deer and a graceful female ibex.[544] May her breasts saturate you all the time; may you continuously be intoxicated by her love.	Let the deer of your love and the colt of your grace converse with you, and consider her your own and let her be with you all the time, because while accommodating in her love you will be increased immeasurably.[545]

Although the meaning of the verse is not exactly the same in the translation, the main thought, i.e., always to be intoxicated by or indulge in love, is expressed in both versions. One can argue whether the LXX translator has provided a completely different rendering but preserved the meaning of the Hebrew text, or whether the Hebrew *Vorlage* of the LXX differed from MT.[546] It might be the case that the LXX translator found the Hebrew expression to be very odd and inconsistent and, therefore, tried to come up with a different rendering of the verse that (a) preserved the initial meaning and (b) preserved the animal imagery found in the Hebrew but modified it to another animal image that suited his

---

544 DCH has translated יַעֲלָה by 'wild she-goat' instead of 'female ibex' (HALOT). I am more inclined to follow DCH rather than HALOT. An ibex can be considered more graceful than a goat.
545 My own translation differs from the NETS translation of Proverbs. Cook did not translate πῶλος by 'colt' but opted for 'foal' which more or less expresses the same thought/meaning.
546 As I have argued elsewhere, on the basis of the different structure and taken into account the ancient scribal practice, the LXX translation of Proverbs was translated from a different Hebrew *Vorlage*. Smaller changes on verse level could possibly be explained due to the creativity and freedom of the translator. See Beeckman, "Trails of a Different Vorlage". Cook will not ascribe major differences to a diverging Hebrew *Vorlage* because there is no extant text that attests this Hebrew text. See Cook, "Contrasting as a Translation Technique," 412.

Greek verse. However, since the LXX version of the verse is significantly different than the MT-version, I am more inclined to ascribe it to a different Hebrew
Vorlage.

II Prov 28:15

MT	LXX
אֲרִי־נֹהֵם וְדֹב שׁוֹקֵק מֹשֵׁל רָשָׁע עַל עַם־דָּל׃	λέων πεινῶν καὶ λύκος διψῶν ὃς τυραννεῖ πτωχὸς ὢν ἔθνους πενιχροῦ.
Like a roaring lion or a charging bear is a wicked ruler over a poor people.	A hungry lion and a thirsty wolf is he who rules a needy nation while he himself is poor.

In Prov 28:15, דֹב (bear) has been rendered by λύκος (wolf). Tova Forti has examined this peculiar rendering in her article entitled *If You Go Down to the Woods
Today: B(e)aring the Text of Proverbs MT and LXX*. She argues that this translation can be explained by a misreading of דב as the Aramaic ד(א)ב, which means
'wolf.'[547] Indeed, it is highly plausible that this is the case.

B Lack of variation
There is only one specific animal name in which the translator shows a potential lack of variation with regard to the Greek equivalent used in his translation.
For the translation of the Hebrew words כְּפִיר (young lion; 19:12; 20:2; 28:1), אֲרִי
(lion; 22:13; 26:23; 28:15), לַיִשׁ (lion; 30:30) and שַׁחַל (lion-cub; 26:13), he always
used the same noun λέων. Although the meaning of those Hebrew lexemes
belong to the same lexical and semantic domain, i.e., lion, there is a nuance in
meaning between the different lexemes: young lion, lion-cub and lion. In what
follows, I will try to investigate whether this difference in meaning is adequately
preserved in the LXX or not.

For the rendering of כְּפִיר the LXX translator could have used the Greek
equivalent σκύμνος as the LXX translators of Isaiah and Ezekiel did in e.g., Isa
5:29; 31:4 and Ezek 19:2.3.[548] However, the rendering of כְּפִיר with λέων was not

547 See Tova Forti, "If You Go Down to the Woods Today: B(e)aring the Text of Proverbs MT
and LXX," in *From Author to Copyist: Essays on the Composition, Redaction, and Transmission
of the Hebrew Bible in Honor of Zipi Talshir*, ed.Cana Werman (Winona Lake, IN: Eisenbrauns,
2015), 103–112, 107.
548 More background surrounding the translation of כְּפִיר by 'young lion,' see Forti, *Animal
Imagery in the Book of Proverbs*, 58.

an uncommon practice in the translation of the LXX. Other LXX books, e.g., Psalms (17[LXX 16]:12; 35[LXX 34]:17XE "Psalms:+35(LXX 34\:17") and Jeremiah (51(LXX 28):38 XE "Jeremiah:51(LXX 28)\:+38"), also attest λέων as translation of כְּפִיר.

The lexemes אֲרִי is adequately rendered as λέων since the LXX translates this noun with λέων in all occurrences of the word in MT.

The rare Hebrew word לַיִשׁ only occurs three times in MT: Job 4:11, Prov 30:30 and Isa 30:6. Both Isaiah and Proverbs render it with σκύμνος λέοντος, whereas Job renders it with the Greek *hapax legomenon* μυρμηκολέων ('antlion').[549] In my opinion, it is very hard to come to a proper solution on whether the LXX translator of Proverbs provided an adequate rendering of the Hebrew noun לַיִשׁ based on this little attestation. I am inclined to think that, because the LXX translator of Ezekiel also translated לַיִשׁ by σκύμνος λέοντος, it might have been the most adequate rendering.

The Hebrew noun שַׁחַל is not translated in LXX. In the Hebrew text, there is a repetition of the same thought in 26:13:

MT	NRSV
אָמַר עָצֵל שַׁחַל בַּדָּרֶךְ אֲרִי בֵּין הָרְחֹבוֹת:	The lazy person says: "There is a lion in the road! There is a lion on the square!"

It is plausible to assume that the LXX translator of Proverbs, who had a rather free approach towards his Hebrew *Vorlage*, found this repetition redundant and therefore omitted one sentence from the verse.

On the basis of the above-mentioned analysis, we can conclude the following. Although the LXX translator exhibits a lack in variation of Greek lexemes with regard to Hebrew animal names concerning the lexical and semantic domain of 'lion,' he tried to give an adequate translation for the corresponding Hebrew animal names he was confronted to while translating his *Vorlage*.

C Missing renderings

As it is clear from the synopsis above, some Hebrew animal names are seemingly not rendered at all. It concerns the words דֹּב (17:12), שַׁחַל (26:13) and עַז (27:27).

---

549 According to LEH this word is a neologism (μύρμηξ + λέων), see LEH, 410. For a more elaborated discussion on the usage of μυρμηκολέων for לַיִשׁ by the LXX translator of Job, see Anna Angelini, "Biblical Translation and Cross-Cultural Communication. A Focus on the Animal Imagery," *Semitica et Classica* 8 (2015): 33–43, 34–35.

I דֹּב (Prov 17:12)

MT	LXX
פָּגוֹשׁ דֹּב שַׁכּוּל בְּאִישׁ וְאַל־כְּסִיל בְּאִוַּלְתּֽוֹ׃	ἐμπεσεῖται μέριμνα ἀνδρὶ νοήμονι, οἱ δὲ ἄφρονες διαλογιοῦνται κακά.
(It is better) to meet a bear robbed of its children by a man and not (to meet) a fool in folly.	Ambition will befall an intelligent man, but fools will consider bad things.

Due to the nature of the LXX translation of this specific verse, it would seem impossible that the translator would not have been able to translate the Hebrew and therefore provided a completely different translation. For this reason, I argue that the LXX version of this verse attests a different Hebrew *Vorlage*.[550] Thus, we cannot ascribe the non-rendering of the Hebrew lexeme דֹּב to the activity of the translator. However, we see that the Greek verse also attests a parallelism (νοήμων/ἄφρων). In that sense, whatever the Hebrew text in the *Vorlage* might have been, the translator nonetheless tried to preserve (or perhaps tried to enhance or create) the parallelism.[551]

II שַׁחַל (Prov 26:13)

See above (inadequate renderings).

III עֵז (Prov 27:27)

MT	LXX
וְדֵי חֲלֵב עִזִּים לְלַחְמְךָ לְלֶחֶם בֵּיתֶךָ וְחַיִּים לְנַעֲרוֹתֶֽיךָ׃	υἱέ, παρ᾽ ἐμοῦ ἔχεις ῥήσεις ἰσχυρὰς εἰς τὴν ζωήν σου καὶ εἰς τὴν ζωὴν σῶν θεραπόντων.

---

550 Forti, on the other hand, ascribes the non-rendering due to a misreading of the Hebrew text by the LXX translator. See Forti, "If You Go Down to the Woods Today," 110–112. This might as well be the case. It is hard to determine whether it concerns a divergent *Vorlage* or a misreading here. However, given the fact that the LXX provides a totally different proverb than MT, the hypothesis of a different *Vorlage* is, in my opinion, more likely.

551 The use of double and related semantic words for contrasting colons and thereby creating parallelism was an aspect of the translation technique of the LXX translator of Proverbs. See Cook, "Contrasting as a Translation Technique," 409 and 414; Cook, "The Ideology of Septuagint Proverbs;" Cook, "Theological/ideological Tendenz," 77; Tauberschmidt, *Secondary Parallelism*.

MT	LXX
And (there will be) enough goats' milk for your food, for the food of your house(hold) and the lives of your maidens.	Son, you have powerful sayings from me for your life and for the life of your servants.

Once again, as argued above, I am more inclined to explain this difference on the basis of a diverging *Vorlage*. Therefore, we cannot draw conclusions with regard to the translation technique of the translator in this specific passage.

D Adequate renderings

For the majority of the renderings of Hebrew animal names, the LXX translator provided an adequate Greek equivalent. These animal names, thus, seem not to have formed a challenge for the translator. The lexical and semantic meaning of the Hebrew words is preserved in the Greek text. Therefore, these Hebrew words were, most likely, known to the translator and therefore he rendered them with an adequate corresponding Greek word. The translator was aware of both the Hebrew names of all the animals attested in Proverbs, as well as the Greek equivalent of the vocabulary.

This observation strengthens the hypothesis postulated by Cook that the translator was a Jew who was well-educated in Greek language.[552] It seems to be unlikely that the translator was Greek and had a profound knowledge in Hebrew. There was no reason for Greeks to learn the Hebrew language. Therefore, the translator, who was familiar with the Hebrew language, must have stood in the Jewish tradition. Moreover, due to his seemingly good knowledge of Greek fauna vocabulary the LXX translator of Proverbs shows himself to be well-versed in the Greek language as well[553]. This enabled him to preserve the mean-

---

552 See, e.g., Cook, "The Dating of Septuagint Proverbs," 399; Cook, "The Law of Moses in Septuagint Proverbs," 461. Cook even states that the translator is a conservative Jew.

553 Cook has stressed the familiarity of the LXX translator of Proverbs with Greek language in multiple publications. See, e.g., Cook, *The Septuagint of Proverbs*, 317; Cook, "The Translator of the Septuagint of Proverbs," 550; Cook, "A Case Study of LXX Proverbs, LXX Job and 4 Maccabees," 64. Soisalon-Soinnen and Raija Sollamo have also indicated that the LXX translator of Proverbs was familiar with Greek language. They come to this conclusion on the basis of the study of the rendering of Hebrew infinitives (Soisalon-Soininnen) and Hebrew semiprepositions (e.g., πρὸ προσώπου) (Rajia Sollamo). See Soisalon-Soininen, *Die Infinitive in der Septuaginta*; Sollamo, *Renderings of Hebrew Semiprepositions in the Septuagint*; Soisalon-Soininen, "Der Gebrauch des genetivus absolutus in der Septuaginta." See also chapter 1 of this monograph. Albert Wifstrand's study on the place of the enclitic personal pronouns in the LXX books

ing of the Hebrew word as adequately as possible. He translated the Hebrew animal names adequately and thus remained faithful to his Hebrew text.[554]

E Conclusion

Having analysed the rendering of Hebrew animal names in the LXX version of Proverbs, we can draw some conclusions with regard to (1) the translation technique and (2) the identity of the LXX translator:

(1) As indicated above in the evaluation of the different renderings, most of the Hebrew lexemes have been adequately rendered by the Greek translator. Some renderings, however, seem to be inadequately rendered at first sight, exhibit a lack of variation or are not rendered at all. After closer investigation, they can be explained due to (a) a different Hebrew *Vorlage* or a misreading in the case of the non-rendered names and inadequate renderings or (b) the only available or best possible Greek equivalent available to the translator with regard to the lack of variation. Overall, the LXX translator of Proverbs tried to render his Hebrew *Vorlage* in an adequate and faithful way with regard to the rendering of Hebrew animal names.

(2) Moreover, by providing an adequate translation of the Hebrew animal names the LXX translator of Proverbs shows himself to be familiar with Greek and Hebrew fauna jargon and thus well-versed in both Hebrew and Greek language. This sheds confirmative light on the identity of the translator of LXX Proverbs, who can be characterised as a Jew who was well-educated in Greek language.

Now that we have analysed the Greek rendering of Hebrew animal names in Proverbs, we will examine this category of words in Job.

2.4.2.2 Evaluation of the Greek rendering of Hebrew animal names in Job

As we did for Proverbs, from the registration table above, we can make some preliminary observations from which we will try to evaluate the different variant readings. These observations are the following: some renderings (a) show a

---

have also led him to the conclusion that LXX Proverbs, together with Job and in a lesser degree Esther, Daniel and I. Ezra, can be characterised as a literary Greek translation. See Albert Wifstrand, *Die Stellung der Enklitischen Personalpronomina bei den Septuaginta*, K. Humanistiska vetenskapssamfundets i Lund Arsberättelse 1949-1950 II (Lund: Gleerup, 1950), 44–70 (esp. 68).

554 On the faithfulness of a translation, see Aejmelaeus, "The Significance of Clause Connectors;" Ausloos and Lemmelijn, "Faithful Creativity".

potential lack of variation, (b) are potential non-adequate renderings, (c) are missing in the Greek text and (d) are adequate translations.

A Potential lack of variation

The Greek noun δράκων occurs six times in LXX Job and is used to render several Hebrew nouns, i.e., כְּפִיר (4:10 and 38:19), תַּנִּין (7:12), פֶּתֶן (20:16), נָחָשׁ (26:13) and לִוְיָתָן (40:25). Erik Eynikel and Katrin Hauspie have examined the use of the noun δράκων in the LXX.[555] Throughout the LXX, the word δράκων is used to translate six different Hebrew lexemes, i.e. כְּפִיר, תַּנִּין, פֶּתֶן, נָחָשׁ, לִוְיָתָן and תַּן. All of these lexemes occur in Job but only five lexemes are rendered by δράκων (תַּן is rendered by σειρήν in LXX Job, see discussion below).

The noun כְּפִיר is attested 31 times in the Hebrew Bible. In most of the cases, it is rendered by λέων and σκύμνος. In Job, however, it is never rendered by these lexemes. Both occurrences of כְּפִיר in LXX Job are rendered by δράκων.[556] According to Eynikel and Hauspie, the translator opted for this odd rendering on the basis of concern for variation within the verse as well as δράκων being a symbol of the impious.[557] The argument of variation might be valid, but why did the translator not opt for the more obvious translation σκύμνος if he wanted to choose a different rendering than λέων as is the case in Psalm 17(LXX 16):12, Isa 5:29 and 31:4? Moreover, for the second argument, they use Psalm 17(LXX 16):12 as one of the examples in favour of the argument of a lion as a symbol for the impious.[558] But why did the LXX translator of Psalms not render כְּפִיר by δράκων in 17(LXX 16):12 but with σκύμνος instead? The Greek lexeme σκύμνος was known to the LXX translator of Job since he has used it as a rendering of וּבְנֵי לָבִיא (σκύμνοι δὲ λεόντων) in Job 4:11. Thus, he could have rendered כְּפִיר by σκύμνος as the LXX translator of Psalms did but instead opted for δράκων. Therefore, it seems that the LXX translator of Job was not familiar with the Hebrew lexeme כְּפִיר and tried to find an appropriate lexeme instead.[559] The most

555 Erik Eynikel and Katrin Hauspie, "The Use of δράκων in the Septuagint," in *Biblical Greek Language and Lexicography*, ed. Bernard A. Taylor, John A. L. Lee, Peter R. Burton and Richard E. Whitake (Grand Rapids, MI: Eerdmans, 2004), 126–135.
556 In my article on the Greek rendering of animal names in Proverbs, I state that כְּפִיר is rendered by λέων. This is a mistake, there should have been Psalms. See Beeckman, "Proverbia de Animalibus," 264.
557 See Eynikel and Hauspie, "The Use of δράκων in the Septuagint," 133.
558 See Eynikel and Hauspie, "The Use of δράκων in the Septuagint," 133.
559 Although contemporary dictionaries always record 'young lion' as translation of כְּפִיר, this was not always the case. In the past, scholars have wondered whether כְּפִיר might have been a 'young lion' or perhaps some sort of serpent. See Charles Taylor, Edward Wells and Augustin

appropriate lexeme to the LXX translator of Job was δράκων because the combination of λέων and δράκων was well-known in classical Greek literature and occurs elsewhere in the Greek Bible, i.e., Sir 25:16; Ps 90(MT 91):13 and Ezek 32:25.[560]

According to Eynikel and Hauspie, the translation of פֶּתֶן by ἀσπίς (20:14) and δράκων (20:16) can be seen as an indication of the translator wanting to put some variation in his translation.[561] However, Job 20:14 is part of the asterisked material and can thus not be taken into consideration for the analysis of the translation technique of LXX Job. Therefore, I tend to doubt Eynikel and Hauspie's conclusion in this respect. The Hebrew ראש פתנים of Job 20:16 has a parallel with Deut 32:33:

MT	LXX
חֲמַת תַּנִּינֶם יֵינֶם וְרֹאשׁ פְּתָנִים אַכְזָר׃	θυμὸς δρακόντων ὁ οἶνος αὐτῶν, καὶ θυμὸς ἀσπίδων ἀνίατος.
Their wine is the poison of serpents, the cruel venom of asps.	Their wine is the wrath of dragons, and the wrath of asps beyond cure.

The LXX version of Job 20:16 also attests θυμὸς δρακόντων. This might be an example of a so-called "anaphoric" or "associative" translation, whereby a passage from elsewhere in the LXX corpus is being transferred into LXX Job, which is often applied by the LXX translator of Job.[562]

Calmet, *Scripture Illustrated by Means of Natural Science, in Botany, in Geology, in Geography, Natural History, Natural Philosophy, Utensils, Domestic and Military, Habiliments, Manners and Customs* (Charlestown: Samuel Etheridge Junior, 1814), 126. According to these authors, כְּפִיר might also be read as some sort of serpent based on Nicander's *Theriac* in which a certain snake is referred to as a 'spotted lion' (λέων αἰόλος) due to its characteristics. See Taylor, Wells and Calmet, *Scripture Illustrated*, 126. For the fragment of Nicander see: Otto Schneider, *Nicandrea. Theriaca et Alexipharmaca* (Leipzig: Teubner, 1856), 246, v. 463. This argument seems to be implausible.

560 See Dhondt, Style and Context of Old Greek Job, 130.
561 See Eynikel and Hauspie, "The Use of δράκων in the Septuagint," 133. In Deut 32:33 the words ἀσπίς and δράκων are paralleled.
562 The term 'anaphoric translations' is applied by Heater whereas Cox prefers 'associative translations' because "it places the translator's approach in a larger framework." See Heater, *A Septuagint Translation Technique*; Claude E. Cox, "The Historical, Social & Literary Context of Old Greek Job," in *XII Congress of the International Organisation for Septuagint and Cognate Studies, Leiden, 2004*, ed. Melvin K. H. Peters, SBLSCS 54 (Atlanta, GA: Society of Biblical Literature, 2006), 105–116, 116 n. 53.

The lexeme נָחָשׁ is mostly rendered by ὄφις and only twice by δράκων (Job 26:13 and Amos 9:13). Although נָחָשׁ bears the meaning of dragon and serpent, it is peculiar that is only rendered twice by δράκων. According to Eynikel and Hauspie, the LXX translators of Amos and Job have opted for the Greek lexeme δράκων because 'it concerns a mythological sea-monster.'[563] However, in the (so-called) Targum scroll of Job found at Qumran (= 11QtgJob) the Hebrew תנין is found. This lexeme is almost always rendered by δράκων (also in Job 7:12).[564] Since this Targum version of Job agrees with the LXX on certain details,[565] the Hebrew *Vorlage* of the LXX translator might have attested תנין. Therefore, the LXX translator rendered it by the common rendering δράκων. This might also be the case in 40:25 where the Targum attests תנין instead of לִוְיָתָן (Leviathan), although the latter is very often translated by δράκων or κῆτος (Job 3:8).[566]

Eynikel and Hauspie conclude that the LXX translator understood all of these Hebrew lexemes, identified them as being animals symbolising evil and adequately rendered them by δράκων which also symbolises evil or evil forces.[567] In other words, the LXX translator cannot be accused of exhibiting a lack of variation in his usage of the Greek lexeme δράκων. Indeed, sometimes the LXX translator has rendered the same Hebrew lexeme by two different Greek lexemes, i.e., לִוְיָתָן - δράκων/κῆτος. For the rendering of תַּנִּין it is rendered by the most adequate Greek equivalent δράκων. This might also be the case for the rendering of נָחָשׁ. However, the latter can probably be ascribed to the Hebrew *Vorlage* of the LXX translator that probably attested תנין instead of נָחָשׁ in verse 26:13. The rendering of פֶּתֶן by δράκων can be ascribed to the translator's transla-

---

563 Eynikel and Hauspie, "The Use of δράκων in the Septuagint," 133.

564 In 12 out of 15 occurrences תנין of it is rendered by δράκων. In Isa 51:9 it is not rendered, in Neh 2:13 it is rendered by τῶν συκῶν and in Gen 1:26 by κῆτος. See Eynikel and Hauspie, "The Use of δράκων in the Septuagint," 130–132 for an elaborated discussion.

565 See Johannes P. M. van der Ploeg, *Le targum de Job de la grotte 11 de Qumran (11QtgJob. Première communication*, Med. KNAW 25.9 (Amsterdam : Noord-Hollandsche Uitgevers Maatschappij, 1962), 553: "Les Septante et le targum de 11Q sont quelquefois d'accord sur certain détails, ce qui prouve, non une dépendance littéraire, mais une tradition exégétique commune" (= van der Ploeg and van der Woude, ed., *Le Targum de Job de la grotte xi de Qumrân*, 7).

566 See Angelini, "Biblical Translation and Cross-Cultural Communication," 40; Eynikel and Hauspie, "The Use of δράκων in the Septuagint," 132.

567 Eynikel and Hauspie, "The Use of δράκων in the Septuagint," 135. Eynikel and Hauspie, however, generalise the LXX translator. They do not draw conclusions with regard to the translation technique of the different LXX translators of the different LXX books but seem to postulate one LXX translator for all books. Most likely this is not their intention. However, they should have nuanced their wording.

tion technique who applied an "anaphoric" or "associative" translation. Only the rendering of כְּפִיר by δράκων seems to be odd. This can, however, be explained due to the possibility that the LXX translator did not know the Hebrew lexeme כְּפִיר.

B Potential non-adequate translations

Some Hebrew animal names might seem to be not adequately rendered. In this section we will evaluate these renderings and see if they are truly non-adequate.

I Semantic domain of 'lion'

The LXX translator of Job renders Hebrew lexemes that belong to the semantic domain of 'lion' by different Greek lexemes: i.e., אַרְיֵה (λέων [4:10]), שַׁחַל (λέαινα [4:10] and λέων [10:16 and 28:8✻]), כְּפִיר (δράκων [4:10; 38:39]), לַיִשׁ (μυρμηκολέων [4:11]), לָבִיא (λέων [4:11; 38:39]). Some of these renderings might seem odd at first sight and might therefore be potential non-adequate renderings.

The rendering of אַרְיֵה by λέων is a common one (53 out of 57 times it is rendered by this Greek lexeme). Therefore, λέων is an adequate equivalent for אַרְיֵה.

In LXX Job שַׁחַל is rendered two times by λέων (10:16 and 28:8✻) and one time by λέαινα (4:10). Although most dictionaries translate this word with 'young lion', some would argue to denote it as a 'lion of some sort' without specifying the nature (young/old; female/male).[568] In Job 4:10 the translator might have opted for the rendering λέαινα for the sake of variation because he has rendered the before-mentioned אַרְיֵה in the same verse by λέων.

The rendering of כְּפִיר by δράκων has been discussed above.

In Job 4:11, the LXX translator rendered לַיִשׁ by the *hapax legomenon* μυρμηκολέων. Later revisions of the LXX have found this translation equivalent odd and rendered it by a different word: λῖς (α´) and ἀνυπόστατος λέων (σ´).

---

568 See Brent A. Strawn, *What is Stronger than a Lion? Leonine Image and Metaphors in the Hebrew Bible and the Ancient Near East*, OBO 212 (Fribourg – Göttingen: Academic Press Fribourg – Vandenhoeck & Ruprecht, 2005), 322 and 324. Sigmund Mowinckel has even suggested that the שַׁחַל in Job 28:8 must be understood as a serpent-like creature, see Sigmund Mowinckel, "שַׁחַל," in *Hebrew and Semitic Studies Presented to Godfrey Rolles Driver. In Celebration of His Seventieth Birthday, 20 august 1962*, ed David W. Thomas and William D. McHardy (Oxford: Clarendon Press, 1963), 95–103. Scott J. Jones has argued that שַׁחַל could connote both 'lion' and 'serpent', the latter esp. in Job 28:8. See Scott J. Jones, "Lions, Serpents, and Lion-Serpents in Job 28:8 and Beyond," *JBL* 130.4 (2011): 663–686. Job 28:8, however, belongs to the asterisked material and will not be discussed because our primary interest is the translational activity of the OG-translator of Job.

Anna Angelini argues that "the translator [probably] knew some traditions concerning the μυρμήκες, lions or ferocious animals that were supposed to live in Arabic lands."[569] She goes on to argue that this noun is attested in other Hellenistic sources such as Strabo, Aelianus and Agatarchides, also in the context of lions as is the case in Job 4:11.[570] Agatarchides lived during the same period when the LXX version of Job was translated (second half of 2nd century BCE) and therefore it is plausible that the LXX translator of Job shared a common background.[571] The neologism that the LXX translator of Job created is not-surprising given the attestations of different Hebrew lexemes denoting a sort of lion in Job 4:10-11. In order to obtain variation, the LXX translator opted for a contraction of two nouns, i.e., μύρμηξ and λέων, and came up with the neologism μυρμηκολέων. Although μύρμηξ might also mean 'ant,' by connecting it with λέων, by the attestation of μυρμηκολέων in connection with lions in other Hellenistic writings and the lion imagery in Job 4:10-11, it must have been clear to the target audience that a sort of lion was intended with μυρμηκολέων.[572]

In all dictionaries, לָבִיא is translated as 'lioness.' Thus, one might think that the LXX translator did not render the Hebrew lexeme adequately and failed to provide a decent translation equivalent which matches the gender of the Hebrew lexeme. However, Brent A. Strawn has argued that לָבִיא does not necessarily denote a female lion but can also denote a male lion.[573] Those who prefer to render לָבִיא with 'lioness' are heavily depending upon previous scholarship that is influenced by the Vulgate which renders לָבִיא with *leaena* in the majority of the cases.[574] Moreover, לָבִיא is a masculine noun and should be translated as

---

569 Angelini, "Biblical Translation and Cross-Cultural Communication," 34.

570 See Angelini, "Biblical Translation and Cross-Cultural Communication," 34. The same remark is made by Gerleman. See Gerleman, *Job*, 46.

571 See, e.g., Agathargides' *De mari Erythreo* section 69: "Τῶν δὲ καλουμένων μυρμήκων οἱ μὲν πλεῖστοι κατὰ τὴν ἰδέαν τῶν λοιπῶν οὐδὲν παραλλάττουσι, τὴν δὲ τῶν αἰδοίων φύσιν ἀπεστραμμένην ἔχουσιν, ἐναντίαν τοῖς ἄλλοις." Karl Müller, *Geographi Graeci minores. Vol. 1* (Paris: Didot, 1855), 158. LSJ translates μύρμηξ by 'ant' but also by 'fabulous animal in India.' See LEH, 71598.

572 Mia I. Gerhardt has also shown that the μυρμηκολέων must have been a sort of lion. In her article she also discusses the reception of this word up until the works of Albert the Great. See Mia I. Gerhardt, "The Ant-lion. Nature Study and The Interpretation of a Biblical Text, From The Physiologus to Albert the Great," *Vivarium* 3 (1965): 1–23.

573 See Strawn, What is Stronger than a Lion?, 317–319.

574 See Strawn, *What is Stronger than a Lion?*, 317–318. In Job 4:11 the Vulgate translates לָבִיא by *leo*, in 38:39 by *leaena*.

such.[575] Therefore, the LXX translator of Job rendered לָבִיא with an adequate equivalent, i.e., λέων.

II פָּרָה/ἐν γαστρὶ ἔχουσα (Job 21:10)

MT	LXX	11QtgJob
שׁוֹרוֹ עָבַר וְלֹא יַגְעִל תְּפַלֵּט פָּרָתוֹ וְלֹא תְּשַׁכֵּל׃	ἡ βοῦς αὐτῶν οὐκ ὠμοτόκησεν, διεσώθη δὲ αὐτῶν ἐν γαστρὶ ἔχουσα καὶ οὐκ ἔσφαλεν.	הריתהון פל]טת
Their bull breeds without fail; their cow calves and never miscarries.	Their cow did not miscarry, and their pregnant one came through safely and did not falter.	Their pregnant (cow) calv[es

In Job 21:10, the Hebrew attests פָּרָה ('cow') whereas the LXX records ἐν γαστρὶ ἔχουσα (the one having in the belly = the pregnant one). The Greek translation is not an exact equivalent since פָּרָה is rendered by βοῦς (e.g., 1 Sam 6:7.10.12 and Isa 11:7) or δάμαλις (Hos 4:16 and Amos 4:1),[576] when a cow is intended. However, in the context of Job 21:10 it pertains to a cow that is pregnant, therefore the LXX translation is not that odd. Moreover, in 11QtgJob we find the following in Job 21:10 instead of פָּרָה: הריתהון (the one of them who is pregnant).[577] The Greek expression ἐν γαστρὶ ἔχουσα seems to be closer to the Targum than the text that is preserved in MT. Moreover, in MT פָּרָה is followed by a suffix 3rd singular (פָּרָתוֹ) but in the Targum it is followed by a 3rd plural. This plural form is also attested in the LXX: αὐτῶν ἐν γαστρὶ ἔχουσα. Thus, the Hebrew *Vorlage* of the LXX translator of Job must have had a similar form as the one that is attested in 11QtgJob.

III תַּן/σειρήν (Job 30:29)

MT	LXX	11QtgJob
אָח הָיִיתִי לְתַנִּים וְרֵעַ לִבְנוֹת יַעֲנָה׃	ἀδελφὸς γέγονα σειρήνων, ἑταῖρος δὲ στρουθῶ.	לבנ]ת יענה [

---

575 See Strawn, What is Stronger than a Lion?, 317–318.
576 α´ has also rendered פָּרָה with δάμαλις.
577 See van der Ploeg and van der Woude, ed., *Le Targum de Job de la grotte xi de Qumrân*, 19. French translation provided in this work: "leur (génisse) pleine." See van der Ploeg and van der Woude, ed., *Le Targum de Job de la grotte xi de Qumrân*, 19.

MT	LXX	11QtgJob
I am a brother of jackals, and a companion of ostriches.	I have become a brother of sirens and a companion of ostriches.	[to the ost]riches.

Where the MT version of Job attests תַּן ('jackal'), the LXX attest the odd rendering σειρήν ('siren, demon of the dead living in the desert'). Various studies have tried to come up with an explanation for this particular rendering,[578] especially because the Greek lexeme σειρήν appears elsewhere in the LXX corpus as a rendering of other animal names: 3x for יַעֲנָה (Mic 1:8; Isa 13:21; Jer 27:39), 1x for בְּנוֹת יַעֲנָה (Isa 34:13) and 2x for תַּן (Job 30:29 and Isa 43:20). Although Norman Henry Snaith has argued that the meaning of σειρήν could be close to the meaning given by Aristotle in his *Historium Animalium*, i.e., solitary bee or wasp,[579] the majority of the scholars identify σειρήν as the siren of Greek mythology[580]. This conclusion seems reasonable given the siren imagery in Greek mythology that depicts sirens often as winged creatures that composed songs and sometimes appear with a musical instrument such as a lyre (κιθάρα). In Job 30:31, there is mention of a κιθάρα (lyre) (ἀπέβη δὲ εἰς πάθος μου ἡ κιθάρα ὁ δὲ ψαλμός μου εἰς κλαυθμὸν ἐμοί). If the LXX translator was alluding to the Greek sirens in Job 30:29 it fits the immediate context of the verse with the mourning and the lyre (30:31). Therefore, I am also inclined to define the meaning of σειρήν in Job

---

578 See esp. Johann H. Kaupel, "'Sirenen' in der Septuaginta," *BZ* 23.2 (1935): 158–165; Norman H. Snaith, "The Meaning of שְׂעִירִים," *VT* 25.1 (1975): 115–118, 115; Manolis Papoutsakis, "Ostriches into Sirens. Towards an Understanding of a Septuagint Crux," *JJS* 55.1 (2004): 25–36; Angelini, "Biblical Translation and Cross-Cultural Communication," 35–37; Peter J. Atkins, "Mythology or Zoology," *Biblical Interpretation* 24 (2016): 48–59, 52–53.

579 See Snaith, "The Meaning of שְׂעִירִים," 115. Reference of Aristotle: HA 9.40.2 (632b) . See David M. Balme (ed.), *Aristotle. Historia Animalium. Volume I. Books I-X: Text*, CCTC 38 (Cambridge: University Press, 2002), 439. However, σειρήν could also denote a small singing-bird as is attested in Hesychius' *Lexicon* (340). See LSJ, 96255.

580 See, e.g., Gerleman, *Job*, 44; Kaupel, "'Sirenen' in der Septuaginta," 163–165; Angelini, "Biblical Translation and Cross-Cultural Communication," 36; Atkins, "Mythology or Zoology," 53. See also Peter Riede, "'Ich bin ein Bruder der Schakale' (Hi 30:29). Tiere als Exponenten der gegenmenschlichen Welt in der Bildsprache der Hiobdialoge", in *Im Spiegel der Tiere. Studien zum Verhältnis von Mensch und Tier im alten Israel*, ed. Peter Riede, OBO 187 (Freiburg – Göttingen: Universitätsverlag Freiburg Schweiz – Vandenhoeck & Ruprecht, 2002), 120–132, 124. However, Peter Riede does not give an explanation on why the LXX opted for the particular rendering of תַּן by σειρήν.

30:29 as an influence of Hellenistic culture, a common background shared by the LXX translator and his target audience.[581]

IV רְאֵם/μονόκερως (Job 39:9)

MT	LXX	11QtgJob
הֲיֹאבֶה רֵּים עָבְדֶךָ אִם־יָלִין עַל־ אֲבוּסֶךָ׃	βουλήσεται δέ σοι μονόκερως δουλεῦσαι ἢ κοιμηθῆναι ἐπὶ φάτνης σου;	היבא ראמ[א ל[מפלחך א]ו היבית על אוריך[
"Is the wild ox willing to serve you? Will it spend the night at your crib?"	"And will the unicorn be willing to be your slave or to lie down at your manger?"	Does [the] wild ox want [to] serve you, o[r] will he spend the night in your stable?

The Hebrew noun רְאֵם denotes an oryx or a wild ox, probably the *bos primigenius Bojanus*, and is rendered by μονόκερως ('unicorn') in Job 39:9. The Greek rendering μονόκερως for רְאֵם is a common translation throughout the LXX corpus, i.e., in Num 23:22; 24:8; Deut 33:17; Ps 22(LXX 21):22; Ps 29(LXX 28):6; Ps 92(LXX 91):11 and Job 39:9. The noun μονόκερως also occurs in other Greek literature, e.g., Aristotle's *Historia Animalium* 499b19 where it is mentioned next to the ox (βοῦς), stag (ἔλαφος), goat (αἴξ) and antelope (ὄρυξ).[582] Indeed, as Angelini has argued, there is no need to postulate a mythical being onto μονόκερως.[583] Certainly given the fact that Aristotle mentions the animal in connection with non-mythical creatures and refers to μονόκερως as ὁ Ἰνδικὸς ὄνος ('the Indian donkey') and the ὄρυξ ('oryx').

Concerning the use of μονόκερως as an equivalent of רְאֵם, Johann J. Hess, who regards רְאֵם as the 'wild ox,' argues that the wild ox (*bos primigenius Bojanus*) was extinct during the time of the LXX translation.[584] Therefore, the LXX translators only knew the wild ox from depictions on steles (such as the Babylonian stelae).[585] On these stelae, the wild ox is depicted with one horn since its

---

581 See Kaupel, "'Sirenen' in der Septuaginta," 163–164: "Nicht verwunderlich, weil gerade in diesem Punkt [= Dämonenglaube] auch das palästinische Milieu nicht der Diaspora nachtsteht, wie es sich überhaupt dem Einfluss des Hellenismus wenigstens zeitweise nicht zu entziehen vermochte." See also Angelini, "Biblical Translation and Cross-Cultural Communication," 33 and 36.

582 See Aristotle HA 499 b19 in Balme, *Aristotle. Historia Animalium*, 93.

583 See Angelini, "Biblical Translation and Cross-Cultural Communication," 37.

584 See Hess, "Beduinisches zum Alten und Neuen Testament," 121.

585 See Hess, "Beduinisches zum Alten und Neuen Testament," 121.

horns appear as one horn when looking at it from aside.[586] Since the LXX translators probably only knew the רְאֵם from these stelae, it is likely that the μονόκερως of the LXX refers to a wild ox instead of the mythological unicorn.[587] Therefore, μονόκερως seems to be an adequate rendering for the Hebrew noun רְאֵם.

C Missing renderings

There are multiple animal names that are not rendered into Greek: דָּג (12:8), פֶּתֶן (20:14), רִמָּה (24:20), תּוֹלֵעָה (25:6), אַיָּה (28:7), שַׁחַל (28:8), עוֹף (28:21), יַעֲלֵי־סָלַע (39:1), אַיָּלָה (39:1), עָרוֹד (39:5), רְנָנִים (39:12), חֲסִידָה (39:18) and אַרְבֶּה (39:20). These will be analysed below.

I Lexemes pertaining to the omitted Hebrew material in LXX Job

The following Hebrew lexemes are not rendered by the LXX translator of Job: דָּג (12:8), פֶּתֶן (20:14), תּוֹלֵעָה (25:6), אַיָּה (28:7), שַׁחַל (28:8), עוֹף (28:21), יַעֲלֵי־סָלַע (39:1), אַיָּלָה (39:1), רְנָנִים (39:12) and חֲסִידָה (39:18). In the ecclesiastical Greek text of Ziegler their Greek translation is indicated with an asterisk. Therefore they do not originate from the LXX translator. The majority consensus on why these verses are not translated by the LXX translator of Job is that the LXX text does not reflect a shorter Hebrew *Vorlage* that differed from MT but that these verses are omitted by the LXX translator.[588]

---

586 See Hess, "Beduinisches zum Alten und Neuen Testament," 121. See also Max Hilzheimer, *Die Wildrinder im alten Mesopotamien*, MOA 2.2 (Leipzig: Verlag von Eduard Pfeifer, 1926), 6–7 (description) and image p. 10 and 14. According to Robert Graves and Raphael Patai, the LXX translators rendered רְאֵם by μονόκερως because the Palestinian רְאֵם was extinct and thus single horns from Arabia were imported to Alexandria. See Robert Graves and Raphael Patai, *Hebrew Myths. The Book of Genesis* (Garden City, NY: Doubleday, 1964), 56.

587 Joachim Schaper, on the other hand, gives a totally different explanation. He argues that μονόκερως is used as a metaphor to enhance messianic imagery in the LXX. See Joachim L. W. Schaper, "The Unicorn in the Messianic Imagery in the Greek Bible," *JTS* 45.1 (1994): 117–136.

588 For an overview of the scholarly debate on whether the LXX text of Job reflects a shorter Hebrew Vorlage than MT see Claude E. Cox, "Does a Shorter Hebrew Parent Text Underlie Old Greek Job?," in *In the Footsteps of Sherlock Holmes. Studies in the Biblical Text in Honour of Anneli Aejmelaeus*, ed. Timothy M. Law, Kristin De Troyer and Marketta Liljeström, CBET 72 (Leuven — Paris — Walpole, MA: Peeters, 2014), 451–462.

II רִמָּה (Job 24:20)

MT	LXX
יִשְׁכָּחֵהוּ רֶחֶם| מְתָקוֹ רִמָּה עוֹד לֹא־יִזָּכֵר וַתִּשָּׁבֵר כָּעֵץ עַוְלָה:	εἶτ᾽ ἀνεμνήσθη αὐτοῦ ἡ ἁμαρτία, ὥσπερ δὲ ὁμίχλη δρόσου ἀφανὴς ἐγένετο· ἀποδοθείη δὲ αὐτῷ ἃ ἔπραξεν, συντριβείη δὲ πᾶς ἄδικος ἴσα ξύλῳ ἀνιάτῳ.
The womb forgets them; the worm finds them sweet; they are no longer remembered; so wickedness is broken like a tree.	Then his sin was remembered, and he disappeared like a dewy mist, but may what he did be paid back to him, and may every unjust person be crushed like an incurable tree!

The Hebrew lexeme רִמָּה appears elsewhere in the book of Job, i.e., Job 7:5; 17:14; 21:26 and 25:6. In these instances the LXX translator has rendered רִמָּה with σκώληξ (7:5) and σαπρία (17:14; 21:6; 25:6). Whereas the σκώληξ ([wood]worm) seems to be the best possible translational equivalent, σαπρία (decay, decayed matter) more or less expresses the same thought, i.e., something that occurs when something is dead.

With regard to the non-rendering of רִמָּה in verse 24:20, Claude Cox argues that this verse as well as the pre- and proceeding verses are obscure in the Hebrew text.[589] Therefore, the LXX translator has tried to come up with a different rendering. This seems to be plausible, given the obscurity of the Hebrew text in 24:18-20.22-25.

III עָרוֹד (Job 39:5)

MT	LXX	11QtgJob
מִי־שִׁלַּח פֶּרֶא חָפְשִׁי וּמֹסְרוֹת עָרוֹד מִי פִּתֵּחַ:	τίς δέ ἐστιν ὁ ἀφεὶς ὄνον ἄγριον ἐλεύθερον, δεσμοὺς δὲ αὐτοῦ τίς ἔλυσεν;	מן שלח פראה ברחרין וחנקי ערדא מן שרא
"Who has let the wild ass go free? Who has loosed the bonds of the swift ass".	"And who is he that let the wild ass go free, and its bonds – who loosed them?"	"Who has set the wild ass free, and the bonds of the onager, who untie them?"

This word is a *hapax legomenon* in the Hebrew bible. It is not rendered in the LXX but it is also attested in 11QtgJob. In the first part of the first the LXX trans-

---

589 See Cox, *Iob* (forthcoming).

lator rendered פֶּרֶא ('zebra, wild donkey') by ὄνος ἄγριος ('wild donkey'). This is an adequate rendering that also occurs in Job 6:5. Although the LXX translator has many Greek lexemes to render 'donkey' or something alike, e.g., ὄνος, ὄνος ἄγριος, ὄνος θήλεια, ὄνος ἐρημίτης and ὑποζύγιον, it seems that the LXX translator did not want to repeat the same animal again and instead rendered it with a pronoun (αὐτοῦ).[590]

IV אַרְבֶּה (Job 39:20)
The whole Greek rendering of Job 39:20 does not align with the Hebrew of MT:

MT	LXX	11QtgJob
הֲתַרְעִישֶׁנּוּ כָּאַרְבֶּה הוֹד נַחְרוֹ אֵימָה:	περιέθηκας δὲ αὐτῷ πανοπλίαν, δόξαν δὲ στηθέων αὐτοῦ τόλμῃ;	[lacuna] התזענה בתקף בסחרוה' אימה ודחלה
Do you make it leap like the locust? Its majestic snorting is terrible.	And did you endow it with full armor and the majesty of its breast with courage?	Can you make him leap with strength [When he { } there is fright and fear.

Our word under discussion, אַרְבֶּה, is not preserved in the Targum fragment. van der Ploeg and van der Woude argue that the *lacuna* found in the manuscript (ca. 13 mm) is big enough to fit the Hebrew word כארבה (as the locust).[591] Thus, we can assume that the Targum goes with MT. Therefore, the LXX translator has probably modified the verse because it did not fit within the context, Job 30:19-25, wherein war and horse imagery is prominent. This imagery is even strengthened in the LXX by the rendering of Job 30:20 and especially by the insertion of the Greek lexeme πανοπλία ('full armor').

D Adequate renderings
Notwithstanding the foregoing cases, one can conclude that most of the Hebrew animal names that are attested in Job have been rendered adequately with a Greek equivalent by the LXX translator. The LXX translator had a profound

---

590 See Verbeke, "Hebrew Hapax Legomena," 329. This is also the case in LXX Prov 26:13 where the Hebrew lexeme שַׁחַל is not rendered due to repetition (אֲרִי). See Beeckman, "Proverbia de Animalibus," 265 and above.

591 See van der Ploeg and van der Woude, ed., *Le Targum de Job de la grotte xi de Qumrân*, 76, n. 1.

knowledge of the Hebrew animal onomastics and rendered most of them adequately. This knowledge can especially be detected in the rendering of Hebrew animal names belonging to the same semantic domain, *e.g.* donkey (ὄνος, ὄνος ἄγριος, ὄνος θήλεια, ὄνος ἐρημίτης and ὑποζύγιον) or lion (λέων, λέαινα and μυρμηκολέων, discussion see above).

E Conclusion

The LXX translator of Job was well-versed in both Hebrew and Greek language. This enabled him to render each Hebrew animal name with an appropriate Greek lexeme. Only the Hebrew lexeme כְּפִיר seems to be unknown to the LXX translator since he has translated it with δράκων.

Although some renderings might seem to reflect a potential lack of variation at first sight, the analysis above has indicated that this is not the case. Moreover, the LXX translator tried to create variation, if this was desirable, by opting for different lexemes pertaining to the same semantic domain (lexemes concerning 'lion' and 'donkey), applying neologisms (μυρμηκολέων; Job 4:11) or by not repeating the same lexeme again (עָרוֹד; Job 39:5).

The analysis of the missing rendering of אַרְבֶּה (Job 39:20) has also indicated that the LXX translator enhanced the (horse and war) imagery found in the immediate context of the verse (Job 39:19-25). By doing so he provided the target audience with a better and more coherent text.

2.4.3 LXX Job and LXX Proverbs: One or two translators?

As stated in the introduction of this excursus, this study also tries to provide an indicative, yet relevant answer to the question of a single translator for LXX Proverbs and LXX Job. The results will be compared on two levels: (a) general conclusions regarding translation technique and (b) Greek translation equivalents for shared Hebrew lexemes.

2.4.3.1 General translation technique with regard to animal names

With regard to the Greek rendering of Hebrew animal names in Proverbs, I have concluded that the LXX translator provided an adequate or best possible rendering for each Hebrew animal name.[592] When a Hebrew animal name is not rendered, we can ascribe this to a different Hebrew *Vorlage* or the avoidance of

---

592 See Beeckman, "Proverbia de Animalibus," 267–268.

repetition.[593] Therefore, the LXX translator was someone who was well-versed in both Hebrew and Greek.[594]

The LXX translator of Job also tries to avoid repetition (cf. Job 39:5), enhances variation by creating neologisms (cf. Job 4:11) and enhanced the imagery that is present in a certain context (cf. Job 39:20). Moreover, he has rendered most Hebrew animal names with an appropriate Greek lexeme. Just as the LXX Proverbs, he had a profound knowledge of both Hebrew and Greek. However, he did not know the meaning of כְּפִיר and therefore did not provide an adequate rendering.

We will now turn to the analysis of the Greek translation equivalents for shared Hebrew lexemes in order to see whether this ignorance is significant or not.

2.4.3.2 Greek translation equivalents for shared Hebrew lexemes

The MT version of Proverbs and Job share 13 unique Hebrew animal lexemes, some of them occur multiple times in both versions.[595] These occurrences and their respective Greek rendering in LXX Proverbs and LXX Job are listed in the table below.

MT	LXX Job	LXX Proverbs[596]
אַיָּלָה (doe of a fallow deer)	/ (39:1)	ἔλαφος (deer, hind) (5:19)
צִפּוֹר (bird)	ὄρνεον (bird) (41:5)	ὄρνεον (bird) (6:5; 7:23; 26:2; 27:8)
שׁוֹר (bull, ox, steer)	βοῦς (cow) (6:5; 21:10; 24:3)	βοῦς (cow) (7:22; 14:4)/ μόσχος (calf) (15:17)
כְּפִיר (young lion)	δράκων (dragon, serpent) (4:10; 38:39)	λέων (lion) (19:12; 20:2; 28:1)
סוּס (horse)	ἵππος (horse) (39:19)	ἵππος (horse) (21:31;26:3)

---

593 See Beeckman, "Proverbia de Animalibus," 268–269.
594 See Beeckman, "Proverbia de Animalibus," 269.
595 As Strawn has noted, the Hebrew lexemes אֲרִי/אַרְיֵה, both translated by LXX Proverbs and LXX Job by λέων, are different lexemes. Therefore, they will not be discussed. See Strawn, *What is Stronger than a Lion?*, 294–295. Also, some Hebrew animal names that have been rendered into Greek are attested in the asterisked material in Job (e.g., אַיָּלָה / ἔλαφος (Prov 5:19; Job 39:1). These will not be presented in the table because our aim is to identify the identity of the OG-translators.
596 A complete list of Hebrew animal names and their Greek rendering in Proverbs, see Beeckman, "Proverbia de Animalibus," 261–262.

MT	LXX Job	LXX Proverbs[596]
נֶשֶׁר (eagle, vulture)	ἀετός (eagle) (39:27)	ἀετός (eagle) (23:5; 30:17.19)
נָחָשׁ (snake)	δράκων (dragon, serpent) (26:13)	ὄφις (snake, serpent) (23:32)
חֲמוֹר (donkey)	ὑποζύγιον (draught animal, beast of burden, ass, mule or horse) (24:3)	ὄνος (donkey) (26:3)
כֶּלֶב (dog)	κύων (dog) (30:1)	κύων (dog) (26:11.17)
שַׁחַל (lion-cub)	λέαινα (lioness) (4:10); λέων (lion) (10:16)	/ (26:13)
כֶּבֶשׂ (young ram)	ἀμνός (lamb) (31:20)	πρόβατον (sheep) (27:26)
עֹרֵב (raven)	κόραξ (raven) (38:41)	κόραξ (raven) (30:17)
אַרְבֶּה (locust)	/ (39:20)	ἀκρίς (locust) (30:27)
לַיִשׁ (lion)	μυρμηκολέων (ant-lion) (4:11)	σκύμνος λέοντος (young lion) (30:30)

Out of the 14 instances, the LXX version of Proverbs and Job share six translation equivalents (צִפּוֹר/ὄρνεον, שׁוֹר/βοῦς, סוּס/ἵππος, נֶשֶׁר/ἀετός, כֶּלֶב/κύων, עֹרֵב/κόραξ). Some renderings that are not aligned are to be explained due to a diverging *Vorlage* (נָחָשׁ / δράκων [Job 26:13; see above]), avoidance of repetition (שַׁחַל [Prov 26:13]),[597] enhancing imagery (אַרְבֶּה [Job 39:20; see above]), enhancing variation (לַיִשׁ/μυρμηκολέων [Job 4:11; see above]) and omission (אַיָּלָה [Job 39:1; see above]).

However, three Hebrew animal names are not rendered by the same Greek equivalent in LXX Proverbs and LXX Job: (1) כְּפִיר/δράκων (Job) - λέων (Proverbs), (2) חֲמוֹר/ὑποζύγιον (Job) - ὄνος (Proverbs) and (3) כֶּבֶשׂ/ἀμνός (Job) - πρόβατον (Proverbs). These renderings might reflect two different translators. Especially the first two lexemes might indicate a different translator. As argued above, the LXX translator of Job was probably not aware of the meaning of כְּפִיר. The LXX translator of Proverbs, on the other hand, certainly was, since he rendered all three occurrences of the word by λέων. For the rendering of the Hebrew lexeme חֲמוֹר, the LXX Job records the Hellenistic word ὑποζύγιον, whereas

597 See Beeckman, "Proverbia de Animalibus," 265.

LXX Proverbs attests the older ὄνος.[598] Therefore, on a lexical level, we cannot speak of a single translator for LXX Proverbs and LXX Job (*contra* Gerleman).[599]

2.4.4 Conclusion

After having analysed the Greek rendering of Hebrew animal names in LXX Proverbs and Job, we can formulate some conclusions on the translation technique of the LXX translator as well as on the question whether or not LXX Job and LXX Proverbs were translated by one and the same person.

With regard to the translation technique, I have concluded that the LXX translator of Proverbs provided an adequate or best possible rendering for each Hebrew animal name When a Hebrew animal name is not rendered, we can ascribe this to a different Hebrew *Vorlage* or the avoidance of repetition.

Regarding LXX Job, we can conclude that the LXX translator of Job was well-versed in both Hebrew and Greek. The majority of Hebrew animal names are rendered by an adequate Greek lexeme. Thus, despite the fact that some renderings might seem to reflect a potential lack of variation at first sight, this is not the case. On the contrary, the LXX translator tried to create variation by opting for different lexemes that belong to the same semantic domain (*e.g.* domain of 'lion' and 'donkey'), creating neologism or by avoiding repetition. Moreover, in Job 39:20 the LXX translator shows himself to be a creative translator by enhancing the imagery found in the immediate context of the verse in order to provide a more coherent text.

When comparing the Greek rendering of Hebrew animal names in LXX Proverbs and Job, we can conclude that both translators show themselves to be excellent translators, e.g., by providing adequate Greek translation equivalents or by avoiding unnecessary repetition. However, since they opt for completely different renderings for some specific Hebrew lexemes, it seems unlikely that the same person has translated both LXX books. This does not exclude, however, that they might stem from the same group of translators.

---

598 See John A. L. Lee, *A Lexical Study of the Septuagint Version of the Pentateuch*, SBLSCS 14 (Chico, CA: Scholars Press, 1983), 140–143.
599 The results of my study on the Greek rendering of Hebrew plant, floral and herb names also reveal two translators instead of one. See Beeckman, "Unitas Vegetabilium?" and Excursus II.

2.5 Excursus II: the Greek rendering of Hebrew floral, plant and herb names in LXX Proverbs and Job

The previous excursus has examined the Greek rendering of Hebrew animal names in both Proverbs and Job in order to come to a better characterisation of the translation technique of both books and to assess whether they were translated by a single translator or not. The results of this study have obtained a clearer picture of their translation technique and also point to a different translator. However, in order to come to a more adequate image of the translation technique of LXX Proverbs and Job and to obtain an even more accurate answer to the question of a single translator, other content- and context-related criteria need to be analysed. Therefore, this excursus will examine the Greek translation of Hebrew floral, herb and plant names in LXX Job and LXX Proverbs in order to arrive at a more nuanced characterisation of the translation technique of both books as well as to give a more substantiated, be it still indicative, answer to the question of a single translator.[600]

First, all the Hebrew plant, herb and floral names and their Greek rendering in both Job and Proverbs will be registered. Afterwards, the Greek rendering of these Hebrew lexemes will be evaluated by book in order to characterize the translation technique of LXX Proverbs and LXX Job. Finally, the results of the evaluation will be compared in order to draw conclusions with regard to the question of a single translator.

---

600 The analysis of the Greek rendering of Hebrew plants, floral and herb names have proven to be of great significance in the characterisation of the translation technique of the different LXX books. Bénédicte Lemmelijn has analysed the Greek translation of Hebrew plants, floral and herb names in LXX Song of Songs. See Lemmelijn, "Flora in Cantico Canticorum," 27–51. This study has indicated that the LXX translator of Song of Songs was not a 'slavish' one, as the majority of scholars assume, but rather a faithful translator who often exhibits a more free approach towards his parent text. See Lemmelijn, "Flora in Cantico Canticorum," 50–51. Gerleman has also pointed at the importance of studying the Greek rendering of Hebrew plant, herb and floral names in order to characterize the translation technique of the LXX translator(s). See Gerleman, *Job*, 32. Recently, Benjamin M. Austin has analysed the Greek rendering of plant metaphors in LXX Isaiah. See Benjamin M. Austin, *Plant Metaphors in the Old Greek of Isaiah*, SBLSCS 69 (Atlanta, GA: SBL Press, 2019).

2.5.1 The registration of Hebrew floral, plant and herb names in Proverbs and Job

In order to evaluate and characterise the translation technique of LXX Job and LXX Proverbs, we will first register all the Hebrew floral, plant and herb names and their Greek rendering in the respective books.[601] The Hebrew attestations of floral, plant and herb names and their respective Greek renderings will be presented in the table below.[602] As Noted before, since we are only interested in the translational activity of the LXX translator, the asterisked material, indicated by the *siglum* '÷' in Ziegler's edition of the Greek text of Job, will be indicated for the sake of completeness but we will not evaluate those renderings since they do not belong the LXX translator. Where applicable, the attestations in the Qumran scrolls (DSS) are attested as well.

2.5.1.1 Registration of Hebrew floral, plant and herb names and their Greek rendering in Proverbs

Verse	MT	LXX	DSS
5:4	לַעֲנָה (wormwood)[603]	χολή (gall (bladder)[604]	/
7:17	מֹר (myrrh)	κρόκος (saffron)[605]	/

---

601 Although several works have listed all the plants, flora and herbs in the Bible, none of them provide the reader with an accurate index concerning the verses wherein each plant, flower or herb is mentioned. See, e.g., Harold N. Moldenke and Alma L. Moldenke, *Plants of the Bible* (Waltham, MA: Chronica Botanica Company, 1952); United Bible Societies and Committee on Translations, *Fauna and Flora of the Bible*, Help for Translators XI (London: United Bible Societies, 1972); Michael Zohary, *Plants of the Bible. A Complete Handbook to All the Plants with 200 Full-Color Plates Taken in the Natural Habitat* (Cambridge – London –New Rochelle, NY – Melbourne: Cambridge University Press, 1982). Only the work of Immanuel Löw has tried to do so, although the index is incomplete and only mentions the most important passages of each book. See Immanuel Löw, *Die Flora der Juden IV. Zusammenfassung – Nachträge – Berichtigungen – Indizes – Abkürzungen* (Hildesheim: Georg Olsm Verlagsbuchhandlung, 1967), 700–703.
602 General terms such as 'tree' or 'fruit' will not be registered. We are interested in more specific names of sorts of fruits, grass, trees, plants and herbs. These specific Hebrew lexemes might have posed a greater difficulty for the LXX translator to render.
603 English translation taken from KBL.
604 English translation from the Greek lexemes based upon LEH.
605 Semitic loanword according to LEH, 356 and Emanuel Tov, "Loan-words, Homophony and Transliterations in the Septuagint," *Biblica* 60.2 (1979): 216–236, 221 (= Emanuel Tov, "Loan-words, Homophony and Transliterations in the Septuagint," in *The Greek and Hebrew Bible*.

Verse	MT	LXX	DSS
7:17	אֲהָלִים (aloewood)	/	/
7:17	קִנָּמוֹן (cinnamon)	κιννάμωμον (a superior kind of cassia, cinnamon)[606]	/
10:26	חֹמֶץ (vinegar)	ὄμφαξ (unripe grape)	/
15:19	חֵדֶק (nightshade, thorn bush)[607]	ἄκανθα (thorny plant, thorn)	/[608]
22:5	צֵן (thorns)[609]	τρίβολος (*tribulus terrestris*, thistle, caltrops)	/
24:31	קִמֹּשׂ (weeds)	χορτομανέω (to run to grass, to grow rank, to be covered with grass)[610]	/
24:31	חָרוּל (chickling, weeds in a field or orchard)[611]	/	/
25:11	תַּפּוּחַ (apple, apple tree)	μῆλον (apple fruit, apple tree)	/
25:20	חֹמֶץ (vinegar)	ὄξος (vinegar)	/
26:9	חוֹחַ (thorns, spiniferous plants)	ἄκανθα (thorny plant, thorn)	/
27:18	תְּאֵנָה (fig tree)	συκῆ (fig tree)	/

Collected Essays on the Septuagint, ed. Emanuel Tov, VTS 72 (Leiden: Brill, 1999), 165–182, 169). However, Bénédicte Lemmelijn and Hans Ausloos have argued that this is not a Semitic loan-word on the basis of its attestations in Homeric works. See Ausloos and Lemmelijn, "Rendering Love," 54; See also Lemmelijn, "Flora in Cantico Canticorum," 46.

606 Semitic loanword according to LEH, 340.

607 KBL only records 'nightshade' as a translation of חֵדֶק. Wilhelm Gesenius *Hebräisches und Aramäisches Handwörterbuch* attests 'thorn bush.' See GESENIUS, 193. It might seem that the LXX translator by rendering חֵדֶק as ἄκανθα exhibits a lack of variation since he uses the same Greek lexeme to render חוֹחַ (Prov 26:9). However, the Hebrew lexeme חֵדֶק only occurs twice in the LXX corpus: Prov 1:9 and Mic 7:4. In Mic 7:4 it is not rendered. One might assume that ἄκανθα is an adequate rendering of חוֹחַ. Critical editions of Proverbs seem to have no difficulties with the Greek rendering of Prov 15:9 since it is not mentioned. See, e.g., d'Hamonville, *Les Proverbes*, 249; Fox, *Proverbs*, 233.

608 The fragment starts with the final word of verse 15:19, i.e., סוללה (MT: סְלֻלָּה). See DJD XVI, 186.

609 KBL translates this lexeme as 'butcher's hook,' although the editors are not certain. See KBL, 808; HALOT, 308. Gesenius, Carl Siegfried and Bernhard Stade render it by 'thorns.' See GESENIUS, 687; Carl Siegfried and Bernhard Stade, *Hebräisches Wörterbuch zum Alten Testamente* (Leipzig: Verlag von Veit & Comp., 1893), 629. Taking the content and context of the verse into account, the rendering proposed by Gesenius, Siegfried and Stade seems the most plausible one.

610 Neologism according to LEH, 666.

611 The latter meaning is only found in the concise HALOT, 116.

Verse	MT	LXX	DSS
27:25	חָצִיר (green gass)	χλωρός (light green of plants, green herbs, herbage)	/
27:25	דֶּשֶׁא (young, new grass)	πόα (grass, herb; kind of grass with cleansing properties, lye)	/
27:25	עֵשֶׂב (herb, herbage, plants of one season)	χόρτος (grass, herb, hay, stubble)	/
31:13	פֵּשֶׁת (flax, linnen)	λίνον (flax, linen cloth, lamp wick)	/

2.5.1.2 Registration of Hebrew floral, plant and herb names and their Greek rendering in Job

Verse	MT	LXX	DSS
5:5	צֵן (thorns)	κακός (bad, evil, wicked)	/
5:25	עֵשֶׂב (herb, herbage, plants of one season)	παμβότανον (all the herbage, grass)[612]	/
8:11	גֹּמֶא (papyrus)	πάπυρος (papyrus)	/
8:11	אָחוּ (marsh-plant, reed)	βούτομον (sedge, reeds, rushes)	/
9:26	אֵבֶה (reed)	/	/
13:25	קַשׁ (stubble, mixed into clay)	χόρτος (grass, herb, hay, stubble)	lacuna
15:33	גֶּפֶן (vine, shrub, plant with tendrils)	/	/
15:33	בֹּסֶר (unripe grape, unripe fruit, be before the proper time, grapes beginning to ripen)	ὄμφαξ (unripe grape)	/
15:33	זַיִת (olive tree)	ἐλαία (olive tree)	/
21:18	תֶּבֶן (ears threshed fine, straw)	ἄχυρον (chaff, straw)	/
24:6	כֶּרֶם (vineyard)	ἀμπελών (vine, grape, vineyard)	/
24:18	כֶּרֶם (vineyard)	/	/
30:4	מַלּוּחַ (a herb tasting salt,	ἅλιμος (plants growing at the	lacuna

---

612 Neologism according to LEH, 458.

Verse	MT	LXX	DSS
	salt-herb)	seashore, salty plants, sea oraches)[613]	
30:4	רֹתֶם (broom)	ξύλον (wood, timber, tree)	[רתמ]ין (broom)[614]
30:7	שִׂיחַ (shrub)	/※	/
30:7	חָרוּל (chickling, weeds in a field or orchard)	φρύγανον ἄγριον (wild brushwood)	/
31:40	חִטָּה (wheat)	πυρός (wheat)	חטא (wheat)
31:40	חוֹחַ (thorns, spiniferous plants)	κνίδη (nettle)	lacuna
31:40	שְׂעֹרָה (the hairy grain plant, barley)	κριθή (barley)	lacuna
31:40	בָּאְשָׁה (malodorous plants)	βάτος (bramble)	באשושה (malodorous plants)[615]
38:27	דֶּשֶׁא (young, new grass)	/※	דתאה (grass)
40:17	אֶרֶז (a kind of tree and its wood used for beams)	κυπάρισσος (cypress, cypress wood)	/
40:21	צֶאֱלִים (thorny shrubs, *Zizyphus lotus*)	παντοδαπὰ δένδρα (trees of every kind)	/
40:21	קָנֶה (reeds)	κάλαμος (reed, calamus)	/
40:22	צֶאֱלִים (thorny shrubs, *Zizyphus lotus*)	δένδρα μεγάλα (big trees)	/
40:22	עֲרָבָה (willow, *Populus euphratica* Oliv.)	ἄγνος (willow, chaste tree)	/
41:21	קָנֶה (reeds)	/※	/

613 According to Dhorme the rendering of מַלּוּחַ as ἅλιμος is an adequate rendering. For an elaborated discussion see Dhorme, *A Commentary on the Book of Job*, 432–433.

614 On the basis of the Targum text made by Paul de Lagarde, van der Woude and van der Ploeg argue that the Targum scroll found at Qumran must have attested רתמין. See van der Ploeg and van der Woude, ed., *Le Targum de Job de la grotte xi de Qumrân*, 41, n. 9. For the Targum edition of Job made by Paul de Lagarde, see Paul de Lagarde, ed., *Hagiographa Chaldaice* (Lipsiae: Teubner, 1873), esp. 107 for Job 30:4. For an overview of the attestation of רתמין in multiple printed editions see David M. Steg, *The Text of the Targum of Job. An Introduction and Critical Edition* AGJU 20 (Leiden – New York, NY – Köln: Brill, 1994), 47. Although this reading might be plausible, the letters ין can hardly be read in the manuscript. See der Ploeg and van der Woude, ed., *Le Targum de Job de la grotte xi de Qumrân*, 113 (fragment 13).

615 Van der Ploeg and van der Woude write: "באשושה désigne une plante puante; c'est évidemment la traduction de TM באשה." der Ploeg and van der Woude, ed., *Le Targum de Job de la grotte xi de Qumrân*, 50, n. 2.

2.5.2 The evaluation of the Greek rendering of Hebrew floral, plant and herb names in Proverbs and Job

Now that we have registered all the plant, floral and herb names in both Job and Proverbs and their Greek rendering in the LXX versions, we will subsequently evaluate these renderings in order to characterize the translation technique of both LXX books more specifically.

2.5.2.1 Evaluation of the Greek rendering of Hebrew plant, floral and herb names in Proverbs

In this section, we will analyse the Greek translation of the 17 Hebrew plant, floral and herb names in Proverbs. From the table above, we can categorize the renderings according to several observations at first sight: (1) non-adequate renderings, (2) missing renderings and (3) adequate renderings. These categories will be discussed below.

A   Non-adequate renderings

Some Hebrew lexemes seem to be inadequately rendered by the LXX translator of Proverbs, i.e., לַעֲנָה/χολή (5:4), מֹר/κρόκος (7:17), חֹמֶץ/ὄμφαξ (10:26) and קִמֹּשׂ/χορτομανέω (24:31).

I   לַעֲנָה/χολή (Prov 5:4)

MT	LXX
וְאַחֲרִיתָהּ מָרָה כַלַּעֲנָה חַדָּה כְּחֶרֶב פִּיּוֹת׃	ὕστερον μέντοι πικρότερον χολῆς εὑρήσεις καὶ ἠκονημένον μᾶλλον μαχαίρας διστόμου.
but in the end she is bitter as wormwood, sharp as a two-edged sword.	Later, however, you will find it more bitter than gall and sharper than a two-edged dagger.

The Hebrew noun לַעֲנָה occurs eight times in MT: Deut 29:17; Prov 5:4; Jer 9:14; 23:15; Lam 3:15.19; Amos 5:7, 6:12. It is rendered five times as χολή (Deut 29:17; Prov 5:4; Jer 9:14; Lam 3:15.19), twice by πικρός (Jer 23:15; Amos 6:12) and once by εἰς ὕψος (Amos 5:7).[616] Thus, all LXX translators understood לַעֲנָה as some-

---

616 α′ renders לַעֲנָה by ἀψίνθιον ('absinth'). See Field, *Origenis Hexaplorum (Tom. II)*, 319. D'Hamonville argues: "[C]ette plante ne fut importée en Égypte que par les Romains, elle n'est pas citée dans les papyri égyptiens avant le IIe siècle de notre ère." d'Hamonville, *Les*

thing bitter. Moreover, the Greek lexeme χολή is the preferred rendering. Although LEH translates χολή as 'gall (bladder),' the *Analytical Lexicon of the Greek New Testament* argues that it can also denote a bitter substance made from wormwood, a plant yielding a bitter-tasting dark-green oil [...]."[617] Therefore, the rendering of χολή for לַעֲנָה seems to be an adequate rendering.

II   מֹר/κρόκος (Prov 7:17)

MT	LXX
נַפְתִּי מִשְׁכָּבִי מֹר אֲהָלִים וְקִנָּמוֹן׃	διέρραγκα τὴν κοίτην μου κρόκῳ, τὸν δὲ οἶκόν μου κινναμώμῳ.
I have perfumed my bed with myrrh, aloes, and cinnamon.	I have sprinkled my bed with saffron and my house with cinnamon.

The Greek lexeme κρόκος only occurs twice in the LXX corpus: Prov 7:17 and Song 4:14. However, in Song 4:14 it is used as an equivalent for כַּרְכֹּם (saffron).[618] Moreover, the Hebrew noun מֹר is often rendered by σμύρνα (myrrh) or στακτή (oil of myrrh).

It seems unlikely that the LXX translator of Proverbs did not know the common Hebrew noun מֹר and could not provide an adequate Greek lexeme as a translation. Tauberschmidt argues that in Prov 7:17 the LXX translator has aimed to create a better parallelism than its Hebrew counterpart.[619] Indeed, the parallelism in the LXX version is clearly better than the one in MT.

Bearing this in mind, the LXX translator might have found it better to render מֹר by κρόκος in order to create a better parallelism with κιννάμωμον since both are actual spices and מֹר is more a liquid sort of oil.

Proverbes, 187. However, the term does occur in writings of authors such as Hippocrates and Xenophon who lived around the 4th century BCE. See LSJ, 19325.

617 Timothy Friberg, Barbara Friberg and Neva F. Miller, *Analytical Lexicon of the Greek New Testament* (Victoria: Trafford, 2005), 409.

618 For an elaborated discussion on the rendering of כַּרְכֹּם as κρόκος in Song 4:14, see, Ausloos and Lemmelijn, "Rendering Love," 54; and esp. Lemmelijn, "Flora in Cantico Canticorum," 46.

619 See Tauberschmidt, *Secondary Parallelism*, 74. See also Gerleman, *Proverbs*, 24.

III חֹמֶץ/ὄμφαξ (Prov 10:26)

MT	LXX
כַּחֹמֶץ ׀ לַשִּׁנַּיִם וְכֶעָשָׁן לָעֵינָיִם כֵּן הֶעָצֵל לְשֹׁלְחָיו:	ὥσπερ ὄμφαξ ὀδοῦσι βλαβερὸν καὶ καπνὸς ὄμμασιν, οὕτως παρανομία τοῖς χρωμένοις αὐτήν.
Like vinegar to the teeth, and smoke to the eyes, so are the lazy to their employers.	As unripe grapes are harmful to the teeth, and smoke is to the eyes, so transgression is to those that practice it.

One would expect that the adequate rendering for חֹמֶץ should be ὄξος ('sour wine') as it is the case in Prov 25:20; Num 6:3 and Ps 69(LXX 68):22. Nonetheless, the LXX translator of Proverbs opted to render חֹמֶץ by ὄμφαξ.[620] This Greek lexeme occurs only six times in the LXX: Prov 10:26; Job 15:33; Isa 18:5; Jer 38:29.30 and Ezek 18:2. Apparently, the image of sour grapes (instead of vinegar) being harmful to the teeth was a common image in Ancient Israel. Both Jeremiah and Ezekiel mention this imagery in connection with a proverb (מָשָׁל/παραβολή) that, as can be observed in the book of Ezekiel, was well-known by the people of Israel.[621] See, e.g., Ezek 18:2:

LXX	NETS
Υἱὲ ἀνθρώπου, τί ὑμῖν ἡ παραβολὴ αὕτη ἐν τοῖς υἱοῖς Ισραηλ λέγοντες Οἱ πατέρες ἔφαγον ὄμφακα, καὶ οἱ ὀδόντες τῶν τέκνων ἐγομφίασαν;[622]	Son of man, why do you have this comparison among the sons of Israel, when they are saying, "The fathers ate unripe grapes, and the teeth of the children had pain?"[623]

---

620 Neither d'Hamonville nor Fox explain this different rendering. See d'Hamonville, *Les Proverbes*, 223; Fox, *Proverbs*, 183.

621 Daniel I. Block argues that the fact "[t]hat Ezekiel's version is virtually identical to that of his contemporary, Jeremiah, suggests that its form had been fairly firmly established." Daniel I. Block, *The Book of Ezekiel. Chapters 1-24*, NICOT (Grand Rapids, MI: Eerdmans, 1997), 560.

622 For the Greek text of Ezekiel, see Joseph Ziegler and Detlef Fraenkel, *Ezechiel*, Septuaginta. Vetus Testamentum Graecum. Auctoritate Academiae Scientiarum Gottingensis editum XVI.1 (Göttingen: Vandenhoeck & Ruprecht, 2006).

623 Translation see Noel J. Hubler, "Iezekiel," in *A New English Translation of the Septuagint And the Other Greek Translations Traditionally Included Under That Title*, ed. Albert Pietersma and Benjamin G. Wright (New York, NY — Oxford: Oxford University Press, 2007), 946–985.

Thus, instead of rendering חֹמֶץ by the adequate rendering ὄξος, the LXX translator of Proverbs opted for ὄμφαξ which conveys an image that was well-known to his Jewish target audience.[624] This argument is strengthened by the rendering of עָצֵל (the lazy) as παρανομία (lawlessness) in Prov 10:26 since Ezek 18:1-25a deals with righteous and lawless behaviour and consequences.[625]

IV קִמּוֹשׂ/χορτομανέω (Prov 24:31)

MT	LXX
וְהִנֵּה עָלָה כֻלּוֹ קִמְּשֹׂנִים כָּסּוּ פָנָיו חֲרֻלִּים וְגֶדֶר אֲבָנָיו נֶהֱרָסָה:	ἐὰν ἀφῇς αὐτόν χερσωθήσεται καὶ χορτομανήσει ὅλος καὶ γίνεται ἐκλελειμμένος, οἱ δὲ φραγμοὶ τῶν λίθων αὐτοῦ κατασκάπτονται.
And see, it was all overgrown with thorns; the ground was covered with nettles, and its stone wall was broken down.	If you leave it alone, it will become barren and will be totally overrun by weeds and neglected, and its stone fences will be broken down.

The Greek lexeme χορτομανέω is a Greek *hapax legomenon* that does not even appear anywhere else in Ancient Greek literature. Prov 24:31 is the only known attestation of the word. The LEH describes it as a neologism. According to d'Hamonville this word is a contraction of χόρτος ('grass, herb') and μαίνομαι ('to be out of one's mind, to be mad, to rage; never done bearing fruit').[626] The first three meanings of μαίνομαι are attested in LEH.[627] The latter meaning is attested in LSJ as a rendering of ἄμπελος μαινομένη ('a vine that is never done bearing fruit') as attested in *e.g.* Aristotle's *Mirabilium auscultationes* (Arist. Mir.846a38).[628] Thus, the connection of some sort of grass/herb with μαίνομαι was not an uncommon practice in antiquity.

Moreover, χορτομανέω seems to be an adequate rendering for the Hebrew קִמְּשֹׂנִים כָּסּוּ (to be covered with weeds/nettles). In the Hebrew version of the verse, there is also mention of חָרוּל ('chickling, weeds in a field or orchard').

---

624 This link between LXX Proverbs and LXX Ezekiel has not been drawn before. Even commentaries on Ezekiel do not mention Proverbs in the context of Ezek 18:2. See, e.g., Block, *The Book of Ezekiel. Chapters 1-24*, 557–561; John W. Olley, *Ezekiel. A Commentary Based on Iezekiēl in Codex Vaticanus*, SCS (Leiden – Boston, MA: Brill, 2009), 345–346.

625 See Olley, *Ezekiel*, 345–354.

626 See d'Hamonville, *Les Proverbes*, 302.

627 See LEH, 666.

628 See Immanuel Bekker, *Aristotelis Opera. Vol. 2* (Berlin: Reimer, 1831) (repr. Berlin: De Gruyter, 1960), 846.

Thus, the LXX translator must have deemed the repetition of two Hebrew nouns expressing weeds redundant and therefore rendered it as a neologism expressing the same thought as the Hebrew verse although much shorter.

B Missing renderings

The LXX version of Proverbs does not render two Hebrew plant, herb or floral names: אֲהָלִים (7:17) and חָרוּל (24:31).

I אֲהָלִים (Prov 7:17)

MT	LXX
נַפְתִּי מִשְׁכָּבִי מֹר אֲהָלִים וְקִנָּמוֹן׃	διέρραγκα τὴν κοίτην μου κρόκῳ, τὸν δὲ οἶκόν μου κινναμώμῳ.
I have perfumed my bed with myrrh, aloes, and cinnamon.	I have sprinkled my bed with saffron and my house with cinnamon.

Both Fox and d'Hamonville argue that the LXX translator of Proverbs has misread the Hebrew אֲהָלִים as אֹהֶל ('tent').[629] Therefore, he has rendered אֲהָלִים by οἶκος. This seems a plausible if not the best possible explanation. Moreover, by neglecting the plural of אֲהָלִים and rendering it as a singular form (οἶκος), the LXX translator created a better parallelism.[630]

II חָרוּל (Prov 24:31)

MT	LXX
וְהִנֵּה עָלָה כֻלּוֹ קִמְּשֹׂנִים כָּסּוּ פָנָיו חֲרֻלִּים וְגֶדֶר אֲבָנָיו נֶהֱרָסָה׃	ἐὰν ἀφῇς αὐτόν, χερσωθήσεται καὶ χορτομανήσει ὅλος καὶ γίνεται ἐκλελειμμένος, οἱ δὲ φραγμοὶ τῶν λίθων αὐτοῦ κατασκάπτονται.
And see, it was all overgrown with thorns; the ground was covered with nettles, and its stone wall was broken down.	If you leave it alone, it will become barren and will be totally overrun by weeds and neglected, and its stone fences will be broken down.

---

629 See Fox, *Proverbs*, 145 and d'Hamonville, *Les Proverbes*, 202.
630 See Fox, *Proverbs*, 145.

As indicated above, the LXX translator wanted to avoid repetition and therefore rendered both Hebrew lexemes expressing 'weeds' (קִמּוֹשׂ and חָרוּל) as well as the accompanying verb (כסה) into the neologism χορτομανέω.

C   Adequate renderings

11 out of 17 Greek renderings of Hebrew plant, floral and herb names seem to be rendered adequately by the LXX translator of Proverbs. Moreover, the lexemes that seem to have been non-adequately rendered at first sight are most of the time adequate renderings after thorough investigation. In these instances the LXX translator tried to enhance parallelism (Prov 7:17), to enhance the image of the verse so that it would be more comprehensible to his target audience (Prov 10:26) or to avoid repetition (Prov 24:31). The Hebrew lexemes that have not been translated by the LXX translator are due to a misreading of the Hebrew lexeme (Prov 7:17) or they present a non-rendering in order to avoid repetition (Prov 24:31).

2.5.2.2 Evaluation of the Greek rendering of Hebrew plant, floral and herb names in Job

After having analysed the Greek rendering of Hebrew plant, floral and herb names in Proverbs, we will now focus our attention on the Greek translation of the Hebrew plant, floral and herb names in Job. Just as for Proverbs, we can categorize the renderings according to several observations at first sight: (1) non-adequate renderings, (2) missing renderings and (3) adequate renderings.

A   Non-adequate renderings

Nine Hebrew lexemes seem to be inadequately rendered by the LXX translator of Job, i.e., צַן/κακός (5:5), עֶשֶׁב/παμβότανον (5:25), אָחוּ/βούτομον (8:11), רֹתֶם/ξύλον (30:4), חָרוּל/φρύγανον ἄγριον (30:7), בְּאֻשָׁה/βάτος (31:40), אֶרֶז/κυπάρισσος (40:17), צֶאֱלִים/παντοδαπὰ δένδρα (40:21), צֶאֱלִים/δένδρα μεγάλα (40:22).

I   צַן/κακός (Job 5:5)

MT	LXX
אֲשֶׁר קְצִירוֹ רָעֵב יֹאכֵל וְאֶל־מִצִּנִּים יִקָּחֵהוּ וְשָׁאַף צַמִּים חֵילָם:	ἃ γὰρ ἐκεῖνοι συνήγαγον δίκαιοι ἔδονται, αὐτοὶ δὲ ἐκ κακῶν οὐκ ἐξαίρετοι ἔσονται, ἐκσιφωνισθείη αὐτῶν ἡ ἰσχύς.

MT	LXX
The hungry eat their harvest, and they take it even out of the thorns; and the thirsty pant after their wealth.	For what they gathered, the upright shall eat, and they will not be excepted from harmful things; may their strength be drained.

According to Edouard Dhorme, the LXX translator has misread וְאֶל־מִצִּנִּים as אֶל־מִצָּרִים and rendered this construction as ἐκ κακῶν οὐκ.[631] The Hebrew plural noun צָרִים stems from צַר ('adversary, foe') and occurs multiple times in Job and is often rendered by ἐχθρός. However, in Job 5:5 it is rendered by κακός.

The rendering of צַר by κακός instead of ἐχθρός seems to fit the context. It would have been weird to opt for ἐχθρός, since the context denotes something edible.

II עֵשֶׂב/παμβότανον (Job 5:25)

MT	LXX
וְיָדַעְתָּ כִּי־רַב זַרְעֶךָ וְצֶאֱצָאֶיךָ כְּעֵשֶׂב הָאָרֶץ:	γνώσῃ δὲ ὅτι πολὺ τὸ σπέρμα σου, τὰ δὲ τέκνα σου ἔσται ὥσπερ τὸ παμβότανον τοῦ ἀγροῦ.
You shall know that your descendants will be many, and your offspring like the grass of the earth.	And you shall know that your descendants will be many, and your offspring shall be as the grass of the field.

The Greek lexeme παμβότανον ('all the herbage;' πᾶς + βοτάνη) is a neologism and is not attested elsewhere in Greek literature. This neologism exists out of a contraction of two existing Greek words. It is therefore not excluded that the word was known in the time when the LXX translation of Job was made. Moreover, even if the word was not known and it was a neologism invented by the translator, his target audience might immediately have understood its meaning.[632] In 5:25, παμβότανον is applied to render the Hebrew lexeme עֵשֶׂב (herb, herbage, plants of one season).

The LXX translator rendered the singular noun עֵשֶׂב as a singular noun παμβότανον. However, by applying the Greek noun παμβότανον, he created a

631 See Dhorme, A Commentary on the Book of Job, 59.
632 See James K. Aitken, "Neologisms: A Septuagint Problem," in *Interested Readers: Essays on the Hebrew Bible in Honor of David J. A. Clines*, ed. James K. Aitken, Christl Maier and Jeremy M. S. Clines (Atlanta, GA: Society of Biblical Literature, 2013), 315–329, 318; 320–321. On neologisms in Job see also Dhont, *Style and Context of Old Greek Job*, 146–148.

better parallelism in Greek: πολύς/πᾶς. Thus, although he did not render עֵשֶׂב by a more common equivalent such as χόρτος, we can argue that the rendering is based upon stylistic considerations.

III אָחוּ/βούτομον (Job 8:11)

MT	LXX
הֲיִגְאֶה־גֹּמֶא בְּלֹא בִצָּה יִשְׂגֶּה־אָחוּ בְלִי־מָיִם:	μὴ θάλλει πάπυρος ἄνευ ὕδατος ἢ ὑψωθήσεται βούτομον ἄνευ πότου;
"Does papyrus grow without water, or sedge become tall without drink?"	"Does papyrus grow without water, or sedge become tall without drink?"

The Hebrew lexeme אָחוּ occurs only three times in the Hebrew Bible: Gen 41:2.18 and Job 8:11. In Genesis, it is transliterated as ἐν τῷ ἄχει. It is probable that the LXX translator of Genesis did not know אָחוּ and therefore opted for a transliteration of the Hebrew. In LXX Job, however, it is rendered by βούτομον, a Greek lexeme that occurs twice in the LXX Job and which is not attested elsewhere in the LXX corpus.[633] The Greek lexeme βούτομον denotes a 'sedge' (*Carex riparia*) and is commonly known as a marsh-plant. So apparently, the LXX translator of Job did know the Hebrew lexeme אָחוּ and rendered it by an adequate equivalent. On the basis of this argumentation, one can argue that Hebrew lexica might opt for the more specific term 'sedge' as a translation of אָחוּ, instead of the more general 'marsh-plant.'

IV רֹתֶם/ξύλον (Job 30:4)

MT	LXX	11QtgJob
הַקֹּטְפִים מַלּוּחַ עֲלֵי־שִׂיחַ וְשֹׁרֶשׁ רְתָמִים לַחְמָם:	οἵτινες ἅλιμα ἦν αὐτῶν τὰ σῖτα, ἄτιμοι δὲ καὶ πεφαυλισμένοι, ἐνδεεῖς παντὸς ἀγαθοῦ, οἳ καὶ ῥίζας ξύλων ἐμασῶντο ὑπὸ λιμοῦ μεγάλου.	ועיקרי רתמ[ין לחמהון]ו
They pick mallow and the leaves of bushes, and to warm themselves the roots of broom.	Who indeed! Saltwort was their food, and they were without honor and disparaged, in want of everything good, who also chewed on tree roots out of great hunger.	[and the root of broom]s was thei[r] bread.

---

633 It is, however, attested in other Greek literature in the works of Aristophanes and Theocritus, according to LSJ.

The Hebrew noun רֹתֶם ('broom, *Retama raetam*') occurs four times in the Old Testament: 1 Kgs 19:4.5; Job 30:4; Ps 120(LXX 119):4. In 1 Kgs 19:4, it is translit-erated as ραθμ, 1 Kgs 19:5 renders it as φυτόν ('plant, bush, thicket') and Ps 120(LXX 119):4 does not render it at all. For Job 30:4, α΄ and θ΄ render it into a more (trans)literal rendering ῥαθαμίν and σ΄ into ξύλων ἀγρίων. It seems that none of the LXX translators knew an adequate Greek lexeme to render רֹתֶם. This is not surprising given the fact that the *Retama raetam* (broom) does only grow in Palestine and Arabia.[634] Since there probably was no adequate Greek noun available to render רֹתֶם, the LXX translators could either transliterate the He-brew or find an alternative rendering that captured the general meaning of the word. The LXX translator of Job did not transliterate the word as the LXX trans-lator of 1 Kgs tended to do. Moreover, he tried to preserve the general meaning of the word by rendering it into the general lexeme ξύλον.[635]

V חָרוּל/φρύγανον ἄγριον (Job 30:7)

MT	LXX
בֵּין־שִׂיחִים יִנְהָקוּ תַּחַת חָרוּל יְסֻפָּחוּ׃	οἳ ὑπὸ φρύγανα ἄγρια διῃτῶντο.
Among the bushes they bray; under the nettles they huddle together.	Who spent their lives under wild bushes.

The Hebrew and Greek of chapter 30 do not align, since there are a lot of aster-isked material in the Greek version that was not attested in Old Greek (OG) Job. The first colon of verse 30:7 is not attested in OG Job and belongs to the aster-isked material.[636] It might be possible that the *Vorlage* of the LXX translator differed and that חָרוּל was not attested in this text. Nevertheless, the choice of the LXX translator to opt for φρύγανον ἄγριον seems to fit the context of the previous verses in the Greek text (Job 30:5-7):

---

634 See United Bible Societies and Committee on Translations, *Fauna and Flora of the Bible*, 100. See also Moldenke and Moldenke, *Plants of the Bible*, 201: "The white broom is a beautiful shrub and is abundant in the Palestinian desert regions, growing on hills, in rocky places, ravines, and sandy situations. It is common around the Dead Sea, in Gilead, in the Jordan valley, on the Syrian desert, in Lebanon, on Mount Carmel, and on all the deserts southwards to Arabia Petraea, Sinai and Egypt."

635 According to Gerleman, the LXX translator of Job's rendering ξύλον is very generalizing as well as simplifying. See Gerleman, *Job*, 33.

636 The asterisked material reads ἀνὰ μέσον εὐήχων βοήσονται.

LXX	NETS
⁵ ἐπανέστησάν μοι κλέπται, ⁶ ὧν οἱ οἶκοι αὐτῶν ἦσαν τρῶγλαι πετρῶν· ⁷ οἳ ὑπὸ φρύγανα ἄγρια διῃτῶντο.	⁵ Thieves have risen up against me, ⁶ whose houses were caves in the rocks, ⁷ who spent their lives under wild bushes.

According to Gerleman, the חָרוּל denotes a sort of thistle of the *Cynara* genus and is rendered by a general term by the LXX translator.[637] However, considering the context of the verse in connection with the previous verses (see above), the LXX translator opted for a plausible rendering. Thieves are more probable to hide under wild bushes than underneath thistles when waiting for a next victim to rob. Therefore, the rendering of חָרוּל into the Greek lexemes φρύγανον ἄγριον seems appropriate in this context.

VI בָּאְשָׁה/βάτος (Job 31:40)

MT	LXX	11QtgJob
תַּחַת חִטָּה ׀ יֵצֵא חוֹחַ וְתַחַת־שְׂעֹרָה בָּאְשָׁה תַּמּוּ דִּבְרֵי אִיּוֹב׃	ἀντὶ πυροῦ ἄρα ἐξέλθοι μοι κνίδη, ἀντὶ δὲ κριθῆς βάτος. Καὶ ἐπαύσατο Ιωβ ῥήμασιν.	תחות חטא] [באשושה ספ]ו
"Let thorns grow instead of wheat, and foul weeds instead of barley." The words of Job are ended.	"Then may nettles come forth to me instead of wheat, and a bramble instead of barley." And Iob ceased speaking.	Instead of weat [ ] rue. Ended [

The Hebrew noun בָּאְשָׁה is a *hapax legomenon* in the Hebrew Bible and is mostly rendered by 'malodorous plant' (from the root באש ['to have a foul smell']).[638] Indeed, as Dhorme argues, the rendering βάτος is based upon the parallelism that is present in the Hebrew and that has not been preserved in the Greek text.[639] Moreover, if בָּאְשָׁה indeed denotes a malodorous plant, then βάτος forms a better parallelism with חוֹחַ/κνίδη ('thorns/nettles').[640] Therefore, although the

---

637 See Gerleman, *Job*, 34.
638 See Dhorme, *A Commentary on the Book of Job*, 467. For an elaborated discussion on the *hapax legomenon*, see Verbeke, "Hebrew Hapax Legomena," 311–312.
639 See Dhorme, A Commentary on the Book of Job, 466.
640 This is not observed by Verbeke in her analysis of the *hapax legomenon* and its Greek rendering. One might also ask the question why the LXX translator of Job opted for the Greek

LXX translator probably did not know the Hebrew noun בְּאֻשָׁה or could not find an appropriate Greek lexeme to render it, he opted for a Greek lexeme which fitted the context and the parallelism and even enhanced the latter.

VII אֶרֶז/κυπάρισσος (Job 40:17)

MT	LXX
יַחְפֹּץ זְנָבוֹ כְמוֹ־אָרֶז גִּידֵי (פְחָדָו) [פַחֲדָיו] יְשֹׂרָגוּ׃	ἔστησεν οὐρὰν ὡς κυπάρισσον, τὰ δὲ νεῦρα αὐτοῦ συμπέπλεκται.
It makes its tail stiff like a cedar; the sinews of its thighs are knit together.	It stood up its tail like a cypress, and its sinews have been interwoven.

According to the *Concise* HALOT, אֶרֶז is "a kind of tree, and its wood, from Lebanon, is used for beams, paneling, pillars; trad[itionally it is rendered by] cedar, [however], *Cedrus Libani Barrel* does not have long enough trunks for building, so that it is more likely the fir, *Abies Cilicica* or another evergreen with long trunk."[641] However, this observation is not correct since the trunk of the cedar might grow to a diameter of 8 feet and length of 120 feet.[642] Moreover, it is often used as masts for ships.[643] Therefore, the traditional rendering of אֶרֶז as 'cedar' seems to be highly plausible.

In an exemplary study on the Greek renderings of אֶרֶז in the LXX, Jacobus A. Naudé and Cynthia L. Miller-Naudé conclude that the rendering of אֶרֶז as κυπάρισσος is used by the LXX translator if he does not want to attribute the positive characteristics or connotations of the word 'ceder' in a given context wherein something negative is being described.[644] For Job 40:17, the LXX translator did not want to use κέδρος, with its positive qualities, in order to describe

---

noun βάτος which only occurs in Exod 3:2.3.4 and Deut 33:16 solely in connection with the image of divine revelation through the burning bush.

641 HALOT, 27.

642 See Moldenke and Moldenke, *Plants of the Bible*, 68. See also the article of Jacobus A. Naudé and Cynthia L. Miller-Naudé on the translation of אֶרֶז in the LXX for the same conclusion but on the basis of a different argumentation: Jacobus A. Naudé and Cynthia L. Miller-Naudé, "Lexicography and the Translation of 'Cedars of Lebanon' in the Septuagint," *HTS Teologiese Studies/Theological Studies* 74.3 (2018): 1–13, 12.

643 See Moldenke and Moldenke, *Plants of the Bible*, 69.

644 See Jacobus A. Naudé and Cynthia L. Miller-Naudé, "Editorial Theory and the Range of Translations for 'Cedars of Lebanon' in the Septuagint," *HTS Teologiese Studies/Theological Studies* 74/3 (2018): 1–12, 3–4.

Behemoth in Job 40:15.[645] Instead, he used κυπάρισσος which does not have the same positive qualities as κέδρος.[646]

VIII צֶאֱלִים/παντοδαπὰ δένδρα (Job 40:21); δένδρα μεγάλα (Job 40:22)

MT	LXX
²¹ תַּחַת־צֶאֱלִים יִשְׁכָּב בְּסֵתֶר קָנֶה וּבִצָּה: ²² יְסֻכֻּהוּ צֶאֱלִים צִלֲלוֹ יְסֻבּוּהוּ עַרְבֵי־נָחַל:	²¹ ὑπὸ παντοδαπὰ δένδρα κοιμᾶται παρὰ πάπυρον καὶ κάλαμον καὶ βούτομον· ²² σκιάζονται δὲ ἐν αὐτῷ δένδρα μεγάλα σὺν ῥαδάμνοις καὶ κλῶνες ἄγνου.
²¹ Under the lotus plants it lies, in the covert of the reeds and in the marsh. ²² The lotus trees cover it for shade; the willows of the wadi surround it.	²¹ Under trees of every kind it lies down, by the papyrus and reed and sedge. ²² And tall trees find themselves in its shade, with limbs, as do the chaste-tree's branches.

The Hebrew lexeme צֶאֱלִים only occurs in these passages. Looking at the rendering of the LXX translator, Gerleman is right in his observation that the LXX translator was probably not familiar with the term.[647] However, although he did not know the term, he took the context into consideration, i.e., plants and shade, and did not destroy the meaning of the Hebrew word although the renderings denote a more general meaning. Moreover, instead of rendering צֶאֱלִים into one Greek lexeme, he opted for two different lexemes and thus created variation.

B Missing renderings
There are six Hebrew plant, floral or herb names that have not been rendered by the LXX translator of Job. These are: אֵבֶה (9:26), גֶּפֶן (15:33), כֶּרֶם (2:18), שִׂיחַ (30:7), דֶּשֶׁא (38:27) and קָנֶה (41:21).

I Lexemes pertaining to the omitted Hebrew material in LXX Job
The following Hebrew lexemes are not rendered by the LXX translator of Job: שִׂיחַ (30:7), דֶּשֶׁא (38:27) and קָנֶה (41:21). In the ecclesiastical Greek text of Ziegler the Greek translation of these verses is indicated with an asterisk. These verses

---

645 See Naudé and Miller-Naudé, "Editorial Theory," 4.
646 See Naudé and Miller-Naudé, "Editorial Theory," 4. This also happens in the LXX version of Ezekiel where κυπάρισσος is often used as a translation of אֶרֶז in order to avoid the positive qualities that go with κέδρος. See Naudé and Miller-Naudé, "Editorial Theory," 3-4.
647 See Gerleman, *Job*, 34.

were not translated by the LXX translator of Job. Scholars agree that they do not reflect a shorter Hebrew *Vorlage* that differed from MT.[648] Moreover, the majority of scholars ascribe these minuses to the translational activity of the LXX translator who omitted them.[649]

II   אֵבֶה (Job 9:26)

MT	LXX
חָלְפוּ עִם־אֳנִיּוֹת אֵבֶה כְּנֶשֶׁר יָטוּשׂ עֲלֵי־אֹכֶל׃	ἦ καὶ ἔστιν ναυσὶν ἴχνος ὁδοῦ ἢ ἀετοῦ πετομένου ζητοῦντος βοράν;
They go by like skiffs of reed, like an eagle swooping on the prey.	Is any trace at all left of a way taken by ships or of an eagle flying in search of prey?

The Hebrew lexeme אֵבֶה is a *hapax legomenon*. According to Cox, the LXX translator of Job probably did not know the meaning of this *hapax* and thus paraphrases the rest of the verse.[650] Moreover, the rendering of אניות אבה as ναυσὶν ἴχνος ὁδοῦ enhances the analogy because like a ship that does not leave a trail, so does Job's life not leave one either.[651]

III   גֶּפֶן (Job 15:33)

MT	LXX
יַחְמֹס כַּגֶּפֶן בִּסְרוֹ וְיַשְׁלֵךְ כַּזַּיִת נִצָּתוֹ׃	τρυγηθείη δὲ ὥσπερ ὄμφαξ πρὸ ὥρας, ἐκπέσοι δὲ ὡς ἄνθος ἐλαίας.
They will shake off their unripe grape, like the vine, and cast off their blossoms, like the olive tree.	But may he be picked like unripe grapes, before his time, and fall off, like an olive blossom.

The Hebrew noun גֶּפֶן is not rendered into an equivalent in the LXX version. Instead, the LXX translator adds πρὸ ὥρας after ὄμφαξ. The rendering of גֶּפֶן as πρὸ ὥρας might seem odd at first sight, but, when taking the previous verse

---

648 See Cox, "Does a Shorter Hebrew Parent Text Underlie Old Greek Job?'
649 See Cox, "Does a Shorter Hebrew Parent Text Underlie Old Greek Job?," 461–462.
650 See Cox, *Iob* (forthcoming). Dhorme argues that אֵבֶה is rendered by ἴχνος ὁδοῦ. See Dhorme, *A Commentary on the Book of Job*, 141. Verbeke argues that the rendering is based upon Proverbs 30:19. See Verbeke, "Hebrew Hapax Legomena," 231-233.
651 See Cox, *Iob* (forthcoming).

(15:32) into account, it might seem to be a deliberate rendering of the LXX translator:

LXX	NETS
³² ἡ τομὴ αὐτοῦ πρὸ ὥρας, φθαρήσεται καὶ ὁ ῥάδαμνος αὐτοῦ οὐ μὴ πυκάσῃ· ³³ τρυγηθείη δὲ ὥσπερ ὄμφαξ πρὸ ὥρας, ἐκπέσοι δὲ ὡς ἄνθος ἐλαίας.	³² His stump will perish before its time, and his branch will provide no cover. ³³ But may he be picked like unripe grapes, before his time, and fall off, like an olive blossom.

It seems to me that the LXX translator wanted to create a better parallel with verse 32 than the Hebrew text. Therefore, he added πρὸ ὥρας in verse 33 since he rendered בְּלֹא־יוֹמוֹ as πρὸ ὥρας in verse 32.

IV כְּרֶם (Job 24:18)

MT	LXX
קַל־הוּא ׀ עַל־פְּנֵי־מַיִם תְּקֻלַּל חֶלְקָתָם בָּאָרֶץ לֹא־יִפְנֶה דֶּרֶךְ כְּרָמִים:	καταραθείη ἡ μερὶς αὐτῶν ἐπὶ γῆς.
"Swift are they on the face of the waters; their portion in the land is cursed; no treader turns toward their vineyards.	"May their earthly portion be cursed".

Some parts of Job 24:18 are rendered into Greek by the LXX translator and some belong to the asterisked material. The asterisked material reads ἐλαφρός ἐστιν ἐπὶ πρόσωπον ὕδατος. Only καταραθείη ἡ μερὶς αὐτῶν ἐπὶ γῆς (may their earthly portion be cursed) is attested in OG Job, being an adequate rendering of תְּקֻלַּל חֶלְקָתָם בָּאָרֶץ. Thus, it seems that the LXX translator of Job had a different *Vorlage* that did not correspond to the Hebrew we know in MT. Moreover, the Hebrew noun כֶּרֶם is adequately rendered by ἀμπελών in Job 24:6. Thus, if the Hebrew noun כֶּרֶם was attested, the LXX translator would have probably rendered it as ἀμπελών as well. The hypothesis of a diverging *Vorlage* is the most plausible argument in this case.

C Adequate renderings

Out of the 27 Hebrew plant, herb and floral in names in Job, 15 are rendered adequately into an appropriate Greek lexeme. However, as we have seen above most of the Greek renderings that seem to be not adequately rendered are in fact adequate renderings. In some cases, the LXX translator of Job rendered the Hebrew plant, herb and floral names (a) by taking context into account (30:7; 31:40; 40:17.21-22), (b) on the basis of stylistic considerations and thus enhancing the parallelism (5:25; 15:33; 31:40) and (c) for the sake of variation (40:21-22). Only once did the LXX translator misread his *Vorlage* (5:5). One missing rendering could be explained due to a diverging *Vorlage* that differed from MT (24:18) and one Hebrew lexeme seems not to have been known to the translator (9:26). However, although this lexeme was not known to the translator, he paraphrased the verse and strengthened the analogy with the previous verses.

2.5.3 The comparison of the results of the examination of the Greek rendering of Hebrew floral, plant and herb names in Proverbs and Job

After having analysed all the Hebrew plant, floral and herb names in Proverbs and Job, we can now compare the results of the said observations in order to answer the question on whether they could have been created by a single translator. The results will be compared on two levels: (a) general conclusions regarding the translation technique and (b) Greek translation equivalents for shared Hebrew lexemes.

2.5.3.1 General observations with respect to the translation technique with regard to plant, floral and herb names

As it is clear from the above analyses, the translator(s) of LXX Job and Proverbs have rendered most Hebrew plant, floral and herb names adequately by an appropriate Greek lexeme. Moreover, both LXX Job and LXX Proverbs seem to have tried to render some Hebrew lexemes in order to enhance parallelism or analogy, thereby improving the stylistic quality of the text (Prov 7:17 and Job 5:25; 9:26; 15:33; 31:40). However, whereas the LXX translator of Proverbs tries to avoid repetition (Prov 24:31) and aims at making the text more comprehensible for his target audience (Prov 10:26), the LXX translator of Job has often taken the context into account (30:7; 31:40; 40:17.21-22) and seems to have tried to create variation (40:21-22).[652]

Although both translations exhibit different techniques to render the Hebrew floral, plant and herb names that were attested in their *Vorlage*, both

---

652 The avoidance of repetition is applied in LXX Job and LXX Proverbs to render specific Hebrew animal names into Greek. See Beeckman, "Proverbia de Animalibus," 265; Beeckman, "Animalia in Libro Iob," 274 –275. See also Excursus I.

translations clearly indicate familiarity with the Greek language and creativity (e.g., by the usage of neologisms) in translating the various Hebrew lexemes with special attention for the (poetic) style of the Greek text.[653]

We will now turn to the lexical equivalency of the Greek rendering of Hebrew plant, floral and herb names in both Proverbs and Job in order to come to a conclusion to the question of a single translator.

2.5.3.2 Greek translation equivalents for shared Hebrew lexemes

The Hebrew MT version of Proverbs and Job share only five Hebrew plant, floral and herb names. These instances as well as and their respective Greek rendering in the LXX versions will be listed in the table below.

MT	LXX Job	LXX Proverbs
צֵן (thorns)	κακός (bad, evil, wicked) (5:5)	τρίβολος (*tribulus terrestris*, thistle, caltrops) (22:5)
חָרוּל (chickling, weeds in a field or orchard)	φρύγανον ἄγριον (wild brushwood) (30:7)	/ (24:31)
חוֹחַ (thorns, spiniferous plants)	κνίδη (nettle) (31:40)	ἄκανθα (thorny plant, thorn) (26:9)
דֶּשֶׁא (young, new grass)	/ (38:27)	πόα (grass, herb; kind of grass with cleansing properties, lye) (27:25)
עֵשֶׂב (herb, herbage, plants of one season)	παμβότανον (all the herbage, grass) (5:25)	χόρτος (grass, herb, hay, stubble) (27:5)

A first look at these instances shows that none of the renderings in LXX Proverbs and LXX Job are identical. However, some of the different renderings can be explained due to the specific translation technique of the translator(s). As indicated above, the rendering of צֵן as κακός is based upon a misreading of the Hebrew by the LXX translator. The odd rendering of חָרוּל in LXX Job can be explained as a contextual rendering and the non-rendering in LXX Proverbs as an avoidance of repetition (see above). The non-rendering of דֶּשֶׁא in LXX Job can be regarded as an omission of the LXX translator (see above).

The Hebrew noun חוֹחַ, nevertheless, is rendered by two different Greek lexemes in both translations. Both Greek lexemes are only attested in one or in the

653 See Beeckman, "Proverbia de Animalibus," 268–269; Beeckman, "Animalia in Libro Iob," 275.

other. LXX Proverbs uses ἄκανθα to render חוֹחַ and חֶדֶק. Moreover, ἄκανθα is often used as a rendering for חוֹחַ (see, e.g., Song 2:2; Hos 9:6; Isa 34:14 [with adjective]), whereas κνίδη (applied by LXX Job) is a Greek *hapax legomenon*.

Concerning the rendering of עֵשֶׂב in both versions, we observe that (a) the neologism παμβότανον of Job is not applied in Proverbs and (b) χόρτος is used in LXX Job to render קַשׁ (13:25). This again might indicate two different LXX translators instead of one.

Thus, the comparison of the common Hebrew plant, herb and floral names seems to reflect a different LXX translator for respectively Job and Proverbs, especially in the latter two instances.

2.5.4 Conclusion

After the analysis of the Greek rendering of the Hebrew plant, floral and herb names in both Proverbs and Job, we can formulate the following observations with regard to the translation technique:

(a) The LXX translator of Proverbs rendered most Hebrew plant, floral and herb adequately. The LXX translator even tried to enhance parallelism (Prov 7:17), to enhance the image of the verse so it would be more comprehensible to his target audience (Prov 10:26) or to avoid repetition (Prov 24:31). Only one Hebrew lexeme has not been translated by the LXX translator due to a misreading (Prov 7:17);

(b) The LXX translator of Job also rendered most Hebrew plant, floral and herb adequately. When rendering these specific names he (a) took into account the context of the verse (30:7; 31:40; 40:17.21-22); (b) he chose Greek lexemes on the basis of stylistic considerations and by doing so, he enhanced the parallelism (5:25; 15:33; 31:40) and (c) he created variation (40:21-22). Only once did the LXX translator misread his *Vorlage* (5:5) and one non-rendering can be explained due to a diverging *Vorlage* (24:18). Moreover, although one Hebrew lexeme was probably not known to the translator, he tried to render it in a certain way in order to improve the analogy with the previous verses (9:26).

After a comparison of the characteristics of the translation technique of both LXX Job and LXX Proverbs on a general and lexical level, we arrive at the following conclusions:

(a) The translation technique in rendering the Hebrew plant, floral and herb names differs in both books. However, both books indicate a translator that rendered most Hebrew lexemes adequately, tried to enhance the Greek (poetic) structure of the verse and handled his *Vorlage* in a free and creative way. Moreover, the application of neologisms are an indication that both were well-versed in Greek language.

(b) On a lexical level, some shared Hebrew plant, floral and herb names are rendered by different Greek lexemes in both LXX books. Some can be explained on the basis of the translation technique. Others, however, indicate different lexical choices for a given Hebrew lexeme.

Re-assessing the question of a single translator for LXX Job and LXX Proverbs, we can conclude, on the basis of this excursus, that LXX Job and LXX Proverbs were translated by two different translators. This conclusion is strengthened by the results of the study on the Greek rendering of Hebrew animal names in Job and Proverbs. Although they were not translated by one and the same translator, we cannot exclude that they might stem from the same group of translators.[654]

2.6 Conclusion

This chapter has examined the Greek rendering of Hebrew *hapax legomena* and animal, plant, floral and herb names in both LXX Proverbs and Job. The results of these studies have exhibited that the translators of Proverbs and Job were highly proficient in Greek language which can be observed by their inclination to make a stylistically good Greek text by means of introducing rhyme (assonance and alliteration) and the enhancement (or creation) of parallelisms. Moreover, not only were they experts in Greek language, they also possessed a great knowledge of Hebrew. This can be observed in the great amount of adequate renderings for Hebrew hapaxes, animal, floral, plant and herb names, which can be considered to be difficult words to translate due to their uniqueness or jargon-defined character. Furthermore, when they did struggle with the Hebrew text, they never resorted to transliteration but, instead, rendered their *Vorlage* by applying a variety of techniques, e.g., contextual exegesis, metathesis and root-linked renderings.

The observation of similar techniques, which was the result of the examination of the Greek rendering of Hebrew *hapax legomena* in both books, resulted in a (preliminary) positive answer to the question of a single translator for Proverbs and Job. However, the results of the examination of the Greek rendering of

---

654 See, e.g., Cox, "The Historical, Social & Literary Context of Old Greek Job," 116; d'Hamonville, *Les Proverbes,* 139–141 (esp. 141).

Hebrew animal, floral, plant and herb names indicate two different translators. Although they exhibit similar techniques to translate their Hebrew *Vorlage* into Greek, they have opted for different Greek lexemes to render the same, specific and jargon-defined, shared vocabulary. A combination of the results of the analyses in this chapter on three content- and context-related criteria steers us into the direction of two different translators (due to the difference in lexical choice for shared jargon-defined vocabulary) who probably came from the same milieu/group (based on their shared translation techniques).

In order to provide a more conclusive answer to this question, this work will not only focus on the lexical level of LXX Proverbs and Job, but will also look at the theological and ideological level of both translations. Therefore, the next chapter will analyse the plusses in LXX Proverbs and Job in which ὁ θεός and ὁ κύριος are attested. The results of the examination of these textual variants in both books will be compared in order to come to a more conclusive answer of a single translator. Moreover, by analysing these variants, the next chapter also hopes to provide more insight into the translation technique and theology of both books.

3 Theological exegesis in verses of LXX Proverbs and LXX Job containing ὁ κύριος and ὁ θεός without any counterpart in MT

As already noted in the introduction of this monograph, interest in the theology of the LXX is vastly growing.[1] The newest volume of the *Handbuch zur Septuaginta* (LXX.H), dealing with the theology of the LXX, is one of the most recent and elaborated efforts to examine whether the theology of the different LXX books differs from the theology of their Hebrew counterparts.[2]

For the LXX version of Proverbs, Johann Cook has argued the LXX of Proverbs reflects a different theology than its Hebrew counterpart.[3] In several studies, he has demonstrated that the translator of LXX Proverbs was a conservative Jew who tried to put more emphasis on the Mosaic Law and tried to warn his readers against foreign (Hellenistic) wisdom.[4] Although Cook has published ample contributions on the question whether LXX Proverbs attests a diverging

---

* This chapter is based on several presentations which have been published or accepted for publication in peer-reviewed journals. The sections dealing with the additional attestations of ὁ κύριος and ὁ θεός in LXX Proverbs have been published in: Bryan Beeckman, "De Nomine Dei: Theological Exegesis in Verses of the Septuagint Version of Proverbs Containing ὁ θεός Without Any Counterpart in the Masoretic Text?," *Louvain Studies* 43.4 (2020): 372–387; Bryan Beeckman, "De Nominibus Sacris: Theological Exegesis in Verses of LXX-Proverbs Containing ὁ κύριος Without Any Counterpart in MT?," *RB* 128.4 (2021): 501–524. The section dealing with the additional attestations of ὁ κύριος and ὁ θεός in LXX Job is accepted for publication, see Bryan Beeckman, "Nomina Sacra in Libro Iob: Theological Exegesis in Verses of LXX Job Containing ὁ θεός and ὁ κύριος Without Any Counterpart in MT?," *VT* (2022): 1–27. The excursus of this chapter, on the minuses of the LXX where MT attests אלוה, is published in *Biblische Zeitschrift*, see Bryan Beeckman, "Absentia Nominum Sacrorum in Libro Iob: The Examination of אֱלוֹהַּ in Job Without Counterpart in the LXX," *BZ* 66.1 (2022): 16–30.
1 For a short overview on the development of the attention for a specific theology of the LXX, see Martin Rösel, "Towards a "Theology of the Septuagint."
2 See Ausloos and Lemmelijn, eds., Die Theologie der Septuaginta / The Theology of the Septuagint.
3 See i.a., Cook, *The Septuagint of Proverbs*; Cook, "Contrasting as a Translation Technique;" Cook, "Exegesis in the Septuagint;" Cook, "Exegesis in the Septuagint of Proverbs;" Cook, "Towards a Formulation of a Theology of the Septuagint;" Cook, "Interpreting the Septuagint."
4 See, i.a., Cook, "The Dating of Septuagint Proverbs," 397; Cook, "The Law of Moses in Septuagint Proverbs," 460; Cook, "The Translator of the Septuagint of Proverbs," 558; Cook, "Towards a Formulation of a Theology of the Septuagint," 635–636.

https://doi.org/10.1515/9783111041582-004

theology than its Hebrew counterpart, he is the only scholar who has tried to answer this question in greater detail.[5]

In order to contribute to a more precise and adequate description of the theology of LXX Proverbs, this chapter will look at the LXX verses in which ὁ κύριος and ὁ θεός are attested and which have no counterpart in MT.[6] Thus, the present study will not look at the rendering of the Hebrew nouns יהוה or אלהים as such. Although the rendering of these nouns might equally reflect the theology of the LXX translator of Proverbs, my reasons not to discuss them are twofold: (1) Looking at all the renderings of יהוה and אלהים by ὁ κύριος and ὁ θεός takes a lot of work and cannot be discussed within the limits of this study, and furthermore, (2) I am of the opinion that looking at the pluses containing ὁ κύριος and ὁ θεός, thus without any equivalent in MT, will reveal more information on an alleged theology of the LXX translator,[7] since it is based on the explicit differences.[8] Thus, the divine name can be considered as a *locus theologicus par excellence* in which a possible 'theology' of the translator, if there is any, can be detected.[9]

Since the present study aims at formulating an answer to the question of a single translator of LXX Proverbs and LXX Job, this chapter will also examine the additional attestations of ὁ κύριος and ὁ θεός in LXX Job without any coun-

---

5 Other scholars have (often briefly) touched upon the religious colouring and theology of LXX Proverbs but not as elaborated as Cook has done. See, e.g., Gerleman, *Proverbs*, esp. chapter II (36-57); d'Hamonville, *Les Proverbes*, 113–128; Fox, *Proverbs*, 43–45. In the *Handbuch zur Septuaginta*, focussing on the theology of the LXX, there are several articles that deal with wisdom literature and thus also with Proverbs: Cook, "Man Before God;" Witte, "Weisheitsschriften;" Ueberschaer, "Weisheit."

6 Martin Rösel has stressed the importance of the study of the Greek rendering of the Hebrew designation of God. See Rösel, "Towards a "Theology of the Septuagint," 245–48; Rösel, "The Reading and Translation of the Divine Name."

7 With the term 'plus,' we denote a sentence or part of a sentence that is attested in the target text (here the LXX) but not in the source text (MT or Hebrew *Vorlage*). When a sentence or part of a sentence is attested in the source text but not in the target text, we talk about a 'minus.' These terms are being used descriptively and do not yet entail, in contrast to the terms 'addition' and 'omission,' any evaluation of a particular textual variant. See Lemmelijn, *A Plague of Texts?*, 23 (n. 84).

8 The focus on differences between MT and the LXX in order to detect a theology of a certain LXX book has been posited by several scholars. See, i.a., Dafni, "Theologie der Sprache der Septuaginta", 327; Aejmelaeus, "Von Sprache zur Theologie;," 30; Cook, "Towards the Formulation of a Theology of the Septuagint," 622; Ausloos, "Sept défis," 249–250; Ausloos and Lemmelijn, "Theology or not?," 32 and 44.

9 See Rösel, "Towards a 'Theology of the Septuagint'," 245–248; Rösel, "Reading and Translation."

terpart in MT. Although some works have already touched upon the theology and more specifically the Hebrew divine names and their Greek rendering in LXX Job,[10] no study has undertaken a systematic analysis of the additional attestations of the Greek divine names in order to determine whether or not the Greek text reflects a distinguished theology differing from its Hebrew counterpart.

It must be noted, however, that although the LXX of Job attests three divine names, e.g., ὁ θεός, ὁ κύριος, and ὁ παντοκράτωρ,[11] this study will only examine the additional attestations of ὁ κύριος and ὁ θεός for the following reasons:

(1) Of the 16 instances where the divine name παντοκράτωρ occurs in LXX Job,[12] it is never a plus and it is always used as a rendering of שׁדי. Since we are

---

10 Studies pertaining to the theology of Job LXX are manifold. See, e.g., Henry S. Gehman, "The Theological Approach of the Greek Translator of Job 1–15," *JBL* 68.3 (1949): 231–40; Donald H. Gard, "The Concept of Job's Character According to the Greek Translator of the Hebrew Text," *JBL* 72.3 (1953): 182–86; Donald H. Gard, *The Exegetical Method of the Greek Translator of the Book of Job*, JBLMS VIII (Philadelphia, PN: SBL Press, 1952 [repr. 1967]); Cook, "Were the LXX Versions of Proverbs and Job Translated by the Same Person?"; Cook, "Towards a 'Theology'." More recent works include JiSeong J. Kwon, "Rewritten Theology in the Greek Book of Job," *Bib* 100.3 (2019): 339–52; Witte, "Weisheitsschriften," esp. 90–93; Ueberschaer, "Weisheit," esp. 139–40; Ludger Schwienhorst-Schönberger, "Weisheit und das Leben vor Gott," in *Die Theologie der Septuaginta / The Theology of the Septuagint*, ed. Hans Ausloos and Bénédicte Lemmelijn, LXX.H 5 (Gütersloh: Gütersloher Verlagshaus, 2020), 337–397. For studies specifically on the divine name and their Greek rendering in Job LXX, see, e.g., Wolf Wilhelm Grafen Baudissin, *Kyrios als Gottesname im Judentum und seine Stelle in der Religionsgeschichte. Erster Teil: Der Gebrauch des Gottesnamens Kyrios in Septuaginta*, Giesen, Otto Eissfeldt, 1929, 246–260; Markus Witte, "The Greek Book of Job," in *Das Buch Hiob und seine Interpretationen. Beiträge zum Hiob-Symposium auf dem Monte Verità vom 14.-19. August 2005*, ed. Thomas Krüger et al., AThANT 88 (Zürich: Theologischer Verlag, 2007), 33–54, esp. 50–52; Dominique Mangin, "Le texte court de la version grecque du livre de Job et la double interprétation du personnage jusqu'au IIᵉ siècle. Tome I" (PhD diss., Université d'Aix-Marseille I, 2005), 25–65 (esp. 46–60).

11 In the asterisked material, one also finds the divine name ἱκανός, as a rendering of שׁדי in Job 21:15; 31:2, and 40:2. More information on this rendering can be found in Georg Bertram, "IKANOΣ in den griechischen Übersetzungen des ATs als Wiedergabe von schaddaj," *ZAW* 70.1 (1958): 20–31; Markus Witte, "Vom El Schaddaj zum Pantokrator. Ein Überblick zur israelitisch-jüdischen Religionsgeschichte," in *Studien zur hebräischen Bibel und ihrer Nachgeschichte. Beiträge der 32. Internationalen Ökumenischen Konferenz der Hebräischlehrenden, Frankfurt a.M. 2009*, ed. Johannes F. Diehl and Markus Witte, KUSATU 12–13 (Kamen: Hartmut Spenner, 2011), 215–241, 230–232. Moreover, the noun δεσπότης (Job 5:8), used as a divine name in Gen 15:8, will also not be examined.

12 See LXX Job 5:17; 8:5; 11:7; 15:25; 22:17.25; 23:16; 27:2.11.13; 32:8; 33:4; 34:10.12; 35:13; 37:22.

only interested in the explicit quantitative differences between MT and the LXX, the lexeme παντοκράτωρ will not be evaluated;[13]

(2) Ever since Gillis Gerleman has postulated a single translator for LXX Job and LXX Proverbs,[14] multiple scholars have tried either to affirm or debunk his hypothesis.[15] However, most studies only briefly touch upon this question without providing a detailed systematic analysis and comparison of the translation technique of both books.[16] Therefore, the results of the study on the additional attestations of ὁ κύριος and ὁ θεός in LXX Job will be compared to the studies on the additional attestations of ὁ κύριος and ὁ θεός in LXX Proverbs in order to formulate an indicative answer to the question of a single translator for both books. Since this study focusses solely on the additional attestations of ὁ κύριος and ὁ θεός and because the lexeme παντοκράτωρ does not occur in LXX Proverbs, παντοκράτωρ will not be examined in this study.

---

13 Although παντοκράτωρ will not be analysed here, this does not imply that it could not tell us something about the theology of the LXX translator. In contrast, it can definitely learn something about the theology of Job LXX. See, e.g., Georg Bertram, "Zur Prägung der biblischen Gottesvorstellung in der griechischen Übersetzung des Alten Testaments. Die Wiedergabe von schadad und schaddaj im Griechischen," *Die Welts des Orients vol. 2* 5.6 (1959): 502–513, 511–513; Witte, "Vom El Schaddaj zum Pantokrator."

14 See Gerleman, *Job*, 15–17; Gerleman, *Proverbs*, 59–60.

15 Among those who have debunked this hypothesis are Gammie, Cook, and Joosten. See Gammie, "The Septuagint of Job," 15; Jan Joosten, "Elaborate Similes – Hebrew and Greek A Study in Septuagint Translation Technique," *Bib* 77.2 (1996): 227–236, 236; Cook, "Aspects of the Relationship between the Septuagint Versions of Proverbs and Job;" Cook, "Were the LXX Versions of Proverbs and Job Translated by the Same Person?" Those scholars who, explicitly or implicitly and contrary to Gammie and Cook, share the same opinion as Gerleman are Dorival, Trebolle Barrera, Kaestli, and Lemmelijn. See Dorival, "L'Achèvement de la Septante dans le Judaïsme," 105; Trebolle Barrera, *Jewish Bible*, 319; Kaestli, "La formation," 106; Lemmelijn, "Greek Rendering," 135. However, Lemmelijn has only examined the Greek rendering of several Hebrew hapaxes in her article and although her conclusion points at similarities concerning the translation technique, her conclusion is preliminary. There are some scholars, e.g., Cox and d'Hamonville, who agree on the fact that both Job LXX and Proverbs LXX were not translated by the same person but who do not exclude the possibility that they originated from the same group of translators. See Cox, "The Historical, Social & Literary Context of Old Greek Job," 116; d'Hamonville, *Les Proverbes*, 139–141, esp. 141.

16 The studies of Cook and Lemmelijn have dealt with the question in a more systematic way by making it part of the research question(s). See, e.g., Cook, "Aspects of the Relationship between the Septuagint Versions of Proverbs and Job"; Cook, "Were the LXX Versions of Proverbs and Job Translated by the Same Person?"; Cook, "Contextuality in Wisdom Literature"; Cook and van der Kooij, *Law, Prophets and Wisdom*; Lemmelijn, "The Greek Rendering of Hebrew Hapax Legomena in LXX Proverbs and Job."

I will first register all the pluses of LXX Proverbs in which ὁ κύριος and ὁ θεός are attested. Secondly, I will evaluate these pluses and try to define whether they (a) are the work of the translator, (b) were already attested in the Hebrew *Vorlage* of the translator and/or (c) whether they are later additions made during the textual transmission of the Greek text. While doing so, we will also examine whether a certain kind of theology can be detected in those cases that can be ascribed to the translational work of the translator. Afterwards, the same methodology will be applied for LXX Job. Finally, the results of the analysis of the pluses of ὁ κύριος and ὁ θεός in LXX Proverbs and LXX Job will be compared with one another in order to discern whether they were translated by the same translator or not.

3.1 The additional attestations of ὁ κύριος and ὁ θεός in LXX Proverbs

3.1.1 The registration of the additional attestations of ὁ κύριος and ὁ θεός in LXX Proverbs

The noun ὁ κύριος is attested 77 times in LXX Proverbs, whereas ὁ θεός occurs 34 times[17]. Compared to the attestation of אלהים (5 times) and יהוה (87 times), it is obvious that the Greek version of Proverbs attests seven more references to God than MT. David-Marc d'Hamonville has provided a list of renderings and attestations of יהוה and אלהים by ὁ θεός and ὁ κύριος in his work *Les Proverbes* within the *Bible d'Alexandrie* series:[18]

Prov 1-9	Prov 10:1-15:27	Prov 15:27a-22:17	Prov 22:17-31:31
יהוה – κύριος 13	יהוה – κύριος 18	יהוה – κύριος 22	יהוה – κύριος 11
יהוה – θεός 5		יהוה – θεός 12	יהוה – θεός 1
אלהים – κύριος 1		יהוה – / (16:3) 1	אלהים – κύριος 2
אלהים – θεός 2			אלוה – θεός 1
0 / – κύριος 4	0 / – κύριος 1	0 / – κύριος 3	0 / – κύριος 5
0 / – θεός 2		0 / – θεός 2	0 / – θεός 5

---

17 D'Hamonville, *Les Proverbes*, 46.

18 Table taken from d'Hamonville, *Les Proverbes*, 46. According to Bibleworks, however, there are 87 attestations of the Tetragrammaton in MT-Proverbs instead of d'Hamonville's 83.

According to d'Hamonville, ὁ κύριος is attested 13 times without a Hebrew counterpart, whereas ὁ θεός is only attested nine times without a Hebrew equivalent.[19] However, d'Hamonville does not indicate the verses in which ὁ κύριος and ὁ θεός are only attested in the LXX and not in MT. Nor does he mention his methodology on how he gathered these data. This makes it difficult to re-trace his steps and to come to the same results. Therefore, I have re-examined the instances in which ὁ κύριος and ὁ θεός are attested in LXX Proverbs without any Hebrew equivalent in MT. My results differ from those of d'Hamonville. Indeed, ὁ κύριος is attested 13 times without a Hebrew counterpart.[20] For ὁ θεός, however, I have found 10 cases instead of the nine that d'Hamonville records. In d'Hamonville's analysis, two instances are recorded in Prov 15:27a-22:17, whereas I record three (Prov 16:7; 21:8 and 22:8). In Prov 21:8 and 22:8, it is obvious that ὁ θεός is not attested in the Hebrew version. Therefore, d'Hamonville must have excluded Prov 16:7 in his analysis. Perhaps, he has taken the LXX version of Prov 16:7 as an equivalent of MT Prov 16:7, although he indicates in his annotation of the translation of LXX Proverbs that the verse is not attested in the Hebrew version.[21] The Hebrew version of Prov 16:7 has a parallel in LXX 15:28.[22]

Taking this into account we arrive at the following verses where the LXX has a plus containing ὁ κύριος and ὁ θεός:

ὁ κύριος (13x)	ὁ θεός (10x)
3:18; 3:34; 7:1; 8:26; 10:6; 16:8; 21:27; 22:11; 23:11; 24:7.12; 27:20 and 29:23.	1:7; 4:27; 16:7; 21:8; 22:8; 30:1.3; 31:1.3 and 31:8.

Now that all pluses of ὁ κύριος and ὁ θεός have been registered, we can start evaluating them. First, the additional attestations of ὁ κύριος in LXX Proverbs will be evaluated, afterwards the additional attestations of ὁ θεός.

---

19 See d'Hamonville, *Les Proverbes*, 46.
20 One could count 14 instances of ὁ κύριος without a Hebrew equivalent. If one is inattentive when looking for such instances, Prov 17:11 might be seen as such an instance. In this verse מַלְאָךְ (messenger) is rendered with ὁ κύριος ἄγγελον (messenger of God). This, however, cannot be regarded as an extra attestation of ὁ κύριος because the Hebrew noun also carries the meaning of God's messenger (see HALOT, 196). The Greek ὁ κύριος ἄγγελον can thus be seen as an adequate translation of the Hebrew מלאך.
21 See d'Hamonville, *Les Proverbes*, 253.
22 See Beeckman, "Trails of a Different Vorlage," 577.

3.1.2 The evaluation of additional attestations of ὁ κύριος in LXX Proverbs

After having registered all the instances of the attestation of ὁ κύριος in LXX Proverbs without any counterpart in MT, 13 in total, we will now evaluate these pluses and examine whether they (a) are the work of the translator, (b) were already attested in the translator's *Vorlage* and/or (c) are later additions made during the textual transmission of the Greek text.

The extra attestations of ὁ κύριος in LXX Proverbs can be subdivided in several categories: (a) explicit reference, (b) nuance, (c) additional verses, (d) different Greek rendering of Hebrew verses and cola and (e) addition of comparison/simile.

3.1.2.1 Explicit references

In a couple of verses in which ὁ κύριος is attested in LXX, MT does not specifically attest the name of God (יהוה or אלהים) but God is, however, referred to as the subject of the clause. This is the case in the following verses: Prov 3:34; 8:26 and 24:12.

A   Prov 3:34

MT	LXX
אִם־לַלֵּצִים הוּא־יָלִיץ (וְלַעֲנָיִים) [וְלַעֲנָוִים] יִתֶּן־חֵן:	**κύριος** ὑπερηφάνοις ἀντιτάσσεται, ταπεινοῖς δὲ δίδωσιν χάριν.
Toward the scorners he is scornful, but to the humble he shows favor.	The Lord resists the arrogant, but he gives grace to the humble.

In Prov 3:34, the LXX version indicates that God is the one who resists the arrogant and gives grace to the humble. In MT, however, the subject is not specified. Although one could derive God as subject from the previous verses in MT, this is not the case when looking at the LXX version:

MT (Prov 3:32-33)	LXX (Prov 3:32-33)
כִּי תוֹעֲבַת יְהוָה נָלוֹז וְאֶת־יְשָׁרִים סוֹדוֹ:	ἀκάθαρτος γὰρ ἔναντι **κυρίου** πᾶς παράνομος,
מְאֵרַת יְהוָה בְּבֵית רָשָׁע וּנְוֵה צַדִּיקִים יְבָרֵךְ:	ἐν δὲ δικαίοις οὐ συνεδριάζει.
	κατάρα θεοῦ ἐν οἴκοις ἀσεβῶν, ἐπαύλεις δὲ δικαίων εὐλογοῦνται.

MT (Prov 3:32-33)	LXX (Prov 3:32-33)
For the perverse are an abomination to the Lord, but the upright are in his confidence. The Lord's curse is on the house of the wicked, but he blesses the abode of the righteous.	For every transgressor is impure be-fore the Lord. and he does not sit in council among the righteous. A divine curse is in the homes of the impious, but the abodes of the just are blessed.

In MT's version of Prov 3:32, the upright (or righteous) are in the confidence of the Lord, whereas the LXX attests that every transgressor (the subject of the first colon) does not sit in council among the righteous. Moreover, in Prov 3:33, the subject of the second colon differs between MT and the LXX as well. In the LXX, the abodes of the just are blessed (passive form) without explicitly mentioning who is blessing. MT, on the other hand, uses a *piel* third masculine singular of ברך, implying that God is the one blessing the abodes of the righteous. Because of the fact that in verse 32 of the LXX version the subject is the transgressor and in verse 33 the one who is blessing is not explicitly mentioned, it would have been hard for the target audience of the LXX translator to know whom the subject of Prov 3:34 is, when only a word-by-word rendering of the MT-version would have been offered, without specifying the subject of the clause. Therefore, this might have led the LXX translator to opt for an explication of ὁ κύριος in Prov 3:34 instead of not specifying the actor of the verse.

B Prov 8:26

MT	LXX
עַד־לֹא עָשָׂה אֶרֶץ וְחוּצוֹת וְרֹאשׁ עָפְרוֹת תֵּבֵל׃	**κύριος** ἐποίησεν χώρας καὶ ἀοικήτους καὶ ἄκρα οἰκούμενα τῆς ὑπ᾽ οὐρανόν.
When he had not yet made earth and fields, or the world's first bits of soil.	The Lord made countries and uninhabited spaces and the habitable heights of that beneath the sky.

The explicit mentioning of ὁ κύριος in Prov 8:26, compared to MT, can be seen against the background of the general theme of creation that is elaborated in Prov 8:20-36. As Johann Cook has already pointed out, "[t]he specification of the subject as, the Lord, could be [a] sign of the translator's intention to stress that

God/the Lord is the sole actor in the creation process."[23] When reading the Hebrew version of the text, the reader might think that wisdom was present with God at the start of creation and that wisdom was creating as well. As Cook has demonstrated in several of his articles, the translator has repeatedly tried to avoid this 'misunderstanding' by changing the aspect and subject of some verbs in 8:20-36.[24]

C   Prov 24:12

MT	LXX
כִּי־תֹאמַר הֵן לֹא־יָדַעְנוּ זֶה הֲלֹא־תֹכֵן לִבּוֹת הוּא־יָבִין וְנֹצֵר נַפְשְׁךָ הוּא יֵדָע וְהֵשִׁיב לְאָדָם כְּפָעֳלוֹ:	ἐὰν δὲ εἴπῃς Οὐκ οἶδα τοῦτον, γίνωσκε ὅτι **κύριος** καρδίας πάντων γινώσκει, καὶ ὁ πλάσας πνοὴν πᾶσιν αὐτὸς οἶδεν πάντα, ὃς ἀποδίδωσιν ἑκάστῳ κατὰ τὰ ἔργα αὐτοῦ.
If you say, "Look, we did not know this"-- does not he who weighs the heart perceive it? Does not he who keeps watch over your soul know it? And will he not repay all according to their deeds?	If you say: "I do not know this person," be aware that the Lord is familiar with the heart of everyone, and he who formed breath for all, he knows everything, he who will render to each according to his deeds.

The LXX version attests a reading that differs from MT. In the LXX version the omniscience of God is stressed (αὐτὸς οἶδεν πάντα) as well as His power to create (ὁ πλάσας πνοὴν πᾶσιν). As was the case in the LXX version of Prov 8:20-36 (see above), the LXX translator stresses that the Lord is the sole creator, because he is the one 'who formed breath for all.' In Gen 2:7, the Greek noun πνοή is also used in connection with the verb πλάσσω (to form/to mold) to denote the formation of the human (אדם/ἄνθρωπος) and the gift of the breath of life (πνοή ζωῆς).[25] This very connection between the noun πνοή and the verb πλάσσω only occurs in LXX Genesis and LXX Proverbs. Therefore, this reference to the creation story, in which only God creates and no mention is made of Wisdom, strengthens Cook's argument that the LXX translator wants to emphasise that God is the sole creator. In this regard, the explicit mentioning of ὁ κύριος can

23 Cook, "Were the LXX Versions of Proverbs and Job Translated by the Same Person?," 152.
24 See Cook, "Were the LXX Versions of Proverbs and Job Translated by the Same Person?," 156.
25 The verb πλάσσω is used only once in LXX Proverbs.

thus be seen as an exegetical activity of the translator in order to put extra emphasis on the Lord (and he alone!) as sole creator as well as omniscient being.

3.1.2.2 Nuancing

Next to the tendency of making the text more explicit in LXX Proverbs, we can also detect three instances wherein ὁ κύριος is being used to nuance the meaning of the verse. These instances are Prov 10:6; 21:27 and 23:11.

A Prov 10:6

MT	LXX
בְּרָכוֹת לְרֹאשׁ צַדִּיק וּפִי רְשָׁעִים יְכַסֶּה חָמָס:	εὐλογία **κυρίου** ἐπὶ κεφαλὴν δικαίου, στόμα δὲ ἀσεβῶν καλύψει πένθος ἄωρον.
Blessings are on the head of the righteous, but the mouth of the wicked conceals violence.	The blessing of the Lord is upon the head of the righteous, but the mouth of the impious will conceal untimely sorrow.

The noun εὐλογία occurs four times in LXX Proverbs: i.e., in Prov 10:8.22; 11:26 and 24:25. Two of the four times, it is followed by the genitive form of κύριος, namely in Prov 10:6 and 10:22.[26] Moreover, in Prov 10:22, the same first colon can be found in the LXX: εὐλογία κυρίου ἐπὶ κεφαλὴν δικαίου. However, the MT-version of the first colon of Prov 10:6 and 10:22 differ from each other:

MT Prov 10:6	MT Prov 10:22
בְּרָכוֹת לְרֹאשׁ צַדִּיק	בִּרְכַּת יְהוָה הִיא תַעֲשִׁיר
Blessings are on the head of the righteous.	The blessing of the Lord is upon the head of the righteous.

The Greek translation of Prov 10:6a differs slightly from the Hebrew: בְּרָכוֹת is rendered with a singular form (εὐλογία) instead of a plural form (εὐλογίαι) and in the LXX the genitive singular of κύριος, i.e., κυρίου, has been added. The Hebrew version of Prov 10:22a attests the divine name יהוה, which is rendered

---

26 In the rest of the LXX corpus, the word pair εὐλογία κυρίου appears three times elsewhere, i.e., Gen 39:5; Deut 12:15; 16:17; 33:13; Ps 128(MT 129):8; Isa 65:8.

into Greek by κυρίου. However, the Greek rendering of Prov 10:22a (εὐλογία κυρίου ἐπὶ κεφαλὴν δικαίου αὕτη πλουτίζει) adds ἐπὶ κεφαλὴν δικαίου, which has no equivalent in MT. Thus, the Greek translation of the first cola of both verses seems to combine the Hebrew of the first cola of both verses.[27]

In Prov 11:26, the same expression of 'putting a blessing on the head of someone' can be found. However, in this verse, the name of God is absent in the Hebrew as well as in the Greek version of the text. If the translator had a specific kind of theology in mind that pertained to the expression εὐλογία κυρίου ἐπὶ κεφαλὴν, he would also have added the genitive singular of κύριος in Prov 11:26. Therefore, I am inclined to ascribe the variant reading in Prov 10:6 and 10:22 to a different Hebrew *Vorlage*. Moreover, the expression εὐλογία κυρίου ἐπὶ κεφαλὴν does not appear in other text in Greek literature, but does appear, however slightly different, elsewhere in the LXX, i.e., Gen 49:26 and Deut 33:16.[28] Both verses are dealing with a blessing coming from God and given to Joseph. The Hebrew version of the text also attests ברך לראש, just as in Prov 10:6.22 and 11:26. The expression 'to bless someone on the head' might thus be a typical Hebrew expression. The Greek rendering of this Hebrew expression, i.e., εὐλογία κυρίου ἐπὶ κεφαλὴν, might thus be seen as a Hebraism. This strengthens the argument in favour of a different Hebrew Vorlage underlying the Greek translation of Prov 10:6 and 10:22.

B Prov 21:27

MT	MT
זֶבַח רְשָׁעִים תּוֹעֵבָה אַף כִּי־בְזִמָּה יְבִיאֶנּוּ׃	θυσίαι ἀσεβῶν βδέλυγμα **κυρίῳ**· καὶ γὰρ παρανόμως προσφέρουσιν αὐτάς.
The sacrifice of the wicked is an abomination; how much more when brought with evil intent.	The sacrifice of the impious is an abomination to the Lord, for they even offer them unlawfully.

The Greek expression βδέλυγμα κυρίῳ is found 15 times in the LXX: 7 times in Deuteronomy (Deut 7:25; 12:1; 17:1; 18:12; 22:5; 23:19; 25:16 and 27:15) and

---

27 This observation has also been made by Peter T.H. Hatton. See Peter T. H. Hatton, *Contradiction in the Book of Proverbs. The Deep Waters of Counsel* (Aldershot: Ashgate, 2008), 97.

28 In Deut 33:16, no specific mention is made of a blessing. However, in Deut 33:13 mention is made of a blessing of the Lord (ברך יהוה/εὐλογία κυρίου). The verses between Deut 33:13 and 33:16 specify the blessing of Joseph's land that rests upon his head.

8 times in Proverbs (Prov 11:20; 12:22; 15:8.9; 15:26; 20:23; 21:27 and 27:20). In all instances, except Prov 21:27 and 27:20, it is used as a translation of תועבה יהוה. This Hebrew expression is found 11 times in Proverbs, namely in Prov 3:32; 11:1; 11:20; 12:22; 15:8.9.26; 16:5; 17:15; 20:10 and 20:23. Not all of these instances have thus been rendered by the expression βδέλυγμα κυρίῳ. The LXX translator did not render this expression systematically by the same corresponding Greek expression. Several instances are rendered by a form of the adjective ἀκάθαρτος instead of βδέλυγμα and some also connect ἀκάθαρτος/βδέλυγμα and κύριος to a preposition such as ἔναντι (Prov 3:32), ἐνώπιον (Prov 11:1 and 20:10) or παρά (in connection with the dative form of θεός) (Prov 16:5 and 17:5). The translator of LXX Proverbs took the freedom to render the Hebrew expression תועבה יהוה. However, what is remarkable is that the LXX translator translated every Hebrew construction of תועבה in a construct form + יהוה by a Greek equivalent, i.e., noun nominative + noun dative or noun nominative + preposition + dative or genitive. The absolute form, as it is attested in Prov 21:27, is the same as the construct form. The LXX translator must have thought that תועבה in Prov 21:27 was a construct form, found it odd that there was no word to which the construct noun could be linked, and must have added a dative form of κύριος as he did in previous verses (e.g., Prov 11:1.20; 15:26, *etc.*). Thus, the addition of κυρίῳ in this verse might be regarded as a misunderstanding of תועבה by the translator.

C   Prov 23:11

MT	LXX
כִּי־גֹאֲלָם חָזָק הוּא־יָרִיב אֶת־רִיבָם אִתָּךְ:	ὁ γὰρ λυτρούμενος αὐτοὺς **κύριος** κραταιός ἐστιν καὶ κρινεῖ τὴν κρίσιν αὐτῶν μετὰ σοῦ.
For their redeemer is strong; he will plead their case against you.[29]	For the Lord who redeems them is strong and he will plead their case with you.

In the Hebrew version of this verse, the redeemer is not specified. In other Old Testament books, God is often referred to as the redeemer (see, e.g., Isa [i.a., 41:14; 43:14; 44:24; 48:17] and Psalms [19:15; 78:35]). The Greek participle of the

---

29 The NRSV translates the preposition אֶת with 'against', whereas the KJV renders it to 'with.' The KJV has a more adequate translation. The preposition אֶת denotes the meaning of 'being together.' See KBL, 100.

verb λυτρόω is in the majority of the instances being used to denote God. In Jer 50(LXX 27):34 we find the same thought as in Prov 23:11:

MT (50:34)	LXX (27:34)
גֹּאֲלָ֣ם ׀ חָזָ֗ק יְהוָ֤ה צְבָאוֹת֙ שְׁמ֔וֹ רִ֥יב יָרִ֖יב אֶת־רִיבָ֑ם לְמַ֙עַן֙ הִרְגִּ֣יעַ אֶת־הָאָ֔רֶץ וְהִרְגִּ֖יז לְיֹשְׁבֵ֥י בָבֶֽל׃	καὶ ὁ λυτρούμενος αὐτοὺς ἰσχυρός, κύριος παντοκράτωρ ὄνομα αὐτῷ κρίσιν κρινεῖ πρὸς τοὺς ἀντιδίκους αὐτοῦ, ὅπως ἐξάρῃ τὴν γῆν, καὶ παροξυνεῖ τοῖς κατοικοῦσι Βαβυλῶνα[30].
Their Redeemer is strong; the LORD of hosts is his name. He will surely plead their cause, that he may give rest to the earth, but unrest to the inhabitants of Babylon.	And he that redeems them is strong; the Lord Almighty is his name. He will judge with judgment against his adversaries, that he may destroy the earth, and for those that inhabit Babylon he will incite[31].

God is explicitly mentioned as the redeemer who will plead the case of the oppressed, i.e., the Judeans and Israelites. In order to avoid misunderstanding of who the redeemer might be, the extra attestation in Prov 23:11 is possibly an addition of the LXX translator to emphasise that the God of Israel is the one and only redeemer.[32] According to Gerhard Tauberschmidt, the explicitation of the subject, such as the addition of κύριος, is a form of participant referencing which is commonly used by the LXX translator of Proverbs.[33]

3.1.2.3 Additional verses and cola
In the LXX version of Proverbs, there are some verses and cola which contain ὁ κύριος and that are absent in the Hebrew version of the text. The following

---

30 Greek text of Jeremiah, taken from Joseph Ziegler, *Jeremias, Baruch, Threni, Epistula Jeremiae*, Septuaginta: Vetus Testamentum graecum XV (Göttingen: Vandenhoeck & Ruprecht, 2006).

31 Translation from Albert Pietersma and Marc Saunders, "Ieremias," in *A New English Translation of the Septuagint. And the Other Greek Translations Traditionally Included under That Title*, ed. Albert Pietersma and Benjamin G. Wright (Oxford: Oxford University Press, 2007), 876–924.

32 Fox also records the specification of the redeemer with κύριος. According to him this addition is unnecessary. See Fox, *Proverbs*, 313.

33 See Tauberschmidt, *Secondary Parallelism*, 19: "[...] [T]he translator of Proverbs is concerned to refer to participants introduced by nouns (or noun phrases) – or if they are not introduced to introduce them first [...] – by using pronouns, the person affix in the verb, or zero reference."

verses have no counterpart in MT: Prov 7:1a; 16:8 and 27:20. We will analyse these verses below.

A Prov 7:1a

MT	LXX
בְּנִי שְׁמֹר אֲמָרָי וּמִצְוֹתַי תִּצְפֹּן אִתָּךְ:	Υἱέ φύλασσε ἐμοὺς λόγους, τὰς δὲ ἐμὰς ἐντολὰς κρύψον παρὰ σεαυτῷ· ¹ᵃ υἱέ τίμα **τὸν κύριον** καὶ ἰσχύσεις, πλὴν δὲ αὐτοῦ μὴ φοβοῦ ἄλλον.
My child, keep my words and store up my commandments with you.	My son, keep my words, and hide my commandments with yourself. ¹ᵃ My son, honor the Lord, and you will grow strong, and fear no other but him.

The Hebrew version of the verse is adequately, and even word-by-word, rendered by the LXX translator. The second colon of the LXX version of the verse, however, is not attested in the Hebrew version. The imperative to honour the Lord (τίμα τὸν κύριον) is also found in Prov 3:9 as a rendering of כבד את־יהוה. The expression ἰσχύσεις, which expresses a future, is also found in 3 Kgdms 2:2, in which David, at the end of his days, is telling his son Salomon to be strong and keep God commandments according to the Law of Moses (3 Kgdms 2:1-3). This is striking because (a) the proverbs in chapter 7 of the Book of Proverbs are also directed from a father to his son (υἱέ),[34] and (b) the book itself is attributed to Solomon (παροιμίαι Σαλωμῶντος υἱοῦ Δαυιδ ὃς ἐβασίλευσεν ἐν Ισραηλ [Prov 1:1]). This insertion of ἰσχύσεις can thus be an extra emphasis on the alleged authorship of Solomon.

The last part of 7:1a commands to fear the Lord and only Him. The Greek expression πλὴν δὲ αὐτου μὴ φοβοῦ ἄλλον does not appear elsewhere in the LXX. Nonetheless, in Deuteronomy, the people of Israel are ordered not the fear their enemies (e.g., Deut 1:29; 3:22; 7:18; 20:1; 31:6) but to only fear the God of Israel (e.g., Deut 13:4; 14:23; 17:19; 31:12). However, in Wisdom literature, e.g., Wisdom of Sirach, Job and Psalms, this fear of the Lord must be understood as

---

34 In Wisdom literature this does not necessarily have to be read in a literal sense. It can be seen as a traditional address from a teacher to his pupil (cf. Wisdom of Sirach).

respect for the Lord.[35] This sapiential thought is repeated and emphasised in the LXX version of Prov 7:1a. Thus, next to the emphasis on the alleged authorship of Solomon, the LXX translator also emphasised that one should only fear (or better: should have respect for) the Lord and no one else but Him.

B   Prov 16:8 (LXX)

LXX	NETS
ὁ ζητῶν **τὸν κύριον** εὑρήσει γνῶσιν μετὰ δικαιοσύνης, οἱ δὲ ὀρθῶς ζητοῦντες αὐτὸν εὑρήσουσιν εἰρήνην.	He who seeks the Lord will find knowledge with righteousness, and they who seek him rightly will find peace.

The MT version of Prov 16:8 corresponds more or less to the LXX version of Prov 15:29a.[36] However, Prov 16:8 in the LXX has no Masoretic counterpart. In secondary literature, no one explains this plus in the LXX version, apart from d'Hamonville who describes this plus as an addition made by the translator without elaborating on the reason why the translator would have added this verse.[37]

Prov 16:8 is located in a section that shows some major differences between MT and the LXX: Prov 15:28-16:9.[38] Several verses have been reordered and transposed. As I have indicated in my article *Trails of a Different Vorlage and a Free Translator in LXX Proverbs: A Text-Critical Analysis of Proverbs 16:1-7*,[39] this transposition can be explained due to a Hebrew *Vorlage* that differed from the order of MT, and this in contrast to Cook who ascribes these transpositions to the translator's translation and interpretational activity.[40] The conclusion of a

---

35 See Bénédicte Lemmelijn, "The Wisdom of Life as Way of Life. The Wisdom of Jesus Sirach as a Case in Point," *OTE* 27.2 (2014): 444–71, 448–449.
36 See, e.g., Fox, *Proverbs*, 246.
37 See d'Hamonville, *Les Proverbes*, 49 and 253–254. Fox mentions the plus of LXX Prov 16:8 but does not indicate why and how does plus came about. He only categorises the MT version of 16:8 as an 'alternative proverb.' See Fox, *Proverbs*, 246–247 and 421.
38 The order of the MT-version of Proverbs and the LXX version differs radically. For an overview of the different order in MT and LXX see Tov, "Recensional Differences," 428, and also the numerous commentaries on Proverbs.
39 See Beeckman, "Trails of a Different Vorlage," 587.
40 See Beeckman, "Trails of a Different Vorlage," 587. For Cook's view on this matter, see, e.g., Cook, "'ishah zarah," 460; Cook, "The Greek of Proverbs," 618; Cook, "The Translator of the

different *Vorlage* can be made taking into account the ancient way of copying and writing on papyri scrolls:

> When one takes note of the writing and copying methods in Antiquity, one has to take into account that papyrus scrolls were used in this period. These scrolls lent themselves to a continuous reading intended for a "start-to-finish"-reading that made it difficult to proceed from one chapter to another. Therefore, it is unlikely that the translator shifted entire verses from one chapter to another. In my opinion, this would have demanded a huge amount of time and effort. It is more convincing to claim that the translator remained faithful to the structure of the chapters and verses as attested in his *Vorlage*.[41]

It is not impossible that the different structure in the LXX version might have also attested verses that are not present in MT. It seems unlikely that the LXX translator, although his translation is often referred to as being extremely free, would have added a complete verse/proverb unless he had good reasons to do so, e.g., emphasis, ideology, theology. Indeed, as my discussion of Prov 7:1a (see above) has indicated, he might have added an extra cola to an already existing proverb. Creating a whole new proverb, however, seems to be highly questionable.

C Prov 27:20

MT	LXX
שְׁאוֹל וַאֲבַדֹּה לֹא תִשְׂבַּעְנָה וְעֵינֵי הָאָדָם לֹא תִשְׂבַּעְנָה׃	ᾅδης καὶ ἀπώλεια οὐκ ἐμπίμπλανται, ὡσαύτως καὶ οἱ ὀφθαλμοὶ τῶν ἀνθρώπων ἄπληστοι.
	[20a] βδέλυγμα **κυρίῳ** στηρίζων ὀφθαλμόν, καὶ οἱ ἀπαίδευτοι ἀκρατεῖς γλώσσῃ.
Sheol and Abaddon are never satisfied, and human eyes are never satisfied.	Hades and destruction are never satisfied; likewise insatiable are the eyes of people.
	[20a] An abomination to the Lord is a person who fixates his eye, also the uneducated, unable to control their tongue.

Septuagint of Proverbs," 547; Cook and van der Kooij, *Law, Prophets, and Wisdom*, 91, 94 and 105.
41 Beeckman, "Trails of a Different Vorlage," 587.

According to Fox, there is not enough evidence in order to tell whether this plus can be ascribed to the translator, a later reviser or a different Hebrew *Vorlage*.[42] However, he does mention that the plus elaborates the thought concerning the eyes expressed in Prov 27:20.[43] d'Hamonville, on the other hand, ascribes this plus to the LXX translator, once again (just as in 16:8) without elaboration.[44]

It is difficult, as Fox has observed, to ascribe this verse to the work of the translator or a different Hebrew *Vorlage*. However, two words might indicate that this plus is an addition made by the translator: (a) ἀπαίδευτοι and (b) ἀκρατεῖς:

(a) The noun ἀπαίδευτος occurs 7 times in LXX Proverbs (Prov 5:23; 8:5; 15:12.14; 17:21; 24:8 and 27:20) and only twice elsewhere (Zeph 2:1 and Isa 26:11). The Greek word is not consistently used to translate one and the same Hebrew lexeme. Moreover, it is used as a translation of a variety of Hebrew lexemes, i.e., אין מוסר (Prov 5:23), כסיל (Prov 8:5 and 15:4), לץ (Prov 15:12). In the other verses in which ἀπαίδευτοι is used, i.e., Prov 15:12; 17:21; 24:8 and 27:20, the LXX translation has a different rendering of the MT-version of the verse (Prov 15:12; 17:21 and 24:8) or has no equivalent in MT (Prov 27:20). The lexeme ἀπαίδευτος thus belonged to the characteristic vocabulary of the LXX translator of Proverbs.

(b) The adjective ἀκρατής (intemperate) is a *hapax legomenon* in the LXX corpus.[45] The LXX translator of Proverbs uses a lot of Greek *hapax legomena* which are not attested elsewhere in the LXX.[46] The multiple use of Greek words that are not attested in the other LXX books seems to be an indication of the translator's profound knowledge of Greek language as well as his rich vocabulary.[47] Therefore, this lexeme might also be a lexeme that is

---

42 See Fox, *Proverbs*, 421 (also n. 3). However, his writing is coloured towards an interpretation that ascribes the plus to the work of a translator or reviser. The words 'inserted' and 'additions' denote the activity of a translator or a later scribe. See Fox, *Proverbs*, 357 and 421. If he is not sure about whether or not to ascribe it to a diverging *Vorlage* or translational/revisional activity, he should have used the neutral word 'plus' which is also used in this monograph.

43 See Fox, *Proverbs*, 357.

44 See d'Hamonville, *Les Proverbes*, 49 and 325.

45 LEH, 23.

46 For an overview of all the Greek *hapax legomena* in LXX Proverbs see Cook, "The Translator(s) of the Septuagint of Proverbs."

47 See also, "The Translator(s) of the Septuagint of Proverbs." In my research on the Greek rendering of Hebrew animal names in LXX Proverbs, I have also concluded that the Greek translator of Proverbs must have had a profound knowledge of the Greek language in order to adequately render the diverse Hebrew animal names that are attested in Proverbs. In the major-

characteristic of the vocabulary of the LXX translator and would thus not stem from a diverging Hebrew *Vorlage*.

Thus, considering the characteristic vocabulary used in this additional verse, the addition of Prov 27:20a can be ascribed to the translational activity of the translator. The LXX translator might have found the original Hebrew verse to vague and elaborated the thought in Prov 27:20a (cf. Fox).

The attestation of βδέλυγμα κυρίῳ, which is a common Greek expression in both LXX Proverbs and LXX Deuteronomy as a rendering of תועבה יהוה (see above Prov 21:27), in Prov 27:20a deals with the wickedness of the eyes and the tongue. The negative connotation given to the eyes and the tongue are also attested elsewhere throughout the book.[48] In the MT-version of Prov 6:16-17, proud eyes and a lying tongue are an abomination to the Lord. However, the LXX version of Prov 6:16 is not identical to MT. There is no mention of an abomination of the Lord in LXX Prov 6:16. In the following verse, i.e., 6:17, however, the LXX agrees again with MT starting to list seven abominations, including the proud eyes and lying lips, which MT has announced in 16:6 and which are elaborated in 6:17-19. Since the explicit reference of wicked eyes and lips as an abomination in the eyes of the Lord is missing from 6:16, it is possible that the LXX translator stressed this thought in Prov 27:20a, which was the perfect place to do so since he was able to elaborate on the vague thought that is conveyed in Prov 27:20.

3.1.2.4 Different Greek rendering of Hebrew verses

Some verses in the LXX version of Proverbs attest a completely different rendering from its Hebrew counterpart in MT. This is the case in verses Prov 22:11; 24:7 and 29:23, in which ὁ κύριος is attested without a Hebrew counterpart in MT. These verses will be analysed below.

---

ity of the cases he has translated them with an adequate Greek equivalent. See Beeckman, "Proverbia de Animalibus."

48 For the negative connotation of the eyes, see, e.g., Prov 4:25; 6:13.17; 10:10; 28:27. For the negative connotation of the tongue, see, e.g., Prov 6:17.24; 15:4; 21:6; 26:28.

A   Prov 22:11

MT	LXX
אֹהֵב (טְהוֹר־)[טְהָר־]לֵב חֵן שְׂפָתָיו רֵעֵהוּ מֶלֶךְ׃	ἀγαπᾷ **κύριος** ὁσίας καρδίας, δεκτοὶ δὲ αὐτῷ πάντες ἄμωμοι· χείλεσιν ποιμαίνει βασιλεύς.
Those who love a pure heart and are gracious in speech will have the king as a friend.	The Lord loves devout hearts, and all the blameless are acceptable to him. A king herds with his lips.

This verse has traditionally been labelled as a 'difficult verse.'[49] In his commentary on Proverbs, William McKane sees the attestation of ὁ κύριος as an addition of the LXX translator instead of something that was already present in the translator's Hebrew *Vorlage*.[50] Moreover, according to Tauberschmidt, "[t]he translator's interest in religious or spiritual interpretation might have played a role in the decision to insert 'Lord'."[51] The attestation of ὁ κύριος might have been a misunderstanding of the LXX translator of אהב as a *qal* third person singular instead of a participle.[52] As the subject in this reading would not have been specified and thus staying vague, the LXX translator added ὁ κύριος – the obvious subject in this case – in order to specify who the subject of the verse is (cf. Prov 21:27 above). This is the same practice of the 'explication of participants' as in Prov 23:11 (see above).[53]

B   Prov 24:7

MT	LXX
רָאמוֹת לֶאֱוִיל חָכְמוֹת בַּשַּׁעַר לֹא יִפְתַּח־פִּיהוּ׃	σοφία καὶ ἔννοια ἀγαθὴ ἐν πύλαις σοφῶν· σοφοὶ οὐκ ἐκκλίνουσιν ἐκ στόματος **κυρίου**.
Wisdom is too high for fools; in the gate they do not open their mouths.	Wisdom and insight are to be found in the gates of the wise, and the wise do not turn away from the mouth of the Lord.

---

49 See Tauberschmidt, *Secondary Parallelism*, 217.

50 See William McKane, *Proverbs. A New Approach*, OTL (Philadelphia, PA: Westminster Press, 1970), 567.

51 Tauberschmidt, *Secondary Parallelism*, 218.

52 See Tauberschmidt, *Secondary Parallelism*, 218.

53 See Tauberschmidt, *Secondary Parallelism*, 218.

The Hebrew and Greek version of this verse differ. Whereas MT focusses on the fools and their lack of wisdom in order to speak as representatives of a community, or settle legal disputes at the gate where such things were being discussed,[54] the LXX version focusses on the wise instead of the fools. According to the parallelism in this verse, which is a better parallelism than in MT, wisdom and insight are connected to the mouth of the Lord. Thus, the Lord is the source of wisdom and insight.

Fox ascribes this variant reading to the LXX translator's activity. In his view, the translator found the Hebrew text odd and changed it to a better proverb.[55] This might be correct, but it does not explain why he opted for this particular rendering. In connection to the other extra attestations of ὁ κύριος which we have analysed thus far, the translator's focus on the Lord as the one who created and brings forth wisdom (see Prov 8:26 above) is emphasised in this verse as well.

C Prov 29:23

MT	LXX
גַּאֲוַת אָדָם תַּשְׁפִּילֶנּוּ וּשְׁפַל־רוּחַ יִתְמֹךְ כָּבוֹד׃	ὕβρις ἄνδρα ταπεινοῖ, τοὺς δὲ ταπεινόφρονας ἐρείδει δόξῃ **κύριος**.
A person's pride will bring humiliation, but one who is lowly in spirit will obtain honour.	Pride humbles a man, but the Lord supports the humble-minded with glory.

The differences between MT and LXX in Prov 29:23 are often ascribed to the translator.[56] This assumption might be strengthened by the usage of the Greek *hapax* ταπεινόφρονας.

In the LXX version of the text, it is the Lord (ὁ κύριος) who is the one who gives glory to those who are humble-minded, whereas in the MT-version, it is not mentioned who gives the glory/honour to the one who is humble in spirit.

---

54 See McKane, *Proverbs*, 398.
55 See Fox, *Proverbs*, 322.
56 See Fox, *Proverbs*, 377; d'Hamonville, Les Proverbes, 336; Hatton, Contradiction in the Book of Proverbs, 91.

Once again, the subject of the verb ἐρείδω, to fix firmly, to support,[57] has been specified by the LXX translator.

Moreover, Fox has observed that the LXX translator was not familiar to the meaning of 'to hold/to grasp' for the Hebrew verb תמך ('to support').[58] Instead, he translated the verb with other Greek verbs:

> G is not familiar with the sense 'grasp', which is required in Prov 3:18 (ἐπερειδομένοι[ς]); 4:4 (ἐρειδέτω), 5:5 (ἐρείδεται); [5:]22 (N-stem; translated σφίγγεται, as required by context); 11:6a (emend to ἐρείδει [...]), [11:]16b (ἐρείδονται [...]); 29:23 (ἐρείδει); and 31:19 (ἐρείδει). Means 'support' in 28:17 and is translated, relevantly, ἐν ἀσφαλείᾳ. G's limited understanding of the meaning of תמך sometimes led to infelicities.[59]

Prov 3:18 (see below) expresses the idea that those who hold fast (תמך) to wisdom will be happy. In the LXX version, תמך is rendered with the verb ἐπερείδω ('to lean upon'),[60] and ὁ κύριος is added as well. Thus, one has to lean upon Wisdom as they do on the Lord. It seems that the LXX translator wanted to convey the message that the Lord is the one (next to Wisdom) upon whom you can lean (Prov 3:18, see elaborated discussion below) and that He is the one who will support you (Prov 29:23), not Wisdom.

3.1.2.5 Addition of comparison/simile
In Prov 3:18, wisdom is honoured and compared to a tree of life, on which one can hold to for support:

MT	LXX
עֵץ־חַיִּים הִיא לַמַּחֲזִיקִים בָּהּ וְתֹמְכֶיהָ מְאֻשָּׁר׃	ξύλον ζωῆς ἐστι πᾶσι τοῖς ἀντεχομένοις αὐτῆς, καὶ τοῖς ἐπερειδομένοις ἐπ᾽ αὐτὴν ὡς ἐπὶ **κύριον** ἀσφαλής.
She is a tree of life to those who lay hold of her; those who hold her fast are called happy.	She is a tree of life to all those who lay claim to her, and she is steadfast to those who lean upon her, as on the Lord.

---

57 LEH, 241–42.
58 See Fox, *Proverbs*, 102.
59 Fox, *Proverbs*, 102.
60 LEH, 223.

As we can see in the LXX version, the following is a minor plus: ὡς ἐπὶ κύριον ἀσφαλής. This plus indicates that one can rely on Wisdom as one does on the Lord. Thus, the Lord is depicted as someone on whom they can count as well, especially because he is the creator (Prov 8), redeemer (Prov 23:11), the one the people of Israel need to fear (e.g., Prov 7:1a [LXX]). As indicated above, the LXX translator emphasised that the Lord is the sole creator (Prov 8:26) and the only redeemer (Prov 23:11). Therefore, the plus in Prov 3:18 can be regarded as an addition by the LXX translator who wanted to emphasise that one is not only able to rely on Wisdom alone but also on God, who is the primordial one on whom humans can always firmly rely.[61]

3.1.2.6 Conclusion
So far, we have examined the 13 extra attestations of ὁ κύριος in LXX Proverbs without any Hebrew counterpart in MT. Two of these instances (i.e., Prov 10:6 and 16:8) can be ascribed to the translator's Hebrew *Vorlage* differing from MT. The other 11 instances can be ascribed to the translator's translational activity. With regard to the translation technique and the theology of the LXX translator of Proverbs, we can make the following observations:

- In most of the cases the LXX translator seems to have tried to specify the subject of the verb, when it is not specified in MT (Tauberschmidt's 'explication of participants'). This is the case in Prov 3:18; 3:34; 8:26; 21:27; 22:11; 24:7.12; 23:11 and 29:23. Sometimes, this has happened due to different reading (or misunderstanding) of the Hebrew verb (Prov 21:27 and 22:11). In several instances, this explication adds a religious nuance by emphasising God (1) as the only redeemer (Prov 23:11), (2) as sole creator (Prov 8:26; 24:7 and 24:12) and (3) as the one to lean on and who will give support (Prov 3:18 and 29:23);
- In the additional verses and cola which can be ascribed to the translator, the translator seems to have tried to emphasise the Solomonic authorship of Proverbs (Prov 7:1a) and the sapiential tradition of God as the one to fear (Prov 7:1a and 27:20).

---

61 Fox has also indicated the LXX version "enhances the religious message" by adding the comparison between Wisdom and God. Fox, *Proverbs*, 101. Tauberschmidt also regards this as an addition from the hand of the translator. See Tauberschmidt, *Secondary Parallelism*, 76 and n. 235. Gillis Gerleman has noted that in this verse, the LXX translator found the Hebrew verse too secular and thus tried to religionise the verse. See Gerleman, *Proverbs*, 38.

Out of these observations we can conclude that the LXX version of Proverbs does not necessarily attest a different theology than MT but nuances and emphasises the theology of MT. Whereas the MT leaves room to interpret Wisdom as a creational actor or the only thing one can confine and lean on for support, the LXX version emphasises that God is the sole creator, the redeemer of the people of Israel and, next to Wisdom, the one to lean on, and who is able to give support to those worthy of receiving it. Moreover, the LXX translator emphasises the Solomonic authorship of Proverbs and the sapiential tradition that focusses on the respect for the Lord. In short, these observations seem to strengthen Cook's hypothesis that the LXX translator of Proverbs must have been a conservative Jew.

3.1.3 The evaluation of additional attestations of ὁ θεός in LXX Proverbs

As can be observed from the registration above, there are 10 additional attestations of ὁ θεός in LXX Proverbs with no counterpart in MT, i.e., in 1:7; 4:27; 16:7; 21:8; 22:8; 30:1.3; 31:1.3 and 31:8. The additional attestations of ὁ θεός can be subdivided into the following categories: additional verses or stichs and different Greek rendering of Hebrew verses.

3.1.3.1 Additional verses or stichs
Several additional attestations of ὁ θεός can be found in verses or stichs that do not have a counterpart in MT. The verses in question are: Prov 1:7; 4:27; 16:7 and 22:8.

A   Prov 1:7

MT	LXX
יִרְאַת יְהוָה רֵאשִׁית דָּעַת חׇכְמָה וּמוּסָר אֱוִילִים בָּזוּ׃	ἀρχὴ σοφίας φόβος **θεοῦ**, σύνεσις δὲ ἀγαθὴ πᾶσι τοῖς ποιοῦσιν αὐτήν· εὐσέβεια δὲ εἰς θεὸν ἀρχὴ αἰσθήσεως, σοφίαν δὲ καὶ παιδείαν ἀσεβεῖς ἐξουθενήσουσιν.
The fear of the LORD is the be-ginning of knowledge; fools despise wisdom and in-struction.	The beginning of wisdom is fear of God, and understanding is good for all those who practice it, and piety upon God is the beginning of perception; the impious, however, will despise wisdom and discipline.

In this verse, the LXX attests two extra lines compared to MT. These lines correspond to the first lines of LXX Ps 110(MT 111):10:

LXX	NETS
ἀρχὴ σοφίας φόβος κυρίου, σύνεσις ἀγαθὴ πᾶσι τοῖς ποιοῦσιν αὐτήν.	Fear of the Lord is wisdom's beginning; a good understanding belongs to all who practice it.[62]

In scholarly literature, the variant reading between MT and LXX Prov 1:7 has been explained in light of the intertextuality between LXX Proverbs and LXX Psalms.[63] Both Cook and Joosten agree on the fact that the LXX version of the Psalter was established first and that the LXX translator of Proverbs must have drawn upon this translation.[64] As a result, the extra attestation of the Greek lines *vis-à-vis* the Hebrew text can be explained by the translator's activity instead of a diverging Hebrew *Vorlage*. Cook explains the addition of the extra lines in function of the theology and ideology of the LXX translator.[65] Indeed, as Cook argues, the option of the LXX translator to insert a Psalter text might be a way to emphasise the Jewishness of the translation as a way to counter the Hellenising trend that was leading Jews away from their own religion.[66]

This being said, no one explicitly explains the shift from ὁ κύριος in LXX Psalms to ὁ θεός in LXX Proverbs. Only Lorenzo Cuppi ascribes this attestation of ὁ θεός to the translation technique of the LXX translator, but he does not explain precisely how this might be so.[67] In my view, however, the choice to change ὁ κύριος to ὁ θεός can be explained by taking the translation technique of the LXX translator of Proverbs into account. The LXX translator frequently

62 Translation from Albert Pietersma, "Psalms (and the Prayer of Manasses)," in *A New English Translation of the Septuagint. And the Other Greek Translations Traditionally Included under That Title*, ed. Albert Pietersma and Benjamin G. Wright (Oxford: Oxford University Press, 2007), 542–620.
63 See, for example, Cook, "Intertextual Relationships between the Septuagint of Psalms and Proverbs"; Lorenzo Cuppi, "Concerning the Origin of the Addition Found in Prov^LXX 1:7," in *XIV Congress of the IOSCS, Helsinki, 2010*, ed. Melvin K. H. Peters, SBLSCS 59 (Atlanta, GA: SBL Press, 2013), 93–103; Jan Joosten, "The Relation of the Septuagint of Proverbs to the Septuagint of Psalms," in *Septuagint, Sages and Scripture. Studies in Honour of Johann Cook*, ed. Randall X. Gauthier, Gideon Kotzé and Gert Steyn, VTS 172 (Leiden: Brill, 2016), 99–107.
64 See Cook, "Intertextual Relationships between the Septuagint of Psalms and Proverbs," 228; Joosten, "The Relation of the Septuagint of Proverbs to the Septuagint of Psalms," 107.
65 See Cook, *The Septuagint of Proverbs*, 61; Cook, "Intertextual Relationships between the Septuagint of Psalms and Proverbs," 228.
66 See Cook, *The Septuagint of Proverbs*, 61.
67 See Cuppi, "Concerning the Origin of the Addition Found in Prov^LXX 1:7," 99–100.

tries to improve the poetic quality of his text by enhancing parallelism.[68] Thus, the option the change ὁ κύριος from LXX Psalms to ὁ θεός in LXX Proverbs can be explained by the translator's concern to provide good parallelism with the attestation of ὁ θεός in following stich.

B Prov 4:27

MT	LXX
אַל־תֵּט־יָמִין וּשְׂמֹאול הָסֵר רַגְלְךָ מֵרָע׃	μὴ ἐκκλίνῃς εἰς τὰ δεξιὰ μηδὲ εἰς τὰ ἀριστερά, ἀπόστρεψον δὲ σὸν πόδα ἀπὸ ὁδοῦ κακῆς· 27a ὁδοὺς γὰρ τὰς ἐκ δεξιῶν οἶδεν **ὁ θεός**, διεστραμμέναι δέ εἰσιν αἱ ἐξ ἀριστερῶν· 27b αὐτὸς δὲ ὀρθὰς ποιήσει τὰς τροχιάς σου, τὰς δὲ πορείας σου ἐν εἰρήνῃ προάξει.
Do not swerve to the right or to the left; turn your foot away from evil.	Do not incline to the right or to the left; rather turn away your foot from an evil way, 27a for God knows the ways on the right, but those on the left are twisted. 27b But it is he who will make your tracks straight, and he will guide your journeys in peace.

The first stich of the Greek version is an interpretation of the Hebrew verse. The following two stichs, containing the reference to ὁ θεός, are not attested in MT. According to Michael V. Fox, these additional stichs should be explained as a later scribal interpretation that reacted to the original translation.[69] However, he does not exactly explain *why* the said scribes added verses in question.[70] Thus, his explanation is unsatisfactory. Moreover, given that the LXX translator often provides an additional explanation of a certain Hebrew verse that could poten-

---

68 See Beeckman, "Trails of a Different Vorlage," 584. The suggestion that enhancing parallelism is a characteristic of the translation technique of the LXX Proverbs has been clearly demonstrated by Tauberschmidt. See Tauberschmidt, *Secondary Parallelism*. See also Fox, *Proverbs*, 52–54.

69 See Fox, *Proverbs*, 113.

70 Crawford H. Toy's explanation is more elaborate than the explanation given by Fox. He argues that the insertion was made by someone who wanted to stress divine supervision. See Toy, *Proverbs*, 99–100.

tially be misunderstood by his audience,[71] the additional verses in Prov 4:27 might be explained as translator's activity. The fact that it is a clarification of the original Hebrew verse and not a completely new proverb supports this idea.

In these additional verses, God is the one who knows the ways 'on the right,' which are implicitly the ways of the righteous, whereas 'those on the left,' the ways of the unrighteous, are crooked. In the last analysis, it is only God who can make the ways of humans straight. Thus, just as in Prov 3:18 and 29:23, in which ὁ κύριος was added by the LXX translator to give emphasis to God being the one to lean on for support,[72] the LXX translator has tried to make God the one who will ultimately make the ways of (wo)men straight instead of the human actors themselves.

C Prov 16:7

LXX	NETS
ἀρχὴ ὁδοῦ ἀγαθῆς τὸ ποιεῖν τὰ δίκαια, δεκτὰ δὲ παρὰ **θεῷ** μᾶλλον ἢ θύειν θυσίας.	The beginning of a good way is to do righteous things, and they are more acceptable with God than to bring sacrifices.

As I have pointed out elsewhere, this verse can be ascribed to a diverging Hebrew *Vorlage*.[73] This view contrasts with Cook, who ascribes every difference (on macro and micro level) to the creative mind of the translator.[74] He does not posit the use of a diverging Hebrew *Vorlage* since we do not have extant evidence of such a text.[75] However, explaining the extensive changes in verse and chapter order on the basis of the LXX translator's creativity is hard to maintain if we account for scribal practice in Antiquity.[76] Accordingly, the extra attestation of ὁ θεός in this verse cannot tell us more about the translation technique or the theology of LXX Proverbs.

---

71 See, for example, the tendency of the translator to explicate the subject and direct object, which are obscure in the Hebrew text. See Tauberschmidt, *Secondary Parallelism*, 116–120.

72 See Beeckman, "De Nominibus Sacris," 521–523.

73 See Beeckman, "Trails of a Different Vorlage," 586–588.

74 See, i.a., Cook, "'ishah zarah," 460; Cook, "The Greek of Proverbs," 618; Cook and van der Kooij, *Law, Prophets, and Wisdom*, 91, 94 and 105.

75 See, e.g., Cook, "Contrasting as a Translation Technique," 412.

76 See Beeckman, "Trails of a Different Vorlage," 587.

D Prov 22:8

MT	LXX
זֹרֵעַ עַוְלָה (יִקְצוֹר־)[יִקְצָר־][אָוֶן וְשֵׁבֶט עֶבְרָתוֹ יִכְלֶה:	ὁ σπείρων φαῦλα θερίσει κακά, πληγὴν δὲ ἔργων αὐτοῦ συντελέσει. ⁸ᵃ ἄνδρα ἱλαρὸν καὶ δότην εὐλογεῖ **ὁ θεός**, ματαιότητα δὲ ἔργων αὐτοῦ συντελέσει.
Whoever sows injustice will reap calamity, and the rod of anger will fail.	He who sows what is cheap will reap what is bad and will complete the impact of his deeds. ⁸ᵃ God blesses a cheerful and generous man, but he will bring to an end the vanity of his deeds.

The LXX attests an additional verse *vis-à-vis* MT. According to Fox, the first part of Prov 22:8a, i.e., ἄνδρα ἱλαρὸν καὶ δότην εὐλογεῖ ὁ θεός,[77] does not constitute part of the Old Greek (OG) text but of a recensional addition, whereas the second part, i.e., ματαιότητα δὲ ἔργων αὐτοῦ συντελέσει, is a reformulation by the translator of ושבט עברתו יכלה (and the rod of anger will fail).[78] BHQ records these additional verses as exegesis and double reading/translations, whereby the first part of the addition is an interpretation of 22:9a.[79]

Indeed, the Greek text of Prov 22:9 also differs from MT:

MT	LXX
טוֹב־עַיִן הוּא יְבֹרָךְ כִּי־נָתַן מִלַּחְמוֹ לַדָּל:	ὁ ἐλεῶν πτωχὸν αὐτὸς διατραφήσεται· τῶν γὰρ ἑαυτοῦ ἄρτων ἔδωκεν τῷ πτωχῷ ⁹ᵃ νίκην καὶ τιμὴν περιποιεῖται ὁ δῶρα δούς, τὴν μέντοι ψυχὴν ἀφαιρεῖται τῶν κεκτημένων.
Those who are generous are blessed, for they share their bread with the poor.	He who has compassion over the poor will himself be nourished, because he gave his own food to the poor. ⁹ᵃ He who hands out gifts secures victory and honor; moreover, he takes away the soul of those who have possessions.

---

77 This verse is also alluded to in 2 Cor 9:7.
78 See Fox, *Proverbs*, 299.
79 See BHQ, 39 and 50.

While the LXX translator of Proverbs is generally depicted as a free translator,[80] it seems unlikely that he was responsible for all these changes. Taking the translation technique of the translator into account, he seems, for the most part, to have changed his text at a micro level, or to have inserted an extra stich in order to emphasise a certain thought or to provide an explanation of the preceding Hebrew stich, which might have been unclear for the target audience.[81] Therefore, the different reading in Prov 22:8-9 must have originated from a diverging Hebrew *Vorlage* and/or changes during the transmission history of the Greek text.

3.1.3.2 Different Greek rendering of Hebrew verses

The LXX frequently offers a different Greek rendering of the Hebrew text. In the following verses, the Greek translation attests ὁ θεός where this has no counterpart in MT: Prov 21:8; 30:1.3; 31:1.3 and 31:8.

A   Prov 21:8

MT	LXX
הַפַּכְפַּךְ דֶּרֶךְ אִישׁ וָזָר וְזַךְ יָשָׁר פָּעֳלוֹ:	πρὸς τοὺς σκολιοὺς σκολιὰς ὁδοὺς ἀποστέλλει **ὁ θεός·** ἁγνὰ γὰρ καὶ ὀρθὰ τὰ ἔργα αὐτοῦ.
The way of the guilty is crooked, but the conduct of the pure is right.	To the crooked God sends crooked ways, for his works are pure and upright.

The Hebrew version of this verse is obscure and may have posed a difficulty for the translator to render.[82] Nevertheless, since the change does not entail the addition of an entire proverb, and since the LXX translator often changes the text at a micro level,[83] this variant reading can be ascribed to the translator. The translator has tried to make the verse more intelligible and has added ἀποστέλλει ὁ θεός (God sends). Interestingly, this verse deals with the 'ways of people' (here the crooked), just as in Prov 4:27. In the analysis of Prov 4:27 (see

---

80 See, e.g., Cook, "The Dating of Septuagint Proverbs," 388: "There is a general consensus that Septuagint Proverbs represents a rather free translation unit."
81 See Beeckman, "Trails of a Different Vorlage," 588; Beeckman, "De Nominibus Sacris," 515–517.
82 See Fox, *Proverbs*, 289.
83 See Cook, *The Septuagint of Proverbs*, 31; Beeckman, "Trails of a Different Vorlage," 585.

above), I argue that the LXX translator wants to emphasise God's agency in making straight the ways of people. In Prov 21:8, the nuance suggests that God himself sends crooked ways to the crooked, thus making God the actor in the LXX.[84] This is further elaborated in the second colon which states that God's works are pure and upright. The general thought expressed in Prov 4:27 and Prov 21:8, therefore, is that it is God who makes straight the ways of the people (especially the righteous, those 'on the right'), whereas he sends crooked ways to those who are crooked (those 'on the left').

B Prov 30:1

MT	LXX
דִּבְרֵי ׀ אָגוּר בִּן־יָקֶה הַמַּשָּׂא נְאֻם הַגֶּבֶר לְאִיתִיאֵל לְאִיתִיאֵל וְאֻכָל׃	τοὺς ἐμοὺς λόγους υἱέ φοβήθητι καὶ δεξάμενος αὐτοὺς μετανόει· τάδε λέγει ὁ ἀνὴρ τοῖς πιστεύουσιν **θεῷ**, καὶ παύομαι.
The words of Agur son of Jakeh. An oracle. Thus says the man: I am weary, O God, I am weary, O God. How can I pre-vail?	My son, fear my words, and repent when you receive them; this is what the man says to those who believe in God: Now I stop.

Remarkably, the reference here to Agur has not been attested in the Greek text. This is not the only instance in which this proper name in the Hebrew text of Proverbs is not present in the LXX. In chapters 30 and 31, no mention is made of Agur or Lemuel in the LXX. Both Ruth Scoralick and Johann Cook suggest that this reflects the translator's theological/ideological motives.[85] Throughout his translation, the translator deliberately omits the Hebrew names of Agur and Lemuel in order to emphasise that Solomon is the sole author of the book of Proverbs.[86] This also results in Proverbs not being a mere collection of different proverbs, but a unity of proverbs originating from Solomon.[87]

---

84 See also Tauberschmidt, *Secondary Parallelism*, 160.
85 See Cook, *The Septuagint of Proverbs*, 307; Scoralick, "Salomos griechische Gewänder," 55–56. Tov does not explain the minus of the proper names of Lemuel and Agur on theological grounds, but merely as a misunderstanding of the *Vorlage* by the LXX translator. See Tov, "Recensional Differences," 430–431.
86 See Cook, *The Septuagint of Proverbs*, 307; Scoralick, "Salomos griechische Gewänder," esp. 55–56 and 72.
87 See Scoralick, "Salomos griechische Gewänder," 56.

This tendency is not only evident in the omissions of proper names, but it can also be observed elsewhere in the LXX translation. As I have already observed above, the translator has emphasised the authorship of Solomon in Prov 7:1a.[88] In this verse, the addition of υἱέ τίμα τὸν κύριον καὶ ἰσχύσεις πλὴν δὲ αὐτοῦ μὴ φοβοῦ ἄλλον, especially the insertion of ἰσχύσεις (which refers to 3 Kgdms 2:2 where David tells his son Solomon to be strong and keep God's commandments according to the Law of Moses), can be seen as an emphasis on the sole authorship of Solomon.[89] The tendency of the translator to emphasise the authorship of Solomon as well as the sacred authority of the text might be a response to the Hellenistic context wherein the LXX translation of Proverbs was made.

C   Prov 30:3

MT	LXX
וְלֹא־לָמַדְתִּי חָכְמָה וְדַעַת קְדֹשִׁים אֵדָע׃	**θεὸς** δεδίδαχέν με σοφίαν, καὶ γνῶσιν ἁγίων ἔγνωκα.
I have not learned wisdom, nor have I knowledge of the holy ones.	God has taught me wisdom, and I have gained knowledge of holy things.

In the LXX, God is depicted as the teacher of wisdom. The negative meaning of the Hebrew is transformed into a positive in Greek. It has been argued by some scholars that the Hebrew text contains irony, which is omitted by the translator in his Greek text.[90] Moreover, since it is Solomon who is speaking in the Greek text instead of Agur (see Prov 30:1 above), this verse enhances the idea of Solomon being a wise man who has gained knowledge of divine things from God.[91] The Greek rendering of this verse thus reveals a translator who wanted to stress the unique authorship of Solomon (see above) as well as Solomon as a personification of a wise man who received his teachings and wisdom from God himself.

Moreover, Ludger Schwienhorst-Schönberger has recently demonstrated that the LXX version of Proverbs exhibits a stronger focus on revelatory wisdom

---

88 See Beeckman, "De Nominibus Sacris," 514–515.
89 See Beeckman, "De Nominibus Sacris," 514.
90 See Tauberschmidt, *Secondary Parallelism*, 140 (also n. 89).
91 See Scoralick, "Salomos griechische Gewänder," 55–56. The idea of Solomon being a wise man is also found in other biblical books; see, for example, 1 Kg 4:29 (LXX 3 Kgdms 5:9).

('Offenbarungsweisheit').[92] This wisdom comes from God and is contrasted or complemented by experiential wisdom ('Erfahrungsweisheit').[93] Wisdom from revelation becomes more explicit throughout the transmission history of the Old Testament wisdom literature.[94] In Prov 30:3, the shift from Agur to Solomon and especially the explicit reference to God can be seen as an attempt on the part of the LXX translator to make revelatory wisdom more explicit.[95]

D Prov 31:1

MT	LXX
דִּבְרֵי לְמוּאֵל מֶלֶךְ מַשָּׂא אֲשֶׁר־יִסְּרַתּוּ אִמּוֹ׃	Οἱ ἐμοὶ λόγοι εἴρηνται ὑπὸ **θεοῦ**, βασιλέως χρηματισμός, ὃν ἐπαίδευσεν ἡ μήτηρ αὐτοῦ.
The words of King Lemuel. An oracle that his mother taught him.	My words have been spoken by God, the oracular response of a king, whom his mother instructed.

The proper name Lemuel is attested twice in the Hebrew text of Proverbs, i.e., Prov 31:1 and 31:4. Nevertheless, as was the case with Agur in Prov 30:1, this proper name is not attested in the LXX. On the one hand, the addition of ὁ θεός in this verse can be explained as a different reading of the name of Lemuel as אֵל לְמוֹ דְּבָרֵי (whereby לְמוֹ is interpreted as ὑπὸ 'by').[96] On the other hand, this reading might be influenced by the translator's concern to emphasise the Solomonic authorship of Proverbs by omitting every proper name of kings in his Greek text. The option to render דברי למואל by οἱ ἐμοὶ λόγοι εἴρηνται ὑπὸ θεοῦ might be a combination of both options. The translator's *Vorlage* lends itself to a reading in which the divine name can be read and the translator's own desire to attribute the book solely to Solomon have resulted in the Greek text we now know.

---

92 See Schwienhorst-Schönberger, "Weisheit und das Leben vor Gott," 342–344.
93 See Schwienhorst-Schönberger, "Weisheit und das Leben vor Gott," 341–342.
94 See Schwienhorst-Schönberger, "Weisheit und das Leben vor Gott," 342. Wisdom from revelation is also present in MT but not as explicit as in the LXX. The LXX translators often make this type of wisdom more explicit in comparison to its attestation in the Hebrew text.
95 See Schwienhorst-Schönberger, "Weisheit und das Leben vor Gott," 343.
96 See also Fox, *Proverbs*, 388 and Cook, *The Septuagint of Proverbs*, 297–298.

E   Prov 31:2

MT	LXX
מַה־בְּרִי וּמַה־בַּר־בִּטְנִי וּמֶה בַּר־נְדָרָי׃	τί, τέκνον, τηρήσεις; τί; ῥήσεις **θεοῦ·** πρωτογενές, σοὶ λέγω, υἱέ· τί, τέκνον ἐμῆς κοιλίας; τί, τέκνον ἐμῶν εὐχῶν;
No, my son! No, son of my womb! No, son of my vows!	What, my child, will you keep? What? Divine sayings. My firstborn, I speak to you, my son. What, child of my womb? What, child of my vows?

The LXX has a reading different from MT. Moreover, this verse refers to Prov 31:1 (see above) and the words uttered by God, thus giving them a divine provenance.[97] As argued above, the LXX translator made the divine provenance of wisdom more explicit in his translation (see Prov 30:3).

F   Prov 31:8

MT	LXX
פְּתַח־פִּיךָ לְאִלֵּם אֶל־דִּין כָּל־בְּנֵי חֲלוֹף׃	ἄνοιγε σὸν στόμα λόγῳ **θεοῦ** καὶ κρῖνε πάντας ὑγιῶς.
Speak out for those who cannot speak, for the rights of all the destitute.	Open your mouth with a divine word, and judge all fairly.

Once again, this verse refers to the previous verses, especially 31:1 and 31:2, in which the emphasis lies on the divine provenance of the teachings.[98]

3.1.3.3 Conclusion

Having registered and analysed the 10 additional attestations of ὁ θεός in LXX Proverbs without counterpart in MT, we can now make the following conclusions with regard to the translation technique and particular theology of the LXX translator:

---

97 See Cook, *The Septuagint of Proverbs*, 299.
98 See Cook, *The Septuagint of Proverbs*, 303.

- The LXX translator has omitted every reference to Lemuel and Agur to whom the proverbial collections in the Hebrew text are ascribed (see Prov 30:1 and 31:1). This seems to have been done in order to stress the authorship of Solomon. Moreover, the translator also emphasises that Solomon received his wisdom from God (Prov 30:3; 31:2 and 31:8). Wisdom in these verses can thus be seen as revelatory wisdom;
- The addition of LXX Ps 110(MT 111):10 in Prov 1:7 can be seen as an emphasis on the Jewishness of the Greek translation. The additional attestation of ὁ θεός in this verse can be explained by the translator's concern to provide good parallelisms;
- The extra attestations of ὁ θεός in Prov 4:27 and 21:8 relate to the theological and ethical dimension. The Hebrew text only mentions human actor(s), whereas the LXX suggests God's agency in making straight the ways of humans (Prov 4:27) or crooked the ways of the crooked (Prov 21:8);
- Some additional attestations of ὁ θεός should not be ascribed to the translator's translation technique, but rather to a diverging *Vorlage* and/or textual transmission (e.g., Prov 16:7 and 22:8).

If we compare these results with the results obtained by examining the additional attestations of ὁ κύριος, we can make the following observations:
- Emphasis on Solomonic authorship can be observed in the translator's additions of both ὁ θεός and ὁ κύριος. However, ὁ θεός is used in verses pertaining to wisdom, whereas ὁ κύριος is used in a verse referring to commandments;
- The explicitation of the subject of the verb – and the religious nuance(s) it introduces – brought about by the LXX translator's addition of ὁ κύριος, is not found in the addition of ὁ θεός. Nor is there any emphasis on the sapiential thought of God as 'one to fear' in the verses containing an addition of ὁ θεός.

The translator's approach in using ὁ θεός or ὁ κύριος thus clearly differs. However, further research into the Greek translation of the Hebrew divine names in LXX Proverbs will be necessary to reach sound conclusions on this point. Nevertheless, and on the basis of these results, it is safe to conclude that the LXX translator of Proverbs endeavoured to emphasise the Jewishness of his translation by stressing the Solomonic authorship of the book. Furthermore, his emphasis on God as an ethical, sapiential and creational actor is also characteristic of the translator's theology. It is thus clear that the LXX version of Proverbs attests to particular 'theological accents or elements,'[99] compared to its Hebrew counterpart. Establishing a complete picture of this distinct theology evidently requires more research into the theology of the LXX.

3.2 The additional attestations of ὁ κύριος and ὁ θεός in LXX Job

Having analysed the pluses of ὁ κύριος and ὁ θεός in LXX Proverbs, we will now conduct the same research on LXX Job. In what follows, we will firstly register and evaluate all the instances where ὁ κύριος and ὁ θεός are attested in LXX Job without a Hebrew counterpart. Afterwards, we will compare the results obtained in the evaluation to the results from the studies on LXX Proverbs.

3.2.1 The registration of the additional attestations of ὁ κύριος and ὁ θεός in LXX Job

In order to evaluate and discern whether the Greek text of Job reflects a theology differing from its Hebrew version, the additional attestations of ὁ κύριος and ὁ θεός in LXX Job will first be registered. In order to do so, some methodological remarks need to be made. Since our research pertains to the translation technique of the Old Greek (OG) translator of Job, the verses marked with an asterisk (※) in Ziegler's edition will not be examined because they belong to the asterisked material in LXX Job and are thus not part of OG Job.[100] Of the 116 attestations of ὁ κύριος and 13 attestations of ὁ θεός, 11 have no counterpart in MT.[101] These additional attestations are found in the following verses: 1:21.22; 7:2; 15:25; 19:3; 33:23; 36:12; 40:4 (ὁ κύριος) and 2:10; 6:10; 34:27 (ὁ θεός). First, the additional attestations of ὁ κύριος will be evaluated, afterwards the additional attestations of ὁ θεός.

---

99 See Ausloos and Lemmelijn, "Theology or not? That's the Question," 45.

100 See Ziegler, *Job*. As noted before, Ziegler's edition of the LXX text of Job is not flawless. Therefore, Peter J. Gentry provided an updated list of the asterisked material in Job LXX. See Gentry, *Asterisked Materials*, 31. The verses in which there is a plus of ὁ κύριος and ὁ θεός but which belong to the asterisked material are 37:2; 40:1, and 42:17.

101 In the asterisked material, there are 4 additional attestations of ὁ κύριος (i.e., 12:9; 37:2; 40:1 and 42:17) and 5 additional attestations of ὁ θεός (i.e., 31:2; 35:10; 39:17; 40:1 and 40:2). In some instances, the critical apparatus indicate that some manuscripts attest ὁ κύριος instead of ὁ θεός and vice versa. However, the main text of Ziegler will be used as a point of departure for the OG of Job.

3.2.2 The evaluation of additional attestations of ὁ κύριος in LXX Job

Eight times does ὁ κύριος occur without any counterpart in MT: Job 1:21.22; 7:2; 15:25; 19:3; 33:23; 36:12, and 40:4.

3.2.2.1 Job 1:21

MT	LXX
וַיֹּאמֶר עָרֹם [יָצָתִי] (יָצָאתִי) מִבֶּטֶן אִמִּי וְעָרֹם אָשׁוּב שָׁמָּה יְהוָה נָתַן וַיהוָה לָקָח יְהִי שֵׁם יְהוָה מְבֹרָךְ:	Αὐτὸς γυμνὸς ἐξῆλθον ἐκ κοιλίας μητρός μου, γυμνὸς καὶ ἀπελεύσομαι ἐκεῖ· ὁ κύριος ἔδωκεν, ὁ κύριος ἀφείλατο· ὡς **τῷ κυρίῳ** ἔδοξεν, οὕτως ἐγένετο· εἴη τὸ ὄνομα κυρίου εὐλογημένον.
He said, "Naked I came from my mother's womb, and naked shall I return there; the Lord gave, and the Lord has taken away; blessed be the name of the Lord".	"I came naked from my mother's womb; naked also shall I return there; the Lord gave; the Lord has taken away; as it seemed good to the Lord, so it turned out; blessed be the name of the Lord".

The Greek text has a plus compared to the Hebrew text: ὡς τῷ κυρίῳ ἔδοξεν οὕτως καὶ ἐγένετο ('as it seemed good to the Lord, so it turned out').[102] Evaluatively, this plus can be ascribed to the LXX translator who seems to have aimed at explaining what has been uttered in the preceding lines of the verse, i.e., ὁ κύριος ἔδωκεν ὁ κύριος ἀφείλατο ('the Lord gave; the Lord has taken away'). Claude E. Cox argues that the plus, which can be regarded as an addition, "is intended to soften the apparently arbitrary actions of the deity, who gives and takes away. It issues from a type of pastoral concern for the audience."[103] Indeed, by adding that the disaster which struck Job was because this seemed good to the Lord, the reader of the Greek text learns about God's motive, something which is lacking in the Hebrew text.[104] Thus, by adding ὡς τῷ κυρίῳ ἔδοξεν οὕτως καὶ ἐγένετο, the LXX translator explained and therefore clarified the Hebrew text which is silent on God's motive.

---

102 See Cox, *Iob* (forthcoming). Markus Witte argues that this plus corresponds to Job 42:6 (διὸ ἐφαύλισα ἐμαυτὸν καὶ ἐτάκην ἥγημαι δὲ ἐμαυτὸν γῆν καὶ σποδόν). However, he does not elaborate this correspondence. See Witte, "Greek Book of Job," 49.
103 Cox, *Iob* (forthcoming).
104 Gerleman also recognises this plus as an exegetical addition of the translator without further explanation. See Gerleman, *Job*, 12.

3.2.2.2 Job 1:22

MT	LXX
בְּכָל־זֹאת לֹא־חָטָא אִיּוֹב וְלֹא־נָתַן תִּפְלָה לֵאלֹהִים:	Ἐν τούτοις πᾶσιν τοῖς συμβεβηκόσιν αὐτῷ οὐδὲν ἥμαρτεν Ἰὼβ ἐναντίον **τοῦ κυρίου** καὶ οὐκ ἔδωκεν ἀφροσύνην τῷ θεῷ.
In all this Job did not sin or charge God with wrongdoing.	In all these things that happened to him Iob did not sin at all before the Lord, and he did not charge God with folly.

In this verse, the plus of ὁ κύριος is made in connection to the preposition ἐναντίον. This preposition occurs 22 times in LXX Job and is used to render 8 different lexemes: מִן (4:17; 32:2), לְ (8:4; 34:37), אֶל (9:4; 13:3; 15:25.26), בְּעֵינֶיךָ (11:4; 15:15; 18:3; 19:15; 25:5; 32:1), אֶל־פָּנָיו (13:15), לִפְנֵי (13:16; 35:14), אֵת (1:9).[105] It is a plus in three instances, i.e., 1:22; 2:10, and 34:26, two of them (1:22 and 2:10) attest a divine title without counterpart in MT.

The plus ἐναντίον τοῦ κυρίου in this verse offers information about the verb חטא/ἁμαρτάνω ('to sin').[106] As Cox argues,[107] questions regarding to whom Job did not sin against might have arisen with the readers of the Hebrew text, since it is not made explicit to whom Job did not sin against or before in MT. Moreover, in each instance in which ἐναντίον is used in the Greek text, it is specified in the Hebrew text against whom Job sinned. Only in the instances where this is not the case, the LXX translator adds this element after the same proposition ἐναντίον, and thus in the genitive form. This can be observed in 1:22; 2:10, and 34:26. Thus, just as was the case in Job 1:21, the LXX translator provided the reader with additional information that is lacking in the Hebrew text.

---

105 See Cox, *Iob* (forthcoming). According to Cook, this addition stresses God's omnipotence. However, he does not elaborate his statement. See Cook and van der Kooij, *Law, Prophets and Wisdom*, 182–183.

106 The preposition ἐναντίον is often used in connection with חטא/ἁμαρτάνω (i.e., in Job 1:22; 2:10, and 8:4). See Dhont, *Style and Context of Old Greek Job*, 138–139. In these instances it is always used with a genitive indicating God (κυρίου [1:22]; θεοῦ [2:10]; αὐτοῦ [8:4]).

107 See Cox, *Iob* (forthcoming).

3.2.2.3 Job 7:2

MT	LXX
כְּעֶבֶד יִשְׁאַף־צֵל וּכְשָׂכִיר יְקַוֶּה פָעֳלוֹ׃	ἢ ὥσπερ θεράπων δεδοικὼς **τὸν κύριον** αὐτοῦ καὶ τετευχὼς σκιᾶς ἢ ὥσπερ μισθωτὸς ἀναμένων τὸν μισθὸν αὐτοῦ.
Like a slave who longs for the shadow, and like laborers who look for their wages.	Or like an attendant who fears his master and finds shadow, or like a wage-earner waiting for his wages?

In this verse, scholars agree that the plus of this verse, i.e., τὸν κύριον αὐτοῦ, is inserted by the LXX translator who has drawn from his own earlier translation, here 3:19.[108] However, there is a discussion whether the plus τὸν κύριον αὐτοῦ pertains to God or just to the master of slaves. Since the word is ambiguous,[109] some scholars do not see the need to see this as an additional attestation of the divine name.[110] Even the ancient scribes had difficulty in judging whether this attestation must be considered a divine name or not.[111]

Therefore, an examination of the usage of the noun θεράπων in the LXX corpus might shed more light on this matter. Θεράπων, meaning 'one devoted to

---

108 See Beer, Der Text des Buches Job, 44; Heater, A Septuagint Translation Technique, 49; Markus Witte and Martina Kepper, "Job/Das Buch Ijob/Hiob," in Septuaginta Deutsch – Erläuterungen und Kommentare: Band 2: Psalmen bis Danielschriften, ed. Martin Karrer and Wolfgang Kraus (Stuttgart: Deutsche Bibelgesellschaft, 2011), 2041–2126, 2081; Dhont, Style and Context of Old Greek Job, 27; Cox, Iob (forthcoming).
109 See Cox, Iob (forthcoming).
110 See Cox, Iob (forthcoming). Also Wolf Wilhelm Grafen Baudissin does not take this additional attestation to be designating a divine name since it is not discussed in his work. See Baudissin, Kyrios als Gottesname im Judentum.
111 It can be observed that Codex Vaticanus (B) and Codex Ephraemi (C) do not record this as a nomen sacrum. However, Codex Sinaiticus (א) and Alexandrinus (A) do. For the verse 3:19, only Codex Sinaiticus attests a nomen sacrum. Codex Vaticanus and Sinaiticus have been consulted online. See https://digi.vatlib.it/view/MSS_Vat.gr.1209; http://codexsinaiticus.org. Since the LXX of Codex Alexandrinus is not available online, a facsimile has been used. See British Museum, The Codex Alexandrinus (Royal MS. 1 D. V–VIII) in Reduced Photographic Facsimile. Old Testament Part IV I Esdra-Ecclesiasticus (London: Trustees of the British Museum, 1957), 4:vi. 22–viii. 3. For Codex Ephraemi a transcription has been consulted. See Constantinus von Tischendorf, Codex Ephraemi Syri Rescriptus sive Fragmenta Veteris Testamenti E Codice Novi Testamenti E Codice Graeco Parisiensi Celeberrimo quinti ut videtur post Christum Seculi eruit atque editit Constantinus Tischendor (Lipsiae: Tauchnitz, 1845), 6.

somebody else's service; (religious) servant,'[112] is used 53x times in the LXX, mostly as a rendering for the noun עֶבֶד ('slave').[113] However, the most common rendering of עֶבֶד is δοῦλος. In LXX Job, δοῦλος is only used once as a rendering for עֶבֶד, namely in 40:28. The other 11 occurrences of the noun עֶבֶד are rendered by παῖς (1:8; 4:18) and θεράπων (2:3; 3:19; 7:2; 19:16; 31:13; 42:7; 42:8 [3x]). The noun θεράπων refers to the attendants/slaves of Job (19:16; 31:13), to Job as the attendant of the Lord (2:3; 42:7; 42:8) and is used twice to refer to undesignated slaves (3:19 and 7:2). In the rest of the LXX corpus, θεράπων is often used in connection with the patriarchs of Israel but especially to Moses (see, e.g., Gen 24:44; Exod 4:10; Num 12:7; Josh 1:2; 1 Chr 16:40). Thus, the meaning of θεράπων as a (religious) servant of the Lord is not uncommon in the LXX writings. It is likely that the LXX translator had the intention to place Job in the same line as Moses and the patriarchs as a loyal servant of God.[114] However, since 3:19 and 7:2 do not refer to Job but are sentences uttered by Job, it is indeed unlikely that the LXX translator wanted to express a divine name. Therefore, the more basic notion of 'master' is the correct interpretation of ὁ κύριος in both verses. Consequently, the plus of ὁ κύριος in 7:2 cannot tell us anything regarding the theology of the LXX translator of Job.

3.2.2.4 Job 15:25

MT	LXX
כִּי־נָטָה אֶל־אֵל יָדוֹ וְאֶל־שַׁדַּי יִתְגַּבָּר׃	ὅτι ἦρκεν χεῖρας ἐναντίον τοῦ κυρίου, ἔναντι δὲ **κυρίου** παντοκράτορος ἐτραχηλίασεν.
Because they stretched out their hands against God, and bid defiance to the Almighty.	Because he lifted his hands against the Lord and stiffened his neck against the Lord Almighty.

---

112 See GELS, 327–28; LEH, 273–274.
113 On the Greek translation equivalents of עֶבֶד, see Arie van der Kooij, "Servant or Slave. The Various Equivalents of Hebrew Ebed in the Septuagint of the Pentateuch," in *XIII Congress of the International Organization for Septuagint and Cognate Studies, Ljubljana, 2007,* ed. Melvin K. H. Peter, SBLSCS 35 (Atlanta, GA: SBL Press, 2008), 225–238; Arie van der Kooij, "Servant or Slave? The Various Equivalents of Hebrew 'Ebed in the Old Greek of Isaiah," in *Die Septuaginta – Themen, Manuskripte,Wirkungen, 7. Internationale Fachtagung veranstaltet von Septuaginta Deutsch (LXX.D), Wuppertal 19.–22. Juli 2018,* ed. Eberhard Bons et al., WUNT 444 (Tübingen: Mohr Siebeck, 2020), 259–271.
114 See Cox, *Iob* (forthcoming).

In Job 15:25, the divine name is attested three times in the Greek text: twice by ὁ κύριος and once by παντοκράτωρ. The plus of the divine name in this verse is the second occurrence of ὁ κύριος.

Recently, Marieke Dhont has argued that this plus can be seen either as (1) a case of double translation by the LXX translator in order to create variety,[115] (2) a reading of אל as a noun instead of a preposition (which she thinks would be unlikely), (3) a case of dittography, or as (4) the introduction of anadiplosis as a stylistic feature.[116] However, it seems that she assumes that παντοκράτωρ is the plus in this verse, since she argues that "[t]he divine name, which is differentiated in the Hebrew text (אל versus שדי), is rendered twice as κύριος."[117] Since παντοκράτωρ is always used as a rendering of שדי when it is attested in the same verse as ὁ κύριος (see 5:17; 8:5; 11:7; 22:17; 23:16; 27:2.11.13; 34:10.12, and 35:13), the plus is (a) not παντοκράτωρ but κύριος and (b) the addition of ὁ κύριος cannot be regarded as a double translation for the sake of variety. Therefore, the explanation of a dittography seems to be the best possible solution.[118] The translator might have read ואל-(אל-)שדי and rendered it by κυρίου ἔναντι δὲ κυρίου παντοκράτορος, a combination he used in 8:5 without ἐναντίον (in the accusative form: πρὸς κύριον παντοκράτορα) and which is also found in other LXX books (e.g., Zechariah, Malachi, Jeremiah, Micah, Judith, Habakkuk, and Haggai).

3.2.2.5 Job 19:3

MT	LXX
זֶה עֶשֶׂר פְּעָמִים תַּכְלִימוּנִי לֹא־תֵבֹשׁוּ תַּהְכְּרוּ־לִי:	γνῶτε μόνον ὅτι **ὁ κύριος** ἐποίησέν με οὕτως· καταλαλεῖτέ μου, οὐκ αἰσχυνόμενοί με ἐπίκεισθέ μοι.
These ten times you have cast reproach upon me; are you not ashamed to wrong me?	Know only that the Lord treated me this way; you speak against me; shamelessly you press upon me.

---

115 For an exploration on several double translations in Job LXX, see Dhont, "Double Translations."

116 See Dhont, Style and Context of Old Greek Job, 236.

117 Dhont, Style and Context of Old Greek Job, 236.

118 This is also observed by Cox. See Cox, *Iob* (forthcoming).

The LXX version of the first part of the verse, i.e., γνῶτε μόνον ὅτι ὁ κύριος ἐποίησέν με οὕτως, attests a different reading than MT.[119] According to Choon-Leong Seow, the LXX would be corrupt.[120] Scholars have explained this variant reading due to the LXX translator's reading of עשה זה ('this he did') instead of זה עשׂר, therefore rendering it to ἐποίησέν με οὕτως.[121] However, Cox argues that the Greek translation does make sense and that the translation is transposed from 19:6, reading:[122]

MT	LXX
דְּעוּ־אֵפוֹ כִּי־אֱלוֹהַ עִוְּתָנִי וּמְצוּדוֹ עָלַי הִקִּיף:	γνῶτε οὖν ὅτι ὁ κύριός ἐστιν ὁ ταράξας, ὀχύρωμα δὲ αὐτοῦ ἐπ᾽ ἐμὲ ὕψωσεν.
Know then that God has put me in the wrong, and closed his net around me.	Know then that it is the Lord who troubles me, and he raised up his stronghold against me.

The similarity between γνῶτε μόνον ὅτι ὁ κύριος (19:3) and γνῶτε οὖν ὅτι ὁ κύριός (19:6) is indeed striking. Only μόνον and οὖν are different, which can be explained due to the usage of μόνος for "expressing rhetorically pre-eminence in an action or quality."[123] However, apart from the stylistic motivations, no scholar gives any further explanation on why γνῶτε μόνον ὅτι ὁ κύριος has been inserted in 19:3. In the Hebrew text, Job is referring to his friends who have humiliated him. In the LXX, this is not the case. The LXX emphasises that it is only God who has made his soul weary and destroyed him with words (see 19:2). It seems that the LXX translator wanted to emphasise God's omnipotence and responsibility and that only God's acts and words could discomfort Job, not the words of his friends.[124]

---

119 θ´ and σ´ read τουτο δεκατον κατησχυνατε σε, a correction towards the Hebrew text. See Ziegler, *Job*, 292.

120 See Seow, *Job 1–21*, 811.

121 See Dhorme, *A Commentary on the Book of Job*, 270; Heater, *A Septuagint Translation Technique*, 67; Witte and Kepper, "Job," 2093.

122 See Cox, *Iob* (forthcoming).

123 LSJ, 70867. See also Cox, *Iob* (forthcoming).

124 That the LXX translator of Job emphasis God's omnipotence has recently been demonstrated by Jiseong J. Kwon. See Kwon, "Rewritten Theology," 347–352.

3.2.2.6 Job 33:23

MT	LXX
אִם־יֵשׁ עָלָיו מַלְאָךְ מֵלִיץ אֶחָד מִנִּי־אָלֶף לְהַגִּיד לְאָדָם יָשְׁרוֹ׃	ἐὰν ὦσιν χίλιοι ἄγγελοι θανατηφόροι, εἷς αὐτῶν οὐ μὴ τρώσῃ αὐτόν· ἐὰν νοήσῃ τῇ καρδίᾳ ἐπιστραφῆναι ἐπὶ **κύριον**, ἀναγγείλῃ δὲ ἀνθρώπῳ τὴν ἑαυτοῦ μέμψιν, τὴν δὲ ἄνοιαν αὐτοῦ δείξῃ.
Then, if there should be for one of them an angel, a mediator, one of a thousand, one who declares a person upright.	If there be a thousand death-bearing angels, not one of them shall wound him; if he purpose with his heart to turn to the Lord and declare to a person his own fault and reveal his folly.

In Job 33:23, the LXX translator has added two additional lines: ἐὰν νοήσῃ τῇ καρδίᾳ ἐπιστραφῆναι ἐπὶ κύριον ('if he purposes with his heart to turn to the Lord') and τὴν δὲ ἄνοιαν αὐτοῦ δείξῃ ('and reveal his folly'). At this juncture, we are interested in the first additional line that attests an additional occurrence of ὁ κύριος without a counterpart in MT.

According to Edouard Dhorme, Homer Heater, and Cox,[125] the LXX translator has drawn from the previous speeches of Eliphaz in chapter 22, more specifically from 22:22–23, to construct this addition, rephrasing the following equivalents:

ἐν καρδίᾳ σου (22:22)	τῇ καρδίᾳ (33:23)
ἔναντι κυρίου (22:23)	ἐπιστραφῆναι ἐπὶ κύριον (33:23)

However, the similarities seem rather weak to postulate that the LXX translator has constructed 33:23 on the basis of 22:22–23. Moreover, as Cox points out,[126] 'to turn with your heart to the Lord' was a common expression throughout the LXX corpus (see, e.g., Deut 30:10; Tob 13:6, and Ps 84:9). Since the addition forms the protasis of a conditional clause which has its apodosis in the following verses, i.e., 33:24–25, the addition should be understood as the condition for (a) saving from death and (b) the renewal of the body and health (33:24–25). This can only be done by turning to the Lord with whole his heart and to declare to

---

125 See Dhorme, *A Commentary on the Book of Job*, 500–501; Heater, *A Septuagint Translation Technique*, 105; Cox, *Iob* (forthcoming).See also Witte and Kepper, "Job," 2112. Beer, however, sees the plus as a paraphrase. See Beer, *Der Text des Buches Job*, 211–212.
126 See Cox, *Iob* (forthcoming).

his own fault. Thus, inserting ἐὰν νοήσῃ τῇ καρδίᾳ ἐπιστραφῆναι ἐπὶ κύριον into the verse causes a shift in meaning compared to the Hebrew text. Whereas in MT the angel is the subject of the verses,[127] it is God in the LXX. Not the angel saves a righteous human from death by mere mercy (= MT), but it is due to commitment to God (τῇ καρδίᾳ ἐπιστραφῆναι ἐπὶ κύριον) and to admit his own fault that God Himself will save a (righteous) person. Thus, in the LXX there is no mediating angel but God himself who helps the suffering man.[128] Moreover, once again, the omnipotence of God is stressed since only God has the power to save humans from death.

3.2.2.7 Job 36:12

MT	LXX	11QtgJob
וְאִם־לֹא יִשְׁמְעוּ בְּשֶׁלַח יַעֲבֹרוּ וְיִגְוְעוּ כִּבְלִי־דָעַת:	ἀσεβεῖς δὲ οὐ διασῴζει παρὰ τὸ μὴ βούλεσθαι εἰδέναι αὐτοὺς **τὸν κύριον** καὶ διότι νουθετούμενοι ἀνήκοοι ἦσαν.	[והן לא ישמע]ון בחרבא יפלח ויאבדון מן מ[נדעא]
But if they do not listen, they shall perish by the sword, and die without knowledge.	But the impious he does not deliver, because they do not wish to know the Lord and because, when they were being admonished, they were unreceptive.	[And if they do not list]en, they shall fall by the sword, and perish without k[n]owledge[129].

The LXX records a different reading than MT and 11QtgJob. Scholars agree that LXX Job 36:12 is a contraction of some parts of 36:12–13.[130] Heater asserts that the phrase παρὰ τὸ μὴ βούλεσθαι εἰδέναι αὐτοὺς τὸν κύριον, in which ὁ κύριος is attested without a Hebrew counterpart in MT, would be an allusion to 21:14 (ὁδούς σου εἰδέναι οὐ βούλομαι):[131]

---

127 According to Witte, God is the subject of this verse in MT. See Markus Witte, *Das Buch Hiob*, ATD 13 (Göttingen: Vandenhoeck & Ruprecht, 2021), 520.

128 Donald H. Gard argues that "[t]he translator apparently wishes to magnify the role of God in this passage." Gard, *The Exegetical Method of the Greek Translator*, 56.

129 English translation of 11Qtg Job is taken from Florentino G. Martínez et al., eds., *Qumran Cave 11 II. 11Q2–18, 11Q20–31*, DJD XXIII (Oxford: Clarendon Press, 1998).

130 See Beer, Der Text des Buches Job, 227; Dhorme, A Commentary on the Book of Job, 542; Cox, Iob (forthcoming).

131 See Heater, A Septuagint Translation Technique, 118.

MT	LXX
וַיֹּאמְרוּ לָאֵל סוּר מִמֶּנּוּ וְדַעַת דְּרָכֶיךָ לֹא חָפָצְנוּ:	λέγει δὲ κυρίῳ ἀπόστα ἀπ᾽ ἐμοῦ ὁδούς σου εἰδέναι οὐ βούλομαι.
They say to God, "Leave us alone! We do not desire to know your ways".	But he says to the Lord, "Stay away from me; I do not wish to know your ways".

Indeed, since 21:14 also deals about the ἀσεβεῖς ('impious', see 21:7), it seems plausible that the LXX translator has repeated the same thought in 36:12. However, the words in 21:14 are uttered by Job, whereas those in 36:12 are uttered by Elihu and directed towards Job. Cox regards this as an implicit accusation against Job.[132] The addition of ὁ κύριος in 36:12 can be explained in the context of 21:14, in which the pronoun σου refers to the ways of the Lord, who has been addressed (κυρίῳ). Since the Lord is not mentioned in the immediate context of 36:12, and thus differently from 21:14, the LXX translator has specified whom the impious did not wish to know, i.e., the Lord (ὁ κύριος).

3.2.2.8 Job 40:4

MT	LXX
הֵן קַלֹּתִי מָה אֲשִׁיבֶךָּ יָדִי שַׂמְתִּי לְמוֹ־פִי:	Τί ἔτι ἐγὼ κρίνομαι νουθετούμενος καὶ ἐλέγχων **κύριον** ἀκούων τοιαῦτα οὐθὲν ὤν; ἐγὼ δὲ τίνα ἀπόκρισιν δῶ πρὸς ταῦτα; χεῖρα θήσω ἐπὶ στόματί μου·
See, I am of small account; what shall I answer you? I lay my hand on my mouth.	Why do I yet contend—being rebuked even while confuting the Lord, hearing such things—when I am nothing? And I, what answer shall I give to these things? I will lay my hand on my mouth.

Verse 4 of chapter 40 in the LXX is a representation of a combination of the Hebrew text of 40:4 and 40:2.[133] The latter verse has no equivalent in the LXX

---

132 See Cox, *Iob* (forthcoming).
133 See Beer, *Der Text des Buches Job*, 246; Dhorme, *A Commentary on the Book of Job*, 615; Witte and Kepper, "Job," 2120.

but only in the asterisked material. The additional attestation of ὁ κύριος in 40:4 likely represents אלוה and/or שדי of MT 40:2:[134]

הֲרֹב עִם־שַׁדַּי יִסּוֹר מוֹכִיחַ אֱלוֹהַּ יַעֲנֶנָּה׃

"Shall a faultfinder contend with the Almighty? Anyone who argues with God must respond".

Thus, what seems to be an additional attestation of ὁ κύριος at first sight is not an actual addition by the translator but probably rather a rendering of the divine name that was present in the LXX translator's *Vorlage* which might have been a combination of MT 40:2 and 40:4.

3.2.3 The evaluation of additional attestations of ὁ θεός in LXX Job

Compared to ὁ κύριος, there are only three instances where the LXX reads ὁ θεός without a Hebrew equivalent in MT. These are found in Job 2:10; 6:10, and 34:27.

3.2.3.1 Job 2:10

MT	LXX
וַיֹּאמֶר אֵלֶיהָ כְּדַבֵּר אַחַת הַנְּבָלוֹת תְּדַבְּרִי גַּם אֶת־הַטּוֹב נְקַבֵּל מֵאֵת הָאֱלֹהִים וְאֶת־הָרָע לֹא נְקַבֵּל בְּכָל־זֹאת לֹא־חָטָא אִיּוֹב בִּשְׂפָתָיו׃	ὁ δὲ ἐμβλέψας εἶπεν αὐτῇ Ὥσπερ μία τῶν ἀφρόνων γυναικῶν ἐλάλησας· εἰ τὰ ἀγαθὰ ἐδεξάμεθα ἐκ χειρὸς κυρίου, τὰ κακὰ οὐχ ὑποίσομεν; ἐν πᾶσιν τούτοις τοῖς συμβεβηκόσιν αὐτῷ οὐδὲν ἥμαρτεν Ἰὼβ τοῖς χείλεσιν ἐναντίον **τοῦ θεοῦ**.
But he said to her, "You speak as any foolish woman would speak. Shall we receive the good at the hand of God, and not receive the bad?" In all this Job did not sin with his lips.	But Iob looked up and said to her, "You have spoken like one of the foolish women. If we received the good things from the Lord's hand, shall we not bear the bad?" In all these things that happened to him Iob did not sin at all with his lips before God.

The phrase οὐδὲν ἥμαρτεν Ιωβ τοῖς χείλεσιν ἐναντίον τοῦ θεοῦ is almost identical with the phrase οὐδὲν ἥμαρτεν Ἰὼβ ἐναντίον τοῦ κυρίου found in Job 1:22

---

134 According to Maria Gorea, it represents both Hebrew lexemes. See Maria Gorea, *Job repensé ou trahi? Omissions et raccourcis de la Septante*, EB.NS 56 (Paris: Gabalda, 2007), 211.

(see above), except for the additional τοῖς χείλεσιν and the difference between τοῦ κυρίου (1:22) and τοῦ θεοῦ (2:10).[135] The same explanation as 1:22 holds here as well. The Hebrew text does not spell out to whom Job did not sin against. Therefore, the LXX translator added the phrase ἐναντίον τοῦ θεοῦ to make clear that Job did not sin against God.[136] This, to clarify to whom Job is not sinning (see Job 1:22, above). Moreover, by doing so, the piety of Job towards God is emphasised.

However, the LXX translator has opted for ὁ θεός instead of ὁ κύριος, most probably to create variation with the preceding stich where he already used ὁ κύριος (τὰ ἀγαθὰ ἐδεξάμεθα ἐκ χειρὸς κυρίου).[137]

3.2.3.2 Job 6:10

MT	LXX
וְתְּהִי עוֹד ׀ נֶחָמָתִי וַאֲסַלְּדָה בְחִילָה לֹא יַחְמֹל כִּי־לֹא כִחַדְתִּי אִמְרֵי קָדוֹשׁ׃	εἴη δέ μου πόλις τάφος, ἐφ᾽ ἧς ἐπὶ τειχέων ἡλλόμην ἐπ᾽ αὐτῆς, οὐ μὴ φείσωμαι· οὐ γὰρ ἐψευσάμην ῥήματα ἅγια **θεοῦ** μου.
This would be my consolation; I would even exult in unrelenting pain; for I have not denied the words of the Holy One.	And may my city, whose walls I used to leap upon, be my grave—I will not spare myself, for I did not belie the holy words of my God.

The plus in this verse pertaining to the divine name is θεοῦ μου. The LXX translator has read קדשׁ instead of אמרי קדושׁ and therefore rendered it with ῥήματα ἅγια.[138] Moreover, he added the θεοῦ μου to indicate that those holy words are the words of God.[139] This would avoid any misunderstanding on the provenance

---

135 Some manuscripts attest κυρίου instead of θεοῦ in this verse, see n. 101.
136 Gard claims that the translator added ἐναντίον τοῦ θεοῦ because the Hebrew text leaves room to think that Job has sinned "inwardly in his thoughts." Gard, *The Exegetical Method of the Greek Translator*, 28. However, if this is the case, I fail to see this how the LXX translator has eliminated this possibility.
137 See also Cox, *Iob* (forthcoming). The translator often opted for a different lexeme for stylistic reasons such as variation. See Beeckman, "Animalia in Libro Iob," 274.
138 See also Cox, *Iob* (forthcoming). Choon-Leong Seow mentions that there is one manuscript that attests this reading without indicating which manuscript it is. See Seow, *Job 1–21*, 475.
139 One could, perhaps, argue that the LXX translator employed a 'double-translation,' i.e., ἅγιος and θεός, to render קדושׁ. However, in order for Greek equivalents to count as a 'double translation,' the Greek equivalents must be independent equivalents of the same Hebrew lexeme. See Zipora Talshir, "Double Translations in the Septuagint," in *VI Congress of the Interna-*

of those holy words (perhaps they could have been uttered by a priest or a prophet as spokesmen of God). Moreover, it reminds the reader of other biblical passages, especially the reading and promulgation of the law and the covenant.[140] See, e.g., LXX Exod 24:3-4a:

LXX	NETS
εἰσῆλθεν δὲ Μωυσῆς καὶ διηγήσατο τῷ λαῷ πάντα τὰ ῥήματα τοῦ θεοῦ καὶ τὰ δικαιώματα· ἀπεκρίθη δὲ πᾶς ὁ λαὸς φωνῇ μιᾷ λέγοντες Πάντας τοὺς λόγους, οὓς ἐλάλησεν κύριος, ποιήσομεν καὶ ἀκουσόμεθα. καὶ ἔγραψεν Μωυσῆς πάντα τὰ ῥήματα κυρίου[141].	And Moyses went in and recounted to the people all God's words and statutes. And all the people answered with one voice, saying, "All the words that the Lord has spoken we will do and heed". And Moyses wrote all the words of the Lord[142].

In these verses, the words of the Lord are mentioned twice: τὰ ῥήματα τοῦ θεοῦ (24:3) and πάντα τὰ ῥήματα κυρίου (24:4a). In other instances, ῥήματα is also often paired with κυρίου.

The addition of the personal pronoun μου in Job 6:10 stresses that it is Job's God, thereby creating a stronger parallelism with the preceding colon εἴη δέ μου πόλις τάφος ἐφ᾽ ἧς ἐπὶ τειχέων ἡλλόμην ἐπ᾽ αὐτῆς, in which the personal pronoun also occurs in the genitive form.[143]

3.2.3.3 Job 34:27

MT	LXX	11QtgJob
אֲשֶׁר עַל־כֵּן סָרוּ מֵאַחֲרָיו וְכָל־דְּרָכָיו לֹא הִשְׂכִּילוּ׃	ὅτι ἐξέκλιναν ἐκ νόμου **θεοῦ**, δικαιώματα δὲ αὐτοῦ οὐκ ἐπέγνωσαν.	אר]חה ובכל שבילוהי לא הסתכ]לו
Because they turned aside	Because they turned aside	His [wa]y, and [they] did not

---

tional Organization for Septuagint and Cognate Studies. Jerusalem 1986, ed. Claude E. Cox, SBLSCS 23 (Scholars Press: Atlanta, GA, 1987), 21–63, 23. In Job LXX, θεός is never used as an equivalent for קדוש. Moreover, throughout the LXX θεός is not used as an equivalent for קדוש. Only in Amos 2:7 θεός is used as a rendering of קֹדֶשׁ that shares the same root as קדוש.

140 The Mosaic Law plays important role in Job LXX and is often emphasised. See Cox, "Job," 395–396.
141 LXX text from Wevers, *Exodus*.
142 LXX translation taken from Perkins, "Exodus."
143 See also Dhont, Style and Context of Old Greek Job, 222.

MT	LXX	11QtgJob
from following him, and had no regard for any of his ways.	from God's law and did not recognize his requirements.	he[ed] any of his paths.

The LXX has a different reading, distinguished from MT and 11QtgJob. Recently, Jiseong J. Kwon has commented on the Greek rendering of this verse stating that the LXX translator "replaces the 'path' imagery of מאחריו and כל־דרכיו with law-related words, so that [the Greek text] stresses those 'who broke God's law' (ἐξέκλιναν ἐκ νόμου θεοῦ) and 'did not recognize his commandments' (δικαιώματα [...] αὐτοῦ οὐκ ἐπέγνωσαν; cfr. Deut 30:16)."[144] However, it is not a complete replacement of what is attested in the Hebrew text; it is rather a refinement from the general to the specific:[145]

General	Specific
Suffix ו	νόμου θεου
דרכיו	δικαιώματα αὐτοῦ

Both nouns, δικαίωμα and νόμος, only occur in this verse in LXX Job. However, they are both attested manifold in the LXX translation of the Pentateuch referring to the law and commandments of God.[146] By doing so, the LXX translator reminds his readers once again of the statutes and commandments of the Lord and the importance of keeping oneself to it (see above Job 6:10).

3.2.4 Conclusion

Having analysed the additional attestations of ὁ κύριος and ὁ θεός in LXX Job, we can draw the following conclusions with regard to the translation technique and the theology of the LXX translator:

---

144 Kwon, "Rewritten Theology," 346.
145 See Cox, *Iob* (forthcoming). See also Gerleman, *Job*, 11. Gerleman only observes that the meaning of the Hebrew is clarified in the Greek text without further explanation. Dhorme sees the rendering of מאחריו by ἐκ νόμου θεοῦ as a mere paraphrase. See Dhorme, *A Commentary on the Book of Job*, 522.
146 For δικαίωμα, see, e.g., Exod 24:3; Num 30:17; Deut 4:1; for νόμος, see, e.g., Exod 18:16; Deut 4:44; Josh 9:2. They even occur together in Num 15:16.

(a) The LXX translator has often inserted an extra divine name in order to clarify or specify the Hebrew text because the latter was rather vague (Job 1:21.22; 2:10; 6:10; 34:27, and 36:12);

(b) In several instances, the extra attestations are of a stylistic nature in the Greek text compared to the Hebrew, creating variation (2:10) or creating a better parallelism (6:10);

(c) With regard to the theology of the LXX of Job, the LXX translator has especially stressed the omnipotence of God in several instances (19:3 and 33:23), emphasised the Law and commandments of God and the importance of observing them (6:10 and 34:27) as well as Job's piety before the Lord (1:22 and 2:10) in a stronger way than the MT;

(d) Three instances of ὁ κύριος that seem to be additional attestations at first sight turn out not to be. They can be explained due to (1) the denotation of the more mundane meaning of lord (7:2), (2) a dittography (15:25), or (3) a Greek rendering of a different Hebrew verse (40:4).

In section 4, these results will be compared to the results obtained in the studies on the additional attestations of ὁ κύριος and ὁ θεός in LXX Proverbs.

3.3 Excursus III: the examination of אלוה in Job without counterpart in the LXX

The examination of the additional attestations of ὁ κύριος and ὁ θεός in LXX Job has proven to be fruitful and has indicated that LXX Job exhibits a different or more nuanced theology. The LXX translator has emphasised God's omnipotence, the piety of Job and the observance of the Mosaic Law. Although this study has shed new light on the theology of LXX Job, research concerning its theology is still in its early stages. Therefore, and in order to contribute to this field of research, this excursus will analyse the minuses in LXX Job where MT records a divine name. Just as is the case with the additional attestations of ὁ κύριος and ὁ θεός, minuses are explicit differences between MT and the LXX and can therefore function as possible *loci theologici* where a diverging theology might be detected. As a preliminary study, I will only examine the minuses in LXX Job of אלוה, since these make up the majority of instances.

First, the minuses in LXX Job where MT reads אלוה will be registered. Afterwards, they will be evaluated in order to investigate whether the LXX of Job reflects a diverging theology than its Hebrew counterpart. By doing so, this excursus aims at contributing to a deeper understanding of the translation technique and theology of the LXX translator of Job.

3.3.1 The registration of the minuses in LXX Job where MT reads אֱלוֹהַּ

In his unpublished doctoral dissertation, Dominique Mangin has listed the Hebrew divine names in Job (יהוה, אלהים, אֵל, אלוה, שׁדי and אדון) and their Greek rendering in the LXX.[147] With regard to the minuses in the LXX version of Job where MT records a divine name, one can find 13 minuses in total:

Divine name	Verse(s)
יהוה	2:1; 42:9
אלהים	1:16
אֵל	13:8; 15:11; 22:17; 33:6
אלוה	6:4; 12:4.6; 21:19; 36:2
שׁדי	29:5
אדון	/

As is evident from this list above, there are 5 instances where the LXX does not have a rendering for אלוה. The divine name אלוה occurs 58 times in the Hebrew Bible. In the 17 instances outside Job,[148] אלוה is always rendered by θεός. In Job it is rendered in a variety of ways:[149]

Rendering	Verse(s)[150]	Distribution
κύριος	3:4; 4:9.17; 5:17; 6:8.9; 10:2; 11:5.6.7; 15:8; 16:20.21; 19:6.21.26; 21:9; 27:8; 31:6; 33:26	20x

---

147 See Mangin, "Le texte court de la version grecque du livre de Job," 25–65 (esp. 46–60).
148 See Deut 32:15.17; 2 Kgs 17:31; 2 Chr 32:15; Neh 9:17; Ps 18(LXX 17):32; Ps 50(LXX 49):22; Ps 114(LXX 113):7; Ps 139(LXX 138):19; Prov 30:5; Isa 44:8; Dan 11:37.38 (2x).39; Hab 1:11; 3:3.
149 For the data, see Mangin, "Le texte court de la version grecque du livre de Job," 54–55. Mangin presents it differently. The table here provides a more readable overview.
150 For the sake of completeness, the verses that are marked with an asterisk (✶) in Ziegler's edition of LXX Job and, thus, do not belong to the OG version of Job, are also presented in the table.

Rendering	Verses[s][150]	Distribution
θεός	3:23; 29:2.4; 31:2 (⁕); 35:10 (⁕); 37:3 (πνεῦμα θεῖον/ ורוח אלוה); 37:15; 39:17 (⁕); 40:2 (⁕)	9x (5x OG/4x ⁕)
παντοκράτωρ	37:22	1x
αὐτός	9:13; 24:12; 27:10	3x
ὁ τὰ ὑψηλὰ ναίων	22:12	1x
εἰς τὸν οὐρανὸν	22:26	1x
ὁ ἐπάνω βροτῶν	33:12	1x
/	6:4; 12:4.6; 21:19; 36:2	5x

Thus, as is clear from the table above, the LXX translator of Job used κύριος more than θεός as a rendering of אלוה, which stands in contrast to the translation in the other LXX books. In six verses LXX Job does not attest a Greek divine name for אלוה but renders it by αὐτός (9:13; 24:12; 27:10),[151] ὁ τὰ ὑψηλὰ ναίων (22:12), εἰς τὸν οὐρανὸν (22:26), ὁ ἐπάνω βροτῶν (33:12).[152] Although an examination of these verses might be interesting as well, we will only focus on the actual minuses in LXX Job since these present a more explicit difference.

In the following section we will evaluate the missing renderings of אלוה in LXX Job in order to discern whether these reflect a diverging theology or not.

3.3.2 The evaluation of the minuses in LXX Job where MT reads אלוה

In this section, the minuses in LXX Job where אלוה is attested in MT, i.e., found in 6:4; 12:4.6; 21:19 and 36:2, will be evaluated in order to discern whether these minuses can be ascribed to the translator's translation technique, a diverging Hebrew *Vorlage* or the textual transmission of the Greek text. Moreover, if they are to be ascribed to the translation technique of the LXX translator, the question whether the translator was motivated by theological motives to provide a different translation than MT will be addressed.

---

151 Kwon wrongly indicates that אֱלֹוַהּ has been deleted by the LXX translator in 9:13 and 24:12. Although the divine name is not rendered with a Greek divine name, it is represented by αὐτός and thus not deleted as Kwon argues. See Kwon, "Rewritten Theology in the Greek Book of Job," 348.

152 See Mangin, "Le texte court de la version grecque du livre de Job," 54-55.

3.3.2.1 Job 6:4

MT	LXX
כִּי חִצֵּי שַׁדַּי עִמָּדִי אֲשֶׁר חֲמָתָם שֹׁתָה רוּחִי בְּעוּתֵי **אֱלוֹהַּ** יַעַרְכוּנִי:	βέλη γὰρ κυρίου ἐν τῷ σώματί μού ἐστιν ὧν ὁ θυμὸς αὐτῶν ἐκπίνει μου τὸ αἷμα ὅταν ἄρξωμαι λαλεῖν κεντοῦσί με.
For the arrows of the Almighty are in me; my spirit drinks their poison; the terrors of God are arrayed against me.	For the arrows of the Lord are in my body; their wrath drinks my blood; when I begin to speak, they pierce me.

In Job 6:4 MT records two divine names: שׁדי and אלוה. The name שׁדי occurs 31 times in Job and is rendered by a variety of Greek lexemes whereby παντοκράτωρ and κύριος constitute the majority of renderings.[153]

Although several scholars have tried to explain the rather strange translation of the Greek,[154] none of the scholars provided an adequate answer to the question why אלוה is not rendered in the LXX. A good example is the explanation on the Greek rendering of 6:4 by Edouard Dhorme.[155] He meticulously examines the whole Hebrew verse and its Greek translation and provides a decent explanation for each translation equivalent. However, for בעותי אלוה, he plainly states: "It is difficult to see how G gets ὅταν ἄρξομαι λαλεῖν from בעותי אלוה,"[156] without further elaboration. Georg Beer does also not provide an explanation on why the LXX translator did not render אֱלוֹהַּ and only argues that the translator misunderstood בעותי.[157] Harry M. Orlinsky, on the other hand, asserts that the LXX translator had a *Vorlage* that differed from MT,[158] which might explain the LXX's different reading. Cox notes an intertextual link (ἄρχω + λαλέω) between Job 6:4 and Gen 18:27,[159] which reads:

---

153 For an exhaustive overview of all the Greek renderings of שַׁדַּי in LXX Job and their distribution, see Mangin, "Le texte court de la version grecque du livre de Job," 52–54.

154 Surprisingly, Homer Heater who has written a monograph on the translation technique of LXX Job does not deal with any of the verses discussed in this excursus. See Heater, *A Septuagint Translation Technique*.

155 See Dhorme, A Commentary on the Book of Job, 76-77.

156 Dhorme, A Commentary on the Book of Job, 76.

157 See Beer, *Der Text des Buches Hiob*, 36: "G hat בעותי ganz verkannt."

158 See Harry M. Orlinsky, "Studies in the Septuagint of the Book of Job: Chapter III (Continued)," *HUCA* 32 (1961): 239–68, 251–252 (esp. 252).

159 See Cox, *Iob* (forthcoming).

MT	LXX
וַיַּעַן אַבְרָהָם וַיֹּאמַר הִנֵּה־נָא הוֹאַלְתִּי לְדַבֵּר אֶל־אֲדֹנָי וְאָנֹכִי עָפָר וָאֵפֶר:	καὶ ἀποκριθεὶς Αβρααμ εἶπεν νῦν ἠρξάμην λαλῆσαι πρὸς τὸν κύριον ἐγὼ δέ εἰμι γῆ καὶ σποδός.[160]
Abraham answered, "Let me take it upon myself to speak to the Lord, I who am but dust and ashes."	And Abraam said in reply, "Now I have begun to speak to the Lord, though I am earth and ashes.[161]

According to him, the context of both verses deal with a mortality motive.[162] Although there is an agreement in the usage of both ἄρχω and λαλέω, the intertextual link seems to be rather weak.

However, there is another possible explanation for the non-rendering of אֱלוֹהַ in Job 6:4. When looking at the Hebrew verbs underlying the Greek ἄρχω in the LXX, there are several instances where it reads a form of the verb יאל ('to be pleased, willing, to undertake, to be determined').[163] This is the case in Gen 18:27; Deut 1:5; Judg 1:27.35; 17:11; 19:6; 2 Sam 7:29; 1 Chr 17:27; Hos 5:11 and also in Job 6:9.[164] The translator (or his *Vorlage*) might have read הואיל or more likely הואל instead of אלוה and בענתי (> ענה, 'to answer, to speak') instead of בעותי and consequently rendered it by ἄρξωμαι λαλεῖν.[165] However, it is hard to discern whether this reading originated from the translator's *Vorlage* (= Orlinsky)

---

160 For the Greek text of Genesis, see John W. Wevers, *Genesis*, Septuaginta. Vetus Testamentum Graecum. Auctoritate Academiae Scientiarum Gottingensis editum I (Göttingen: Vandenhoeck & Ruprecht, 1974).

161 English translation taken from nets, see Robert J. V. Hiebert, "Genesis," in *A New English Translation of the Septuagint. And the Other Greek Translations Traditionally Included under That Title*, ed. Albert Pietersma and Benjamin G. Wright (Oxford: Oxford University Press, 2007), 1–42.

162 See Cox, *Iob* (forthcoming).

163 See DCH, vol. IV, 71.

164 Josh 17:12 has ἤρχετο as a rendering of יאל. However, on the basis of its parallel with Judg 1:27, one could argue that Josh 17:12 read ἤρξατο (> ἄρχω) instead of ἤρχετο (> ἔρχομαι). Judg 1:27 reads καὶ ἤρξατο ὁ Χαναναῖος κατοικεῖν ἐν τῇ γῇ ταύτῃ, whereas Josh 17:12 reads καὶ ἤρχετο ὁ Χαναναῖος κατοικεῖν ἐν τῇ γῇ ταύτῃ. For Josh 17:12, codex Alexandrinus (A) does attest ἤρξατο. For Judg 1:27 no textual variants are listed. See Rahlfs, *Septuaginta*, 386 and 409. Thus, it seems reasonable to assume that Josh 17:12 read ἤρξατο (> ἄρχω) instead of ἤρχετο.

165 The reading of בענתי is proposed by Cox. See Cox, *Iob* (forthcoming). I agree with his argument concerning this reading.

or a misreading by the translator himself. Nevertheless, there is no need to resort to explanations entailing theological motives or intertextuality.[166]

3.3.2.2 Job 12:4

MT	LXX
שְׂחֹק לְרֵעֵהוּ אֶהְיֶה קֹרֵא לֶאֱלוֹהַּ וַיַּעֲנֵהוּ שְׂחוֹק צַדִּיק תָּמִים׃	δίκαιος γὰρ ἀνὴρ καὶ ἄμεμπτος ἐγενήθη εἰς χλεύασμα.
I am a laughingstock to my friends; I, who called upon God and he answered me, a just and blameless man, I am a laughingstock.	A just and blameless man, you see, has become a laughingstock.

Several scholars have tried to come up with an explanation on the different rendering of the LXX and minus of אלוה. Donald H. Gard argues that the different reading and especially the absence of the divine name in the Greek text is due to the translator who wanted to avoid the notion of injustice with regard to God's affairs with man.[167] However, he also notes and recognises the possibility of homoeoarchy with the double attestation of שְׂחוֹק in the Hebrew text.[168] This is exactly what other scholars assert without making reference to theological motivations of the translator. Marieke Dhont, for example, argues that the LXX of this verse represents a paraphrastic rendering of the Hebrew due to the repetition of שְׂחֹק ('laughter').[169] Similar to Dhont's argumentation, Dhorme notes that the translator skipped from the first שְׂחוֹק to the second.[170] Orlinsky uses verse 12:4 as an example to illustrate his thesis that the LXX translator simply reproduced his Hebrew *Vorlage* faithfully without any theological motives involved.[171]

---

166 This in contrast to Gehman who takes Job 6:4 as an example of a theological nuance in LXX Job whereby the LXX translator softens down what might have seemed offensive. However, his analysis is brief and lacks sufficient explanation. See Gehman, "The Theological Approach of the Greek Translator of Job 1-15," 234–235.

167 See Gard, *The Exegetical Method of the Greek Translator*, 25. Gard's book deals with the theological character of LXX Job. According to him the omission of the divine name in LXX Job is often used to get rid of offensive ideas towards God. However, it is interesting to note that he does not examine Job 6:4 (see above) in this context.

168 See Gard, The Exegetical Method of the Greek Translator, 25.

169 See Dhont, *Style and Context*, 203–204.

170 See Dhorme, *A Commentary on the Book of Job*, 169. Seow agrees with Dhorme. See Seow, *Job 1-21*, 630–631.

171 See Orlinsky, "Chapter III (Continued)," 262.

However, he does not explain how the translator rendered the strikingly different Hebrew verse into Greek and simply states that "the LXX — for whatever reason — has an abbreviated version of [the Hebrew]. Yet the translation is more blunt, and uncomplimentary, so far as God is concerned."[172]

Looking at the Greek translation, it seems that the LXX translator has only rendered the second stich of the verse, i.e., שְׂחוֹק צַדִּיק תָּמִים. He has rendered the lexeme שְׂחֹק ('laughter, laughingstock') by the hapax χλεύασμα ('target of scoffing, object of mockery'),[173] צַדִּיק ('righteous, right, innocent') by δίκαιος ἀνήρ ('righteous man') and תָּמִים ('complete, perfect, blameless') by ἄμεμπτος ('irreproachable, blameless'),[174] since he read תָּמִים as תָּם ('completeness, perfection, blamelessness, innocence') which is rendered four times by the same Greek lexeme ἄμεμπτος in LXX Job (i.e., 1:1.8; 2:3; 9:20).[175] Since only the second stich is represented by the LXX,[176] the first stich, where אלוה is attested, was either overlooked by the translator due to the repetition of שְׂחוֹק (= homoeoarchy), as argued especially by Dhont and Dhorme (see above), or not present in the his *Vorlage*. The former one seems to be the most probable explanation.

3.3.2.3 Job 12:6

MT	LXX
יִשְׁלָיוּ אֹהָלִים׀ לְשֹׁדְדִים וּבַטֻּחוֹת לְמַרְגִּיזֵי אֵל לַאֲשֶׁר הֵבִיא אֱלוֹהַּ בְּיָדוֹ:	οὐ μὴν δὲ ἀλλὰ μηδεὶς πεποιθέτω πονηρὸς ὢν ἀθῷος ἔσεσθαι ὅσοι παροργίζουσιν τὸν κύριον ὡς οὐχὶ καὶ ἔτασις αὐτῶν ἔσται.
The tents of robbers are at peace, and those who provoke God are secure, who bring their god in their hands.	Nonetheless, let the wicked not trust that he will be guiltless – as many as provoke the Lord – as if indeed there will be no scrutiny of them.

In Job 12:6, the LXX attests a free rendering of its Hebrew text. In the Hebrew, two divine names are attested: אֵל and אלוה. אֵל is rendered by its common

---

172 Orlinsky, "Chapter III (Continued)," 262.
173 See DCH, vol. VIII, 120; GELS, 733; LEH, 664.
174 See resp. DCH, vol. VII, 75–78; DCH, vol. VIII, 643–44; GELS, 32; LEH, 32.
175 See DCH, vol. VIII, 638–39.
176 According to Markus Witte, this rendering emphasises the righteousness of Job and alludes to Job 1:1 more than its Hebrew counterpart. See Witte, "The Greek Book of Job,", 49.

equivalent in LXX Job, i.e., κύριος,[177] whereas אלוה is not represented in the Greek text.

The divine name אֱלוֹהַ occurs in the third stich of the verse which reads לאשר הביא אלוה בידו and is rendered in the LXX by ὡς οὐχὶ καὶ ἔτασις αὐτῶν ἔσται. Gard explains the minus of אלוה in the LXX text as an omission by the translator because "[t]he concept of the Hebrew that God acts capriciously [was] objectionable to the translator."[178] According to Gillis Gerleman, the LXX translator was also motivated by theological motives and has neutralised blasphemous speech in several verses.[179] For 12:6, however, he does not indicate how this neutralizing occurs and simply notes that the Greek "is probably a paraphrase without exact correspondence in the original."[180] Indeed, scholars have noted the difficult and probably corrupt Hebrew of the verse which led them to emend the text.[181] In one of his studies, Orlinsky has commented upon the occurrence of the divine names אֵל, אלוה and אלהים in parallel stichs.[182] These names do not occur together in parallel stichs[183]. If another divine name is attested, it is always with שׁדי.[184] There are only two verses where this is not the case: 12:6 (אֵל/אלוה) and 20:29 (אֵל/אלוה).[185] According to Orlinsky, the Hebrew of these verses is corrupt:[186]

---

177 For the distribution of the Greek equivalents of אֵל in LXX Job, see Mangin, "Le texte court de la version grecque du livre de Job," 48–52.

178 Gard, The Exegetical Method of the Greek Translator, 49.

179 See Gerleman, *Job*, 54. Verbeke also briefly mentions that the LXX translator probably omitted אֱלוֹהַ in 12:6 for theological reasons. However, she does not elaborate her statement. See Verbeke, "Hebrew Hapax Legomena," 241 and 410.

180 Gerleman, *Job*, 54. Orlinsky does not agree with Gerleman and suspends any judgement on the Greek rendering of 12:6. See Orlinsky, "Chapter III (Continued)," 262.

181 Several scholars have, therefore, emended the Hebrew text. See, e.g., Bernhard Duhm, *Das Buch Hiob*, KHC 16 (Tübingen: Mohr-Siebeck, 1897), 66–67; Beer, *Der Text des Buches Hiob*, 73. Seow argues that these emendations are not supported by textual evidence and not necessary. See Seow, *Job 1-21*, 632.

182 See Orlinsky, "Studies in the Septuagint of the Book of Job: Chapter V. The Hebrew Vorlage of the Septuagint of Job: The Text and the Script," *HUCA* 35 (1964): 57–78, 62.

183 See Orlinsky, "Chapter V," 62.

184 See Orlinsky, "Chapter V," 62. Orlinsky also notes the references where אֵל, אֱלוֹהַ and אֱלֹהִים is paralleled with שַׁדַּי. See Orlinsky, "Chapter V," 62.

185 Orlinsky records 20:9 which is a mistake, it is 20:29. See Orlinsky, "Chapter V," 62.

186 Orlinsky even suggests emending Samuel Driver and George Gray's text that reads "Where in each line of a distich a divine name is used ... a marked preference is shown for שׁדי as one of the two" to "... ידש is always one of the two." See Samuel R. Driver and George B. Grey, *A Critical and Exegetical Commentary on the Book of Job: Together With a New Translation*, ICC (Edinburgh: T&T Clark, 1964), xliii; Orlinsky, "Chapter V," 62 (n. 17). By doing so, he clearly indi-

[...] [T]hese exceptions are only apparent, since scholars have long agreed — on grounds other than for the names of God — that the text of both verses is suspect; indeed, not only is the text difficult per se but the LXX differs from the preserved Hebrew text, among other places, precisely where the terms for God are concerned.[187]

On the basis of these arguments, i.e., the corrupted Hebrew of MT and the distribution of divine names in parallel stichs, one can conclude that the Hebrew *Vorlage* must have differed from the text preserved in MT. Once more, the translator did not render the Hebrew on the basis of theological motivations.

3.3.2.4 Job 21:19

MT	LXX
אֱלוֹהַ יִצְפֹּן־לְבָנָיו אוֹנוֹ יְשַׁלֵּם אֵלָיו וְיֵדָע׃	ἐκλίποι υἱοὺς τὰ ὑπάρχοντα αὐτοῦ.
You say, 'God stores up their iniquity for their children.' Let it be paid back to them, so that they may know it.	May his possessions fail his sons.

Only the first part of the verse, i.e., אלוה יצפן־לבניו אונו, is rendered by the LXX translator. The other stich of the Hebrew verse, i.e., ישלם אליו וידע, is not rendered by the LXX translator but is represented in the asterisk material as ἀνταποδώσει πρὸς αὐτὸν καὶ γνώσεται. In the LXX, אלוה is not represented. However, θ΄ does represent אלוה by ὁ θεός.

Once again, Gard explains the Greek rendering of this verse on the basis of the theology of the translator. According to him, the וה of אלוה is intentionally deleted by the translator in order to remove "[t]he idea that God harbours punishment for the children of guilty fathers."[188] Beer notes that the LXX translator has intentionally skipped the divine name without providing further information.[189] However, most scholars agree that the translator read אֶל instead of

---

cates that the Hebrew of MT is corrupt and that the LXX translator probably had a diverging *Vorlage*.

187 Orlinsky, "Chapter V," 62.

188 Gard, *The Exegetical Method of the Greek Translator*, 51. He even states that the Hebrew text of 21:19b is also intentionally omitted by the LXX translator because it depicts a vengeful God. See Gard, *The Exegetical Method of the Greek Translator*, 80.

189 See Beer, *Der Text des Buches Hiob*, 141. By stating that the LXX *omitted* אֱלוֹהַ, Dhorme also seems to suggest that the LXX translator did not render the divine name on purpose. See Dhorme, *A Commentary on the Book of Job*, 316.

אלוה in his parent text.[190] Even Gard, who provides a theological explanation, admits (in a footnote!) that the LXX translator might have had אֵל in his Hebrew *Vorlage* and even indicates that אֵל is metrically better than אֱלוֹהַ in this verse.[191] Moreover, BHS also proposes אֵל instead of אלוה in the critical apparatus.[192] Thus, the non-rendering of אלוה in 12:6 can be explained due to a diverging *Vorlage* that read אֵל instead of the divine name.

3.3.2.5 Job 36:2

MT	LXX
כַּתַּר־לִי זְעֵיר וַאֲחַוֶּךָ כִּי עוֹד לֶאֱלוֹהַ מִלִּים:	μεῖνόν με μικρὸν ἔτι ἵνα διδάξω σε ἔτι γὰρ ἐν ἐμοί ἐστιν λέξις.
"Bear with me a little, and I will show you, for I have yet something to say on God's behalf".	"Wait for me a little longer so that I may teach you, for there is still more speech in me".

The last minus of אלוה in LXX Job is found in stich b of 36:2. The LXX renders כִּי עוֹד לאלוה מלים by ἔτι γὰρ ἐν ἐμοί ἐστιν λέξις. Thus, it seems that the LXX has translated לֶאֱלוֹהַ by the construction ἐν ἐμοί which only occurs here in LXX Job.[193] In the recensions of the LXX, only σ΄ presents a different reading that does attest the divine name: [ἔ]τι γὰρ περὶ θεοῦ [εἰ]σὶ λόγοι.[194]

Dhorme argues that the Greek representation of לאלוה with ἐν ἐμοί is a "theological correction."[195] However, as was the case for 6:4 (see above), he does not provide additional explanation. As was to be expected, Gard sees the theology of the translator at play.[196] He asserts that the Hebrew was offensive to the LXX translator because he considers saying something on God's behalf to be disre-

---

190 See, e.g., Duhm, *Das Buch Hiob*, 111; Seow, *Job 1-21*, 886.

191 See Gard, *The Exegetical Method of the Greek Translator*, 51 (n. 1). Driver and Gray have also suggested that אֵל is rhythmically better. See Driver and Grey, *A Critical and Exegetical Commentary*, 148.

192 See BHS, 1249.

193 Three times elsewhere in the asterisked material, i.e., 7:8; 16:8 and 28:14.

194 This reading is not attested in Ziegler's edition but is recorded and discussed in John D. Meade's critical edition of the Hexaplaric fragments of Job 22-42. See John D. Meade, *A Critical Edition of the Hexaplaric Fragments of Job 22–42*, Origen's Hexapla: A Critical Edition of the Extant Fragments (Leuven: Peeters, 2020), 231–232.

195 Dhorme, A Commentary on the Book of Job, 538.

196 See Gard, The Exegetical Method of the Greek Translator, 24.

spectful.[197] Cox, on the other hand, is more cautious in ascribing the minus of אלוה to the theology of the LXX translator. He argues that Dhorme might be correct but that it is more probable that the translator has opted for ἐν ἐμοί in order to nuance Elihu's character as someone who has a lot to say and who sees himself as Job's teacher (ἵνα διδάξω σε).[198] Indeed, in 36:1-4 of the LXX, Elihu is speaking about himself and the knowledge he possesses. Only in verse 5, he starts to exalt God:

MT 36:1-5	LXX 36:1-5
¹ וַיֹּסֶף אֱלִיהוּא וַיֹּאמַר:	¹ προσθεὶς δὲ Ελιους ἔτι λέγει
² כַּתַּר־לִי זְעֵיר וַאֲחַוֶּךָּ כִּי עוֹד לֶאֱלוֹהַּ מִלִּים:	² μεῖνόν με μικρὸν ἔτι ἵνα διδάξω σε ἔτι γὰρ ἐν
³ אֶשָּׂא דֵעִי לְמֵרָחוֹק וּלְפֹעֲלִי אֶתֵּן־צֶדֶק:	ἐμοί ἐστιν λέξις
⁴ כִּי־אָמְנָם לֹא־שֶׁקֶר מִלָּי תְּמִים דֵּעוֹת עִמָּךְ:	³ ἀναλαβὼν τὴν ἐπιστήμην μου μακρὰν ἔργοις
⁵ הֶן־אֵל כַּבִּיר וְלֹא יִמְאָס כַּבִּיר כֹּחַ לֵב:	δέ μου δίκαια ἐρῶ
	⁴ ἐπ' ἀληθείας καὶ οὐκ ἄδικα ῥήματα ἀδίκως συνίεις
	⁵ γίγνωσκε δὲ ὅτι ὁ κύριος οὐ μὴ ἀποποιήσηται τὸν ἄκακον δυνατὸς ἰσχύι καρδίας
¹ Elihu continued and said:	¹ Now Elious added still more and said:
² "Bear with me a little, and I will show you, for I have yet something to say on God's behalf.	² "Wait for me a little longer so that I may teach you, for there is still more speech in me.
³ I will bring my knowledge from far away, and ascribe righteousness to my Maker.	³ Having fetched my knowledge from afar, yes, in my efforts I will speak what is just,
⁴ For truly my words are not false; one who is perfect in knowledge is with you.	⁴ in truth, and not unjust words; you understand wrongly!
⁵ "Surely God is mighty and does not despise any; he is mighty in strength of understanding.	⁵ "But know that the Lord will not reject the innocent.

Even the omission of ולפעלי in LXX 36:4 can be understood against this background. The actual exaltation of God by Elihu only starts at verse 5. In the LXX, Elihu confirms his (self-)acclaimed role as teacher without referring to God. The words spoken by Elihu in verses 2-4 and, consequently, his appraisal of God are coming from Elihu himself and are not ascribed to or coming from God. The LXX translator has indeed emphasised Elihu's role as Job's teacher in verses 1-4 compared to the Hebrew text.

---

197 See Gard, The Exegetical Method of the Greek Translator, 24.
198 See Cox, Iob (forthcoming).

Since there is no textual evidence to support a diverging *Vorlage* and/or a misreading seems impossible, the LXX translator must have omitted אֱלוֹהַּ in 36:2 deliberately in order the emphasis Elihu's role as teacher.

3.3.3 Conclusion

Having analysed the verses in LXX Job that record a minus where אלוה is attested in MT, we can draw following conclusions:

(a) In four instances, i.e., 6:4; 12:4.6 and 21:19, the minus in the LXX was not a deliberate omission on the part of the translator. For 12:6 and 21:19, it has been argued that the *Vorlage* of the LXX translator differed from the text attested in MT. Either the Hebrew of MT is corrupted (12:6) or the *Vorlage* read אֶל instead of אלוה (21:19). In 12:4, the LXX translator has overlooked the stich of the verse wherein אלוה was attested due to homoeoarchy. For 6:4, the translator has either misread his *Vorlage* (הואל instead of אלוה) or the Hebrew of the *Vorlage* differed from MT. However, on the basis of the extant textual material, it is hard to judge which explanation is more correct;

(b) Only in one instance, i.e., 36:2, did the LXX translator deliberately chose not to render אלוה, this in order to emphasise Elihu's role as Job's teacher in the context of chapter 36 and especially verses 2-4.

Thus, compared to the examination of the additional attestations of ὁ κύριος and ὁ θεός in LXX Job where a distinct theology can be found,[199] the analysis of the minuses in the LXX where MT records אלוה did not elicit a nuanced or different theology in the LXX *vis-à-vis* MT. It seems that the LXX translator was more conservative in preserving the Hebrew divine name into Greek than he was in adding divine names where there is none in the Hebrew text. However, in this excursus only the missing renderings of אלוה have been discussed. In order to come to a more complete image of the way in which the LXX translator rendered his Hebrew *Vorlage* into Greek and to examine whether the LXX text exhibits a different theology than MT, the other divine names that record a minus in the LXX (i.e., יהוה, אלהים, אֶל and שדי) need to be analysed. New (theological?) research endeavours await!

---

199 See Beeckman, "Nomina Sacra in Libro Iob."

3.4 The comparison of the translation technique and theology of LXX Proverbs and LXX Job with regard to the additional attestations of ὁ κύριος and ὁ θεός

As outlined in the introduction of this chapter, this chapter on the additional attestations of ὁ κύριος and ὁ θεός in LXX Proverbs and LXX Job also strives at formulating an indicative answer on the question of a single translator for both books. Therefore, the results of the analysis of the additional attestations of ὁ κύριος and ὁ θεός without any counterpart in MT will be compared in both books respectively. First, the amount of additional attestations of both lexemes in both books will be compared. Afterwards, a comparison of their evaluation and the results pertaining to the translation technique with regard and the theology will be made.

3.4.1 The amount of additional attestations of ὁ κύριος and ὁ θεός in LXX Job and LXX Proverbs

The amount of additions of ὁ κύριος and ὁ θεός in both books compared to the overall amount of attestations is presented in the table below:

	LXX Proverbs	LXX Job
κύριος	13/79	6/116[200]
θεός	10/34	3/13

LXX Proverbs records more pluses containing ὁ κύριος and ὁ θεός compared to MT. However, this does not necessarily shed more light on the translation technique or theology of both translators. The only thing we might perhaps conclude from these numbers is that the LXX translator of Job was apparently more conservative or sparse with the extra usage of the divine name than the LXX translator of Proverbs. However, a comparison of the evaluation of the additional attestations is necessary.

---

200 The plus containing ὁ κύριος in 7:2; 15:25, and 40:4 are not accounted for since they cannot be seen as additional attestations of ὁ κύριος, see above.

3.4.2 The evaluation of additional attestations of ὁ κύριος and ὁ θεός in LXX Proverbs and LXX Job

When comparing the results of the evaluation of the additional attestations of ὁ κύριος and ὁ θεός in LXX Proverbs and LXX Job, some differences and similarities can be observed.

(a) Differences
- As indicated above in the evaluation of 2:10 of LXX Job, the LXX translator of Job opted for a different Greek lexeme denoting the divine name when confronted with another divine name in the verse or in the immediate context of the verse. By doing so, he created variation. The LXX translator of Proverbs did not introduce this kind of variation as can be observed in 1:7 where ὁ θεός is used twice.
- The LXX translator of Proverbs often specified or clarified the subject of the verb where MT does not specify it (see, e.g., Prov 3:34; 8:26; 24:26; 29:13). The translator of LXX Job applied a similar technique, i.e., specifying when MT is vague: in 1:21.22; 2:10; 6:10, 34:27 and 36:12. However, the additions in LXX Proverbs used to specify the Hebrew text are always explications of the subject of the verb and thus, they always occur in the nominative form. This is never the case in LXX Job.
- Some peculiarities pertaining to the theology of LXX Proverbs are not present in LXX Job and *vice versa*, since they belong to the characteristics of Job and Proverbs which are not shared by both books. Examples thereof are the emphasis on the Solomonic authorship in Proverbs (e.g., 7:1; 30:1, and 31:1) and Job's piety before the Lord (1:22 and 2:10)·
- Moreover, there are some different theological nuances when comparing the two translations. LXX Proverbs emphasises the sapiential tradition of God as the one to fear (see, e.g., Prov 7:1a and 27:20) which is not present and even discarded in LXX Job (see, e.g., Job 4:6; 6:14, and 28:28).

(b) Similarities
- In the evaluation of the additional attestations of ὁ κύριος and ὁ θεός in LXX Job, it became clear that the divine law has been emphasised by the LXX translator (Job 6:10 and 34:27). Although this is not observed in the studies on Proverbs as to ὁ κύριος and ὁ θεός, it has been observed in other studies that this is also the case in LXX Proverbs.[201] However, this similarity

---

201 See Cook, "Law of Moses in Septuagint Proverbs."

might be an attitude of the translators to prompt their readers to observe the Thora in a Hellenistic context, in which both of them can be situated.

- In both translations, the power of God is stressed either by emphasising his omnipotence (Job 19:3 and 33:23) or by highlighting his role as the sole redeemer (Prov 23:11), the one to lean on (Prov 3:18 and 29:23), and the sole creator (Prov 8:26; 24:7, and 24:12). Although the latter is not found in the evaluation of additional attestations of ὁ κύριος and ὁ θεός in LXX Job, it has been stressed similarly by Cook and more recently by Kwon.[202]

3.5 Conclusion

This chapter has examined the additional attestations of ὁ κύριος and ὁ θεός in LXX Proverbs and LXX Job in order to come to a more nuanced characterisation of the translation technique of the LXX translator, to examine a possible diverging theology and to formulate an indicative answer to the question of a single translator for both books. On the basis of this study, the following concluding remarks can be made:

(1) Translation technique and theology of LXX Proverbs

- Regarding the translation technique of LXX Proverbs, the examination of the additional attestations of ὁ κύριος and ὁ θεός have pointed at a translator who specified the subjects of the verse when this information was lacking in MT (e.g., 3:34; 8:26; 24:26; 23:11). This has its influence on the theology of the LXX text since the specification emphasises the omnipotence of God (e.g., 3:18; 8:26; 23:11; 24:7). Also, the LXX translator provided a better parallelism in 1:7, which is a recurring trait of his translation technique.
- Concerning the theology of LXX Proverbs, it has been noted that the LXX text emphasises the Solomonic authorship (7:1a; 30:1 and 31:1) and Jewishness (1:7) of the translation. Moreover, God's omnipotence is stressed (e.g., 4:27; 23:11; 8:26; 21:8; 24:7.12) and wisdom is portraited as revelatory wisdom (30:3; 31:2 and 31:8).

---

202 See Cook, "Were the LXX Versions of Proverbs and Job Translated by the Same Person?," 146; Cook, "Aspects of the Relationship between the Septuagint Versions of Proverbs and Job," 323; Kwon, "Rewritten Theology," 351–52.

(2) Translation technique and theology of LXX Job

- With regard to the translation technique of LXX Job, the additional attestations of ὁ κύριος and ὁ θεός reflect a translator who created variation (2:10), enhanced parallelism (6:10) and clarified his source text when the latter was vague (Job 1:21.22; 2:10; 6:10; 34:27, and 36:12). By doing so, he ameliorated the stylistic nature of the Greek compared to the Hebrew and made it more comprehensible for his target audience. Three instances in which ὁ κύριος is a plus compared to MT cannot be regarded as such after close examination, due to the denotation of the more mundane meaning of lord (7:2), dittography (15:25) and/or a Greek rendering of a different Hebrew verse (40:4).
- The LXX of Job reflects a different theology than MT. The LXX translator has emphasised God's omnipotence (19:3 and 33:23), the piety of Job (1:22 and 2:10) and the observance of the Mosaic Law (6:10 and 34:27).

(3) Single translator LXX Proverbs and LXX Job?

- With regard to the question of a single translator for LXX Job and LXX Proverbs it can be observed that both books rather indicate a different translator with regard to the translation technique. LXX Job's urge for variation when using the divine name is absent in LXX Proverbs. Also, when clarifying the Hebrew text, LXX Proverbs always uses the nominative form whereas this is not the case in LXX Job.
- The nuances in theology in both books show some similarities (emphasis on divine Law and God's omnipotence) and differences (differences pertaining to the book itself and the focus of Proverbs on God as the one to fear). However, some similarities might be explained due to a common (Hellenistic-Jewish) context in which the two books were translated.
- Thus, the results of the comparison point to a different translator for both books. However, we cannot exclude the possibility that they might stem from the same milieu.[203] Thus, the question of a common environment remains open.

Although the additional attestations of ὁ κύριος and ὁ θεός in both LXX Proverbs and LXX Job have now been examined, in order to come to an even more

---

203 See, e.g., Cox, "The Historical, Social & Literary Context of Old Greek Job,", 116; d'Hamonville, *Les Proverbes,* 139–41, esp. 141.

accurate description of their translation technique and theology, the minuses in the LXX where MT attests a divine name as well as the attestations of ὁ κύριος and ὁ θεός that have been rendered from Hebrew into Greek could or should be examined. An initial examination on the minuses in the LXX where MT reads אלוה in Job has already been presented in the excursus of this chapter.[204] Although the results of this study have not shed light on a diverging theology of the LXX of Job,[205] the examination of the other minuses in the LXX of Job, as well as Proverbs, where MT attests a divine name might shed light on the theology of the LXX. Consequently, these results could thereafter also be compared in order to strengthen or debunk the hypothesis of a different translator for both books.

---

204 See Beeckman, "Absentia Nominum Sacrorum in Libro Iob."

205 Other studies, focusing on the non-standard renderings יהוה/θεός and אלהים/κύριος in LXX Proverbs and the minuses of יהוה, אלהים, אֵל and שׁדי in LXX Job, did also not shed light on a distinct theology. See resp., Bryan Beeckman, "Theologica Variatio? An Examination of the Variation in the Greek Rendering of יהוה and אלהים in LXX Proverbs," *HTS Teologiese Studies/Theological Studies* 78.1 (2022): 1–6; Bryan Beeckman, "Absentia Nominum Sacrorum in Libro Iob (Part II): The Examination of the Minuses of יהוה, אלהים, אֵל and שׁדי in LXX Job," *Bib* 103.4 (2023): 481-498.

4 General conclusion

This monograph has tried to come to a more nuanced characterisation of the translation technique of the LXX translator of Proverbs and Job. In addition to this, it has also aimed at answering the contemporary question whether or not the LXX of both books attests a diverging theology than their Hebrew counterpart as well as the question of a single translator for Proverbs and Job. The conclusions with regard to these aims will be summarised in the next sections.

4.1 Translation technique

After providing a detailed *status quaestionis* regarding the translation technique of LXX Proverbs in chapter 1, we have examined the translation technique of LXX Proverbs and Job by analysing the Greek rendering of Hebrew *hapax legomena* in chapter 2. Additionally, the Greek rendering of Hebrew animal, plant, floral and herb names has also been analysed in two excursuses. This study was the first of its kind to examine these so-called content- and context-related criteria in Proverbs and also, apart from Verbeke's study, in Job. Since these criteria might be considered as possible difficult semantic situations to render into Greek, their investigation has shed more light on the translation technique of both Proverbs and Job.

4.1.1 LXX Proverbs

The translator of LXX Proverbs has shown himself to be highly proficient in both Hebrew and Greek. The tendency to provide adequate Greek lexemes for Hebrew hapaxes, animal, floral, plant and herb names, as well as the usage of Greek neologisms as well as Greek *hapax legomena* to render Hebrew hapaxes, testify of his knowledge of both languages. Next to this, he also wanted to make a literary Greek text. This trait can be observed in his tendency to enhance parallelism (e.g., 7:16; 29:21), introducing rhyme, e.g., by means of alliteration and assonance (e.g., 16:30; 17:22.25; 21:8; 22:29), and the avoidance of repetition and therefore creating variation (e.g., 7:18; 8:13; 23:29; 25:11). In some instances (3:26; 4:24; 26:11), the translator elaborated the image preserved in the Hebrew verse in order to make the image more understandable for his target audience. The elaboration or specification of the Hebrew text can also be observed in the additions of the divine names.

https://doi.org/10.1515/9783111041582-005

Although the majority of Hebrew lexemes has been rendered by an adequate Greek equivalent, it seems that the translator struggled to translate several Hebrew hapaxes as well as jargon-defined lexemes. Nonetheless, he never resorted to transliteration but tried to come up with a translation which fitted to context of the verse (i.e., contextual exegesis) (e.g., 4:24; 8:6.18; 15:19; 16:26; 22:29; 23:2.29; 25:28). In the case of (non-absolute) *hapax legomena*, he often provided root-linked renderings (e.g., 9:13; 12:2.15.18; 19:15; 21:8; 23:34; 25:18; 31:27). Although root-linked renderings might be an indication of the translator's ignorance of the meaning of a certain word, it is more plausible that they reveal a translator who either knew the word or took the context into consideration since these renderings fit the context of the verse. These techniques are an indication of the translator's creativity to deal with semantical difficult situations.

Only a handful of words have been misread (e.g., 11:2; 22:21; 29:21; 30:31; 31:19) or have not been rendered by the translator (e.g., 5:19; 16:1; 26:18). Some of these can be explained by a diverging *Vorlage*, other due to the application of contextual exegesis, stylistic motivations or metathesis. Metathesis could be either a (indeliberate) misreading of the translator or a deliberate technique to make sense of the word (or verse) attested in his Hebrew *Vorlage*. In the verses wherein metathesis occurs (e.g., 15:19; 16:27; 23:28), the latter seems to most plausible one.

4.1.2 LXX Job

The LXX translator of Job was, just as the LXX translator of Proverbs, well-taught in Greek and Hebrew. He also provided a corresponding Greek lexeme for the hapaxes and jargon-defined vocabulary discussed in this dissertation. He never transliterated the Hebrew text. Moreover, next to his excellent knowledge of Greek and Hebrew, he also shares the same techniques with LXX Proverbs to make his text a decent piece of Greek literature, *i.e.* enhancement of parallelism (e.g., 36:18; 37:9), imagery (e.g., 8:14), creating variation (4:11), harmonisation (e.g., 20:22) and neologisms (4:11). Moreover, in several verses, he clarified the verse which can be considered vague in Hebrew. This in order to make his target text more comprehensible for his target audience.

When confronted with a difficult Hebrew word, he resorted to root-linked renderings (e.g. 33:9; 34:25.36 and 37:16) or applied contextual exegesis (e.g., 15:24.29; 37:16) to render his Hebrew *Vorlage*. The words which he probably did not fully understand were translated by a double translation (33:16) or he provided one Greek equivalent for two Hebrew lexemes (20:22).

Often, a word has not been rendered. Some non-renderings can be explained by a diverging Hebrew *Vorlage* (e.g., 18:3; 33:25) and some by the translator's need to skip a certain word on the basis of stylistic motivations which were often defined by context (e.g., 8:14; 33:24; 20:22; 36:18; 37:9).

4.2 Theology

Chapter 3 has examined whether the LXX of Proverbs and Job attest of a different theology than MT by applying a new and innovative methodology: the examination of the pluses in the LXX containing ὁ θεός and ὁ κύριος. Being explicit differences between the Greek and Hebrew text, these pluses, that contain theological markers (i.e., divine names), might shed light on a possible characteristic theology of the LXX. As has been convincingly demonstrated by the analyses of the additional attestations of the divine names, these pluses can indeed be considered as *loci theologici* where a diverging theology *vis-à-vis* MT can be found.

4.2.1 LXX Proverbs

Throughout Proverbs, it has been observed that the LXX translator often added the divine name in order to specify the subject of the verse which is lacking in the Hebrew. Often, this created a religious nuance which emphasised God's omnipotence, i.e., God as being the sole redeemer (8:26; 24:7.12), only creator (8:26), the one who makes straight the ways of humans and crooked those of the wicked (4:27) and the one to lean on and who will grant support (3:18; 29:23). Moreover, the LXX translator emphasises the Solomonic authorship of Proverbs by omitting every reference to Lemuel and Agur and adding references to God (30:1; 31:1). In the LXX, it is also emphasised that Solomon receives his wisdom directly from God (30:3; 31:2.8). By doing so, wisdom is characterised as revelatory wisdom. Furthermore, LXX Proverbs also emphasises the sapiential tradition that focusses on the respect for the Lord (7:1a; 27:20).

The stress on the Solomonic authorship of Proverbs, the sapiential tradition which focusses on the respect of the Lord as well as an intertextual reference to LXX Psalms, seem to indicate the translator's tendency to highlight the Jewishness of the translation. These observations point to a translator who wanted to preserve Jewish thought and tradition. This might be an argument in favour of Cook's hypothesis that the translator of Proverbs was a conservative Jew.

4.2.2 LXX Job

The LXX translator of Job has also added the divine name to clarify the Hebrew text when it could be considered vague. Some of the added divine names have led to a religious emphasis. In LXX Job the omnipotence of God (i.e., only God's acts and words can discomfort Job and God is the only saviour of humans) (e.g., 19:3; 33:23), the importance of observing the Law and the commandments (6:10; 34:27) and Job's piety are stressed (1:22; 2:10). These observations also point to a translator who wanted to stress Jewish tradition and the Jewishness of the translation for his target audience.

This hypothesis is strengthened by the examination of the minuses in the LXX where אֱלוֹהַּ is attested in MT. This study has indicated that these minuses do not shed light on a diverging theology. Only in one case did the translator deliberately omit the divine name in order to emphasise Elihu's role as Job's teacher (36:2). The (preliminary) conclusions of the examination of minuses in LXX Job were MT attests a divine name point to a translator who was more conservative in preserving the Hebrew divine name into Greek than he was in adding divine names where there is none in the Hebrew text.

4.3 Single translator?

In order to solve the question whether LXX Proverbs and Job were translated by the same person, a comparison of the results obtained in both books has been made.

The results of the Greek rendering of Hebrew *hapax legomena* have indicated that both translators share the same techniques to render the hapaxes present in their *Vorlage*. Even though several techniques were not detected in one book but were detected in the other after the examination of hapaxes (*e.g.* metathesis, double translation, rhyme and harmonisation), scholars have noted examples of these techniques elsewhere in the book where these techniques are not applied to render hapaxes. Thus, from the study on Hebrew *hapax legomena* and their Greek rendering in the LXX, we concluded that both books were translated by the same translator or the same group of translators.

However, when looking at the Greek translation of Hebrew animal, plant, floral and herb names, we arrived at a different conclusion. Indeed, the same techniques for both books as the ones observed for the rendering of hapaxes were applied. However, in both books, different Greek lexemes have been used to render the same Hebrew lexeme. Given the unique nature of animal, floral, plant and herb names, this is an indication that we are dealing with two translators. Nonetheless, given the fact that they exhibit similar techniques, a shared milieu cannot be excluded.

The examination of the pluses containing the divine name in both books aimed to draw conclusions not only with regard to the translation technique, but primarily on the theology of LXX Proverbs and Job. The results of this study have indicated that both translators have added the divine name to make the text more comprehensible and explicit. However, this type of clarifications in Proverbs are always explications of the subject of the verb, in the nominative form, which is absent in LXX Job. Moreover, the LXX translator of Job opted for a different divine name when confronted with another divine name in the verse or in the immediate context of the verse. This variation is absent in Proverbs that does not shun to use the same divine name twice in the same verse (Prov 1:7). However, both translators have stressed the Jewishness of their work by stressing the importance of the divine law and the omnipotence of God. Nonetheless, also here some differences can be detected. First of all, there are differences in theology which pertain to the content of the book itself. However, this does not tell us anything with regard to the question of a single translator. More importantly is the second difference, i.e., LXX Proverbs which emphasises the sapiential tradition of God as the one to fear, whereas this is absent and even discarded in LXX Job (e.g., Job 4:6; 6:14 and 28:28).

On the basis of the results, we can conclude that LXX Proverbs and LXX Job were not translated by the same translator, thus *unum et unum sunt duo*. This can be observed in their choice to render shared jargon-defined vocabulary by different Greek lexemes and their different approach on dealing with divine names (*i.e.* variation vs no variation) and some particular theological nuances which are present in the one book but absent in the other. However, although both books were translated by a different translator, they probably stemmed from the same milieu or group of translators. This hypothesis is strengthened by their shared techniques, i.a., enhancement of the literary character of the Greek text, avoidance of repetition and creating variation, the elaboration of imagery, the explicitation of the Hebrew text, root-linked renderings, etc. Also the stress on the Jewishness of the translation and their excellent knowledge of both Greek and Hebrew point in the direction of a same milieu or group.

4.4 *Quo vadis?*

This research has examined several content- and context-related criteria to come to a more nuanced image of the translation technique of LXX Proverbs and Job. However, a more complete characterisation of their translation technique can be obtained by analysing other content- and context-related criteria such as Hebrew wordplay, parallelism and aetiologies. Consequently, the results of those studies in both books can also be compared to one another to either debunk or corroborate my hypothesis of two different translators stemming from the same milieu/group.

Concerning the theology of LXX Proverbs and LXX Job, this study has already examined the minuses in LXX Job where MT attests אֱלוֹהַּ. A study pertaining to the minuses where MT records the other divine names might be a worthwhile endeavour in order to see whether these minuses reveal a diverging theology between LXX and MT. With regard to pluses and minuses in the LXX, a study analysing all the pluses and minuses in a systematic way has not yet been conducted for LXX Proverbs. However, such a study can shed more light on the translation technique, Hebrew *Vorlage*, textual transmission and theology LXX Proverbs. This is even more true given the fact that scholarship does not agree whether a certain plus or minus or the transposition of verses and chapters in Proverbs belong to a diverging Hebrew *Vorlage*, the translator's technique and ideology/theology or the textual transmission of the text. Therefore, a systematic study of the pluses and minuses in LXX Proverbs is worth undertaking.

Finally, the new methodologies applied in this research, i.e., Hebrew animal names as a content-and context-related criterion and pluses and minuses of (Greek and Hebrew) divine names, can be applied in other LXX books to achieve a better understanding of their translation technique and (possible diverging) theology.

When one door closes, another opens. *Quo vadis? Ego procedo.*

Bibliography

1 Texts, editions and facsimiles

Alexander, Philip S. and Geza Vermes, ed.. *Qumran Qave 4 XIX. Serek Ha-Yahad and Two Relat-ed Texts*. DJD XXVI. Oxford: Clarendon Press, 1998.

Attridge, Harold et al., ed., *Qumran Cave 4 VIII. Parabiblical Texts, Part* 1. DJD XIII. Oxford: Clarendon Press, 1994.

Baillet, Maurice, Jozef T. Milik and Roland de Vaux, ed. *Les 'petites grottes' de Qumrân*. DJD III. Oxford: Clarendon Press, 1962.

Balme, David M., ed. *Aristotle. Historia Animalium. Volume I. Books I-X: Text*. CCTC 38. Cambridge: University Press, 2002.

Baumgarten, Jospeh M. *Qumran Cave 4 XIII. The Damascus Document (4Q266-273)*. DJD XVIII. Oxford: Clarendon Press, 1996.

Beentjes, Pancratius C. The Book of Ben Sira in Hebrew. A Text Edition of All Extant Hebrew Manuscripts and a Synopsis of All Parallel Hebrew Ben Sira Texts. SVT 68. Leiden: Brill, 1997.

Bekker, Immanuel. *Aristotelis Opera. Vol. 2*. Berlin: Reimer, 1831 (repr. Berlin: De Gruyter, 1960).

British Museum. The Codex Alexandrinus (Royal MS. 1 D. V–VIII) in Reduced Photographic Facsimile. Old Testament Part IV I Esdra-Ecclesiasticus. London: Trustees of the British Museum, 1957.

de Lagarde, Paul, ed. *Hagiographa Chaldaice*. Lipsiae: Teubner, 1873.

de Vaux, Roland and Jozef T. Milik, ed. Qumrân grotte 4. II. I. Archéologie; II. Tefellin, Mezuzot et Targums (4Q128-4Q157). DJD VI. Oxford: Clarendon Press, 1977.

de Waard, Jan, ed. *Proverbs*. BHQ 17. Stuttgart: Deutsche Bibelgesellschaft, 2008.

Elliger, Karl et al. *Biblia Hebraica Stuttgartensia*. Stuttgart: Deutsche Bibelstiftung, ⁵1977.

Field, Frederick, ed. Origenis Hexaplorum quae supersunt sive veterum interpretum Graecorum in totum vetus testamentum fragmenta. Tomus 2 Jobus – Malachias. Oxonii: Typographeo Clarendoniano, 1875.

Fischer, Bonfiatius et al., ed. *Biblia Sacra. Iuxta Vulgatam Versionem. Tomus II: Proverbia – Apocalypsis*. red. Robert Weber. Stuttgart: Württembergische Bibelanstalt, 1969.

Fox, Michael V. Proverbs. An Eclectic Edition with Introduction and Textual Commentary. HBCE 1. Atlanta, GA: SBL Press, 2015.

García Martínez, Florentino, Eibert Tigchelaar and Adam S. van der Woude, ed. *Qumran Cave 11 II. 11Q2–18, 11Q20–31*. DJD XXIII. Oxford: Clarendon Press, 1998.

Gorfinkle, Joseph I. *The Sayings of the Jewish Fathers. Pirkei Abot* (July 2003). http://www.gutenberg.org/cache/epub/8547/pg8547-images.html.

Hagedorn, Ursula and Dieter Hagedorn, ed. *Olympiodor, Diakon von Alexandria – Kommentar zu Iob*. PTS 24. Berlin: De Gruyter, 1984.

Hanhart, Robert. *Esther*. Septuaginta. Vetus Testamentum Graecum. Auctoritate Academiae Scientiarum Gottingensis editum VIII.3. Göttingen: Vandenhoeck & Ruprecht, 1966.

McCarthy, Carmel. *Deuteronomy*. BHQ 5. Stuttgart: Deutsche Bibelgesellschaft, 2007.

Metso, Sarianna. *The Community Rule. A Critical Edition with Translation*. EJL 51. Atlanta, GA: SBL Press, 2019.

https://doi.org/10.1515/9783111041582-006

Milik, Jozef T. Qumrân grotte 4 II. Tefillin, Mezuzot et Targums (4Q128–4Q157). DJD VI. Oxford: Clarendon Press, 1977.

Müller, Karl. *Geographi Graeci minores. Vol. 1.* Paris: Didot, 1855.

Rahlfs, Alfred, ed. *Septuaginta. Id est Vetus Testamentum Graece iuxta LXX Interpretes.* Stuttgart: Deutsche Bibelgesellschaft, 2006.

Schneider, Otto. *Nicandrea. Theriaca et Alexipharmaca.* Leipzig: Teubner, 1856.

Schuller, Eileen M. and Carol A. Newsom. *The Hodayot (Thanksgiving Psalms): A Study Edition of 1QH^a.* SBLEJIL 36. Atlanta, GA: Society of Biblical Literature, 2012.

Skehan, Patrick W., Eugene Ulrich, and Judith E. Sanderson, ed. *Qumran Cave 4 IV. Palaeo-Hebrew and Greek Biblical Manuscripts.* DJD IX. Oxford: Clarendon Press, 1992.

Steg, David M. *The Text of the Targum of Job. An Introduction and Critical Edition.* AGJU 20. Leiden – New York, NY – Köln: Brill, 1994.

Ulrich, Eugene et al., ed. *Qumran Cave 4, XI. Psalms to Chronicles.* DJD XVI. Oxford: Clarendon Press, 2000.

van der Horst, Pieter W. The Sentences of Pseudo-Phocylides with Introduction and Commentary. SVTP 4. Leiden: Brill, 1978.

van der Ploeg, Johannes P. M. and Adam S. van der Woude, ed. *Le Targum de Job de la grotte xi de Qumrân.* Leiden : Brill, 1971.

von Tischendorf, Constantin, ed. Bibliorum Codex Sinaiticus Petropolitanus. III Veteris Testamenti pars posterior. Hildesheim: Georg Olms Verlag, 1969.

von Tischendorf, Constantin, Codex Ephraemi Syri Rescriptus sive Fragmenta Veteris Testamenti E Codice Novi Testamenti E Codice Graeco Parisiensi Celeberrimo quinti ut videtur post Christum Seculi eruit atque editit Constantinus Tischendor. Lipsiae : Tauchnitz, 1845.

Wevers, John W. *Deuteronomium.* Septuaginta. Vetus Testamentum Graecum. Auctoritate Academiae Scientiarum Gottingensis editum III.2. Göttingen: Vandenhoeck & Ruprecht, 1977.

Wevers, John W. *Exodus.* Septuaginta. Vetus Testamentum Graecum. Auctoritate Academiae Scientiarum Gottingensis editum II.1. Göttingen: Vandenhoeck & Ruprecht, 1991.

Wevers, John W. *Genesis.* Septuaginta. Vetus Testamentum Graecum. Auctoritate Academiae Scientiarum Gottingensis editum I. Göttingen: Vandenhoeck & Ruprecht, 1974.

Yadin, Yigael. *The Temple Scroll. Volume Two: Text and Commentary.* Jerusalem: The Israel Exploration Society – The Institute of Archaeology of the Hebrew University of Jerusalem – The Shrine of the Book, 1983.

Ziegler, Joseph. *Jeremias, Baruch, Threni, Epistula Jeremiae.* Septuaginta. Vetus Testamentum Graecum. Auctoritate Academiae Scientiarum Gottingensis editum XV. Göttingen: Vandenhoeck & Ruprecht, 2006.

Ziegler, Joseph. *Job.* Septuaginta. Vetus Testamentum Graecum. Auctoritate Academiae Scientiarum Gottingensis editum XI.4. Göttingen: Vandenhoeck & Ruprecht, 1982.

Ziegler, Joseph. *Sapientia Salomonis.* Septuaginta. Vetus Testamentum Graecum. Auctoritate Academiae Scientiarum Gottingensis editum XII.1. Göttingen: Vandenhoeck & Ruprecht, 1962.

Ziegler, Joseph and Detlef Fraenkel. *Ezechiel.* Septuaginta. Vetus Testamentum Graecum. Auctoritate Academiae Scientiarum Gottingensis editum XVI.1. Göttingen: Vandenhoeck & Ruprecht, 2006.

2 Dictionaries and concordances

Bons, Eberhard, ed. Historical and Theological Lexicon of the Septuagint. Volume I: Alpha – Gamma. Tübingen: Mohr Siebeck, 2020.

Brown, Francis, Samuel R. Driver and Charles A. Briggs. The New Brown – Driver – Briggs – Genesius Hebrew and English Lexicon with an Appendix Containing the Biblical Aramaic. Peabody, MA: Hendrickson Publishers, 1979.

Clines, David J. A. *The Dictionary of Classical Hebrew Volume I–IX*. Sheffield: Sheffield Academic Press, 1993–2016.

Cook, Edward M. *Dictionary of Qumran Aramaic*. University Park, PA: Penn State University Press, 2015.

Friberg, Timothy, Barbara Friberg and Neva F. Miller. *Analytical Lexicon of the Greek New Testament*. Victoria: Trafford, 2005.

Gesenius, Wilhelm. *Hebräischen und Aramäischen Handwörterbuch*. Leipzig: Verlag von F. C. W. Vogel, [17]1921.

Hatch, Edwin and Henry A. Redpath. A Concordance to the Septuagint. And the Other Greek Versions of the Old Testament (Including the Apocryphal Books). Second Edition. Grand Rapids, MI: Baker Book House Company, 1998.

Holladay, William L. A Concise Hebrew and Aramaic Lexicon of the Old Testament. Based upon the Lexical Work of Ludwig Koehler and Walter Baumgartner. Leiden — Boston —Köln: Brill, 2000.

Koehler, Ludwig and Walter Baumgartner. Hebräisches und Aramäisches Lexikon zum Alten Testament. Unveranderter Nachdruck der Dritten Auflage (1967–1995). Leiden – Boston: Brill, 2004.

Liddell, Henry G., Robert Scott and Henry S. Jones. *A Greek-English Lexicon*. Oxford: Clarendon Press, 1996.

Liddell, Henry G., Robert Scott and Henry S. Jones. *Greek-English Lexicon. A Supplement*. Edited by E. A. Barber with the Assistance of P. Maas, M. Scheller and M. L. West. Oxford: Clarendon Press, 1968.

Lisowsky, Gerhard. *Konkordanz zum hebräischen Alten Testament*. Stuttgart: Württembergische Bibelanstalt, 1958.

Lust, Johan, Erik Eynikel and Katrin Hauspie. *Greek-English Lexicon of the Septuagint. Third Corrected Edition*. Stuttgart: Deutsche Bibelgesellschaft, 2015.

Montanari, Franco. *The Brill Dictionary of Ancient Greek*. Brill: Leiden, 2015.

Muraoka, Takamitsu. *A Greek-English Lexicon of the Septuagint*. Leuven: Peeters, 2009.

Siegfried, Carl and Bernhard Stade. *Hebräisches Wörterbuch zum Alten Testamente*. Leipzig: Verlag von Veit & Comp., 1893.

3 Other research tools

BibleWorks 10.0 (BibleWorks. Software for Biblical Exegesis and Research, 2016).

CATSS. Computer Assisted Tools for Septuagint Studies (http://ccat.sas.upenn.edu/gopher/text/religion/biblical/parallel/).

Dead Sea Scrolls Digital Library (https://www.deadseascrolls.org.il/)

The Online Liddell-Scott-Jones Greek-English Lexicon (http://stephanus.tlg.uci.edu/lsj/)

Thesaurus Linguae Graecae (http://stephanus.tlg.uci.edu/index.php).

4 Secondary literature

Abercrombie, John R. "A Computer-Assisted Study of A Textual Family in the Book of Ruth." *Textus* 13 (1986): 95–110.

Aejmelaeus, Anneli "Introduction." Pages XIII–XVIII in *On the Trail of the Septuagint Translators. Collected Essays*. Edited by Anneli Aejmeleaus. CBET 50 (Leuven — Paris — Dudley, MA: Peeters, 2007).

Aejmelaeus, Anneli, ed. *On the Trail of the Septuagint Translators. Collected Essays*. CBET 50. Leuven — Paris — Dudley, MA: Peeters, 2007.

Aejmelaeus, Anneli. "Oti Causale in Septuaginal Greek." Pages 115–132 in *La Septuaginta en la Investigación Contemporánea (V Congreso de la IOSCS)*. Edited by Natalio Fernández Marcos. TECC 34. Madrid: Instituto "Arias Montano," 1985 (= Aejmelaeus, Anneli. "Oti Causale in Septuagintal Greek." Pages 11–29 in *On the Trail of the Septuagint Translators. Collected Essays*. Edited by Anneli Aejmelaeus. CBET 50. Leuven — Paris — Dudley, MA: Peeters, 2007).

Aejmelaeus, Anneli. "Oti Recitativum in Septuagintal Greek." Pages 74–82 in *Studien zur Septuaginta. Robert Hanhart zu Ehren: aus Anlaß seines 65. Geburtstages*. Edited by Detlef Fraenkel, Udo Quast and John W. Wevers. MSU 20. Göttingen: Vandenhoeck & Ruprecht, 1990 (= Aejmelaeus, Anneli. "Oti Recitativum in Septuagintal Greek." Pages 30–41 in *On the Trail of the Septuagint Translators. Collected Essays*. Edited by Anneli Aejmelaeus. CBET 50. Leuven — Paris — Dudley, MA: Peeters, 2007).

Aejmelaeus, Anneli. "Participium Coniunctum as a Criterion of Translation Technique." *VT* 32 (1982): 385–393 (= Aejmelaeus, Anneli. "Participium Coniunctum as a Criterion of Translation Technique." Pages 1–10 in *On the Trail of the Septuagint Translators. Collected Essays*. Edited by Anneli Aejmelaeus. CBET 50. Leuven — Paris — Dudley, MA: Peeters, 2007).

Aejmelaeus, Anneli. "The Significance of Clause Connectors in the Syntactical and Translation-Technical Study of the Septuagint." Pages 43–57 in *On the Trail of the Septuagint Translators. Collected Essays*. Edited by Anneli Aejmelaeus. CBET 50. Leuven — Paris — Dudley, MA: Peeters, 2007.

Aejmelaeus, Anneli. "Translation Technique and the Intention of the Translator." Pages 59–69 in *On the Trail of the Septuagint Translators. Collected Essays*. Edited by Anneli Aejmelaeus. CBET 50. Leuven — Paris — Dudley, MA: Peeters, 2007.

Aejmelaeus, Anneli. "Von Sprache zur Theologie. Methodologische Überlegungen zur Theologie der Septuaginta." Pages 21–48 in *The Septuagint and Messianism*. Edited by Michael A. Knibb. BETL 195. Peeters: Leuven, 2006.

Aejmelaeus, Anneli. "What Can We Know about the Hebrew Vorlage of the Septuagint?" Pages 71–106 in *On the Trail of the Septuagint Translators. Collected Essays*. Edited by Anneli Aejmelaeus. CBET 50. Leuven — Paris — Dudley, MA: Peeters, 2007.

Aejmelaeus, Anneli. " What We Talk About When We Talk About Translation Technique." Pages 205–222 in *On the Trail of the Septuagint Translators. Collected Essays*. Edited by Anneli Aejmelaeus. CBET 50. Leuven — Paris — Dudley, MA: Peeters, 2007 (= Aejmelaeus, Anneli. "What We Talk About When We Talk About Translation Technique." Pages 531–552 in *X Congress of the International Organization for Septuagint and Cognate Studies. Oslo, 1998*. Edited by Bernard A. Taylor. SBLSCS 51. Atlanta, GA: Society of Biblical Literature).

Aitken, James K. "Neologisms: A Septuagint Problem." Pages 315–329 in *Interested Readers: Essays on the Hebrew Bible in Honor of David J. A. Clines*. Edited by James

K. Aitken, Christl Maier and Jeremy M. S. Clines. Atlanta, GA: Society of Biblical Literature, 2013.

Altschüller, M.A. "Einige textkritische Bemerkungen zum Alten Testamente." *ZAW* 6.1 (1886): 211–213.

Angelini, Anna. "Biblical Translation and Cross-Cultural Communication. A Focus on the Animal Imagery." *Semitica et Classica* 8 (2015): 33–43.

Atkins, Peter J. "Mythology or Zoology." *BibInt* 24 (2016): 48–59.

Ausloos, Hans. "Hapax Legomena, the Septuagint, and Hebrew Lexicography." Pages 291–300 in *XIV Congress of the International Oganization for Septuagint and Cognate Studies. Helsinki, 2010*. Edited by Melvin K. H. Peters. SBLSCS 51. Atlanta, GA: SBL, 2013.

Ausloos, Hans. "LXX's Rendering of Hebrew Proper Names and the Characterization of the Translation Technique of the Book of Judges". Pages 53–71 in *Scripture in Transition. Essays on Septuagint, Hebrew Bible, and Dead Sea Scrolls in Honour of Raija Sollamo*. Edited by in Ansi Voitila and Jutta Jokiranta. SJSJ 126. Leiden: Brill, 2008.

Ausloos, Hans. "Sept défis posés à une theologie de la Septante." Pages 228–250 in *Congress Volume IOSOT Stellenbosch 2016* (SVT, 177). Edited by Louis C. Jonker, Gideon R. Kotzé and Christl M. Maier. Leiden – Boston, MA: Brill, 2017.

Ausloos, Hans. "The Septuagint's Rendering of Hebrew Hapax Legomena and the Characterization of Its 'Translation Technique': The Case of Exodus." *Acta Patristica et Byzantina* 20 (2009): 360–376.

Ausloos, Hans. "The Septuagint's Rendering of Hebrew Toponyms as an Indication of the Translation Technique of the Book of Numbers." Pages 35–50 in *Florilegium Complutense. Textual Criticism and Dead Sea Scrolls Studies in Honour of Julio Trebolle Barrera*. Edited by Andrés Piquer Otero and Pablo Torijano Morales. SJSJ 157. Leiden: Brill, 2012.

Ausloos, Hans and Bénédicte Lemmelijn. "Characterizing the LXX Translation of Judges on the Basis of Content-Related Criteria. The Greek Rendering of Hebrew Absolute Hapax Legomena in Judg 3,12-30." Pages 171–192 in *After Qumran. Old and Modern Editions of the Biblical Texts — The Historical Books*. Edited by Hans Ausloos, Bénédicte Lemmelijn and Julio Trebolle Barrera. BETL 246. Leuven — Paris — Dudley, MA: Peeters, 2012.

Ausloos, Hans and Bénédicte Lemmelijn. "Content-Related Criteria in Characterising the LXX Translation Technique." Pages 356–376 in *Die Septuaginta. Texte, Theologien und Einflüsse. 2. Internationale Fachtagung veranstaltet von Septuaginta Deutsch (LXX.D), Wuppertal 23.-27. Juli 2008*. Edited by Wolfgang Kraus, Martin Karrer and Martin Meiser. WUNT 252. Tübingen: Mohr Siebeck, 2010.

Ausloos, Hans and Bénédicte Lemmelijn, ed. *Die Theologie der Septuaginta / The Theology of the Septuagint*. LXX.H 5. Gütersloh: Gütersloher Verlagshaus, 2020.

Ausloos, Hans and Bénédicte Lemmelijn. "Etymological Renderings in the Septuagint." Pages 193–201 *Die Sprache der Septuaginta*. Edited by Eberhard Bons and Jan Joosten. LXX.H 4. Gütersloh: Gütersloher Verlag, 2016.

Ausloos, Hans and Bénédicte Lemmelijn. "Faithful Creativity Torn Between Freedom and Literalness in the Septuagint's Translations." *JNSL* 40.2(2014): 53–69.

Ausloos, Hans and Bénédicte Lemmelijn. "Rendering Love. Hapax Legomena and the Characterisation of the Translation Technique of Song of Songs." Pages 43–61 in *Translating a Translation. The LXX and its Modern Translations in the Context of Early Judaism*. Edited by Hans Ausloos et al. BETL 213. Leuven — Paris — Dudley, MA: Peeters, 2008.

Ausloos, Hans and Bénédicte Lemmelijn. "Theology or not? That's the Question. Is There Such a Thing as 'The Theology of the Septuagint'?" Pages 19–45 *Die Theologie der Septuaginta*

/ *The Theology of the Septuagint.* Edited by Hans Ausloos and Bénédicte Lemmelijn. LXX.H 5. Gütersloh: Gütersloher Verlagshaus, 2020.

Ausloos, Hans, Bénédicte Lemmelijn and Valérie Kabergs. "The Study of Aetiological Wordplay as a Content-Related Criterion in the Characterization of LXX Translation Technique." Pages 273–294 in *Die Septuaginta. Entstehung, Sprache, Geschichte. 3. Internationale Fachtagung veranstaltet von Septuaginta Deutsch (LXX.D), Wuppertal 22.-25.7.2010.* Edited by Wolfgang Kraus and Martin Karrer. WUNT 286.Tübingen: Mohr Siebeck, 2012.

Austin, Benjamin M., *Plant Metaphors in the Old Greek of Isaiah.* SBLSCS 69. Atlanta, GA: SBL Press, 2019.

Barr, James. *The Typology of Literalism in Ancient Biblical Translations.* MSU 15. Göttingen: Vandenhoeck & Ruprecht, 1979.

Barr, James. "Words for Love in Biblical Greek." Pages 3–18 in *The Glory of Christ in the New Testament. Studies in Christology in Memory of George Bradford Caird.* Edited by Lincoln D. Hurst and Nicholas T. Wright. Oxford: Clarendon Press, 1987.

Barthélemy, Dominique. *Critique textuelle de l'Ancien Testament. Tome 5: Job, Proverbes, Qohélet et Cantique des Cantiques.* OBO 50.5. Fribourg – Göttingen: Academic Press – Vandenhoeck & Ruprecht, 2015.

Baudissin, Wolf W. G. Kyrios als Gottesname im Judentum und seine Stelle in der Religiongeschichte. Erster Teil: Der Gebrauch des Gottesnamens Kyrios in Septuaginta. Giessen: Otto Eissfeldt, 1929.

Baumgartner, Antoine Jean. "Étude critique sur l'état du texte du livre des Proverbes d'après les principals traductions anciennes." PhD diss., University of Leipzig, 1890.

Beeckman, Bryan. "Absentia Nominum Sacrorum in Libro Iob: The Examination of אֱלֹהַּ in Job Without Counterpart in the LXX." *BZ* 66.1 (2022): 16–30.

Beeckman, Bryan. "Absentia Nominum Sacrorum in Libro Iob (Part II): The Examination of the Minuses of יהוה, אלהים, אֵל and שדי in LXX Job." *Bib* 103.4 (2023): 481-498.

Beeckman, Bryan. "Apologetics Against the Devaluation of the Mosaic Law in Early Judaism? An Indication of An Anti-Hellenistic Stance in LXX Proverbs and the Works of Philo of Alexandria." *Scriptura* 117.1 (2018): 1–10.

Beeckman, Bryan. "Animalia in Libro Iob: The Greek Rendering of Hebrew Animal Names in LXX Job." Pages 255–284 in *XVII Congress of the International Organisation for Septuagint and Cognate Studies, Aberdeen, 2019.* Edited by Michael van der Meer, Martin Rösel and Gideon Kotzé. Atlanta, GA: SBL Press, 2022.

Beeckman, Bryan. "De Nomine Dei: Theological Exegesis in Verses of the Septuagint Version of Proverbs Containing ὁ θεός Without Any Counterpart in the Masoretic Text?" *Louvain Studies* 43.4 (2020): 372–387.

Beeckman, Bryan. "De Nominibus Sacris: Theological Exegesis in Verses of LXX-Proverbs Containing ὁ κύριος Without Any Counterpart in MT?" *RB* 128.4 (2021): 501–524.

Beeckman, Bryan. "De (Pro)verb(i)is Raris: The Greek Rendering of Hebrew Absolute Hapax Legomena in LXX-Proverbs." Pages 153–174 in *The Septuagint South of Alexandria.* Edited by Johann Cook and Gideon Kotzé. VTS 193. Leiden: Brill, 2022.

Beeckman, Bryan. "Nomina Sacra in Libro Iob: Theological Exegesis in Verses of LXX Job Containing ὁ θεός and ὁ κύριος Without Any Counterpart in MT?" *VT* 73.1 (2023): 1–27.

Beeckman, Bryan. "Proverbia de Animalibus. The Greek Rendering of Hebrew Animal Names in Proverbs." *ZAW* 131.2 (2019): 257–270.

Beeckman, Bryan. "Theologica Variatio? An Examination of the Variation in the Greek Rendering of יהוה and אלהים in LXX Proverbs." *HTS Teologiese Studies/Theological Studies* 78.1 (2022): 1–6.

Beeckman, Bryan. "Traces of Proverbs in Patristic Writings. Tracing Back Proverbs' Greek Rendered Hebrew Hapax Legomena in the Commentary on the Book of Proverbs Attributed to John Chrysostom." *JECH* 7.2 (2017): 40–53.

Beeckman, Bryan. "Trails of a Different Vorlage and A Free Translator in Proverbs. A Text-Critical Analysis of Prov 16:1-7." *OTE* 30.3 (2017): 571–591.

Beeckman, Bryan. "Unitas Vegetabilium? The Greek Rendering of Hebrew Floral, Plant and Herb Names in LXX-Proverbs and LXX-Job." *JSCS* 53 (2020): 19–41.

Beeckman, Bryan. "Verba Rara Amicorum Iob: The Greek Rendering of Hebrew Absolute Hapax Legomena in the Speeches of Eliphaz, Bildad and Elihu in LXX Job." *HTS Teologiese Studies/Theological Studies* 77.1 (2021): 1–8.

Beeckman, Bryan. "Voorbij vergeving? Een introductie in het boek Spreuken." *Ezra* 47 (2016): 109–119.

Beer, Georg. *Der Text des Buches Job*. Marburg: N. G. Elwertsche Verlagsbuchandlung, 1897.

Ben-Ḥayyim, Ze'ev. *The Book of Ben Sira. Text, Concordance and an Analysis of the Vocabulary*. The Historical Dictionary of the Hebrew Bible. Jerusalem: The Academy of the Hebrew Language and the Shrine of the Book, 1973.

Bertheau, Ernst. *Die Sprüche Salomo's*. Leipzig: Verlag von S. Hirzel, 1883.

Bertram, Georg. "ΙΚΑΝΟΣ in den griechischen Übersetzungen des ATs als Wiedergabe von schaddaj." *ZAW* 70.1 (1958): 20–31.

Bertram, Georg. "Zur Prägung der biblischen Gottesvorstellung in der griechischen Übersetzung des Alten Testaments. Die Wiedergabe von schadad und schaddaj im Griechischen." *Die Welts des Orients vol. 2* 5.6 (1959): 502–513.

Block, Daniel I. *The Book of Ezekiel. Chapters 1-24*. NICOT. Grand Rapids, MI: Eerdmans, 1997.

Büchner, Dirk L. "Leuitikon." Pages 82–106 in *A New English Translation of the Septuagint And the Other Greek Translations Traditionally Included Under That Title*. Edited by Albert Pietersma and Benjamin G. Wright. New York, NY — Oxford: Oxford University Press, 2007.

Casanowicz, Immanuel M. et al. "Hapax Legomena. Biblical Data." *The Jewish Encyclopedia* 6 (1904): 226–229.

Clines, David J. A. *Job 21-37b*. WBC 18a. Mexico City: Thomas Nelson, 2006.

Clifford, Richard J. "Observations on the Text and Versions of Proverbs." Pages 47–61 in *Wisdom, You Are My Sister. Studies in Honour of Roland E. Murphy, O.Carm., on the Occasion of His Eightieth Birthday*. Edited by Michael L. Barré. CBQMS 29. Washington, DC: The Catholic Biblical Association of America, 1997.

Clifford, Richard J. *Proverbs. A Commentary*. OTL. Louisville: KY, Westminster John Knox Press, 1999.

Cook, Johann. "A Case Study of LXX Proverbs, LXX Job and 4 Maccabees." Pages 59–77 in Die Septuaginta. Orte und Intentionen. 5. Internationale Fachtagung veranstaltet von Septuaginta Deutsch (LXX.D), Wuppertal 24.-27. Juli 2014. Edited by Siegfried Kreuzer et al. WUNT 361. Tübingen: Mohr Siebeck, 2016.

Cook, Johann. "A Comparison of Proverbs and Jeremiah in the Septuagint." *JNSL* 20.1 (1994): 49–58.

Cook, Johann. "Apocalyptic Terminology in Septuagint Proverbs." *JNSL* 25.1 (1999): 251–264.

Cook, Johann. "Aspects of the Relationship between the Septuagint Versions of Proverbs and Job." Pages 309–328 in *IX Congress of the International Organization for Septuagint and*

Cognate Studies, Cambridge, 1995. Edited by Bernard A. Taylor. SBLSCS 45. Atlanta, GA: Scholars Press, 1997.

Cook, Johann. "Aspects of the Translation Technique Followed by the Translator of LXX Proverbs." *JNSL* 22.1 (1996): 143–153.

Cook, Johann. "Contextual Exegetical Interpretations in the Septuagint Proverbs." *JNSL* 25.2 (1999): 132–146.

Cook, Johann. "Contrasting as a Translation Technique in the LXX of Proverbs." Pages 403–414 in *The Quest for Context and Meaning. Studies in Biblical Intertextuality in Honor of James A. Sanders*. Edited by Craig Evans and Shemaryahu Talmon. Leiden: Brill, 1997.

Cook, Johann. "Exegesis in the Septuagint." *JNSL* 30.1 (2004): 1–19.

Cook, Johann. "Exegesis in the Septuagint of Proverbs." Pages 187–198 in Stimulation from Leiden. Collected Communications to the XVIIIth Congress of the International Organisation for the Study of the Old Testament, Leiden 2004. Edited by Hermann M. Niemann and Matthias Augustin. BEATAJ 54. Peter Lang: Frankfurt am Main, 2006.

Cook, Johann. "Following the Septuagint Translators." *JNSL* 22.2 (1996): 181–190.

Cook, Johann. "Hellenistic Influence in the Septuagint Book of Proverbs." Pages 341–353 in *VII Congress of the International Organization for Septuagint and Cognate Studies. Leuven, 1989*. Edited by Claude E. Cox. SBLSCS 31. Atlanta, GA: Scholars Press.

Cook, Johann. "Ideology and Translation Technique. Two Sides of the Same Coin?" Pages 195–210 in *Helsinki Perspectives on the Translation Technique of the Septuagint*. Edited by Raija Sollamo and Seppo Sipilä. Helsinki: Finnish Exegetical Society; Göttingen: Vandenhoeck & Ruprecht, 2001.

Cook, Johann. "Interpreting the Septuagint." Pages 1–22 in *Congress Volume Stellenbosch 2016*. Edited by Louis C. Jonker, Gideon R. Kotzé and Christl M. Maier. VTS 177. Leiden – Boston, MA: Brill, 2017.

Cook, Johann. "Intertextual Relationships Between the Septuagint of Psalms and Proverbs." Pages 218–228 in *The Old Greek Psalter. Studies in Honour of Albert Pietersma*. Edited by Robert V. J. Hiebert, Claude E. Cox and Peter J. Gentry. JSOTSS 332. Sheffield: Sheffield Academic Press, 2001.

Cook, Johann. "'ishah zarah (Proverbs 1-9 Septuagint): A Metaphor for Foreign Wisdom?" *ZAW* 106.3 (1994): 458–476.

Cook, Johann. "Lexical Issues Septuagint of Proverbs." *JNSL* 26.2 (2000): 163– 173.

Cook, Johann. "Man Before God." Pages 301–335 in *Die Theologie der Septuaginta / The Theology of the Septuagint*. Edited by Hans Ausloos and Bénédicte Lemmelijn. LXX.H 5. Gütersloh: Gütersloher Verlagshaus, 2020.

Cook, Johann. "Proverbs." Pages 621–647 in *A New English Translation of the Septuagint. And the Other Greek Translations Traditionally Included under That Title*. Edited by Albert Pietersma and Benjamin G. Wright. New York, NY — Oxford: Oxford University Press, 2007.

Cook, Johann. "Septuagint Proverbs and Canonization." Pages 79–91 in Canonization & Decanonization. Papers Presented to the International Conference of the Leiden Institute for the Study of Religions (LISOR) Held at Leiden 9-10 January 1997. Edited by Arie van der Kooij and Karel van der Toorn. Leiden: Brill, 1998.

Cook, Johann. "Textual Problems in the Septuagint of Proverbs." *JNSL* 26.1 (2000): 163–173.

Cook, Johann. "The Dating of Septuagint Proverbs." *ETL* 69.4 (1993): 383–399.

Cook, Johann. "The Greek of Proverbs. Evidence of a Recensionally Deviating Hebrew Text?" Pages 605–618 in *Emanuel. Studies in Hebrew Bible, Septuagint, and Dead Sea Scrolls in*

Honor of Emanuel Tov. Edited by Shalom M. Paul, Robert A. Kraft, Lawrence R. Schiffman and Weston W. Fields. Leiden – Boston: Brill, 2003.

Cook, Johann. "The Hexaplaric Text, Double Translation and Other Textual Phenomena in the Septuagint (Proverbs)." *JNSL* 22.2 (1996): 129–140.

Cook, Johann. "The Ideology of Septuagint Proverbs." Pages 463–479 in B*X Congress of the International Organization for Septuagint and Cognate Studies. Oslo, 1998.* Edited Bernard A. Taylor. SBLSCS 51. Atlanta, GA: Society of Biblical Literature, 2001.

Cook, Johann. "The Law in the Septuagint Proverbs." *JNSL* 23.1 (1997): 211–223.

Cook, Johann. "The Law of Moses in Septuagint Proverbs." *VT* 49.4 (1999): 448– 461.

Cook, Johann. "Theological/Ideological Tendenz in the Septuagint. LXX Proverbs a Case Study." Pages 65–79 in *Interpreting Translation. Studies on the LXX and Ezekiel in Honour of Johan Lust.* Edited by Florentino García Martínez and Marc Vervenne. BETL 192. Leuven: University Press – Peeters, 2005.

Cook, Johann. "The Relationship Between the LXX Versions of Proverbs and Job." Pages 145–155 in *Text-Critical and Hermeneutical Studies in the Septuagint.* Edited by Johann Cook and Hermann-Josef Stipp. VTS 157. Leiden – Boston, MA: Brill, 2012.

Cook, Johann. "The Relationship Between the Wisdom of Jesus Ben Sira and the Septuagint Version of Proverbs." Pages 11–26 in Construction, Coherence and Connotations: Studies on the Septuagint, Apocryphal and Cognate Literature. Papers Presented at the Association for the Study of the Septuagint in South Africa International Conference at the Faculty of Theology, North-West University, Potchefstroom, South Africa (28-30 August 2015). Edited by Pierre J. Jordaan and Nicholas P. L. Allen. DCLS 34. Berlin – Boston, MA: De Gruyter, 2016.

Cook, Johann. "The Relevance of Exegetical Commentaries on the Septuagint. LXX Proverbs 1:1-7 as an Example." *OTE* 23.1 (2010): 28–43.

Cook, Johann. "The Septuagint as Contextual Bible Translation. Alexandria or Jerusalem as Context for Proverbs?" *JNSL* 19 (1993): 25–39.

Cook, Johann. The Septuagint of Proverbs. Jewish and/or Hellenistic Proverbs? Concerning the Hellenistic Colouring of LXX Proverbs. SVT 69. Leiden – New York – Köln: Brill, 1997.

Cook, Johann. "The Septuagint Proverbs as a Jewish-Hellenistic Document." Pages 349–365 in *VIII Congress of the International Organization for Septuagint and Cognate Studies.* Edited by Leonard J. Greenspoon and Olivier Munnich. SBLSCS 41. Atlanta, GA: Scholars Press, 1995.

Cook, Johann. "The Text-Critical Value of the Septuagint of Proverbs." Pages 409–419 in *Seeking Out the Wisdom of the Ancients. Essays in Honor of Michael V. Fox on the Occasion of His Sixty-Fifth Birthday.* Edited by Ronald L. Troxel, Kelvin G. Friebel and Dennis R. Magary. Winona Lake, IN: Eisenbrauns, 2005.

Cook, Johann. "The Theory and Practice of Textual Criticism. Reconstructing the Old Greek of Proverbs 8." *OTE* 17.4 (2004):531–543.

Cook, Johann. "The Translator of the Septuagint of Proverbs. Is His Style the Result of Platonic and/or Stoic Influence?" Pages 559–571 in *Die Septuaginta. Texte, Kontexte, Lebenswelten. Internationale Fachtagung veranstaltet von Septuaginta Deutsch (LXX.D), Wuppertal 20.-23. Juli 2006.* Edited by Martin Karrer, Wolfgang Kraus and Martin Meiser. WUNT 219. Tübingen: Mohr Siebeck, 2008.

Cook, Johann. "The Translator(s) of the Septuagint of Proverbs." *TC: A Journal of Biblical Textual Criticism* 7 (2002): http://rosetta.reltech.org/TC/v07/Cook2002.html.

Cook, Johann. "Towards a Computerised Exegetical Commentary of the Septuagint Version of Proverbs." Pages 421–433 in Computer and Bible. The Stellenbosch AIBI-6 Conference: Proceedings of the Association Internationale Bible et Informatique 'From Alpha to Byte', University of Stellenbosch 17-21 July, 2002. Edited by Johann Cook. Leiden: Brill, 2002.

Cook, Johann. "Towards a Formulation of a Theology of the Septuagint." Pages 621–640 in *Congress Volume Ljubljana 2007*. Edited by André Lemaire. VTS 133. Leiden – Boston, MA: Brill, 2010.

Cook, Johann. "Unit Delimitation in the Book of Proverbs. In the Light of the Septuagint of Proverbs." Pages 46–65 in *Studies in Scriptural Unit Division*. Edited by Marjo Korpel and Josef M. Oesch. Pericope 3. Assen: Royal Van Gorcum, 2002.

Cook, Johann. "Were the LXX Versions of Proverbs and Job Translated by the Same Person?" *HS* 51 (2010): 129–156.

Cook, Johann and Arie van der Kooij. Law, Prophets, and Wisdom. On the Provenance of Translators and their Books in the Septuagint Version. CBET 68. Leuven: Peeters, 2012.

Cox, Claude E. "Does a Shorter Hebrew Parent Text Underlie Old Greek Job." Pages 451–462 in *In the Footsteps of Sherlock Holmes. Studies in the Biblical Text in Honour of Anneli Aejmelaeus*. Edited by Timothy M. Law, Krsitin De Troyer and Marketta Liljeström. CBET 72. Leuven – Paris – Walpole, MA: Peeters, 2014.

Cox, Claude E. *Iob*. SBLCS (forthcoming).

Cox, Claude E. "Iob." Pages 667–696 in *A New English Translation of the Septuagint. And the Other Greek Translations Traditionally Included under That Title*. Edited by Albert Pietersma and Benjamin G. Wright. New York, NY – Oxford: Oxford University Press, 2007.

Cox, Claude E. "Job." Pages 385–400 in *The T&T Clark Companion to the Septuagint*. Edited by James K. Aitken. London – New York, NY: Bloomsbury T&T Clark, 2015.

Cox, Claude E.. "Some Things Biblical Scholars Should Know about the Septuagint." *ResQ* 56 (2014): 85–98.

Cox, Claude E. "The Historical, Social & Literary Context of Old Greek Job." Pages 105–116 in *XII Congress of the International Organisation for Septuagint and Cognate Studies, Leiden, 2004*. Edited by Melvin K. H. Peters. SBLSCS 54. Atlanta, GA: Society of Biblical Literature, 2006.

Croy, N. Clayton. *3 Maccabees*. SCS. Leiden: Brill, 2006.

Cuppi, Lorenzo. "Concerning the Origin of the Addition Found in Prov^{LXX} 1:7." Pages 93–103 in *XIV Congress of the IOSCS, Helsinki, 2010*. Edited by Melvin K. H. Peters. SBLSCS 59. Atlanta, GA: SBL Press, 2013.

Cuppi, Lorenzo. "Long Doublets in the Septuagint of the Book of Proverbs: With a History of the Research on the Greek Translations." PhD diss. University of Durham, 2012.

Dafni, Evangelia."Theologie der Sprache der Septuaginta." *TZ* 58 (2002): 315–328.

Debel, Hans. "Rewritten Bible, Variant Literary Editions and OriginalText(s). Exploring the Implications of a Pluriform Outlook on the Scriptural Tradition." Pages 65–91 in *Changes in Scripture: Rewriting and Interpreting Authoritative Traditions in the Second Temple Period*. Edited by Hanne von Weissenberg, Marko Martilla and Juha Pakkala. BZAW 419. Berlin – New York, NY: Walter de Gruyter, 2011.

de Joode, Johan. Metaphorical Landscapes and the Theology of the Book of Job. An Analysis of Job's Spatial Metaphors. VTS 179. Leiden – Boston, MA: Brill, 2018.

de Lagarde, Paul. Anmerkungen zur Griechischen Übersetzung der Proverbien/ Leipzig: F. A. Brockhaus, 1863.

Delitzsch, Frank J. *Biblical Commentary on the Proverbs of Solomon. Vol. II.* Translated by Matthew George. Easton – Edinburgh: T&T Clark, 1875.

Derrenbacker, Robert A. *Ancient Compositional Practices and the Synoptic Problem.* BETL 186. Leuven — Paris — Dudley, MA: Peeters, 2005.

de Waard, Jan. "Difference in Vorlage or Lexical Ignorance: a Dilemma in the Old Greek of Proverbs." *JSJ* 38.1 (2007): 1–8.

de Waard, Jan. "Indices phonétiques hébreux dans et derrière le grec de la Septante de Proverbs." Pages 105–117 in *L'apport de la Septante aux études sur l'Antiquité.* Edited by Jan Joosten and Philippe Le Moigne. Lectio Divina. Paris: Les Éditions du Cerf, 2005.

de Waard, Jan. "Lexical Ignorance and the Ancient Versions of Proverbs." Pages 261–268 in *Sôfer Mahîr. Essays in Honour of Adrian Schenker Offered by the Editors of Biblia Hebraica Quinta.* Edited by Yohanan A. P. Goldman, Arie van der Kooij and Richard D. Weis. SVT 110. Leiden – Boston, MA: Brill, 2006.

de Waard, Jan. "Metathesis as a Translation Technique?" Pages 249–260 in *Traducere navem: Festschrift für Katharina Reiß zum 70. Geburtstag.* Edited by Justa Holz-Mänttäri and Christiane Nord. Studia translatologica 3. Tampere: Finland, University of Tampere, 1993.

de Waard, Jan. "Some Unusual Translation Techniques Employed by the Greek Translator(s) of Proverbs." Pages 185–193 in *Helsinki Perspectives. On the Translation Technique of the Septuagint.* Edited by Raija Sollamo and Seppo Sipilä. PFES 82. Göttingen: Vandenhoeck & Ruprecht, 2001.

de Waard, Jan. "The Septuagint of Proverbs as a Translational Model?" *BT* 50.3 (1999): 304–314.

Deysel, Lesley C. F. "Animal Names and Categorisation in the Hebrew Bible. A Textual and Cognitive Approach." Phd. diss., University of Pretoria, 2017.

d'Hamonville, David-Marc. *Les Proverbes.* BA 17. Paris: Les Éditions du Cerf, 2000.

Dhont, Marieke. "Double Translations in Old Greek Job." Pages 475–490. in Die Septuaginta – Orte und Intentionen. 5. Internationale Fachtagung veranstaltet von Septuaginta Deutsch (LXX.D), Wuppertal 24.–27. Juli 2014. Edited by Siegfried Kreuzer et al. WUNT 361. Tübingen: Mohr Siebeck, 2016.

Dhont, Marieke. *The Language and Style of Old Greek Job in Context.* PhD diss., UCLouvain–KU Leuven, 2016.

Dhont, Marieke. *Style and Context of Old Greek Job.* SJSJ 183. Leiden – Boston: MA, Brill, 2017.

Dhorme, Edouard. *A Commentary on the Book of Job.* London: Thomas Nelson & Sons, 1967.

Dick, Michael B. "The Ethics of the Old Greek Book of Proverbs." Pages 20–50 in *The Studia Philonica Annual. Studies in Hellenistic Judaism Volume II 1990.* Edited by David T. Runia. Brown Judaic Studies 226. Atlanta, GA: Scholars Press, 1991.

Dorival, Gilles. "L'Achèvement de la Septante dans le Judaïsme. De la faveur au rejet." Pages 83–125 in *La bible grecque des Septante. Du judaïsme hellénistique au christianisme ancient.* Edited by Margueritte Harl, Gilles Dorival and Olivier Munnich. ICA. Paris: Cerf, 1988.

Doughty, Charles M. *Travels in Arabia Deserta.* London: Jonathan Cape – The Medici Society Limited, 1924.

Driver, Samuel R. and George B. Grey. A Critical and Exegetical Commentary on the Book of Job: Together With a New Translation. ICC. Edinburgh: T&T Clark, 1964.

Duhm, Bernhard. *Das Buch Hiob.* KHC 16. Freiburg – Leipzig – Tübingen: Mohr-Siebeck, 1897.

Ehrlich, Arnold B. Randglossen zur hebräischen Bibel. Textkritisches, sprachliches und sachliches. Sechter Band: Psalmen, Spruche und Hiob. Hildesheim: Georg Olms Verlagbuchhandlung, 1968.

Eve, Eric C. S., "The Synoptic Problem Without Q?" Pages 551–570 in *New studies in the Synoptic Problem. Oxford conference, April 2008. Essays in Honour of Christopher M. Tuckett.* Edited by Paul Foster et al. BETL 239. Leuven – Paris – Walpole, MA: Peeters, 2011.

Eynikel, Erik and Katrin Hauspie "The Use of δράκων in the Septuagint." Pages 126–135 in *Biblical Greek Language and Lexicography.* Edited by Bernard A. Taylor, John A. L. Lee, Peter R. Burton and Richard E. Whitake. Grand Rapids, MI: Eerdmans, 2004.

Feldman, Louis H. Jew and Gentile in the Ancient World. Attitudes and Interactions from Alexander to Justinian. Princeton: Princeton University Press, 1993.

Feldman, Louis H. *Judaism and Hellenism Reconsidered.* SJSJ 107. Leiden – Boston: Brill, 2006.

Forti, Tova L.. *Animal Imagery in the Book of Proverbs.* VTS 118. Leiden – Boston: Brill, 2008.

Forti, Tova L. "Animal Images in the Book of Proverbs." *Bib* 77.1 (1996): 48–63.

Forti, Tova L. "If You Go Down to the Woods Today: B(e)aring the Text of Proverbs MT and LXX." Pages 103–112 in *From Author to Copyist: Essays on the Composition, Redaction, and Transmission of the Hebrew Bible in Honor of Zipi Talshir.* Edited by Cana Werman. Winona Lake, IN: Eisenbrauns, 2015.

Fritsch, Charles T. "The Treatment of the Hexaplaric Signs in the Syro-Hexaplar of Proverbs." *JBL* 72.3 (1953): 169–181.

Gammie, John G. "The Septuagint of Job. Its Poetic Style and Relationship to the Septuagint of Proverbs." *CBQ* 49.1 (1987): 14–31.

Gard, Donald H. "The Concept of Job's Character According to the Greek Translator of the Hebrew Text." *JBL* 72.3 (1953): 182–186.

Gard, Donald H. *The Exegetical Method of the Greek Translator of the Book of Job.* JBLMS VIII. Philadelphia, PN: SBL, 1952 (repr. 1967).

Gehman, Henry S.. "Theological Approach of the Greek Translator of Job 1–15." *JBL* 68.3 (1949): 231–240.

Gentry, Peter J. *The Asterisked Materials in the Greek Job.* SBLSCS 38. Atlanta, GA: Scholars Press, 1995.

Gerhardt, Mia I. "The Ant-lion. Nature Study and The Interpretation of a Biblical Text, From The Physiologus to Albert the Great." *Vivarium* 3 (1965): 1–23.

Gerleman, Gillis. *Studies in the Septuagint. I. The Book of Job.* LUA 43.2. Lund: Gleerup, 1946.

Gerleman, Gillis. Studies in the Septuagint. III. The Book of Proverbs. LUA 52.3. Lund: Gleerup, 1956.

Giese, Ronald L. "Strength Through Wisdom and the Bee in LXX Prov 6,8^{a-c}." *Bib* 73.3 (1992): 404–411.

Gorea, Maria. Job repensé ou trahi? Omissions et raccourcis de la Septante. EB.NS 56. Paris: Gabalda, 2007.

Graves, Robert and Raphael Patai. *Hebrew Myths. The Book of Genesis.* Garden City, NY: Doubleday, 1964.

Greenspahn, Frederick E. Hapax Legomena in Biblical Hebrew. A Study of the Phenomenon and Its Treatment Since Antiquity with Special Reference to Verbal Forms. SBLDS 74. Chico, CA: Scholars Press, 1984.

Grignac, Francis T. *A Grammar of the Greek Papyri of the Roman and Byzantine Periods. Volume I: Phonology.* Testi e documenti per lo studio dell'antichità, 55. Milan: Instituto Editoriale Cisalpino – La Goliardica, 1976.

Hatton, Peter T. H. Contradiction in the Book of Proverbs. The Deep Waters of Counsel. Aldershot: Ashgate, 2008.

Healey, John F. The Targum of Proverbs. Introduction, Apparatus, and Notes. ArBib 15. Edinburgh, T&T Clark, 1991.

Heater, Homer. A Septuagint Translation Technique in the Book of Job. CBQMS 11. Washington, DC: The Catholic Biblical Association of America, 1982.

Hess, Johann J.. "Beduinisches zum Alten und Neuen Testament." ZAW 35 (1915): 120–36.

Hiebert, Robert J. V. "Genesis." Pages 1–42 in A New English Translation of the Septuagint. And the Other Greek Translations Traditionally Included under That Title. Edited by Albert Pietersma and Benjamin G. Wright. New York, NY — Oxford: Oxford University Press, 2007.

Hilzheimer, Max. Die Wildrinder im alten Mesopotamien. MOA 2.2. Leipzig: Verlag von Eduard Pfeifer, 1926.

Hoffmann, Johann G. E. Hiob. Kiel: C. F. Haeseler, 1891.

Hubler, Noel J. "Iezekiel." Pages 946–985 in A New English Translation of the Septuagint. And the Other Greek Translations Traditionally Included under That Title. Edited by Albert Pietersma and Benjamin G. Wright. New York, NY — Oxford: Oxford University Press, 2007.

Jäger, Johann G. Observationes in Proverbiorum Salomonis versionem Alexandrinam. Meldorpi et Lipsiae: Apud Reinhold Iacob Boie, 1788.

Jones, Scott J. "Lions, Serpents, and Lion-Serpents in Job 28:8 and Beyond." JBL 130.4 (2011): 663–686.

Joosten, Jan. "Elaborate Similes – Hebrew and Greek A Study in Septuagint Translation Technique." Bib 77.2 (1996): 227–236.

Joosten, Jan. "The Relation of the Septuagint of Proverbs to the Septuagint of Psalms." Pages 99–107 in Septuagint, Sages and Scripture. Studies in Honour of Johann Cook. Edited by Randall X. Gauthier, Gideon Kotzé and Gert Steyn. VTS 172. Leiden, Brill: 2016.

Kabergs, Valérie. "Creativiteit in het spel? De Griekse weergave van expliciet Hebreeuws woordspel op basis van eigennamen in Pentateuch en Twaalf Profeten." PhD diss., KU Leuven, 2014.

Kabergs, Valérie and Hans Ausloos. "Paronomasia or Wordplay? A Babylonian Confusion. Towards A Definition of Hebrew Wordplay." Bib 93.1 (2012): 1–20.

Kaestli, Jean-Daniel, "La formation et la structure du canon biblique. Que peut apporter l'étude de la septante." in The Canon of Scripture in Jewish and Christian Tradition. Le Canon des Écritures dans les traditions juive et chrétienne. Edited by Philip S. Alexander and Jean-Daniel Kaestli. PIRSB 4. Lausanne : Les Éditions du Zèbre, 2007.

Kaupel, Johann H. "'Sirenen' in der Septuaginta." BZ 23.2 (1935): 158–165.

Kraft, Robert A. and Emanuel Tov. "Computer-Assisted Tools for Septuagint Studies." BIOSCS 14 (1981): 22–40.

Kuhn, Gottfried. Beiträge zur Erklärung des Salomonischen Spruchbuches. BWANT III.16. Stuttgart: W. Kohlhammer Verlag, 1931.

Kühn, Karl G. "De musculorum dissectione ad tirones." Pages 925–1026 in Claudii Galeni Opera Omnia. Edited by Karl G. Kühn. Cambridge: Cambridge University Press.

Kwon, Jiseong J. "Rewritten Theology in the Greek Book of Job." Bib 100.3 (2019): 339–352.

Lee, John A. L. A Lexical Study of the Septuagint Version of the Pentateuch. SBLSCS 14. Chico, CA: Scholars Press, 1983.

Lemmelijn, Bénédicte. A Plague of Texts? A Text-Critical Study of the So-Called 'Plague Narrative' in Exodus 7,14-11,10. OTS 56. Leiden — Boston, Brill: 2009.

Lemmelijn, Bénédicte. "Flora in Cantico Canticorum. Towards a More Precise Characterisation of Translation Technique in the LXX of Song of Songs." Pages 27–51 in *Scripture in Transition. Essays on Septuagint, Hebrew Bible, and Dead Sea Scrolls in Honour of Raija Sollamo*. Edited by in Ansi Voitila and Jutta Jokiranta. SJSJ 126. Leiden: Brill, 2008.

Lemmelijn, Bénédicte. "Textual Criticism." Pages 709–721 in *Oxford Handbook of the Septuagint*. Edited by Alison G. Salvesen and Timothy M. Law. Oxford: Oxford University Press, 2021.

Lemmelijn, Bénédicte. "The Greek Rendering of Hebrew Hapax Legomena in LXX Proverbs and Job. A Clue to the Question of a Single Translator?" Pages 133–150 in *In the Footsteps of Sherlock Holmes. Studies in the Biblical Text in Honour of Anneli Aejmelaeus*. Edited by Timothy M. Law, Kristin De Troyer and Marketta Liljeström. CBET 72. Leuven — Paris — Walpole, MA: Peeters, 2014.

Lemmelijn, Bénédicte. "The Wisdom of Life as Way of Life. The Wisdom of Jesus Sirach as a Case in Point." *OTE* 27.2 (2014): 444–471.

Lemmelijn, Bénédicte. "Two Methodological Trails in Recent Studies on the Translation Technique of the Septuagint." Pages 43–63 in *Helsinki Perspectives. On the Translation Technique of the Septuagint*. Edited by Raija Sollamo and Seppo Sipilä. PFES 82. Göttingen: Vandenhoeck & Ruprecht, 2001.

Lemmelijn, Bénédicte and Hans Ausloos. "Septuagint Studies in Louvain." Pages 144–158 in The Present State of Old testament Studies in the Low Countries. A Collection of Old Testament Studies Published on the Occasion of the Seventy-Fifth Anniversary of the Oudtestamentisch Werkgezelschap. Edited by Klaas Spronk. OTS 69. Leiden: Brill, 2016.

Likeng, Paul B. "Animal Imagery in Proverbs." *BT* 49.2 (1998): 225–232.

Löw, Immanuel. Die Flora der Juden IV. Zusammenfassung – Nachträge – Berichtigungen – Indizes – Abkürzungen. Hildesheim: Georg Olsm Verlagsbuchhandlung, 1967.

Lust, Johan. "Syntax and Translation Greek." *ETL* 77.4 (2001): 395–401.

Mangan, Céline. *The Targum of Job*. ArBib 15. Edinburgh: T&T Clark, 1991.

Mangin, Dominique. "Le texte court de la version grecque du livre de Job et la double interprétation du personnage jusqu'au IIe siècle. Tome I." PhD diss., Université d'Aix-Marseille I, 2005.

Marquis, Galen. "Consistency of Lexical Equivalents as a Criterion for the Evaluation of Translation Technique as Exemplified in the LXX of Ezekiel." Pages 405–424 in *VI Congress of the International Organization for Septuagint and Cognate Studies. Jerusalem, 1986*. Edited by Claude E. Cox. SBLSCS 23. Atlanta, G:, Scholars Press, 1987, 405- 424.

Marquis, Galen. "Word Order as a Criterion for the Evaluation of Translation Technique in the LXX and the Evaluation of Word-order Variants as Exemplified in LXX Ezekiel." *Textus* 13 (1986): 59–84.

McKane, William. *Proverbs. A New Approach*. OTL. Philadelphia, PA: Westminster Press, 1970.

Meade, John D. *A Critical Edition of the Hexaplaric Fragments of Job 22-42*. Origen's Hexapla: A Critical Edition of the Extant Fragments. Leuven: Peeters, 2020.

Meecham, Henry G. The Letter of Aristeas. A Linguistic Study with Special Reference to the Greek Bible. Manchester: Manchester University Press, 1935.

Modrzejewski, Joseph M. *The Jews of Egypt. From Ramses II to Emperor Hadrian*. Princeton: Princeton University Press, 1995.

Moldenke, Harold N. and Alma L. Moldenke. *Plants of the Bible*. Waltham, MA: Chronica Botanica Company, 1952.

Mowinckel, Sigmund. "שׁחל." Pages 95–103 in *Hebrew and Semitic Studies Presented to God-frey Rolles Driver. In Celebration of His Seventieth Birthday, 20 august 1962*. Edited by David W. Thomas and William D. McHardy. Oxford: Clarendon Press, 1963.

Muraoka, Takamitsu. "Hebrew Hapax Legomena and Septuagint Lexicography." Pages 205–222 in *VII Congress of the International Organization for Septuagint and Cognate Studies. Leuven, 1989*. Edited by Claude E. Cox. SBLSCS 31. Atlanta, GA: Scholars Press, 1991, 205-222.

Naudé, Jacobus A. and Cynthia L. Miller-Naudé. "Editorial Theory and the Range of Translations for 'Cedars of Lebanon' in the Septuagint." *HTS Teologiese Studies/Theological Studies* 74.3 (2018): 1–12.

Naudé, Jacobus A. and Cynthia L. Miller-Naudé. "Lexicography and the Translation of 'Cedars of Lebanon' in the Septuagint." *HTS Teologiese Studies/Theological Studies* 74.3 (2018): 1–13.

Nowack, Wilhelm G. H. *Sprüche, Prediger und Hoheslied überzetst und erklärt*. HKAT II.3. Göttingen: Vandenhoeck & Ruprecht, 1989.

Olivero, Vladimir. "A Genealogy of Lust. The Use of Hesiod's Theogony in the LXX Translation of the Book of Proverbs." *Textus* 30 (2021): 28–42.

Olley, John W. Ezekiel. A Commentary Based on Iezekiël in Codex Vaticanus. SCS. Leiden – Boston, MA: Brill, 2009.

Olofsson, Staffan. "Consistency as a Translation Technique." Pages 50–66 in *Translation Technique and Theological Exegesis. Collected Essays on the Septuagint Version*. Edited by Staffan Olofsson. CBOTS 57. Winona Lake, IN: Eisenbrauns, 2009, 50-66.

Olofsson, Staffan. The LXX Version. A Guide to the Translation Technique of the Septuagint. CBOTS 30. Stockholm: Almqvist och Wiksell, 1990.

Orlinsky, Harry M. "Studies in the Septuagint of the Book of Job: Chapter III (Continued)." *HUCA* 32 (1961): 239–268.

Orlinsky, Harry M.. "Studies in the Septuagint of the Book of Job: Chapter V. The Hebrew Vorlage of the Septuagint of Job: The Text and the Script." *HUCA* 35 (1964): 57–78.

Papoutsakis, Manolis. "Ostriches into Sirens. Towards an Understanding of a Septuagint Crux." *JJS* 55.1 (2004): 25–36.

Perkins, Larry J. "Exodus." Pages 43–81 in *A New English Translation of the Septuagint. And the Other Greek Translations Traditionally Included under That Title*. Edited by Albert Pietersma and Benjamin G. Wright. New York, NY — Oxford: Oxford University Press, 2007.

Peters, Melvin K. H. "Deuteronomion." Pages 141–173 in *A New English Translation of the Septuagint. And the Other Greek Translations Traditionally Included under That Title*. Edited by Albert Pietersma and Benjamin G. Wright. New York, NY — Oxford: Oxford University Press, 2007.

Pietersma, Albert. "Psalms (and the Prayer of Manasses)." Pages 542–620 in *A New English Translation of the Septuagint. And the Other Greek Translations Traditionally Included under That Title*. Edited by Albert Pietersma and Benjamin G. Wright. New York, NY — Oxford: Oxford University Press, 2007.

Pietersma, Albert and Marc Saunders. "Ieremias." Pages 876–924 620 in *A New English Translation of the Septuagint. And the Other Greek Translations Traditionally Included under That Title*. Edited by Albert Pietersma and Benjamin G. Wright. New York, NY — Oxford: Oxford University Press, 2007.

Pope, Marvin H. *Song of Songs. An New Translation with Introduction and Commentary*. AB 7c. New York, NY — London — Toronto — Sydney — Auckland: Doubleday, 1977.

Puech, Émile. "Le targum de Job de la grotte 4: 4Q157 = 4QtgJob." *RevQ* 32.1 (2020): 135–141.

Reed, Annette Y. "Job as Jobab: The Interpretation of Job in LXX Job 42:17b-e." *JBL* 120.1 (2001): 31–55.

Renaud, Silly. *Les grands mystères de la sagesse. Proverbes de Salomon 8 & 9 dans la version des Septante*. Paris: Les Belles Lettres, 2020.

Riede, Peter. "'Ich bin ein Bruder der Schakale' (Hi 30,29). Tiere als Exponenten der gegenmenschlichen Welt in der Bildsprache der Hiobdialoge." Pages 120–132 in *Im Spiegel der Tiere. Studien zum Verhältnis von Mensch und Tier im alten Israel*. Edited by Peter Riede. OBO 187. Freiburg – Göttingen: Universitätsverlag Freiburg Schweiz – Vandenhoeck & Ruprecht, 2002.

Rösel, Martin. "The Reading and Translation of the Divine Name in the Masoretic Tradition and the Greek Pentateuch – with an Appendix: Frank Shaw's Book on IAΩ." Pages 291–315 in *Tradition and Innovation. English and German Studies on the Septuagint*. Edited by Martin Rösel. SBLSCS 70. Atlanta, GA: SBL 2018.

Rösel, Martin. "Towards a 'Theology of the Septuagint'." Pages 239–252 in *Septuagint Research. Issues and Challenges in the Study of the Greek Jewish Scriptures*. Edited by Wolfgang Kraus and R. Glenn Wooden. SBLSCS 53. Atlanta, GA: SBL, 2006. (= Rösel, Martin, "Towards a 'Theology of the Septuagint'." Pages 253–272 in *Tradition and Innovation. English and German Studies on the Septuagint*. Edited by Martin Rösel. SBLSCS 70. Atlanta, GA: SBL 2018).

Satterthwaite, Philip E. "Judges." Pages 195–238 in *A New English Translation of the Septuagint. And the Other Greek Translations Traditionally Included under That Title*. Edited by Albert Pietersma and Benjamin G. Wright. New York, NY — Oxford: Oxford University Press, 2007.

Schaper, Joachim L. W. "The Unicorn in the Messianic Imagery in the Greek Bible." *JTS* 45.1 (1994): 117–136.

Schechter, Solomon. "A Further Fragment of Ben Sira. Prefatory Note." *JQR* 12.3 (1900): 456–465.

Schwienhorst-Schönberger, Ludwig. "Weisheit und das Leben vor Gott." Pages 337–397 in *Die Theologie der Septuaginta / The Theology of the Septuagint*. Edited by Hans Ausloos and Bénédicte Lemmelijn. LXX.H 5. Gütersloh: Gütersloher Verlagshaus, 2020.

Schultens, Albert. *Liber Jobi: cum nova versione ad Hebraeum fontem et commentario perpetuo*. Lugduni Batavorum: apud J. Lusac, 1737.

Scoralick, Ruth. "Salomos griechische Gewänder. Beobachtungen zur Septuagintafassung des Sprichwörterbuches." in *Rettendes Wissen. Studien zum Fortgang weisheitlichen Denkens im Frühjudentum und im frühen Christentum*. Edited by Karl Löning and Martin Faßnacht. AOAT 300. Münster: Ugarit-Verlag, 2002, 43-75.

Seow, Choon-Leong. *Job 1-21. Interpretation and Commentary*. Illuminations. Grand Rapids, MI – Cambridge: Eerdmans, 2013.

Seow, Choon-Leong. "Putative Hapax Legomena in the Book of Job." Pages 145–182 in Studien zur hebräischen Bibel und ihrer Nachgeschichte. Beiträge der 32. Internationalen Ökumenischen Konferenz der Hebräischlehrenden, Frankfurt a.m. 2009. Edited by Johannes F. Diehl and Markus Witte. KUSATU 12.13. Kamen: Hartmut Spenner, 2011.

Snaith, Norman H. "The Meaning of שְׂעִירִים." *VT* 25.1 (1975): 115–118.

Soisalon-Soininen, Ilmari. "Der Gebrauch des genetivus absolutus in der Septuaginta." Pages 175–180 in *Studien zur Septuaginta-Syntax*. Edited by Ilmari Soisalon-Soininen, Anneli

Aemelaeus and Raija Sollamo. AASF Series B 237. Helsinki: Suomalainen Tiedeakatemia, 1987.

Soisalon-Soininen, Ilmari. "Die Auslassung des Possessivpronomens im griechischen Pentateuch." Pages 86–103 in *Studien zur Septuaginta-Syntax*. Edited by Ilmari Soisalon-Soininen, Anneli Aemelaeus and Raija Sollamo. AASF Series B 237. Helsinki: Suomalainen Tiedeakatemia, 1987.

Soisalon-Soininen, Ilmari. *Die Infinitive in der Septuaginta*. AASF Series B 132. Helsinki: Suomalainen Tiedeakatemia, 1965.

Soisalon-Soininen, Ilmari. "Einleitung." Pages 11–18 in *Studien zur Septuaginta-Syntax*. Edited by Ilmari Soisalon-Soininen, Anneli Aemelaeus and Raija Sollamo. AASF Series B 237. Helsinki: Suomalainen Tiedeakatemia, 1987.

Soisalon-Soininen, Ilmari. "Methodologische Fragen der Erforschung der Septuaginta-Syntax." Pages 40–52 in *Studien zur Septuaginta-Syntax*. Edited by Ilmari Soisalon-Soininen, Anneli Aemelaeus and Raija Sollamo. AASF Series B 237. Helsinki: Suomalainen Tiedeakatemia, 1987.

Soisalon-Soininen, Ilmari. "Renderings of Hebrew Comparative Expressions with מן in the Greek Pentateuch." Pages 141–153 in *Studien zur Septuaginta-Syntax*. Edited by Ilmari Soisalon-Soininen, Anneli Aemelaeus and Raija Sollamo. AASF Series B 237. Helsinki: Suomalainen Tiedeakatemia, 1987.

Sollamo, Raija. "Pleonastic Use of the Pronoun in Connection with the Relative Pronoun in the LXX of Leviticus, Numbers and Deuteronomy." Pages 43–62 in *VIII Congress of the International Organization for Septuagint and Cognate Studies*. Edited by Leonard J. Greenspoon and Olivier Munnich. SBLSCS 41. Atlanta, GA: Scholars Press, 1995.

Sollamo, Raija. *Renderings of Hebrew Semiprepositions in the Septuagint*. AASFDHL 19. Helsinki: Suomalainen Tiedeakatemia, 1979.

Sollamo, Raija. *Repetition of the Possessive Pronouns in the Septuagint*. SCS 40. Atlanta, GA: Scholars Press, 1995.

Sollamo, Raija. "Some 'Improper' Prepositions, such as ἐνώπιον, ἐναντίον, ἔναντι etc., in the Septuagint and Early Koine Greek." *VT* 25.4 (1975): 773–782.

Sollamo, Raija. "The LXX Renderings of the Infinitive Absolute Used with a Paronymous Finite Verb in the Pentateuch." Pages 101–113 in *La Septuaginta en la Investigación Contemporánea (V Congreso de la IOSCS)*. Edited by Natalio Fernández Marcos. Textos y Estudios 'Cardinal Cisneros' 34. Madrid: Instituto "Arias Montano," 1985.

Sollamo, Raija. "The Study of Syntax and the Study of Translation Technique - What is the Difference?." Pages 32–41 in *Helsinki Perspectives on the Translation Technique of the Septuagint*. Edited by Raija Sollamo and Seppo Sipilä. Helsinki: Finnish Exegetical Society; Göttingen: Vandenhoeck & Ruprecht, 2001.

Strawn, Brent A. *What is Stronger than a Lion? Leonine Image and Metaphors in the Hebrew Bible and the Ancient Near East*. OBO 212. Fribourg – Göttingen: Academic Press Fribourg – Vandenhoeck & Ruprecht, 2005.

Swinn, S. Paul. "ἀγαπᾶν in the Septuagint." Pages 49–82 in *Melbourne Symposium on Septuagint Lexicography*. Edited by Takamitsu Muraoka. SBLSCS 28. Atlanta, GA: Scholars Press, 1990.

Talshir, Zipi. "Double Translations in the Septuagint." Pages 21–63 in *VI Congress of the International Organization for Septuagint and Cognate Studies. Jerusalem 1986*. Edited by Claude E. Cox. SBLSCS 23. Atlanta, GA: Scholars Press, 1987.

Tauberschmidt, Gerhard. Secondary Parallelism. A Study of Translation Technique in LXX Proverbs. AcBib 15. Leiden: Brill, 2004.

Taylor, Charles, Edward Wells and Augustin Calmet. Scripture Illustrated by Means of Natural Science, in Botany, in Geology, in Geography, Natural History, Natural Philosophy, Utensils, Domestic and Military, Habiliments, Manners and Customs. Charlestown: Samuel Etheridge Junior, 1814.

Tigchelaar, Eibert. "Spreuken." Pages 357–370 in *De Bijbel literair. Opbouw en gedachtegang van de bijbelse geschriften en hun onderlinge relaties*. Edited by Jan Fokkelman and Wim Weren. Zoetermeer: Meinema; Kapellen: Pelckmans, 2003.

Tov, Emanuel. "A Computerized Database for Septuagint Research." Pages 31–51 in *The Greek and Hebrew Bible. Collected Essays on the Septuagint*. Edited by Emanuel Tov. VTS 72. Leiden, Brill, 1999.

Tov, Emanuel. "A Textual-Exegetical Commentary on Three Chapters in the Septuagint." Pages 275–290 in *Scripture in Transition. Essays on Septuagint, Hebrew Bible, and Dead Sea Scrolls in Honour of Raija Sollamo*. Edited by in Ansi Voitila and Jutta Jokiranta. SJSJ 126. Leiden: Brill, 2008.

Tov, Emanuel. "Did the Septuagint Translators Always Understand Their Hebrew Text?." Pages 203–218 in *The Greek and Hebrew Bible. Collected Essays on the Septuagint*. Edited by Emanuel Tov. SVT 72. Leiden — Boston, MA — Köln: Brill, 1999.

Tov, Emanuel. "Loan-words, Homophony and Transliterations in the Septuagint." in *Bib* 60.2 (1979): 216–236 (= Tov, Emanuel. "Loan-words, Homophony and Transliterations in the Septuagint." Pages 165–182 in *The Greek and Hebrew Bible. Collected Essays on the Septuagint*. Edited by Emanuel Tov. VTS 72. Leiden, Brill, 1999).

Tov, Emanuel. "Recensional Differences Between the Masoretic Text and the Septuagint of Proverbs." Pages 43–56 in Of Scribes and Scrolls. Studies on the Hebrew Bible, Intertestamental Judaism, and Christian Origins Presented to John Strugnell on the Occasion of His Sixtieth Birthday. Edited by Harold W. Attridge, John J. Collins and Thomas H. Tobin. CTSRR 5. Lanham, MD: University Press of America, 1990.

Tov, Emanuel. *Textual Criticism of the Hebrew Bible*. Minneapolis, MN: Fortress Press; Assen, Royal Van Gorcum, 1992².

Tov, Emanuel. "The Accordance Search Program for the MT, LXX, and the CATSS Database." *BIOSCS* 30 (1997): 36–44.

Tov, Emanuel. "The CATSS Project. A Progress Report." Pages 157–163 in *VII Congress of the International Organization for Septuagint and Cognate Studies*. Edited by Claude E. Cox. SBLSCS 31. Atlanta, GA: Scholars Press, 1991.

Tov, Emanuel. "The Representation of the Causative Aspects of the Hiph'il in the LXX A Study in Translation Technique." *Bib* 63.3 (1982): 417–424.

Tov, Emanuel. The Text-Critical Use of the Septuagint in Biblical Research. Revised and Enlarged Second Edition. JBS 8. Jerusalem: Simor LTD., ²1997.

Tov, Emanuel. The Text-Critical Use of the Septuagint in Biblical Research. Third Edition, Completely Revised and Enlarged. Winona Lake, IN: Eisenbrauns, 2015.

Tov, Emanuel. "The Use of Computers in Biblical Research." Pages 228–246 in *Hebrew Bible, Greek Bible, and Qumran*. Edited by Emanuel Tov. TSAJ 121. Tübingen: Mohr Siebeck, 2008.

Tov, Emanuel and Benjamin G. Wright. "Computer-Assisted Study of the Criteria for Assessing the Literalness of Translation Units in the LXX." *Textus* 12 (1985): 149–187 (= Tov, Emanuel and Benjamin G. Wright. "Computer- Assisted Study of the Criteria for Assessing the Literalness of Translation Units in the LXX." Pages 219–237 in *The Greek and Hebrew Bible. Collected Essays on the Septuagint*. Edited by Emanuel Tov. VTS 72. Leiden: Brill, 1999).

Toy, Crawford H. A Critical and Exegetical Commentary on The Book of Proverbs. ICC. Edinburgh: T&T Clark, ²1904.

Treat, Jay C. "Song of Songs." Pages 657–666 in *A New English Translation of the Septuagint And the Other Greek Translations Traditionally Included Under That Title*. Edited by Albert Pietersma and Benjamin G. Wright. New York, NY — Oxford: Oxford University Press, 2007.

Trebolle Barrera, Julio. *The Jewish Bible and the Christian Bible. An Introduction to the History of the Bible*. Leiden — New York, NY — Köln: Brill; Grand Rapids, MI — Cambridge: Eerdmans, 1998.

Ueberschaer, Frank. "Weisheit." Pages 137–147 in *Die Theologie der Septuaginta / The Theology of the Septuagint*. Edited by Hans Ausloos and Bénédicte Lemmelijn. LXX.H 5. Gütersloh: Gütersloher Verlagshaus, 2020.

United Bible Societies and Committee on Translations. *Fauna and Flora of the Bible*. Help for Translators XI. London: United Bible Societies, 1972.

van der Kooij, Arie. "Servant or Slave? The Various Equivalents of Hebrew 'Ebed in the Old Greek of Isaiah." Pages 259–271 in Die Septuaginta – Themen, Manuskripte, Wirkungen, 7. Internationale Fachtagung veranstaltet von Septuaginta Deutsch (LXX.D), Wuppertal 19.–22. Juli 2018. Edited by Eberhard Bons et al. WUNT 444. Tübingen: Mohr Siebeck, 2020.

van der Kooij, Arie. "Servant or Slave. The Various Equivalents of Hebrew Ebed in the Septuagint of the Pentateuch." Pages 225–238 in *XIII Congress of the International Organization for Septuagint and Cognate Studies, Ljubljana, 2007*. Edited by Melvin K. H. Peters. SBLSCS 35. Atlanta, GA: SBL Press, 2008.

van der Louw, Theo A. W. Transformations in the Septuagint. Towards an Interaction of Septuagint Studies and Translation Studies. CBET 47. Leuven — Paris — Walpole, MA: Peeters, 2007.

van der Meer, Michael. "The Use and Non-Use of the Particle οὖν in the Septuagint." Pages 151–170 in *In the Footsteps of Sherlock Holmes. Studies in the Biblical Text in Honour of Anneli Aejmelaeus*. Edited by Timothy M. Law, Kristin De Troyer and Marketta Liljeström. CBET 72. Leuven — Paris — Walpole, MA: Peeters, 2014.

van der Ploeg, Johannes P. M. *Le targum de Job de la grotte 11 de Qumran (11QtgJob. Première communication*. Med. KNAW 25.9. Amsterdam : Noord-Hollandsche Uitgevers Maatschappij, 1962.

Verbeke, Elke. "Hebrew Hapax Legomena and their Greek Rendering in LXX Job." PhD. diss., KU Leuven, 2011.

Verbeke, Elke. "The Use of Hebrew Hapax Legomena in Septuagint Studies. Preliminary Remarks on Methodology" Pages 507–521 in *Florilegium Lovaniense. Studies in Septuagint and Textual Criticism in Honour of Florentino García Martínez*. Edited by Hans Ausloos, Bénédicte Lemmelijn and Marc Vervenne. BETL 224. Leuven — Paris — Dudley, MA: Peeters, 2008.

Voitila, Ansi. "Μέλλω-Auxiliary Verb Construction in the Septuagint." Pages 195–216 in *In the Footsteps of Sherlock Holmes. Studies in the Biblical Text in Honour of Anneli Aejmelaeus*. Edited by Timothy M. Law, Kristin De Troyer and Marketta Liljeström. CBET 72. Leuven — Paris — Walpole, MA: Peeters, 2014.

Walters, Peter. *The Text of the Septuagint. Its Corruptions and their Emendation*. Edited by David W. Gooding. Cambridge: University Press, 1973.

Waltke, Bruce K. *The Book of Proverbs 15-31*. NICOT. Grand Rapids, MI – Cambridge: Willam B. Eerdmans Publishing Company, 2005.

Wevers, John W. *Notes on the Greek Text of Deuteronomy*. SCS 39. Altlanta, GA: Scholars Press, 1995.

Wifstrand, Albert. *Die Stellung der Enklitischen Personalpronomina bei den Septuaginta*. K. Humanistiska vetenskapssamfundets i Lund Arsberättelse 1949-1950 II. Lund: Gleerup, 1950.

Wildeboer, Gerrit D. *Die Sprüche*. KHC. Freiburg – Leipzig – Tübingen: Mohr Siebeck, 1897.

Witte, Markus. *Das Buch Hiob*. ATD 13. Göttingen: Vandenhoeck & Ruprecht, 2021.

Witte, Markus. "The Greek Book of Job." Pages 33–54 in *Das Buch Hiob und seine Interpretationen. Beiträge zum Hiob-Symposium auf dem Monte Verità vom 14.-19. August 2005*. Edited by Thomas Krüger et al. ATANT 88. Zürich: Theologischer Verlag, 2007.

Witte, Markus. "Vom El Schaddaj zum Pantokrator. Ein Überblick zur israelitisch-jüdischen Religionsgeschichte." Pages 215–241 in *Studien zur hebräischen Bibel und ihrer Nachgeschichte. Beiträge der 32. Internationalen Ökumenischen Konferenz der Hebräischlehrenden, Frankfurt a.M. 2009*. Edited by Johannes F. Diehl and Markus Witte. KUSATU 12–13. Kamen: Hartmut Spenner, 2011.

Witte, Markus. "Weisheitsschriften." Pages 83–98 in *Die Theologie der Septuaginta / The Theology of the Septuagint*. Edited by Hans Ausloos and Bénédicte Lemmelijn. LXX.H 5. Gütersloh: Gütersloher Verlagshaus, 2020.

Witte, Markus and Martina Kepper. "Job/Das Buch Ijob/Hiob." Pages 2041–2126 *Septuaginta Deutsch – Erläuterungen und Kommentare: Band 2: Psalmen bis Danielschriften*. Edited by in Martin Karrer and Wolfgang Kraus. Stuttgart: Deutsche Bibelgesellschaft, 2011.

Wolters, Al. Proverbs. A Commentary Based on Paroimiai in Codex Vaticanus. SCS. Leiden – Boston, MA: Brill, 2020.

Wright, Benjamin G. *No Small Difference. Sirach's Relationship to its Hebrew Parent Text*. SCS 26. Atlanta, GA: Scholars Press, 1989.

Wright, Benjamin G. The Letter of Aristeas. 'Aristeas To Philocrates' Or 'On the Translation of the Law of the Jews.' CEJL. Berlin: De Gruyter, 2015.

Wright, Benjamin G. "The Quantitative Representation of Elements. Evaluating 'Literalism' in the LXX." Pages 311–335 in *VI Congress of the International Organization for Septuagint and Cognate Studies. Jerusalem, 1986*. Edited by Claude E. Cox. SBLSCS 23. Atlanta, GA: 1987.

Young, Douglas. "Some Types of Scribal Error in Manuscripts of Pindar." *GRBS* 6.4 (2002): 247–273.

Ziegler, Joseph. *Der textkritische Wert der Septuaginta des Buches Job*. Miscellaneis Biblicis II. Pontifico Instituto Biblico: Rome, 1934.

Zohary, Michael. Plants of the Bible. A Complete Handbook to All the Plants with 200 Full-Color Plates Taken in the Natural Habitat. Cambridge – London –New Rochelle, NY – Melbourne: Cambridge University Press, 1982.

Index of Sources

1. Scripture references

Genesis
- 1:1, 22
- 1:26, 225
- 2:7, 270
- 18:27, 312
- 22:12, 146
- 24:44, 299
- 29:27, 142
- 39:5, 271
- 41:2, 250
- 41:18, 250
- 46:4, 146
- 49:26, 272

Exodus
- 4:10, 299
- 7:4, 146
- 9:31, 77
- 12:4, 77
- 16:14, 76
- 16:31, 77
- 18:16, 308
- 23:7, 201
- 24:4-3, 308
- 30:34, 77
- 24:3-4a, 307

Leviticus
- 4:11, 203
- 24:12, 187
- 24:22, 35

Numbers
- 6:3, 245
- 12:7, 299
- 15:16, 308
- 23:22, 230
- 24:8, 230
- 25:8, 130
- 30:17, 308

Deuteronomy
- 1:5, 313
- 1:29, 275
- 3:22, 275
- 4:1, 308
- 4:34, 197
- 4:44, 308
- 7:18, 275
- 7:25, 272
- 8:20, 146
- 11:25, 197
- 12:1, 272
- 12:15, 271
- 12:18, 146
- 13:4, 275
- 14:23, 275
- 15:10, 146
- 16:17, 271
- 17:1, 272
- 17:19, 275
- 18:12, 272
- 20:1, 275
- 22:5, 272
- 23:19, 272
- 25:16, 272
- 26:8, 197
- 27:15, 272
- 28:8, 146
- 28:20, 147
- 29:17, 243
- 30:10, 302
- 30:16, 308
- 31:6, 275
- 31:12, 275
- 32:10, 142
- 32:15, 310
- 32:17, 310
- 32:33, 224
- 33:13, 271, 272
- 33:16, 272
- 33:17, 230

https://doi.org/10.1515/9783111041582-007

2. Dead sea scrolls

3. Ancient authors